UNIVERSITY OF WOLVERHAMPTON

Harrison Learning Centre

News:

A Reader

News:
A Reader

Edited by
Howard Tumber

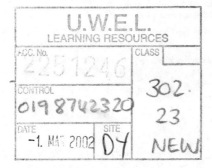

OXFORD
UNIVERSITY PRESS

OXFORD
UNIVERSITY PRESS

Great Clarendon Street, Oxford ox2 6dp
Oxford University Press is a department of the University of Oxford.
It furthers the University's objective of excellence in research, scholarship,
and education by publishing worldwide in

Oxford New York

Athens Auckland Bangkok Bogotá Buenos Aires Calcutta
Cape Town Chennai Dar es Salaam Delhi Florence Hong Kong Istanbul
Karachi Kuala Lumpur Madrid Melbourne Mexico City Mumbai
Nairobi Paris São Paulo Singapore Taipei Tokyo Toronto Warsaw
with associated companies in Berlin Ibadan

Oxford is a registered trade mark of Oxford University Press
in the UK and certain other countries

Published in the United States
by Oxford University Press Inc., New York

Introduction, editorial arrangement and selection Howard Tumber © 1999

British Library Cataloguing in Publication Data
Data available

Library of Congress Cataloging in Publication Data
News: a reader / edited by Howard Tumber.
Includes bibliographical references and index.
1. Journalism—Social aspects. I. Tumber, Howard.
PN4749.N49 1999   302.23—dc21   99–15284

ISBN 0–19–874231–2

3 5 7 9 10 8 6 4

Typeset in Minion
by Jayvee, Trivandrum, India
Printed in Great Britain
on acid-free paper by
Bookcraft Ltd.,
Midsomer Norton, Somerset

HARVEY MOLOTCH AND MARILYN LESTER 'News as Purposive Behavior' from *American Sociological Review* (February 1974), reprinted by permission of American Sociological Association and Harvey Molotch.

ROBERT E. PARK 'News as a Form of Knowledge' from *American Journal of Sociology* (1940), reprinted by permission of The University of Chicago Press.

ROBERT G. PICARD 'Global Communications Controversies' from *Global Journalism* by John C. Merrill, (1991), reprinted by permission of Addison Wesley Educational Publishers, Inc.

BERNARD ROSHCO extract from *Newsmaking*, reprinted by permission of The University of Chicago Press and the author.

ANTHONY SAMPSON 'The Crisis At the Heart of Our Media', from *British Journalism Review*, Vol. 7, No. 3 (1996), reprinted by permission of the *British Journalism Review*.

PHILIP SCHLESINGER extract from *Putting 'Reality' Together*, © 1978 Philip Schlesinger (First published in 1978 by Constable & Co Ltd, first published as a University Paperback in 1987 by Methuen & Co Ltd, published in the USA by Methuen & Co. in association with Methuen, Inc), reprinted by permission of the author.

PHILIP SCHLESINGER AND HOWARD TUMBER extract from *Reporting Crime: The Media Politics of Criminal Justice*, © 1994 Philip Schlesinger and Howard Tumber, reprinted by permission of Oxford University Press.

MICHAEL SCHUDSON extract from *Discovering the News*, © Basic Books 1978, reprinted by permission of Basic Books.

PAMELA J. SHOEMAKER extracts from *Gatekeeping* (Sage Publications 1991), reprinted by permission of the author.

LEON V. SIGAL extract from *Reporters and Officials: The Organization and Politics of Newsmaking* (D.C. Heath and Company, 1973).

LEE SIGELMAN 'Reporting the News' from *American Journal of Sociology*, Vol. 79, No. 1 (1973), reprinted by permission of The University of Chicago Press and the author.

JOHN SOLOSKI 'News Reporting and Professionalism: Some Constraints on the Reporting of the News' from *Media, Culture and Society*, Vol. 11 (1989), reprinted by permission of Sage Publications Ltd.

GAYE TUCHMAN 'Objectivity as Strategic Ritual: An Examination of Newsmen's Notions of Objectivity' from *American Journal of Sociology*, Vol. 77, No. 4 (1972), reprinted by permission of The University of Chicago Press and the author.

JEREMY TUNSTALL 'World News Duopoly' from *The Anglo-American Media Connection* (Oxford University Press, 1999), reprinted by permission of Oxford University Press and the author.

DAVID MANNING WHITE 'The "Gatekeeper": A Case Study in the Selection of

In memory of
my parents

Acknowledgements

THANKS ARE DUE especially to Amanda Goodall for her energy, good humour, and efficiency in organizing footnotes and bibliographies; also to George Gantzias for assistance in gathering material; to Philip Schlesinger for initial discussions about the project and continual support; to Brian Winston, editor of the series, for his insights and suggestions. Thanks also to editors at Oxford University Press: Andrew Lockett, Michael Belson, Matthew Hollis, Tom Chandler, and Angela Griffin. Much gratitude to Sheila Munton and Pam Smith of City University library for assistance way beyond the call of duty. Other colleagues at various times have been both encouraging and supportive: Michele Barrett, Jeremy Tunstall, Ali Rattansi, Michael Bromley, David Morrison, Steve Miller, Frank Webster, and Barbie Zelizer, to all of them—thank you.

The Editor and Publisher gratefully acknowledge permission to reprint the following:

BEN H. BAGDIKIAN extract from *The Media Monopoly*, 5th edition, © 1997 Ben H. Bagdikian, reprinted by permission of Beacon Press, Boston.

CHARLES R. BANTZ 'News Organizations: Conflicts as a Crafted Cultural Norm' from *Communication*, Vol. 8, (1985), reprinted by permission of Gordon and Breach Publishers.

JO BARDOEL 'Beyond Journalism: A Profession between Information Society and Civil Society' from *European Journal of Communication*. © Sage Publications 1996, reprinted by permission of the publisher.

DANIEL J. BOORSTIN extract from *The Image*, © 1961 by Daniel J. Boorstin, reprinted by permission of Scribners, a division of Simon & Schuster, Inc.

WARREN BREED 'Social Control in the Newsroom: A Functional Analysis' from *Social Forces*, Vol. 33 (1955), reprinted by permission of *Social Forces*.

DANIEL DAYAN AND ELIHU KATZ extract from *Media Events: The Live Broadcasting History*, © 1992 by the President and Fellows of Harvard College, reprinted by permission of Harvard University Press.

RICHARD V. ERICSON, PATRICIA M. BARANEK, AND JANET B. L. CHAN extract from *Negotiating Control: A Study of News Sources* (Open University Press, 1989), reprinted by permission of the authors; extract from *Visualizing Deviance: A Study of News Organization*, reprinted by permission of University of Toronto Press and the authors.

MARK FISHMAN extract from *Manufacturing the News*, © 1980, reprinted by permission of the University of Texas Press.

JOHAN GALTUNG AND MARI HOLMBOE RUGE 'The Structure of Foreign [News]' *Journal of International Peace Research*, 1 (1965), 64–90. Reprinted wi[th] permission.

HERBERT J. GANS extract from *Deciding What's News*, © 1979 Herbert [J.] Gans, reprinted by permission of the publisher, Pantheon Books, a div[ision] of Random House Inc.

WALTER GIEBER 'News is what Newspapermen Make It' from *People, So[ciety] and Mass Communication* by Lewis Anthony Dexter and David Mannin[g] White, © 1964 The Free Press, reprinted by permission of The Free Pres[s], Division of Simon & Schuster, Inc.

TODD GITLIN extract from *The Whole World is Watching: Mass Media in the Making and the Unmaking of the New Left*, © 1980 The Regents of the University of California, reprinted by permission of University of Californi[a] Press.

PETER GOLDING AND GRAHAM MURDOCK 'Culture, Communications, and Political Economy' from *Mass Media and Society* edited by James Curran and Michael Gurevitch, © 1991 Peter Golding and Graham Murdock, reprinted by permission of Edward Arnold.

PETER GOLDING AND PHILIP ELLIOTT extract from *Making the News* (1979), reprinted by permission of Addison Wesley Longman Ltd.

STUART HALL, CHAS CRITCHER, TONY JEFFERSON, JOHN CLARKE, AND BRIAN ROBERTS extract from *Policing the Crisis: Mugging, The State, and Law and Order* (Macmillan, 1978).

DANIEL C. HALLIN extract from *The 'Uncensored War': The Media and Vietnam*, © 1986 Daniel Hallin, reprinted by permission of Oxford University Press, Inc.

EDWARD S. HERMAN AND NOAM CHOMSKY extract from *Manufacturing Consent* (Vintage, 1988), reprinted by permission of Random House UK Ltd, for British Commonwealth excluding Canada.

PENN KIMBALL extract from *Downsizing the News: Network Cutbacks in the Nation's Capital*, © 1994, reprinted by permission of The Johns Hopkins University Press.

WALTER LIPPMANN extract from *Public Opinion*, © 1922, renewed 1949 Walter Lippmann, reprinted by permission of The Free Press, a division of Simon & Schuster Inc.

MAXWELL E. McCOMBS AND DONALD L. SHAW, 'The Agenda-Setting Function of Mass Media' from *Public Opinion Quarterly*, 36 (Summer 1972).

JOHN H. McMANUS 'The Nature of News Reconsidered' from *Market Driven Journalism: Let the Citizen Beware*, reprinted by permission of the author.

DAVIS MERRITT extracts from *Public Journalism and Public Life: Why Telling the News is Not Enough*, © 1995 Davis Merritt, reprinted by permission of the publisher, Lawrence Erlbaum Associates.

News', from *Journalism Quarterly*, Vol. 27 (1950), reprinted by permission of *Journalism Quarterly*.

BARBIE ZELIZER 'CNN, the Gulf War, and Journalistic Practice' from *Journal of Communication*, 42 (1) (1992), reprinted by permission of Oxford University Press.

Despite every effort to trace and contact copyright holders before publication this has not been possible in a few cases. If notified, the publisher will be pleased to rectify any errors or omissions at the earliest opportunity.

Contents

Introduction

News: A Reader is a collection of pieces on news by authors who attempt in various ways to address the problems of definition, process, power, and ideology.

The main aim of the book is to provide readers with a selection of work on news that highlights some of the main themes and debates surrounding the issues of news since the beginnings of mass communication research. The articles in the reader are brought together to provide a mapped insight into the emergence of news research. Each piece has been very carefully edited to enable readers to enjoy the essence of each one and provide the theoretical and/or empirical kernel of the work. Despite changes in the focus of research on news during the years when these pieces were written many of the articles included in this reader have an enduring quality. Students are often reluctant to search through old volumes of journals often kept in store. Providing an accessible, edited volume, enables a 'new' reading of these pieces by young scholars and a critical revaluation of their standing in the field.

This book is divided into five parts organized mainly thematically but also historically. All the pieces are fully discussed in the introductions to each of the five parts later in the reader. The reason for the division is to provide a framework for readers to comprehend the debates about the nature of news and its production process.

Part One, 'Definitions of News', brings together early and recent work on the characterizations of stories and events as news. The seven pieces provide a flavour of the attempts, over the last seventy years, to define news. The first and earliest piece by Walter Lippmann illustrates the concern that journalists as well as academic researchers exhibit in the quest to understand what makes a good story. Robert Park argues that news makes people talk, can be characterized like a public document but is not history. Instead it deals with isolated events and unlike history does not place them in causal sequences. Time has always been a key element in definitions of news and Bernard Roshco illustrates how the three aspects of recency, immediacy, and currency operate in regard to the type of news that is considered for publication. This ephemeral nature of news characterizes its difference from knowledge which in contrast strives for permanency. Many studies have attempted to define the factors that influence the flow of news. Johan Galtung and Mari Holmboe Ruge provide a systematic description of factors that are important in this process. Looking at crisis coverage in four foreign newspapers, Galtung and Ruge hypothesize the degree of importance of the factors in relation to one another. The nature of events is a theme examined in the pieces by Daniel Boorstin; Harvey Molotch and Marilyn Lester; and Daniel Dayan and Elihu Katz. Boorstin views news as man-made events often orchestrated by PR campaigns. These pseudo-events, as he labels them, provide the material in the mass media to fill the expectations of the public.

In an influential piece Molotch and Lester attempt to show how events reflect not a world out there but instead are the results of the activities of those with power to determine the experience of the audience. Dayan and Katz attempt a definition of media events by looking at the live broadcasting of events. They provide a different insight into the continual debate over definitions of news.

Part Two, 'Production of News', changes the emphasis from attempts to define news to how it is produced. Gatekeeping is a famous term in mass media research on news. As one of the earliest models its place in history is assured, though its relevance and credence is somewhat tarnished. Its importance derives from David Manning White's empirical assessment that definitions of news, issues, and events should include the preferences of journalists. Whilst the gatekeeper concept has subsequently been both refined and dismissed it provides an important nail in the 'news is a mirror of reality' coffin. Pamela Shoemaker attempts to impose a more sophisticated embrace of the gatekeeping model. The lone copy-editor immortalized in White's study is replaced by multiple staff gatekeepers controlling different aspects of the process, each possessing the power to exercise both their own selection routines and shape of message. The articles by Warren Breed, Lee Sigelman, and Charles Bantz examine the socialization of journalists into the news organization. These studies are important in revealing aspects of journalistic culture that emerge from reporters' engagement with their editors and peers. Breed, for example, shows how journalists' values are defined in relation to the news organizational group whilst Sigelman demonstrates how supportive institutional values are structured so that the belief of a free and democratic press is not diminished. Even when conflicts may emerge in the organization these can often be normalized. Bantz suggests that the incompatibility in news organizations, particularly television, of professional norms and business norms inevitably results in conflict. This expectation or predictability makes conflict acceptable and even appropriate. The pieces by Mark Fishman; Peter Golding and Philip Elliott; and Philip Schlesinger represent examples of the 'golden' period of media production studies conducted during the 1970s in the UK and US. Some of these studies were based on Ph.D. research or research grants and involved interviews with news organization personnel and observation in newsrooms. They provide insights and observations of the production of news with the emphasis on the operation of organizational constraints and the social construction of reality in social systems. The titles of these three works and of others conducted during the period clearly indicate this position: 'Putting "Reality" Together', 'Manufacturing the News', 'Making the News'. A decade later Richard Ericson, Patricia Baranek, and Janet Chan provide a useful diagrammatical account of the news production process, indicating the different roles of the various personnel.

Part Three, 'Economics of News', shifts the emphasis from social organization to economics. The seven pieces included in this section demonstrate in various ways how ownership and control of news organizations affect the news produced. The early political economy approaches to the study of news in particular and the mass media more generally painted an instrumentalist portrait of capitalist ownership, producing media content that reflected the values and ideas of the ruling class. One of the criticisms of this approach argued that ownership is now more widespread and therefore could not be equated with control of editorial content. However, Ben Bagdikian clearly demonstrates the growth of the new media cartel. He argues that the growth of monopoly and the changes in ownership within the communications industries are leading to serious problems for news workers who have to comply with corporate interests. The work of Peter Golding and Graham Murdock mirrors the development of the political economy approach to media organizations. The piece included in the reader is relatively far removed from their initial work produced twenty years earlier. Whilst acknowledging economic dynamics in some crucial form, they absolve it as a total answer for the understanding of communication activity. The model of the news media produced in the writings of Edward Herman and Noam Chomsky is often referred to as an extreme version of the political economy approach. Their propaganda model of journalistic production is based on an analysis of various examples where the news media act as conduits in ideologically mobilized campaigns. The model has a predictive quality that can forecast the manner in which the media will report future events. John McManus's piece represents an important development, showing how news is a commodity refined to the determinates of the market. McManus researched four television stations affiliated to a major network in the US and describes how the market place has explicitly entered the newsroom. Simply, journalism is being designed to serve the market. Jeremy Tunstall shows the commercial imperative that has led to the dominance of Associated Press and Reuters in the control of news flowing around the world. He also suggests that the financialization of news is leading to conflicts of interest amongst these big players, who may eschew reporting detrimental stories about their wealthy clients. Market-led news and its consequences are the briefs of Anthony Sampson and Penn Kimball. Both talk about the downsizing of news. Sampson concentrates on the British press whilst Kimball presents a pessimistic picture of broadcasting in the US. Tabloidization of news is now a common term to describe the trend of late twentieth-century journalism product.

Part Four of the book, 'Sources of News', moves the sociology of news to a different focus. Much of the discussion in the research on news over the years has centred on the degree of autonomy that journalists enjoy. The articles in this part concentrate on influence exerted by outside interests rather than control directed from editorial or proprietorial authority. Walter Gieber acknowledges the pressures from the news bureaucracy and outside sources. Unlike White, who focuses solely on the copy-editor as gatekeeper, Gieber, in addition, examines the role of the source as gatekeeper and compares the values of both. All the other pieces acknowledge the importance of the journalist–source relationship in the production of news. Leon Sigal concentrates on the US capital and provides empirical evidence to show the heavy reliance by journalists on official government sources. In a further example of the observation studies of newsrooms conducted in the 1970s Herbert Gans sees news as information flowing from sources, via journalists who mould it into a suitable product, to audiences. Whilst Stuart Hall *et al.* use a structural analysis to acknowledge the role that certain social groups, due to their institutional power, exert in the definition of events represented by the media, Philip Schlesinger and Howard Tumber argue that other less powerful groups play a part in the battle to define the news. A similar position is adopted by Richard Ericson *et al.* in a study conducted in Canada in which the processes of negotiation between sources and journalists is examined. All these three studies look at the reporting of crime and deviancy to explore source power. Todd Gitlin examines the anti-war protest against Vietnam rather than crime to demonstrate the development of authoritative sources emerging out of the student movement. Gitlin provides examples of news organizations' construction of news and their codes of practice to achieve objectivity and balance.

The pieces that comprise Part Five, 'Objectivity and Ideology of News', look at different aspects of bias arising from journalism culture. All the authors examine the nature of professionalism and objectivity. Michael Schudson neatly analyses historically the way objectivity has been adopted by journalists as an ideal that metaphorically licences their profession. Gaye Tuchman asserts the idea of objectivity as a strategic ritual applied by reporters primarily as a defensive response to the threat of censure emanating from accusations of bias. John Soloski, in an examination of the newsroom, provides a recent addition to the studies conducted by Breed and Sigelman reproduced in Part Two. He shows how ideas of objectivity enable social control to be maintained in the newsroom, thereby negating the necessity of formal control mechanisms. In a landmark study Maxwell McCombs and Donald Shaw seek to research the relationship between the mass media and its audience. The main hypothesis postulates that readers learn from the press not only about an issue but the degree of importance to give to that issue from the amount of information provided and its position in a news story. The media may not tell the public what to think but may play an important role in informing them of what to think about. Since the initial research some thirty years ago numerous other agenda-setting studies have been conducted that develop the initial ideas and also explore how the media agenda is set and how the public agenda can influence the policy agenda. Daniel Hallin, using the reporting of the Vietnam War as an empirical case study, provides a model for comprehending how the commitment to the routines of objective journalism by the media was prevalent throughout the conflict, irrespective of the degree of support they gave to the war. Ten years later Barbie Zelizer shows how the Gulf War is part of a long line of major events that offer journalists a forum for examining their profession. It is these special incidents that enable an introspection of journalistic practice and reassessment of news values. In describing the global communications debates Robert Picard traces the western domination of international news and attempts by international organizations to counteract the bias endemic in the image of the developing world. Dissent with traditional western news values is the subject of Davis Merritt's piece. The professional idea of objectivity with its emphasis on balance leads to deficiencies of accuracy. Public journalism is a new movement that aims to fill the gap between citizens and government. The intention is to serve local communities by adopting a public bias. In this way journalists may be able to reclaim an authority largely dissipated over recent years. Debate about cyberculture and the role journalists could play in the new virtual environment is the theme addressed by Jo Bardoel. Predicting the future at an early stage of the development of online media is a rather risky enterprise but Bardoel captures some of the important questions about traditional forms of journalism. How will the professional values and ideas of objectivity survive in the new unmediated environment?

It is impossible to be entirely comprehensive when presenting only a personalized selection from the wealth of research and comment emanating from this area of mass communication research. Inevitably, due to space constraints, difficult decisions have to be made. But it is hoped that readers will find the selection relevant and enjoyable in understanding the news process.

1

Definitions of News

PART ONE

Definitions of News

Introduction to Part I: Definitions of News

TWO OF THE enduring questions of the sociology of news and journalism are 'what is news' and 'what makes news' and the pieces in part one provide some answers. The long time-span over which they were written emphasizes the continuing efforts and obsessions of mass communications scholars to define news. Walter Lippmann, in attempting to identify the nature of news, was one of the first people this century to see news as a product of journalistic routines and standardized procedures. He argues that by the time it reaches its readers, the news is the result of a series of selections. These choices are made from news organization conventions rather than applying objective standards.

Robert Park, a journalist like Lippmann, writing nearly twenty years later uses a formulation of knowledge to argue that news increases in importance compared to history. Park addresses the essence of news suggesting that it is more than 'acquaintance with' (common sense) but less than 'knowledge about' (formal knowledge) an event. News occupies a space or point along a continuum and is characterized by its 'transient' and 'ephemeral' quality.

Daniel Boorstin (writing in the early 1960s) sees news as a series of pseudo-events. Interestingly Boorstin talks about public relations and news, a subject of increasing interest over the last decade. His work is acknowledged in many studies but it is quite rare to find chapters or extracts from his work. He is concerned to move away from the idea of news as 'God-made events' to those that are man-made or pseudo-events. He takes a number of events including political/public ones and illustrates how various occurrences are arranged for the convenience of the mass media. The success of the PR campaign that accompanies the events can then be assessed by how widely the event is reported. Boorstin argues that the public has a demand for inclusion—they demand more than the world can provide and something has to be made up to fill the gap of this deficiency. The public's expectations is that newspapers, television, and radio have to be full of news, and if there is no news visible to the reporter or the citizen the successful reporters of news organizations are still expected to provide the story. It is this kind of political synthetic novelty which Boorstin labels pseudo-events.

Galtung and Ruge's much-cited article addresses the general problem of identifying various factors having a bearing on the flow of foreign news. The key question they ask is 'how do events become news'. Based on their idea that consideration of an event is culturally determined they describe the factors affecting the selection process and the degree of importance of various factors in relation to each other. Eight factors held to be culture free, in that they do not expect these factors to vary significantly along north-south or east-west axes are identified, along with four culture bound factors that influence the transition from events to news. The relevance of Galtung and Ruge's model is its predictive quality in determining patterns of news. In many later studies similar factors were identified as important characteristics of news reports, not only of foreign news but also of domestic and other specialist news.

Bernard Roshco discusses the difficulty of defining news. Whilst confirming many of the factors identified by Galtung and Ruge, Roshco stresses the importance of time and timeliness in the news production process and in the determination of whether an item of news actually gets published. He claims an understanding of the definitions of news that permits a comprehension of the newsmaking process. Regardless of the social and political values of individual journalists, he argues, conflict and crisis are the main ingredients of front-page stories in the press rather than ones of friendship and success.

The final pieces in this section examine the nature of events. Molotch and Lester argue that the public develops a conception of news as a social construction. Events exist because of the practical purposes they serve rather than from any ideas of objective importance. The news produced by media organizations results from practical, purposive, and creative processes on the part of news promoters, assemblers, and consumers. At each stage of an event's generation the main features are built within the context of previous and anticipated occurrences. The role of sources in predicting events is of great importance and the manner in which access is accomplished can change and vary, and lead Molotch and Lester to create a typology of event types. By so doing they hope to reveal the stratification of the way society is organized.

The concluding piece by Daniel Dayan and Elihu Katz examines the design and broadcasting of historic events. They pose a number of questions about the nature of these events, for example, whether they are world rituals or modern-day versions of the political spectacle. They explore the idea that ceremonial politics provide a sense of solidarity and equality engendering a sense of occasion, a coming together of nations. Broadcasters, in deciding which ceremonies qualify for the big production into a media event, provide a form of protection against the establishment that may favour coverage of all ceremonial politics. They examine a number of public spectacles including the Olympic Games, the wedding of Charles and Diana, and the Kennedys' funerals and explore the potential for live television to act as a powerful social force in the transformation of society.

1

Public Opinion

Walter Lippmann

The Nature of News

ALL THE REPORTERS in the world working all the hours of the day could not witness all the happenings in the world. There are not a great many reporters. And none of them has the power to be in more than one place at a time. Reporters are not clairvoyant, they do not gaze into a crystal ball and see the world at will, they are not assisted by thought-transference. Yet the range of subjects these comparatively few men manage to cover would be a miracle indeed, if it were not a standardized routine.

Newspapers do not try to keep an eye on all mankind.[1] They have watchers stationed at certain places, like Police Headquarters, the Coroner's Office, the County Clerk's Office, City Hall, the White House, the Senate, House of Representatives, and so forth. They watch, or rather in the majority of cases they belong to associations which employ men who watch 'a comparatively small number of places where it is made known when the life of anyone . . . departs from ordinary paths, or when events worth telling about occur. For example, John Smith, let it be supposed, becomes a broker. For ten years he pursues the even tenor of his way and except for his customers and his friends no one gives him a thought. To the newspapers he is as if he were not. But in the eleventh year he suffers heavy losses and, at last, his resources all gone, summons his lawyer and arranges for the making of an assignment. The lawyer posts off to the County Clerk's office, and a clerk there makes the necessary entries in the official docket. Here in step the newspapers. While the clerk is writing Smith's business obituary a reporter glances over his shoulder and a few minutes later the reporters know Smith's troubles and are as well informed concerning his business status as they would be had they kept a reporter at his door every day for over ten years.'[2]

When Mr Given says that the newspapers know 'Smith's troubles' and 'his business status', he does not mean that they know them as Smith knows them, or as Mr Arnold Bennett would know them if he had made Smith the hero of a three volume novel. The newspapers know only 'in a few minutes' the bald facts which are recorded in the County Clerk's Office. That overt act 'uncovers' the news about Smith. Whether the news will be followed up or

---

Source: Walter Lippmann, *Public Opinion* (New York: Free Press, 1965; orig. published 1922), 214–25.

1 See the illuminating chapter in Mr John L. Given's book on 'Uncovering the News', ch. 5.

2 Ibid. 57.

What determines a news [handwritten marginalia]

not is another matter. The point is that before a series of events become news they have usually to make themselves noticeable in some more or less overt act. Generally too, in a crudely overt act. Smith's friends may have known for years that he was taking risks, rumours may even have reached the financial editor if Smith's friends were talkative. But apart from the fact that none of this could be published because it would be libel, there is in these rumours nothing definite on which to peg a story. Something definite must occur that has unmistakable form. It may be the act of going into bankruptcy, it may be a fire, a collision, an assault, a riot, an arrest, a denunciation, the introduction of a bill, a speech, a vote, a meeting, the expressed opinion of a well-known citizen, an editorial in a newspaper, a sale, a wage-schedule, a price change, the proposal to build a bridge. . . . There must be a manifestation. The course of events must assume a certain definable shape, and until it is in a phase where some aspect is an accomplished fact, news does not separate itself from the ocean of possible truth.

Naturally there is room for wide difference of opinion as to when events have a shape that can be reported. A good journalist will find news oftener than a hack. If he sees a building with a dangerous list, he does not have to wait until it falls into the street in order to recognize news. It was a great reporter who guessed the name of the next Indian Viceroy when he heard that Lord So-and-So was inquiring about climates. There are lucky shots but the number of men who can make them is small. Usually it is the stereotyped shape assumed by an event at an obvious place that uncovers the run of the news. The most obvious place is where people's affairs touch public authority. *De minimis non curat lex*. It is at these places that marriages, births, deaths, contracts, failures, arrivals, departures, lawsuits, disorders, epidemics and calamities are made known.

News and sociology [handwritten marginalia]

In the first instance, therefore, the news is not a mirror of social conditions, but the report of an aspect that has obtruded itself. The news does not tell you how the seed is germinating in the ground, but it may tell you when the first sprout breaks through the surface. It may even tell you what somebody says is happening to the seed under ground. It may tell you that the sprout did not come up at the time it was expected. The more points, then, at which any happening can be fixed, objectified, measured, named, the more points there are at which news can occur. [. . .]

Wherever there is a good machinery of record, the modern news service works with great precision. There is one on the stock exchange, and the news of price movements is flashed over tickers with dependable accuracy. There is a machinery for election returns, and when the counting and tabulating are well done, the result of a national election is usually known on the night of the election. In civilized communities deaths, births, marriages, and divorces are recorded, and are known accurately except where there is concealment or neglect. The machinery exists for some, and only some, aspects of industry and government, in varying degrees of precision for securities, money and staples, bank clearances, realty transactions, wage scales. It exists for imports and exports because they pass through a custom house and can be directly recorded. It exists in nothing like the same degree for internal trade, and especially for trade over the counter.

It will be found, I think, that there is a very direct relation between the

certainty of news and the system of record. If you call to mind
which form the principal indictment by reformers against the press
they are subjects in which the newspaper occupies the position of th   ...pire
in the unscored baseball game. All news about states of mind is of this character: so are all descriptions of personalities, of sincerity, aspiration, motive,
intention, of mass feeling, of national feeling, of public opinion, the policies
of foreign governments. So is much news about what is going to happen. So
are questions turning on private profit, private income, wages, working conditions, the efficiency of labour, educational opportunity, unemployment,[3]
monotony, health, discrimination, unfairness, restraint of trade, waste,
'backward peoples', conservatism, imperialism, radicalism, liberty, honour,
righteousness. All involve data that are at best spasmodically recorded. The
data may be hidden because of a censorship or a tradition of privacy, they
may not exist because nobody thinks record important, because he thinks it
red tape, or because nobody has yet invented an objective system of measurement. Then the news on these subjects is bound to be debatable, when it
is not wholly neglected. The events which are not scored are reported either
as personal and conventional opinions, or they are not news. They do not
take shape until somebody protests, or somebody investigates, or somebody
publicly, in the etymological meaning of the word, makes an *issue* of them.

This is the underlying reason for the existence of the press agent. The enormous discretion as to what facts and what impressions shall be reported is
steadily convincing every organized group of people that whether it wishes to
secure publicity or to avoid it, the exercise of discretion cannot be left to the
reporter. It is safer to hire a press agent who stands between the group and the
newspapers. Having hired him, the temptation to exploit his strategic position is very great. [. . .] 'The great corporations have them, the banks have
them, the railroads have them, all the organizations of business and of social
and political activity have them, and they are the media through which news
comes. Even statesmen have them.'[4]

Were reporting the simple recovery of obvious facts, the press agent would
be little more than a clerk. But since, in respect to most of the big topics of
news, the facts are not simple, and not at all obvious, but subject to choice
and opinion, it is natural that everyone should wish to make his own choice
of facts for the newspapers to print. The publicity man does that. And in
doing it, he certainly saves the reporter much trouble, by presenting him a
clear picture of a situation out of which he might otherwise make neither
head nor tail. But it follows that the picture which the publicity man makes
for the reporter is the one he wishes the public to see. He is censor and propa-
gandist, responsible only to his employers, and to the whole truth responsible only as it accords with the employers' conception of his own interests.

The development of the publicity man is a clear sign that the facts of
modern life do not spontaneously take a shape in which they can be known.
They must be given a shape by somebody, and since in the daily routine
reporters cannot give a shape to facts, and since there is little disinterested

3 Think of what guesswork went into the Reports of Unemployment in 1921.

4 Address by Mr Frank Cobb before the Women's City Club of New York, Dec. 11, 1919. Reprinted,
New Republic, Dec. 31, 1919, p. 44.

organization of intelligence, the need for some formulation is being met by the interested parties. [. . .]

Let us suppose the conditions leading up to a strike are bad. What is the measure of evil? A certain conception of a proper standard of living, hygiene, economic security, and human dignity. The industry may be far below the theoretical standard of the community, and the workers may be too wretched to protest. Conditions may be above the standard, and the workers may protest violently. The standard is at best a vague measure. However, we shall assume that the conditions are below par, as par is understood by the editor. Occasionally without waiting for the workers to threaten, but prompted say by a social worker, he will send reporters to investigate, and will call attention to bad conditions. Necessarily he cannot do that often. For these investigations cost time, money, special talent, and a lot of space. To make plausible a report that conditions are bad, you need a good many columns of print. In order to tell the truth about the steel worker in the Pittsburgh district, there was needed a staff of investigators, a great deal of time, and several fat volumes of print. It is impossible to suppose that any daily newspaper could normally regard the making of Pittsburgh Surveys, or even Interchurch Steel Reports, as one of its tasks. News which requires so much trouble as that to obtain is beyond the resources of a daily press.[5]

The bad conditions as such are not news, because in all but exceptional cases, journalism is not a first-hand report of the raw material. It is a report of that material after it has been stylized. Thus bad conditions might become news if the Board of Health reported an unusually high death rate in an industrial area. Failing an intervention of this sort, the facts do not become news until the workers organize and make a demand upon their employers. Even then, if an easy settlement is certain the news value is low, whether or not the conditions themselves are remedied in the settlement. But if industrial relations collapse into a strike or lockout the news value increases. If the stoppage involves a service on which the readers of the newspapers immediately depend, or if it involves a breach of order, the news value is still greater. [. . .]

It follows that in the reporting of strikes, the easiest way is to let the news be uncovered by the overt act, and to describe the event as the story of interference with the reader's life. That is where his attention is first aroused, and his interest most easily enlisted. A great deal, I think myself the crucial part, of what looks to the worker and the reformer as deliberate misrepresentation on the part of newspapers, is the direct outcome of a practical difficulty in uncovering the news, and the emotional difficulty of making distant facts interesting unless, as Emerson says, we can 'perceive (them) to be only a new version of our familiar experience' and can 'set about translating (them) at once into our parallel facts'.[6]

---

5 Not long ago Babe Ruth was jailed for speeding. Released from jail just before the afternoon game started, he rushed into his waiting automobile, and made up for time lost in jail by breaking the speed laws on his way to the ball grounds. No policeman stopped him, but a reporter timed him, and published his speed the next morning. Babe Ruth is an exceptional man. Newspapers cannot time all motorists. They have to take their news about speeding from the police.

6 From his essay entitled *Art and Criticism*. The quotation occurs in a passage cited on p. 87 of Professor R. W. Brown's, *The Writer's Art*.

If you study the way many a strike is reported in the press, you will find, very often, that the issues are rarely in the headlines, barely in the leading paragraphs, and sometimes not even mentioned anywhere. A labour dispute in another city has to be very important before the news account contains any definite information as to what is in dispute. The routine of the news works that way, with modifications it works that way in regard to political issues and international news as well. The news is an account of the overt phases that are interesting, and the pressure on the newspaper to adhere to this routine comes from many sides. It comes from the economy of noting only the stereotyped phase of a situation. It comes from the difficulty of finding journalists who can see what they have not learned to see. It comes from the almost unavoidable difficulty of finding sufficient space in which even the best journalist can make plausible an unconventional view. It comes from the economic necessity of interesting the reader quickly, and the economic risk involved in not interesting him at all, or of offending him by unexpected news insufficiently or clumsily described. All these difficulties combined make for uncertainty in the editor when there are dangerous issues at stake, and cause him naturally to prefer the indisputable fact and a treatment more readily adapted to the reader's interest. The indisputable fact and the easy interest are the strike itself and the reader's inconvenience.

All the subtler and deeper truths are, in the present organization of industry, very unreliable truths. They involve judgements about standards of living, productivity, human rights that are endlessly debatable in the absence of exact record and quantitative analysis. And as long as these do not exist in industry, the run of news about it will tend, as Emerson said, quoting from Isocrates, 'to make of moles mountains, and of mountains moles'.[7] Where there is no constitutional procedure in industry, and no expert sifting of evidence and the claims, the fact that is sensational to the reader is the fact that almost every journalist will seek. Given the industrial relations that so largely prevail, even where there is conference or arbitration, but no independent filtering of the facts for decision, the issue for the newspaper public will tend not to be the issue for the industry. And so to try disputes by an appeal through the newspapers puts a burden upon newspapers and readers which they cannot and ought not to carry. As long as real law and order do not exist, the bulk of the news will, unless consciously and courageously corrected, work against those who have no lawful and orderly method of asserting themselves. The bulletins from the scene of action will note the trouble that arose from the assertion, rather than the reasons which led to it. The reasons are intangible. [. . .]

Every newspaper when it reaches the reader is the result of a whole series of selections as to what items shall be printed, in what position they shall be printed, how much space each shall occupy, what emphasis each shall have. There are no objective standards here. There are conventions. Take two newspapers published in the same city on the same morning. The headline of one reads: 'Britain pledges aid to Berlin against French aggression; France openly backs Poles.' The headline of the second is 'Mrs Stillman's Other Love'. Which you prefer is a matter of taste, but not entirely a matter of the

---

7 Ibid.

editor's taste. It is a matter of his judgement as to what will absorb the half hour's attention a certain set of readers will give to his newspaper. Now the problem of securing attention is by no means equivalent to displaying the news in the perspective laid down by religious teaching or by some form of ethical culture. It is a problem of provoking feeling in the reader, of inducing him to feel a sense of personal identification with the stories he is reading. News which does not offer this opportunity to introduce oneself into the struggle which it depicts cannot appeal to a wide audience. The audience must participate in the news, much as it participates in the drama, by personal identification. Just as everyone holds his breath when the heroine is in danger, as he helps Babe Ruth swing his bat, so in subtler form the reader enters into the news. In order that he shall enter he must find a familiar foothold in the story, and this is supplied to him by the use of stereotypes. They tell him that if an association of plumbers is called a 'combine' it is appropriate to develop his hostility; if it is called a 'group of leading businessmen' the cue is for a favourable reaction.

It is in a combination of these elements that the power to create opinion resides. Editorials reinforce. Sometimes in a situation that on the news pages is too confusing to permit of identification, they give the reader a clue by means of which he engages himself. A clue he must have if, as most of us must, he is to seize the news in a hurry. A suggestion of some sort he demands, which tells him, so to speak, where he, a man conceiving himself to be such and such a person, shall integrate his feelings with the news he reads. [. . .]

This is the plight of the reader of the general news. If he is to read it at all he must be interested, that is to say, he must enter into the situation and care about the outcome. But if he does that he cannot rest in a negative, and unless independent means of checking the lead given him by his newspaper exists, the very fact that he is interested may make it difficult to arrive at that balance of opinions which may most nearly approximate the truth. The more passionately involved he becomes, the more he will tend to resent not only a different view, but a disturbing bit of news. That is why many a newspaper finds that, having honestly evoked the partisanship of its readers, it cannot easily, supposing the editor believes the facts warrant it, change position. If a change is necessary, the transition has to be managed with the utmost skill and delicacy. Usually a newspaper will not attempt so hazardous a performance. It is easier and safer to have the news of that subject taper off and disappear, thus putting out the fire by starving it.

2

News as a Form of Knowledge: A Chapter in the Sociology of Knowledge

Robert E. Park

KNOWLEDGE ABOUT, SO far at least as it is scientific, becomes in this way a part of the social heritage, a body of tested and accredited fact and theory in which new increments, added to the original fund, tend to check up, affirm, or qualify, first of all, in each special science and, finally, in all the related sciences, all that has been contributed by earlier investigators.

On the other hand, acquaintance with, as I have sought to characterize it, so far as it is based on the slow accumulation of experience and the gradual accommodation of the individual to his individual and personal world, becomes, as I have said, more and more completely identical with instinct and intuition.

Knowledge about is not merely accumulated experience but the result of systematic investigation of nature. It is based on the answers given to the definite questions which we address to the world about us. It is knowledge pursued methodically with all the formal and logical apparatus which scientific research has created. [. . .]

What is here described as 'acquaintance with' and 'knowledge about' are assumed to be distinct forms of knowledge—forms having different functions in the lives of individuals and of society—rather than knowledge of the same kind but of different degrees of accuracy and validity. They are, nevertheless, not so different in character or function—since they are, after all, relative terms—that they may not be conceived as constituting together a continuum—a continuum within which all kinds and sorts of knowledge find a place. In such a continuum news has a location of its own. It is obvious that news is not systematic knowledge like that of the physical sciences. It is rather, in so far as it is concerned with events, like history. Events, because

Source: Robert E. Park, 'News as a Form of Knowledge: A Chapter in the Sociology of Knowledge', *American Journal of Sociology* 45 (1940), 669–86.

they are invariably fixed in time and located in space, are unique and cannot, therefore, be classified as is the case with things. Not only do things move about in space and change with time but, in respect to their internal organization, they are always in a condition of more or less stable equilibrium.

News is not history, however, and its facts are not historical facts. News is not history because, for one thing among others, it deals, on the whole, with isolated events and does not seek to relate them to one another either in the form of causal or in the form of teleological sequences. History not only describes events but seeks to put them in their proper place in the historical succession, and, by doing so, to discover the underlying tendencies and forces which find expression in them. In fact, one would not be far wrong in assuming that history is quite as much concerned with the connections of events—the relation between the incidents that precede and those that follow—as it is with the events themselves. On the other hand, a reporter, as distinguished from a historian, seeks merely to record each single event as it occurs and is concerned with the past and future only in so far as these throw light on what is actual and present. [. . .]

News, as a form of knowledge, is not primarily concerned either with the past or with the future but rather with the present—what has been described by psychologists as 'the specious present'. News may be said to exist only in such a present. What is meant here by the 'specious present' is suggested by the fact that news, as the publishers of the commercial press know, is a very perishable commodity. News remains news only until it has reached the persons for whom it has 'news interest'. Once published and its significance recognized, what was news becomes history.

This transient and ephemeral quality is of the very essence of news and is intimately connected with every other character that it exhibits. Different types of news have a different time span. In its most elementary form a news report is a mere 'flash,' announcing that an event has happened. If the event proves of real importance, interest in it will lead to further inquiry and to a more complete acquaintance with the attendant circumstances. An event ceases to be news, however, as soon as the tension it aroused has ceased and public attention has been directed to some other aspect of the habitat or to some other incident sufficiently novel, exciting, or important to hold its attention.

The reason that news comes to us, under ordinary circumstances, not in the form of a continued story but as a series of independent incidents becomes clear when one takes account of the fact that we are here concerned with the public mind—or with what is called the public mind. In its most elementary form knowledge reaches the public not, as it does the individual, in the form of a perception but in the form of a communication, that is to say, news. Public attention, however, under normal conditions is wavering, unsteady, and easily distracted. When the public mind wanders, the rapport, grapevine telegraph, or whatever else it is that insures the transmission of news within the limits of the public ceases to function, tension is relaxed, communication broken off, and what was live news becomes cold fact.

A news item, as every newspaperman knows, is read in inverse ratio to its length. The ordinary reader will read a column and a half of two- or three-line items about men and things in the home town before he will read a column article, no matter how advertised in the headlines, unless it turns out to be not merely news but a story, i.e. something that has what is called technically 'human interest'.

News comes in the form of small, independent communications that can be easily and rapidly comprehended. In fact, news performs somewhat the same functions for the public that perception does for the individual man; that is to say, it does not so much inform as orient the public, giving each and all notice as to what is going on. It does this without any effort of the reporter to interpret the events he reports, except in so far as to make them comprehensible and interesting.

The first typical reaction of an individual to the news is likely to be a desire to repeat it to someone. This makes conversation, arouses further comment, and perhaps starts a discussion. But the singular thing about it is that, once discussion has been started, the event under discussion soon ceases to be news, and, as interpretations of an event differ, discussions turn from the news to the issues it raises. The clash of opinions and sentiments which discussion invariably evokes usually terminates in some sort of consensus or collective opinion—what we call public opinion. It is upon the interpretation of present events, i.e. news, that public opinion rests. [...]

Freeman, the historian, has said that history is past politics and politics is present history. This puts a great deal of truth into a few words, even if the statement in practice needs some enlargement and some qualification. News, though intimately related to both, is neither history nor politics. It is, nevertheless, the stuff which makes political action, as distinguished from other forms of collective behaviour, possible. [...]

There is a proverbial saying to the effect that it is the unexpected that happens. Since what happens makes news, it follows, or seems to, that news is always or mainly concerned with the unusual and the unexpected. Even the most trivial happening, it seems, provided it represents a departure from the customary ritual and routine of daily life, is likely to be reported in the press. This conception of news has been confirmed by those editors who, in the competition for circulation and for advertising, have sought to make their papers smart and interesting, where they could not be invariably either informing or thrilling. In their efforts to instil into the minds of reporters and correspondents the importance of looking everywhere and always for something that would excite, amuse, or shock its readers, news editors have put into circulation some interesting examples of what the Germans, borrowing an expression from Homer, have called *geflügelte Wörter*, 'winged words'. The epigram describing news which has winged its way over more territory and is repeated more often than any other is this: 'Dog bites man'—that is not news. But 'Man bites dog'—that is. *Nota bene*! It is not the intrinsic importance of an event that makes it newsworthy. It is rather the fact that the event is so unusual that if published it will either startle, amuse, or otherwise excite the reader so that it will be remembered and repeated. For news is always finally, what Charles A. Dana described it to be, 'something that will make people talk', even when it does not make them act. [...]

In order that a report of events current may have the quality of news, it should not merely circulate—possibly in circuitous underground channels—but should be published, if need be by the town crier or the public press. Such publication tends to give news something of the character of a public document. News is more or less authenticated by the fact that it has been exposed to the critical examination of the public to which it is addressed and with whose interests it is concerned.

The public which thus, by common consent or failure to protest, puts the stamp of its approval on a published report does not give to its interpretation the authority of statement that has been subjected to expert historical criticism. Every public has its local prejudices and its own limitations. A more searching examination of the facts would quite possibly reveal to a more critical and enlightened mind the naïve credulity and bias of an unsophisticated public opinion. [. . .]

If it is the unexpected that happens, it is the not wholly unexpected that gets into the news. The events that have made news in the past, as in the present, are actually the expected things. They are characteristically simple and commonplace matters, like births and deaths, weddings and funerals, the conditions of the crops and of business, war, politics, and the weather. These are the expected things, but they are at the same time the unpredictable things. They are the incidents and the chances that turn up in the game of life.

The fact is that the thing that makes news is news interest, and that, as every city editor knows, is a variable quantity—one that has to be reckoned with from the time the city editor sits down at his desk in the morning until the night editor locks up the last form at night. The reason for this is that the news value is relative, and an event that comes later may, and often does, diminish the value of an event that turned up earlier. In that case the less important item has to give way to the later and more important.

The anecdotes and 'believe it or nots' which turn up in the news are valuable to the editor because they can always be lifted out of the printer's form to make way for something hotter and more urgent. In any case it is, on the whole, the accidents and incidents that the public is prepared for; the victories and defeats on the ball field or on the battlefield; the things that one fears and things that one hopes for—that make the news. It is difficult to understand, nevertheless, considering the number of people who are killed and maimed annually by automobile accidents (the number killed in 1938 was 32,600) that these great losses of life rarely make the front page. The difference seems to be that the automobile has come to be accepted as one of the permanent features of civilized life and war has not.

News, therefore, at least in the strict sense of the term, is not a story or an anecdote. It is something that has for the person who hears or reads it an interest that is pragmatic rather than appreciative. News is characteristically, if not always, limited to events that bring about sudden and decisive changes. It may be an incident like that of the coloured family in Philadelphia, Frances and Ben Mason, who won a fortune in the Irish sweepstakes recently.[1] It may be a tragic incident like the battle off the coast of Uruguay which resulted in the destruction of the German battleship, the *Graf Spee*, and the suicide of its captain. These events were not only news—that is, something that brought a sudden decisive change in the previously existing situation—but, as they were related in the newspapers and as we reflected upon them, they tended to

---

1 See *Time*, 25 Dec. 1939, p. 12.

assume a new and ideal significance: the one a story of genuine human interest, the other that of tragedy, something, to use Aristotle's phrase, to inspire 'pity and terror'. Events such as these tend to be remembered. Eventually they may become legends or be recorded in popular ballads. Legends and ballads need no date line or the names of persons or places to authenticate them. They live and survive in our memories and in that of the public because of their human interest. As events they have ceased to exist. They survive as a sort of ghostly symbol of something of universal and perennial interest, an ideal representation of what is true of life and of human nature everywhere.

Thus it seems that news, as a form of knowledge, contributes from its record of events not only to history and to sociology but to folklore and literature; it contributes something not merely to the social sciences but to the humanities. [...]

In the modern world the role of news has assumed increased rather than diminished importance as compared with some other forms of knowledge, history, for example. The changes in recent years have been so rapid and drastic that the modern world seems to have lost its historical perspective, and we appear to be living from day to day in what I have described earlier as a 'specious present'. Under the circumstances history seems to be read or written mainly to enable us, by comparison of the present with the past, to understand what is going on about us rather than, as the historians have told us, to know 'what actually happened'.

Thus Elmer Davis in a recent article in the *Saturday Review* announces as 'required reading' for 1939 two volumes: Hitler's *Mein Kampf* and Thucydides' *History of the Peloponnesian War* (431 BC). He recommends the history of the Peloponnesian War because, as he says, 'Thucydides was not only a brilliant analyst of human behavior both individual and collective' but was at the same time 'a great reporter'.[2]

One notes, also, as characteristic of our times, that since news, as reported in American newspapers, has tended to assume the character of literature, so fiction—after the newspaper the most popular form of literature—has assumed more and more the character of news.[3]

Emile Zola's novels were essentially reports upon contemporary manners in France just as Steinbeck's *The Grapes of Wrath* has been described as an epoch-making report on the share-cropper in the United States.

Ours, it seems, is an age of news, and one of the most important events in American civilization has been the rise of the reporter.

---

2 'Required Reading', *Saturday Review of Literature*, 14 Oct. 1939.

3 See Helen MacGill Hughes, *News and the Human Interest Story* (Chicago: University of Chicago Press, 1940).

3
The Image

From News Gathering to News Making: A Flood of Pseudo-Events

A PSEUDO-EVENT IS a happening that possesses the following characteristics:

1. It is not spontaneous, but comes about because someone has planned, planted, or incited it. Typically, it is not a train wreck or an earthquake, but an interview.

2. It is planted primarily (not always exclusively) for the immediate purpose of being reported or reproduced. Therefore, its occurrence is arranged for the convenience of the reporting or reproducing media. Its success is measured by how widely it is reported. Time relations in it are commonly fictitious or factitious; the announcement is given out in advance 'for future release' and written as if the event had occurred in the past. The question, 'Is it real?' is less important than, 'Is it newsworthy?'

3. Its relation to the underlying reality of the situation is ambiguous. Its interest arises largely from this very ambiguity. Concerning a pseudo-event the question, 'What does it mean?' has a new dimension. While the news interest in a train wreck is in *what* happened and in the real consequences, the interest in an interview is always, in a sense, in *whether* it really happened and in what might have been the motives. Did the statement really mean what it said? Without some of this ambiguity a pseudo-event cannot be very interesting.

4. Usually it is intended to be a self-fulfilling prophecy. The hotel's thirtieth-anniversary celebration, by saying that the hotel is a distinguished institution, actually makes it one.

In the last half century a larger and larger proportion of our experience, of what we read and see and hear, has come to consist of pseudo-events. We expect more of them and we are given more of them. They flood our consciousness. Their multiplication has gone on in the United States at a faster rate than elsewhere. Even the rate of increase is increasing every day. This is true of the world of education, of consumption, and of personal relations. It is especially true of the world of public affairs. [...]

We begin to be puzzled about what is really the 'original' of an event. The authentic news record of what 'happens' or is said comes increasingly to seem to be what is given out in advance. More and more news events become dramatic performances in which 'men in the news' simply act out more or less well their prepared script. The story prepared 'for future release' acquires an authenticity that competes with that of the actual occurrences on the scheduled date.

In recent years our successful politicians have been those most adept at using the press and other means to create pseudo-events. President Franklin Delano Roosevelt, whom Heywood Broun called 'the best newspaperman who has ever been President of the United States', was the first modern master. While newspaper owners opposed him in editorials which few read, F. D. R. himself, with the collaboration of a friendly corps of Washington correspondents, was using front-page headlines to make news read by everybody. He was making 'facts'—pseudo-events—while editorial writers were simply expressing opinions. It is a familiar story how he employed the trial balloon, how he exploited the ethic of off-the-record remarks, how he transformed the Presidential press conference from a boring ritual into a major national institution which no later President dared disrespect, and how he developed the fireside chat. Knowing that newspapermen lived on news, he helped them manufacture it. And he knew enough about news-making techniques to help shape their stories to his own purposes. [. . .]

Nowadays a successful reporter must be the midwife—or more often the conceiver—of his news. By the interview technique he incites a public figure to make statements which will sound like news. During the twentieth century this technique has grown into a devious apparatus which, in skilful hands, can shape national policy.

The pressure of time, and the need to produce a uniform news stream to fill the issuing media, induce Washington correspondents and others to use the interview and other techniques for making pseudo-events in novel, ever more ingenious and aggressive ways. [. . .]

In many subtle ways, the rise of pseudo-events has mixed up our roles as actors and as audience—or, the philosophers would say, as 'object' and as 'subject'. Now we can oscillate between the two roles. [. . .]

An admirable example of this new intertwinement of subject and object, of the history and the historian, of the actor and the reporter, is the so-called news 'leak'. By now the leak has become an important and well-established institution in American politics. It is, in fact, one of the main vehicles for communicating important information from officials to the public.

A clue to the new unreality of the citizen's world is the perverse new meaning now given to the word 'leak'. To leak, according to the dictionary, is to 'let a fluid substance out or in accidentally: as, the ship leaks'. But nowadays a news leak is one of the most elaborately planned ways of emitting information. It is, of course, a way in which a government official, with some clearly defined purpose (a leak, even more than a direct announcement, is apt to have some definite devious purpose behind it) makes an announcement, asks a question, or puts a suggestion. It might more accurately be called a 'sub rosa announcement', an 'indirect statement', or 'cloaked news'.

The news leak is a pseudo-event par excellence. In its origin and growth, the leak illustrates another axiom of the world of pseudo-events: pseudo-events produce more pseudo-events. [. . .]

Pseudo-events spawn other pseudo-events in geometric progression. This is partly because every kind of pseudo-event (being planned) tends to become ritualized, with a protocol and a rigidity all its own. As each type of pseudo-event acquires this rigidity, pressures arise to produce other, derivative, forms of pseudo-event which are more fluid, more tantalizing, and more interestingly ambiguous. Thus, as the press conference (itself a pseudo-event) became formalized, there grew up the institutionalized leak. As the leak becomes formalized still other devices will appear. Of course the shrewd politician or the enterprising newsman knows this and knows how to take advantage of it. Seldom for outright deception; more often simply to make more 'news', to provide more 'information', or to 'improve communication'. [...]

These pseudo-events which flood our consciousness must be distinguished from propaganda. The two do have some characteristics in common. But our peculiar problems come from the fact that pseudo-events are in some respects the opposite of the propaganda which rules totalitarian countries. Propaganda—as prescribed, say, by Hitler in *Mein Kampf*—is information intentionally biased. Its effect depends primarily on its emotional appeal. While a pseudo-event is an ambiguous truth, propaganda is an appealing falsehood. Pseudo-events thrive on our honest desire to be informed, to have 'all the facts', and even to have more facts than there really are. But propaganda feeds on our willingness to be inflamed. Pseudo-events appeal to our duty to be educated, propaganda appeals to our desire to be aroused. While propaganda substitutes opinion for facts, pseudo-events are synthetic facts which move people indirectly, by providing the 'factual' basis on which they are supposed to make up their minds. Propaganda moves them directly by explicitly making judgements for them.

In a totalitarian society, where people are flooded by purposeful lies, the real facts are of course misrepresented, but the representation itself is not ambiguous. The propaganda lie is asserted as if it were true. Its object is to lead people to believe that the truth is simpler, more intelligible, than it really is. [. . .] But in our society, pseudo-events make simple facts seem more subtle, more ambiguous, and more speculative than they really are. Propaganda oversimplifies experience, pseudo-events overcomplicate it.

At first it may seem strange that the rise of pseudo-events has coincided with the growth of the professional ethic which obliges newsmen to omit editorializing and personal judgements from their news accounts. But now it is in the making of pseudo-events that newsmen find ample scope for their individuality and creative imagination.

In a democratic society like ours—and more especially in a highly literate, wealthy, competitive, and technologically advanced society—the people can be flooded by pseudo-events. For us, freedom of speech and of the press and of broadcasting includes freedom to create pseudo-events. Competing politicians, competing newsmen, and competing news media contest in this creation. They vie with one another in offering attractive, 'informative' accounts and images of the world. They are free to speculate on the facts, to bring new facts into being, to demand answers to their own contrived questions. Our 'free market place of ideas' is a place where people are confronted by competing pseudo-events and are allowed to judge among them. When we speak of 'informing' the people this is what we really mean. [...]

Here are some characteristics of pseudo-events which make them over-shadow spontaneous events:

1. Pseudo-events are more dramatic. A television debate between candidates can be planned to be more suspenseful (for example, by reserving questions which are then popped suddenly) than a casual encounter or consecutive formal speeches planned by each separately.

2. Pseudo-events, being planned for dissemination, are easier to disseminate and to make vivid. Participants are selected for their newsworthy and dramatic interest.

3. Pseudo-events can be repeated at will, and thus their impression can be re-enforced.

4. Pseudo-events cost money to create; hence somebody has an interest in disseminating, magnifying, advertising, and extolling them as events worth watching or worth believing. They are therefore advertised in advance, and rerun in order to get money's worth.

5. Pseudo-events, being planned for intelligibility, are more intelligible and hence more reassuring. Even if we cannot discuss intelligently the qualifications of the candidates or the complicated issues, we can at least judge the effectiveness of a television performance. How comforting to have some political matter we can grasp!

6. Pseudo-events are more sociable, more conversable, and more convenient to witness. Their occurrence is planned for our convenience. The Sunday newspaper appears when we have a lazy morning for it. Television programs appear when we are ready with our glass of beer. In the office the next morning, Jack Paar's (or any other star performer's) regular late-night show at the usual hour will overshadow in conversation a casual event that suddenly came up and had to find its way into the news.

7. Knowledge of pseudo-events—of what has been reported, or what has been staged, and how—becomes the test of being 'informed'. News magazines provide us regularly with quiz questions concerning not what has happened but concerning 'names in the news'—what has been reported in the news magazines. Pseudo-events begin to provide that 'common discourse' which some of my old-fashioned friends have hoped to find in the Great Books.

8. Finally, pseudo-events spawn other pseudo-events in geometric progression. They dominate our consciousness simply because there are more of them, and ever more. [...]

A perfect example of how pseudo-events can dominate is the recent popularity of the quiz show format. Its original appeal came less from the fact that such shows were tests of intelligence (or of dissimulation) than from the fact that the situations were elaborately contrived—with isolation booths, armed bank guards, and all the rest—and they purported to inform the public.

The application of the quiz show format to the so-called 'Great Debates' between Presidential candidates in the election of 1960 is only another example. These four campaign programmes, pompously and self-righteously advertised by the broadcasting networks, were remarkably successful in reducing great national issues to trivial dimensions. With appropriate vulgarity, they might have been called the $400,000 Question (Prize: a $100,000-a-year job for four years). They were a clinical example of the pseudo-event, of how it is made, why it appeals, and of its consequences for democracy in America.

In origin the Great Debates were confusedly collaborative between politicians and news makers. Public interest centered around the pseudo-event itself: the lighting, make-up, ground rules, whether notes would be allowed, etc. Far more interest was shown in the performance than in what was said. The pseudo-events spawned in turn by the Great Debates were numberless. People who had seen the shows read about them the more avidly, and listened eagerly for interpretations by news commentators. Representatives of both parties made 'statements' on the probable effects of the debates. Numerous interviews and discussion programmes were broadcast exploring their meaning. Opinion polls kept us informed on the nuances of our own and other people's reactions. Topics of speculation multiplied. Even the question whether there should be a fifth debate became for a while a lively 'issue'.

The drama of the situation was mostly specious, or at least had an extremely ambiguous relevance to the main (but forgotten) issue: which participant was better qualified for the Presidency. Of course, a man's ability, while standing under *klieg* lights, without notes, to answer in two and a half minutes a question kept secret until that moment, had only the most dubious relevance—if any at all—to his real qualifications to make deliberate Presidential decisions on long-standing public questions after being instructed by a corps of advisers. The great Presidents in our history (with the possible exception of F. D. R.) would have done miserably; but our most notorious demagogues would have shone. [. . .]

Pseudo-events thus lead to emphasis on pseudo-qualifications. Again the self-fulfilling prophecy. If we test Presidential candidates by their talents on TV quiz performances, we will, of course, choose presidents for precisely these qualifications. In a democracy, reality tends to conform to the pseudo-event. Nature imitates art.

We are frustrated by our very efforts publicly to unmask the pseudo-event. Whenever we describe the lighting, the make-up, the studio setting, the rehearsals, etc., we simply arouse more interest. One newsman's interpretation makes us more eager to hear another's. One commentator's speculation that the debates may have little significance makes us curious to hear whether another commentator disagrees.

Pseudo-events do, of course, increase our illusion of grasp on the world, what some have called the American illusion of omnipotence. Perhaps, we come to think, the world's problems can really be settled by 'statements', by 'Summit' meetings, by a competition of 'prestige', by overshadowing images, and by political quiz shows.

Once we have tasted the charm of pseudo-events, we are tempted to believe they are the only important events. Our progress poisons the sources of our experience. And the poison tastes so sweet that it spoils our appetite for plain fact. Our seeming ability to satisfy our exaggerated expectations makes us forget that they are exaggerated.

4

The Structure of Foreign News

Johan Galtung and Mari Holmboe Ruge

IMAGINE THAT THE world can be likened to an enormous set of broadcasting stations, each one emitting its signal or its programme at its proper wavelength. (Another metaphor might be of a set of atoms of different kinds emitting waves corresponding to their condition.) The emission is continuous, corresponding to the truism that something is always happening to any person in the world. Even if he sleeps quietly, sleep is 'happening'[1]—what we choose to consider an 'event' is culturally determined. The set of world events, then, is like the cacophony of sound one gets by scanning the dial of one's radio receiver, and particularly confusing if this is done quickly on the medium-wave or short-wave dials. Obviously this cacophony does not make sense, it may become meaningful only if one station is tuned in and listened to for some time before one switches on to the next one.

Since we cannot register everything, we have to select, and the question is what will strike our attention. This is a problem in the psychology of perception and the following is a short list of some obvious implications of this metaphor:

F_1: If the frequency of the signal is outside the dial it will not be recorded.

F_2: The stronger the signal, the greater the amplitude, the more probable that it will be recorded as worth listening to.

F_3: The more clear and unambiguous the signal (the less noise there is), the more probable that it will be recorded as worth listening to.

F_4: The more meaningful the signal, the more probable that it will be recorded as worth listening to.

Source: Johan Galtung and Mari Holmboe Ruge, 'The Structure of Foreign News', *Journal of International Peace Research*, 1 (1965), 64–90. This is a much revised and extended version of a paper presented at the First Nordic Conference on Peace Research, Oslo, 4–8 January 1963 and as a guest lecture at Danmarks Journalisthöjskole, Århus, May, 1964, here published as Peace Research Institute, Oslo publication No. 14–2. The authors wish to express their gratitude to the Institute for Social Research, the Norwegian Research Council for Science and the Humanities, and the Norwegian Council for Research on Conflict and Peace for financial support; to stud.mag.art. Marit Halle and stud.mag.art. Elisabeth Bögh for assistance with the data-collection and to our friends and colleagues at PRIO and particularly to Einar Östgaard for stimulating criticism and suggestions.

1 For an impression of what sociologists can get out of the condition of sleeping see Vilhelm Aubert and Harrison White, 'Sleep: A Sociological Interpretation', *Acta Sociologica*, 4/2: 46–54 and 4/3: 1–16.

F_5: The more consonant the signal is with the mental image of what one expects to find, the more probable that it will be recorded as worth listening to.

F_6: The more unexpected the signal, the more probable that it will be recorded as worth listening to.

F_7: If one signal has been tuned in to the more likely it will continue to be tuned in to as worth listening to.

F_8: The more a signal has been tuned in to, the more probable that a very different kind of signal will be recorded as worth listening to next time.

Some comments on these factors are in order. They are nothing but common-sense perception psychology translated into radio-scanning and event-scanning activities. The proper thing to do in order to test their validity would be to observe journalists at work or radio listeners operating with the dial—and we have no such data. For want of this the factors should be anchored in general reasoning and social science findings. [. . .]

The first factor is trivial when applied to radio sets, less so when applied to events in general. Since this is a metaphor and not a model we shall be liberal in our interpretation of frequency and proceed as follows. By the 'frequency' of an event we refer to the time-span needed for the event to unfold itself and acquire meaning. For a soldier to die during a battle this time-span is very short; for a development process in a country to take place the time-span may be very long. Just as the radio dial has its limitation with regard to electro-magnetic waves, so will the newspaper have its limitations, and the thesis is that *the more similiar the frequency of the event is to the frequency of the news medium, the more probable that it will be recorded as news by that news medium.* A murder takes little time and the event takes place between the publication of two successive issues of a daily, which means that a meaningful story can be told from one day to the next. But to single out one murder during a battle where there is one person killed every minute would make little sense—one will typically only record the battle as such (if newspapers were published every minute the perspective could possibly be changed to the individual soldier). Correspondingly, the event that takes place over a longer time-span will go unrecorded unless it reaches some kind of dramatic climax (the building of a dam goes unnoticed but not its inauguration). Needless to say, this under-reporting of trends is to some extent corrected by publications with a lower frequency. A newspaper may have a habit of producing weekly 'reviews', there are weeklies and monthlies and quarterlies and yearbooks—and there are *ad hoc* publications. If we concentrate on dailies, however, the thesis is probably valid and probably of some heuristic value when other aspects of news communication are to be unravelled.

The second thesis is simply that there is something corresponding to the idea of 'amplitude' for radio waves. What this says is only that the bigger the dam, the more will its inauguration be reported *ceteris paribus*; the more violent the murder the bigger the headlines it will make. It says nothing about what has greater amplitude, the dam or the murder. It can also be put in a more dichotomous form: there is a threshold the event will have to pass before it will be recorded at all.[2] This is a truism, but an important one.

The third hypothesis is also trivial at the radio level but not at the news level. What is 'signal' and what is 'noise' is not inherent; it is a question of convention,[3] as seen clearly when two radio stations are sending on the same frequency. Clarity in this connection must refer to some kind of one-dimensionality, that there is only one or a limited number of meanings in what is received. Thus interpreted the hypothesis says simply the following: the less ambiguity the more the event will be noticed. This is not quite the same as preferring the simple to the complex, but one precization of it rather; an event with a clear interpretation, free from ambiguities in its meaning, is preferred to the highly ambiguous event from which many and inconsistent implications can and will be made.[4]

The fourth hypothesis also deals with meaning but not with its ambiguity. 'Meaningful' has some major interpretations. One of them is 'interpretable within the cultural framework of the listener or reader' and all the thesis says is that actually some measure of *ethnocentrism* will be operative: there has to be *cultural proximity*. That is, the event-scanner will pay particular attention to the familiar, to the culturally similar, and the culturally distant will be passed by more easily and not be noticed. It is somewhat like the North European radio listener in say, Morocco: he will probably pass by the Arab music and speech he can get on his dial as quaint and meaningless and find relief in European music and French talk.

The other dimension of 'meaningful' is in terms of *relevance*: an event may happen in a culturally distant place but still be loaded with meaning in terms of what it may imply for the reader or listener. Thus the culturally remote country may be brought in via a pattern of conflict with one's own group.[5]

2   This, of course, is a fundamental idea in the psychology of perception. Actually there are two separate ideas inherent here: the notion of an absolute level that must not be too low, and the notion of the increase needed to be noticed—the 'just noticeable differences' (jnd's). The jnd increases with increasing absolute level; the stronger the amplitude, the more difference is needed to be noticed (whether this is according to Weber's principle or not). This principle probably applies very explicitly to news communication: the more dramatic the news, the more is needed to add to the drama. This may lead to important distortions. The more drama there already is, the more will the news media have to exaggerate to capture new interest, which leads to the hypothesis that there is more exaggeration the more dramatic the event—i.e. the less necessary one might feel it is to exaggerate.

3   N. R. Ashby in *An Introduction to Cybernetics* (New York: Wiley, 1957) defines noise simply as distortion that may create differences in interpretation at the sender and receiver ends of a communication channel. But one may just as well say that the signal distorts the noise as vice versa.

4   B. Berelson and G. A. Steiner in their *Human Behaviour: An Inventory of Scientific Findings* (New York: Harcourt, Brace & World, 1963) mention a number of principles under 'Perceiving', and two of them are (p. 112 and p. 100):
   B7: The greater the ambiguity of the stimulus, the more room and need for interpretation.
   B3.3a: There may also be decreased awareness of stimuli if it is important *not* to see (perceptual defence).
   What we have been doing is to combine these theorems (but not deductively) into the idea of defence against ambiguity. There are several reasons for this. Modern newspapers are mass media of communication, at least most of them, and publishers may feel (justifiably or not) that increase in ambiguity may decrease the sales. Moreover, to the extent that news shall serve as a basis for action orientation ambiguity will increase rather than reduce the uncertainty and provide a poorer basis for action.

5   The common factor behind both dimensions of what we have called 'meaningfulness' is probably 'identification'.

The fifth hypothesis links what is selected to the mental pre-image, where the word 'expects' can and should be given both its cognitive interpretation as 'predicts' and its normative interpretation as 'wants'. A person *predicts* that something will happen and this creates a mental matrix for easy reception and registration of the event if it does finally take place. Or he *wants* it to happen and the matrix is even more prepared, so much so that he may distort perceptions he receives and provide himself with images consonant with what he has wanted. In the sense mentioned here 'news' are actually 'olds', because they correspond to what one expects to happen—and if they are too far away from the expectation they will not be registered, according to this hypothesis of consonance.[6]

The sixth hypothesis brings in a corrective to the fourth and fifth. The idea is simply that it is not enough for an event to be culturally meaningful and consonant with what it expected—this defines only a vast set of possible news candidates. Within this set, according to the hypothesis, the more unexpected have the highest chances of being included as news. It is the unexpected *within the meaningful and the consonant* that is brought to one's attention, and by 'unexpected' we simply mean essentially two things: *unexpected* or *rare*. Thus, what is regular and institutionalized, continuing and repetitive at regular and short intervals, does not attract nearly so much attention, *ceteris paribus*, as the unexpected and *ad hoc*—a circumstance that is probably well known to the planners of summit meetings.[7] Events have to be unexpected or rare, or preferably both, to become good news.

The seventh hypothesis is the idea that once something has hit the headlines and been defined as 'news', then it will *continue* to be defined as news for some time even if the amplitude is drastically reduced.[8] The channel has been opened and stays partly open to justify its being opened in the first place, partly because of inertia in the system and partly because what was unexpected has now also become familiar. Thus F_7 is, in a sense, deducible from F_3 and F_6.

The eighth and final hypothesis refers to the *composition* of such units as evening entertainment for the family around the radio set, the front page of a newspaper, the newscast on radio, the newsreel on TV or in the cinema, and so on. The idea is this: imagine the news editor of a broadcasting station has received only news from abroad and only of a certain type. Some minutes before he is on the air he gets some insignificant domestic news and some foreign news of a different kind. The hypothesis is that the threshold value for these news items will be much lower than would otherwise have been the

---

6 Again, some findings from Berelson and Steiner are useful (*Human Behaviour*, 101 and 529):

B3.2: With regard to expectations, other things being equal, people are more likely to attend to aspects of the environment they anticipate than to those they do not, and they are more likely to anticipate things they are familiar with.

B3.3: With regard to motives, not only do people look for things they need or want; but the stronger the need, the greater the tendency to ignore irrelevant elements.

A1: People tend to see and hear communications that are favourable to their predispositions; they are more likely to see and hear congenial communications than neutral or hostile ones. And the more interested they are in the subject, the more likely is such selective attention.

7 For a discussion of this see Johan Galtung, 'Summit Meetings and International Relations', *Journal of Peace Research* (1964), 36–54.

8 For a discussion of this factor see Östgaard, 'Factors Influencing the Flow of News', *Journal of Peace Research*, 1 (1965), 151.

case, because of a desire to present a 'balanced' whole. Correspondingly, if there are already many foreign news items the threshold value for a new item will be increased.

As mentioned, these eight factors are based on fairly simple reasoning about what facilitates and what impedes perception. They are held to be culture-free in the sense that we do not expect them to vary significantly with variations in human culture—they should not depend much on cultural parameters. More particularly, we would not expect them to vary much along the east-west, north-south or centre-periphery axes which we often make use of to structure the world. In particular, these factors should be relatively independent of some other major determinants of the press. A newspaper may vary in the degree to which it caters to mass circulation and a free market economy. If it wants a mass circulation, all steps in the news chain will probably anticipate the reaction of the next step in the chain and accentuate the selection and distortion effects in order to make the material more compatible with their image of what the readers want. Moreover, a newspaper may vary in the degree to which it tries to present many aspects of the situation, or, rather, like the partners in a court case, try to present only the material that is easily compatible with its own political point of view. In the latter case selection and distortion will probably be accentuated and certainly not decrease.

But there is little doubt that there are also culture-bound factors influencing the transition from events to news, and we shall mention four such factors that we deem to be important at least in the north-western corner of the world. They are:

F_9 : The more the event concerns élite nations, the more probable that it will become a news item.

F_{10}: The more the event concerns élite people, the more probable that it will become a news item.

F_{11}: The more the event can be seen in personal terms, as due to the action of specific individuals, the more probable that it will become a news item.

F_{12}: The more negative the event in its consequences, the more probable that it will become a news item.

Again, some comments are in order.

That news is *élite-centred*, in terms of nations or in terms of people, is hardly strange. The actions of the élite are, at least usually and in short-term perspective, more consequential than the activities of others: this applies to élite nations as well as to élite people. Moreover, as amply demonstrated by the popular magazines found in most countries, the élite can be used in a sense to tell about everybody. A story about how the king celebrates his birthday will contain many elements that could just as well have been told about anybody, but who in particular among ordinary men and women should be picked for the telling of the story? Elite people are available to serve as objects of general identification, not only because of their intrinsic importance. Thus in an élite-centred news communication system ordinary people are not even given the chance of representing themselves. *Mutatis mutandis*, the same should apply to nations.

More problematic is the idea of *personification*. The thesis is that news has a tendency to present events as sentences where there is a subject, a named person or collectivity consisting of a few persons, and the event is then seen as a consequence of the actions of this person or these persons. The alternative would be to present events as the outcome of 'social forces', as structural more than idiosyncratic outcomes of the society which produced them. In a structural presentation the names of the actors would disappear much as they do in sociological analysis and much for the same reason—the thesis is that the presentation actually found is more similar to what one finds in traditional personified historical analysis. To the extent that this is the case the problem is *why*, and we have five different explanations to offer:

1. Personification is an outcome of *cultural idealism* according to which man is the master of his own destiny and events can be seen as the outcome of an act of free will. In a culture with a more materialistic outlook this should not be the case. Structural factors should be emphasized, there will be more events happening to people or with people as instruments than events caused by people.

2. Personification is a consequence of the need for meaning and consequently for *identification*: persons can serve more easily as objects of positive and negative identification through a combination of projection and empathy.

3. Personification is an outcome of the *frequency-factor*: persons can act during a time-span that fits the frequency of the news media, 'structures' are more difficult to pin down in time and space.

4. Personification can be seen as a direct consequence of the *élite-concentration* but as distinct from it.

5. Personification is more in agreement with modern techniques of news gathering and news presentation. Thus, it is easier to take a photo of a person than of a 'structure' (the latter is better for movies—perhaps), and whereas one interview yields a necessary and sufficient basis for one person-centred news story, a structure-centred news story will require many interviews, observation techniques, data gathering, etc. Obviously, there is an egg-chicken argument implied here since it may also be argued that personification came first and that techniques, the whole structure of news communication, were developed accordingly.

We only offer those explanations without choosing between them; first of all because there is no reason to choose as long as they do not contradict each other, and secondly because we have neither data nor theory that can provide us with a rational basis for a choice. It is our hunch that future research will emphasize that these factors reinforce each other in producing personification.

When we claim that *negative* news will be preferred to positive news we are saying nothing more sophisticated than what most people seem to refer to when they say that 'there is so little to be happy about in the news', etc. But we can offer a number of reasons why this state of affairs appears likely, just as we did for the factor of personification. We shall do so using the other factors relatively systematically:

1. Negative news enters the news channel more easily because it satisfies the *frequency* criterion better. There is a *basic asymmetry* in life between the positive, which is difficult and takes time, and the negative, which is much easier and takes less time—compare the amount of time needed to bring up and socialize an adult person and the amount of time needed to kill him in an accident: the amount of time needed to build a house and to destroy it in a fire, to make an aeroplane and to crash it, and so on. The positive cannot be too easy, for then it would have low scarcity value. Thus, a negative event can more easily unfold itself completely between two issues of a newspaper and two newscast transmissions—for a positive event this is more difficult and specific. Inaugurating or culminating events are needed. A PR-minded operator will, of course, see to that—but he is not always present.

2. Negative news will more easily be *consensual and unambiguous* in the sense that there will be agreement about the interpretation of the event as negative. A 'positive' event may be positive to some people and not to others and hence not satisfy the criterion of unambiguity. Its meaning will be blurred by other overtones and undertones.

3. Negative news is said to be more *consonant* with at least some dominant pre-images of our time. The idea must be that negative news fulfils some latent or manifest needs and that many people have such needs. Of the many theories in this field we prefer the cognitive dissonance version because it is falsifiable. The theory, however, presupposes a relatively high level of general anxiety to provide a sufficient matrix in which negative news can be embedded with much consonance. This should be the case during crises,[9] so a test of this theory would be that during crises news that is not related to the crisis tends to be more negative and not more positive (as a theory of compensation rather than of dissonance/reduction would predict).

4. Negative news is more *unexpected* than positive news, both in the sense that the events referred to are more rare, and in the sense that they are less predictable. This presupposes a culture where changes to the positive, in other words 'progress', are somehow regarded as the normal and trivial thing that can pass under-reported because it represents nothing new. The negative curls and eddies rather than the steady positive flow will be reported. The test of this theory would be a culture with *regress* as the normal, and in that case one would

---

9 Festinger has a very interesting account of how Indians selected rumours following an earthquake, and consistent with the fear provoked by the earthquake: 'Let us speculate about the content of the cognition of these persons. When the earthquake was over they had this strong, persistent fear reaction but they could see nothing different around them, no destruction, no further threatening things. In short, a situation had been produced where dissonance existed between cognition corresponding to the fear they felt and the knowledge of what they saw around them which, one might say, amounted to the cognition that there was nothing to be afraid of. The vast majority of the rumours which were widely circulated were rumours which, if believed, provided cognition consonant with being afraid. One might even call them "fear-provoking" rumours, although, if our interpretation is correct, they would more properly be called "fear justifying" rumours.' Leon Festinger, 'The Motivating Effect of Cognitive Dissonance', in Gardner Lindzey (ed.), *Assessment of Human Motives* (New York: Grove Press, 1958), 72.

predict over-reporting of positive news. This is exemplified by news about the illness of an important person: the slightest improvement is over-reported relative to a steady decline.

Again we do not have sufficient theory to make a choice between these possible explanations—nor do we have to do so since they do not exclude each other.

As to these last four factors it was mentioned that they seem to be of particular importance in the northwestern corner of the world. This does not mean that they are not operating in other areas, but one could also imagine other patterns of relationship between the set of events and the set of news. Table 1 shows some examples.

TABLE 1. *Some patterns of news structure*

Pattern	F_9 nation	F_{10} people	F_{11} personification	F_{12} negativization
1	élite centred	élite centred	person centred	negative centred
2	élite centred	élite centred	structure centred	positive centred
3	élite centred	élite centred	both	negative centred
4	non-élite centred	élite centred	person centred	positive centred

Pattern 1 is the pattern we have described above. Pattern 2 would, where the last two aspects are concerned, be more in agreement with socialist thinking, and where the first two are concerned, with big-power thinking. It might fit the news structure of the Soviet Union, but with the important proviso that one would probably use Pattern 3 to describe Western powers. Similarly, a newly independent developing nation might use Pattern 4 for itself, but also receive pattern 3 for former colonial powers. But all this is very speculative.[10]

Let us then list systematically the twelve factors we have concentrated on in this analysis; with subfactors:

Events become news to the extent that they satisfy the conditions of:

F_1 : frequency
F_2 : threshold
$F_{2.1}$: absolute intensity

---

10 As an example some impressions can be given from three months' systematic reading of the Moroccan newspaper *Le Petit Marocain*. In very summarized form: the first page contained news about progress in Morocco, the second about decadence, murder, rape, and violence in France—so that anybody could draw his conclusion. Of course, such things will depend rather heavily on the value-systems of the editorial staff—but we nevertheless postulate the existence of general patterns. Ola Mårtensson, in a mimeographed report (in Swedish) of a content analysis of three major papers in the USSR, indicates both personification and élite concentration. Ola Mårtensson, *Pravda, Izvestija och Krasanaja Zvezda under våren hösten 1964* (Lund: Institute for Political Science, Lund University, Sweden, 1965), 26 pp. mimeo.

$F_{2.2}$: intensity increase
F_3 : unambiguity
F_4 : meaningfulness
$F_{4.1}$: cultural proximity
$F_{4.2}$: relevance
F_5 : consonance
$F_{5.1}$: predictability
$F_{5.2}$: demand
F_6 : unexpectedness
$F_{6.1}$: unpredictability
$F_{6.2}$: scarcity
F_7 : continuity
F_8 : composition
F_9 : reference to élite nations
F_{10} : reference to élite people
F_{11} : reference to persons
F_{12} : reference to something negative

As mentioned, these twelve factors are not independent of each other: there are interesting interrelations between them. However, we shall not attempt to 'axiomatize' on this meagre basis.

Let us now imagine that all these factors are operating. This means, we hypothesize, three things:

1. The more events satisfy the criteria mentioned, the more likely that they will be registered as news (selection).

2. Once a news item has been selected what makes it newsworthy according to the factors will be accentuated (distortion).

3. Both the process of selection and the process of distortion will take place at all steps in the chain from event to reader (replication).

Thus the longer the chain, the more selection and distortion will take place according to this—but the more material will there also be to select from and to distort if one thinks of the press agencies relative to special correspondents. In other words, we hypothesize that every link in the chain reacts to what it receives fairly much according to the same principles. The journalist scans the phenomena (in practice to a large extent by scanning other newspapers) and selects and distorts, and so does the reader when he gets the finished product, the news pages, and so do all the middle-men. And so do, we assume, people in general when they report something, and, for instance, diplomats when they gather material for a dispatch to their ministry—partly because they are conditioned by their psychology and their culture, partly because this is reinforced by the newspapers.

In general this means that the cumulative effects of the factors should be considerable and produce an image of the world different from 'what really happened'—for instance in the ways indicated by Östgaard.[11] However, since we have no base-line in direct reports on 'what really happened' on which this can be tested we shall proceed in a different direction. Our

---

11 Östgaard, 'Factors Influencing the Flow of News', 52 ff.

problem is how the factors relate to each other in producing a final outcome. [...]

The policy implications of this article are rather obvious: try to counteract all twelve factors. More specifically, this means:

1. More emphasis on build-up and background material in the total media output. Journalists should be better trained to capture and report on long-term development, and concentrate less on 'events'.

2. Occasional reports on the trivial even if it does not make 'news', to counterbalance the image of the world as composed of strings of dramatic events.

3. More emphasis on complex and ambiguous events, not necessarily with any effort to interpret them.

4. More reports from culturally distant zones even if the content has no immediate relevance for oneself. Experiments with newspapers in different countries exchanging local columns might prove even more interesting than reprinting what was said in the newspaper fifty or a hundred years ago.

5. More emphasis on the dissonant, on that which does not fit stereotypes. Training of journalists to increase their insights into their own stereotypes so as to facilitate their awareness of the consonance factor.

6. More emphasis given to the predictable and frequent, for the same reason as under 2 above.

7. More awareness of the continuity factor—and at the same time more emphasis on follow-ups even if the chain of events has been interrupted for some time. Often one has the impression that one hears about something negative that has happened but not about how it has been counteracted, if the time-span is so long that the continuity has been broken.

8. More awareness of the composition factor in order not to create news artefacts.

9. More coverage of non-élite nations.

10. More coverage of non-élite people.

11. More reference to non-personal causes of events. Special training is probably needed here.

12. More reference to positive events.

These implications work on one factor at a time and would, if implemented, reduce the effects of the factors. However, the combined effects of the factors might still persist even if the effect of any one factor is reduced.

One might say that all or much of this is what the élite paper tries to do, and that is probably true. However, élite papers are probably mainly read by élite people and this may increase the distance between centre and periphery where international perspective is concerned.

Hence one additional need is for a more widely dispersed style of news communication in agreement with these principles. It should be emphasized, however, that the present article hypothesizes rather than demonstrates the presence of these factors, and hypothesizes rather than demonstrates that these factors, if present, have certain effects among the audience.

5

Newsmaking

Bernard Roshco

The Difficulty of Defining News

NEWS IS MORE easily pursued than defined, a characteristic it shares with such other enthralling abstractions as love and truth. The difficulty that newsmen have in defining the product for which they are responsible is exemplified in this statement by a former editor of the *New York Times*, who told a television interviewer, 'My own definition of news is that it is something you didn't know before, had forgotten, or didn't understand.'[1] In that case, looking up a word in the dictionary is a way of getting the latest news. Equating news with every kind of freshly acquired information does more to becloud than to clarify what is distinctive about the information published as news. Such a definition casts no light on the criteria that editors necessarily employ, each day, to decide which news to offer their audiences.

Efforts to define news tend to dissolve into lists of newsmaking events. The best-known definition only describes what is alleged to be an unmistakable news event: 'When a dog bites a man, that is not news; but when a man bites a dog, that is news.'[2] If a cub reporter brought his editor this exemplary news story, he would inevitably be asked: 'Who was the man?' He might also be asked, 'Who was the dog?' An ordinary citizen who nibbled on a nameless canine might rate a paragraph.[3] Such an act by an inmate of a mental institution would not, in all likelihood, be reported at all. But, if either of these anonymous humans bit a notable canine, such as Lassie, the occurrence would blossom in importance as news. Similarly, when a notable human, President Lyndon Johnson, merely pulled his dog's ears on the White House lawn, that act made the front pages.

Source: Bernard Roshco, *Newsmaking* (Chicago and London: University of Chicago Press, 1975).

1 Attributed to Turner Catledge, former executive editor of the *New York Times*, in Dennis J. Chase, 'The Aphilosophy of Journalism', *The Quill* 59 (Sept. 1971), 16.

2 Attributed to John B. Bogart, city editor of the *New York Sun* (c.1880), in Burton Stevenson (ed.), *The Home Book of Proverbs, Maxims and Familiar Phrases* (New York: Macmillan, 1948), 1682. The statement has been attributed to various journalists including, as this reference notes, Charles A. Dana, editor of the *Sun* at that time.

3 A comparable 'story,' of man saving rescue-dog, rated a paragraph in the *New York Times* under the headline, 'Man Rescues St Bernard':
GLENS FALLS, N.Y. (AP)—They were the right subjects for a winter rescue story—a man and a St Bernard dog—but the rest of the saga was a little twisted. Duchess, the St Bernard, was discovered struggling in the icy waters of nearby Glen Lake by Dick Tomb. Mr Tomb, who was walking to work, plunged into the water and rescued the 125-pound dog. (*New York Times*, 1 June 1971, city edn. p. 60.)

Answers to the question, 'Who bit whom?' do not constitute a definition of news; rather, they form a scale of news value and recall another well-known maxim of journalism, 'Names make news'. Why 'names' make news and what they must do in order to make news are questions that cannot be confronted until news itself has been more closely examined.

A definition of news should encompass both 'negative' and 'positive' news, making possible an explanation of why an armistice has as much news value as a declaration of war and why a moon-landing rates as large a banner headline as the dropping of an atomic bomb.[4] Such a definition promotes understanding of the newsmaking process. It also provides insight into why, in daily practice, conflict and crisis are the stuff of front-page stories more often than amity and success, regardless of the social and political values of individual journalists. [...]

Any division of labour requires individuals to inform themselves about the activities of others, making news an inherent part of organized social life. The technology of modern communication did not change the intrinsic nature of news. But it did enlarge the quantity of news that is collected and disseminated, speed the pace at which it is transmitted, and create diverse means of presenting it to the public. Yet, in a sense, broadcasting is an extension of the oldest means of circulating news, passing it by word of mouth.

News in general cannot, therefore, be defined in terms of news media, having existed long before any institution for disseminating it. In the fifth century BC, Sophocles wrote, in *Antigone*, a line anticipating some of the press's contemporary critics: 'No man delights in the bearer of bad news.'[5] Shakespeare has characters in several of his plays inquiring for the latest news: In *King John*, 'What's the news?'[6] In *The Merchant of Venice*, 'What's news of the Rialto?'[7]

News is continually sought and offered in the course of social communication because it is a necessary, and therefore valuable, commodity of social exchange. The urgent need for news arises in every social organization, from the nuclear family to a complex bureaucracy. Within groups, up-to-date information regarding adherence to social norms is a requisite for exercising social control and maintaining social cohesion. Between groups, either conflict or co-operation is dependent upon news of the attitudes and behaviour of groups with whom there is interaction.

News is a consequence of the human desire—and need—to know the state of the surrounding social and physical environment. 'What's the news?' is a concise way of asking either of two questions: 'What has happened that I didn't anticipate?' or, 'What is likely to happen that I haven't anticipated?' News is relevant to current situations. Its concern with the past, or the future, is in terms of the present assessments that knowing the news makes possible. [...]

4 When the 'negative' becomes the rule, the 'positive' exception makes news, as witness the following headline: 'No Cabbies Slain Here Last Year.' The story began: 'Not one driver of a medallion cab here was murdered in 1971, the first full year without a homicide in 15 years. In 1970, seven drivers of yellow cabs were slain, the Metropolitan Taxicab Board of Trade said yesterday' (*New York Times*, 14 January 1972, p. 35).

5 Stevenson, *Proverbs*, 1682. Cited as line 277 of the play; translator unnoted.

6 *King John*, v. vi.

7 *Merchant of Venice*, I. iii.

News can be only partly defined, however, in terms of the functions it performs for someone receiving it. A new resident of a community, for example, needs orientation to his changed environment. Still, what is new and vital information for him may be folk wisdom to his neighbours. *Timeliness* is inherent in the concept of news, which is distinguished from other kinds of information by the intimation that it is shared as soon as possible after it is learned.[8]

Time is a fundamental and complex aspect of all news and becomes a crucial concern in determining whether an item of news shall be published. The newspaper 'extra' and the radio or television 'bulletin' are devices for underscoring the freshness of the proffered information. So is the reportorial convention of inserting the adjective 'yesterday' or 'today' in every account to indicate how recently the news 'broke'. The format of the press release, which is postdated, submitted to the press in advance of the occasion it reports, and then 'released' just prior to publication, further illustrates the role of time in the newsmaking process.

Time can be conceived as having three aspects with regard to news being considered for publication by the daily press; together, they constitute what herein is termed 'timeliness'. For an item of information to be timely, in the sense employed here, requires the conjunction of: (1) *recency* (recent disclosure); (2) *immediacy* (publication with minimal delay); (3) *currency* (relevance to present concerns). To speak of news as timely information, therefore, is to imply the existence and interaction of a news source, a news medium, and a news audience.

Recency is a matter of recent disclosure rather than of recent occurrence. News is based on the announcement, 'It was just learned' rather than 'It just happened'. Bringing to light information that had been lost or overlooked confers recency upon it. Events that belong to history become news if they have just become known to contemporary scholars. The contents of the Dead Sea Scrolls made news after two millennia because they were recently discovered and deciphered. Similarly, it is news when a scientist finally announces an invention, even though he has tested prototypes for years. At any time during that interval, the first announcement would have been news to any colleagues who learned of it. Thus, insiders' old information becomes news to successively larger publics, as a story moves from specialized to more popular news media.

Immediacy is the correlative of recency. In past times, when a single messenger might be the sole news medium for a report affecting an entire nation, immediacy was a matter of the time required for the courier to convey his message. (Recall the twenty-six-mile run from Marathon to Athens that brought news of the Persian defeat in 490 BC.) In this age of multiple news media, with much of the news gathered by open exchanges between a news source and assembled reporters, the immediacy with which news is reported

---

8 'Since news has immediate relevance to action that is already under way, it is perishable. This suggests that news is not merely something new; it is information that is timely. Even if it is about events long past, the information is necessary for current adjustment; it relieves tension in the immediate situation' (Tamotsu Shibutani, *Improvised News: A Sociological Study of Rumor* (Indianapolis: Bobbs-Merrill, 1965), 41). Shibutani discusses the characteristics of news on pp. 39–46.

depends upon the interplay between communication technology and the institutional practices of the news media.

Competition for public attention makes immediacy significant to the media; the laggard in news, like the laggard in love, tends to lose to rivals the esteem and attention of his audience. The effort to achieve immediacy reflects a medium's concern that it not publish as 'news' information made stale because fresher data were published by a rival. Newspapers have been forced to acknowledge broadcasting's greater immediacy in publishing headline items; the print media now emphasize the greater fullness of their news reports, thereby attaining immediacy for what broadcasting omits.

Like recency, immediacy is measurable only on a comparative basis. News becomes more immediate to the extent that the interval shrinks between the time an event occurs and the time it is reported. The 'scoop', though infrequent, exemplifies the value to a news medium of maximizing immediacy. If a newspaper or a network acquires 'exclusive' information, it maximizes both recency and immediacy because the event is not revealed to the press until news of it is published. The fact of publication becomes part of the news.[9] [. . .]

Immediacy links recent events and the media that report them; currency links these events to segments of the public. Recency makes an item of information into an item of news; currency, which is based on audience interest, gives that news item its news value. News is not an absolute, and currency is as relative as the other aspects of timeliness. When an editor speaks of exercising 'news judgement' in assessing the 'news value' of a report, he is applying his criteria of currency to the available items of recent information from which a news presentation can be assembled.

Weather reports illustrate how currency reflects news value. On any news broadcast, the most recent weather conditions and the next day's predicted readings are both of high current interest to the audience in the affected area; therefore, both sets of data have high news value. The long-term prediction for the next several days, despite its low certainty, is the best current information about a situation that interests the audience; therefore, it has a good deal of news value. The report of the day before yesterday, having been superseded by more recent information, has minimal currency; therefore, it has little news value.

Currency is the 'local angle' in the broadest sense, which is why emergencies that acutely affect local audiences are a news staple for local media. Because such situations are urgent, and therefore obtrusive, they quickly become visible to newsmen, attain high currency among the news audience, and remain highly newsworthy until the emergency is resolved. Currency does not, however, depend on the objective characteristics of events but on subjective reactions to those events. Currency is not, therefore, correlated with significance, as a commentator on the press indicated:

> One day in November of 1968, 55 reporters and cameramen waited for three hours in a cold rain to see Jacqueline Kennedy Onassis get off an

---

9 This was clearly illustrated in the case of the so-called 'Anderson Papers', when syndicated columnist Jack Anderson became the rest of the Press's source of news about White House policy-making during the India–Pakistan war. See e.g. the *New York Times*, from 3 Jan. 1972.

airplane on her return to New York after marrying Aristotle Onassis. That evening, the news programs showed us her arrival in detail and the next morning, the *New York Times* gave 19 paragraphs and two three-column pictures to the story, starting on page one. . . . Of all the national media, only the *Times* covered a press conference the same day by a relief worker who predicted that two million Biafran children might die in the following months. That news was reported by the *Times* in five paragraphs on page 20. On the television news programs, there was silence.[10]

Individuals whose decisions affect large sectors of the public may be ignored by newsmen because the significance of their activities is unknown or unrecognized. On the other hand, the doings of celebrities have currency not because of their impact upon public affairs but because an audience has become interested in their behaviour. An editor may choose to present his unconcerned audience with news he considers significant, hoping they will waken to its relevance. Or, he may decide to withhold information of assured interest because he deems publication impolitic or inappropriate.[11] The *New York Times*'s well-known slogan, 'All the News That's Fit to Print', asserts the editor's occupational prerogative, which is to exercise his own judgement as to what is appropriate for publication in his medium for his audience.

Public knowledge is no longer news, so far as the press is concerned, demonstrating that the correlative of timeliness is perishability. When a report ceases to be news, it becomes not a part of history but of an archive. [. . .] It is hard to discern a trend or infer a principle from discrete facts, which is why they provide only the raw material of historical knowledge. As newsprint yellows, history begins to supply its own evaluation of the relevance of events. A contemporary American historian implicitly distinguished between news judgement and the judgement of history when he noted:

> Big turning points in history are rare. Some cast a shadow in advance, as did both the start and end of World War II. Others pass unnoticed until long afterward when, looking back, men can detect some slower ebb or flow beneath the froth of everyday events.[12]

Because news is timebound, and therefore ephemeral, it differs fundamentally from knowledge that aspires to longevity.

---

10 Robert Stein, 'Telling It Like It Is', *Television Quarterly* 10 (Winter 1973), 49.

11 Reasons for not publishing may range from obeisance to an executive's personal prejudices, as when the Hearst newspapers omitted all references to Orson Welles because of his Hearst-like portrait of 'Citizen Kane', to self-censorship of news believed to endanger national interests, as when the *New York Times* played down its knowledge of the imminent Bay of Pigs invasion. For a pioneering analysis of how considerations of policy affect news judgement, see Warren Breed, 'Social Control in the Newsroom'.

12 William H. McNeill, 'What to Expect in 1972', *New York Times*, 31 Dec. 1971, p. 19.

6

News As Purposive Behaviour: On the Strategic Use of Routine Events, Accidents, and Scandals

Harvey Molotch and Marilyn Lester

EVERYONE NEEDS NEWS. In everyday life, news tells us what we do not experience directly and thus renders otherwise remote happenings observable and meaningful. Conversely, we fill each other in with news. Although those who make their living at newswork (reporters, copy editors, publishers, typesetters, etc.) have additional needs for news, all individuals, by virtue of the ways they attend to and give accounts of what they believe to be a pre-given world, are daily newsmakers.

News is thus the result of this invariant need for accounts of the unobserved, this capacity for filling-in others, and the production work of those in the media. This paper seeks to understand the relationships between different kinds of news needs and how it is that news needs of people differently situated *vis à vis* the organization of news work produce the social and political 'knowledge' of publics.[1] [. . .]

Career Lines of Public Events

In the career pattern of a public event, an occurrence passes through a set of agencies (individuals or groups), each of which helps construct, through a distinctive set of organizational routines, what the event *will have turned*

Source: Harvey Molotch and Marilyn Lester, 'News as Purposive Behavior', *American Sociological Review*, 39 (Feb. 1974), 101–12. The authors would like to thank Aaron Cicourel, Mark Fishman, Lloyd Fitts, Richard Flacks, Eliot Friedson, Richard Kinane, Milton Mankoff, Hugh Mehan, Linda Molotch, Milton Olin, Charles Perrow, Michael Schwartz, David Street, Gaye Tuchman, John Weiler, Eugene Weinstein and Don Zimmerman. Financial support was provided through a faculty senate grant, University of California, Santa Barbara.

1 The term 'public' throughout this essay is used in the sense John Dewey used it: a political grouping of individuals brought into being as a social unit through mutual recognition of common problems for which common solutions should be sought. Information thus does not merely *go to* publics, it *creates* them. See Dewey (1927).

out to be using as resources the work of agencies who came before and anticipating what successive agencies 'might make out of it'.[2]

For simplicity, we view events as being constituted by three major agencies.[3] First, there are the *news promoters*—those individuals and their associates who identify (and thus render observable) an occurrence as special, on some ground, for some reason, for others. Second, there are the *news assemblers* (newsmen, editors, and rewritemen) who, working from the materials provided by the promoters, transform a perceived finite set of promoted occurrences into public events through publication or broadcast. Finally, there are the *news consumers* (e.g. readers) who analogously attend to certain occurrences made available as resources by the media and thereby create in their own minds a sense of public time. Each successive agency engages in essentially the same kind of constructing work, based on purposes-at-hand which determine given event needs. But the work accomplished at each point closes off or inhibits a great number of event-creating possibilities. In this closing off of possibilities lies the power of newswork and of all accounting activity.

■ **1. Promoting**

There are interests in promoting certain occurrences for public use, as well as interests in preventing certain occurrences from becoming public events. By 'promoting' we merely mean that an actor, in attending to an occurrence, helps to make that occurrence available to still others. In some instances, the promoting may be direct, crass, and obvious—as in public relations work (cf. Boorstin 1961) or transparently political activity (e.g. a candidate's press conference). In others, promotion work is less crassly self-serving as when a citizen tries to publicize a health danger. Commonly, promotion work revolves around one's own activity which like all social activity is accomplished with its prospective and retrospective potential uses in mind. Thus, the press conference is held for the benefits which its public impact are assumed to provide; a protest demonstration is, in the same way, geared for its selection as an event (cf. Myerhoff 1972). Similarly, a decision to bomb North Vietnam is conducted with what-will-be-made-of-it and what-it-really-was-all-along (e.g. its deniability) as two of its constituent features. In our language, then, doing and promoting are part of the same process; indeed, the career of the occurrence will, in the end, constitute what was 'done'. That is, if the bombing is not widely reported or is reported as 'bombing selected military targets', the nature of the act itself, from the perspective of the agent (Nixon), will radically differ from the result of prominent and widespread coverage which stipulates 'indiscriminate massive bombing'.

---

2 Cicourel (1968) makes an analogous argument with respect to the creation of a juvenile delinquent. A delinquent is constituted by a set of accounts produced by a series of law enforcement agencies motivated by the need to appear rational to others in the processing system. Any youth's activities will be made (through a course of accounting work) to tally with or violate some law. Thus a delinquent is an accomplishment of a chain of processing agencies who need to do a competent-job-for-all-practical-purposes. That is, what the act, the person (or event), 'really is'—is as it is attended to through members' practical work. This view departs fundamentally from the gatekeeping theory of newswork which sees the self-same happening as acted upon by a series of newsworkers (cf. Shibutani 1966). For a discussion of 'gatekeeping', see White (1965), Gieber (1964).

3 These agencies, as here presented, are generally consistent with Holsti's six 'basic elements': source, encoding process, message, channel of transmission, recipient, decoding process (see Holsti 1969: 24).

Although promoters often promote occurrences for which they themselves are responsible, they also have access (within limits) to promote the activities of others—including individuals whose purposes are opposed to their own. Thus, a political candidate can 'expose' the corrupt occurrence work of a political rival or take credit for its beneficent consequences. [. . .] The richness and irony of political life is made up of a free-wheeling, skilled competition among people having access to the media, trying to mobilize occurrences as resources for their experience-building work.

■ 2. Assembling

Media personnel form a second agency in the generation of public events. From their perspective, a finite number of things 'really happen', of which the most special, interesting, or important are to be selected. Their task involves 'checking a story out' for worthiness, a job which may involve months of research or a fleeting introspection or consultation with a colleague. The typical conception of the media's role, then, at least in western, formally uncensored societies, is that the media stand as reporter-reflector-indicators of an objective reality 'out there', consisting of knowably 'important' events of the world. Armed with time and money, an expert with a 'nose for news' will be led to occurrences which do, indeed, index that reality. Any departure from this ideal tends to be treated as 'bias' or some other pathological circumstance.

To suggest the view that assemblers' own events need help to constitute public events, is also to imply the importance of the organizational activities through which news is generated. The nature of the media as formal organization, as routines for getting work done in newsrooms, as career mobility patterns for a group of professionals, as profit-making institutions, all become inextricably and reflexively tied to the content of published news.[4] The extent to which news organizations generate event needs among news assemblers that vary from those of occurrence promoters is the extent to which the media have an institutionally patterned independent role in newsmaking. How then does the construction work of the media coincide or conflict with the construction work of promoters? Assemblers' purposes-at-hand, as they contrast or coincide with the purposes-at-hand of different types of promoters, will determine the answers to such a question.

Powerful promoters may attempt to increase the correspondence between their event needs and those of assemblers by pressuring media into altering their work routines. The sanctions which the powerful exercise to control media routines may be direct and crude (e.g. threatening speeches, advertising boycotts, anti-trust suits against broadcasters) or subtle (e.g. journalism awards, and the encouragement, through regularized interviews, leaks and press conferences of newsroom patterns which inhibit follow-up, experimentation and deviation). Thus, for example, all television networks have abandoned their habit of 'instant analysis' of presidential speeches, as a response, we assume, to White House pressure. What may eventually evolve as a journalistic 'professional canon' will have been historically grounded in

---

4 Breed (1955), Gieber (1964; 1956) and Tuchman (1972a; 1972b; 1973) have provided important insights into the assembling process.

an attempt by the institutionally powerful to sustain ideological hegemony. In this instance, the event needs of assemblers come to closely resemble those of promoters who affect journalistic work routines.

In societies having a formally controlled press, the substantive relationship between news promoters and assemblers is less obscured. In such societies, media are organized to serve a larger purpose (e.g. creating socialist man or maintaining a given regime). Validity thus tends to be equated with utility. Presumably, career advancement and survival depend on one's ability to mesh one's 'nose for news' with the bosses' conceptions of the general social purpose and thus of the utility of a given occurrence.

Because western conceptions of news rely on the assumption that there is a reality out-there-to-be-described, the product of any system which denies this premise is termed 'propaganda'. Thus, in the western mind, the distinction between news and propaganda lies in the premise seen to be embedded in the assemblers' work: those with purposes produce propaganda; those whose only purpose is to reflect reality, produce news. [...]

■ 3. Consuming   Members of publics, glutted with the published and broadcasted work of the media, engage in the same sort of constituting activity as news assemblers. A residue of biography, previous materials made available by media, and present context, all shape the consumer's work of constructing events. Their newswork is procedurally identical with that of promoters and assemblers, but with two important differences: the stock of occurrences available as resources has been radically truncated through the newswork of other agencies; and, unlike assemblers, they ordinarily have no institutional base from which to broadcast their newswork.

A Typology of
Public Events

Despite the overarching similarity of individuals' and organizations' methods of newsmaking, we find it useful to describe certain substantive differences in the ways in which occurrences are promoted to the status of public event.[5]

In using this typology, we are imposing ideal types on data. Consistent with that fact, any event which we may pull from a newspaper's front page for illustrative purposes may be seen to contain some features of each event type. Similarly, the category which any kind of event 'fits' may similarly shift with changing features or schemes of interpretation, which may lead to a revision of what 'really happened'.

We distinguish between events by the circumstances of the promotion work which makes them available to publics. The answers to two questions which can be asked of any event provide the basis for our typology. First: did the underlying happening come into being through intentional or unintentional human activity? And second: does the party promoting the occurrence

---

5 That is, following the ethnomethodological instruction, we have heretofore attempted to suspend our belief in a normative order. However, to extend our analysis to a common-sensically useful approach to news and to provide tools of concise description for mundane, practical work, we enter the 'attitude of everyday life' in this section of the essay.

into an event appear to be the same as the party who initially accomplished the happening upon which the event is based? The relevance of these questions will become clearer as each event type is described.

■ **Routine Events** Routine events are distinguishable by the fact that the underlying happenings on which they are presumably based are purposive accomplishments and by the fact that the people who undertake the happening (whom we call 'effectors') are identical with those who promote them into events. The prototypical routine event is the press conference statement, but the great majority of stories appearing in the daily press fall in this category; hence, on grounds of frequency, we term them 'routine'.[6]

Whether or not a given promoter is the 'same' as the effector can be difficult to determine in some instances. It is clear, for example, that if Richard Nixon's Press Secretary promotes the President's trip to China or Russia, the effector (Nixon) and the promoter (Press Secretary) can be taken as identical for all intents and purposes. If, however, Nixon reads a letter on TV written to him by a POW's wife, the degree of identity between Nixon, the promoter, and POW wife, as effector, is less clear. To the extent to which it can be assumed that both party's purposes are identical—e.g. to bring public attention to POWs and/or to mobilize support for the war—the promoter and agent can be deemed identical and the written letter as a public event can be classified as routine. Of course, it may be that Nixon wants to bring attention to the POWs for other long-range ('ulterior') purposes not shared by the POW wife. In such a case, Nixon is not merely using his position to advance the effector's public event needs, but is fostering a new occurrence of his own and promoting it as a public event. After noting that kind of constructing work, the 'new' occurrence is analytically the same as any other.

While all routine events share certain features, elucidating those features does not tell us what makes for a successful routine event. Each day a multitude of activities is done with a view to creating routine events. But those intentions must complement the work done by news assemblers if a public event is to result. The success of a potential routine event is thus contingent on the assembler's definition of an occurrence as a 'story'. Put another way, those who seek to create public events by promoting their activities (occurrences) must have access to that second stage of event-creation. With respect to this accessibility, various subtypes of routine events can be discussed. [. . .]

(a) Habitual Access As the term implies, habitual access exists when an individual or group is so situated that their own event needs routinely coincide with the newsmaking activities of media personnel. Thus, for example, the President of the United States is always assumed to say 'important' things. This 'importance' is taken-for-granted, and a Washington reporter who acts on the opposite assumption will probably lose his job. Habitual access is likely limited in this country to high government officials, major corporate figures, and, to a lesser extent, certain glamour personalities (cf. Tuchman 1972*b*). Such people,

---

6 Manela (1971), in an analogous typology of events, treats events as objective phenomena which are categorized in terms of how well they fit ongoing formal organization rules and routines.

especially those in political life, must be concerned with keeping their podia alive and organizing the news so that their goals do not suffer in the continuing competition to create publics. That competition may involve occasional struggles with other powerful figures, or, on the other hand, with insurgent groups seeking to provide a different set of public experiences. Intra- or inter-group competitions notwithstanding, habitual access is generally found among those with extreme wealth or other institutionally-based sources of power. Indeed, this power is both a result of the habitual access and a continuing cause of such access. Routine access is one of the important sources and sustainers of existing power relationships. [...]

Although news assemblers commonly act upon the assumption that those with official authority are the most newsworthy (Tuchman 1972b), other individuals and groups are occasionally in the position to generate events. Yet, whereas the US President's access to the media continues across time and issue, the access of other groups—e.g. spokespeople for women's rights, civil rights, and youth will ebb and flow over time and place (cf. Molotch and Lester 1973). For this reason, the ideal-typical routine event is taken to be the generating of a public experience by those in positions to have continual access to asserting the importance and factual status of 'their' occurrences.

(b) Disruptive Access

Those lacking habitual access to event-making who wish to contribute to the public experience, often come to rely on disruption (cf. Myerhoff 1972). They must 'make news' by somehow crashing through the ongoing arrangements of newsmaking, generating surprise, shock, or some more violent form of 'trouble'. Thus, the relatively powerless disrupt the social world to disrupt the habitual forms of event making. In extreme cases, multitudes are assembled in an inappropriate place to intervene in the daily schedule of occurrence and events. Such activities constitute, in a sense, 'anti-routine' events. This 'obvious' disruption of normal functioning and its challenge to the received social world prompts the coverage of the mass media.

The disruptive occurrence becomes an event because it is a problem for the relatively powerful. We would argue that a protest event—e.g. a student sit-in—receives media play precisely because it is thought to be an occurrence which 'serious people' need to understand. What does a sit-in mean? Have students gone berserk? Will secretaries be raped? Is order in jeopardy? People interested in maintaining the ongoing process need to answer these questions before developing strategy and plans for restoration of order. The coverage which results typically speaks to these implications—not to the issues which raised the protest in the first place. Thus, to the extent that student protest activity continues as an issue, it does so because important parties disagree about what the protest means and how it should best be handled. [...]

We would argue that coverage of student protest fades as the event needs of one or the other important party declines. The mystery of the student protest declines as the scenario becomes increasingly typified through repetition: buildings are taken—speeches made—administrations respond—cops are called—heads are cracked—ringleaders arrested—trials proceed. No rapes, little destruction, token reform (maybe). People can go back to their everyday activities; the strategic need to know is satisfied.

There is a second reason this type of routine event declines in usefulness to important people. The very reporting on the occurrence may come to be seen as precipitating the creation of more such occurrences. Thus, an interest develops in eliminating such events from the news—either by taking actions to prevent them (e.g. softening resistence to student demands) or by agreeing not to report them. Police, for example, may bar reporters from the sites of ghetto riots, and be supported in doing so by politicians, civic leaders, and publishers as well. Certain canons of the 'responsibility of the press' are readily available to editors who choose to bypass anti-routine events. The purposiveness underlying all routine events can be selectively perceived at appropriate moments to justify cancelling a story because it is viewed as promoted precisely for its media effects.[7] When important people see a potential event as too costly, given their purposes-at-hand, there are various resources for eliminating it.

(c) Direct Access   Some news stories are generated by assemblers who go out and 'dig up' the news. Feature stories are often of this sort but many 'straight news' articles can be of the same type. For example, assemblers in scrutinizing the police blotter may detect that 'crime is rising' or may interview or poll a population for attitude shifts. This newswork is routine in that creating the occurrence (e.g. record checking, attitude polling) is a purposive activity promoted as a public event by the effector. It is distinctive, however, in that the promoter and the assembler are identical. When this identity is sufficiently transparent, the media involved may be castigated for lacking 'objectivity' or for engaging in 'muckraking' or 'yellow journalism'. A tenet of the 'new journalism' is that such newsmaking is indeed appropriate. This controversy is, in our terms, a conflict over whether or not media personnel can legitimately engage in transparent news promotion, or whether they must continue to appear to be passively reporting that which objectively happens.[8]

■ **Accidents**   An accident differs from a routine event in two respects: (1) the underlying happening is not intentional, and (2) those who promote it as a public event are different from those whose activity brought the happening about. In the case of accidents people engage in purposive activity which leads to unenvisioned happenings which are promoted by others into events. Accidents thus rest upon miscalculations which lead to a breakdown in the customary order.

Events such as the Santa Barbara oil spill, the Watergate arrests, the release of nerve gas at Dugway Proving Ground, and the inadvertent US loss of hydrogen bombs over Spain all involve 'foul ups' in which the strategic

---

7 In response to a complaint that his newspaper was holding back an important story, a reporter for the *Los Angeles Times* wrote Molotch the following defense: 'We have not run an extensive story on   because of the judgment of my editors that because the   case has not become an issue of major proportions enveloping the campus community, we might be accused of creating an issue if we give it full-blown treatment at this point in time. It is not a case of holding back information, but the concern that my editors have for trying to avoid the situation where something becomes a major issue *because* a large daily newspaper has written about it at length'. Personal communication to the author, 8 Jan. 1971.

8 What is or is not a transparently nonobjective technique changes historically. Fishman (forthcoming) details how the use of interview in straight news came as a radical departure from objective news coverage. The technique was introduced as part of the yellow journalism movement and was denounced by the more traditional papers.

purpose of a given activity (e.g. oil production, political espionage, gas research, national defence) becomes unhinged from its consequences.

The accident tends to have results which are the opposite of routine events. Instead of being a deliberately planned contribution to a purposely developed social structure (or in the language of the literature, 'decisional outcome'), it fosters revelations which are otherwise deliberately obfuscated by those with the resources to create routine events.

For people in everyday life, the accident is an important resource for learning about the routines of those who ordinarily possess the psychic and physical resources to shield their private lives from public view. The Ted Kennedy car accident gave the public access to that individual's private activities and dispositions. As argued elsewhere (Molotch 1970), an accident like the Santa Barbara oil spill provided the local public analogous insights into the everyday functioning of American political and economic institutions.

When accidents surface as public events, they do so in 'error'; we can expect that, unless the needs of powerful people differ, routine event-making procedures subsequently and increasingly come into play to define the accident out of public politics. But the suddenness of the accident and its unanticipated nature means that event makers are initially not ready and thus the powerful could give uncoordinated, mutually contradictory accounts. This process of accidental disruption, followed by attempts to restore traditional meanings can, we have found, be observed empirically; and thus, *we take accidents to constitute a crucial resource for the empirical study of event-structuring processes.*[9]

In their realization as events, accidents are far less contingent than are routine events on the event needs of the powerful. Given the inherent drama, sensation, and atypicality of accidents, it is difficult to deny their existence; and typically nonimportant groups can more easily hold sway in the temporal demarcation process. Thus, the outflow of a small sea of oil on the beaches of California is for 'anybody' a remarkable occurrence; and a reporter or newspaper which ignored it would, owing to the physical evidence widely available to direct experience, be obviously 'managing the news'. That is, if newsmaking results in published accounts considered by a multitude to differ from 'what happened' as determined by their own event needs, the legitimacy of newsmaking as an objective enterprise is undermined. Of course, not all accidents become public events. Oil spills off the Gulf of Mexico, almost as large as the Santa Barbara spill, received far less coverage; similarly, the massive escape of nerve gas at Dugway Proving Ground (cf. Hirsch 1969) could easily be conceived as far more disastrous to the natural environment and to human life than any oil spill; yet again, relatively little coverage occurred (cf. Lester 1971). All this attests to the fact that all events are socially constructed and their 'newsworthiness' is not contained in their objective features.

---

9 It is precisely these forms of events which tend to be excluded in community power research using the decisional technique (cf. Banfield 1962). By uncritically accepting those stories which appear in newspapers over an extensive time period as corresponding to the basic local political conflicts, use of the decisional technique guarantees that only those matters on which the elites do internally disagree will emerge as study topics. Thus, pluralistic findings are guaranteed through the mode of case selection.

■ Scandals   Scandals share features of both accidents and routine events but differ from both as well. A scandal involves an occurrence which becomes an event through the intentional activity of individuals (we call them 'informers') who for one reason or another do not share the event-making strategies of the occurrence effectors. Like a routine event, the precipitating happening is intended and the event is promoted; but unlike a routine event, the promoting is not done by those who originally brought about the happening. In fact, the event's realization typically comes as a surprise to the original actors. Thus, Ronald Reagan deliberately paid no state income tax 1970–1, but did not expect, in so doing, to read about it in newspapers. [. . .] A scandal requires the willing cooperation of at least one party having power and legitimacy which derive either from first-hand experience (the eyewitness) or position in the social structure (e.g. a 'leaker' of memos or Pentagon papers). The more both circumstances are fulfilled, the greater the capacity to generate a scandal. Again, this capacity is disproportionately in the hands of elites, but their trusted hirelings are also strategically well situated. Like the accident, the scandal reveals normally hidden features of individual lives or institutional processes.

The My Lai massacre is one of the more dramatic examples of scandal. It is not a routine event in that those originally involved in making it happen—whether defined as the troops in the field or the President and Generals—did not intend that the mass murder become a recorded phenomenon. The tortuous route the occurrence followed (it was twenty months becoming a public event) has been elucidated in some detail.[10] My Lai was originally reported as a successful, routine offensive against Viet Cong soldiers; only later was it transformed into a 'massacre'. In other scandals, high status people 'fink' on each other—as, for example, when political reformers expose 'the machine', or when political leaders wage internecine war to eliminate opponents. Of course, scandals can also occur when statuses are more asymmetrical; it may have been a clerk who exposed Reagan; it was an Army corporal who exposed My Lai. Also, when the informer is of relatively low status and unsupported by a group with power, the scandal-making business can be quite arduous (e.g. My Lai) and often a complete failure. Frequently, an accident can stimulate a series of scandals, as in the instance of the Santa Barbara oil spill, and in the McCord and Dean testimony in the aftermath of the Watergate arrests.

■ Serendipity   A fourth type of event, the serendipity event, shares features of both the accident and the routine. The serendipity event has an underlying happening which is unplanned (as with accidents) but is promoted by the effector himself (as with routine events). Examples of the serendipitous event are hard to come by precisely because one of its features is that the effector/promoter disguises it to make it appear routine. Self-proclaimed heroes are perhaps a variant of those who effect serendipitous events: one inadvertently performs a given act which results in the accomplishment of some courageous and socially-desired task. Thus, through self-promotion (or at least tacit approval), one converts an accident into a deliberate act.

---

10 See *New York Times*, 20 November 1969; *The Times* (London), 20 November 1969.

TABLE 1. *Event Classificatory Scheme*

	Happening accomplished intentionally	Happening accomplished not intentionally
Promoted by Effector	Routine	Serendipity
Promoted by Informer	Scandal	Accident

Unlike the accident, the underlying happening in the serendipity event remains unobserved and perhaps unobservable for members of publics. Because the agent can transform the unintended happening into a routine event through his promotion activities, people are not given the kinds of information which accidents and scandals afford. Because serendipity events are difficult to differentiate from routine events, they are as unretrievable for sociological investigation as accidents are retrievable. They are the least sociologically useful of any event type.

By way of summary, Table 1 displays the four event types, distinguished by the degree to which their underlying happening is accomplished intentionally and by whether the occurrence effector or an informer does the promotion work.

Summary Discussion

Consistent with Gans's (1972) urgings, we attempt a new departure for the study of news. We see media as reflecting not a world out there, but the practices of those having the power to determine the experience of others. Harold Garfinkel made a similar point about clinical records he investigated; rather than viewing an institution's records as standing ideally for something which happened, one can instead see in those records the organizational practices of people who make records routinely. Garfinkel concludes that there are 'good organizational reasons for bad clinical records'. And those 'good reasons' are the topic of research because they spell out the clinic's social organization.

We think that mass media should similarly be viewed as bad clinical records. Following Garfinkel, our interest in its 'badness' does not rest in an opportunity for criticism and depiction of irony, but rather in the possibility of understanding how the product comes to look like it does, i.e. what the 'good reasons' are. We advocate examining media for the event needs and the methods through which those with access come to determine the experience of publics. We can look for the methods through which ideological hegemony is accomplished by examining the records which are produced.

Seen in this way, one approach to mass media is to look not for reality, but for purposes which underlie the strategies of creating one reality instead of another. For the citizen to read the newspaper as a catalogue of the important happenings of the day, or for the social scientist to use the newspaper for uncritically selecting topics of study, is to accept as reality the political work by which events are constituted by those who happen to currently hold power. Only in the accident, and, secondarily, in the scandal, is that routine political work transcended to some significant degree, thereby allowing access to information which is directly hostile to those groups who typically manage public event making. Future research on media and on the dynamics of power would be strengthened by taking this 'second face of power' (cf. Bachrach and Baratz 1962; Edelman 1964) into consideration. More profoundly, sociologists who habitually take their research topics and conceptual constructs as they are made available through mass media and similar sources may wish to extricate their consciousnesses from the purposive activities of parties whose interests and event needs may differ from their own.

References

BACHRACH, PETER, and MORTON BARATZ (1962), 'The Two Faces of Power', *American Political Science Review*, 56 (Dec.): 947–52.

BANFIELD, EDWARD (1962), *Political Influence* (New York: Free Press).

BOORSTIN, DANIEL (1961), *The Image: A Guide to Pseudo Events in America* (New York: Harper and Row).

BREED, WARREN (1955), 'Social control in the newsroom', *Social Forces* 33 (May): 326–35.

CICOUREL, AARON (1968), *The Social Organization of Juvenile Justice* (New York: Wiley).

DEWEY, JOHN (1927), *The Public and Its Problems* (New York: Holt, Rinehart).

EDELMAN, MURRAY (1964), *The Symbolic Uses of Politics* (Urbana: University of Illinois Press).

FISHMAN, MARK (Forthcoming) *News of the World: What Happened and Why* (Unpublished doctoral dissertation, Department of Sociology, University of California, Santa Barbara).

GANS, HERBERT (1972), 'The Famine in American Mass Communications Research: Comments on Hirsch, Tuchman and Gecas', *American Journal of Sociology*, 77 (Jan.): 697–705.

GIEBER, WALTER (1964), 'News Is What Newspapermen Make It', in L. A. Dexter and D. M. White (eds.), *People, Society and Mass Communication* (New York: Free Press), 173–80.

—— (1956), 'Across the desk: A Study of 16 Telegraph editors', *Journalism Quarterly*, 43 (Fall): 423–32.

HIRSCH, SEYMOUR (1969), 'On Uncovering the Great Nerve Gas Cover-Up', *Ramparts*, 3 (July): 12–18.

LESTER, MARILYN (1971), *Toward a Sociology of Public Events* (Unpublished Masters Paper, University of California, Santa Barbara).

MANELA, ROGER (1971), 'The Classification of Events in Formal Organizations' (Ann Arbor: Institute of Labour and Industrial Relations, mimeo.).

MILLER, GEORGE, EUGENE GALANTER, and KARL PRIBRAM (1960), *Plans and the Structure of Behavior* (New York: Holt, Rinehart and Winston).

MOLOTCH, HARVEY and MARILYN LESTER (1972), 'Accidents, Scandals and Routines', presented at the American Sociological Association meetings, New Orleans.

—— —— (n.d.) 'The Great Oil Spill as Local Occurrence and National Event' (Thesis).

MYERHOFF, BARBARA (1972), 'The Revolution as a Trip: Symbol and Paradox', in Philip G. Altbach and Robert S. Laufer (eds.), *The New Pilgrims: Youth Protest in Transition* (New York: David McKay), 251–66.

ROTH, JULIUS (1963), *Timetables: Structuring the Passage of Time in Hospital Treatment and Other Careers* (New York: Bobbs-Merrill).

SHIBUTANI, TAMOTSU (1966), *Improvised News* (New York: Bobbs-Merrill).

TUCHMAN, GAYE (1972*a*), 'Objectivity as Strategic Ritual', *American Journal of Sociology*, 77 (Jan.) 660–79.

—— (1972*b*), 'News as Controlled Conflict and Controversy', New York: Department of Sociology, Queens College (mimeo.).

—— (1973), 'Making News by Doing Work: Routinizing the Unexpected', *American Journal of Sociology*, 79 (July): 110–31.

WHITE, D. M. (1964), 'The Gatekeeper: A Case Study in the Selection of News', in L. A. Dexter and D. M. White (eds.), *People, Society and Mass Communications* (New York: Free Press), 160–72.

7

Media Events

Daniel Dayan and Elihu Katz

Defining Media Events

THE MOST OBVIOUS difference between media events and other formulas or genres of broadcasting is that they are, by definition, not routine. In fact, they are *interruptions* of routine; they intervene in the normal flow of broadcasting and our lives. Like the holidays that halt everyday routines, television events propose exceptional things to think about, to witness, and to do. Regular broadcasting is suspended and pre-empted as we are guided by a series of special announcements and preludes that transform daily life into something special and, upon the conclusion of the event, are guided back again. In the most characteristic events, the interruption is *monopolistic*, in that all channels switch away from their regularly scheduled programming in order to turn to the great event, perhaps leaving a handful of independent stations outside the consensus. Broadcasting can hardly make a more dramatic announcement of the importance of what is about to happen.

Moreover, the happening is *live*. The events are transmitted as they occur, in real time; the French call this *en direct*. They are therefore unpredictable, at least in the sense that something can go wrong. Even the live broadcast of a symphony orchestra contains this element of tension. Typically, these events are *organized outside the media*, and the media serve them in what Jakobson (1960) would call a phatic role in that, at least theoretically, the media only provide a channel for their transmission. By 'outside' we mean both that the events take place outside the studio in what broadcasters call 'remote locations' and that the event is not usually initiated by the broadcasting organizations. This kind of connection, in real time, to a remote place—one having major importance to some central value of society, as we shall see—is credited with an exceptional value, by both broadcasters and their audiences (Vianello 1983). Indeed, the complexity of mounting these broadcasts is such, or is thought to be such, that they are hailed as 'miracles' by the broadcasters, as much for their technological as for their ceremonial triumphs (Sorohan 1979; Russo 1983).[1]

Source: Daniel Dayan and Elihu Katz, *Media Events* (Cambridge, Mass., and London: Harvard University Press, 1992).

---

1 Russo's (1983) dissertation sketches the organizational and technological solutions to the problems of the live broadcasting of special events from remote locations. He shows, for example, how the series of space shots stimulated important developments in video technology that were subsequently employed in quite different contexts, such as coverage of the Kennedy assassination and funeral. We shall repeatedly draw on Russo's work.

The organizers, typically, are public bodies with whom the media cooperate, such as governments, parliaments (congressional committees, for example), political parties (national conventions), international bodies (the Olympics committee), and the like. These organizers are well within the establishment. They are part of what Shils (1975) calls the center. They stand for consensual values and they have the authority to command our attention. It is no surprise that the Woodstock festival—the landmark celebration of protesting youth in the 1960s—was distributed as a film rather than as a live television event.

Thus, the League of Women Voters and the two major political parties organized the presidential debates in 1976 and 1980; the palace and the Church of England planned and 'produced' the royal wedding; the Olympics are staged by the International Olympics Committee. There may be certain exceptions to this rule: the European Broadcasting Union organizes the annual Eurovision Song Contest, for example, and the Super Bowl—the American football championship—involves a direct organizational input on the part of American broadcasters. But on the whole, these events are not organized by the broadcasters even if they are planned with television 'in mind'. The media are asked, or ask, to join.

Of course, there may well be collusion between broadcasters and organizers, as was evident in the Gerald Ford–Jimmy Carter debate in Philadelphia, for example, when the TV sound failed and the ostensibly local meeting in a hired hall was suspended until the national broadcast could be resumed. And a state-operated broadcasting system (Poland, for example; *not* England or Israel) may be indistinguishable from the organizers. But the exceptions only serve to prove the rule.

These events are *preplanned*, announced and advertised in advance. Viewers—and, indeed, broadcasters—had only a few days notice of the exact time of Sadat's arrival in Jerusalem (Cohen 1978); Irish television advertised the Pope's visit to Ireland a few weeks in advance (Sorohan 1979); the 1984 Los Angeles Olympics were heralded for more than four years. Important for our purpose is that advance notice gives time for anticipation and preparation on the part of both broadcasters and audiences. There is an active period of looking forward, abetted by the promotional activity of the broadcasters.

The conjunction of *live* and *remote*, on the one hand, and *interrupted* but *preplanned*, on the other, takes us a considerable distance toward our definition of the genre. Note that live and remote excludes routine studio broadcasts that may originate live, as well as feature programmes such as 'Roots' or 'Holocaust'. The addition of interruption excludes the evening news, while preplanned excludes major news events—such as the attempted assassination of a pope or a president, the nuclear accident at Three Mile Island, and, at first glance (but we shall reconsider this), the so-called television revolutions in Romania and Czechoslovakia. In other words, our corpus is limited to ceremonial occasions.

Returning to the elements of definition, we find that these broadcast events are presented with *reverence* and *ceremony*. The journalists who preside over them suspend their normally critical stance and treat their subject with respect, even awe. Garry Wills (1980) called media coverage of the Pope, including that of the written press, 'falling in love with love' and 'The

Greatest Story Ever Told'. He was referring to the almost priestly role played by journalists on the occasion, and we find a reverential attitude characteristic of the genre as a whole. We have already noted that the broadcast transports us to some aspect of the sacred center of the society (Shils 1975).

Of course, the very flow of ceremonial events is courtly and invites awe. There is the playing of the national anthem, the funereal beat of the drum corps, the diplomatic ceremony of being escorted from the plane, the rules of decorum in church and at Senate hearings. The point is that in media events television rarely intrudes: it interrupts only to identify the music being played or the name of the chief of protocol. It upholds the definition of the event by its organizers, explains the meaning of the symbols of the occasion, only rarely intervenes with analysis and almost never with criticism. Often advertising is suspended. There are variations: the live broadcast of Sadat's arrival in Jerusalem was treated differently by Israeli television than by the American networks, which had more explaining to do (Zelizer 1981). While we shall have occasion to point out these differences, they are outweighed by the similarities.

Even when these programmes address conflict—as they do—they celebrate not conflict but *reconciliation*. This is where they differ from the daily news events, where conflict is the inevitable subject. Often they are ceremonial efforts to redress conflict or to restore order or, more rarely, to institute change. They call for a cessation of hostilities, at least for a moment, as when the royal wedding halted the street fighting in Brixton and the terror in Northern Ireland. A more permanent truce followed the journeys of Sadat to Jerusalem and the Pope to Argentina. These events applaud the *voluntary* actions of great personalities. They celebrate what, on the whole, are establishment initiatives that are therefore unquestionably *hegemonic*. They are proclaimed *historic*.

These ceremonials *electrify very large audiences*—a nation, several nations, or the world. They are gripping, enthralling. They are characterized by a *norm of viewing* in which people tell each other that it is mandatory to view, that they must put all else aside. The unanimity of the networks in presenting the same event underlines the worth, even the obligation, of viewing. They cause viewers to *celebrate* the event by gathering before the television set in groups, rather than alone. Often the audience is given an active role in the celebration. Figuratively, at least, these events induce people to dress up, rather than dress down, to view television. These broadcasts *integrate* societies in a collective heartbeat and evoke a *renewal of loyalty* to the society and its legitimate authority.

■ **A More Parsimonious Approach to Definition**   Despite its heaviness, we shall argue that the elements in our definition are 'necessary', and that no subset of them is 'sufficient' without the others.[2] This hypothesis does not mean that the elements cannot exist without one another, but they are not then what we call media events; they are something else.

2 Huizinga (1950) and Caillois (1961) face the same sort of problem with their multifaceted definition of play. Their definition is an overview of the different types of games. Thus, play is an activity (1) entered voluntarily (except when ceremonial roles or social pressures force participation); (2) situated 'outside' ordinary life and accompanied by an awareness of its 'unreality'; (3) intensely absorbing to the participants; (4) bounded in time and space; (5) governed by rules of order;

Consider, for example, the *live* broadcasting of an event which is not *pre-planned*—say, the live reporting of the leaking atomic energy plant at Three Mile Island (Veron 1981). The leakage is a great *news* event, but not one of the great *ceremonial* events that interest us. Thus, we are interested here in the Kennedy funeral—a great ceremonial event—and not the Kennedy assassination—a great news event. The messages of these two broadcasts are different, their effects are different, they are presented in quite a different tone. Great news events speak of accidents, of disruption; great ceremonial events celebrate order and its restoration. In short, great news events are another genre of broadcasting, neighbour to our own, that will help to set the boundaries of media events.[3]

Consider an event that fails to *excite* the public or one that is not presented with *reverence* by the broadcasters. Such events do not qualify according to the definition, but they are particularly interesting because they suggest a pathology of media events, of which the former is an event 'manqué' and the latter an event 'denied' by the broadcasters.

Performing Media Events: Television as Wedding Photographer

Television's commitment to an event is, first of all, definitional. It recognizes the event, conveys its distinctive features, and exposes what Searle (1971) would call its constitutive rules. A second aspect of definition is 'hermeneutic'. Beyond identifying the event, television explores what the event is about and offers 'instant interpretation' (Nora 1972). One might say that television proposes the event's 'ascribed' meaning, as opposed to the meaning the event will eventually 'achieve' through the retrospective assessment of historians. Third, television is protective of the event. It makes clear the event's absolute priority and, in particular, its precedence over other news of all sorts. It gives resonance to the event's specific mood. An aesthetic watchdog, television makes sure that the event's unity of tone and action are preserved from interference.

■ Upholding Definition

Unlike physical objects, ceremonies are self-defining; their performance consists in the proclamation of their identity. Television serves to relay the pertinent features through which this identity is proclaimed, allowing viewers to identify the nature of the event. Given the contractual character of public events and the equally important role of principals and public, these features are to be found both in the realm of reaction and in the realm of performance.

The very nature of a ceremony implies the existence of a response. Television underlines this response, first by highlighting the reactions of the

---

(6) uncertain of outcome; and (7) promoting the formation of social groupings. Some of these elements also define media events; others are characteristics of ordinary television viewing (Stephenson 1967). The problems of specifying the social conditions that give rise to play, the types of play, and the function of play for individual and society are closely related to the problems that confront the present project.

3 Russo (1983: 42) distinguishes three genres of television news—regular news, documentaries, and special events—but does not make the distinction between major news events and major ceremonial events that is central to our argument. 'Special events broadcasting', Russo's subject, 'refers to a genre or type of news coverage which deals with live origination of a major news story'.

audience of spectators who are present at the event in person. Directors select the 'relevant' reactions for transmission and emulation.[4] They stress the communal nature of the experience, the unanimous adhesion of the crowd to the values and symbols being celebrated. What is stressed is not only unanimity, but unanimity within diversity. Consensus is portrayed as a process, as an overcoming of differences. The event requires that rivals suspend their feuds and strangers their particularisms to join in the effusive, contagious mood of the moment. As in the Roman Adventus—the ceremonial welcome of a distinguished visitor at the town gate—care is taken to assure the presence of representatives of all groups that are constituent of the community; the absence of any group might seem to imply rejection or defiance.[5] The event must therefore be shown to be adequately representative of the entire community.

Television also provides means for identifying the event through the tone and cadence of the narrator's voice. Some presenters have become famous—indeed, some have become indispensable—for their specialization in the narration of public events. Their reverent tone, eloquent silences, strangled or contained voices, are essential elements of the event. Like the cheering crowd, they have over the years become part of the event's prerequisites. In fact, narration and cheering are so similar in function that one can be substituted for the other. In the coverage of the royal wedding by both British channels, the roaring of the crowds was permitted virtually to drown out the voice of the presenter, as if the narration was but a more articulate form of cheering.

The absence of a responding crowd, and in some extreme cases the unavailability of a narration, may leave viewers in doubt about what type of reaction is called for, and ultimately about what is going on. Recalling an earlier example, the decision by Polish television to focus on the Pope's ritual functions and (deliberately) to play down public reactions resulted in a blurring of the event's definition as the reunion between a people and the representative of the spiritual heritage from which it was forcibly separated. Technical instruction in the nature of Catholic liturgy was not what Polish viewers needed from television. Similarly, the funeral of President Sadat caused obvious embarrassment (and hardly disguised irritation) to the narrator of the event's French broadcast. Ambiguity concerning the type of response expected, and uncertainty about whether any response at all was expected, ultimately backfired on the performance itself, casting doubt on the nature of what was taking place. In this particular case, the event remained 'mute'. While lending a hand to the technical tasks of burying his president, Hosni Mubarak abstained from making any decisive statement, thus further preventing the burial from becoming a 'full' public event and, as such, the state funeral of an assassinated leader. Television was unable to uphold a definition which the event itself was reluctant to provide.

When events are less ambiguous, television can come to the rescue of their self-definition, reiterating the features by which their organizers wish them

---

4 Eco (1989) addresses this point and other aspects of the aesthetics of live broadcasting in a 1964 essay, recently translated into English.

5 We have elaborated on this point in Dayan, Katz, and Kerns (1984), basing ourselves on Brown (1981). See also Dupront (1973).

to be identified. Emotional displays, for example, are not supposed to be part of a hero's funeral. In the case of Lord Mountbatten's funeral, therefore, British television resisted the temptation to display 'private' emotions: the fact that Prince Charles was apparently fighting back a tear during his reading of scripture was not shown in close-up. Emotion, however, is quite compatible with the ethos of a wedding. Therefore, when the expression of emotion took the form of a newlywed kiss on the balcony of Buckingham Palace, it was perceived and presented by television as a public gesture.[6]

With respect to the definition of the royal wedding, television deliberately overlooked not only the deviations of the performers from their scenarios, but also the antics of the would-be performers among the spectators. The carnival ambiance which could be observed along the procession route led many observers (including novelist John Fowles) to comment on the contrast between what they perceived as English playfulness (that of the crowd) versus British arrogance (the procession), and between Elizabethan jocularity (street behaviour) and Victorian etiquette (behaviour of the principals). Only the Victorian or British in tone survived the broadcast, leaving little place for the ironic dimension of many a patriotic gesture. Chaney (1983) notes this same tendency—and its social and moral cost—in the BBC's preference for military formalism over civilian expressiveness in its live broadcast of the victory parade after World War II. The spontaneity and universalistic mood of the informal marchers was sacrificed thereby. Tact, good taste, and restraint guide the BBC broadcasters as custodians of an event's definition.

Loyalty to definition is probably the essence of that which makes broadcasters performers rather than observers. As loyalty often does, it may render the broadcasters blind to the non-scripted aspects of the very event they are transmitting. This was strikingly illustrated at the queen's silver jubilee, when a mock attempt on the life of the queen was noticed by those present at the event but not by the television team which was unwittingly recording it. Of course, the dilemma of whether to transmit an aberration or a 'hijacking' of an event (such as Sadat's review of troops turned assassination, or the Munich Olympics turned massacre) involves an uneasy editorial choice. As we have seen, it requires a decision to violate the integrity of the contractually agreed event by reintroducing journalistic considerations that may go beyond the authority and competence of the special teams charged with the broadcasting of ceremonial events.

■ **Providing Interpretation**

Television serves as a guide to the meanings of which the event is a carrier. It does so first by imposing a narrative coherence on the event, by endowing it with a story line; indeed, it constrains even its organizers to think of the event as a whole. Its participants are invested with roles and attributes which interpret and add depth to the identity of the event.

Television also relies on connotations by highlighting those elements—generally nonverbal ones—which illuminate the 'why' of an event from the perspective of its organizers. The ostensible discovery by the cameras of

6 Both broadcasting organizations inadvertently missed the cue.

visual messages 'inlaid' in the faces of participants or the windows of the cathedral tends to mask the fact that such messages are made available by a deliberate decision. Television's reading is, thus, more 'expositive' than interpretive. In a sense, it is an exercise in authority.

These two processes take place simultaneously; they reinforce each other and are often indistinguishable. Consider the royal wedding once more. The messages of the wedding were organized in eloquent dramaturgies and spelled out in the articulate voice of the Archbishop of Canterbury. Television's performance joined that of the archbishop and the other organizers—palace, church, armed forces, police—in a way so strikingly complementary that while the three performances were organized independently, so we were told, there lingers an insistent feeling of 'collusion'—call it teamwork. The archbishop explicated the themes which the organizers tried to communicate in protocol and ceremony. The messages later made articulate in the archbishop's speech were also visually or gesturally offered to the spectators throughout the occasion, in flickering, discontinuous cueings.

The archbishop's speech fulfilled an editorial function. Constituting an event within the event, it referred to the main themes of the occasion and, in the process, proposed additional messages of its own. Reciprocally, television abandoned its role as observer and commentator, and reverently assumed an 'observant' role. Organizers, for their part, pre-empted the directorial role, planted photo opportunities, and offered a choreographed ceremony, anticipating the metamorphosis of the heroes of the day into televised images. In short, the organizers were putting on a show; the priest was commenting upon it; television was leading the amens.

We perceive television as a chorus, underlining on the surface of the event the messages the archbishop spoke from its depths. While the meanings proposed by the archbishop were authentic by virtue of his authority over the event (because, in a 'performative' act, he simply made them so), the meanings proposed by television were not openly ascribed to the event but rather revealed during its unravelling. It is striking that, with the exception of one message, these several meanings were identical.

The archbishop firmly established the fairy tale theme in the very act of brushing it aside. 'Here is the stuff of which fairy tales are made', he began. Having thus ushered in Cinderella, the archbishop continued by rejecting the sufficiency of the metaphor. He dismissed the idea that the time had come for the newlyweds to live happily ever after.

Cinderella, however, was much on the minds of the organizers, who made sure that Lady Diana would be accompanied to Saint Paul's by ordinary policemen, but be escorted back to Buckingham Palace by the household cavalry. The same organizers dutifully displayed the roommates of her brief working career now seated in the church's front pews, where television cameras could easily underline their presence. The narrators continued from that point. Announcing that the bride's gown was a 'fairy tale' gown, that the state carriage in which she rode was a 'glass carriage' (indeed, there were windows), they evoked a narrative metamorphosis which, for a moment, demoted the granddaughter of Lady Fermoy to a fairy tale 'commoner'. She was a kindergarten teacher, an Earl's Court boarder—the better to celebrate her promotion.

The archbishop's second theme redirected attention from the institution of royalty to the institution of family. Pulling an aristocratic, wealthy, and outrageously privileged couple out of its leisure class, the orator pointed to it as an embodiment of the universal image of youth and of the drama of every-man's marriage. 'There is an ancient Christian tradition', said the arch-bishop, 'that every bride and groom, on their wedding day, are regarded as a royal couple'. The archbishop thus translated the extraordinary status of this particular couple into something equally extraordinary, but no longer 'above' ordinary: the universally shared, but once-in-a-lifetime experience of marriage. In Turnerian (1969) terms, the archbishop transposed the origin-ality of the event from the realm of 'structure' into that of 'antistructure'. He switched from particular to universal in order to recognize the ceremony of marriage as the foundation of the institution of family, and to proclaim that family holds the potential for social change. 'Our faith sees a wedding day, not as a place of arrival, but as the place where the adventure really begins...'

Obviously, there is a difference between the progression of royal family events and soap operas, in that the former have a public face offered only intermittently and in ceremonial settings, while the latter expose private life as a continuous performance. Both, however, deal with the interaction between individuals and norms; both are concerned with the fate of families and the transmission of values from generation to generation. The organizers of this event did not need to emphasize its family dimension—it was visible through-out. Television's performance echoed this attitude, highlighting the arch-bishop's concern. BBC close-ups subtly stressed the theme, pointing rapidly to a worried mother, a proud father, an emotional grandmother. These domes-tic figures told a story that paralleled that of the royal personae, providing a frame which, at least superficially, competed with the Cinderella story.

The third theme stressed the power of marriage to improve society in accordance with God's will. 'We, like them, are agents of creation', said the archbishop, to indicate the similarity between a 'we' (the people) and a 'them' (the princely couple). The statement 'We are like them', or more exactly, 'We, like them, are agents of creation', invited the overcoming of distance. But despite the overcoming, distance was maintained. The royals will move closer, but only if you imitate them. Their approachability is not physical but moral. They are approachable insofar as they are embodiments of norms to which any one of us may subscribe. The archbishop's rhetorical gesture was particularly interesting in that it offered a solution to the paradox highlighted by Blumler *et al.* (1971) in their analysis of the contradictory attitude of the British public toward the royal family. The royal family, in the Blumler study, was expected to meet the impossible requirements of both dropping and maintaining decorum; of abolishing protocol and perpetuating it; of keeping its distinctiveness, while renouncing the thought of being different.

The event's organizers catered to this ambivalence of the British public *vis-à-vis* monarchical distance, but less subtly than the archbishop. The rhetorical core of the event consisted in a series of back and forth motions stressing two antithetical themes: 'Now they are like us . . . Now they are not . . .' Relayed by television, the pomp and pageantry served to establish distance, but they were also used as a continuous background for discrete signs of approachability. Such was the 'Just Married' sign painted in lipstick and naughtily stuck on the back of the state carriage, together with a flock of balloons echoing those in the hands of myriads of well-wishers, or the departure at Waterloo Station, where cameras showed the honeymooners delivered into the realm of public transportation from a six-horse carriage on a red carpet.

Television was faithful to the organizers' view of the problem of monarchical distance. Humanizing devices were stressed as often as possible against the background of the event's definitional grandeur. The 'Just Married' sign received full attention. Royal children were celebrated as childlike, the princely couple as young, and biology was generally allowed to obliterate caste. Such details may seem pedestrian, compared to the archbishop's elevated message. They provide a translation of its gist, however. Television highlighted messages that were in fact the wedding's *raison d'être*, proving itself something more than a reliable wedding photographer.

To take an example from another event, consider President Sadat's arrival at Ben Gurion Airport. The particular way in which he disembarked was hailed by almost every narrator as 'symbolic' of the trip as a whole. While crew members opened the door of the Boeing aircraft, impressively decorated with the emblem of the Arab Republic of Egypt, an El Al gangway was pushed alongside. Unthinkable until that very minute, this juxtaposition was the paradigmatic example of what the television teams were there to film. Missing that image would have been a minor catastrophe (as it was for ITV to have missed the royal kiss on Buckingham Palace's balcony, and for the BBC to have failed to show it in close-up).

Television directors are constantly on the lookout for situations which express the purpose of an event in a condensed way. Television narrators have to make sure that the significance of such images will not pass unnoticed and will be correctly assessed. In other terms, television's interpretive function consists in making sure (1) at the image level, that the significant features of the event, its visual messages, are properly highlighted; and (2) at the narration level, that these features, once noticed, are correctly interpreted— that is, within a frame of reference consonant with that of the organizers.

The highlighting process has an importance which goes far beyond its technical achievement. It diminishes the role of exhortations and announcements emanating from the organizers of the event or its principals while exalting the event's visual or gestural aspects. By displacing audience focus from explicit statements to visual clues, television 'naturalizes' the event; it authenticates its inlaid message, transforming the performative aspects of ceremonies (utterances emanating from figures of power) into visual anecdotes. It also makes audiences active partners in the reading of the event by inviting interpretation, by encouraging hermeneutic pleasure in the deciphering of indexes and the scrutiny of 'symbols'. Television converts pronouncements of authority into exercises in seduction.

■ Protecting Tone and Prerogative

Unlike the roving glance of the cynical journalist, the glance of the media-event broadcaster is stubbornly focused. Unlike the equally single-minded glance of the security agent, the broadcaster's glance is participatory, actively involved in the official meaning of the event, busy endorsing and conveying its definition. The security glance is blind to meanings.[7] The journalistic glance is cynically receptive to all meanings. The broadcaster's glance, helping the event to spell its name, enacts its meaning. The event is given absolute priority over all other programmes; it is placed above all competing concerns and tightly protected from any interference with its political content, its temporal sequence, its tone, its mood.

Television's power lies not only in the way it structures the flow of daily life, but in its consequent ability to interrupt this flow. Media events are an example of this interruptive dimension. They cancel all other programmes, bring television's clock to a stop, and while they are on the air, cannot themselves be interrupted. Their performance belongs to 'sacred time', bringing all social activity to a standstill. For a while, the event occupies society's 'centre'. No matter what happens, the event has to go on. Thus the riots at Toxteth during the royal wedding ceremonies are not mentioned until the ceremonial occasion is over. This protectiveness toward the event goes to such extremes that it inspires plans for the continuation of the broadcast even if a terrorist incident were to affect some of the principals. The BBC preparation for the royal wedding included contingency plans and alternative editing routes. The occasion can go on while the crisis is being dealt with.

The only reality which can compete with a media event is another media event. We have already noted how one major American channel chose to commute between the Rose Bowl and Sadat's arrival in Jerusalem. The result was that both events were robbed of their symbolic resonance, of their mood. The Jerusalem event looked unbearably slow and pompous; the American event looked gratuitously frenetic.[8] Television's double commitment in this case failed to protect an essential dimension of such events: their tone.

While anthropologists keep stressing the messy and often chaotic dimensions of rituals they have attended, media events are characterized by an almost pedantic concern with unity: unity of time (related to the duration of the live broadcast) and, of course, unity of action. Only in news broadcasts—never in media events—does one juxtapose and give equal importance to, say, the peace moves of President Sadat and the bellicose declarations of rejection-front leaders among the Arabs.

The Dallas assassination of President Kennedy was a 'tragedy', and as such, an occasion to invoke fate and to turn the youngest President into an effigy of human suffering, the central figure of a 'tableau': *Pietà* in a convertible. But tragedy was also an aesthetic concern. Television's homage to the departed

---

7 The glance of journalists may be characterized by distance and, within distance, by mobility. It is typically concerned with recontextualizing the event by situating it in larger frames. It is always alert to possible departures from the announced script, since such departures constitute information. With respect to the royal wedding, for example, the British trade magazine *Broadcast* notes: 'There is another, less happy purpose in the dual feed, about which our sources are naturally circumspect. If anything untoward were to happen anywhere, it would be possible to continue transmitting the planned picture while also feeding back the unexpected event to Television Centre for recording and assessment there by Philip Lewis and if circumstances develop that require a journalistic decision, by Dick Francis' (Griffin-Beale 1981). The security glance, by contrast, is little interested in context. Now a familiar feature of media events, the perpetually shifting eyes of unidentified characters surrounding the principals reveal security people scanning the event for possible sources of disruption.

8 This example illustrates the limits of what Newcomb (1974) has described as television 'dialogism', whereby TV programmes are thought to comment on each other and to reframe each other. The present instance is less a mutual commentary than it is a mutual annihilation.

President stressed the dignified stoicism of the principals, particularly the Hecuba-like composure adopted by Jacqueline Kennedy after a few seconds of petit-bourgeois dismay. Once this tone was established, it had to be maintained throughout the event. Hence the uneasiness felt by television teams over the assassination of Lee Harvey Oswald and expressed in the CBS tribute to Kennedy, 'Four Dark Days'. There were now two assassinations, two corpses, two funerals. The second corpse could not be brushed aside for the duration of television's requiem. A stylistic problem received a rhetorical solution: if the first assassination was a tragedy, the second would be a farce, a caricature, a travesty. Illustrious examples notwithstanding, Kennedy's crucifixion could not take place in bad company. Genres are not to be mixed.

Television's protective role stems from the fact that it is not reporting an event, but actively performing it. In view of this fact, one can hardly expect broadcast journalists to display a penelopean abnegation and to coldly dissect what is largely their own creation. They are not simply transmitting an event or commenting upon it; they are bringing it into existence. Thus, broadcasters double as monument makers or apostles.[9]

Something takes place in the symbolic realm which might affect reality. This something is akin to the medieval dramaturgy of 'mysteries'. Giving media-event status to a proposed event implies a belief in its mystery. As in all religious rites, attendance cannot be neutral and uncommitted. Television here is not simply an observer or a producer. Its presence reactivates an ancient function: the act of attending, of 'being there', and of being an eventual propagator, a subsequent medium. Those present at early Christian events were used as such 'media'. They were called 'witnesses', or, in Greek, 'martyrs'.

Agreeing to promote a political occasion to media-event status thus implies a willingness on the part of television organizations to accept an apostolic mission. It involves an endorsement of the event's goals and an affirmative assessment of the event's power to achieve these goals. This power inheres in the ceremony—in its appeal and evocative character—and in the ability of the media to produce the ceremony. This is still show business, of course: producers have to assess the potential of an event before placing their bets.

Once the commitment is made, it is not easy to switch back again to journalism, as in the hijacking of an event. In the face of media events, the journalistic paradigm of objectivity and neutrality is simply irrelevant. The choice is either to maintain an agonistic role, treating the event as 'news' and addressing it within a news broadcast, or to enter the mode of media ceremonial and become the event's witness. A journalist assigned to a media event must undergo a temporary conversion, one which is not always to his liking (Levy 1981).

---

9 For this reason in part, media events are often made the responsibility of sports units or 'special-events' units (Russo 1983). Still, how can one avoid bringing in journalists, when the event has news value and political or diplomatic implications? Why should a network deprive itself of its experts, precisely when they are most needed? And yet the problem remains that this is not quite journalism. Unlike the news, media events are not descriptive of a state of affairs, but symbolically instrumental in bringing about that state of affairs. They do have some of the qualities inherent in primitive rituals with which they share, in particular, a pragmatically oriented reliance on magical evocation: media events display symbolically what they wish to achieve.

References   Blumler, J. G., *et al.* (1971), 'Attitudes to the Monarchy: Their Structure and Development during a Ceremonial Occasion', *Political Studies*, 19/2: 149–71.

Chaney, D. (1983), 'A Symbolic Mirror of Ourselves: Civic Ritual in Mass Society', *Media, Culture, and Society*, (5)3: 119–35.

Cohen, N. (1978), 'President Sadat's Visit to Jerusalem: Broadcasting Aspects', *EBU Review*, 29: 8–12.

Jakobson, R. (1960), 'Linguistics and Poetics', in T. Sebeok (ed.), *Style in Language*, New York: Wiley.

Levy, M. (1981), 'Disdaining the News', *Journal of Communication*, 31/3: 24–31.

Nora, P. (1972), 'L'événement monstre', *Communications*, 18: 162–72.

Russo, M. A. (1983), 'CBS and the American Political Experience: A History of the CBS News Special Events and Election Units, 1952–1968', Ph.D. dissertation, New York University; Ann Arbor: University microfilm.

Searle, R. (1971), *Philosophy of Language*, Oxford: Oxford University Press.

Shils, E. (1975), *Center and Periphery: Essays in Macrosociology*, Chicago: University of Chicago Press.

Sorohan, J. (1979), 'Pulling off a Broadcasting Miracle with Nine Weeks' Notice', *Irish Broadcasting Review*: 46–7.

Turner, V. (1969), *The Ritual Process: Structure and Antistructure*, Ithaca: Cornell University Press. Reprint edn. 1977.

Veron, E. (1981), *Construire l'événement: les médias et l'accident de Three Mile Island*, Paris: Minuit. (With the collaboration of J. Dana and A. F. de Ferrière.)

Vianello, R. (1986), 'The Power Politics of Live Television', *Journal of Film and Video*, 37/3: 26–40.

Wills, G. (1980), 'The Greatest Story Ever Told', *Columbia Journalism Review*, 18: 25–33.

Zelizer, B. (1981), 'The Parameters of Broadcast of Sadat's Arrival in Jerusalem'. Master's thesis, Communications Institute, Hebrew University of Jerusalem.

2

PART TWO

Production of News

Introduction to Part II: Production of News

PART 2 BEGINS with David Manning White's 1950 study of the gatekeeper. Hoping to gain an insight into the roles the gatekeeper plays in the news production process, he investigated how a wire editor of a morning newspaper on an industrialized mid-west city rejected or accepted stories. Although the gatekeeper theory has been refined and criticized since White's original study, it provides an insight into the subjective nature of the news production process. It also indicates the degree of reliance on judgements, experiences, and attitudes of the participants of the news process. White's copy-editor, 'Mr Gates' as he has come to be known, had twenty-five years experience as a journalist working as a reporter and copy-editor. Gates decided to print about 10 per cent of the copy that was available to him and to assist White, Gates recorded his reasons for rejecting stories and selecting others.

Over the years the gatekeeping process underwent a more sophisticated development and Pamela Shoemaker reveals its complexity. Whilst the individual editor/gatekeeper has his or her own preferences about events, decision-making strategies and values determining his or her rejection or selection of an item, there is an acknowledgement that the gatekeeper works within the constraints and bureaucratic routines of the news organization. Shoemaker identifies various psychological processes affecting the gatekeeping process and acknowledges that news organizations relate very strongly to the social system in which they operate.

Warren Breed, in a classic piece first published in 1955, examines how young journalists are socialized into the norms of their jobs. He outlines six factors creating conformity and preventing potentially deviant staff from acting in a way contrary to the norms and policies of the news organizations. He also posits five factors relevant to the reporter's ability to circumvent news organization policy. Breed's study is important in eschewing notions of conspiracy. He analyses the way the socialization processes in news organizations occur and points to areas of potential bias. Breed shows how compliance by reporters and journalists is rewarded amongst their colleagues and superiors rather than by the readers, so instead of appealing to both societal and professional ideals, values are redefined to the more pragmatic level of the newsroom group. Any change, therefore, towards a more democratic press has to arise from possible judgements made on the owners who set out the policy and the senior editors who co-ordinate it.

Lee Sigelman continues the theme of the organizational approach in his observation and investigation of local political journalists working for two opposing political and ideological metropolitan newspapers in the south-eastern USA. To understand the nature of bias, he conducted a study of the newspapers' recruitment, socialization, and control processes. Sigelman focuses on two of the main planks on which organizations implicate attitudes among their employees, namely selective recruitment and socialization. The two newspapers devoted relatively little time to recruiting new reporters and ensuring that new recruits were socialized into the norms of the organization. In addition they did not even ensure applicants were in general agreement with the editorial policies of the newspaper. Nevertheless, Sigelman found a number of ways in which the socialization process operates, for example editorial revisions, informal contacts with more experienced newsmen and perhaps of more importance the editorial conference. What was (and continues to be) fascinating about Sigelman's observations was the discovery that owners and editors were just as bound up as the reporters and new recruits in the myths of a free and democratic and responsible press and a belief in the idea of objective reporting. It meant, therefore, they were very reluctant to provide an overt or conspiratorial way of indoctrinating new members with their own political views. Newspapers did not need to be very diligent in their recruiting and selection processes since there was a large element of self-selection on the part of journalists as to which newspapers they chose to work for. The processes are so structured that supporting attitudes of journalists are assured without any 'violation of the institutional mythology' of a free and democratic press.

The short extract by Ericson, Baranek, and Chan is the first of two pieces in the reader from their three-volume epic study of crime coverage in Canada. It provides a flavour of the way news production typically occurs in newspaper and television newsrooms and gives a diagrammatical account of the news production process illustrating the different roles of the reporters and editors. The study, conducted in the late 1980s in Canada, is similar to the classic observation and organization studies of a decade earlier. The 1970s were a very fruitful period in mass communications research on news organizations and the following three pieces come from studies conducted during that period.

The first by Mark Fishman looks at the different beats that journalists cover and how news generates from their general assignments. He examines the way a reporter detects, investigates, and formulates a story from his or her beat. Fishman's study identifies the way the world is bureaucratically organized for journalists enabling the reporter to detect stories and events and providing him or her with a way of locating knowledge of happenings already occurred. For example, Fishman gives the story of a large fire in a warehouse. The journalist knows the local fire department is in a position to have the information. Similarly if a crime is committed, the journalist knows the police are in a position to provide the details. Officials and authorities are thus in a structural position aware of events happening. Fishman argues that bureaucratic consciousness is invaluable for detecting news. It indicates the position reporters should adopt to discover happenings not yet known. For the beat or specialist reporter, under pressure to produce large amounts of daily news, it means they can generate large and reliable quantities of information by focusing on these bureaucratic information generators.

Golding and Elliott's work is based on an international comparison of newsrooms in Ireland, Sweden, and Nigeria. News production is a very competitive, predictable, and strongly patterned routine that varies only marginally from country to country. It is a regulated process and any bias detected in the product is an unintended but nevertheless inevitable result of the organizational routines. Golding and Elliott suggest that news is the transmission of ideology of particular social groups arising out of the production process and the identified demands of the audience. The organized production of news results in a transmission of values similar to those of the ideology. General consensus forms around social conflicts and the professional norms operating within the news environment provide a consensus of views rather than any kind of opposition or alternative ones. The study is very useful in providing descriptions of various elements of the production cycle and how these operate in forming this consensus.

The piece by Philip Schlesinger comes from a study conducted of BBC news in the late 1970s. The chapter selected here from his book *Putting 'Reality' Together* engages with the question of time in the news cycle. As he points out himself, whilst the importance of time in the news production cycle is often signalled it is rarely given the time for separate analysis. Schlesinger shows how the concepts of production are determined by the constraints of time and the implication this has for the kind of news the public receives. He demonstrates how the bias towards immediacy is not just a response to competition and other market factors, but is something inherent in the way that newsmen have become obsessional about time. The dynamics of the production process shows the ephemeral and perishable nature of stories leading to a framing of the news out of any historical or textual manner and a reduction of understanding of events.

The final piece in Part 2 by Charles Bantz examines various forms of social conflict as a way of understanding behaviour in news organizations, in particular television news. Bantz identifies various factors to illustrate how organizational cultures in news organizations normalize the occurrence of conflict. Professional and business norms, often viewed as being incompatible, may result in conflict becoming ordinary and routine, and perhaps even in a valuable outcome.

8

The 'Gatekeeper': A Case Study in the Selection of News

David Manning White

IT WAS THE LATE Kurt Lewin, truly one of the great social scientists of our time, who applied the term 'gatekeeper' to a phenomenon which is of considerable importance to students of mass communications. In his last article,[1] before his untimely death, Dr Lewin pointed out that the traveling of a news item through certain communication channels was dependent on the fact that certain areas within the channels functioned as 'gates'. Carrying the analogy further, Lewin said that gate sections are governed either by impartial rules or by 'gatekeepers,' and in the latter case an individual or group is 'in power' for making the decision between 'in' or 'out'.

To understand the functioning of the 'gate', Lewin said, was equivalent to understanding the factors which determine the decisions of the 'gate-keepers', and he rightly suggested that the first diagnostic task is the finding of the actual 'gatekeepers'.

The purpose of this study is to examine closely the way one of the 'gatekeepers' in the complex channels of communication operates his 'gate'.

Wilbur Schramm made an observation central to this whole study when he wrote that 'no aspect of communication is so impressive as the enormous number of choices and discards which have to be made between the formation of the symbol in the mind of the communicator, and the appearance of a related symbol in the mind of the receiver'.[2] To illustrate this in terms of a news story let us consider, for example, a Senate hearing on a proposed bill for federal aid to education. At the hearing there will be reporters from the various press associations, Washington correspondents of large newspapers which maintain staffs in the capital, as well as reporters for local newspapers. All of these form the first 'gate' in the process of communication. They have to make the initial judgement as to whether a story is 'important' or not. One

Source: David Manning White, 'The Gatekeeper', *Journalism Quarterly*, 27 (1950), 383–90. The author acknowledges the suggestions of Dr Wilbur Schramm during the preparation of this paper, also the assistance of Mr Raymond F. Stewart.

1 Kurt Lewin, 'Channels of Group Life', *Human Relations*, 1/2: 145.

2 Wilbur Schramm, *Mass Communications* (Urbana: University of Illinois Press, 1949), 289.

has only to read the Washington stories from two newspapers whose general editorial attitudes differ widely on such an issue as federal aid to education to realize from the beginning of the process the 'gatekeepers' are playing an important role. The appearance of the story in the Chicago *Tribune* and the Chicago *Sun-Times* might well show some differences in treatment. It is apparent that even the actual physical event of the Senate hearing (which we might call the *criterion event*) is reported by two reporters in two different perceptual frameworks and that the two men bring to the 'story' different sets of experience, attitudes and expectations.

Thus a story is transmitted from one 'gatekeeper' after another in the chain of communications. From reporter to rewrite man, through bureau chief to 'state' file editors at various press association offices, the process of choosing and discarding is continuously taking place. And finally we come to our last 'gatekeeper,' the one to whom we turn for the purpose of our case study. This is the man who is usually known as the wire editor on the non-metropolitan newspaper. He has charge of the selection of national and international news which will appear on the front and 'jump' pages of his newspaper, and usually he makes up these pages.

Our 'gatekeeper' is a man in his middle 40s, who after approximately 25 years' experience as a journalist (both as reporter and copy-editor) is now the wire editor of a morning newspaper of approximately 30,000 circulation in a highly industrialized mid-west city of 100,000. It is his job to select from the avalanche of wire copy daily provided by the Associated Press, United Press, and International News Service what 30,000 families will read on the front page of their morning newspapers. He also copy-edits and writes the headlines for these stories. His job is similar to that which newspapermen throughout the country hold in hundreds of non-metropolitan newspapers.[3] And in many respects he is the most important 'gatekeeper' of all, for if he rejects a story the work of all those who preceded him in reporting and transmitting the story is negated. It is understood, of course, that the story could have 'ended' (insofar as its subsequent transmission is concerned) at any of the previous 'gates'. But assuming the story has progressed through all the 'gates', it is obvious that this wire editor is faced with an extremely complicated set of decisions to make regarding the limited number of stories he can use.

Our purpose in this study was to determine some preliminary ideas as to why this particular wire editor selected or rejected the news stories filed by the three press associations (and transmitted by the 'gatekeeper' above him in Chicago) and thereby gain some diagnostic notions about the general role of the 'gatekeeper' in the areas of mass communications.

The problem of finding out what Mr Gates selected from the mass of incoming wire copy was not difficult, for it appeared on the front and 'jump' pages of his newspaper each morning. Actually, we were far more concerned with the copy that did not get into the paper. So for the week of 6–13 February 1949, Mr Gates saved every piece of wire copy that came to his desk. [. . .] Mr Gates went through every piece of copy in the

---

3 By far the majority of the approximately 1,780 daily newspapers in this country are in the smaller cities not on the main trunk wires of the press associations. Their reliance on the single wire 'state' operations which emanate from the larger cities thus places great responsibility in the hands of the wire-editor.

'reject' box and wrote on it the reason why he had initially rejected it, assuming that he could recall the reason. In the cases where no ascertainable reason had occurred to him he made no notations on the copy. [...]

Assuming that five lines of wire copy are equivalent to a column inch in a newspaper, Mr Gates received approximately 12,400 inches of press association news from the AP, UP, and INS during the week. Of this he used 1,297 column inches of wire news, or about *one-tenth*, in the seven issues we measured. Table 1 shows a breakdown by categories of the wire news received and used during the week.

TABLE 1. *Amounts of Press Association news Mr Gates received and used during seven-day period*

Category	Wire Copy Received		Wire Copy Used	
	Col. In.*	% of Total	Col. In.*	% of Total
Crime	527	4.4	41	3.2
Disaster	405	3.4	44	3.4
Political				
State	565	4.7	88	6.8
National	1722	14.5	205	15.8
Human Interest	4171	35.0	301	23.2
International				
Political	1804	15.1	176	13.6
Economic	405	3.4	59	4.5
War	480	4.0	72	5.6
Labour	650	5.5	71	5.5
National				
Farm	301	2.5	78	6.0
Economic	294	2.5	43	3.3
Education	381	3.2	56	4.3
Science	205	1.7	63	4.9
TOTAL	11,910	99.9	1,297	100.1

* Counting five lines of wire copy as one column inch.

It is only when we study the reasons given by Mr Gates for rejecting almost nine-tenths of the wire copy (in his search for the one-tenth for which he has space) that we begin to understand how highly subjective, how reliant upon value-judgements based on the 'gatekeeper's' own set of experiences, attitudes and expectations the communication of 'news' really is. In this particular case the 56 wordings given may be divided into two main categories: (1) rejecting the incident as worthy of being reported, and (2) selecting from many reports of the same event. (See Table 2.)

Thus we find him rejecting one piece of wire copy with the notation, 'He's too Red'. Another story is categorically marked 'Never use this'. [...] Thus we see that many of the reasons which Mr Gates gives for the rejection of the stories fall into the category of highly subjective value-judgements.

TABLE 2. *Reasons for rejection of Press Association news given by Mr Gates during seven-day period*

Reason	Number of times given
Rejecting incident as worthy of reporting	423
Not interesting (61); no interest here (43)	104
Dull writing (51); too vague (26); drags too much (3)	80
No good (31); slop (18); B. S. (18)	67
Too much already on subject (54); used up (4); passed—dragging out*; too much of this; goes on all the time; dying out	62
Trivial (29); would ignore (21); no need for this; wasted space; not too important; not too hot; not too worthy	55
Never use this (16); never use (7)	23
Propaganda (16); he's too red; sour grapes	18
Wouldn't use (11); don't care for suicide stories; too suggestive; out of good taste	14
Selecting from reports of the same event	910
Would use if space (221); no space (168); good—if space (154); late—used up (61); too late—no space (34); no space—used other press service; would use partially if space	640
Passed for later story (61); waiting for later information (48); waiting on this (33); waiting for this to hatch (17); would let drop a day or two (11); outcome will be used—not this; waiting for later day progress	172
Too far away (24); out of area (16)	40
Too regional (36)	36
Used another press service: Better story (11); shorter (6); this is late; lead more interesting; meatier	20
Bannered yesterday	1
I missed this one	1

* In this and other cases where no number follows the reason that reason was given only once.

The second category gives us an important clue as to the difficulty of making choices of one piece of copy over another. No less than 168 times, Mr Gates makes the notation 'No space.' In short, the story (in his eyes) has merit and interest, he has no 'personal' objections to it, but space is at a premium. It is significant to observe that the later in the evening the stories came in, the higher was the proportion of the 'no space' or 'would use' type of notation. As the evening progresses the wire editor's pages become more and more filled up. A story that has a good chance of getting on the front page at 7.30 or 8 o'clock in the evening may not be worth the precious remaining space at 11 o'clock. [. . .] Other reasons which fall into the mechanical category are 'Used INS—shorter' or 'Used UP—this is late'. Even in this category, though, we find subjective value-judgements such as 'Used AP—better story' or 'Used INS—lead more interesting'.

Now that we have some preliminary knowledge of the manner in which Mr Gates selects or rejects news for his front and 'jump' pages, it might be interesting to examine his performance for a specific day. In Table 3 the amount and type of news which appeared on the front and 'jump' pages edited by Gates for 9 February 1949 is presented. Table 4 shows the total number of dispatches (classified as to type of story) received but not used.

During this particular week the Cardinal Mindzenty trial was receiving wide play from newspapers throughout the land and the press associations were filing many stories covering all phases of the case. So in making a comparison of the dispatches received and the stories which appeared it should not be surprising to note that Human Interest news was used most. [. . .]

TABLE 3. *Column inches devoted to content categories in 9 February 1949 issue*

Category		Front Page and Jump
Local		3.50
Crime		5.00
Disaster		9.75
Political		41.25
Local	9.75	
State	19.50	
National	12.00	
Human Interest		43.75[a]
International		23.00
Political	11.50	
Economic	11.50	
War	—	
National		24.25
Labour	19.25	
Farm	—	
Economic	5.00	
Education		—
Science		6.00[b]

[a] About one-half of this amount were Cardinal Mindzenty stories, which, because of the human appeal, were classed as Human Interest.

[b] Three column picture not included.

Political news enjoyed the second largest play. Here we begin to have an indication of preference, as political news ranked only fifth in the 'dispatches received' department. Political news seems to be a favourite with Mr Gates, for even if we subtract the almost ten inches given to a local political story it ranks second in play.

TABLE 4. *Number of pieces of Press Association releases received but not used 9 February 1949*

Category	Received before Front Page Was Made Up	Received after Front Page Was Made Up	Total Received For Day
Local	3		3
Crime	32	1	33
Disaster	15		15
Political			22
Local	1	2	
State	10	2	
National	6	1	
Human Interest	65	14	79
International			46
Political	19	5	
Economic	9	1	
War	10	2	
National			37
Farm	2		
Labour	13	1	
Economic	17	4	
Education	3	2	5
Science	5	2	7
Total for Day	210	37	247

While a total of 33 crime stories was received, only five column inches of crime appeared on the front and 'jump' pages of Mr Gates's paper. The obvious conclusion is that crime news, as such, does not appeal to this wire editor. But it should be noted that no 'big' crime stories broke that day.

As one examines the whole week's performance of Mr Gates, as manifested in the stories he chose, certain broad patterns become apparent. What do we know, for example, about the kinds of stories that he selected in preference to others from the same category? What tests of subject matter and way-of-writing did Mr Gates seem to apply? In almost every case where he had some choice between competing press association stories Mr Gates preferred the 'conservative'. I use this expression not only in terms of its political connotations, but also in terms of the style of writing. Sensationalism and insinuation seemed to be avoided consistently.

As to the way-of-writing that he preferred, Mr Gates showed an obvious dislike for stories that had too many figures and statistics. In almost every case where one news agency supplied a story filled with figures and statistics and the competing agency's story was an easier going, more interpretative than statistical type of story, the latter appeared in the paper. An indication of his standards for writing is seen in Table 2, where 26 stories were rejected as being 'too vague', 51 rejected for 'dull writing', and 61 for being 'not interesting'.

Another question that should be considered in this study (and subsequent ones) is: does the category really enter into the choice? That is, does the wire editor try to choose a certain amount of crime news, human interest news, etc.? Are there some other divisions of subject matter or form which he chooses in this manner, such as a certain number of one-paragraph stories?

Insofar as this 'gatekeeper' is representative of wire editors as a whole, it does not appear that there is any conscious choice of news by categories. [...] It would be most interesting and valuable to ascertain how a wire editor determines what one issue or type of story is 'the' story of the week. Many times that decision is made by 'gatekeepers' above him, or by 'gatekeepers' in competing media. Can a wire editor refuse to play a story 'up' when his counterpart in the local radio station is playing it to the hilt? Likewise, can a wire editor play down a story when he sees competing papers from nearby metropolitan areas coming into his city and playing up the story? These factors undoubtedly have something to do in determining the wire editor's opinion as to what he should give the reading public the next morning. This brings up the rather obvious conclusion that theoretically all of the wire editor's standards of taste should refer back to an audience who must be served and pleased. [...]

It is a well known fact in individual psychology that people tend to perceive as true only those happenings which fit into their own beliefs concerning what is likely to happen. It begins to appear (if Mr Gates is a fair representative of his class) that in his position as 'gatekeeper' the newspaper editor sees to it (even though he may never be consciously aware of it) that the community shall hear as a fact only those events which the newsman, as the representative of his culture, believes to be true.

This is the case study of one 'gatekeeper', but one, who like several hundred of his fellow 'gatekeepers', plays a most important role as the terminal 'gate' in the complex process of communication. Through studying his overt reasons for rejecting news stories from the press associations we see how highly subjective, how based on the 'gatekeeper's' own set of experiences, attitudes and expectations the communication of 'news' really is.

9

Gatekeeping

Pamela J. Shoemaker

**A New
Gatekeeping
Model**

FIGURES 1, 2, AND 3 summarize and integrate what is known about gatekeeping, based on the theoretical approaches we have discussed. Figures 2 and 3 are not independent models but represent enlargements of portions of Figure 1. The overall process is shown in Figure 1 but without detail within communication organizations and within individual gatekeepers. Figure 2 shows the gatekeeping processes within a communication organization, and Figure 3 shows the intra-individual psychological processes within one gatekeeper. In Figure 1 (see Figs. 2 and 3 for more detail), circles represent individual gatekeepers, vertical bars in front of gatekeepers are gates, and the arrows in front of and behind each gate represent the forces that affect a message's entrance into the gate and what happens to it afterwards. The large squares are communication organizations, and small rectangles represent social and institutional factors. One or more channels lead to and from each gate and gatekeeper, each carrying one or more messages or potential messages.

The process starts with a variety of potential messages travelling through multiple channels to any of several types of communication organizations, such as a wire service, a public relations agency, a newspaper, or a television network. An organization may have multiple staff members operating in boundary role input positions, each with the power to control which potential messages actually enter the organization and the power to shape the message.

Moving to the organizational enlargement (Fig. 2), we see that, within a complex organization, the boundary role gatekeepers in charge of inputs may channel selected messages to one or more internal gatekeepers, who may exert their own selection processes and who also may shape the message in a variety of ways. The surviving, shaped messages are then transmitted to boundary role gatekeepers for final shaping, selection, and transmission directly to the audience or to another communication organization (see Fig. 1). As the feedback loop from organization 2 to organization 1 (and from the audience to organization 2) indicates, selection of messages for outputting is heavily influenced by the selection criteria of the receiver. As Figure 2 shows, the gatekeeping processes internal to the organization are embedded in the organization's communication routines and characteristics, which affect the

Source: Pamela J. Shoemaker, *Gatekeeping* (Newbury Park, Calif., London, and New Delhi: Sage Publications, 1991).

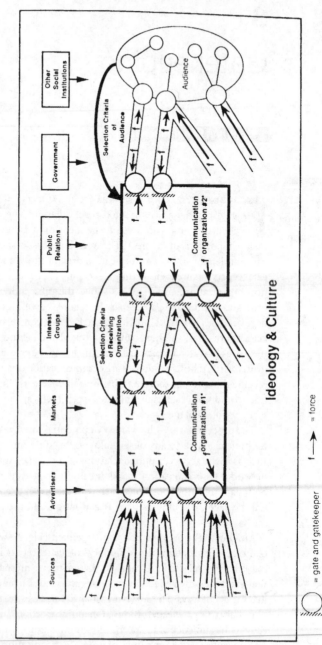

Figure 1.
Gatekeeping between organizations is embedded in social system ideology and culture and is influenced by social and institutional factors.

Note: As an example, communication organizations could include wire services, public relations agencies, television networks, or newspapers.
* See Fig. 2 for a detailed version of gatekeeping within an organization.
** See Fig. 3 for a detailed version of gatekeeping within an individual.

decisions organizational gatekeepers make. Figure 2 also provides for the 'groupthink' phenomenon (Janis 1983), particularly among socially cohesive groups of gatekeepers.

Figure 3 identifies various psychological processes and individual characteristics that can affect the gatekeeping process, including cognitive heuristics, models of thinking, socialization, second-guessing, values, attitudes,

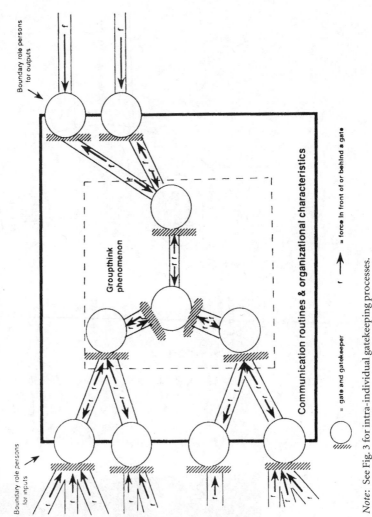

Figure 2.
Gatekeeping within an organization is embedded in communication organizational characteristics.

decision-making strategies, role conceptions, and type of job. Just as the broader gatekeeping model (Fig. 1) is embedded in social system ideology and culture, and within-organization gatekeeping (Fig. 2) is embedded in communication routines and organizational characteristics, individual-level gatekeeping processes (Fig. 3) are embedded in the individual's life experiences.

Thus we see the complexity of the gatekeeping process. The individual gatekeeper has likes and dislikes, ideas about the nature of his or her job, ways of thinking about a problem, preferred decision-making strategies, and values that all impinge on the decision to reject or select (and shape) a message. But the gatekeeper is not totally free to follow a personal whim; he or she must operate within the constraints of communication routines to do things this way or that. All of this also must occur within the framework of the communication organization, which has its own priorities but also is

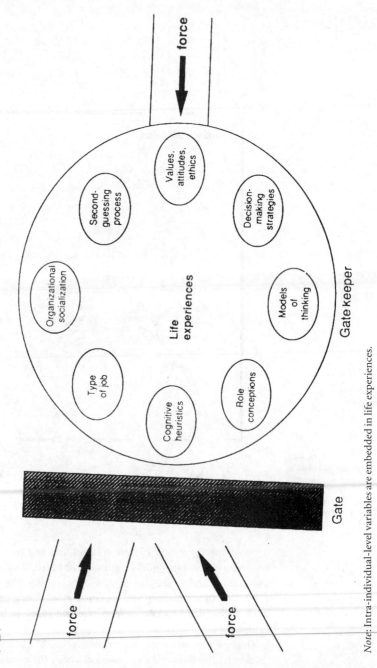

Figure 3.
Intra-individual
gatekeeping processes.

Note: Intra-individual-level variables are embedded in life experiences.

continuously buffeted by influential forces from outside the organization. And, of course, none of these actors—the individual, the routine, the organization, or the social institution—can escape the fact that it is tied to and draws its sustenance from the social system.

Future Research Even a multiple-level model such as is shown in Figures 1–3 still leaves many questions unanswered. Although the gatekeeping literature covers nearly fifty years and scores of studies, more can be done. This final section will suggest directions for future studies.

First, scholars would be well advised to consider the roles that gatekeeping can play on multiple levels of analysis. Some studies include variables from more than one level—for example, personal attitudes (individual level) with communication routines; this is in principle an advantage because it increases the richness of the study. However, if variables from multiple levels are combined in one analysis, this could confuse interpretation of the results.

Second, the linkages between levels could particularly benefit from study. Exactly what is the mechanism through which social system variables affect social institutions, and how do these influence communication organizations? In what ways do communication organizations and their routines influence gatekeeping processes within individuals?

Third, the relative power of the levels should be addressed. One line of thought holds that individual-level influences are least important, being effectively controlled by communication routines and influences from higher levels. As we indicated earlier, however, some studies (Sasser and Russell 1972; Stempel 1985) suggest that communication routines override individual influences in some circumstances but not in others. As Hirsch (1977: 21) points out, gatekeeping studies are primarily interested in 'subjective bias', and this can operate at more than the individual level of analysis. If an individual gatekeeper wants to base decisions on his or her personal attitudes, to what extent can this be done? How much autonomy and power do individual gatekeepers have to impose their own agendas on media content? What conditions would be conducive to the exercise of personal judgement over more structural constraints?

Fourth, study of the individual needs to progress beyond simple questions of attitudes or bias. We have suggested a variety of intra-individual approaches (e.g. models of thinking, cognitive heuristics, second-guessing, decision making) that could help identify the extent to which individual-level processes are important.

Fifth, the extension of gatekeeping into the higher levels of analysis allows us to use some theoretical approaches that are not generally applied to gatekeeping and presents many ideas for research. The boundary roles perspective (Adams 1980) seems particularly fruitful, suggesting new interpretations of old studies, as suggested above. If Adams is correct, the wire services may use their own criteria to select input messages but use criteria from the receiving organizations to select outputs. This reverses the assumed causal direction in several gatekeeping studies and suggests that the media get from wire services what they want rather than what the wire services want them to have.

Sixth, studies should do more with the gates themselves and the forces surrounding them. Does the number of items in front of or behind a gate affect the polarity and strength of the force exerted? Must forces always change polarity? Is movement through a gate always unidirectional or could some items move 'backwards'? What would cause them to do so? Are some gates 'lower' than others?

Seventh, the study of gatekeeping ought to be broadened beyond mere selection to the shaping, display, timing, withholding, or repetition of messages (Donohue *et al.* 1972). We ought to investigate particularly the role of pre- and postgate forces in these processes of non-selection.

Eighth, more can be done with characteristics of the messages. Nisbett and Ross (1980) have suggested that vivid messages would be more likely than pallid messages to pass through a gate, but this idea has not been used in gatekeeping research. We need to progress beyond a categorization of messages (e.g. human interest, economy, international issues) to develop a number of continuous dimensions on which messages can be measured. This will add much to our ability to predict whether and in what form a message will pass through a gate.

Ninth, we might compare the gatekeeping activities of various types of communication organizations, such as television networks and local stations, newspapers, radio stations, advertising agencies, public relations agencies, and magazines. How do communication routines differ? How do the differing goals of these organizations affect inputs and outputs not just in terms of selection but also in terms of how the messages are shaped?

References   ADAMS, J. S. (1980), 'Interorganizational Processes and Organizational Boundary Spanning Activities', in B. M. Staw and L. L. Cummings (eds.), *Research in organizational behavior* (Greenwich, Conn.: JAI), ii. 321–55.

DONOHUE, G. A., TICHENOR, P. J., and OLIEN, C. N. (1972), 'Gatekeeping: Mass Media Systems and Information Control', in F. G. Kline and P. J. Tichenor (eds.), *Current Perspectives in Mass Communication Research* (Beverly Hills, Calif.: Sage), 41–70.

HIRSCH, P. M. (1977), 'Occupational, Organizational and Institutional Models in Mass Media Research: Toward an Integrated Framework', in P. M. Hirsch, P. V. Miller, and F. G. Kline (eds.), *Strategies for Communication Research* (Beverly Hills, Calif.: Sage).

JANIS, I. L. (1983), *Groupthink: Psychological Studies of Policy Decisions and Fiascoes* (Boston: Houghton Mifflin).

NISBETT, R., and ROSS, L. (1980), *Human Inference: Strategies and Shortcomings of Social Judgment* (New York: Prentice-Hall).

SASSER, E. L., and RUSSELL, J. T. (1972), 'The Fallacy of News Judgment', *Journalism Quarterly, 49*: 280–4.

STEMPEL, G. H., III. (1985), 'Gatekeeping: The Mix of Topics and the Selection of Stories', *Journalism Quarterly, 62*: 791–6, 815.

10

Social Control in the Newsroom: A Functional Analysis

IDEALLY, THERE WOULD be no problem of either 'control' or 'policy' on the newspaper in a full democracy. The only controls would be the nature of the event and the reporter's effective ability to describe it. In practice, we find the publisher does set news policy, and this policy is usually followed by members of his staff. Conformity is *not* automatic, however, for three reasons: (1) the existence of ethical journalistic norms; (2) the fact that staff subordinates (reporters, etc.) tend to have more 'liberal' attitudes (and therefore perceptions) than the publisher and could invoke the norms to justify anti-policy writing; and (3) the ethical taboo preventing the publisher from commanding subordinates to follow policy. How policy comes to be maintained, and where it is bypassed, is the subject of this paper. [...]

Every newspaper has a policy, admitted or not.[1] The central question will be: How is policy maintained, despite the fact that it often contravenes journalistic norms, that staffers often personally disagree with it, and that executives cannot legitimately command that it be followed? [...]

How the Staffer Learns Policy

The first mechanism promoting conformity is the 'socialization' of the staffer with regard to the norms of his job. When the new reporter starts work he is not told what policy is. Nor is he ever told. Yet all but the newest

Source: Warren Breed, 'Social Control in the Newsroom: A Functional Analysis', *Social Forces*, 33 (1955), 326–35.

1 It is extremely difficult to measure the extent of objectivity or bias. One recent attempt is reported in Nathan B. Blumberg, *One-Party Press?* (Lincoln: University of Nebraska Press, 1954), which gives a news count for 35 papers' performance in the 1952 election campaign. He concluded that 18 of the papers showed 'no evidence of partiality', 11 showed 'no conclusive evidence of partiality', and 6 showed partiality. His interpretations, however, are open to argument. A different interpretation could conclude that while about 16 showed little or no partiality, the rest did. It should be noted; too, that there are different areas of policy depending on local conditions. The chief difference occurs in the deep South, where frequently there is no 'Republican' problem and no 'union' problem over which the staff can be divided. Colour becomes the focus of policy.

staffers know what policy is.[2] On being asked, they say they learn it 'by osmosis'. Sociologically, this means they become socialized and 'learn the ropes' like a neophyte in any subculture. Basically, the learning of policy is a process by which the recruit discovers and internalizes the rights and obligations of his status and its norms and values. [...]

Reasons for Conforming to Policy

There is no one factor which creates conformity-mindedness, unless we resort to a summary term such as 'institutionalized statuses' or 'structural roles'. Particular factors must be sought in particular cases. The staffer must be seen in terms of his status and aspirations, the structure of the newsroom organization and of the larger society. He also must be viewed with reference to the operations he performs through his workday, and their consequences for him. The following six reasons appear to stay the potentially intransigent staffer from acts of deviance—often, if not always.[3]

1. Institutional Authority and Sanctions

The publisher ordinarily owns the paper and from a purely business standpoint has the right to expect obedience of his employees. He has the power to fire or demote for transgressions. This power, however, is diminished markedly in actuality by three facts. First, the newspaper is not conceived as a purely business enterprise, due to the protection of the First Amendment and a tradition of professional public service. Secondly, firing is a rare phenomenon on newspapers. [...] It is true, however, that staffers still fear punishment; the myth has the errant star reporter taken off murders and put on obituaries—'the Chinese torture chamber' of the newsroom. Fear of sanctions, rather than their invocation, is a reason for conformity, but not as potent a one as would seem at first glance.

Editors, for their part, can simply ignore stories which might create deviant actions, and when this is impossible, can assign the story to a 'safe' staffer. In the infrequent case that an anti-policy story reaches the city desk, the story is changed; extraneous reasons, such as the pressure of time and space, are given for the change.[4] Finally, the editor may contribute to the durability of policy by insulating the publisher from policy discussions. He may reason that the publisher would be embarrassed to hear of conflict over

---

2 While the concept of policy is crucial to this analysis, it is not to be assumed that newsmen discuss it fully. Some do not even use the word in discussing how their paper is run. To this extent, policy is a latent phenomenon; either the staffer has no reason to contemplate policy or he chooses to avoid so doing. It may be that one strength of policy is that it has become no more manifest to the staffers who follow it.

3 Two cautions are in order here. First, it will be recalled that we are discussing not all news, but only policy news. Second, we are discussing only staffers who are potential non-conformers. Some agree with policy; some have no views on policy matters; others do not write policy stories. Furthermore, there are strong forces in American society which cause many individuals to choose harmonious adjustment (conformity) in any situation, regardless of the imperatives. See Erich Fromm, *Escape From Freedom* (New York: Farrar and Rinehart, 1941), and David Riesman, *The Lonely Crowd* (New Haven: Yale, 1950).

4 Excellent illustration of this tactic is given in the novel by an experienced newspaperwoman: Margaret Long, *Affair of the Heart* (New York: Random House, 1953), ch. 10. This chapter describes the framing of a Negro for murder in a middle-sized southern city, and the attempt of a reporter to tell the story objectively.

policy and the resulting bias, and spare him the resulting uneasiness; thus the policy remains not only covert but undiscussed and therefore unchanged.[5]

2. Feelings of Obligation and Esteem for Superiors

The staffer may feel obliged to the paper for having hired him. Respect, admiration and gratitude may be felt for certain editors who have perhaps schooled him, 'stood up for him', or supplied favours of a more paternalistic sort. Older staffers who have served as models for newcomers or who have otherwise given aid and comfort are due return courtesies. Such obligations and warm personal sentiments toward superiors play a strategic role in the pull to conformity.

3. Mobility Aspirations

In response to a question about ambition, all the younger staffers showed wishes for status achievement. There was agreement that bucking policy constituted a serious bar to this goal. In practice, several respondents noted that a good tactic toward advancement was to get 'big' stories on Page One; this automatically means no tampering with policy. Further, some staffers see newspapering as a 'stepping stone' job to more lucrative work: public relations, advertising, free-lancing, etc. The reputation for troublemaking would inhibit such climbing. [...]

4. Absence of Conflicting Group Allegiance

The largest formal organization of staffers is the American Newspaper Guild. The Guild, much as it might wish to, has not interfered with internal matters such as policy. It has stressed business unionism and political interests external to the newsroom. As for informal groups, there is no evidence available that a group of staffers has ever 'ganged up' on policy.

5. The Pleasant Nature of the Activity

(a) *In-groupness in the newsroom.* The staffer has a low formal status *vis-a-vis* executives, but he is not treated as a 'worker'. Rather, he is a co-worker with executives; the entire staff co-operates congenially on a job they all like and respect: getting the news. The newsroom is a friendly, first-namish place. Staffers discuss stories with editors on a give-and-take basis. Top executives with their own offices sometimes come out and sit in on newsroom discussions.[6]

(b) *Required operations are interesting.* Newsmen like their work. Few voiced complaints when given the opportunity to gripe during interviews. The operations required—witnessing, interviewing, briefly mulling the meanings of events, checking facts, writing—are not onerous.

(c) *Non-financial perquisites.* These are numerous: the variety of experience, eye-witnessing significant and interesting events, being the first to know, getting 'the inside dope' denied laymen, meeting and sometimes

---

5 The insulation of one individual or group from another is a good example of social (as distinguished from psychological) mechanisms to reduce the likelihood of conflict. Most of the factors inducing conformity could likewise be viewed as social mechanisms. See Talcott Parsons and Edward A. Shils, 'Values, Motives and Systems of Action', in Parsons and Shils (eds.), *Toward A General Theory of Action* (Cambridge, Mass.: Harvard University Press, 1951), 223–30.

6 Further indication that the staffer–executive relationship is harmonious came from answers to the question, 'Why do you think newspapermen are thought to be cynical?' Staffers regularly said that newsmen are cynical because they get close enough to stark reality to see the ills of their society, and the imperfections of its leaders and officials. Only two, of forty staffers, took the occasion to criticize their executives and the enforcement of policy. This displacement, or lack of strong feelings against executives, can be interpreted to bolster the hypothesis of staff solidarity. (It further suggests that newsmen tend to analyse their society in terms of personalities, rather than institutions comprising a social and cultural system.)

befriending notables and celebrities (who are well-advised to treat newsmen with deference). Newsmen are close to big decisions without having to make them; they touch power without being responsible for its use. From talking with newsmen and reading their books, one gets the impression that they are proud of being newsmen.[7] There are tendencies to exclusiveness within news ranks, and intimations that such near out-groups as radio newsmen are entertainers, not real newsmen. Finally, there is the satisfaction of being a member of a live-wire organization dealing with important matters. The newspaper is an 'institution' in the community. People talk about it and quote it; its big trucks whiz through town; its columns carry the tidings from big and faraway places, with pictures.

Thus, despite his relatively low pay, the staffer feels, for all these reasons, an integral part of a going concern. His job morale is high. Many newsmen could qualify for jobs paying more money in advertising and public relations, but they remain with the newspaper.

6. News Becomes a Value.

Newsmen define their job as producing a certain quantity of what is called 'news' every 24 hours. This is to be produced *even though nothing much has happened.* News is a continuous challenge, and meeting this challenge is the newsman's job. He is rewarded for fulfilling this, his manifest function. A consequence of this focus on news as a central value is the shelving of a strong interest in objectivity at the point of policy conflict. Instead of mobilizing their efforts to establish objectivity over policy as the criterion for performance, their energies are channeled into getting more news. The demands of competition (in cities where there are two or more papers) and speed enhance this focus. Newsmen do talk about ethics, objectivity, and the relative worth of various papers, but not when there is news to get. News comes first, and there is always news to get.[8] They are not rewarded for analysing the social structure, but for getting news. It would seem that this instrumental orientation diminishes their moral potential. A further consequence of this pattern is that the harmony between staffers and executives is cemented by their common interest in news. Any potential conflict between the two groups, such as slowdowns occurring among informal work groups in industry, would be dissipated to the extent that news is a positive value. The newsroom solidarity is thus reinforced.

The six factors promote policy conformity. To state more exactly how policy is maintained would be difficult in view of the many variables contained in the system. The process may be somewhat better understood, however, with the introduction of one further concept—the reference group.[9] The

---

7 There is a sizeable myth among newsmen about the attractiveness of their calling. For example, the story: 'Girl: "My, you newspapermen must have a fascinating life. You meet such interesting people." Reporter: "Yes, and most of them are newspapermen." ' For a further discussion, see Warren Breed, 'The Newspaperman, News and Society' (Ph.D. diss., Columbia University, 1952), ch. 17.

8 This is a variant of the process of 'displacement of goals', newsmen turning to 'getting news' rather than to seeking data which will enlighten and inform their readers. The dysfunction is implied in the nation's need not for more news but for better news—quality rather than quantity. See R. K. Merton, *Social Theory and Social Structure* (Glencoe: Free Press, 1949), 154–5.

9 Whether group members acknowledge it or not, 'if a person's attitudes are influenced by a set of norms which he assumes that he shares with other individuals, those individuals constitute for him a

staffer, especially the new staffer, identifies himself through the existence of these six factors with the executives and veteran staffers. Although not yet one of them, he shares their norms, and thus his performance comes to resemble theirs. He conforms to the norms of policy rather than to whatever personal beliefs he brought to the job, or to ethical ideals. All six of these factors function to encourage reference group formation. [. . .]

The process of learning policy crystallizes into a process of social control, in which deviations are punished (usually gently) by reprimand, cutting one's story, the withholding of friendly comment by an executive, etc. [. . .] To further specify the conformity-deviation problem, it must be understood that newspapering is a relatively complex activity. The newsman is responsible for a range of skills and judgments which are matched only in the professional and entrepreneurial fields. Oversimplifications about policy rigidity can be avoided if we ask, '*Under what conditions* can the staffer defy or bypass policy?' We have already seen that staffers are free to argue news decisions with executives in brief 'news conferences', but the arguments generally revolve around points of 'newsiness', rather than policy as such.[10] Five factors appear significant in the area of the reporter's power to by-pass policy:

1. The norms of policy are not always entirely clear, just as many norms are vague and unstructured. Policy is covert by nature and has large scope. The paper may be Republican, but standing only lukewarm for Republican Candidate *A* who may be too 'liberal' or no friend of the publisher. Policy, if worked out explicitly, would have to include motivations, reasons, alternatives, historical developments, and other complicating material. Thus a twilight zone permitting a range of deviation appears.[11]

2. Executives may be ignorant of particular facts, and staffers who do the leg (and telephone) work to gather news can use their superior knowledge to subvert policy. On grounds of both personal belief and professional codes, the staffer has the option of selection at many points. He can decide whom to interview and whom to ignore, what questions to ask, which quotations to note, and on writing the story which items to feature (with an eye toward the headline), which to bury, and in general what tone to give the several possible elements of the story.

3. In addition to the 'squeeze' tactic exploiting executives' ignorance of minute facts, the 'plant' may be employed. Although a paper's policy may proscribe a certain issue from becoming featured, a staffer, on getting a good story about that issue may 'plant' it in another paper or wire service through a friendly staffer and submit it to his own editor, pleading the story is now too big to ignore.

4. It is possible to classify news into four types on the basis of source of

reference group', Theodore M. Newcomb, *Social Psychology* (New York: Dryden, 1950), 225. Williams states that reference group formation may segment large organizations; in the present case, the reverse is true, the loyalty of subordinates going to their 'friendly' superiors and to the discharge of technical norms such as getting news. See Robin M. Williams, *American Society* (New York: Knopf, 1951), 476.

10 The fullest treatment of editor–reporter conferences appears in Charles E. Swanson, 'The Mid-City Daily' (Ph.D. diss., State University of Iowa, 1948).

11 Related to the fact that policy is vague is the more general postulate that executives seek to avoid formal issues and the possibly damaging disputes arising therefrom. See Chester I. Barnard, *Functions of the Executive* (Cambridge, Mass.: Harvard University Press, 1947).

origination. These are: the policy or campaign story, the assigned story, the beat story, and the story initiated by the staffer. The staffer's autonomy is larger with the latter than the former types. With the campaign story (build new hospital, throw rascals out, etc.), the staffer is working directly under executives and has little leeway. An assigned story is handed out by the city editor and thus will rarely hit policy head on, although the staffer has some leverage of selection. When we come to the beat story, however, it is clear that the function of the reporter changes. No editor comes between him and his beat (police department, city hall, etc.), thus the reporter gains the 'editor' function. It is he who, to a marked degree, can select which stories to pursue, which to ignore. [...] The fourth type of story is simply one which the staffer originates, independent of assignment or beat.

5. Staffers with 'star' status can transgress policy more easily than cubs. This differential privilege of status was encountered on several papers. [...]

Summary

The problem, which was suggested by the age-old charges of bias against the press, focused around the manner in which the publisher's policy came to be followed, despite three empirical conditions: (1) policy sometimes contravenes journalistic norms; (2) staffers often personally disagree with it; and (3) executives cannot legitimately command that policy be followed. Interview and other data were used to explain policy maintenance. It is important to recall that the discussion is based primarily on study of papers of 'middle' circulation range, and does not consider either non-policy stories or the original policy decision made by the publishers.

The mechanisms for learning policy on the part of the new staffer were given, together with suggestions as to the nature of social controls. Six factors, apparently the major variables producing policy maintenance, were described. The most significant of these variables, obligation and esteem for superiors, was deemed not only the most important, but the most fluctuating variable from paper to paper. Its existence and its importance for conformity led to the sub-hypothesis that reference group behaviour was playing a part in the pattern. To show, however, that policy is not iron-clad, five conditions were suggested in which staffers may by-pass policy.

Thus we conclude that the publisher's policy, when established in a given subject area, is usually followed, and that a description of the dynamic socio-cultural situation of the newsroom will suggest explanations for this conformity. The newsman's source of rewards is located not among the readers, who are manifestly his clients, but among his colleagues and superiors. Instead of adhering to societal and professional ideals, he redefines his values to the more pragmatic level of the newsroom group. He thereby gains not only status rewards, but also acceptance in a solidary group engaged in interesting, varied, and sometimes important work. Thus the cultural patterns of the newsroom produce results insufficient for wider democratic needs. Any important change toward a more 'free and responsible press' must stem from various possible pressures on the publisher, who epitomizes the policy-making and co-ordinating role.

11

Reporting the News: An Organizational Analysis¹

Lee Sigelman

THIS CASE STUDY focuses on local political reporters for two news-papers in 'Southeast City', a metropolitan area in the south-eastern United States. A series of propositions developed by organization the-orists guides our examination of relations between the local political reporter and his newspaper hierarchy. By examining the newspapers' recruitment, socialization, and control processes, we hope to better understand newsman–news leadership relationships and achieve a better perspective on the complex and timely question of media bias.

Institutional Mythology

In their periodic introspections, American newspapermen reveal a morally conditioned 'public regardingness', a self-imposed obligation to watch over the public's business. Perhaps the most persistent proponent of this doctrine is columnist James Reston: 'The first article of the Bill of Rights was placed there as a pledge of safety to the *people*, and . . . therefore the primary obli-gation of the newspaper in general and of the reporter in particular is *to the people*. . . . He does not owe that primary allegiance to the owner of his news-paper, or to his managing editor, or to his government, or to the sources of his information; he owes it to the people' (1945: 93–4).

Philip Selznick fathered the concept of the 'institutional myth', which he defined as an effort to 'state in language of uplift and idealism, what is dis-tinctive about the aims and methods of the enterprise' (1957: 151). Clearly, the position enunciated by Reston (and enshrined in the 'Canons of Journal-ism') is American newspaper journalism's reigning institutional myth. [. . .]

Newsmen, then, tend to view their role in terms of dramatically stated symbols of their mission in society.² As an operational corollary to this role,

Source: Lee Sigelman, 'Reporting the News: An Organizational Analysis', *American Journal of Sociology*, 79/1 (1973), 132–51.

1 Data for this study were gathered by participant observation and taped interviews undertaken while the author was an American Political Science Association intern in state and local government. Special thanks are due to Carol K. Sigelman and Gary I. Wamsley.

2 'I share with thousands of others in journalism a sense of mission that I have seen in only two other professions,' proclaims Barry Bingham, editor of the prestigious Louisville *Courier-Journal*. 'One of

an instrumental myth—'objectivity'—also figures prominently in journalistic role definition. As a tribune of the people, the myth runs, the reporter is duty bound to present the public with a fair, disinterested account of political happenings. This is not to say that the newsman feels that he can achieve total objectivity on any question. In the representative words of one reporter: 'I don't think there's any such thing as a truly objective story, because if there were three reporters covering the same story, you'd have three different stories on the same incident. All of them would feel that they were objective in their own way, I'm sure.'[3] But it is clear that Southeast City reporters view objectivity as a goal to be pursued, even if never attained (a view which should not be altogether unfamiliar to social scientists). One reporter's comments were typical: 'You know, we like to think we're doing an honest job. You have to report the full stream. You can't pick what you want and leave out what you want.'[4]

These two myths of newspaper journalism—the primary one of the reporter's public function, the operational one of disinterested objectivity—form a general backdrop for the present study. If these myths were simply actualized, the newspaper would be a fairly passive chronicle of the day's events, and its political role would be readily understandable. [...]

One enters the two Southeast City dailies through the front door of the building the newspapers share. Upon entering, one can either turn left and enter the offices of the morning *Sun*, or turn right to the newsroom of the evening *Star*. The choice of direction, fittingly enough, is also ideological. The newspapers have a long and colourful history of maintaining their ideological positions on national and international issues (during World War I, for example, the *Sun's* publisher even crusaded editorially to have the foreign-born *Star* publisher interned as an enemy alien), with the *Sun* pleading the liberal cause while the *Star* adheres to a staunchly conservative philosophy. In local affairs, they are also constantly opposed, though the split tends to be factional as well as doctrinal.

The papers' news columns convey radically divergent pictures of the political community, to an extent which can be gauged from their handling of a local conference on race relations coverage. The *Star* headlined its story, 'Perception Cited in Modern Journalism'; the *Sun* captioned its story on the same conference, 'Racial News Coverage Held Lacking'. And disagreements between the two papers are not usually restricted to the editorial pages.[5]

---

them is teaching and the other is the ministry' (Bingham 1960: 105). Such idealistic conceptions of journalism may underlie the very decision to choose journalism as a career. High school students who intend to become journalists rate the field very high in interest of the work and its usefulness to society and much lower in financial rewards and economic security (Kimball and Lubell 1960).

3 Reminiscent of the preacher, the geologist, and the cowboy who were viewing the Grand Canyon for the first time. 'One of the wonders of God,' said the preacher. 'One of the wonders of science,' said the geologist. 'What a hell of a place to raise a cow,' said the cowboy.

4 As might be suspected, 'objectivity' is also used as a defensive shield against outside criticism. In Gaye Tuchman's words: 'Attacked for a controversial presentation of "facts", newspapermen invoke their objectivity almost the way a Mediterranean peasant might wear a clove of garlic around his neck to ward off evil spirits' (1972: 660).

5 In the words of Edith Efron: 'Although a liberal publication and a conservative publication will both cover the "universally significant" issues, they tend necessarily to cover different secondary issues. And in the "universal" issues they often present different sets of political facts, cite the opinions of different sets of people, offer different causal interpretations and transmit different solutions' (1971: 12).

Their biases are evident throughout their pages: the *Star* favours front-page editorials lambasting its opponents, while the *Sun* saturates its pages with pictures of its favourites. So evident, in fact, are these biases that a local Committee for a Fair Press has denounced both for 'excessive, distorted, and slanted news of political events', charging that 'for too long the two newspapers have indulged in political deception and at times, outright journalistic demagoguery'.

Far from acting as detached observers of the political scene, then, the papers are consistently at one another's throats—to the point that they have built up a public expectation that they will be at odds in their support for and coverage of political issues and personalities. According to a locally famous story, the papers have even disagreed about the time of day. Several years ago, when the papers split over daylight saving time, each face of the two-faced clock at the entrance to the building the papers share was set to correspond to the preference of the paper whose offices it faced—one on standard time, the other on daylight saving time.

Why are the newspapers as they are politically? According to reporters, their policies are simply extensions of the political philosophies of the newspapers' publishers. One reporter stated: 'I think naturally the publisher's view is going to filter down through the whole organization of any newspaper, whether it be the *Sun*, the *Star*, or the *New York Times*. . . . Naturally, the publisher's feelings are going to be favoured, when and if there's a choice.' Another put it this way: 'Any newspaper, it seems to me, with a single ownership . . . reflects the thinking of the publisher and his philosophy. . . . To a great extent, the publisher *is* the newspaper and the newspaper *is* the publisher.'

But what about the mythology of free and untrammelled reporting? Reviewing 84 studies of biased news, Ben Bagdikian (1972) found a very high correlation between editorial policy and news bias; in only three of the 84 cases did news bias contravene editorial position. Moreover, David Bowers (1967) reported on the basis of a survey of more than 600 dailies that publishers are most active in directing news on local, as opposed to state, regional, national, or international issues. If policy guidelines influence local coverage so greatly, how do reporters cope with the disparity between myth and reality? How, in organizations whose members claim to be deeply committed to the professional goal of objectivity, do the publishers' political views affect the coverage of local politics?

According to Herbert Simon's classic study of organizational behaviour, superiors can win influence over an employee by 'establishing in the operative employee himself attitudes, habits, and a state of mind which lead him to reach that decision which is advantageous to the organization,' and by 'imposing on the operative employee decisions reached elsewhere in the organization' (Simon 1957: 11). Applying Simon's propositions to the newspapers, news policy should move from top to bottom by active promotion of attitudes which render reporters favourable to newspaper policies ('attitude promotion') and by imposition of policies on reporters by means of hierarchical authority ('organizational control').

Attitude Promotion

In their studies of how organizations seek to inculcate certain attitudes among their employees, organization analysts have focused on two mechanisms: selective recruitment and socialization. If newspapers resemble other organizations with respect to attitude promotion, they should select recruits known to be in accord with newspaper policies and devote resources to centrally directed socialization of news reporters into favourable attitudes.

■ Selective Recruitment

The two Southeast City dailies devote little time or effort to recruiting new reporters. Most newspapers are wholly dependent on voluntary applications in filling their positions and house no formally organized personnel departments (Lindley 1958). The Southeast City papers are no exception, for in the overwhelming majority of cases, the initial contact was made by the recruit himself; in none of these instances was an opening even advertised. One reporter described his hiring as follows: 'I came up here and was interviewed. It was the common statement: "We don't have any openings now, but we'll call you when we do." So that same week the managing editor called me and told me they had a vacancy.' [. . .]

Even though the papers play such a passive role in attracting new reporters, they might nonetheless take pains to insure that applicants are in general accord with editorial policies. But in describing their job interviews, not a single reporter mentioned any discussion of political views. The following responses are representative: 'It was just more or less a standard application, background information, and why I wanted to be a reporter.' 'There weren't many questions . . . I had some clippings with me when I was interviewed. Mostly what happened was they went over my qualifications with me a little bit more and read a few of my stories and discussed salary and whether or not I had any friends or relatives in Southeast City. The executive editor said he was impressed with my character or something—I don't remember which. It didn't last very long. And then they told me they'd let me know if they had an opening.' To a man, reporters resolutely denied that there had been any political discussion in their interviews. Rather, interviews centred on qualifications, experience, and working conditions. Further, reporters doubted that the newspapers 'had done any other checking on you'. [. . .]

■ Socialization

What is more, the newspapers make no formal provisions for inculcating job or policy norms. Rather, the socialization process is highly diffuse and extremely informal.

The neophyte reporter is typically put on 'general assignment', where he may log most of his time covering fires and writing obituaries. Or, if he begins immediately with political reporting, his stories are likely to be humdrum affairs, reporting specific 'non-policy' events. As one older newsman explained it, the young reporter working on an assignment 'doesn't have to know anything about policy or anything else. All he's got to know—he's got to have an ability to get the facts and get 'em in there and put 'em into some reasonable form'.

Reporters felt that learning policy is simply 'a process that takes place over time'. Gradually, reporters 'just begin to know' what policy is. An unobtrusive measure of the elusiveness of the newspapers' socialization process is the faltering nature of responses to the question: 'How do you find out what the paper's policy is?' One said: 'Well, you don't—just kind of have—by just kind of being involved. It's . . . more or less something that you just know. As far as the newspaper coming out with a policy telling reporters, "Now this is going to be our policy," we don't have any written, set policy guidelines to go by.' [. . .]

The reporters did, however, hint at some of the concrete means by which they are able to assimilate policy. They stressed informal contacts with more experienced newsmen. Unquestionably, a process of 'anticipatory socialization' is at work, with cub reporters attempting to tailor their own performances to the patterns set by their role models, the veterans.[6] These contacts solidify the cub's general outlook on the reporter's role as well as his specific attitudes about organization members and processes. Since veteran members of organizations typically have attitudes which are highly supportive of organizational policies (Downs 1967: 230), it should come as no surprise that contacts with successful senior reporters breed attitudes which are also highly supportive of the newspaper.

Editorial revisions are another socialization mechanism. One newsman indicated that 'you can anticipate how they would want you to cover something, after a while'. Another recalled that he had submitted what he considered fair, accurate accounts of political rallies but continually found small changes in his copy—especially concerning crowd reactions and sizes (always more favourable to the paper's candidate, less so to the opposition). 'After a while', he sighed, 'I just began making the changes myself, to save them the time and trouble.'[7]

One further socialization mechanism is the editorial conference, open to only the most experienced reporters. In these conferences, veteran reporters and newspaper management meet to discuss news coverage. As one reporter put it: 'The publisher is a very positive and articulate gentleman. He doesn't mince words about what the newspaper's policies are. If you sit in on an editorial conference with him over an extensive period of time, you're going to know what the policy is, because he expresses it very definitely and frequently.'

Of all these mechanisms, the editorial conference is surely the most organized, coherent, continuing, and centralized process; but it is directed at veterans rather than new recruits. In general, the newspapers appear to devote few resources to centrally insuring that new members are socialized into favourable attitudes.

■ **Attitude Promotion Reconsidered**   Neither of the propositions distilled from the organizational literature concerning 'attitude promotion' is supported by the experiences of Southeast City political reporters. How can this inattention to such attitude-shaping processes as recruitment and socialization be explained?

6 Irwin Smigel (1964) makes the same observation for young lawyers in Wall Street firms.

7 Directly parallel to an incident recounted by Walter Gieber: 'One reporter working on a metropolitan said he is certain his paper is anti-Negro and related this experience: "When I covered a fire or police story in the slum area the desk asked: 'Is this a Nigger story?' If I said yes, they told me to forget it. . . . After a while I didn't bother" ' (1960: 80).

Publishers and editors are certainly no less caught up in the institutional mythology of a 'free and responsible press' and its concomitant of objective reporting than are the newsmen. In this sense, it would be surprising indeed if those high in command were to make any heavy-handed, overt moves to drum their own political philosophies into new members.

More significantly, it is clear that the newspapers simply need not be highly selective politically in their recruiting and need not utilize any systematic socialization processes. Why? Even though recruitment of Southeast City reporters is not politically selective, this requirement is nonetheless fulfilled in effect by the self-selection of newsmen. Conservative newsmen seem naturally to gravitate to the *Star*, liberal reporters to the *Sun*.[8]

Newsmen were asked to characterize their fellow workers politically. In every case, the vast majority of co-workers were identified as corresponding to the employing newspaper's political stance—a congruence which every reporter explained in terms of self-selection. [. . .] A *Star* reporter made the same point in much more colourful terms: 'Usually, if a person applies for a job on the *Star*, or on the *Sun*, or on any other newspaper, they pretty well know what they're doing when they come here. I don't think some long-haired beatnik with a beard and dark glasses, wearing beads and a fringed jacket, is going to come to the *Star* and offer himself as a reporter feeling that he was going to fit in. He'd probably go someplace else.'

Political criteria, then, do play a significant role in recruitment—but it is the recruits, not the newspapers, who actually apply them. Because they do, the newspapers, secure in their knowledge of the self-selection phenomenon, are free to apply achievement criteria in recruiting.

The socialization process is also fundamentally shaped by newsman self-selection. Etzioni has stated the principle that 'if the organization can recruit participants who have the characteristics it requires, it does not have to develop these characteristics through training or education' (1961: 158). Because of self-selection, the *Sun* and the *Star* are not faced with the distasteful task of overhauling the recruit's political outlook. Socialization in these circumstances means cuing the recruit to matters of organizational style—developing in him a sense of the limits of organizational tolerance, a more or less explicit theory of how people 'make it' in the organization, and a general conception of organizational purposes and methods (Long 1962: 142–3)—along with building the recruit's sense of belonging, of group solidarity. The key agents of this process are not those who are high on the organization chart, but are rather the experienced reporters who are used by the recruit as information sources and role models.

What emerges is a picture of recruitment and socialization as processes which perform the dual function of attitude promotion and myth maintenance. That is, these processes are so structured that favourable attitudes among newsmen are assured without violation of the institutional

---

8 Other analysts have noticed the self-selection process at work in different organizational contexts. Robert McMurry (1958) detected a functional relationship between the structured, routinized character of bank operations and the high dependency needs of bank employees—a congruence which McMurry felt resulted from a simple self-selection process. William Scott (1965) also used self-selection to help explain congruence between the value patterns of new pledges and their fraternities.

mythology. The recruit's application of political criteria performs a winnowing function for the newspaper, effectively insuring that the reporter is favourably predisposed toward newspaper policies; the newspaper's application of achievement criteria performs a legitimating function for the reporter, allowing him to retain his faith in the institutional myths. By the same token, the recruit's willingness to tailor his own behaviour to the pattern set by more experienced reporters performs a socializing function for the newspapers, insuring continued reportorial observance of policy norms; but the very diffuseness, voluntarism, and decentralization of the socialization process help maintain the myth of free and untrammeled reporting. [. . .]

Organizational Control

For a number of reasons the newsman enjoys a measure of autonomy in reporting local politics. But how can all this reportorial autonomy be reconciled with the dramatic differences between the two papers in their political coverage? Is the reporter really a free agent, or do important organizational control mechanisms intervene?

The most obvious incentives to reporters, as to employees of any work organization, are monetary and normative. Southeast City newsmen are conscious of a linkage between financial and policy control. As one reporter phrased it: 'The publisher holds the purse strings.' 'Of course, you are conscious of the fact that the publisher owns the paper,' another commented. 'You are conscious of the policies of the paper.' Nor should the significance of normative symbols and social relations be understated. Most *Sun* and *Star* reporters are fiercely loyal to their employers. One judges that his paper (the *Sun*) is 'the best newspaper in the country', adding that what he likes best about working for the *Sun* is 'the paper itself, and the people responsible'. Where such sentiments prevail and can be effectively manipulated, the incidence of policy conflict is bound to be low.

But it is in the very technology of reporting that some of the most significant control mechanisms are located. Newsmen are in an important sense hypothesis testers, whose newsgathering procedures consist of checking the empirical validity of their preconceptions (Bartley 1971). The *Star*'s senior reporter, for instance, scarcely ever asks a question during one of his interviews. He is more likely to launch a series of assertions about the topic at hand and reserve time for the interviewee to react. Other reporters, to be sure, may rely more heavily upon their sources to structure a story; but all, to a significant extent, are guided by a set of explicit or implicit hypotheses.

Describing reporters as hypothesis testers raises some important questions. Whose hypotheses do they test? Who specifies how the hypotheses will be tested? Most reporters most of the time cover stories which have been assigned to them by superiors—by star reporters, editors, or even, in the exceptional case, by the publisher himself. The superior, in determining which stories will be covered (and therefore which will not), exercises an initial and fundamental control over what appears in the newspaper. Once he has determined that a story should be covered, his ability to choose which reporter will cover the story refines his control over content. Further, the assignment is apt to specify not only what will be covered and who will cover it, but also the 'play' the story will receive and the perspective from which it will be approached.[9]

Nor does the control process stop at this point. Reporters submit their stories to an editor who has some revisionary powers. This process presents the news hierarchy with a built-in 'quality-control check' on reporters' performances. Significantly, both reporters and their superiors emphasize that revision is intended to improve a story stylistically. [...] But editors nonetheless can and sometimes do use their power of revision to change important substantive aspects, even the entire thrust, of a news story. One reporter gave an example of this process.

> We had a young reporter that was just starting here, and in a governor's race several years ago we were supporting one candidate—however, we were covering all the candidates. It got to the point that he was swayed by the candidate he was covering, which was not the one we were supporting. He definitely wanted to write this story one way, and the paper didn't want it that particular way. They didn't necessarily—they positively didn't want any of the facts changed. They wanted to use the facts of the story, but facts can be changed around, and still be factual as hell, but with an entirely different meaning. And it was just that this reporter wanted to write a very favourable story on this particular candidate, and the paper didn't want it that way.... The reporter wrote the story, turned it in, and the city desk said, 'This is not what we want. We want this particular point down here on the lead, and we want to start from there.' It was a short argument, and the reporter ended up doing it like the city desk wanted it.

This and other similar cases demonstrate that, although editing is rationalized in narrow, technical terms, it carries a definite substantive impact. One newsman vehemently denied that such policy considerations enter the editing process, but his very description of the process indicates its control potential: 'Well, things are rewritten, but you have other people with opinions, and it's a matter of preference of how you want to tell a story. That doesn't change the story. It might change the emphasis, it might change the direction of it, but it's not killing the story.' Surely the ability to change the emphasis and direction of a news story is a substantial mechanism of control. Combined with the other mechanisms detailed above, it means that the newsman operates within the constraining boundaries of a fairly elaborate set of organizational control structures and processes.

Previous analysts of the organizational context of news reporting have examined the means by which news organizations impose their policies on reporters and by which reporters avoid such imposition (Breed 1955; Stark 1962; Warner 1971). Where one begins one's analysis by asking 'How is policy imposed and avoided?' one is inevitably led to a picture of the newsman–newspaper relationship as a zero-sum game—antagonistic and inherently conflict ridden.

But is this a safe assumption? Is the relationship between reporter and newspaper inevitably conflictual? A new generation of organization theorists

9 See Efron (1971: 8–9) for a parallel statement of the range of choice in television reporting.

and researchers has begun to question the assumption of conflict between professional and organization (Hall 1967). They have argued that there is always a potential for conflict, but that this potential will be tapped only in certain circumstances: when the newsman feels that he is being treated non-professionally, or when newspaper leaders become disenchanted with the newsman's output. Conversely, if the newsman feels that his professional prerogatives are being respected, and if newspaper leaders are content with reportorial performance, the situation should be one of harmony, not conflict.

But, realistically, can both reporter and newspaper hierarchy be content with the same state of affairs? Or are their goals so divergent that conflict is, for all practical purposes, inevitable? As was the case with recruitment and socialization, the picture which emerges of the control structures of the Southeast City dailies is of a tension-avoidance process—a process which insures favourable performances without violating institutional mythology.

Many significant decisions about a story may have been made well before the reporter even begins his coverage. In this case, the reporter is restricted to the technical, administrative task of constructing a story to general specifications drawn elsewhere. His autonomy may realistically consist of little more than his freedom to manoeuvre within the constraining bounds of his assignment. But the reporter's perception of his role is sufficiently narrow and technical that he does not feel that his functional autonomy is jeopardized. His task, as he sees it, consists of writing the best story he can within a given framework; his is more a feat of engineering than of architecture.[10] In fact, far from trying to avoid his newspaper's policies, the reporter may actually seek them out. Walter Gieber found that the reporters in his study did not complain of too much policy (1964: 178). They accepted news policy as part of 'bureaucratic structuring', and were more apt to complain of too little policy, or of policy which was so vague or inconsistent that it could not serve as a reliable guide for their behaviour.

In most instances, the leaders of the *Sun* and the *Star* follow what Matejko calls the 'praxeological principle of minimum intervention': 'Meddle as little as possible with the course of events, achieve your ends by interfering as little as possible, and wherever possible without your own intervention' (1967: 64). The resulting looseness and informality of the newspapers' control structures, along with the narrowness of the reporters' role definitions and the respect they have for their superiors,[11] make for a situation in which

---

10 This technical orientation is highlighted in Flegel and Chaffee's (1971) study of reporters for two papers in Madison, Wisconsin. Unlike the situation in Southeast City, some consistent and rather broad gaps divide Madison reporters and their editors politically. But, significantly, Madison reporters do not perceive that the opinions of editors impinge on their reporting; they are much more likely to cite the technical 'intrinsic news values' of a story as influencing their coverage than editors' opinions, readers' opinions, or even their own opinions.

11 According to a survey undertaken by Per Holting, when television news directors question the competence and knowledgeability of their station managers, friction is likely to ensue. Of the news directors who reported friction, only 8 per cent said their manager had a news background, compared with 42 per cent for the nonfriction group. One news director summarized the frustrations of dealing with a manager who lacks a news background: 'Neither the manager of this station, nor any of the directors has ever had any news experience. Asking them to form an editorial policy, for example, is like asking Rocky Marciano to play Lady Macbeth . . . they just don't know from nothing' (Holting 1957, p. 357).

Southeast City reporters are not presented with a conflict between their professional and organizational commitments. On the other side of the coin, sufficient mechanisms exist within the control system to enable the newspaper hierarchies to exert meaningful control over reportorial performance.

There is simply no reason, then, to assume that all newspapers resemble the one depicted by Stark—to assume, that is, that conflict between reporter and newspaper is inevitable. In fact, if one had to assume anything, he might well be safer in assuming harmony than conflict. [...]

Implications for Media Bias

What are the implications of this case study for our understanding of media bias? Before hazarding any conclusions, it is necessary to address a prior issue. Do the findings of this case study carry beyond the borders of Southeast City? Is it not possible that they obtain only for the Southeast City dailies and not for other newspapers? Just how representative are the *Sun* and the *Star*?

An attempt has been made throughout this study to note points of convergence between the *Sun* and the *Star* and other organizations. At the very least, it can be said that the Southeast City dailies are not so peculiar that their recruitment, socialization, and control processes are unique; rather a wide variety of other organizations share many of their salient organizational features. [...]

The Southeast City newspapers present biased news not because organizational mechanisms allow newspaper leaders to ride roughshod over reporters. Reporters in Southeast City are neither cowering sheep, huddled against the onslaught of policy directives; cynical prostitutes, resigned to the seamy business of selling out their professionalism; nor scheming Machiavellis, plotting endless ways of skirting news policy. Bias is the product not of a simple policy imposition–policy avoidance calculus, but of a far more complex and subtle organizational process. As the late V. O. Key recognized, 'conspiracy theories' of the mass media—theories which paint pictures of shadowy executive committees who ensure that only certain political content will pass through media channels—are hopelessly naïve (1961: 380). The key to understanding bias lies not in conspiracies, not in conflict, but in co-operation and shared satisfactions.

The political news carried by the Southeast City newspapers, and hence the political biases which appear in the papers, is the result of a particular matrix of organizational processes—processes which commence in the recruitment of the reporter, carry on through his socialization, and culminate in his working arrangements. These processes are structured not for policy maintenance—insuring that newspaper leaders will win battles against reporters; nor even for conflict management—keeping conflict within manageable bounds; but rather for conflict avoidance—insuring that the stage will not be set for conflict. We saw above that recruitment, socialization, and control are all structured in such a way that they preserve for the reporter the institutional mythology of objective reporting, while they also assure newspaper leaders of favourable attitudes and performances. What is truly significant about the case of the *Sun* and the *Star* is precisely the extent to which these organizational mechanisms intercede between the potential for conflict and its actualization. If this is the case elsewhere, then newspaper bias is far more subtle and complex, and far less easily eradicable, than had previously been assumed.

References

BAGDIKIAN, BEN H. (1972), 'The Politics of American Newspapers'. *Columbia Journalism Review*, 10 (March/April): 8–13.

BARTLEY, ROBERT L. (1971), 'The Press: Adversary, Surrogate Sovereign, or Both?' Paper delivered at the Annual Meeting of the American Political Science Association, Chicago.

BINGHAM, BARRY (1960), 'The Responsibilities of a Free Press', in Raymond English (ed.), *The Essentials of Freedom* (Gambier, Oh.: Kenyon College).

BOWERS, DAVID R. (1967), 'A Report on Activity by Publishers in Directing Newsroom Decisions', *Journalism Quarterly*, 44 (Spring): 43–52.

DOWNS, ANTHONY (1967), *Inside Bureaucracy*. Boston: Little, Brown.

EFRON, EDITH (1971), *The News Twisters*. Los Angeles: Nash.

ETZIONI, AMITAI (1961), *A Comparative Analysis of Complex Organizations* (New York: Free Press).

FLEGEL, RUTH C., and STEVEN H. CHAFFEE (1971), 'Influence of Editors, Readers, and Personal Opinions on Reporters', *Journalism Quarterly*, 48 (Winter): 645–51.

GIEBER, WALTER (1960), 'Two Communicators of the News: A Study of the Roles of Sources and Reporters', *Social Forces*, 39 (Oct.): 76–83.

—— (1964), 'News Is What Newspapermen Make It', in Lewis A. Dexter and David M. White (eds.), *People, Society, and Mass Communication* (New York: Free Press).

GREENWOOD, ERNEST (1957), 'Attributes of a Profession', *Social Work*, 2 (July): 44–55.

HALL, RICHARD H. (1967), 'Some Organizational Considerations in the Professional Organizational Relationship', *Administrative Science Quarterly*, 12 (Dec.): 461–78.

HOLTING, PER (1957), 'Where Does Friction Develop for TV News Directors?', *Journalism Quarterly*, 34 (Summer): 355–9.

JUDD, ROBERT P. (1961), 'The Newspaper Reporter in a Suburban City', *Journalism Quarterly*, 38 (Winter): 35–42.

KEY, V. O., Jr. (1961), *Public Opinion and American Democracy* (New York: Knopf).

KIMBALL, PENN T., and SAMUEL LUBELL (1960), 'High School Students' Attitudes toward Journalism as a Career, II', *Journalism Quarterly*, 37 (Summer): 413–22.

LINDLEY, WILLIAM R. (1958), 'Recruiting of News-Editorial Personnel by US Newspapers', *Journalism Quarterly*, 35 (Fall): 474–5.

LINDSTROM, CARL E. (1960), *The Fading American Newspaper* (New York: Doubleday).

LONG, NORTON E. (1962), 'Administrative Communication', in Sidney Mallick and Edward Van Ness (eds.), *Concepts and Issues in Administrative Behavior* (Englewood Cliffs, N.J.: Prentice-Hall).

McMURRY, ROBERT N. (1958), 'Recruitment, Dependency, and Morale in the Banking Industry', *Administrative Science Quarterly*, 3 (June): 87–117.

MATEJKO, ALEKSANDER (1967), 'Newspaper Staff as a Social System', *Polish Sociological Bulletin*, (1): 58–68.

RESTON, JAMES (1945), 'The Job of the Reporter', in *The Newspaper: Its Making and Its Meaning*, by members of the staff of the *New York Times* (New York: Scribner's).

SCOTT, WILLIAM A. (1965), *Values and Organizations* (Chicago: Rand McNally).

SELZNICK, PHILIP (1957), *Leadership in Administration* (New York: Harper & Row).

SIMON, HERBERT A. (1957), *Administrative Behaviour* (2nd edn. New York: Free Press).

SMIGEL, IRWIN (1964), *The Wall Street Lawyer* (New York: Free Press).

TUCHMAN, GAYE (1972), 'Objectivity as Strategic Ritual: An Examination of Newsmen's Notions of Objectivity', *American Journal of Sociology*, 77 (Jan.): 660–79.

12

Visualizing Deviance: A Study of News Organization

Richard V. Ericson, Patricia M. Baranek, and Janet B. L. Chan

Newsrooms and Journalists' Cultures

OUR OVERVIEW OF a newspaper newsroom is based on the city news desk at one newspaper. A senior executive described the city desk as '*the* basic department. That's where you put your young reporters. When they get experienced and when they get good, then you move them off on to bureaux so that a lot of the training function is there, most of the investigative stuff is there, a lot of the issue-oriented stuff is there. That's where the generic beats are: health, education, welfare, law, labour.'

At the time of our research there was a city editor, assistant city editor, night city editor, and staff of thirty-six reporters operating from the city desk. Approximately one-third of these reporters were on general assignment, while two-thirds were on special-topic (e.g. law, labour, welfare) or special-beat (e.g. courts, city hall, provincial legislature) assignment. The assistant city editor was the assignment editor, beginning his day at about 10.00 a.m. and staying on until the 6.00 p.m. deadline for filed stories. His hours overlapped with those of the night editor, who came in at 5.00 p.m. to discuss the schedule of stories that had been produced during the day. The reporters also worked from about 10.00 a.m. to 6.00 p.m. According to one editor, anywhere from 15 to 35 stories were filed each day on the city desk. The newspaper's first edition came together at around 7.30 to 8.00 p.m., was into production by 8.30 p.m., and was on the streets between 10.00 and 11.00 p.m. The night editing staff worked on alterations for the morning edition, and their work was usually completed by midnight.

City-desk personnel worked in an open office plan with the exception of the city editor who had a closed office situated alongside the offices of the assistant managing editor and the managing editor. The assistant city editor (assignment editor) was located between a row of desks belonging to city-desk reporters, and another set of desks from which the slot editors worked. Thus, there was open access among assignment, reporting, and editing

Source: R. V. Ericson, P. M. Baranek, and J. B. L. Chan, *Visualizing Deviance: A Study of News Organization* (Toronto: University of Toronto Press, 1987).

personnel to discuss story assignments, developments, angles, editing suggestions or problems, and so on.

Our overview of processes and roles in a television newsroom is based on one television station. The operation of this newsroom in most respects paralleled that of the city-desk of the newspaper, covering general assignments as well as the police, court, city-hall, and provincial-legislature beats, and a few specializations (minorities, citizen advocate). At the time of our research the newsroom was headed by an executive producer, and his production team also included a producer, assignment editor, lineup editor, and an assistant producer for the night show. There were a dozen reporters, and about the same number of film or video crew members, although on any given day shift the number was usually fewer. There were also two video technicians and several film technicians available for the editing stages. Additional personnel monitored news-service feeds from VisNews and US television networks, as well as print wire services, to fit items into the lineup with locally produced stories. The two anchorpersons came in mid-day to examine the lineup, prepare for any feature interviews they themselves were to conduct, and to rehearse their scripts.

The assignment editor began his day at about 8.00 a.m., staying on until mid-afternoon at which time he was replaced by the assistant producer for the night show. The reporters and crews came in around 9.00 a.m., and worked until their items were ready for the 6.00 p.m. newscast, which was usually between 5.00 and 6.00 p.m. Each reporter filed one story, although occasionally a reporter ended up not producing a story, and very occasionally a reporter would manage to file two stories.

The newsroom was an open plan, with the exception of administrative officers, the executive producer, producer, and two anchorpersons, who had closed offices. The assignment editor had a desk off to one corner, but the rows of reporters' desks were near and there was easy access for discussion and consultation. The executive producer and producer were directly and actively involved in all aspects of the process, beginning with assignment ideas and preliminary schedule right through to giving studio directions for the broadcast. The crews had separate rooms, as did the film and video technicians who were located on the floor above the newsroom, but they sometimes sat in the newsroom, chatting or discussing ideas with reporters, editors and producers.

The news-production process is represented schematically in Figure 1. At the hub of the process initially is the assignment editor, whose job does not differ in any significant respect across news organizations and media. The assignment editor was responsible for developing the schedule of news events to be covered for the day. He assigned reporters to particular items and he was supposed to keep in touch with story developments. Reporters on beats were supposed to call in at least once during the day to indicate what they are working on, their angles, and what and how much they expected to file by the deadline. The assignment editor was also a consultant regarding story angles and developments, and an educator to the inexperienced reporter. The assignment editor worked more closely with the reporter if the reporter was inexperienced, was working on an important or controversial matter, or was involved in an item that originated with more senior levels of the news organization.

The assignment editor attended news conferences, although in the newspaper it was on behalf of the city editor, who sometimes attended himself. The main newspaper conference was in the early afternoon. It was presided over by the managing editor, or the assistant managing editor in his absence.

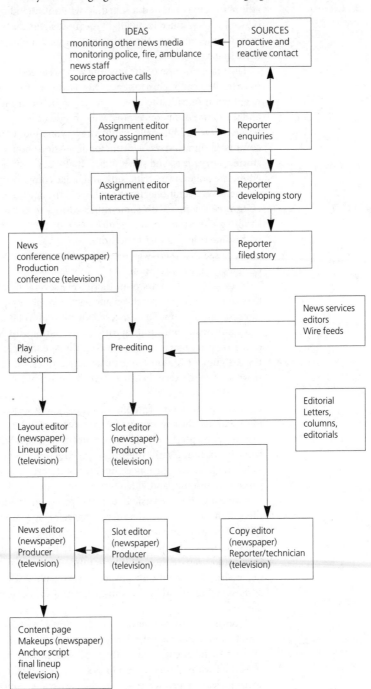

Figure 1
The news-production
process

It was attended by the assistant managing editor, news editor, executive editor, makeup editor, art/photography editor, and editors from each news desk (city, national, international, business, sport, lifestyle, entertainment). Each desk editor circulated his schedule of stories to the others, while the features editor simply submitted a schedule without attending the meeting. Each desk editor was asked to highlight the most significant stories on his respective schedule, and sometimes also made a special plea for prominent play or extra space.

The main purpose of the meeting was to suggest to the news editor what were the best candidates for Page One. However, there was also considerable negotiation outside the news conference between individual desk editors and the news editor concerning what should be on page one. The news conference served additionally to inform everyone about prospects for the forthcoming edition, and was a forum for discussion about important continuing stories, story ideas, and story angles. It also allowed the managing editor to enunciate policy, offer criticisms, and make comparisons with competitors.

There were additional meetings later in the day. At 5.30 p.m. the national-edition editor met with some other editors to consider what city stories should go into the national edition. At 8.00 p.m. the managing editor met with some other editors to scrutinize the page proofs, and later the actual copy, to see that there were no major errors or problems, and to consider changes for the later edition.

In the television newsroom there were several meetings during the day between the executive producer and particular persons whose work he had to direct or know about. These meetings were not formal, and much of the work was done by ongoing and repeated consultations throughout the day. The executive producer met with the assignment editor early in the day to grasp the assignment outlook and make suggestions. As the lineup, including news-service material, became clear, the executive producer and producer met with a graphic artist to develop the graphics for the show. According to the artist, the number of graphics averaged about six to eight per show. In our observations, the suggestions for graphics came mainly from the executive producer and producer, who sometimes drew rough sketches for the artist to work from. In the early afternoon a production meeting was held with the executive producer, producer, lineup editor, script assistants, night assistant producer, and film and video technicians. The schedule was distributed at this meeting, and the basic lineup was prepared including decisions about the leading stories and what news-service or 'fire' stories were available as fillers. This was also a key meeting for informing the technical editing staff of what items were from news services, on ENG (video) or DSS (film), so that they could prepare their editing resources accordingly. The executive producer also met with the anchorpersons, consulted with reporters on scripts and film editing, and held planning meetings with relevant staff during the day.

Reporters used interviewing, observational, and documentary methods, with the television reporter having the additional task of acquiring suitable visuals. As just mentioned, in the process of producing a story the reporter consulted with editors or producers. The reporter usually had to make a special plea for greater space in the newspaper (more than 15 column inches), although the newspaper-editing process allowed for flexibility in this respect. In the case of television, a longer item (more than about 90 seconds) could affect whether colleagues' items got into the show and was a matter that required the attention of the lineup editor and producers at the earliest possible stage.

The newspaper story was prepared on a word processor, and the reporter usually took a copy of his filed story for his own records and to compare with what was published. The assistant city editor or city editor checked filed stories for their overall content and watched for anything that might cause legal problems. The slot desk received the filed story on the word-processing system and assigned it to a copy editor. The slot editor worked with the news editor, quality editor, and makeup personnel, tailoring the length of the item to the space available for city-desk stories, including what city-desk stories had been taken for the front page or might be used as fillers elsewhere. The assistant city editor, city editor, and slot editor decided which stories were worthy of the reporter's byline, the most important symbolic recognition of good work available on a daily basis. A night editor was also available to check the copy further, and there were further checks at the night meeting in which the managing editor and other editors scrutinized the page proofs and first printed copies.

The television story was initially prepared in the form of a written script, which was examined and edited by the producer or executive producer. The script included the 'roll-up' or lead of the anchorperson into the story, the reporter's own words, and an indication of where actuality clips or the 'talking heads' of sources were used. It also included an indication of the overall time, and the timing of each segment within the item. Upon approval of the script, the reporter prepared the item in accordance with the visuals he had gathered. In this task the reporter was the producer and editor of his own item, directing the film or video technician to edit as the reporter saw fit. Occasionally the producer or executive producer participated, especially if there was a technical problem or the deadline was approaching. It was possible to continue editing the item right up to show time, and even into the show, as the producer could juggle the lineup to accommodate the need to put the finishing touches on a particular news item. The executive producer and producer controlled the show as a whole, including its themes across items, anchor scripts, and linkages, but the reporter had considerable autonomy in the production of his individual item.

13

Manufacturing the News

Mark Fishman

Exposure to the Newsworld

■ The Beat

IN THIS SOCIETY the most widely recognized function of newspapers is to report news, to report happenings in the world. There are many conceivable ways one could organize a group of individuals to do this, but for at least the past one hundred years American newspapers have settled on one predominant mode of coverage known as 'the beat'.[1] As a matter of fact, the beat system of news coverage is so widespread among established newspapers that *not* using beats is a distinctive feature of being an experimental, alternative, or underground newspaper.[2]

Ever since its establishment in the 1920s the Purissima *Record* depended heavily on beats to cover local news. By the time of the present study, the *Record*'s editorial department was thoroughly organized around a system of beats. Over two-thirds of the *Record*'s reporting manpower was devoted to covering some fourteen different beats, from the city hall beat to the nature beat.

Reporters who do not generate news from a beat work on what is called general assignment. They are stationed in the newsroom, and either the city editor (the immediate boss of the local reporting staff) assigns them stories to research and write, or they suggest their own stories and get clearance from the city editor. In contrast, reporters working a beat are rarely assigned stories. They are expected to generate news from their beat on their own initiative. Routinely they spend more time stationed at their beat locations than in the newsroom. In comparison with general assignment reporters, beat reporters work autonomously. Removed from the city editor's direct supervision most of the day, the beat reporter is largely responsible for deciding what to cover and how to cover it.

Source: Mark Fishman, *Manufacturing the News* (Austin, Tex., and London: University of Texas Press, 1980).

1 The beat system of news coverage not only is typical of small newspapers like the Purissima *Record* but also is dominant on large prestigious dailies like the Washington *Post* and *New York Times* (Sigal 1973: 119–30). However, the situation is more complex in broadcast journalism. Few television journalists seem to work from beats in the sense that print journalists do (Epstein 1973: 135–8). This does not mean, however, that in broadcast journalism most occurrences are detected and interpreted by reporters working on general assignment. Both network and local television news organizations heavily depend on the print media for their sense of newsworthy events (Epstein 1973: 141–3; Fishman 1978). Thus, newspaper and wire service reporters, who largely work beats, indirectly determine what most of the newsworthy events are for television journalists.

2 Purissima's alternative newspaper did not utilize beats and prided itself upon that fact. But as the paper began to expand its local coverage its staff debated whether beats should be instituted. Interestingly, it was decided they should not be used precisely on the grounds that to do so would cause the newspaper to shift from its distinctive 'alternative' character.

Although I have been speaking as if it were perfectly obvious what a beat is, in fact it is rather difficult to define and clearly distinguish beats from other phenomena of newswork. The beat is a journalist's concept, grounded in the actual working world of reporters. As such I can never absolutely distinguish a beat from, for example, an area of expertise that an individual reporter brings to the job and uses in writing stories. Nevertheless, from observations of work on what the *Record*'s reporters recognized as beats, I can outline several key concepts that clarify what a beat is and what makes beat reporting a distinctive system for covering news.

1. A beat has a history in the news organization that outlives the organizational histories of the individuals who work the beat. The *Record*'s city hall beat was covered by four different reporters in the past decade, but as an organizational structure for news coverage the city hall beat is perceived as substantially the same beat.

2. Superiors assign reporters to their beats. The reporter is responsible for, and has jurisdiction over, covering the beat. But the reporter does not own that beat. Insofar as the person is a reporter, the beat is theirs to be covered. Insofar as a reporter is anything else (a single woman, a grandfather, a gourmet), it is inappropriate to use that beat in connection with those other identities.[3] The beat is an office in Weber's sense (1947: 330–2).

3. The beat is a complex *object of reporting* consisting of a domain of activities occurring outside the newsroom. This object, this domain of activities, is coherent. The coherence of a beat simply means that a beat consists of something more than random assortments of activities. The people who produce the activities occurring within a beat territory, and the reporter who covers them, see these actions as sensibly connected in specific ways. Take the police beat, for example. One day the desk sergeant tells the police reporter that a prostitution ring has been busted; another day the reporter sees an arrest report concerning a prostitution case; another day he sees in the court calendar a preliminary hearing for a prostitution case, and so on. These occurrences are all connected: they comprise the judicial career of the same prostitution case. The police and the courts produce these connections; the reporter sees them.

Moreover, sequences of activities themselves are related to other sequences. Beat reporters, and others, see the relations among sequences in two ways. These turn out to be two alternative ways of defining the beat as an object of coverage. First of all, a beat reporter sees that a number of sequences of activities are all part of the same topic. For example, the police reporter not only perceives a single criminal case underlying and connecting all its various appearances, but the reporter also sees it topically, e.g. as a case of prostitution or as an instance of 'the recent crackdown on victimless crime'. Connected activities form topics which arise again and again within the beat. Over time, these topics define the beat.

Second, reporters see sequences of activities as related because they occur in the same physical locations, they are enacted by the same people, and they

---

3 During my period of study, the police reporter cited for me a striking example of this inappropriateness. The reporter's predecessor on the beat was caught sleeping with a police officer on the beat. The next day the reporter was abruptly transferred to general assignment reporting.

are subject to the same standard operating procedures. Here the beat is territorially defined, as a situated entity with stable locations, stable actors, and stable actions.

The topical and territorial ways of defining the beat represent a genuine duality in the journalist's concept of the beat. This distinction is apparent in the two ways newsworkers talk about their beats: as places to go and people to see or as a series of topics one is responsible for covering.

This duality is even more striking in the phenomenon of overlapping beats. In fact, it makes such overlapping possible. Both Wieder and I observed several cases where two beat reporters' jurisdictions for coverage coincided on the same specific news story, suddenly making it legitimate to ask something that had never needed to be asked: who should cover it? This happened whenever a topic associated with one beat moved into the territory of another beat.

To cite one example, the Nopal Valley beat reporter had been covering the issue of annexing Nopal to the city of Purissima for the preceding three years. One day the issue was coming up before the weekly meeting of the county board of supervisors, which is part of the territory of the county government beat. The Nopal reporter had topical jurisdiction; the county reporter had territorial jurisdiction. The reporters involved had to decide who should cover the story. The beat-as-a-territory and the beat-as-a-set-of-topics offered equally good grounds for claiming jurisdiction. The actual decision of who should do the coverage was always made on other grounds ad hoc, as each ambiguous case arose.[4]

The overlap of beats, while not unusual, is not a matter of constant attention among reporters. Journalists see the social world as so organized that topics and territories tend to coincide, i.e. there are stable locations in which certain topics stably reside. The newspaper's system of beats relies upon this perceived order to organize its coverage of the world. At the same time, the newspaper's system of beats helps sustain this view of social organization in American society.

4. The beat is a *social setting* to which the reporter belongs. The reporter becomes part of the network of social relations which is the beat. Within this network the reporter makes friends and enemies, passes gossip and shares secrets, conducts business, and goofs off. Like everyone else inside the beat, the reporter has a niche: a desk, a typewriter, sometimes a mailbox, and even a coffee mug. But unlike other insiders, being an insider is expressly part of the reporter's job.

This adds an interesting twist to my preliminary picture of the beat. Even though the reporter takes the social setting of the beat as the object of reporting, reporters are part of that object. They participate in the activities that they report. Ethnomethodologically speaking, reporters and their beats are *reflexively* related. On the one hand, reporters inquire into the beat as a 'subject' inquires into an 'object'. On the other hand, the very grounds upon which the reporter does an inquiry are from 'within' the beat and hence are

4 The phenomenon of jurisdictional ambiguity and the conflict it can induce within news organizations are discussed in Tuchman (1978a: 25–31) and Sigal (1973: 21–23). Also see Crouse (1974: 114, 260–261).

part of the activities that make the beat what it is. The consequences of this reflexivity for both the methods of beat coverage and the products of that work will be discussed later.

■ **The Detection of Events**

How are events detected? How does the reporter know where to look for potentially newsworthy happenings on the beat? For that matter, how does the reporter recognize something as an event in the first place?

These questions have rarely been asked about media news production. Past literature and research on newswork have been predicated upon a set of common sense assumptions that steered investigators away from the entire issue of event detection because the topic appeared to be uninteresting, obvious, or trivial. Examining these presuppositions of event detection is worthwhile not simply because they are so widely held, but also because they are plausible hypotheses worthy of empirical validation or invalidation. These presuppositions can be stated as five principles.

1. Events are assumed to be self-evident. Reporters come to know events in ways so obvious as to be trivial: events are immediately given in perception. This means that reporters have practically no methods at all for detecting events. Newsworkers simply put themselves in a position to be exposed to occurrences, and events 'jump out' at them. Provided they are exposed to events directly (in person) or symbolically (through talking with a news source), reporters 'just know' events for what they really are.

2. Events are assumed to exist independently of their knowers. Whether the event is known or unknown in no way affects its existence. Who it is that knows the event in no way affects what it really is. The event and its detection stand independently of one another.

3. The methods for detecting an event are assumed not to create, alter, or otherwise affect the event as it is discovered. Specifically, the object of the reporter's coverage is intransigent to however the journalist may discover it or whatever the journalist may think of it. The methods of detection do not affect the object of detection.

4. An event is assumed to occur logically and temporally before the detection of that event. First the event happens, and then the newsworker detects what has happened. To suggest that reporters might know what has happened before its happening, or simultaneously with its happening, would be to defy common sense or to accuse the journalist of creating events out of thin air (which is to say journalists are not detecting anything at all).[5]

This fourth assumption is quite important because if it were not valid, then the second and third assumptions would also be invalid. An event could no longer be assumed to exist independently of its detection if events could occur within the same process by which they were detected.

The next and fifth presupposition is a 'master assumption', an assumption about the previous four.

5. All of the above presuppositions hold under the assumption that the newsworker or an informant is not venal, corrupt, biased, or otherwise a defective observer. Knowingly or unknowingly, defective observers will filter,

---

5 Boorstin (1961) accuses journalists of just this sort of illogical and corrupt practice after pointing out how modern news reports often precede the events they pretend to report.

distort, or make up what they perceive, or they will fabricate events in the process of searching for them. The above presuppositions are only valid for professionally and socially competent, well-intentioned reporters.

This last principle is particularly interesting. It implies that anyone who even questions whether journalists detect events in the manner suggested by the first four principles is someone embarking on a criticism of reporters as venal, corrupt, biased, or defective. The fifth principle is a first line of defence against doubting the other four assumptions: inquiry toward the presuppositions is turned into a debate over the corruption and bias of the news media. This is a trap. It deflects a manageable inquiry into a controversy which has no end. (Is objectivity possible? Should fairness be the journalistic standard instead of objectivity? Are journalists doing the best job possible under the circumstances? Etc.)

I point out this characteristic of the fifth principle for two reasons. First, because the presuppositions of event detection are critically analyzed, it is likely that some readers will misinterpret my remarks as accusations of venality, corruption, and bias within the ranks of the news media. That is how the fifth principle works to deflect an inquiry of newswork into a debate over the moral quality of newsworkers. My intention is simply to uncover what journalists' actual methods of event detection are. Second, the set of principles I have outlined is an excellent example of an ideology. I mean ideology in the sense that Smith (1972) defines it, as a scheme for interpreting a factual domain which contains procedures for *not knowing* certain things. We have seen how the fifth principle can close off inquiry into the other four. It can blind us from very real forces at work in the media, namely, newsworkers' actual methods for detecting events. [. . .]

■ The Bureaucratic Foundations of News Exposure

Just what are newsworkers systematically exposing themselves to by following a routine round of activities?

In the case of the justice reporter, the answer is clear: his information sources almost exclusively have a formally organized, governmental bureaucratic character. This generalization holds for the selectivity of the reporter's exposure at two different levels. First of all, at the broad-scale institutional level, the reporter regularly visited only bureaucratically organized settings. [. . .]

Second, focusing on the more concrete level of the journalist's specific sources of information, reporters expose themselves only to settings in which formally organized transactions of official business appear. That is, within the selected bureaucratic agencies that they do expose themselves to, again, the round selectively brings reporters before only bureaucratically organized presentations of activities. Within each agency, the justice reporter followed a very specific path that routed him to particular files, agency officials, and courtrooms. [. . .]

The justice reporter regularly exposed himself to only a few strategic points in each agency which were organizational foci of information within the criminal justice system. That is, the police, sheriffs, and courts all contained their own reporting systems, and the journalist routinely relied upon the products of these systems for doing his own work. The justice reporter routinely exposed himself to arrest and investigation reports, coroner's documents, traffic accident records, crime boards, newslines, court calendars, and court case files. Each of these were files recording the daily volumes of business received and processed by the police, sheriffs, and courts. From the reporter's point of view, he did not have to, nor would it necessarily have been possible to, witness the commission of crimes or the operations of law enforcement. The police, sheriffs, and courts recounted these events for him. Nor did the reporter need to ride in squad cars, observe autopsies, or be present at every court hearing. The police, sheriffs, and courts reported on what transpired in these places too. The reporter conveniently predicated his routine coverage on the fact that he could cash in on work already done for him by his beat agencies.

The informational foci of each agency are not only files, however. There are two other kinds of 'centres' within agencies where diverse pieces of information are brought together or concentrated for the reporter. One of these information centres is in the form of a person: a member of the agency variously called the information officer, the community relations man, or the media contact. It is the job of such a person to approach the reporter routinely with potentially newsworthy information and to stand ready to consult with the reporter on information the journalist requires. [...]

Another kind of informational focus included in the reporter's round is 'the meeting'. On each beat there are particular meeting places where formally organized, prescheduled activities take place which have the effect of concentrating diverse sources of information within a short period. In other words, when reporters routinely do expose themselves to ongoing activities (instead of exposing themselves to records of those activities), they invariably do so only in a place which guarantees that information formerly scattered throughout dozens of other settings will be brought together before them in that one setting. The city council meetings of the city hall reporter, the county board of supervisors' meeting of the county government reporter, and the District I Courtroom hearings of the justice reporter were all meetings which served this purpose and which were all obligatory stopping points on the reporters' rounds.

Whether their exposure consists of perusing particular files, talking with key agency personnel, or attending specific meetings, beat reporters cover an institutional locale by stationing themselves at those points at which masses of information collect. Governmental bureaucratic work is so organized that it makes observable to the reporter the topics of the beat, which were enacted in diverse parts of the beat territory, in a few centralized locations. [...]

If we can assume that beat rounds get established in this manner (and, admittedly, the data are sparse on this subject), then we can see why those rounds invariably lead the reporter through bureaucratically organized concentrations of information. Of critical importance in explaining this is the general search procedure for establishing new information networks. The procedure continually invites reporters to treat all phenomena of interest as bureaucratically organized. It inevitably leads them to incorporate larger bureaucratic settings exclusively into their beat rounds. Novel tasks are routinized in a way that weds reporters to the largest bureaucratic reporting systems they can find. Thus, there is good reason to suspect that the historical development of reporters' routine beat rounds closely parallels the historical development of bureaucracy and its self-reporting apparatus. [...]

The justice, city hall, and county beat reporters were not exceptional in their systematic exposure to bureaucratic settings. It simply made no difference what the topic of beat coverage was. For instance, the environment beat occupied its reporter in meetings as much as the city hall and county government beats did. Even the *Record*'s nature beat, which produced stories about the local mountain area, forests, and wildlife, depended on the Forestry Service for its news. When it turned out that even rocks, trees, and squirrels are made available to the newspaper through official agencies, then it is no exaggeration to say that *the world is bureaucratically organized for journalists*.

The journalist's view of the society as bureaucratically structured is the very basis upon which the journalist is able to detect events. Such a perspective on the newsworld provides the reporter with a means for locating knowledge of particular happenings in the society that have already occurred. Upon hearing of a large warehouse fire, one knows that the local fire department is in a position to have the information. Upon being notified of a double suicide, one knows that the police are in a position to know the details. Whatever the happening, there are officials and authorities in a structural position to know.

But more importantly, this perspective of a bureaucratically structured society provides the journalist, in advance of any particular occurrence, with a map of relevant knowers for any topic of newsworthy happenings. Suppose the topic is criminality and law enforcement. Who would be in a position to know such happenings once they occurred? The police and the courts. Suppose the topic is nuclear attack. Who then would be in a position to know? The city and county civil defence agencies. Once newsworkers see the community as bureaucratically structured, they have at their disposal a powerful perspective which informs them of who is in a position to know virtually anything they want to know. This bureaucratic consciousness is invaluable for detecting news because it indicates where the reporters should position themselves to discover happenings not yet known.

Moreover, these structural locations provide for the continuous detection of events. This is quite important to the newsworker. Remember that reporters are under a relentless obligation to produce dependable quantities of news daily, no matter how much or how little they feel is happening. In practical terms this means that beat reporters need stable sources which generate reliable quantities of information. This is precisely what a bureaucratic self-reporting apparatus assures. Through thick and thin, day after day, journalists know where and when they can get information, and they know there will be fresh material there.

It is quite understandable, then, why the beat round so heavily focuses on bureaucratic 'fountains of information'.[6] The reporter can expect these fountains to flow reliably because their operation is normatively enforced within the agencies the reporter observes. It is as much a part of the

---

6 This phrase is taken from the programmatic statement of Benjamin Harris in his first issue of *Publick Occurances* (25 Sept. 1690), America's first newspaper: '. . . nothing shall be entered [in this newspaper], but what we have reason to believe is true, repairing to the best fountains of our information' (as quoted by J. M. Lee 1923: 10).

bureaucrat's job to report on things that they do as it is to do those things in the first place. Thus, the same way in which the readers of a newspaper can depend on predictable quantities of news reports day after day, reporters can depend on the bureaucratic reporting apparatus for their raw materials. The dependability of the operations of both reporting systems, bureaucratic and journalistic, is normatively enforced within the organizations that encompass them.

The structure of the reporter's news gathering work (the round) is shaped by the bureaucratic organization of the activities within the beat territory. The substance of what reporters gather (bureaucratically packaged activities) is produced within the agencies they cover. Whatever the sphere of human activity or natural occurrences, as long as it is systematically covered through the beat, the newsworker sees it from a round and knows it through officials and authorities, their files, and their meetings. Quite literally the domain of coverage is produced for the newsworker in formally organized settings by clerks, forest rangers, policemen, stockbrokers, council-men, morticians, and judges—all certified status incumbents in structural positions of knowledge. In and by their work these organizational actors establish structures of knowledge consisting of what there is to know in the first place (possible knowledge) and who knows what, where, and when (distributed knowledge). These local structures of knowledge are what reporters must understand, take into account, and manipulate, not only to guide themselves through their beat, but also to interpret what they are exposed to. [. . .]

The Practice and Politics of Newswork

It is useful to think of news as the outcome of two systems which produce accounts: a system of journalistic accounts and, underlying this, a system of bureaucratic accounts. How can we characterize the relationship between these two systems in the overall news production process?

The entire news production process occurs in several successive 'levels', stretching from the earliest formulated account of something on up to the reporter's written news story. For example, the accounting process which underlies any one crime story can be traced through successive levels of accounts. Only the top level consists of the police reporter's work of detecting, interpreting, investigating, and formulating the story. Behind the news story, inside the agencies through which the reporter first sees the story, are the bureaucratically produced accounts upon which the news will be based.

Within any single agency, the account production process occurs (and is displayed in case files) in successive stages or levels corresponding to the phases of the case in its agency career. Layer upon layer of accounts are built up for the case. Each layer is partially based on accounts from previous layers (i.e. the records of the case produced in previous bureaucratic stages) and is partially based on recently completed accounting work (e.g. new interviews with the 'client').

Moreover, the entire process often extends beyond a single agency. Any one agency adopts in whole, in part, or in a summarized version the previous agency's multilayered accounts. These become the foundation for a new account-building process for the case. For example, on the basis of police files (investigation reports, search warrants, arrest warrants, arrest reports, etc.), the courts begin to build their own layers of accounts generated from preliminary hearings, arraignments, plea bargains, and so forth. Thus, the bureaucratic account production process can be extremely complex, involving several different but interlinked agencies, each of which, for their own purposes, code and recode the case, adding new layers of accounts to the already accumulated case file.

Up to this point I have been describing newswork as just another level in the news production process. This is not quite true, because the journalistic level of account production has priority over all other levels. Ultimately, it is the journalist's work which defines and determines the chains of accounts which lead up to the published news story. Reporters follow rounds which expose them only to bureaucratically produced accounts, and they apply agency schemes of interpretation and relevance to these accounts. By doing so, the reporter makes the successive levels of bureaucratic account production the foundation for a news story. A journalist can change the sources upon which a story is based (i.e. shift from one underlying account production system to another) simply by shifting the emphasis of what the story will be about.

The newsworker can also produce accounts not based upon the prior accounts of bureaucrats. For example, the police reporter could detect, investigate, and formulate crime news without relying on the record-keeping apparatus of the police. [. . .]

Under the constraints of daily story quotas and deadlines the newsworker needs 'fountains of information' that dependably produce reliable quantities of raw materials every day. Bureaucracies are so organized that their account-producing systems meet these constraints in ways that other kinds of news sources cannot or do not. In other words, there appear to be no other modes of account production in this society that can provide daily newspapers with the scope, variety, dependability, and quantity of information that bureaucracies can deliver—and deliver in a scheduled, predictable way. Newspapers need bureaucracies because the journalistic system of account production is itself bureaucratically organized. The news organization needs reliable, predictable, scheduled quantities of raw materials because it is set up to process these in reliable, predictable, scheduled ways in order to turn out a standard product (the newspaper) at the same time every day. Only another bureaucratically organized system of account production could meet these needs by virtue of its self-regulated, reliable, predictable, scheduled activities.

This can be termed the principle of bureaucratic affinity: only other bureaucracies can satisfy the input needs[7] of a news bureaucracy. Whether one is turning lumber into toothpicks, people into clients, or court files into news stories, the flow of raw materials must be controlled or at least made predictable. News is made by routinizing the unexpected (Tuchman 1973). Thus, every newsworker acknowledges as a fact of life that news is slow on weekends because bureaucracies are shut down. More importantly,

---

7 Notice that, within the bureaucratic logic of news organizations, news becomes just another input to the production process, like newsprint or ink.

they can count on it. Thus, management gears down the news operation accordingly.[8]

Taken to its extreme the bureaucratic logic of news reporting would lead a news organization to bring the flow of the raw materials for news stories thoroughly under its control.[9] Curiously, this would mean eliminating such inputs altogether. All shortages and unpredictable variations in the flow of raw news could ultimately be avoided if the materials upon which news stories were based could be internally generated by the news organization. Thus, the internal pace of producing a set of news stories would no longer have to speed up, slow down, or halt because of the availability of externally generated raw materials for news.

In effect, this means newsworkers would create stories based on what they already knew about something, plus a little imagination. To a limited extent, this already goes on. Every newsroom has as part of its folklore the story about the reporter who missed the mayor's speech or the ground-breaking but wrote it up anyway based on a press release and a good guess. Interestingly, such stories often contain a punch line: the mayor gave a different speech or the ground-breaking was rained out.

That newsworkers attach a moral to such stories indicates that these practices are frowned upon. Good news practices entail going out in the world to get stories. Anything else is seen as a matter of crass expediency or downright cheating.[10] There is, thus, a normative element in newswork which, at least up until the present, has placed limits on the extreme tendencies of the bureaucratic logic of news reporting.

References   ALTHEIDE, DAVID (1976), *Creating Reality: How TV News Distorts Events* (Beverly Hills: Sage).

BOORSTIN, DANIEL (1961), *The Image: A Guide to Pseudo-Events in America* (New York: Harper & Row).

CROUSE, TIMOTHY (1974), *The Boys On The Bus* (New York: Ballantine).

EPSTEIN, EDWARD (1973), *News From Nowhere* (New York: Random House).

FISHMAN, MARK (1978), 'Crime Waves as Ideology', *Social Problems*, 25 (June): 531–43.

LEE, J. M. (1923), *History of Journalism in America* (Boston: Houghton Mifflin).

SIGAL, LEON V. (1973), *Reporters and Officials* (Lexington, Mass.: D. C. Heath).

TUCHMAN, GAYE (1978), *Making News: A Study in the Construction of Reality* (New York: Free Press).

8 This is undoubtedly why crime news is more frequent on weekends. The police never close. (See Altheide 1976: 70.)

9 This is simply an extension of the process of vertical integration whereby corporations seek to own or control everything from the extraction of raw materials to the marketing of finished products. While huge industrial concerns such as multinational oil companies typify this process, large newspaper corporations (e.g. Times–Mirror) already own forests, paper mills, truck fleets, and so forth.

10 Apparently some scandal sheets employ writers to make up a story of what happened based on a grisly photo of an automobile accident. Needless to say, these publications are not held in high repute by professional newsworkers.

14

Making the News

Peter Golding and Philip Elliott

The Production of Broadcast News

■ **The Structure of News Production**

AS IN ANY industry news production is a sequence of gathering raw material, processing it into the required product, and distributing the product to an intended market. The major formal distinction among journalists therefore is between the gatherers and processors. Distribution is important as a determinant of the way the product is made, but it concerns us less here since it is not carried out by journalists.

Because of the sheer technology and productive capacity required by television news it tends to be a more passive, more production-orientated medium than newspapers. [...]

Moving from the formal to the informal structure of news making we find that the production cycle consists essentially of four elements:

1. Planning. In the long term fixed predictable events are selected for coverage and resources allocated. Overall policy is to a greater or lesser extent discussed. In the short term daily news coverage is arranged and men and machines matched to events.

2. Gathering. News material is actively collected by reporters and correspondents, and brought into the newsroom.

3. Selection. Material is collated from reporters, and correspondents, culled from agencies and sifted down to a select number of items for final transmission.

4. Production. The selected items are put in order, treated for suitable presentation and a package prepared to make up a programme or bulletin for broadcasting.

Planning Central among journalistic beliefs is the idea of news as random and unpredictable events tracked down by the skills of journalistic anticipation and circumspection. In fact much time is spent in the newsroom reducing the uncertainty of the task by plotting events in advance and determining which are to become news. Long-term planning considers general themes and policies to be included in news coverage and, often, its relationship to other broadcasting. More important, because closer to and more a determinant of daily news production, is short-term planning. Two mechanisms achieve this: the diary and the editorial conference.

Source: Peter Golding and Philip Elliott, *Making the News* (London and New York: Longman, 1979).

The diary is a key document in any news office. It records predictable events that automatically merit coverage by their unquestionable public importance. It is also a register of less significant events vying for inclusion in the 'automatic' category. In a sense production of the diary is news production in advance, except that it is based on the mere knowledge that events will occur, not on observation of them unfolding. The diary is the implicit script of news. The contents range from the formalities of politics (planned visits by politicians, coronations, elections, expected legislation, official reports and the like) to cultural, religious, social or sporting occasions (the Spring Show in Dublin, the end of Ramadan, the Nobel prize-giving, and so on).

The diary is written from the press releases and invitations which flow into the newsroom, and from the past record of routine coverage. It is a newspaper practice much scorned for the 'soft' nature of the news it promotes, and because it stifles initiative, inventiveness and journalistic enterprise. [...]

On the other hand there's something about the special nature of broadcasting, its monopoly situation and quasi-official status, that makes the recording of such events a matter of duty. Television news becomes a broadcast 'journalism of record'. Many Nigerian journalists took pride in the diary as evidence of the professionalism with which their work was conducted, and took it as a sign of the improved status of the occupation that they were invited to such events. However, many were sceptical of its value, and voiced the conventional dislike of diary stories as dull, repetitive, and undemanding. This distaste for diary stories is universal, suggesting that their persistence is due to organizational imperatives more powerful than the taste or choice of journalists. These imperatives are the unchanging definitions of newsworthy events and the need for pre-planning in an essentially cumbersome operation.

The daily routine of planning is conducted at editorial conferences; gatherings of variable formality which ritually celebrate the limited discretion involved in news selection. Editorial conferences signify on the one hand the degree to which news is arranged and selected *a priori*, while on the other hand their repetitiveness from day to day and limited outcome point up the unchanging nature of these *a priori* choices. [...]

If news is about the unpredictable, its production is about prediction. Both the diary and the editorial conference are aimed at plotting the flow of events in the world and marking them for manufacture into 'stories'. Of course there is a strong awareness that the excitement and more exotic skills of the craft are about the indeterminate. But this comes to be defined in limited ways. Thus one Nigerian sports reporter indignantly pointed out that: 'we do have unexpected stories. Like this afternoon there's the launching of the Western States Racquets Association at Governor's House. We only got the press release this morning. Mind you, we'll have to drop the Ibadan v. Legon game to cover it.' While another observed that: 'we don't do many diary stories really. Like today we had two accidents and one surprise arrival at the airport.'

Of course airport arrivals are a standard source of news film, so an unexpected passenger is a surprise variation on an established theme, just as the accidents are rude shocks to their victims, but not to the news audience. The point of emphasizing the planned and unchanging nature of news production is not to imply the potential superiority of a sensational journalism of accidents, shock deaths, and bizarre intrusions into the calm order of life. It is intended to illustrate the ordered routine of broadcast journalism and its focused attention on those kinds of events and institutional areas which have come to occupy the centre of the social world it portrays.

Gathering

Among the most common of sentiments in the newspaper world is the 'pride in being a reporter', a pride often articulated in deliberate reaction to the lowly status of the news-gatherer by the side of the leader-writer or bylined correspondent. The sentiment lives on in broadcasting, but is stunted by the limited opportunities for active foot-in-the-door sleuth journalism offered by the medium. First, broadcast journalism actually produces far fewer stories per day than newspaper journalism; there is just not the space for a large volume of reportage. Second, the demand for film or tape accessories to a story puts a premium on swift, individual reporting, and at its most cumbersome involves a full team of reporter, cameraman, sound-man, lighting man and associated equipment which cannot possibly be as mobile or flexible as one man and a note pad. Third, as we have argued, broadcast journalism is inherently passive because of the labour and resources required for processing, as opposed to gathering news. Only a minority of stories can be covered by newsroom-based reporters or correspondents. The number of reporter-assignments each day varied from three or four in the Nigerian newsrooms to one or two in Sweden; bulletins contained between ten and sixteen items on average (Rapport's policy of news in depth produced the exceptional average figures of seven items per programme).

Many journalists were well aware that compared to newspapermen they had limited scope for news-gathering. [. . .] News-gathering in fact revolves around fixed points of news-making, covered first by correspondents concerned with particular geographical areas or specific subjects, second by 'stringers', especially for provincial and foreign news, and third by regular contact with reliable and productive sources of news or news 'beats'.

Specialization of correspondents is the highest level of job differentiation in the newsroom and attracts the highest prestige both to the correspondents themselves and to the newsroom with the largest array of specialists at its command. [. . .]

Newsrooms in all three countries used a system of home-based reporters travelling to cover stories as they arose. This is cheaper than permanent foreign postings, though still very expensive, and inevitably a great rarity in Nigeria, infrequent at RTE, rather more common at SR. Foreign coverage has to depend almost entirely upon the news agencies either for complete information, or as a guide and warning system about stories in their initial stages which might warrant the outlay of travel and subsistence funds for newsroom staff to go themselves. Thus having an area specialist in the newsroom enlarges the capability of the organization to react to news of a foreign event by mobilizing his expertise and background knowledge. But it does not change the surveillance techniques which discover those events or evaluate their newsworthiness to begin with. Such surveillance is left, by default, to the agencies whose primary *raison d'etre* is, after all, to spread costs in the collection and distribution of foreign news.

Subject specialization is an interesting index of the way news values are translated into organizational practice. The traditional specializations in foreign, diplomatic and political news have been extended in recent years to include a shifting range of subjects seen to require the expertise and undivided attention of a 'correspondent'. In the context of British journalism Tunstall has shown how this reflects changing notions of audience requirements and, in commercial media, of subject areas likely to attract large audiences and therefore advertising (Tunstall 1971: ch. 3). [. . .]

In turn news will tend to reflect this staffing structure; specialists cannot be left idle, and just as news from news capitals flows steadily because there is someone there to produce it, so subjects graced with a specialist will be guaranteed a regular place in bulletins. [. . .]

News gathering, then, taps some of the core elements of journalism's occupational ideology; the journalist as newshound, the outward orientation of journalism as an active collector of information, the independence of journalist from source. In practice broadcast journalism is relatively limited in the gathering it can do, and the production of television news is, in large part, the passive processing of news the newsroom cannot avoid. Gathering is possible in proportion to resources available, but remains the icing on the cake. Even in highly equipped and financed news organizations there is enormous reliance on the news gathering of agencies and on a few prominent institutional sources, most notably government.

Selection
Before looking at the criteria which are used in the selection of news stories we can describe the actual process of compilation. The sifting and moulding of material coming into the newsroom is the process of converting observed events into stories. The skills involved are largely those of 'sub-editing'; that is editing, but with less power of discretion than a newspaper editor. In practice these skills range from the correction of style and grammar to conform with standard practice, to complete responsibility for the final product.

First among eligible stories for selection are those produced by reporters and correspondents working for the newsroom. The fact that these are normally produced in response to a desk request adds to the likelihood that they will be used. In Nigeria it was common to hear the complaint that there was just not enough news, and it was rare for a reporter to have his story spiked unless it was totally unusable. In practice it was usual for whole bulletins to be written by one man, usually the duty editor or chief sub.

Traditionally reporters and sub-editors are in permanent conflict. To the reporter the sub is an unfeeling butcher hacking fine prose for unworthy ends. To the sub the reporter is callow and undisciplined, unaware of the overall needs of the product. Like many mythologies created in the newspaper world this carries over into broadcasting but is much muted. The opportunities for conflict are few; there is little chance for extensive writing on which to wield the axe, most stories prepared are used, and many other restraints apart from the sub-editor are apparent to the reporter, including technical ones. [. . .]

The second source of material for selection is the news agencies, the international wire agencies, Eurovision, and the news film agencies. We have already hinted at the enormous influence of the agencies on selection and the wire agencies in particular are an example of a supply which creates and shapes its own demand. [...]

There are three significant aspects of the use of the wire agencies in news compilation. First, despite reservations about the suitability of their material, the agencies are essential sources of foreign news. Indeed, they are quite literally irreplaceable. The cost of foreign correspondents is infinitely greater than agency subscriptions. [...] For less well off organizations support of foreign correspondents is beyond their budgets. For them the regionalized services of the agencies, often at scaled-down subscription rates, are the only feasible source of foreign news. [...]

The second feature of agency use is the global uniformity of news definitions their use imposes on newsrooms. Selections can only be made from the material available, and clear guidance is given as to the importance and relative significance of news items. 'Nightleads', midday summaries, 'splashes', 'snaps' are provided as cues for copy- and sub-editors. In remoter stories for which the newsroom cannot supply its own expertise agency interpretation is not lacking. We are not examining here the values implicit in agency journalism, but suggesting that such values do exist and are influential in news production. Uniformity is inevitable since three or four agencies are providing the basis for foreign news coverage in every newsroom in the world. The tyranny of supply is nowhere clearer than in this dependence.

This leads to the third aspect of agency significance. Although newsrooms clearly have an autonomy, to a greater or lesser extent, in their choice and treatment of foreign stories, these choices tend to be influenced by the sheer authority of the agencies (Harris 1976). One agency may be despised for providing Hollywood gossip and baseball scores, but the subscription continues. Another is derided for its lingering British imperial undertones, but again it remains. Agency coverage alerts the newsrooms to world news events, and it is around this knowledge that newsrooms build their own coverage. So even those newsrooms able to send out teams to foreign stories will depend on agency selection for notice of which stories to consider. The agencies are thus an early warning service for newsrooms whose actions are determined by the observations in agency wires.

A second source of material for compilation in the European newsrooms is Eurovision. This is enormously important in a visual medium as it is a source of news film. Eurovision itself was set up in 1954, though the news exchanges did not begin until 1961. The growth of the system has been rapid and it plays a central part in the foreign coverage of European newsrooms. [...] Of course, EVN is not a separate news agency but merely an exchange for items produced by the individual member organizations. [...]

Because of the development of the Eurovision exchanges, the third source of foreign material for selection, air freighted agency news films, has declined in importance for the European stations. By and large it is kept for archival use or the occasional emergency. Outside Europe, however, such material is enormously significant. For the vast majority of non-European television newsrooms it is their only source of foreign news film. This was the case in Nigeria, discounting the embassy handouts and commercial publicity films which occasionally come in.

As with Eurovision, unavoidable use of the agency film is tempered by

…servations about its quality. Nigerian journalists are sceptical of the western orientation of both the selection of items they receive and the tone and language of the commentaries that accompany them. A subscription to a news film agency brings a daily package of about half a dozen news films, ranging in length from a minute to perhaps four or five minutes. [...]

The final, and probably least important sources of materials in compilation are the press releases and hand-outs delivered to the newsrooms. The occupational attitude to this is well-defined; they must be treated with mistrust as an attempt to manipulate the journalist and sway his professional judgement. Official and governmental releases are mistrusted because they interfere with the established journalistic task of teasing out the political truth. Commercial releases are despised as pure advertisement, beneath the contempt of true journalism. Most press releases are derided for their poor technical quality, for not having the information a journalist needs in the crisp well-ordered style and language he prefers. In addition, press releases attract the same weary antagonism as diary stories; they lack the topicality, excitement, unpredictability or depth of the best news stories. Finally they confirm tangibly a dependence on sources which is quite antipathetic to professional self-respect. For all these reasons press releases are very seldom used, except as a starting point. They are used much more, however, than the occupational belief system would suggest.

There are sometimes particular reasons for this. The producers of press releases are usually journalists, and often former colleagues of those to whom their work is addressed. The journalist and PRO know each other's problems and are willing to scratch each other's backs where possible. Often a press release is better than no information at all. [...]

Commercial press releases are far less important than governmental ones, and we shall discuss these below in the context of general governmental influence, after looking at the final stage in the production cycle.

Presentation Simply stated, news gathering is most concerned with news sources, news processing with the audience. This is an over-simplification, but the presentation of news is, of all the production processes, the most hedged around with trade lore about what audiences will and will not accept, comprehend or enjoy. We are interested here in the way this lore is called upon in the daily production of news bulletins.

Consideration of the audience affects production first by influencing the selection of items which become news, second in suggesting ways in which those items may be presented. There are many ways in which journalists can discover the views and demands of audiences, the most formalised being to read the information available to them in audience research reports. [...]

The kind of research journalists see as most useful is on comprehension; examining whether audiences can cope with the vocabulary of bulletins, or have a sufficient general knowledge of people and organizations to understand stories. Such research tends to confirm their worst fears that audience abilities are generally over-estimated. This only reaffirms that strain in the occupational ideology which sees journalism as educative; simplifying and explaining the complexities of life for an audience inadequately equipped to understand them. In this lies the professional skill of journalism.

Any other response to knowledge about the audience is felt to be potentially dangerous, since this would compromise professional autonomy to the demand of the market place. Apparent distaste for the sordid realities of marketing the product is of course common in monopoly broadcasting. A considerable amount of research has described professional broadcasters' distance from and ignorance of their audience (McQuail 1969; Golding 1974: 68–73). The broadcast journalist has an awkward dilemma to resolve. Journalistic responsibility is held to entail detailed knowledge of the needs and interests of the audience. On the other hand professional integrity and autonomy prohibit pandering to these needs and interests. The solution tends to be an assertion that audience requirements are well understood by the journalist by virtue of his wide-ranging experience and daily contacts with a wide selection of audience members. For some this means a cynical contempt, perhaps tinged with regret, for their audience. [. . .]

The only audience research journalists can commonly quote is that showing their rating in a competition with alternative programmes or organizations (see similarly Schlesinger 1978: 111–15; Epstein 1973: 91–100). Audience views could be called upon to support any approach to production. Demands for more background and explanation could be supported by pointing out the lack of knowledge amongst the public. The same 'ignorance' could be used as evidence that the news should stick to a bald narrative of facts, rather than risk going over the heads of viewers.

These kinds of concern about audiences involve social values. But day-to-day production has no time to consider social values, and relies on news values to guide selection and presentation. Presentation is the skill of turning taken-for-granted news values into rules of production. In assessing audience response journalists have to rely on accepted definitions of news, what makes a good or a not so good story. Journalistic notions of what is and is not news have been forged in the workshops of a commercial press serving historically particular needs and interests. It is in this process that news values are created.

■ News Values and News Production

Discussions of news values usually suggest they are surrounded by a mystique, an impenetrable cloud of verbal imprecision and conceptual obscurity. Many academic reports concentrate on this nebulous aspect of news values and imbue them with far greater importance and allure than they merit. We have stressed that news production is rarely the active application of decisions of rejection or promotion to highly varied and extensive material. On the contrary, it is for the most part the passive exercise of routine and highly regulated procedures in the task of selecting from already limited supplies of information. News values exist and are, of course, significant. But they are as much the resultant explanation or justification of necessary procedures as their source.

News values are used in two ways. They are criteria of selection from material available to the newsroom of those items worthy of inclusion in the final product. Second, they are guidelines for the presentation of items, suggesting what to emphasise, what to omit, and where to give priority in the preparation of the items for presentation to the audience. News values are thus working rules, comprising a corpus of occupational lore which implicitly and often expressly explains and guides newsroom practice. It is not as true as often suggested that they are beyond the ken of the newsman, himself unable and unwilling to articulate them. Indeed, they pepper the daily exchanges between journalists in collaborative production procedures. Far more they are terse shorthand references to shared understandings about the nature and purpose of news which can be used to ease the rapid and difficult manufacture of bulletins and news programmes. News values are qualities of events or of their journalistic construction, whose relative absence or presence recommends them for inclusion in the news product. The more of such qualities a story exhibits, the greater its chances of inclusion. Alternatively, the more different news values a story contains, the greater its chances of inclusion (see Galtung and Ruge 1965). News values derive from unstated or implicit assumptions or judgements about three things:

1. The audience. Is this important to the audience or will it hold their attention? Is it of known interest, will it be understood, enjoyed, registered, perceived as relevant?

2. Accessibility—in two senses, prominence and ease of capture. Prominence: to what extent is the event known to the news organization, how obvious is it, has it made itself apparent. Ease of capture: how available to journalists is the event, is it physically accessible, manageable technically, in a form amenable to journalism, is it ready-prepared for easy coverage, will it require great resources to obtain?

3. Fit. Is the item consonant with the pragmatics of production routines, is it commensurate with technical and organizational possibilities, is it homologous with the exigencies and constraints in programme making and the limitations of the medium? Does it make sense in terms of what is already known about the subject?

In other words, news values themselves derive from the two immediate determinants of news making, perceptions of the audience and the availability of material. Historically news values come to imbue the necessities of journalism with the lustre of good practice. They represent a classic case of making a virtue of necessity. This particularly applies to the broader values we have subsumed under the title of the occupational ideology—impartiality, objectivity, accuracy and so on. [...]

■ **Summary** In this chapter we have described the process by which news is produced. Our description suggests broadcast journalism is by no means random reaction to random events. On the contrary, it is a highly regulated and routine process of manufacturing a cultural product on an electronic production line. In stages of planning, gathering, selection and production broadcast news is moulded by the demands of composing order and organization within a daily cycle. The news is made, and like any other product it carries the marks of the technical and organizational structure from which it emerges.

References Epstein, E. J. (1973), *News from Nowhere: Television and the News* (New York: Random House).

Galtung, J., and Ruge, M. (1965), 'The Structure of Foreign News', *Journal of Peace Research*, 1: 64–90.

Golding, P. (1974), *The Mass Media* (London: Longman).

Harris, P. (1976), 'International News Media Authority and Dependence', *Instant Research on Peace and Violence*, 6/4: 148–59.

McQuail, D. (1969), 'Uncertainty about the Audience and the Organisation of Mass Communications', in P. Halmos (ed.), *The Sociology of Mass Media Communicators* (Sociological Review: Monograph no. 13, Keele), 75–84.

Schlesinger, P. (1978), *Putting 'Reality' Together: BBC News* (London: Constable).

Tunstall, J. (1970), *The Westminster Lobby Correspondents* (London: Routledge and Kegan Paul).

—— (1971), *Journalists at Work* (London: Constable).

15

Putting 'Reality' Together: BBC News

Philip Schlesinger

A Stop-Watch Culture

IN THE OCCUPATIONAL mythology of the newsman time looms large among the wicked beasts to be defeated daily in the battle of production. This chapter considers the nature and consequences of the broadcasting newsman's obsession with duration and sequence. As a feature of journalistic work it cannot be ignored, and not only because journalists themselves assert its importance.[1] Rather, it is because much of our sense of what is relevant, and therefore our awareness of the passage of time, is structured by mass media production cycles.

While the structuring role of the time-factor in production cycles is almost invariably mentioned by sociologists who have studied journalists at work, this theme is rarely singled out for separate analytical treatment.[2] What is mainly considered here is the way in which newsmen's production concepts are shaped by the constraints of time, and the implications of this for the form and content of news. In considering this feature of newsmen's occupational ideology we are in the domain of the sociology of knowledge. For, as Gurvitch has pointed out, 'the question of the ways to grasp intuitively, perceive, symbolize and know time in . . . different frameworks' is a 'central problem' of this field.[3]

■ The Time Factor in Context

There are two contexts which must be outlined in order to understand the particular production system examined.

The more immediate context is the occupational culture of the broadcasting journalist engaged in daily production—one which lays a particular emphasis on the stop-watch and the deadline as crucial features of work. In general, journalists are among those occupational groups in industrialized societies for whom precision in timing, and consequently an exacting time-consciousness, is necessary. Railwaymen are another.[4] Such an obsession

Source: Philip Schlesinger, *Putting 'Reality' Together* (London and New York: Methuen, 1978).

1 Wintour 1972: ch. 1; Priestland 1973.

2 Cf. however, Tuchman 1969: ch. 4; Bensman and Lilienfeld 1971; Park 1940.

3 Gurvitch 1964: 14.

4 Cottrell 1939.

with the passage of time is notable among those operating communication and transportation systems, which are dominated by a need for the exact co-ordination and synchronization of activities.[5]

To say that such groups are obsessed by time is but to point to exemplary cases of what is held to be a widely diffused fixation in Western cultures with the passage of the finer gradations of clock-time.[6] It is easy for us to understand such fixations as we are members of a society whose activities, notably work, are generally closely regulated by the clock. If it is true that 'the clock is surely the crucial machine of an industrial civilization'[7] then our looking at newsmen is simply a case of us, the clock-conscious, watching the most clock-conscious. Our common denominator is an all too great familiarity with abstract time-reckoning which it is too easy to overlook, since it is taken for granted.

For cultures and societies which are not regulated by clock-time, the concepts and actions of newsmen must appear curious and alien, and probably quite pathological.

An apt instance came from one assistant editor in Television News who had spent a year teaching news production techniques in Libya on secondment from the BBC. The news was supposed to be transmitted at 9.00 p.m. each night, at the insistence of the Minister of Information. On one occasion, the programme before the news overran, so the news was forced to go on the air at 9.10 p.m. In keeping with the Minister of Information's instruction it officially went out at 9 p.m. This feat was achieved by the simple act of turning back the studio clock. The assistant editor had found it very hard to 'get them to take fast news seriously. They don't care about time there.'

Stories such as this underline the relative singularity of the value placed on time in developed Western societies[8] which, it is argued, has derived in part from the time-discipline progressively exerted upon the labour force with the growing dominance of industrial capitalism.[9] As Weber observed, time became just another commodity traded on the market-place, a further extension of rationality.[10]

This, then, is one possible framework for situating journalistic work: that of an occupation dominated by rationalized time-keeping within a society similarly so dominated. Within this context, newsmen travel along an astonishingly fast 'time track'.[11] This follows a regular cycle each day, the pace of which is governed by a series of deadlines.

A second, related context is that of the market for news in a capitalist society. As Raymond Williams has pointed out:

5 Sorokin and Merton 1937.

6 Hall 1959; for a counter-argument see Clark 1976.

7 Moore 1963a: 163.

8 Marcus 1960–61; Bohannan 1953; Evans-Pritchard 1940: ch. 3.

9 Moore 1963b; Thompson 1967.

10 Weber 1968: 157–8.

11 Lyman and Scott 1970.

The newspaper was the creation of the commercial middle class, mainly in the nineteenth century. It served this class with news relevant to the conduct of business, and as such established itself as a financially independent institution.[12]

These commercial market origins still inform the production routines of the press, and by extension, broadcasting. The production system described above, which is organized on the principle of delivering outputs at set times during the newsday, should be seen in relation to its market. Formally, at least, BBC News operates in a duopolistic market, in which competition is provided by the commercial radio and television stations of the Independent Broadcasting Authority.

Competition in production proceeds through each daily cycle. For the BBC's News Division, success in 'breaking' a story quickly or exclusively is principally assessed in relation to the outputs of the commercial network's national news produced by ITN. Newspapers are more of a source than a competitor.

■ **Newsmen:** *Both my organism and my society impose upon me, and upon my inner*
Victims or *time, certain sequences of events that involve waiting. . . .*
Controllers? *(Berger and Luckmann)*[13]

There are long periods of doing fuck all, and then all hell breaks loose.
(Television Newsman)

In an illuminating article, Lyman and Scott contrast two basic attitudes towards time. They write, on the one hand, of 'humanistic time tracks' where individuals feel they have mastery or control of their activities. By way of contrast, they point to 'fatalistic time tracks' where the feeling is rather one of compulsion and obligation.

Both these attitudes are exhibited by newsmen in their working lives. The reason for this lies in the peculiar situational constraints posed by producing news. News, despite much coverage that is pre-planned, is nonetheless felt by the newsman to be full of capriciousness. By definition, the unforeseen lies just around the corner. Newsmen are apt, therefore, to describe themselves and their work fatalistically. They see themselves as victims attendant upon events, and tell this kind of story:

The newsroom is quiet, activity controlled and routine. Then, 'the shit starts to hit the fan': a big story has broken; resources have to be mobilized and plans abandoned.

The tale is told in a way which reflects the way in which the operation is felt to move into top gear, suddenly, electrifyingly. The pace of work becomes frenetic, all-absorbing in its demands. Reporters find they must suddenly leave on an assignment—to report a bank robbery, an aircrash, to conduct an interview. Editors find they must make rapid selections. 'Everything is happening' in an episode of quick-fire activity. Utterances are clipped,

12 Williams 1965: 197.

13 Berger and Luckmann 1971: 41.

sometimes rude; movements deft; the atmosphere tense; the noise level rises steadily. Sub-editors rush between newsroom and cutting-room, snatch a few words with the editor of the day and dictate their copy to typists. The TV news rehearsal takes place at a breathtaking pace. For reporters there is a great qualitative contrast between preparation ('fixing' interviews and 'doorstepping' sources), which involves waiting and holding back, and the act of reporting or interviewing, which is seen as the really authentic part of the job.

Newsmen oscillate, then, from victim to controller. From the valued, authentic aspects of news production—notably the hour before bulletin transmission—comes an idealized image of work as all-consuming action. From the direct experience of the structure of work at a given point in the production cycle the *entire* operation comes to be characterized as a feverish drama.

Such emphasis on action is an important feature of media professionalism. It is professional to be in control of the action rather than to be victimized by the pace at which it must, sometimes, be carried out. But oddly enough, being victimized is also something to be welcomed, as it is seen as what true newsmen feel in coping with an erratic force.

To be professional in this way is not simply to fulfil certain shared criteria of competence. It is as much a question of feeling certain things, of 'having the old adrenalin run'. Newsmen have, therefore, a specific cultural interpretation of the real meaning of their work, basic to it being the excitement and danger which arise from meeting tight deadlines. To become a controller, thereby transcending the victim-creating capriciousness of the news, is what makes newsmen's work so exciting.

The rhetoric employed by newsmen in describing their activities diverges, however, from the observed reality. In general, production is far from chaotic at anything other than a superficial level. Its rationale is to aim at control and prediction, while those who work the system celebrate its relatively rare contingencies. Indeed, there is a strange irony in the last-minute rush to fill the slot. Mostly, the intake of news items occurs during the last hour by design, as the later they arrive the more immediate they are. This means that anxious newsmen are working a system which can only exacerbate their anxieties. The contingencies are in fact created by the newsday cycle itself, and those values which stress immediacy.

■ **Immediacy and Competition**

We become most clearly aware of the emphatic bias towards rapid turnover in broadcast new production when considering the key concept of 'immediacy'.

This is a temporal concept which refers to the time which has elapsed between the occurrence of an event and its reporting as a news story. Logistically, it relates to the speed with which coverage can be mounted. The pure type of immediacy, therefore, is 'live' broadcasting. In such cases, a TV camera or radio car is at the scene of the event as it happens, and the event is transmitted immediately to the viewer or listener. An added implication is the notion that the audience for news, can, via the technical means of communication, be present at the event. This idea is obviously fostered by contemporary broadcasting technology and the possibility of providing up-to-date actuality.

The very fact of having the technology can produce a spurious immediacy which is by now a familiar cliché. The rain-soaked industrial or political correspondent stands outside TUC Headquarters or No. 10 Downing Street and assures us that negotiations are going on at that moment. At this point, when X tells us that he is at a particular spot, and if he has a television OB unit, actually shows that he is there, we enter the realms of the absurd. But it is an absurdity which is broadcasting's own. Newspapers, by comparison, cannot be 'immediate' in this sense. They can, however, try to approach the ideal of rapid turn-over by rapidly updating stories in successive editions.

Immediacy acts as a yardstick for perishability. News is 'hot' when it is most immediate. It is 'cold', and old, when it can no longer be used during the newsday in question. Today's occurrences, those of this morning, afternoon, night, now, are what the broadcasting newsman wants to know about. Yesterday's story, in his view, belongs to the dustbin of history: the news archive. [. . .]

As immediacy is so central to news production as presently conceived it provides newsmen with a standard of logistical success. An apt instance occurred during fieldwork in 1972. There had been a dramatic aircrash in the London area. BBC Television News received an early tip-off about this occurrence and managed to send a film crew to the scene of the tragedy straight away. The main competitor, ITN, did not arrive so quickly, and the BBC team therefore scooped the story. The following assessment by the News Editor is immensely revealing of the dominant attitude towards the time-factor in news production (and also of news values):

> Professionally speaking, we were pleased that we were on the scene ahead of ITN, and got the film when the plane was starting to catch fire. . . .
> *When you've got news you should give it at its earliest.* You can't know all the contingencies.

This view was endorsed at the highest level in TV News. The Editor sent a congratulatory memorandum to the newsroom, commending the film crew in question 'for our extremely successful effort to get the Trident crash story to the screen. We gave a fuller and speedier news service than any other'.[14] From a professional viewpoint, this success in coverage was assessed as evidence of competitive competence based on speedy reactions:

> ITN had no early coverage at all.   (Foreign duty editor, Television News)
>
> We *had* to pull out the stops to beat ITN.   (Duty editor, Television News)

Immediacy, however, is in potential conflict with the value of accuracy. In the corporately cautious news judgement of the BBC, haste leading to mistakes, and thence to a loss of public esteem, ought to be avoided. This caution is given something of a public service gloss, as, for example, in the words of Donald Edwards, a former Editor, News and Current Affairs:

> Sometimes we get hold of a piece of news which we know would interest the audience, but we are not absolutely certain of its accuracy. We have to hold it while we check. It is agony to a newsman to miss a bulletin, *but*

14 Memorandum from Editor, Television News, to News Staff, 18 June 1972.

reliability and accuracy are more important than speed. . . . It is not enough to interest the public. You have to be trusted.[15]

The tension is a basic one, giving us an insight into the way in which journalistic values (competition, speed) may conflict with a paramount organizational value (accuracy). In a context where the pace of output is rigidly governed by a certain number of time-slots, holding back a story until confirmation comes through means that the competition may well beat you to the draw.

The above quotation from Donald Edwards is echoed by the BBC's *News Guide* which lays down 'one-hundred-per-cent accuracy at all times' as the corporate ideal, notes that this 'must remain forever beyond our grasp' due to the 'fallibility' of people and therefore advises that 'If after checking as far as you can, you still have doubts about something, then leave it out.' This kind of policy is a practical counter-measure to what, to judge from the language cited above, is almost a state of original sin: the innate tendency to get the facts wrong. 'Accuracy' has characterized the BBC from its earliest days.[16] Being accurate, and therefore reliable, should be seen in the general context of the caution which characterizes the approach of broadcast news, not just in Britain, but elsewhere.[17] Such caution is manifest in the taking up of stories which have already entered the public domain via the press, or by steering away from some stories altogether. [. . .]

■ **Time Slots and News Values**

Each newsday consists of a number of time-slots, each of which is clearly demarcated. The existence of news slots is public knowledge (available from newspapers, *The Radio Times, The TV Times*). For the news producers the existence of such slots poses a problem: they have to be 'filled' with news. A slot presents newsmen with a *goal.* On the other hand, on days when a lot is happening (in news terms), they might find that they have too much news on hand. The slot is also, therefore, a *constraint.*[18] Thus, time-slots carve up the day, presenting a set of formal targets for the production team. To cope with time-slots newsmen have first to meet their deadlines.

News stories are ranked according to estimates of their news value. This is at the same time a process of according a story a time-value. Time-values take two forms: they slot a story into a sequence, and fix a particular duration. Such time-valuing goes on throughout the production process.

A story's duration in a news bulletin therefore indicates its newsworthiness. As slots cannot generally be exceeded, the editor of the day is forced to express his news judgement through rather rigid *temporal* directives to sub-editors and reporters. Thus, he might ask for 'a one-minute piece on the

---

15 Edwards 1964: 6, 7; emphasis added.

16 Cf. Briggs 1965: 153; Briggs 1970: 180; Halloran *et al.* 1970: 185–6 have also noted the particular BBC concern with 'accuracy'.

17 Cf. Golding and Elliott 1976; Epstein 1973.

18 Slots are products of complex intra-organizational bargaining between the heads of particular departments in the BBC and the Controllers of the channels. As the scheduling of the entire broadcasting day depends on the stability of slots, it is not surprising that they are rarely tampered with. News slots are extended where a special need can be shown: e.g. to cover the shock resignation of Harold Wilson and its immediate implications.

industrial situation', or for 'Twenty seconds on the Queen'. The limit posed by the slot is thus always vividly present.

Editorial instructions to sub-editors and reporters set a time-framework for the newsman. Each individual contribution to a bulletin emerges from the experience of working within a temporal constraint, for every newsman knows that his 'piece' is part of the available total time-slot, and that to exceed it, or to fall below it, would prejudice the overall balance of the bulletin. In practice, not all stories remain statically within their initial duration: as a story grows in importance its time-value increases, and it will decrease if the story is deemed less newsworthy. The BBC's *News Guide*, a codification of desired news practice, ordains: 'Each sentence, each word, must be made to count, We learn to handle words as if they were gold. . . .'[19] A news bulletin takes a serial form, in which each sequence of words to be spoken by the newsreader and reporters has to be precisely timed. It is a standard assumption in the BBC newsrooms that the newsreader's pace of delivery will be at a regular three words-per-second. This might seem a ridiculously crude way of pacing such a technically sophisticated production as a television news bulletin, but it does in fact lie at the basis of the broadcasts we see and hear. Again, the time-slot operates in an intimate and personal way to control individual output in the direction of economy and precision. The practical importance of this rule was observed when one television newsreader was vociferously criticized as being 'hard to write for': his offence lay in a tendency to alter his pace of delivery, which 'threw out' the timing of the entire bulletin, and made a nervous wreck of the studio director. The incident illustrated the collective nature of production, and the reliance placed on accurate timing if it is to run smoothly.

There is a link between the story allocated to a newsman and his estimation of his own status. The stories which lead the bulletin, or are given the longest duration, go to the most senior sub-editors, and reportorial pickings to the specialist correspondents. Prestige is conditioned by two factors: duration and placement in the 'running order'. The longer the story time, the greater the possibility for the newsman to exercise his skills in combining words, graphics, sounds, photographs, film. Given that news is seen as inherently unstable, with one established story being often superseded by a more immediate later one, there is an element of fragility about the status structure on any given day. The time-value of a story has important consequences for the satisfaction experienced by individual newsmen.

Concerning time-value, one senior news executive observed: 'What we leave out is what in our judgement doesn't rank as news in the context of limited time and space.' This remark is revealing, for it shows how scarcity of time may work as a defence: newsmen claim their own prerogative to decide what stories are worth. This tactic was used, on one occasion, by a reporter negotiating the relationship between his source and the Television News Department. His interviewee, the Minister of Transport, complained that a previous interview had not been used. The reporter replied that he was not in ultimate editorial control, and that anyway there could never be any guarantees as time was always short. Moreover, the Minister was told that as it was

---

19 *News Guide*, 1972: 8.

Sunday (with a short main news bulletin) the interview would have to be kept inside one minute. Again, the time-consciousness of the newsman can be seen to have a striking effect on his basic practices.

As has so far been indicated, there is a constant problem of controlling the work processes to meet output times, and of keeping within the slot. There is a detectable element of goal-displacement at times, when slot-filling becomes an end in itself. This was given archetypal voice by one editor of the day who said to his team: 'I'm in the shit length-wise. What've you got?' At such moments newsmen are trying hard to be controllers rather than victims. Although being a victim is quite enjoyable since it makes life authentically tense.

The two senior newsroom editors are supposed to have an over-view of the entire programme. As bulletin time approaches, what tends to happen—notably in television where the programmes are longer and their constituents more complex and numerous—is a shifting of the editor's focus from the content of the programme to its sequence and duration. One senior duty editor noted in an amused way that the timing dominated his thoughts in those last minutes: 'The question you're asking yourself is "What can I drop?" ' He also drew attention to the adding and subtracting of minutes and seconds both before and during the transmission, which he felt was 'primitive', when he was trying to convey complex information. By the time production is at an advanced stage, newsmen no longer 'see' or 'hear' the programme due to their involvement in getting it on the air. As one editor of the day put it: 'You come out [of the studio] and ask "How was it?" You've an idea how you'd *like* it to be, but you don't know what's happening while you're coping with the problems arising.'

■ Time and Newsmen's Language

Newsmen make fine conceptual distinctions concerning time. This is only to be expected as the temporal dimension of their occupational culture is highly elaborated. A brief account of some of their most important working ideas follows.

The Immediacy Cluster

There is a cluster of notions derived from, and related to, 'immediacy', which suggest upheaval, suddenness, unpredictability. Whenever new information on a story comes into the newsroom it is up-dated. New facts and interpretations have to be integrated into the story, if it is to be used, prior to transmission. Such revision is a continual process, and contributes to the feeling that news is naturally without a resting place. Hence, news stories are talked of as 'breaking'. Ideally, they should break well before the deadline to be covered.

It is highly important to newsmen that stories have this apparent capacity to rupture the skein of existing expectations. And they have ways of signalling this to the news audience. Some stories, in their view, just cannot wait until the next scheduled bulletin. For these the 'newsflash' is used: the news item is given separate treatment in its own time, which confers an aura of urgency and importance on it. [...]

In general, though, the tendency towards immediacy is contained within regular time-slots. However, since a 'late' story is always prone to appear, there is an ever-present danger of disturbance. While this could unbalance the existing bulletin, immediacy is so valued as authentic, that the upset, stress, excitement, and drama created by the arrival of 'late' news is not only desired, but also regarded as ideal. It is possible to accommodate an unexpected story by leaving the sequence intact and by prefacing it with 'We've just heard that . . .' This formula stresses the immediacy of the new story. A further way of handling this type of occurrence is for the newsreader to say 'And now some late news . . .' just before the close of bulletin. Honour is saved: the story may be simply a few brute facts served without dressing, but the temporal imperative has been obeyed.

A further, quite distinct, way of coping with stories which are both immediate and 'big' is for the editor of the day to request an extension of the time-slot. Thus, for example, when the Watergate Affair first broke in Britain, ITN's *News At Ten* added a third quarter of an hour to accommodate reports from Washington as well as the rest of the news, the newscaster making it clear why the slot has been extended. A similar extension took place on the *Nine O'Clock News* when the BBC obtained an exclusive interview with President Idi Amin of Uganda following the raid on Entebbe airport by Israeli commandos.

Given the expectation that there might always be a new lead story heading down the wires, we find that the immediate story is treated almost reverentially, being full of potential, at least in principle.

Outside Immediacy   Stories which are unexpected and unplanned for are called 'spot news', and concern events which are of their nature unforeseeable: aircrashes, collisions at sea, rail disasters, fires, assassinations, political coups, earthquakes, deaths. These are distinguished from 'diary' stories which might be known of months in advance: news conferences, space shots, state occasions and visits, elections, budgets. All of these are predictable 'future events' for which early arrangements can be made. Spot news, by contrast, involves 'instant' editorial decisions. It is very important to be sure that the means exist to cover such stories, to know that, for example, reporters and film crews are available who have not been committed to other stories.

Rapid decision-making and the atmosphere of upheaval which both derive from responding to the spot news story contribute to the general evaluation of this kind of story as nearest the bone of true news activity. Diary stories are often denigrated as 'set piece', or as simply routine with no element of surprise.

The Running Story   Another relevant category reflecting working patterns is the 'running story'. This category embraces all stories which transcend a given newsday cycle, and are pursued on subsequent ones. Examples are: The Watergate Affair, The Cod War, The (Lambton) Call Girl Affair, The Lebanese Civil War. A running story is one which is expected to be covered for a number of days at least. It appears for a sequence of days on the News Departments' planning documents. The best example of how a particular category is embedded in day-to-day planning is the 'Ulster Crisis'. During fieldwork this was a permanent category in the planning documents, indicating that the newsmen had become sensitized to both Northern Ireland and Eire as news-source areas. It was firmly expected that things would happen there in the future because of regular incidents (bombings, assassinations, demonstrations, etc.) in the past. This example provides a limiting case. One cynical old hand observed: 'It's been a crisis for so long you can't call it a crisis any more.' The concept of the running story reflects a tendency in production for some newsworthy items, on some occasions, for periods ranging from days to months, or even years, to become institutionalized. But, as with other stories, what one is likely to find on any given day of the running story are the most immediate 'facts' about it.

■ **Time, and News as Cultural Form**

Broadcast news has a specific cultural form.[20] Time concepts can play a role in structuring the presentation and style of news bulletins.

A key idea is that of 'pace'. As broadcasters are in a capitalist market situation, where success is, in the last resort, determined by the size of audience they can attract, they feel themselves impelled to try and 'hook' the audience's attention. Bulletins, they argue, have to be so constructed as to achieve this goal. Orchestrating an interesting sequence of news items becomes, therefore, a dominant aim in production.

Each news bulletin is structured according to a concept of the right pace. Thus, for example, one editor of the day said that he approached the problem of constructing his programme by thinking in terms of a 'dramatic concept', according to which there would be 'peaks and troughs' during the course of the broadcast. He observed: 'You have to keep the interest moving: it's no good doing a flat 2-D newspaper. You have to give presentation some thought.' The kind of style adopted is thus justified by an appeal to the presumed psychology of the audience.

This style is closely linked to the concept of news as today's happenings. The idea of 'moving it along' has a temporal basis: dramatic items are placed in a sequence according to *when* it is thought the audience's interest is likely to flag. This view, it should be noted, expresses an ideal as, given the stress on immediacy, it is always possible the most balanced presentation will be upset by later developments. It is clear, though, that the rhythm of presentation is seen as needing judicious control.

Newsmen's approach to pace is based on this broadcaster's axiom: 'the audience can't go back over what it's just seen or heard'. Frequent contrasts are drawn with print journalism: the newspaper reader may re-read a paragraph or sentence if it is not at first understood, but the broadcast word perishes on the instant. Because news bulletins have a serial form, it is felt that their content has to be grasped at the moment of transmission. Newsmen are therefore aware of the broadcast media themselves as creating inherent difficulties.

Problems of pace are more acute in television news production than in radio. This stems directly from the time-slots available to each of the two media. The longest BBC radio bulletin lasts for fifteen minutes (on Radio 4); the longest television bulletin (on BBC-1) has a 25-minute slot, and, as TV newsmen never tire of saying, is seen as well as heard, and thus, they argue, needs to possess a sustained visual interest.

Changes of pace are provided in various ways. One relatively simple means

20 Williams 1974: ch. 3.

of changing the focus of the audience's attention is to use two newsreaders as joint presenters. ITN's *News at Ten*, following American network news style, has used this technique since 1967. BBC's *Nine O'Clock News* introduced a slightly different version in November 1972, dropping it in March 1976.

Pace is also varied by the placement of stories. Thus, in television news, film stories will be spaced out during the sequence so that they do not 'bunch': they might alternate with the 'talking head' studio-based reports of correspondents. In radio, variability is provided by the interspersing of the newsreader's monologue with the voices of reporters and interviewees, and also 'natural sound'.

There are, in addition, more formal ways of structuring the bulletin. One convention is the 'headline' through which newsmen extract the main story angle, and present it in very brief compass. The headline is a dramatic presentational device. It varies the pace at both the beginning and end of the bulletin, and also rules it off from other programmes.

Another device is the 'catchline' which serves to break up the flow of the bulletin. Thus: 'Industrial News', 'The Commons', 'The Watergate Affair' are all phrases intended to swiftly cue in the audience to the content of the next story, while making the assumption that people are sufficiently familiar with its past developments to comprehend present ones. Catchlines contribute to a news style which both looks and sounds economical. It is easy to see, in view of the foregoing, why newsmen should take it for granted that 'A combination of simplicity, clarity, and urgency is the only possible style.'[21]

These ideas define and limit both the form and the content of news. The basic cultural form is framed by the conventions current in the existing occupational ideology. News is seen as distinct from 'current affairs' and from 'documentary', where immediacy is not such an overweening criterion.[22] News is virtually all foreground with very little background.

■ Conclusion   This chapter illustrates an important aspect of newsmen's occupational ideology. The emphasis on speed in bulletin production is quite clearly derived from the overall constraint of producing news for a market based on the concept of the newsday. There are therefore systematic links between the newsman's time-perspective and the demands created by the organization of work. The newsman's emphatic bias towards immediacy, though, is more than just a response to market conditions. It is a form of fetishism in which to be obsessional about time is to be professional in a way which newsmen have made peculiarly their own. To make this point clearly is important for any sociology of the journalist's occupational knowledge.

Production is so organized that its basic dynamic emphasizes the perishability of stories. Where a story carries over from one day to the next, it is assumed that the audience will, after one day's exposure, be adequately familiar with the subject-matter to permit the 'background' to be largely taken for granted. It is always *today's* developments which occupy the foreground.

---

21 Tyrrell 1972: 19.

22 Swallow 1966: 83.

The corollary of this point is that there is an inherent tendency for the news to be framed in a discontinuous and a historical way, and this implies a truncation of 'context', and therefore a reduction of meaningfulness. Where an 'historical' element is purposely introduced this largely means the utilization of materials which are ready to hand, and which accord only a sketchy chronology to the story. It is hardly to be argued that this kind of practice constitutes an adequate attempt at explanation. But then 'news' as it is currently conceived is not intended to be primarily explanatory.

Such strictures may be thought to be excessive. For news is, after all, not history. It is, if anything, history's antithesis. It is only by such observations about the nature of its form, however, that we grasp its inherent limitations.

References

BENSMAN, JOSEPH, and LILIENFELD, ROBERT (1971), 'The Journalistic Attitude', in Bernard Rosenberg and David Manning White (eds.), *Mass Culture Revisited* (New York: Van Nostrand).

BERGER, PETER, and LUCKMANN, THOMAS (1971), *The Social Construction of Reality* (Harmondsworth: Penguin).

BOHANNAN, PAUL (1953), 'Concepts of Time among the Tiv of Nigeria', *South-western Journal of Anthropology*, 251–61.

BRIGGS, ASA (1965), *The Golden Age of Wireless: The History of Broadcasting in the United Kingdom*, vol. ii (London: Oxford University Press).

—— (1970), *The War of Words: The History of Broadcasting in the United Kingdom*, vol. iii (London: Oxford University Press).

COTTRELL, W. F. (1939), 'Of Time and the Railroader', *American Sociological Review*, 190–8.

EDWARDS, DONALD (1964), *BBC News and Current Affairs*, BBC Lunchtime Lectures Series 2, 12 December.

EPSTEIN, EDWARD JAY (1973), *News from Nowhere: Television and the News* (New York: Random House).

EVANS-PRITCHARD, E. E. (1940), *The Nuer* (Oxford).

GOLDING, PETER, and ELLIOTT, PHILIP (1976), *Making the News* (University of Leicester: Centre for Mass Communication Research).

GURVITCH, GEORGES (1964), *The Spectrum of Social Time* (Dordrecht, Holland: D. Reidel).

HALL, EDWARD T. (1959), *The Silent Language* (New York: Doubleday).

HALLORAN, JAMES D., ELLIOTT, PHILIP, and MURDOCK, GRAHAM (1970), *Demonstrations and Communication: A Case Study* (Harmondsworth: Penguin).

LYMAN, STANFORD M., and SCOTT, MARVIN B. (1970), *A Sociology of the Absurd* (New York: Appleton, Century, Crofts).

MARCUS, JOHN T. (1960–1), 'Time and the Sense of History: East and West', *Comparative Studies in Society and History*, 123–39.

MOORE, WILBERT E. (1963*a*), 'The Temporal Structure of Organizations', in Edward A. Tiryakian (ed.), *Sociological Theory, Values and Sociocultural Change* (London).

—— (1963*b*), *Man, Time and Society* (New York and London: John Wiley and Sons Inc.).

PARK, ROBERT E. (1970), 'News as a Form of Knowledge: A Chapter in the Sociology of Knowledge', *American Journal of Sociology*, 1940, reprinted in Charles S. Steinberg (ed.), *Mass Media and Communication* (New York).

SOROKIN, PITIRIM A., and MERTON, ROBERT K. (1937), 'Social Time: A Methodological and Functional Analysis', *American Journal of Sociology*, 615–29.

SWALLOW, NORMAN (1966), *Factual Television* (London: The Focal Press).

THOMPSON, E. P. (1967), 'Time, Work-Discipline and Industrial Capitalism', *Past and Present*, 56–97.

TUCHMAN, GAYE (1969), *News: The Newsman's Reality*, Ph.D. dissertation, Department of Sociology, Brandeis University.

TYRRELL, ROBERT (1972), *The Work of the Television Journalist* (London and New York: The Focal Press).

WEBER, MAX (1968), *The Protestant Ethic and the Spirit of Capitalism* (London: George Allen and Unwin).

WILLIAMS, RAYMOND (1965), *The Long Revolution* (Harmondsworth: Penguin).

—— (1974), *Television: Technology and Cultural Form* (London: Fontana/Collins).

WINTOUR, CHARLES (1972), *Pressures on the Press: an editor looks at Fleet Street* (London: André Deutsch).

16

News Organizations: Conflict as a Crafted Cultural Norm

Charles R. Bantz

ANALYSES OF NEWS organizations have engaged a variety of perspectives. This essay utilizes a cultural viewpoint identifying five factors that suggest the proposition that the organizational cultures in newswork, particularly in television news, should 'normalize' the occurrence of conflict. That is, the incompatibilities of factors such as professional norms and business norms result in conflict becoming ordinary, routine, perhaps even valuable. In news organizations, conflict, disputes, disagreements are to be expected and defined as appropriate. Further, the interaction of these factors makes such a finding even more likely. The essay makes no claim as to the relative frequency of conflict in news organizations compared to other organizations; rather it outlines the rationale for predicting that news organizational cultures make conflict acceptable within organizational norms. [. . .]

The proposition that television news organizations are cultures that normalize conflict is based on five major factors and the interaction of those factors: (1) newsworkers' distrust of and disputing of individuals who propagate a point of view; (2) conflicts between professional norms and business norms; (3) conflicts between professional norms and entertainment norms; (4) controlled competition among newsworkers and among news organizations; and (5) the structure of television news messages. Considered together these factors suggest that television news organizations are cultures where conflict is a pattern of expected behaviour and conflict is, therefore, ordinary, routine, and reasonable. In fact, the culture's normalization of conflict may even require accounts to justify co-operative behaviour (cf. Tunstall 1970: ch. 7; 1971: ch. 6). This pattern is simultaneously created and maintained by newsworkers and influences the newsworkers' definition of the culture. Thus these factors contribute to the normalization of conflict in the culture by organizational members and that culture in turn influences organizational members as they exist in and reconstitute that culture.

Source: Charles R. Bantz, 'News Organizations: Conflict as a Crafted Cultural Norm',
Communication, 8 (1985), 225–44.

**News Worker
Distrust and
Dispute**

Tuchman (1978) argues that the pattern of newsgathering typically leads to support for the status quo; Altheide (1984) argues there is a tendency for journalists to cast themselves in opposition to the focus of the status quo. It is not necessary to accept either position to find that newsworkers are characterized by a scepticism of sources in general, but are likely to be distrustful of persons obviously presenting a point of view. Johnstone, Slawski, and Bowman's (1976) newsworkers reported a commitment to public responsibility. When the intentions of sources become apparent and the source's intentions are seen by journalists as being inconsistent with their conception of public responsibility, newsworkers are likely to distrust and dispute the sources. For example, newsworkers are very aware and somewhat accepting that the news secretaries of political candidates attempt to present their candidate in a positive light. When, however, news secretaries appear to be deliberately deceiving and obfuscating to protect their candidates for what newsworkers deemed inappropriate reasons, newsworkers may become extraordinarily distrustful (e.g. the attacks on Richard Nixon's news secretary Ron Ziegler during Watergate, see Rather 1978: chs. 11, 12, 13).

Journalists' expectations concerning interaction with news sources depends upon the meanings shared about the relationship between journalists and those sources. If the relationship developed as an open exchange with obvious motivations for interaction, the expectations for behaviour are likely to be clear. For example, the reporters and news secretaries may develop detailed norms that regulate asking questions, answers and parries, follow-up, and leaks (see Sigal 1973: ch. 3). The specific interaction norms will be influenced by many factors, including national and regional culture. Hence the norms are likely to vary from country to country (e.g. Israel vs. United States) and within countries on a number of dimensions (e.g. community homogenity; see Tichenor, Donohue, and Olien 1980). In the US, one assumption guiding the interaction is that some incompatibility between the newsworkers' goals and the sources' goals is accepted, but that incompatibility is managed within mutually defined meanings and expectations. The range of those meanings (e.g. interaction as an agreement to disagree) and expectations (e.g. to be civil) is established over time. However, if one party to the exchange perceives a shift in the relationship that seems inconsistent with prior shared meanings and expectations (e.g. instead of the exchange being sport, it is war) then the level of dispute may escalate dramatically. For example, former US Vice President Agnew's vitriolic attacks on the media seemed to alter the previous definition of media–administration relations and seemed to polarize journalists (see Schorr 1977: ch. 3).

When sources and reporters have interacted for an extended period or where sources have great power over reporters, the interaction between sources and reporters may be routinized as a non-conflict interaction. This is often the case when reporters on beats build long-term relationships—e.g. the police reporter 'goes native' or the political reporter becomes a political actor (see Sigal 1973: ch. 3). Even in those cases, professional norms may support the assumption that there are circumstances where a more conflictive interaction is appropriate. That is, the newsworker can imagine a circumstance, where despite long-established non-conflict relationships, she or he would necessarily confront a source (e.g. a major crisis occurs when the reporter faces a deadline). In other words, newsworkers utilize a calculus that includes the legitimate value of disputing sources and conflict when balancing their relationship with sources and the demands for work. The calculus is only made more complex by factors of professionalism, isolation, and group norms, which are discussed below.

Professional Norms vs. Business Norms

News organizations employ a large number of individuals who work within a set of journalistic professional norms, even though not all employed by those organizations were trained as journalists (Johnstone *et al.* 1976: ch. 3). Professional norms affect the prevalence of organizational conflict in a number of ways. There may, for example, be an inconsistency between professional norms and other norms within a news organization (e.g. business norms or what Ritzer (1977: ch. 5) refers to as bureaucratic norms). If the culture of a news organization includes a set of organizational meanings (e.g. quality means completeness) and consequent norms (e.g. workers should be very thorough) that are consistent with journalistic professional norms, there should be less incidence of endemic organizational conflict within the culture (see the characterization of *The Interpreter* in Lester 1980). If, however, the news organization has built a set of organizational meanings (e.g. good work is efficient work) and consequent expectations (e.g. workers should work quickly and produce high volume) that are inconsistent with professional norms, then there should be greater incidence of endemic organizational conflict. In the television news organization studied by Bantz, McCorkle, and Baade (1980), we found 'an organization that mechanizes [newsworkers'] work, emphasizes worker interchangeability, encourages rapidity in production, has high employee turnover and seldom offers qualitative evaluation of work' (p. 64). We found an organizational culture dominated by business norms, populated by news workers who appeared to follow professional norms, and characterized by conflict. (In contrast, Gans (1979) found little conflict, while Stark (1962) found much conflict, but the conflict was over newspaper policy and professional autonomy.)

The incompatibility of professional and business norms can produce a variety of effects: (1) workers leave the workplace, seeking work in organizations that seem to have developed norms more consistent with their training, (2) workers may alter their meanings and expectations to become more consistent with the workplace they currently are in, or (3) workers may make the conflict between professional norms and existent organizational norms (e.g. business norms) itself an expected occurrence—i.e. make conflict a norm. Stark (1962) observed all three of these patterns. In the third pattern, workers may use the professional community as a reference group to provide input to their meanings and expectations for work and may characterize the newsworker's role as one of upholding professional norms in the face of competing normative pressures. The work on cosmopolitans and locals (Merton 1968: ch. 12), as well as pressures toward group conformity (Festinger 1950), and the development of group cultures (Bormann 1975: ch. 10) detail these processes and the resulting consequences. Stark's (1962) use of the cosmopolitan (he calls them pros) and local distinction demonstrates how groups developed norms that produced conflict—as the pros looked to their professional peers for standards, felt mobile, and tried to finesse the system, while locals identified with the organization, felt a lack of mobility, and accepted the system. The incompatibility of these world views and group affiliations contributed both to intraorganizational conflict and inter group conflict. Even if such an occurrence is an extreme, the inconsistency between professional norms of newsworkers and business norms of managers is likely to yield an organizational culture with less consistency and endemic conflict.

Professional Norms vs. Entertainment Norms

News organizational cultures must manage the conflict between entertainment norms and professional norms. That conflict is manifested in a number of ways. Three interrelated ways are developed here: (1) the source of information for decision-making; (2) internal organizational inconsistency as to which set of norms is primary; and (3) differing definitions of performance.

Television news organizations particularly need to cope with a fundamental difference in source of information for decision-making as defined by professional and entertainment norms. Professional norms place responsibility both for providing information and making decisions in the hands of professionals. For example, both physicians and reporters generate information as well as make decisions on the best way to interpret that information (although reporters are probably second-guessed more often—by editors, see Dunwoody 1981; Sigal 1973: ch. 3). Entertainment norms make the audience the principal source of information for decision-making, with entertainment specialists taking major responsibility for interpretation and decision-making. In entertainment norms (especially when connected to a business norm), no matter how much the decision-maker likes a product, if the audience continues voting 'no', sooner or later the decision-makers' answer will also be 'no'. The contrast between professionals and entertainment decision-making norms is apparent in the frequency with which entertainment specialists ask audiences for judgements concerning programmes and the infrequency of professionals asking the clients for their judgement (e.g. how often do surgeons ask patients their opinion of surgical techniques?). Different organizational cultures are likely to develop different weights for the professional and entertainment norms, and a study of how those different patterns develop could be extremely interesting. However, when the two sets of norms exist in one media organization the likelihood of endemic conflict is great.

The norms of entertainment and professionalism, which affect decision-making in all news organizations, are most likely to collide in television news. Television has been dominated by entertainment norms in the majority of its schedule and throughout most of its history, while newspapers, taken as a whole—scandal sheets and newspapers of record—seem to have had a more balanced tension between entertainment and professional norms. As a result, television news organizations, as part of larger organizations (stations and groups of stations) that create and transmit programming, find themselves the representatives of professional norms in arenas of entertainment. The newsworkers are often professionally oriented; news directors tend to be professionally oriented; the organization as a whole tends to be entertainment and business oriented. The station's culture often exerts entertainment norms on the news organization; news departments are major profit centres of television stations, so management often utilizes business norms in judging news departments; newsworkers are likely, however, to be professionally oriented. As a consequence, newsworkers may define conflict as positive when it is used to defend professional norms from encroachment by entertainment and business norms (see Friendly 1967: ch. 9).

This conflict of professional versus entertainment norms is most apparent in the paradox of the on-air newsworker—a paradox reflected in the various names given that person: reader, anchorperson, managing editor, or talent. The on-air person is often judged by entertainment standards: attractiveness, delivery style, dress, vocal quality, age, and timing. As a consequence of the application of entertainment standards a critical evaluative test of the on-air person is the *appearance of performance.* The appearance of performance is captured in the ability to be perfect (i.e. make no visible errors in pronunciation, delivery), to be in control, and to be durable. The audience's judgement of performance is one based on appearance while broadcasting, and the audience's judgement is to entertainment norms. Thus the on-air person is judged in the entertainment mode through the appearance of performance, a phrase that suggests both the elusive nature of performance *per se* and the value placed on appearance for the on-air person. Thus the on-air person, the most publicly visible member and in the most professionally prestigious position (in US television news), is likely to be judged on entertainment norms. Yet the on-air person works in a news organization where professional norms are typically held. Thus the on-air person illustrates the ongoing conflict between the two sets of norms: should she strive to meet professional norms and satisfy journalistic colleagues or strive to meet entertainment norms and satisfy management?

Controlled Competition

Competition in news is a managed form of conflict. There are pressures both towards competition and towards co-operation in newswork (see Dunwoody 1981; Tunstall 1971). The balancing of those pressures seems to produce a controlled competition with 'rules' limiting both how intense competition may become and how close co-operation can become.

Both professional and business norms may stimulate the organization toward competition with other news organizations. The professional norms associated with getting the story before the other station or paper does (getting the scoop, getting a beat), generates competition between journalists and between their organizations. Research on negotiation and bargaining indicates that when negotiations are more competitive and hence more conflictive (see Kriesberg 1973: chs. 1, 2; Smith 1972). Given an organizational demand to provide a more complete or a unique story, the relationship between news organizations can become win-lose. Further, given a limited number of rewards in newswork (positions, income) and given that performance (or the appearance of performance) may gain access to those rewards, reporters with mobility aspirations may become competitive with reporters within their own organization as well as with reporters in other organizations.

This conflict is intensified by business norms that often characterize the competition between organizations as warfare (the prevalence of military and war metaphors in organizations has often been commented on; see Pondy 1983). In addition to the professional competition between reporters, news competition may escalate into interorganizational conflict where television stations compete for stories, newsworkers, prestige, and ratings as well as advertiser dollars. Commentators have often noted that editors and managers compare their product with their competitor's and criticize newsworkers who 'miss' a story or story element (see Darnton 1975; Dunwoody 1981; Sigal 1973).

What makes competition in newswork so intriguing is that it is controlled and its management may include collegial co-operation. Reporters often work well side-by-side and do collaborate (see Crouse 1973; Darnton 1975; Dunwoody 1981; Sigal 1973: ch. 3; Tiffen 1978: ch. 5, 6; Tunstall 1970: ch. 7; 1971: ch. 6). Reporters seem to learn a set of expectations about how one manages the conflict between newsworkers—particularly when the newsworkers find themselves on a beat or in a confined situation (e.g. campaign coverage, war coverage, foreign correspondents—this latter circumstance is illustrated in the 1983 film *The Year of Living Dangerously*). In such situations, the reporter's reference group is likely to be the professional journalist rather than the business organization. Further, the professionals working together will develop a pattern of small group interaction and its concomitant norms (see Bormann 1975). Both factors facilitate the newsworkers developing patterns to manage the competition between themselves. While different groups will develop different norms, the development of such group norms may permit reporters to provide competitors with factual information (something publicly available and the withholding of which would be seen as petty) or even to delegate one member the task of gathering all the information for sharing (Darnton 1975). At the same time, the reporters may subtly compete for additional details that will differentiate their story from their colleagues.

The competition between news organizations and between journalists means conflict is defined as *necessary* and *useful*. Defining conflict as such creates the expectation that newsworkers will seek to do better than their competitor-colleagues and their organizations. However, the newsworkers, particularly when spending time in groups, may elaborate the meaning and expectations of competition. By invoking professional norms and developing group norms they define conflict as controlled and establish the expectation that the competition will be constrained by those professional and group norms. Working within the cultural definition of competition and conflict, the newsworkers thus reconstruct the pressures toward competition, thereby illustrating the reflexivity of organizational culture. It must be noted, however, that just as the norm of co-operation develops through interaction, the actions of individuals who violate the co-operative norms (e.g. seeking exclusives) and institutional action (e.g. rotation of beats) can weaken the pressures towards co-operation and intensify competitive pressures.

Structure of Television News Messages

The final factor contributing to a culture of conflict is the nature of the product. The product of the television journalist is a story. A 'story' suggests that television news casts events in a dramatic format (see Epstein 1973: ch. 5). In fact, Epstein quotes *NBC Evening News*'s executive producer, Reuven Frank, as instructing his staff that news stories should have the structure of drama—including conflict (1973: 4–5). Television news stories often present events that are conflicts by definition and frequently present non-conflict events in that social conflict (conflicts among social groups over ideas and goals) constitutes 35 per cent of US television news (Adoni 1984). Further, the structural form of television newscasts often presents stories as dramatic conflicts between two or more parties (see Bantz, Robinson, and Ewbank 1984).

The relevance of this pattern for television news organizations is highly speculative. However, within the skein of factors that normalize conflict within an organizational culture, it is quite likely that when newsworkers construct their daily product in a form that is predicated upon conflict, conflict's meaning is seen as *ordinary, everyday, routine*, and perhaps *essential to social life*. The daily creation of nonfiction drama, which is supposed to be the reconstitution of reality, utilizing a conflictive form is likely to encourage the newsworker to view the everyday world (including the world of the news organization) through the frame of conflict. In other words, newsworkers who constitute stories about extra-organizational events in conflict terms are likely to constitute stories about organizational events using a conflict form. The use of this form of storytelling by newsworkers to understand social life contributes to an organizational culture where conflict is a normal occurrence and a typical interpretive framework.

Interaction of the Five Factors

The five factors outlined contribute to the development of organizational cultures in newswork where conflict is normative, that is, defined as ordinary and viewed as appropriate. Organizational culture theory would argue that no matter what the factors, the cultures of similar organizations would *not* be the same; however, my argument is that systematic patterns associated with a type of organization make a particular cultural pattern likely. Individually, the five factors (newsworker distrust, professional norms vs. business norms, professional norms vs. entertainment norms, controlled competition, and the structure of televised news messages) contribute to news organization cultures where the meaning of conflict is *routine, everyday, necessary, valuable*, and *ordinary*. Consequently, conflictive behaviour is defined as acceptable (i.e. normative) behaviour. In addition, the interaction of the five factors increases the likelihood of a conflict culture. Three such possible interactions are suggested below.

First, as a result of the interaction of business norms and professional norms, newsworkers who are based in the organization itself and whose contact with newsworkers in competing organizations is limited in duration are likely to see their organization in competition with other organizations. Conversely, when newsworkers are based outside their organization, are not closely supervised, and are in close contact with workers from competing organizations the development of professional group norms will hamper the interaction between business norms and professional norms. From these two we would predict (1) competition will operate within professional group constraints when newsworkers are physically separate from their news organization but close to their competitor-colleagues, and (2) conflict should be more unbridled when newsworkers are more closely tied to their organizations (Tiffen (1978: ch. 4) contrasts different news organizations on the autonomy granted foreign correspondents; see also Dunwoody 1981; Stark 1962; Tunstall 1970, 1971).

Second, the journalist's tendency to distrust and dispute sources may be exaggerated when the reporter works in a medium that utilizes conflict as a structural form for its product—i.e. television news. Thus the television reporter may try to generate conflict, whether by confrontation or artful questioning, so the resultant story will contain the requisite elements of conflict. It probably is not coincidental that in the US the reporters with the most combative reputations are television reporters (e.g. Dan Rather, Sam Donaldson, Mike Wallace).

Third, the entertainment norms embodied in television's appearance of performance notion should mesh with the business norms of profit in such a powerful way that newsworkers holding professional norms experience an on-going conflict between entertaining and informing.

There is every reason to believe that meanings and expectations learned in one realm have the potential to affect other realms. The newsworker thus functions in and helps create an organization where conflict between news organizations is appropriate, where part of the newsworker's job is to be in conflict with those who wish to withhold information, where professional, entertainment, and business norms collide daily. All these experiences contribute to an organizational culture in which conflict is *necessary, ordinary, valuable, routine* and such expectations make conflict legitimate. In news organizations we can expect frequent disagreements and individuals are unlikely to be reprimanded for disagreeing as long as conflict is maintained within a 'normal range'. Similarly, the organizational culture of newsrooms is likely to be constituted by stories of conflict, though they will be typically heroic rather than tragic tales. Obviously there are limits to these expectations—as the discussion of beat reporters indicates—but if my proposition is valid, conflict should be an integral part of the cultural fabric of news organizations.

References ADONI, H. (1984), 'The Dimensions of Social Conflict in TV News', Paper presented at the International Communication Association convention, San Francisco (May).

ALTHEIDE, D. (1984), 'Media Hegemony: A Failure of Perspective', *Public Opinion Quarterly*, 48: 476–90.

BANTZ, C. R., MCCORKLE, S., and BAADE, R. C. (1980), 'The News Factory', *Communication Research*, 7: 45–68.

—— D. C. ROBINSON, and EWBANK, A. (1984), 'Social Conflict on Television News: Actors, Roles, and Bias', Paper presented to the International Communication Association convention, San Francisco (May).

BORMANN, E. G. (1972), 'Fantasy and Rhetorical Vision: The Rhetorical Criticism of Social Reality', *Quarterly Journal of Speech*, 58: 396–407.

—— (1975), *Discussion and Group Methods: Theory and Practice* (2nd edn. New York: Harper & Row).

CROUSE, T. (1973), *The Boys on the Bus* (New York: Random House).

DARNTON, R. (1975), 'Writing News and Telling Stories', *Daedalus*, 104: 175–94.

DUNWOODY, S. (1981), 'The Science Writing Inner Club: A Communication Link between Science and the Lay Public', in G. C. Wilholt and H. de Book (eds.), *Mass Communication Review Yearbook*, ii (Beverly Hills: Sage; originally published, 1980).

EPSTEIN, E. J. (1973), *News from Nowhere: Television and the News* (New York: Random House).

FESTINGER, L. (1950), 'Informal Social Communication', *Psychological Review*, 57: 271–282.

FRIENDLY, F. W. (1967), *Due to Circumstances Beyond our Control* (New York: Vintage/Random House).

GANS, H. J. (1979), *Deciding What's News: A Study of* CBS Evening News, NBC Nightly News, Newsweek, *and* Time. New York: Pantheon.

JOHNSTONE, J. W. C., SLAWSKI, E. J., and BOWMAN, W. W. (1976), *The News People: A Sociological Portrait of American Journalists and their Work* (Urbana: University of Illinois Press).

KRIESBERG, L. (1973), *The Sociology of Social Conflict* (Englewood Cliffs, NJ: Prentice-Hall).

LESTER, M. (1980), 'Generating Newsworthiness: The Interpretive Construction of Public Events', *American Sociological Review*, 45: 984–94.

MERTON, R. K. (1968), *Social Theory and Social Structure* (1968 enlarged edn., New York: Free Press).

PONDY, L. R. (1983), 'The Role of Metaphors and Myths in Organizations and the Facilitation of Change', in L. R. Pondy, P. J. Frost, G. Morgan, and T. C. Dandridge (eds.), *Organizational Symbolism* (Greenwich, Conn.: JAI Press).

RATHER, D., with HERSKOWITZ, M. (1978), *The Camera Never Blinks: Adventures of a TV Journalist* (New York: Ballantine Books; originally published, 1977).

RITZER, G. (1977), *Working: Conflict and Change* (2nd edn.). Englewood Cliffs, NJ: Prentice-Hall).

SCHORR, D. (1977), *Clearing the Air* (Boston: Houghton Mifflin).

SIGAL, L. V. (1973), *Reporters and Officials: The Organization and Politics of Newsmaking* (Lexington, Mass.: D. C. Heath).

SMITH, D. H. (1972), 'Applications of Behavioral Research to Speech Fundamentals: Applications from Research on Bargaining and Negotiation', paper presented to the Central States Speech Association (April).

STARK, R. (1962), 'Policy and the Pros: An Organizational Analysis of a Metropolitan Newspaper', *Berkeley Journal of Sociology*, 7: 11–31.

TICHENOR, P. J., Donohue, G. A., and Olien, C. N. (1980), *Community Conflict and the Press* (Beverly Hills: Sage).

TIFFEN, R. (1978), *The News from Southeast Asia: The Sociology of Newsmaking* (Singapore: Institute of Southeast Asian Studies).

TUCHMAN, G. (1978), *Making News: A Study in the Construction of Reality* (New York: Free Press).

TUNSTALL, J. (1970), *The Westminster Lobby Correspondents: A Sociological Study of National Political Journalism* (London: Routledge & Kegan Paul).

—— (1971), *Journalists at Work: Specialist Correspondents: Their News Organizations, News Sources, and Competitor-Colleagues* (Beverly Hills: Sage).

3

PART THREE

Economics of News

PART THREE

3

Economics of News

Introduction to Part III: Economics of News

THE FIRST PIECE in Part 3 is the preface to the fifth edition of Ben Bagdikian's book *The Media Monopoly*, and examines the new communications cartel arising during the 1990s. From the first edition published in 1983, and throughout succeeding editions, Bagdikian traces and analyses the changes occurring in the ownership and control of the American mass media. Bagdikian's warning, voiced in the first edition, that media power is political power, is shown to be more accentuated in the development of monopoly and the effects of corporate media control on the news and entertainment industries. The new media cartel includes corporations now owning news organizations for the first time in their history and this accelerates the problems facing news. The consequences for journalism in having to produce news coverage designed to promote the corporate owners are extremely serious.

Golding and Murdoch are pioneers of the political economy approach to the media. Their original article in 1973 stressed the role of the capitalist state and the economic determination of the media. Since then they have revised their views and in the article reproduced here provide a critical political economy of communications. Whilst accepting economic determination as an initial, and perhaps powerful, constraint on media organization activity and the production of news, they provide an analysis that acknowledges the structured relations between owners and editors and journalists, but also the relationships between journalists and their sources.

In contrast to Golding and Murdock whose analysis avoids 'the twin temptations of instrumentalism and structuralism', Herman and Chomsky develop a propaganda model in which the American news media are able to determine public perceptions by managing public opinion through regular propaganda campaigns. In this piece the main constituents of the propaganda model are introduced. The model investigates how money and power are able to filter out the news fit to print, consent is marginalized and the government and dominant private interests are allowed to get their messages across to the public. The raw material of news passes through a set of five news filters and the end news product is then in a fit state to be printed. This is the essential ingredient of the propaganda model. Their analysis argues that the élite domination of the media and the marginalization of dissidents occurs naturally whilst the people working in news organizations are misled into believing they are acting objectively and operating through accepted journalistic news values.

In *Market Driven Journalism* John McManus looks at local television news. By examining how news organizations organize their resources, he shows the most important function is the maintenance and maximization of return to shareholders. The emphasis on dividend and capital growth affects the quality of the news product produced. McManus acknowledges the changes that have taken place in the ownership and corporate structure of news organizations and provides a model of commercial news production. In contemporary journalism, news produced by a sub-unit of a media company is not an independent organization that generates its own income but one that reports back to the parent organization. He shows that even the term news organization is a misnomer nowadays as it is often a very small part of a much larger media entertainment conglomerate. Calling newspapers or television stations news organizations overemphasizes the importance of that function whilst neglecting examination from the media organization's other activities. McManus shows how journalists and editors work within the constraints set by others, demonstrating few of the independent characteristics of other professionals such as doctors or lawyers. He concludes rather pessimistically that news is a commodity—acquiescing to competition in order to fit the demands of the market.

Jeremy Tunstall's research into world news is a subject that readers familiar with his work will recognize as a scene returned to on numerous occasions. In this chapter from his latest book, Tunstall demonstrates that the US and Britain dominate the flow of news around the world. The dominance is shared by Associated Press and Reuters. Senior executives exhibit certain vagueness about the meaning of domination of world news and are defensive and reluctant to admit a duopoly exists. Tunstall notes that both Reuters and AP are the leading suppliers of news whether it is text stories used for newspapers or pictures, graphics, video material and financial news. He shows how the Anglo-American duopoly developed and assesses recent developments of all news television networks like CNN. Senior personnel of these main players who were interviewed deny 'complex non-profit motivation'. They are in it for the money and the idea of prestige on the world news stage has disappeared.

The last two pieces in Part 3 provide an American and British perspective on the perceived crisis of news brought about by intensive competition in the news. Anthony Sampson is concerned about the 'dumbing down' of the British Press. Over the last fifteen years the gap between the quality broadsheet papers and the popular tabloid papers has all but disappeared. As competition intensifies, the quality broadsheets co-opt a more sensationalist veneer to the news product. The broadsheets compete for the same market as the tabloids; an interchange of editors between the tabloids and the quality broadsheets takes place and a downmarket product is established. The crisis, Sampson argues, is due to the competition for advertising and more expensive newsprint leading to a lack of interest in both foreign news and investigative journalism. The decline in the amount of foreign news is the most serious charge against the broadsheet papers and television. The subsequent lack of serious analysis, whilst increasing a human interest for it, is providing a retreat from the world. Despite the increase in television outlets, the news is now a processed product and another branch of entertainment. Sampson's ray of hope is radio, seen as a credible purveyor of world news and a possible buffer against the trivialization of news.

Penn Kimball, writing about network television in the United States, comes to similar conclusions as Sampson. A redefinition of news, financially driven, has taken place. Like McManus, Kimball argues that the separation between the business of news organizations and the product side is now joined. His analysis points to a serious curtailment of newsgathering by the television networks. The 'downsizing of news' on television is accompanied by a downgrading among federal employees in Washington who traditionally aided the news media as sources. He points to the decline in importance of political coverage, particularly of the State Department, and the reduction in the number of correspondents covering the different world regions. In addition news and television coverage of Congress is truncated with the result that the public is starved politically of the workings of the democratic system. Correspondents are demoralized by the changes and Kimball suggests we are witnessing the end of an era in broadcast history. The cable subsidiaries can provide cheap news programmes at a profit, a feat not possible by the trad-itional network news organizations. He ends on an even more pessimistic note. Whilst the old news standards are becoming a prize that network television can ill afford, the television audience might not know the difference, and even if they did, might not be bothered.

17

The Media Monopoly

Ben H. Bagdikian

**Preface to the
Fifth Edition:
The New
Communications
Cartel**

I N THE LAST five years, a small number of the country's largest industrial corporations has acquired more public communications power—including ownership of the news—than any private businesses have ever before possessed in world history.

Nothing in earlier history matches this corporate group's power to penetrate the social landscape. Using both old and new technology, by owning each other's shares, engaging in joint ventures as partners, and other forms of co-operation, this handful of giants has created what is, in effect, a new communications cartel within the United States.

At issue is not just a financial statistic, like production numbers or ordinary industrial products like refrigerators or clothing. At issue is the possession of power to surround almost every man, woman, and child in the country with controlled images and words, to socialize each new generation of Americans, to alter the political agenda of the country. And with that power comes the ability to exert influence that in many ways is greater than that of schools, religion, parents, and even government itself.

Aided by the digital revolution and the acquisition of subsidiaries that operate at every step in the mass communications process, from the creation of content to its delivery into the home, the communications cartel has exercised stunning influence over national legislation and government agencies, an influence whose scope and power would have been considered scandalous or illegal twenty years ago.

The new communications cartel has been made possible by the withdrawal of earlier government intervention that once aspired to protect consumers and move toward the ideal of diversity of content and ownership in the mass media. Government's passivity has emboldened the new giants to boast openly of monopoly and their ability to project news, commercial messages, and graphic images into the consciousness and subconscious of almost every American.

Strict control of public information is not new in the world, but historical dictatorships lacked the late twentieth century's digital multimedia and distribution technology. As the country approaches the millennium, the new cartel exercises a more complex and subtle kind of control.

Source: Ben H. Bagdikian, *The Media Monopoly* (5th edn., Boston: Beacon Press, 1997; orig. pub. 1983).

Michael Eisner, chairman and chief executive officer of the second largest media firm in the world, Disney/ABC/Capital Cities, put it succinctly:

'It doesn't matter whether it comes in by cable, telephone lines, computer, or satellite. Everyone's going to have to deal with Disney.'[1]

In his imperial euphoria, Eisner neglected to mention what for centuries used to be the only mass medium, words printed on paper, as in newspapers, books, and magazines, though these, too, are an important part of the Disney empire.

Even though the new interlocked system of giants is entirely private, it promotes itself as a triumph of patriotic national power. The editor of *Vanity Fair*, a magazine owned by one of the large media corporations (Advance), wrote with evident pride:

'The power centre of America . . . has moved from its role as military-industrial giant to a new supremacy as the world's entertainment-information superpower.'[2]

It is not an idle boast. By almost every measure of public reach—financial power, political influence, and multiple techniques—the new conglomerates have more influence over what Americans see and hear than private firms have ever before possessed.

Because each of the dominant firms has adopted a strategy of creating its own closed system of control over every step in the national media process, from creation of content to its delivery, no content—news, entertainment, or other public messages—will reach the public unless a handful of corporate decision-makers decide that it will. Smaller independents have always helped provide an alternative and still do, but they have become ever more vulnerable to the power of the supergiants. As the size and financial power of the new dominant firms have escalated, so has their coercive power to offer a bothersome smaller competitor a choice of either selling out at once or slowly facing ruin as the larger firm uses its greater financial resources to undercut the independent competitor on price and promotion. In the process, consumers have become less influential than ever.

Financial news still is full of the sounds of clashes between giants. But the new media leaders compete only over marginal matters: their imperial borders, their courtship of new allies, and their acquisitions of smaller firms. Underneath these skirmishes, they are interlocked in shared financial ownership and a complex of joint ventures. With minor exceptions, they share highly conservative political and economic values. Most also own interests in other industries—defence, consumer products and services; firms like General Electric, Westinghouse, and the country's cash-rich telephone companies—and have shown little hesitation in using their control of the news to support the fortunes of their other subsidiaries.

The new cyberspace revolution typified by the Internet and the World Wide Web has been held out as offering the promise of altering our definition of 'mass' in the phrase 'mass media'. Individuals operating from their own home computers connected to telephone lines can communicate with other individual computers. But by the mid-1990s fewer than 15 per cent of

---

1 *Vanity Fair*, September 1955, 272–3.

2 Editor's note in a special issue on 'Leaders of the Information Age', *Vanity Fair*, September 1995, 271.

American households were equipped with modems that connect computers to phone lines. That number will undoubtedly grow, but even now, in the Internet's infancy, concerted corporate efforts are turning the Internet into the most direct mass merchandizing vehicle ever invented, with much of the sales promotion directed at children.

An IBM executive in charge of computer networking has said that by the year 2000 he expects that the Internet will be 'the world's largest, deepest, fastest and most secure marketplace . . . worth $1 trillion annually'.[3]

Perhaps the most troubling power of the new cartel is its control of the main body of news and public affairs information. The reporting of news has always been a commercial enterprise and this has always created conflicts of interest. But the behaviour of the new corporate controllers of public information has produced a higher level of manipulation of news to pursue the owners' other financial and political goals. In the process, there has been a parallel shrinkage of any sense of obligation to serve the noncommercial information needs of public citizenship.

The idea of government interceding to protect consumers is contrary to the ideology of most of the media cartel's leaders, who, with few exceptions, pursue the conservative political and economic notion of an uninhibited free market that operates without social or moral obligations.

Many members of the cartel now show open contempt for their own professional journalists. News tradition has always proclaimed the goal of 'separation of Church and State'—trying to keep news coverage of civic needs and events uninfluenced by the business ambitions of the owners of the news.[4] The complete separation has always been a struggle because owners of the news varied widely in their respect for the tradition.

But today some of the leading members of the media cartel openly order their journalists to report news with an eye to helping advertisers and promoting their owners' other nonjournalistic goals. In an invited speech at the 1995 convention of the Newspaper Association of America, a major advertiser criticized the country's reporters for being reluctant to redefine news as part entertainment and an aid to advertisers.[5] And in 1996, Malcolm Forbes, Jr., admitted that his magazine *Forbes* scheduled or altered editorial articles to favour advertisers.[6] If one insists on silver linings, the new openness at least removes hypocrisy.

Emergence of the new cartel does not change the basic impact of media conglomeration on society. But earlier, it was possible to describe the dominant firms in each separate medium—daily newspapers, magazines, radio, television, books, and movies. With each passing year and each new edition of this book, the number of controlling firms in all these media has shrunk: from fifty corporations in 1984 to twenty-six in 1987, followed by twenty-three in 1990, and then, as the borders between the different media began to

---

3 Robert W. McChesney, 'The Global Struggle for Democratic Communication', *Monthly Review*, May 1996, in manuscript (unpaged).

4 *New York Times*, 1 May 1995, C-10.

5 Ibid.

6 *The Nation*, 22 January 1996, 10.

blur, to less than twenty in 1993. In 1996 the number of media corporations with dominant power in society is closer to ten. In terms of media possessions and resources, the newest dominant ten are Time Warner, Disney, Viacom, News Corporation Limited (Murdoch), Sony, Tele-Communications, Inc., Seagram (TV, movies, cable, books, music), Westinghouse, Gannett, and General Electric.

Ironically, some of the American media giants that have cowed our own government are restrained in their foreign operations by the governments of other democratic nations more serious than the United States about preventing monopolies.

Some of the firms powerful within the United States are based outside the country, like Murdoch's News Corporation (Australia), Thomson (Canada), and Bertelsmann (Germany). Some must meet more stringent rules against monopoly in their own countries than those imposed upon their United States operations.

The warning expressed in the first edition of this book—'media power is political power'—has come to pass to a degree once considered unthinkable. [. . .]

Advertisers continue to enjoy privileged access to the news. Both the ABC and CBS news staffs were forced by their managements to apologize or censor stories on deceptions and possible perjury by tobacco industry leaders.[7] (Tobacco is no longer advertised on television, but tobacco companies now own major food and other firms that do advertise heavily on television, a connection not lost on broadcast executives.) A Marquette University poll of newspaper editors in 1992 found that 93 per cent of them said advertisers tried to influence their news, a majority said their own management condoned the pressure, and 37 per cent of the editors polled admitted that they had succumbed. A recent Nielson survey showed that 80 per cent of television news directors said they broadcast corporate public relations films as news 'several times a month'.[8] [. . .]

In the reign of the new media cartel, the integrity of much of the country's professional news has become more ambiguous than ever. The role of journalists within news companies has always been an inherent dilemma for reporters and editors. Reporters are expected by the public and by reportorial standards to act like independent, fair-minded professionals. But reporters are also employees of corporations that control their hiring, firing, and daily management—what stories they will cover and what part of their coverage will be used or discarded. It is a harsh newsroom reality that never seems to cause conservative critics to speculate why their corporate colleagues who own the news, and have total control over both their reporters' careers and the news that gets into their papers, would somehow delight in producing 'liberal bias'.

The new media conglomerates have exacerbated the traditional problems of professional news. The cartel includes some industries that have never before owned important news outlets. Some of the new owners find it bizarre

---

7 *Editor & Publisher*, 16 January 1993, 17.

8 Richard Crawford, 'Perspectives', Centre for Environment Movement, 2.

that anyone would question the propriety of ordering their employee-journalists to produce news coverage designed to promote the owner's corporation.

Seeing their journalists as obedient workers on an assembly line has produced a growing incidence of news corporations demanding unethical acts. There are more instances than ever of management contempt and cruelty toward their journalists.[9]

The change began in the mid-1980s, when all three major broadcast networks were taken over by outside industries that closed most of the networks' foreign bureaux. One of these new industrial entries into major journalism was the takeover of the National Broadcasting Company by General Electric.

When Murdoch's Fox became a fourth network, its news budget was about a quarter of the size of those spent by each of the three other networks. His initial 'news' show was something called 'A Current Affair', a programme devoted mostly to gossip and scandals about celebrities.[10] Only 59 of the 163 Fox affiliates had any local newscasts.

In 1995, after Disney announced plans to acquire Capital Cities/ABC, ABC fired Robert Anson, editor of Capital Cities' *Los Angeles Magazine*, presumably, like other Eisner sensitivities, because Anson had once written criticisms of Michael Eisner, head of Disney.[11] With the advent of Disney ownership, ABC also fired commentator Jim Hightower. Hightower also had been critical of Disney in the past. After the merger, Hightower said his boss was now Mickey Mouse: 'I work for a rodent.'[12]

These are not the isolated acts of a money-losing industry. Contrary to traditional cries of poverty by news proprietors and to falling circulation as a percentage of all households, the daily newspaper business, for instance, remains one of the most profitable in the country. Profit level of daily newspapers is two to three times higher than average profits of the Fortune 500 top corporations, according to John Morton of Morton Research, an authoritative source on newspaper economics.[13] According to *Standard and Poor's Media Industry Survey*, in 1994, not a banner year in the news industry, the average profit for publicly traded news companies was 20 per cent.[14]

The Times Mirror Corporation is, among other things, a book publishing house and the publisher of seven newspapers, including the largest and most influential daily on the West Coast, the *Los Angeles Times*.[15] In 1995, when it hired a new chairman, Mark Willis, he cut more jobs than ever seen before in a news company—3,000 jobs in the Times Mirror papers overall. He closed one of the company's papers, *New York Newsday* and ordered the editor of the *Los Angeles Times* to move his office to the corporate floor, away from the editor's traditional place in the newsroom. At a lunch, Willis also told

9 *New York Times*, 13 February 1995, C-1.

10 *Wall Street Journal*, 29 March 1995, 1.

11 *Wall Street Journal*, 9 May 1996, B-1.

12 *EXTRA! Update*, December 1995, 4.

13 Morton Research, personal communication with the author.

14 *Standard and Poor's Media Industry Survey 1994*, M-20.

15 *New York Times*, 26 June 1996, C-1.

reporters that they ought to spend more time associating socially with the paper's advertising sales staff. The startled reporters looked to their editor, Shelby Coffey III, for defence against this open breach of the idea of journalistic independence from financial conflict of interest, but the editor remained silent. Times Mirror Company annual dividends rose 67 per cent.

The new brutality and gratuitous shock treatment was used by the Singleton chain when it took over a group of California newspapers, peremptorily firing experienced journalists and hiring new, less experienced reporters at lower salaries.[16] In 1996, when the same paper fired a popular editor and columnist who had worked on the paper for sixteen years, he was escorted out of the building by security guards and told he would have to make an appointment if he wanted to return to get his personal effects from his desk.

The *Winston-Salem Journal*, once regarded as one of the country's better medium-sized dailies, ordered its news staff reduced and told surviving reporters and editors that they would be 'graded' on how closely they followed new orders mandating that a page-one story should be six inches or less, and that a reporter should 'take 0.9 hours to do each story' and write a minimum of forty stories a week.[17]

In Des Moines, the editor and managing editor of the *Des Moines Register* resigned in protest over increasing interference in the paper's news coverage by its business office, reported in the *New York Times* as 'a battle between news professionals and business executives that is raging behind closed doors at many of the country's newspapers'.[18]

In 1996, a California newspaper issued forms to its reporting staff that made it official policy that any story involving a local business must be cleared by the paper's advertising department, telling the reporters and subeditors, 'The . . . advertisers make it possible for us to pay our bills and meet our payroll. You might say they make your job possible'.[19]

Letting advertisers influence the news is no novelty in less respected papers, but in the past it was usually done by innuendo, or quiet editing, reassignment, or firing. It has seldom before been so boldly stated and practiced in ways that typify the new contempt that some news companies feel for the professional independence of their journalists—and for the news audience. The trend typifies a growing attitude that reporting the news is just another business.

Local alternative news weeklies have always been publications that monitor their local dailies and broadcast stations and provide alternative information and opinion.[20] They still do. But even this field has seen the growth of chains, the franchising of weekly papers, and the creeping influence of impersonal corporate management.

Ironically, the lowering of standards by many of our new proprietors flies into the face of history. In the long run, quality news has paid off in survival

---

16 *Columbia Journalism Review*, July/August 1996, 15.

17 *University of North Carolina Journalist*, Winter 1995, 3.

18 *New York Times*, 13 February 1995, C-1.

19 Copy of form provided to the author by various staff members of the paper.

20 *In These Times*, 'Alternative, Inc.', 21 August 1995, 14.

against new competitors and new media, usually accompanied by steady profits. The *New York Times*, the *Wall Street Journal*, and a family of high-quality medium-sized papers have been around more than a century while the 1920s tabloids and skimpy local papers have died or retreated to the supermarket check-out counters. In broadcasting, CBS News, since the 1930s the radio leader in serious news over the air, maintained profit as well as enduring audience leadership for more than thirty years. But like many other American industries since the uninhibited free market policies of the 1980s, CBS and the other networks have recently adopted quick, short-term profit strategies.

Gene Roberts, managing editor of the *New York Times* and former senior vice president and executive editor of the *Philadelphia Inquirer* (a paper he transformed from one of the least impressive to one of the most successful metropolitan dailies in the country), is one of the most respected and successful editors in the country. In a public lecture at Riverside, California, in February 1996, Roberts recounted the depredations occurring in mainstream newsrooms around the country.[21] He entitled his lecture 'Corporatism versus Journalism: Is It Twilight for Press Responsibility?'

---

21 From manuscript of Roberts's address.

18

Culture, Communications, and Political Economy

Peter Golding and Graham Murdock

What is Critical Political Economy?

C RITICAL POLITICAL ECONOMY differs from mainstream economics in four main respects. First, it is holistic. Second, it is historical. Third, it is centrally concerned with the balance between capitalist enterprise and public intervention. Finally, and perhaps most importantly of all, it goes beyond technical issues of efficiency to engage with basic moral questions of justice, equity, and the public good.

Whereas mainstream economics sees the 'economy' as a separate and specialized domain, critical political economy is interested in the interplay between economic organization and political, social and cultural life. In the case of the cultural industries we are particularly concerned to trace the impact of economic dynamics on the range and diversity of public cultural expression, and its availability to different social groups. These concerns are not of course exclusive to critical commentators. They are equally central to political economists on the Right. The difference lies in the starting points of the analysis.

Liberal political economists focus on exchange in the market as consumers choose between competing commodities on the basis of the utility and satisfaction they offer. The greater the play of market forces, the greater the 'freedom' of consumer choice. Over the last decade, this vision had gained renewed credence with the governments of a variety of ideological hues. Born again in their faith in Adam Smith's hidden hand of 'free' competition, they have pushed through programmes of privatization designed to increase consumer choice by extending the scale and scope of market mechanisms. Against this, critical political economists follow Marx in shifting attention from the realm of exchange to the organization of property and production, both within the cultural industries and more generally. They do not deny that cultural producers and consumers are continually making choices, but they do so within wider structures.

Where mainstream economics focuses on the sovereign individuals of capitalism, critical political economy starts with sets of social relations and

Source: Peter Golding and Graham Murdock, 'Culture, Communications, and Political Economy', in James Curran and Michael Gurevitch (eds.), *Mass Media and Society* (London, New York, Melbourne, and Auckland: Edward Arnold, 1991), 15–32.

the play of power. It is interested in seeing how the making and taking of meaning is shaped at every level by the structured asymmetries in social relations. These range from the way news is structured by the prevailing relations between press proprietors and editors or journalists and their sources, to the way that television viewing is affected by the organization of domestic life and power relations within the family. These concerns are of course widely shared by researchers who are not political economists. What marks critical political economy is that it always goes beyond situated action to show how particular micro contexts are shaped by general economic dynamics and the wider structures they sustain. It is especially interested in the ways that communicative activity is structured by the unequal distribution of material and symbolic resources.

Developing an analysis along these lines means avoiding the twin temptations of instrumentalism and structuralism. Instrumentalists focus on the ways that capitalists use their economic power with a commercial market system to ensure that the flow of public information is consonant with their interests. They see the privately owned media as instruments of class domination. This case is vigorously argued in Edward S. Herman and Noam Chomsky's work, *Manufacturing Consent: The Political Economy of the Mass Media* (1988). They develop what they call a 'propaganda model' of the American news media, arguing that 'the powerful are able to fix the premises of discourse, to decide what the general populace is allowed to see, hear and think about, and to "manage" public opinion by regular propaganda campaigns' (1988: xi). They are partly right. Government and business élites do have privileged access to the news; large advertisers do operate as a latter-day licensing authority, selectively supporting some newspapers and television programmes and not others; and media proprietors can determine the editorial line and cultural stance of the papers and broadcast stations they own. But by focusing on these kinds of strategic interventions they overlook the contradictions in the system. Owners, advertisers and key political personnel cannot always do as they would wish. They operate within structures which constrain as well as facilitate, imposing limits as well as offering opportunities. Analysing the nature and sources of these limits is a key task for a critical political economy of culture.

At the same time, it is essential to avoid the forms of structuralism which conceive of structures as building-like edifices, solid, permanent and immovable. Instead, we need to see them as dynamic formations which are constantly reproduced and altered through practical action. Although some studies confine themselves to the structural level of analysis, it is only part of the story we need to tell. Analysing the way that meaning is made and remade through the concrete activities of producers and consumers is equally essential to the perspective we are proposing here. The aim is 'to explain how it comes about that structures are constituted through action, and reciprocally how action is constituted structurally' (Giddens 1976: 161).

This in turn, requires us to think of economic determination in a more flexible way. Instead of holding on to Marx's notion of determination in the *last* instance, with its implication that everything can eventually be related directly to economic forces, we can follow Stuart Hall in seeing determination as operating in the *first* instance (Hall 1983: 84). That is to say we can think of economic dynamics as defining the key features of the general environment within which communicative activity takes place, but not as a complete explanation of the nature of that activity.

Critical political economy is also necessarily historical, but historical in a particular sense. In the terms coined by the great French historian, Fernand Braudel, it is interested in how 'the fast-moving time of events, the subject of traditional narrative history' relates to the 'slow but perceptible rhythms' which characterize the gradually unfolding history of economic formations and systems of rule (Burke 1980: 94). Four historical processes are particularly central to a critical political economy of culture; the growth of the media; the extension of corporate reach; commodification; and the changing role of state and government intervention.

What Thompson describes as 'the general process by which the transmission of symbolic forms becomes increasingly mediated by the technical and institutional apparatuses of the media industries' (1990: 3–4) makes the media industries the logical place to begin an analysis of contemporary culture.

Media production in turn has been increasing, commandeered by large corporations and moulded to their interests and strategies. This has long been the case, but the reach of corporate rationales has been considerable, extended in recent years by a push towards 'privatization' and the declining vitality of publicly funded cultural institutions. Corporations dominate the cultural landscape in two ways. First, an increasing proportion of cultural production is directly accounted for by major conglomerates with interests in a range of sectors, from newspapers and magazines, to television, film, music and theme parks. Second, corporations which are not directly involved in the cultural industries as producers, can exercise considerable control over the direction of cultural activity through their role as advertisers and sponsors. The financial viability of commercial broadcasting, together with a large section of the press, depends directly on advertising revenue, whilst more and more of the other 'sites where creative work is displayed' such as museums, galleries and theatres 'have been captured by corporate sponsors' and enlisted in their public relations campaigns (Schiller 1989: 4).

The extension of corporate reach reinforces a third major process—the commodification of cultural life. A commodity is a good which is produced in order to be exchanged at a price. Commercial communications corporations have always been in the business of commodity production. At first, their activities were confined to producing symbolic commodities that could be consumed directly, such as novels, newspapers, or theatrical performances. Later, with the rise of new domestic technologies such as the gramophone, telephone and radio set, cultural consumption required consumers to purchase the appropriate machine (or 'hardware') as a condition of access. This compounded the already considerable effect of inequalities in disposable income, and made communicative activity more dependent on ability to pay. Before they could make a telephone call or listen to the latest hit record at home, they needed to buy the appropriate hardware. The higher a household's income, the more likely it is to own key pieces of equipment—a telephone, a video recorder, a home computer—and hence the greater its communicative choices.

At first sight, advertising-supported broadcasting seems to be an exception to this trend, since anyone who has a receiving set has access to the full range of programming. Consumers do not have to pay again. However, this analysis ignores two important points. First, audiences do contribute to the costs of programming in the form of additions to the retail price of heavily advertised goods. Second, within this system, audiences themselves are the primary commodity. The economics of commercial broadcasting revolves around the exchange of audiences for advertising revenue. The price that corporations pay for advertising spots on particular programmes is determined by the size and social composition of the audience it attracts. And in prime-time, the premium prices are commanded by shows that can attract and hold the greatest number of viewers and provide a symbolic environment in tune with consumption. These needs inevitably tilt programming towards familiar and well-tested formulae and formats and away from risk and innovation, and anchor it in common-sense rather than alternative viewpoints. Hence the audience's position as a commodity serves to reduce the overall diversity of programming and ensure that it confirms established mores and assumptions far more often than it challenges them.

The main institutional counter to the commodification of communicative activity has come from the development of institutions funded out of taxation and oriented towards providing cultural resources for the full exercise of citizenship. The most important and pervasive of these have been the public broadcasting organizations, typified by the British Broadcasting Corporation (the BBC) which has distanced itself from the dynamics of commodification by not taking spot advertising and by offering the full range of programming equally to everyone who had paid the basic annual licence fee. As the BBC's first Director General, John Reith, put it; public broadcasting 'may be shared by all alike, for the same outlay, and to the same extent . . . there need be no first and third class' (Reith 1924: 217–8). This ideal has been substantially undermined in the last decade as the Corporation has responded to a fall in the real value of the licence fee by expanding its commercial activities in an effort to raise money. In a marked departure from the historic commitment to universal and equal provision, these include plans to launch subscription channels for special interest groups.

At the same time, the Corporation has also come under intensified political pressure, particularly in the areas of news and current affairs. Its always fragile independence from government has been challenged by a series of moves, ranging from well publicized attacks on the 'impartiality' of its news coverage to police seizures of film, and a government ban on live interviews with members of a range of named organizations in Northern Ireland, including the legal political party, Sinn Fein.

These attempts to narrow the field of public discourse and representation are part of a wider historical process whereby the state in capitalist societies has increasingly assumed a greater role in managing communicative activity. From its inception, political economy has been particularly interested in determining the appropriate scope of public intervention. It is therefore inevitably involved in evaluation of competing policies. It is concerned with changing the world as well as with analysing it. Classical political economists and their present-day supporters start from the assumption that public intervention ought to be minimized and market forces given the widest possible freedom of operation. Critical political economists on the other hand point to the distortions and inequalities of market systems and argue that these deficiencies can only be rectified by public intervention, though they disagree on the forms that this should take.

Arguments within political economy on the proper balance between public and private enterprise are never simply technical, however. They are always underpinned by distinctive visions of what constitutes the 'public good'. Adam Smith ended his career as a professor of moral philosophy. He saw markets, not simply as more efficient, but as morally superior, because they gave consumers a free choice between competing commodities; only those goods that provided satisfaction would survive. At the same time, he saw very clearly that the public good was not simply the sum of individual choices, and that private enterprise would not provide everything that a good society required. He saw particular problems in the sphere of culture, and recommended various public interventions to increase the level of public knowledge and provide wholesome entertainment. Critical political economy takes this line of reasoning a good deal further, linking the constitution of the good society to the extension of citizenship rights.

The history of the modern communications media is not only an economic history of their growing incorporation into a capitalist economic system, but also a political history of their increasing centrality to the exercise of full citizenship. In its most general sense, citizenship is 'about the conditions that allow people to become full members of the society at every level' (Murdock and Golding 1989: 182). In an ideal situation, communications systems would contribute to these conditions in two important ways. First, they would provide people with access to the information, advice and analysis that would enable them to know their rights and to pursue them effectively. Second, they would provide the broadcast possible range of information, interpretation and debate on areas that involve political choices, and enable them to register dissent and propose alternatives. This argument has been elaborated by the German theorist, Jurgen Habermas, in his highly influential notion of the 'public sphere'. [. . .]

The Production of Meaning as the Exercise of Power

A focal question for the political economy of communications is to investigate how changes in the array of forces which exercise control over cultural production and distribution limit or liberate the public sphere. In practice this directs attention to two key issues. The first is the pattern of ownership of such institutions and the consequences of this pattern for control over their activities. The second is the nature of the relationship between state regulation and communications institutions. We can briefly review each of these in turn.

The steadily increasing amount of cultural production accounted for by large corporations has long been a source of concern to theorists of democracy. They saw a fundamental contradiction between the ideal that public media should operate as a public sphere and the reality of concentrated private ownership. They feared that proprietors would use their property rights to restrict the flow of information and open debate on which the vitality of democracy depended. These concerns were fuelled by the rise of the great press barons at the turn of the century. Not only did proprietors like Pulitzer and Hearst in the United States and Northcliffe in the United Kingdom own chains or newspapers with large circulations, but they clearly had no qualms about using them to promote their pet political causes or to denigrate positions and people they disagreed with.

These long-standing worries have been reinforced in recent years by the emergence of multi media conglomerates with significant stakes across a range of central communications sectors. [. . .]

The rise of communications conglomerates adds a new element to the old debate about potential abuses of owner power. It is no longer a simple case of proprietors intervening in editorial decisions or firing key personnel who fall foul of their political philosophies. Cultural production is also strongly influenced by commercial strategies built around 'synergies' which exploit the overlaps between the company's different media interests. The company's newspapers may give free publicity to their television stations or the record and book divisions may launch products related to a new movie released by the film division. The effect is to reduce the diversity of cultural goods in circulation. Although in simple quantitative terms there may be more commodities in circulation, they are more likely to be variants of the same basic themes and images.

In addition to the power they exercise directly over the companies they own, the major media moguls also have considerable indirect power over smaller concerns operating in their markets or seeking to break into them. They establish the rules by which the competitive game will be played. They can use their greater financial power to drive new entrants out of the marketplace by launching expensive promotional campaigns, offering discounts to advertisers, or buying up key creative personnel. Firms that do survive compete for market share by offering similar products to the leading concerns and employing tried and tested editorial formulae.

Historically, the main interruptions to this process have come from state intervention. These have taken two main forms. First, commercial enterprises have been regulated in the public interest with the aim of ensuring diversity of cultural production, including forms that would be unlikely to survive in pure market conditions. British commercial television companies for example are required to make a range of minority interest programmes, even though they are not profitable. Second, cultural diversity has been further underwritten by various forms of public subsidy.

Over the last two decades however, this system has been substantially altered by privatization policies. Major public cultural enterprises, such as the French TF1 television network, have been sold to private investors. Liberalization policies have introduced private operators into markets which were previously closed to competition, such as the broadcasting systems of a number of European countries. And regulatory regimes have been altered in favour of freedom of operations for owners and advertisers. The net effect of these changes has been to increase greatly the potential reach and power of the major communications companies and to reinforce the danger that public culture will be commandeered by private interests. Charting these shifts in the balance between commercial and public enterprise and tracing their impact on cultural diversity is a key task for a critical political economy.

There are several dimensions to this process. First, state agencies such as the army and police have become major users of communications technologies both for surveillance and for their own command and control systems. Second, governments and state departments have become increasingly important producers of public information in a variety of forms ranging from official statistics and daily press briefings to public advertising campaigns. Third, governments have extended their regulatory functions in relation to, both the structure of the media industries (through restrictions on ownership and pricing for example), and the range of permissible public expression (through regulations relating to areas such as obscenity, incitement to racial hatred, and 'national security'). Finally, and most importantly, liberal democratic governments have widened the range of cultural activities that they subsidize out of the public purse, either indirectly, by not charging value added tax on newspapers for example, or directly, through various forms of grants. These range from the monies provided for museums, libraries and theatres to the compulsory annual licence fee for television set ownership which funds the BBC. [...]

The contribution of political economy to this debate is to analyse how and in what ways the relation between the media and the state has consequences for the range of expression and ideas in the public arena. For example, what have been the consequences of the effective detachment of the BBC from market forces? [...]

However, the state is not only a regulator of communications institutions. It is itself a communicator of enormous power. How this power is exercised is of major interest to a political economy of culture. Governments are inevitably anxious to promote their own views of the development of policy, and to ensure that legislative initiatives are properly understood and supported. [...]

The production of communications, however, is not merely a simple reflection of the controlling interests of those who own or even control the broad range of capital plant and equipment which make up the means by which cultural goods are made and distributed. Within the media are men and women working within a range of codes and professional ideologies, and with an array of aspirations, both personal and social. These ambitions can be idealized; much cultural production is routine, mundane, and highly predictable. But the autonomy of those who work within the media is a matter of substantial interest to political economists. Their aim is to discover how far this autonomy can be exercised given the consequences of broad economic structure we have described above, and to what extent the economic structure of the media prevents some forms of expression from finding a popular outlet and audience. [...]

The political economy of cultural production, then, is concerned with the concrete consequences for the work and nature of making media goods of the broad patterns of power and ownership which are their backdrop.

Political Economy and Textual Analysis

Research in cultural studies has been particularly concerned with analysing the structure of media texts and tracing their role in sustaining systems of domination. As it has developed, this work decisively rejected the notion that the mass media act as a transmission belt for a dominant ideology and developed a model of the communications system as a field or space, in which contending discourses, offering different ways of looking and speaking, struggle for visibility and legitimacy. But outside of televised political speeches, discourses are seldom available for public consumption in their 'raw' state. They are reorganized and recontextualized to fit the particular expressive form being used. Discourses about AIDS for example, might well feature in a variety of television programmes, ranging from public health advertisement, to news items, investigative reports, studio discussion programme, or episodes of soap operas or police series. Each of these forms has a major impact on what can be said and shown, by whom, and from what point of view. In short, cultural forms are mechanisms for regulating public discourse. We can distinguish two dimensions to this process. The first has to do with the range of discourses that particular forms allow into play, whether they are organized exclusively around official discourses, or whether they provide space for the articulation of counter-discourses. The second concerns the way that the available discourses are handled within the text, whether they are arranged in a clearly marked hierarchy of credibility which urges the audience to prefer one over the others, or whether they are treated in a more even-handed and indeterminate way which leaves the audience with a more open choice.

If cultural studies is primarily interested in the way these mechanisms work within a particular media text or across a range of texts, critical political economy is concerned to explain how the economic dynamics of production structure public discourse by promoting certain cultural forms over others. Take for example, the increasing reliance on international co-production agreements in television drama production—these arrangements impose a variety of constraints on form, as the partners search for subject matter and narrative styles that they can sell in their home markets. The resulting bargain may produce an Americanized product which is fast moving, based on simple characterizations, works with a tried and tested action format, and offers an unambiguous ending. Or it may result in a variant of 'televisual tourism' which trades on the familiar forms and sights of the national cultural heritage (Murdock 1989a). Both strategies represent a narrowing of the field of discourse and inhibit a full engagement with the complexities and ambiguities of the national condition. The first affects a closure around dominant transatlantic forms of story-telling with their clearly marked boundaries and hierarchies of discourse. The second reproduces an ideology of 'Englishness' which excludes or marginalizes a whole range of subordinate discourses.

This general perspective, with its emphasis on the crucial mediating role of cultural forms, has two major advantages. First, it allows us to trace detailed connections between the financing and organization of cultural production and changes in the field of public discourse and representation in a non reducible way, that respects the need for a full analysis of textual organization.

Indeed, far from being secondary, such an analysis is central to the full development of the argument. Second, by stressing the fact that media texts vary considerably in their degree of discursive openness, it offers an approach to audience activity that focuses on structured variations in response. However, in contrast to recent work on audience activity produced within cultural studies, which concentrates on the negotiation of textual interpretations and media use in immediate social settings, critical political economy seeks to relate variations in people's responses to their overall location in the economic system (Murdock 1989*b*). Of course, this cannot explain everything we need to know about the dynamics of response, but it is a necessary starting point.

Consumption— Sovereignty or Struggle?

For political proponents of a free market philosophy communications goods are like any other. Since the best way of ensuring adequate distribution and production of the general commodities people want is through the market, so too, the argument follows, is this true for cultural goods. It is the truth or otherwise of this proposition that provides the analytical target for a political economy of cultural consumption.

Curiously, an influential version of this free market philosophy has had considerable currency in much work within recent cultural studies. In an attempt to contest the apparent simplistic determinism of a view which sees audiences as the passive dupes of all powerful media, some writers have asserted the sovereignty of viewers and readers, to impose their own meanings and interpretations on material which is 'polysemic'—that is capable of generating a variety of meanings. This analysis has tempted writers of very varying political or social presuppositions. For liberal pluralists it has refurbished the view that the checks and balances of cultural supply and demand, though admittedly uneven, are far from bankrupt. The customer, though perhaps a little bruised, is still ultimately sovereign. For writers with more critical or radical instincts, it is a view which has unleashed a populist romance in which the downtrodden victims caricatured by crude economic determinists are revealed as heroic resistance fighters in the war against cultural deception.

Consumer sovereignty is in any total sense clearly impossible—nobody has access to a complete range of cultural goods as and when they might wish, without restriction. The task of political economy, then, is to examine the barriers which limit such freedom. It construes such barriers being of two kinds, material and cultural.

Where communications goods and facilities are available only at a price there will be a finite capacity to have access to them, limited by the disposable spending power of individuals and households. [. . .] As the range of hardware required for such activities grows, however, so too does the demand on private expenditure necessary to participate in them. [. . .]

The disposable spending power of different groups in the population is significantly polarized. Such goods require regular updating and replacement, disadvantaging groups with limited spending power and cumulatively advantaging the better off. Owning video or computer hardware requires expenditure on software, owning a phone means spending money on using it. Thus limited spending power is a deterrent not only to initial purchase but to regular use.

However not all expenditure on communications goods involves expensive acquisition of equipment. Television programmes can be viewed once you have a set to watch them on, as most people do, while many cultural materials are available as public goods; they are paid for from taxation as a common resource—public library books, for example. This is not a static situation, however. For political economists a shift in the provision and distribution of cultural goods from being public services to private commodities signals a substantial change in the opportunity for different groups in the population to have access to them. If television channels, or individual programmes, are accessible by price, then consumption of television programmes will be significantly governed by the distribution of household incomes. Similar considerations would come into play if, for example, public libraries were to make greater use of powers to charge. By imposing the discipline of price on cultural goods they acquire an artificial scarcity which makes them akin to other goods of considerably greater scarcity. It is for this reason that the political economy of cultural consumption has to be especially concerned with material inequalities.

Critical political economy is not only concerned with material barriers to cultural consumption, however. It is also interested in the ways in which social location regulates access to the cultural competences required to interpret and use media materials in particular ways. One of the strongest empirical traditions within cultural studies—running from studies of youth subcultures to research on differential 'readings' of television texts—has concerned itself with how social locations provide access to cultural repertoires and symbolic resources that sustain differences of interpretation and expression (Morley 1983). This emphasis on social experience as a cultural resource is important, but it can be oversold. Consumption practices are clearly not completely manipulated by the strategies of the cultural industries but they are, equally clearly, not completely independent of them. Rather we need to see cultural commodities as the site of a continual struggle over uses and meanings between producers and audiences and between different consumer groups. [. . .]

References   BURKE, PETER (1980), *Sociology and History* (London: George Allen and Unwin).

GIDDENS, ANTHONY (1976), *New Rules of Sociological Method* (London: Hutchinson).

HALL, STUART (1983), 'The Problem of Ideology—Marxism without Guarantees', in B. Matthews (ed.), *Marx: A Hundred Years On* (London: Lawrence and Wishart), 57–85.

HERMAN, EDWARD, S., and CHOMSKY, NOAM (1988), *Manufacturing Consent: The Political Economy of The Mass Media* (New York: Pantheon Books).

MORLEY, DAVID (1983), 'Cultural Transformations: The Politics of Resistance', in H. Davis and P. Walton (eds.), *Language, Image, Media* (Oxford: Basil Blackwell), 104–17.

MURDOCK, GRAHAM (1989*a*), 'Televisual Tourism', in Christian W. Thomsen (ed.),

Cultural Transfer or Electronic Colonialism? (Heidelberg: Carl Winter-Universitatsverlag), 171–83.

—— (1989*b*), 'Audience Activity and Critical Inquiry', in Brenda Dervin *et al.* (eds.), *Rethinking Communication*, ii, *Paradigm Exemplars* (London: Sage Publications), 226–49.

—— and GOLDING, PETER (1989), 'Information Poverty and Political Inequality: Citizenship in the Age of Privatized Communications', *Journal of Communication*, 39/3 (Summer): 180–95.

REITH, JOHN (1924), *Broadcast Over Britain* (London: Hodder and Stoughton).

SCHILLER, HERBERT, I. (1989), *Culture Inc: The Corporate Takeover of Public Expression* (New York: Oxford University Press).

THOMPSON, JOHN, B. (1990), *Ideology and Modern Culture: Critical Social Theory in the Era of Mass Communication* (Oxford: Polity Press).

19
Manufacturing Consent

Edward S. Herman and Noam Chomsky

A Propaganda Model

THE MASS MEDIA serve as a system for communicating messages and symbols to the general populace. It is their function to amuse, entertain, and inform, and to inculcate individuals with the values, beliefs, and codes of behaviour that will integrate them into the institutional structures of the larger society. In a world of concentrated wealth and major conflicts of class interest, to fulfil this role requires systematic propaganda.

In countries where the levers of power are in the hands of a state bureaucracy, the monopolistic control over the media, often supplemented by official censorship, makes it clear that the media serve the ends of a dominant élite. It is much more difficult to see a propaganda system at work where the media are private and formal censorship is absent. This is especially true where the media actively compete, periodically attack and expose corporate and governmental malfeasance, and aggressively portray themselves as spokesmen for free speech and the general community interest. What is not evident (and remains undiscussed in the media) is the limited nature of such critiques, as well as the huge inequality in command of resources, and its effect both on access to a private media system and on its behaviour and performance.

A propaganda model focuses on this inequality of wealth and power and its multilevel effects on mass-media interests and choices. It traces the routes by which money and power are able to filter out the news fit to print, marginalize dissent, and allow the government and dominant private interests to get their messages across to the public. The essential ingredients of our propaganda model, or set of news 'filters', fall under the following headings: (1) the size, concentrated ownership, owner wealth, and profit orientation of the dominant mass-media firms; (2) advertising as the primary income source of the mass media; (3) the reliance of the media on information provided by government, business, and 'experts' funded and approved by these primary sources and agents of power; (4) 'flak' as a means of disciplining the media; and (5) 'anti-Communism' as a national religion and control mechanism. These elements interact with and reinforce one another. The raw material of news must pass through successive filters, leaving only the cleansed residue fit to print. They fix the premises of discourse and interpretation, and the definition of what is newsworthy in the first place, and they explain the basis and operations of what amount to propaganda campaigns.

Source: Edward S. Herman and Noam Chomsky, *Manufacturing Consent: The Political Economy of the Mass Media* (London: Vintage, 1988).

The élite domination of the media and marginalization of dissidents that results from the operation of these filters occurs so naturally that media news people, frequently operating with complete integrity and goodwill, are able to convince themselves that they choose and interpret the news 'objectively' and on the basis of professional news values. Within the limits of the filter constraints they often are objective; the constraints are so powerful, and are built into the system in such a fundamental way, that alternative bases of news choices are hardly imaginable. In assessing the newsworthiness of the US government's urgent claims of a shipment of MIGs to Nicaragua on 5 November 1984, the media do not stop to ponder the bias that is inherent in the priority assigned to government-supplied raw material, or the possibility that the government might be manipulating the news,[1] imposing its own agenda, and deliberately diverting attention from other material. It requires a macro, alongside a micro- (story-by-story), view of media operations, to see the pattern of manipulation and systematic bias.

Let us turn now to a more detailed examination of the main constituents of the propaganda model. [...]

■ 1. Size, Ownership, and Profit Orientation of the Mass Media: The First Filter

The first filter—the limitation on ownership of media with any substantial outreach by the requisite large size of investment—was applicable a century or more ago, and it has become increasingly effective over time.[2] In 1986 there were some 1,500 daily newspapers, 11,000 magazines, 9,000 radio and 1,500 TV stations, 2,400 book publishers, and seven movie studios in the United States—over 25,000 media entities in all. But a large proportion of those among this set who were news dispensers were very small and local, dependent on the large national companies and wire services for all but local news. Many more were subject to common ownership, sometimes extending through virtually the entire set of media variants.[3] [...]

1 Media representatives claim that what the government says is 'newsworthy' in its own right. If, however, the government's assertions are transmitted without context or evaluation, and without regard to the government's possible manipulative intent, the media have set themselves up to be 'managed'. Their objectivity is 'nominal', not substantive.

In early October 1986, memos were leaked to the press indicating that the Reagan administration had carried out a deliberate campaign of disinformation to influence events in Libya. The mass media, which had passed along this material without question, expressed a great deal of righteous indignation that they had been misled. To compound the absurdity, five years earlier the press had reported a CIA-run 'disinformation programme designed to embarrass Qaddafi and his government', along with terrorist operations to overthrow Quaddafi and perhaps assassinate him (*Newsweek*, 3 Aug. 1981; P. Edward Haley, *Qaddafi and the United States since 1969* (New York: Praeger, 1984), 272). But no lessons were learned. In fact, the mass media are gulled on an almost daily basis, but rarely have to suffer the indignity of government *documents* revealing their gullibility. With regard to Libya, the media have fallen into line for each propaganda ploy, from the 1981 'hit squads' through the Berlin discotheque bombing, swallowing each implausible claim, failing to admit error in retrospect, and apparently unable to learn from successive entrapment—which suggests willing error. See Noam Chomsky, *Pirates & Emperors* (New York: Claremont, 1986), ch. 3. As we show throughout the present book, a series of lies by the government, successively exposed, never seems to arouse scepticism in the media regarding the next government claim.

2 Note that we are speaking of media with substantial outreach—mass media. It has always been possible to start small-circulation journals and to produce mimeographed or photocopied news letters sent around to a tiny audience. But even small journals in the United States today typically survive only by virtue of contributions from wealthy financial angels.

3 In 1987, the Times-Mirror Company, for example, owned newspapers in Los Angeles, Baltimore, Denver, and Hartford, Connecticut, had book publishing and magazine subsidiaries, and owned cable systems and seven television stations.

It has long been noted that the media are tiered, with the top tier—as measured by prestige, resources, and outreach—comprising somewhere between ten and twenty-four systems.[4] It is this top tier, along with the government and wire services, that defines the news agenda and supplies much of the national and international news to the lower tiers of the media, and thus for the general public.[5] Centralization within the top tier was substantially increased by the post-World War II rise of television and the national networking of this important medium. Pre-television news markets were local, even if heavily dependent on the higher tiers and a narrow set of sources for national and international news; the networks provide national and international news from three national sources, and television is now the principal source of news for the public.[6] The maturing of cable, however, has resulted in a fragmentation of television audiences and a slow erosion of the market share and power of the networks. [...]

Many of the large media companies are fully integrated into the market, and for the others, too, the pressures of stockholders, directors, and bankers to focus on the bottom line are powerful. These pressures have intensified in recent years as media stocks have become market favourites, and actual or prospective owners of newspapers and television properties have found it possible to capitalize increased audience size and advertising revenues into multiplied values of the media franchises—and great wealth.[7] This has encouraged the entry of speculators and increased the pressure and temptation to focus more intensively on profitability. Family owners have been increasingly divided between those wanting to take advantage of the new

4 David L. Paletz and Robert M. Entman, *Media. Power. Politics* (New York: Free Press, 1981), 7; Stephen Hess, *The Government/Press Connection: Press Officers and Their Offices* (Washington: Brookings, 1984), pp. 99–100.

5 The four major Western wire services—Associated Press, United Press International, Reuters, and Agence-France-Presse—account for some 80 per cent of the international news circulating in the world today. AP is owned by member newspapers; UPI is privately owned; Reuters was owned mainly by the British media until it went public in 1984, but control was retained by the original owners by giving lesser voting rights to the new stockholders; Agence-France-Presse is heavily subsidized by the French government. As is pointed out by Jonathan Fenby, the wire services 'exist to serve markets', and their prime concern, accordingly, 'is with the rich media markets of the United States, Western Europe, and Japan, and increasingly with the business community'. They compete fiercely, but AP and UPI 'are really US enterprises that operate on an international scale. . . . Without their domestic base, the AP and UPI could not operate as international agencies. With it, they must be American organizations, subject to American pressures and requirements' (*The International News Services* (New York: Schocken, 1986), 7, 9, 73–4). See also Anthony Smith, *The Geopolitics of Information: How Western Culture Dominates the World* (New York: Oxford University Press, 1980), ch. 3.

6 The fourteenth annual Roper survey, 'Public Attitudes toward Television and Other Media in a Time of Change' (May 1985), indicates that in 1984, 64 per cent of the sample mentioned television as the place 'where you usually get most of your news about what's going on in the world today . . .' (p. 3). It has often been noted that the television networks themselves depend heavily on the prestige newspapers, wire services, and government for their choices of news. Their autonomy as newsmakers can be easily exaggerated.

7 John Kluge, having taken the Metromedia system private in a leveraged buyout in 1984 worth $1.1 billion, sold off various parts of this system in 1985–6 for $5.5 billion, at a personal profit of some $3 billion (Gary Hector, 'Are Shareholders Cheated by LBOs?' *Fortune*, 17 Jan. 1987, p. 100). Station KDLA-TV, in Los Angeles, which had been bought by a management-outsider group in a leveraged buyout in 1983 for $245 million, was sold to the Tribune Company for $510 million two years later (Richard Stevenson, 'Tribune in TV Deal for $510 Million', *New York Times*, 7 May 1985). See also 'The Media Magnates: Why Huge Fortunes Roll Off the Presses', *Fortune*, 12 October 1987.

opportunities and those desiring a continuation of family control, and their splits have often precipitated crises leading finally to the sale of the family interest.[8]

This trend toward greater integration of the media into the market system has been accelerated by the loosening of rules limiting media concentration, cross-ownership, and control by non-media companies.[9] There has also been an abandonment of restrictions—previously quite feeble anyway—on radio-TV commercials, entertainment-mayhem programming, and 'fairness doctrine' threats, opening the door to the unrestrained commercial use of the airwaves.[10]

The greater profitability of the media in a deregulated environment has also led to an increase in takeovers and takeover threats, with even giants like CBS and Time, Inc., directly attacked or threatened. This has forced the managements of the media giants to incur greater debt and to focus ever more aggressively and unequivocally on profitability, in order to placate owners and reduce the attractiveness of their properties to outsiders.[11] They have lost some of their limited autonomy to bankers, institutional investors,

8 A split among the heirs of James E. Scripps eventually resulted in the sale of the *Detroit Evening News*. According to one news article, 'Daniel Marentette, a Scripps family member and a self described "angry shareholder", says family members want a better return on their money. "We get better yields investing in a New York checking account", says Mr Marentette, who sells race horses' (Damon Darlin, 'Takeover Rumors Hit Detroit News Parent', *Wall Street Journal*, 18 July 1985). The Bingham family division on these matters led to the sale of the *Louisville Courier-Journal*; the New Haven papers of the Jackson family were sold after years of squabbling, and 'the sale price [of the New Haven papers], $185 million, has only served to publicize the potential value of family holdings of family newspapers elsewhere' (Geraldine Fabrikant, 'Newspaper Properties, Hotter Than Ever', *New York Times*, 17 Aug. 1986).

9 The Reagan administration strengthened the control of existing holders of television-station licences by increasing their term from three to five years, and its FCC made renewals essentially automatic. The FCC also greatly facilitated speculation and trading in television properties by a rule change reducing the required holding period before sale of a newly acquired property from three years to one year.

The Reagan era FCC and Department of Justice also refused to challenge mergers and takeover bids that would significantly increase the concentration of power (GE-RCA) or media concentration (Capital Cities-ABC). Furthermore, beginning 2 April 1985, media owners could own as many as twelve television stations, as long as their total audience didn't exceed 25 per cent of the nation's television households; and they could also hold twelve AM and twelve FM stations, as the 1953 '7-7-7 rule' was replaced with a '12-12-12 rule'. See Herbert H. Howard, 'Group and Cross-Media Ownership of Television Stations: 1985' (Washington: National Association of Broadcasters, 1985).

10 This was justified by Reagan-era FCC chairman Mark Fowler on the grounds that market options are opening up and that the public should be free to choose. Criticized by Fred Friendly for doing away with the law's public-interest standard, Fowler replied that Friendly 'distrusts the ability of the viewing public to make decisions on its own through the marketplace mechanism. I do not' (Jeanne Saddler, 'Clear Channel: Broadcast Takeovers Meet Less FCC Static, and Critics Are Upset', *Wall Street Journal*, 11 June 1985). Among other problems, Fowler ignores the fact that true freedom of choice involves the ability to select options that may not be offered by an oligopoly selling audiences to advertisers.

11 CBS increased its debt by about $1 billion in 1985 to finance the purchase of 21 per cent of its own stock, in order to fend off a takeover attempt by Ted Turner. The *Wall Street Journal* noted that 'With debt now standing at 60 per cent of capital, it needs to keep advertising revenue up to repay borrowings and interest' (Peter Barnes, 'CBS Profit Hinges on Better TV Ratings', 6 June 1986). With the slowed-up growth of advertising revenues, CBS embarked on an employment cutback of as many as 600 broadcast division employees, the most extensive for CBS since the loss of cigarette advertising in 1971 (Peter Barnes, 'CBS Will Cut up to 600 Posts in Broadcasting', *Wall Street Journal*, July 1, 1986). In June 1986, Time, Inc., embarked on a programme to buy back as much as 10 million shares, or 16 per cent of its common stock, at an expected cost of some $900 million, again to reduce the threat of a hostile takeover (Laura Landro, 'Time Will Buy as Much as 16 per cent of Its Common', *Wall Street Journal*, 20 June 1986).

and large individual investors whom they have had to solicit as potential 'white knights'.[12] [. . .]

These investors are a force helping press media companies toward strictly market (profitability) objectives. So is the diversification and geographic spread of the great media companies. Many of them have diversified out of particular media fields into others that seemed like growth areas. Many older newspaper-based media companies, fearful of the power of television and its effects on advertising revenue, moved as rapidly as they could into broadcasting and cable TV. Time, Inc., also, made a major diversification move into cable TV, which now accounts for more than half its profits. Only a small minority of the twenty-four largest media giants remain in a single media sector.[13]

The large media companies have also diversified beyond the media field, and non-media companies have established a strong presence in the mass media. [. . .]

Another structural relationship of importance is the media companies' dependence on and ties with government. The radio-TV companies and networks all require government licences and franchises and are thus potentially subject to government control or harassment. This technical legal dependency has been used as a club to discipline the media, and media policies that stray too often from an establishment orientation could activate this threat.[14] [. . .]

In sum, the dominant media firms are quite large businesses; they are controlled by very wealthy people or by managers who are subject to sharp constraints by owners and other market-profit-oriented forces;[15] and they are closely interlocked, and have important common interests, with other major corporations, banks, and government. This is the first powerful filter that will affect news choices. [. . .]

---

12 In response to the Jesse Helms and Turner threats to CBS, Laurence Tisch, of Loews Corporation, was encouraged to increase his holdings in CBS stock, already at 11.7 per cent. In August 1986, the Loews interest was raised to 24.9 per cent, and Tisch obtained a position of virtual control. In combination with William Paley, who owned 8.1 per cent of the shares, the chief executive officer of CBS was removed and Tisch took over that role himself, on a temporary basis (Peter Barnes, 'Loews Increases Its Stake in CBS to Almost 25%', *Wall Street Journal*, 12 Aug. 1986).

13 For the interests of fifteen major newspaper companies in other media fields, and a checklist of other fields entered by leading firms in a variety of media industries, see Benjamin Compaine *et al.*, *Anatomy of the Communications Industry* (White Plains, NY: Knowledge Industry Publications, 1982), tables 2.19 and 8.1, pp. 11 and 452–3.

14 On the Nixon–Agnew campaign to bully the media by publicity attacks and threats, see Marilyn Lashner, *The Chilling Effect in TV News* (New York: Praeger, 1984). Lashner concluded that the Nixon White House's attempt to quiet the media 'succeeded handily, at least as far as television is concerned' (p. 167). See also Fred Powledge, *The Engineering of Restraint: The Nixon Administration and the Press* (Washington: Public Affairs Press, 1971), and William E. Porter, *Assault on the Media: The Nixon Years* (Ann Arbor: University of Michigan Press, 1976).

15 Is it not possible that if the populace 'demands' programme content greatly disliked by the owners, competition and the quest for profits will cause them to offer such programming? There is some truth in this, and it, along with the limited autonomy of media personnel, may help explain the 'surprises' that crop up occasionally in the mass media. One limit to the force of public demand, however, is that the millions of customers have no means of registering their demand for products that are not offered to them. A further problem is that the owners' class interests are reinforced by a variety of other filters that we discuss below.

■ **2. The Advertising Licence to do Business: The Second Filter**

Before advertising became prominent, the price of a newspaper had to cover the costs of doing business. With the growth of advertising, papers that attracted ads could afford a copy price well below production costs. This put papers lacking in advertising at a serious disadvantage: their prices would tend to be higher, curtailing sales, and they would have less surplus to invest in improving the salability of the paper (features, attractive format, promotion, etc.). For this reason, an advertising-based system will tend to drive out of existence or into marginality the media companies and types that depend on revenue from sales alone. With advertising, the free market does not yield a neutral system in which final buyer choice decides. The *advertisers'* choices influence media prosperity and survival.[16] The ad-based media receive an advertising subsidy that gives them a price-marketing-quality edge, which allows them to encroach on and further weaken their ad-free (or ad-disadvantaged) rivals.[17] Even if ad-based media cater to an affluent ('upscale') audience, they easily pick up a large part of the 'down-scale' audience, and their rivals lose market share and are eventually driven out or marginalized. [...]

The successful media today are fully attuned to the crucial importance of audience 'quality': CBS proudly tells its shareholders that while it 'continuously seeks to maximize audience delivery', it has developed a new 'sales tool' with which it approaches advertisers: 'Client Audience Profile, or CAP, will help advertisers optimize the effectiveness of their network television schedules by evaluating audience segments in proportion to usage levels of advertisers' products and services.'[18] In short, the mass media are interested in attracting audiences with buying power, not audiences per se; it is affluent audiences that spark advertiser interest today, as in the nineteenth century. The idea that the drive for large audiences makes the mass media 'democratic' thus suffers from the initial weakness that its political analogue is a voting system weighted by income!

The power of advertisers over television programming stems from the simple fact that they buy and pay for the programmes—they are the 'patrons' who provide the media subsidy. As such, the media compete for their patronage, developing specialized staff to solicit advertisers and necessarily having to explain how their programmes serve advertisers' needs. The choices

16 '[P]roducers presenting patrons [advertisers] with the greatest opportunities to make a profit through their publics will receive support while those that cannot compete on this score will not survive' (Joseph Turow, *Media Industries: The Production of News and Entertainment* (New York: Longman, 1984), 52).

17 Noncommercial television is also at a huge disadvantage for the same reason, and will require a public subsidy to be able to compete. Because public television does not have the built-in constraints of ownership by the wealthy, and the need to appease advertisers, it poses a threat to a narrow élite control of mass communications. This is why conservatives struggle to keep public television on a short leash, with annual funding decisions, and funding at a low level (see Barnouw, *The Sponsor*, 179–82). Another option pursued in the Carter-Reagan era has been to force it into the commercial nexus by sharp defunding.

18 *1984 CBS Annual Report*, p. 13. This is a further refinement in the measurement of 'efficiency' in 'delivering an audience'. In the magazine business, the standard measure is CPM, or 'costs per thousand', to an advertiser to reach buyers through a full-page, black-and-white ad. Recent developments, like CBS's CAP, have been in the direction of identifying the special characteristics of the audience delivered. In selling itself to advertisers, the *Soap Opera Digest* says: 'But you probably want to know about our first milestone: today *Soap Opera Digest* delivers more women in the 18–49 category at the lowest CPM than any other women's magazine' (quoted in Turow, *Media Industries*, 55).

of these patrons greatly affect the welfare of the media, and the patrons become what William Evan calls 'normative reference organizations',[19] whose requirements and demands the media must accommodate if they are to succeed.[20]

For a television network, an audience gain or loss of one percentage point in the Nielsen ratings translates into a change in advertising revenue of from $80 to $100 million a year, with some variation depending on measures of audience 'quality'. The stakes in audience size and affluence are thus extremely large, and in a market system there is a strong tendency for such considerations to affect policy profoundly. [...]

In addition to discrimination against unfriendly media institutions, advertisers also choose selectively among programmes on the basis of their own principles. With rare exceptions these are culturally and politically conservative.[21] Large corporate advertisers on television will rarely sponsor programmes that engage in serious criticisms of corporate activities, such as the problem of environmental degradation, the workings of the military–industrial complex, or corporate support of and benefits from Third World tyrannies. [...]

Advertisers will want, more generally, to avoid programmes with serious complexities and disturbing controversies that interfere with the 'buying mood'. They seek programmes that will lightly entertain and thus fit in with the spirit of the primary purpose of programme purchases—the dissemination of a selling message. [...]

Television stations and networks are also concerned to maintain audience 'flow' levels, i.e. to keep people watching from programme to programme, in order to sustain advertising ratings and revenue. Airing programme interludes of documentary-cultural matter that cause station switching is costly, and over time a 'free' (i.e. ad-based) commercial system will tend to excise it. Such documentary–cultural–critical materials will be driven out of secondary media vehicles as well, as these companies strive to qualify for advertiser interest, although there will always be some cultural-political programming trying to come into being or surviving on the periphery of the mainstream media.

■ **3. Sourcing Mass-Media News: The Third Filter**

The mass media are drawn into a symbiotic relationship with powerful sources of information by economic necessity and reciprocity of interest. The media need a steady, reliable flow of the raw material of news. They have daily news demands and imperative news schedules that they must meet. They cannot afford to have reporters and cameras at all places where important stories may break. Economics dictates that they concentrate their resources where significant news often occurs, where important rumours

---

19 William Evan, *Organization Theory* (New York: Wiley, 1976), 123.

20 Turow asserts that 'The continual interaction of producers and primary patrons plays a dominant part in setting the general boundary conditions for day-to-day production activity' (*Media Industries*, 51).

21 According to Procter & Gamble's instructions to their ad agency, 'There will be no material on any of our programmes which could in any way further the concept of business as cold, ruthless, and lacking in all sentiment or spiritual motivation.' The manager of corporate communications for General Electric has said: 'We insist on a programme environment that reinforces our corporate messages' (quoted in Bagdikian, *Media Monopoly*, 160). We may recall that GE now owns NBC-TV.

and leaks abound, and where regular press conferences are held. The White House, the Pentagon, and the State Department, in Washington, DC, are central nodes of such news activity. On a local basis, city hall and the police department are the subject of regular news 'beats' for reporters. Business corporations and trade groups are also regular and credible purveyors of stories deemed newsworthy. These bureaucracies turn out a large volume of material that meets the demands of news organizations for reliable, scheduled flows. Mark Fishman calls this 'the principle of bureaucratic affinity: only other bureaucracies can satisfy the input needs of a news bureaucracy'.[22]

Government and corporate sources also have the great merit of being recognizable and credible by their status and prestige. This is important to the mass media. [. . .]

The magnitude of the public-information operations of large government and corporate bureaucracies that constitute the primary news sources is vast and ensures special access to the media. The Pentagon, for example, has a public-information service that involves many thousands of employees, spending hundreds of millions of dollars every year and dwarfing not only the public-information resources of any dissenting individual or group but the *aggregate* of such groups. [. . .]

To consolidate their pre-eminent position as sources, government and business-news promoters go to great pains to make things easy for news organizations. They provide the media organizations with facilities in which to gather; they give journalists advance copies of speeches and forthcoming reports; they schedule press conferences at hours well-geared to news deadlines;[23] they write press releases in usable language; and they carefully organize their press conferences and 'photo opportunity' sessions.[24] It is the job of news officers 'to meet the journalist's scheduled needs with material that their beat agency has generated at its own pace'.[25]

In effect, the large bureaucracies of the powerful *subsidize* the mass media, and gain special access by their contribution to reducing the media's costs of acquiring the raw materials of, and producing, news. The large entities that provide this subsidy become 'routine' news sources and have privileged access to the gates. Non-routine sources must struggle for access, and may be ignored by the arbitrary decision of the gatekeepers. It should also be noted that in the case of the largesse of the Pentagon and the State Department's Office of Public Diplomacy,[26] the subsidy is at the taxpayers' expense, so that,

---

22 Mark Fishman, *Manufacturing the News* (Austin: University of Texas Press, 1980), 143.

23 The April 14, 1986, US bombing of Libya was the first military action timed to pre-empt attention on 7 p.m. prime-time television news. See Chomsky, *Pirates & Emperors*, 147.

24 For the masterful way the Reagan administration used these to manipulate the press, see 'Standups', *The New Yorker*, 2 December 1985, 81 ff.

25 Fishman, *Manufacturing the News*, 153.

26 Its nine regional offices also had some public information operations, but personnel and funding are not readily allocable to this function. They are smaller than the central office aggregate.
   The AFSC aggregate public information budget is about the same size as the contract given by the State Department to International Business Communications (IBC) for lobbying on behalf of the contras ($419,000). This was only one of twenty-five contracts investigated by the GAO that 'the Latin American Public Diplomacy office awarded to individuals for research and papers on Central America, said a GAO official involved in the investigation' (Rita Beamish, 'Pro-contra Contracts are Probed,' *Philadelphia Inquirer*, July 22, 1987, p. 4A).

in effect, the citizenry pays to be propagandized in the interest of powerful groups such as military contractors and other sponsors of state terrorism.

Because of their services, continuous contact on the beat, and mutual dependency, the powerful can use personal relationships, threats, and rewards to further influence and coerce the media. The media may feel obligated to carry extremely dubious stories and mute criticism in order not to offend their sources and disturb a close relationship.[27] It is very difficult to call authorities on whom one depends for daily news liars, even if they tell whoppers. Critical sources may be avoided not only because of their lesser availability and higher cost of establishing credibility, but also because the primary sources may be offended and may even threaten the media using them.

Powerful sources may also use their prestige and importance to the media as a lever to deny critics access to the media. [. . .] Perhaps more important, powerful sources regularly take advantage of media routines and dependency to 'manage' the media, to manipulate them into following a special agenda and framework. Part of this management process consists of inundating the media with stories, which serve sometimes to foist a particular line and frame on the media (e.g. Nicaragua as illicitly supplying arms to the Salvadoran rebels), and at other times to help chase unwanted stories off the front page or out of the media altogether (the alleged delivery of MIGs to Nicaragua during the week of the 1984 Nicaraguan election). This strategy can be traced back at least as far as the Committee on Public Information, established to co-ordinate propaganda during World War I, which 'discovered in 1917–18 that one of the best means of controlling news was flooding news channels with "facts", or what amounted to official information'.[28]

The relation between power and sourcing extends beyond official and corporate provision of day-to-day news to shaping the supply of 'experts'. The dominance of official sources is weakened by the existence of highly respectable unofficial sources that give dissident views with great authority. This problem is alleviated by 'co-opting the experts'[29]—i.e. putting them on the payroll as consultants, funding their research, and organizing think tanks that will hire them directly and help disseminate their messages. In this way bias may be structured, and the supply of experts may be skewed in the direction desired by the government and 'the market'.[30] [. . .]

---

27 On 16 Jan. 1986, the American Friends Service Committee issued a news release, based on extended Freedom of Information Act inquiries, which showed that there had been 381 navy nuclear-weapons accidents and 'incidents' in the period 1965–77, a figure far higher than that previously claimed. The mass media did not cover this hot story directly but through the filter of the navy's reply, which downplayed the significance of the new findings and eliminated or relegated to the background the AFSC's full range of facts and interpretation of the meaning of what they had uncovered. A typical heading: 'Navy Lists Nuclear Mishaps: None of 630 Imperilled Public, Service Says', *Washington Post*, 16 Jan. 1986.

28 Stephen L. Vaughn, *Holding Fast the Inner Lines* (Chapel Hill: University of North Carolina Press, 1980), 194.

29 Bruce Owen and Ronald Braeutigam, *The Regulation Game: Strategic Use of the Administrative Process* (Cambridge, Mass.: Ballinger, 1978), 7.

30 See Edward S. Herman, 'The Institutionalization of Bias in Economics', *Media, Culture and Society* (July 1982), 275–91.

■ 4. Flak and the Enforcers: the Fourth Filter

'Flak' refers to negative responses to a media statement or programme. It may take the form of letters, telegrams, phone calls, petitions, lawsuits, speeches and bills before Congress, and other modes of complaint, threat, and punitive action. It may be organized centrally or locally, or it may consist of the entirely independent actions of individuals.

If flak is produced on a large scale, or by individuals or groups with substantial resources, it can be both uncomfortable and costly to the media. Positions have to be defended within the organization and without, sometimes before legislatures and possibly even in courts. Advertisers may withdraw patronage. Television advertising is mainly of consumer goods that are readily subject to organized boycott. During the McCarthy years, many advertisers and radio and television stations were effectively coerced into quiescence and blacklisting of employees by the threats of determined Red hunters to boycott products. Advertisers are still concerned to avoid offending constituencies that might produce flak, and their demand for suitable programming is a continuing feature of the media environment.[31] If certain kinds of fact, position, or programme are thought likely to elicit flak, this prospect can be a deterrent.

The ability to produce flak, and especially flak that is costly and threatening, is related to power. Serious flak has increased in close parallel with business's growing resentment of media criticism and the corporate offensive of the 1970s and 1980s. Flak from the powerful can be either direct or indirect. The direct would include letters or phone calls from the White House to Dan Rather or William Paley, or from the FCC to the television networks asking for documents used in putting together a programme, or from irate officials of ad agencies or corporate sponsors to media officials asking for reply time or threatening retaliation.[32] The powerful can also work on the media indirectly by complaining to their own constituencies (stockholders, employees) about the media, by generating institutional advertising that does the same, and by funding right-wing monitoring or think-tank operations designed to attack the media. They may also fund political campaigns and help put into power conservative politicians who will more directly serve the interests of private power in curbing any deviationism in the media.

Along with its other political investments of the 1970s and 1980s, the corporate community sponsored the growth of institutions such as the American Legal Foundation, the Capital Legal Foundation, the Media Institute, the Centre for Media and Public Affairs, and Accuracy in Media (AIM). These may be regarded as institutions organized for the specific purpose of producing flak. Another and older flak-producing machine with a broader design is Freedom House. [. . .]

Freedom House, which dates back to the early 1940s, has had interlocks with AIM, the World Anticommunist League, Resistance International, and US government bodies such as Radio Free Europe and the CIA, and has long served as a virtual propaganda arm of the government and international right wing. It sent election monitors to the Rhodesian elections staged by

---

31 See above, n. 21.

32 See 'The Business Campaign Against "Trial by TV" ', *Business Week*, 22 June 1980, 77–9; William H. Miller, 'Fighting TV Hatchet Jobs', *Industry Week*, 12 Jan. 1981, 61–4.

Ian Smith in 1979 and found them 'fair', whereas the 1980 elections won by Mugabe under British supervision it found dubious. Its election monitors also found the Salvadoran elections of 1982 admirable.[33] It has expended substantial resources in criticizing the media for insufficient sympathy with US foreign-policy ventures and excessively harsh criticism of US client states. Its most notable publication of this genre was Peter Braestrup's *Big Story*, which contended that the media's negative portrayal of the Tet offensive helped lose the war. The work is a travesty of scholarship, but more interesting is its premise: that the mass media not only should support any national venture abroad, but should do so with enthusiasm, such enterprises being by definition noble. In 1982, when the Reagan administration was having trouble containing media reporting of the systematic killing of civilians by the Salvadoran army, Freedom House came through with a denunciation of the 'imbalance' in media reporting from El Salvador.[34]

Although the flak machines steadily attack the mass media, the media treat them well. They receive respectful attention, and their propagandistic role and links to a larger corporate programme are rarely mentioned or analysed.

The producers of flak add to one another's strength and reinforce the command of political authority in its news-management activities. The government is a major producer of flak, regularly assailing, threatening, and 'correcting' the media, trying to contain any deviations from the established line. News management itself is designed to produce flak. In the Reagan years, Mr Reagan was put on television to exude charm to millions, many of whom berated the media when they dared to criticize the 'Great Communicator'.[35]

■ 5. Anti-Communism as a Control Mechanism

A final filter is the ideology of anti-Communism. Communism as the ultimate evil has always been the spectre haunting property owners, as it threatens the very root of their class position and superior status. The Soviet, Chinese, and Cuban revolutions were traumas to Western élites, and the ongoing conflicts and the well-publicized abuses of Communist states have contributed to elevating opposition to Communism to a first principle of Western ideology and politics. This ideology helps mobilize the populace against an enemy, and because the concept is fuzzy it can be used against anybody advocating policies that threaten property interests or support accommodation with Communist states and radicalism. It therefore helps fragment the left and labour movements and serves as a political-control mechanism. If the triumph of Communism is the worst imaginable result, the support of fascism abroad is justified as a lesser evil. Opposition to social

33 For an analysis of the bias of the Freedom House observers, see Edward S. Herman and Frank Brodhead, *Demonstration Elections: US-Staged Elections in the Dominican Republic, Vietnam, and El Salvador* (Boston: South End Press, 1984), appendix 1, 'Freedom House Observers in Zimbabwe Rhodesia and El Salvador'.

34 R. Bruce McColm, 'El Salvador: Peaceful Revolution or Armed Struggle?' *Perspectives on Freedom*, I (New York: Freedom House, 1982); James Nelson Goodsell, 'Freedom House Labels US Reports on Salvador Biased', *Christian Science Monitor*, 3 Feb. 1982.

35 George Skelton, White House correspondent for the *Los Angeles Times*, noted that in reference to Reagan's errors of fact, 'You write the stories once, twice, and you get a lot of mail saying, "You're picking on the guy, you guys in the press make mistakes too." And editors respond to that, so after a while the stories don't run anymore. We're intimidated' (quoted in Hertsgaard, 'How Reagan Seduced Us').

democrats who are too soft on Communists and 'play into their hands' is rationalized in similar terms.

Liberals at home, often accused of being pro-Communist or insufficiently anti-Communist, are kept continuously on the defensive in a cultural milieu in which anti-Communism is the dominant religion. If they allow Communism, or something that can be labelled Communism, to triumph in the provinces while they are in office, the political costs are heavy. Most of them have fully internalized the religion anyway, but they are all under great pressure to demonstrate their anti-Communist credentials. This causes them to behave very much like reactionaries. Their occasional support of social democrats often breaks down where the latter are insufficiently harsh on their own indigenous radicals or on popular groups that are organizing among generally marginalized sectors. [...]

The Kennedy liberals were enthusiastic about the military coup and displacement of a populist government in Brazil in 1964.[36] A major spurt in the growth of neo-Fascist national-security states took place under Kennedy and Johnson. In the cases of the US subversion of Guatemala, 1947–54, and the military attacks on Nicaragua, 1981–87, allegations of Communist links and a Communist threat caused many liberals to support counterrevolutionary intervention, while others lapsed into silence, paralyzed by the fear of being tarred with charges of infidelity to the national religion.

It should be noted that when anti-Communist fervour is aroused, the demand for serious evidence in support of claims of 'Communist' abuses is suspended, and charlatans can thrive as evidential sources. Defectors, informers, and assorted other opportunists move to center stage as 'experts', and they remain there even after exposure as highly unreliable, if not downright liars.

The anti-Communist control mechanism reaches through the system to exercise a proposed influence on the mass media. In normal times as well as in periods of Red scares, issues tend to be framed in terms of a dichotomised world of Communist and anti-Communist powers, with gains and losses allocated to contesting sides, and rooting for 'our side' considered an entirely legitimate news practice. The ideology and religion of anti-Communism is a potent filter.

■ **6.**
Dichotomization and Propaganda Campaigns

The five filters narrow the range of news that passes through the gates, and even more sharply limit what can become 'big news', subject to sustained news campaigns. By definition, news from primary establishment sources meets one major filter requirement and is readily accommodated by the mass media. Messages from and about dissidents and weak, unorganized individuals and groups, domestic and foreign, are at an initial disadvantage in sourcing costs and credibility, and they often do not comport with the ideology or interests of the gatekeepers and other powerful parties that influence the filtering process.[37]

36 Jan K. Black, *United States Penetration of Brazil* (Philadelphia: University of Pennsylvania Press, 1977), 39–56.

37 Where dissidents are prepared to denounce official enemies, of course, they can pass through the mass-media filtering system, in the manner of the ex-Communist experts described in §5 'Anti-Communism as a Control Mechanism'.

Thus, for example, the torture of political prisoners and the attack on trade unions in Turkey will be pressed on the media only by human-rights activists and groups that have little political leverage. The US government supported the Turkish martial-law government from its inception in 1980, and the US business community has been warm toward regimes that profess fervent anti-Communism, encourage foreign investment, repress unions, and loyally support US foreign policy (a set of virtues that are frequently closely linked). Media that chose to feature Turkish violence against their own citizenry would have had to go to extra expense to find and check out information sources; they would elicit flak from government, business, and organized right-wing flak machines, and they might be looked upon with disfavour by the corporate community (including advertisers) for indulging in such a quixotic interest and crusade. They would tend to stand alone in focusing on victims that from the standpoint of dominant American interests were *unworthy*.[38]

In marked contrast, protest over political prisoners and the violation of the rights of trade unions in Poland was seen by the Reagan administration and business élites in 1981 as a noble cause, and, not coincidentally, as an opportunity to score political points. Many media leaders and syndicated columnists felt the same way. Thus information and strong opinions on human-rights violations in Poland could be obtained from official sources in Washington, and reliance on Polish dissidents would not elicit flak from the US government or the flak machines. These victims would be generally acknowledged by the managers of the filters to be *worthy*. The mass media never explain *why* Andrei Sakharov is worthy and José Luis Massera, in Uruguay, is unworthy—the attention and general dichotomization occur 'naturally' as a result of the working of the filters, but the result is the same as if a commissar had instructed the media: 'Concentrate on the victims of enemy powers and forget about the victims of friends.'[39]

---

38 Of interest in the Turkish case is the Western press's refusal to publicize the Turkish government's attacks on the press, including the US press's own reporters in that country. UPI's reporter Ismet Imset, beaten up by the Turkish police and imprisoned under trumped-up charges, was warned by UPI not to publicize the charges against him, and UPI eventually fired him for criticizing their badly compromised handling of his case. See Chris Christiansen, 'Keeping In With The Generals', *New Statesman*, 4 Jan. 1985.

39 We believe that the same dichotomization applies in the domestic sphere. For example, both British and American analysts have noted the periodic intense focus on—and indignation over—'welfare chisellers' by the mass media, and the parallel de-emphasis of and benign attitudes toward the far more important fraud and tax abuses of business and the affluent. There is also a deep-seated reluctance on the part of the mass media to examine the structural causes of inequality and poverty. Peter Golding and Sue Middleton, after an extensive discussion of the long-standing 'criminalization of poverty' and incessant attacks on welfare scroungers in Britain, point out that tax evasion, by contrast, is 'acceptable, even laudable', in the press, that the tax evader 'is not merely a victim but a hero'. They note, also, that 'The supreme achievement of welfare capitalism' has been to render the causes and condition of poverty almost invisible (*Images of Welfare: Press and Public Attitudes to Poverty* (Oxford: Martin Robertson, 1982), 66–7, 98–100, 186, 193).

   In a chapter entitled 'The Deserving Rich', A. J. Liebling pointed out that in the United States as well, 'The crusade against the destitute is the favourite crusade of the newspaper publisher', and that 'There is no concept more generally cherished by publishers than that of the Undeserving Poor' (*The Press* (New York: Ballantine, 1964), 78–9). Liebling went into great detail on various efforts of the media to keep welfare expenses and taxes down 'by saying that they [the poor] have concealed assets, or bad character, or both' (p. 79). These strategies not only divert, they also help split the employed working class from the unemployed and marginalized, and make these all exceedingly uncomfortable about participating in a degraded system of scrounging. See Peter Golding and Sue Middleton, 'Attitudes to Claimants: A Culture of Contempt', in *Images of Welfare*, 169 ff. President

Reports of the abuses of worthy victims not only pass through the filters; they may also become the basis of sustained propaganda campaigns. If the government or corporate community and the media feel that a story is useful as well as dramatic, they focus on it intensively and use it to enlighten the public. This was true, for example, of the shooting down by the Soviets of the Korean airliner KAL 007 in early September 1983, which permitted an extended campaign of denigration of an official enemy and greatly advanced Reagan administration arms plans. As Bernard Gwertzman noted complacently in the *New York Times* of 31 August 1984, US officials 'assert that worldwide criticism of the Soviet handling of the crisis has strengthened the United States in its relations with Moscow'. In sharp contrast, the shooting down by Israel of a Libyan civilian airliner in February 1973 led to no outcry in the West, no denunciations for 'cold-blooded murder',[40] and no boycott. This difference in treatment was explained by the *New York Times* precisely on the grounds of utility: 'No useful purpose is served by an acrimonious debate over the assignment of blame for the downing of a Libyan airliner in the Sinai peninsula last week.'[41] There was a very 'useful purpose' served by focusing on the Soviet act, and a massive propaganda campaign ensued.[42]

Reagan's fabricated anecdotes about welfare chisellers, and his complete silence on the large-scale chiselling of his corporate sponsors, have fitted into a long tradition of cynical and heartless greed.

40 For a full discussion of this dichotomized treatment, see Edward S. Herman, 'Gatekeeper versus Propaganda Models: A Critical American Perspective', in Peter Golding, Graham Murdock, and Philip Schlesinger (eds.), *Communicating Politics* (New York: Holmes & Meier, 1986), 182–94.

41 Editorial, 1 March 1973. The Soviets apparently didn't know that they were shooting down a civilian plane, but this was covered up by US officials, and the false allegation of a knowing destruction of a civilian aircraft provided the basis for extremely harsh criticism of the Soviets for barbaric behaviour. The Israelis openly admitted knowing that they were shooting down a civilian plane, but this point was of no interest in the West in this particular case.

42 The *New York Times Index*, for example, has seven full pages of citations to the KAL 007 incident for September 1983 alone.

20

Market Driven Journalism: Let the Citizen Beware

John H. McManus

A Model of Commercial News Production

HOW CAN WE make sense of such a news production process? Here's a model, or explanation, of news production—in both local television and newspapers.[1]

Although the vast majority of news consumed by Americans of all latitudes, Europeans, and, since the fall of the Soviet Union, many Asians, is produced by profit-making businesses, no comprehensive model of news production has included the concept of markets. And none have used economics to explain what happens in newsrooms. The present model is a first attempt at filling both gaps.

Joseph Turow's analysis of the influences on production in any mass media industry provides a useful starting point for such a model because, unlike much media theorizing, it features a full cast of primary players. There are roles for news sources, revenue sources, consumers, investors, corporate executives, and the news department with its reporters and editors.[2] Turow defined the relationships among these players using a theory called 'resource dependence'—the notion that parties seek to avoid depending on other actors while increasing others' reliance upon themselves. In a news context, resource dependence would predict that a news source, say a city councilwoman, would try to make a media firm, such as a local TV station, depend upon her for certain types of information. As supplier of information she would exercise some control over what the public learns, an obvious advantage to a politician. At the same time she might cultivate reporters at other stations so she wouldn't have to depend upon the one station for access to the public via the evening news. For its part, the news department tries to make the councilwoman need the station more than the station needs her.

Rather than resource dependence, I'll use a similar, but broader, theory—exchange. There are three reasons: First, *exchange* better describes the relationships between media firms and outside actors such as consumers, sources, advertisers, and potential investors. Such relationships are more

Source: John H. McManus, *Market Driven Journalism: Let the Citizen Beware* (Thousand Oaks, Calif.: Sage, 1994), ch. 2, 'The Nature of News Reconsidered'.

1 Network news follows similar logic, but has several additional players.

2 Turow 1984, 1992.

often co-operative than the power struggle resource dependence implies. Second, because so much news is commercially produced, there must be an underlying economic logic to its production. Third, because what constitutes resource dependence is not as well understood as what constitutes exchange. An entire subdivision of social science is devoted to the latter—micro-economics. [. . .]

This model uses economic reasoning as an integrating concept: that each independent person and organization in the model attempts with a logic that varies in sophistication to increase its supply of what it sees as valuable by trading with others. This is not to argue that such reasoning is the *only* explanation of news production. In each relationship described, other factors enter. But what is common and central to all the relationships in the model, I contend, is a way of reasoning that is essentially economic. In other words, there is a 'bottom line' to each of these relationships, even if the participants choose to operate at a higher level.

Introducing the Players

Interactions among the nine parties in the model (see Figure 1) are powerfully shaped by the enduring values of the culture in which they take place, by laws such as those on libel and privacy, and by regulations such as those covering a station's licence renewal, and by the available technology. This relationship is reciprocal. The norms of culture, laws and regulations, even the direction of technology are all influenced by what does and doesn't become news.

■ The Environment

■ Investors

These are the owners of the media firm or its parent corporation. Because most US news media belong to 'chains' or to larger conglomerate corporations, and most of those are publicly traded on Wall Street, most investors are stockholders.[3] Stockholders exercise their will through election of, or participation on, the corporation's board of directors. The election differs from the democratic model of one person one vote. Since a stockholder's vote is weighted by the number of shares held, the greater the proportion of a company owned by a stockholder, the more influence that person has over the board of directors.

■ Parent Corporation

The parent corporation owns and oversees several media firms and perhaps non-media businesses as well. The Gannett Company, for example, owns *USA Today*, nearly ninety local daily newspapers, several broadcasting stations and a national billboard company.[4] Through the stock market, the parent corporation sells shares in the company to investors. One or more top executives of the parent corporation are usually non-elected members of the board of directors, by virtue of their position. The parent corporation's top managers serve at the pleasure of the board but often nominate board candidates who are voted upon by shareholders. Parent corporation executives

3 Bagdikian 1990.

4 Ibid.

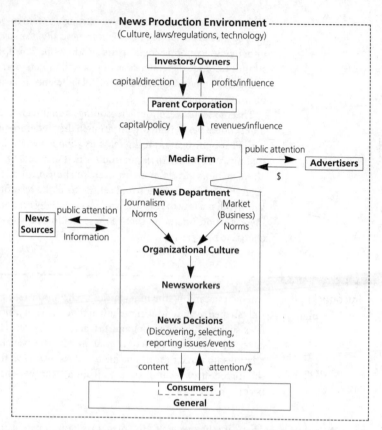

Figure 1.
A Model of Commercial
News Production

may also become substantial stockholders through options and performance clauses. These executives direct the operation of subsidiary companies by formulating policy and selecting their top managers.

■ **Media Firm**

The media firm is the local branch of the parent corporation, a single station or newspaper. It is directed by a general manager in television and a publisher in newspapers. These chief local executives are responsible to parent corporation managers and serve at their pleasure. The media firm includes a variety of departments: production, syndication, advertising sales, news, distribution, public relations, and so forth.

■ **News**
Department

This division produces the news within a given media firm and depends upon it for resources. I have chosen to use the word 'department' rather than the more common terms 'news organization' or 'news firm', because I think it's more accurate. In contemporary commercial journalism, the news is produced by a sub-unit of a media firm; not an independent company that generates its own income and reports back to the parent corporation or investors. The news director in a TV station works at the pleasure of the station's general manager. The managing editor of a newspaper works for the publisher.

In addition to being a subordinate unit of the media firm, the news department is not large enough in employee numbers nor in content production to represent the whole station or newspaper. About 90 per cent of the broadcast day for a local station is entertainment programming. Calling the station a *news* organization because of the remaining 10 per cent is misleading. Although newspaper people may consider their product to be news-centered, most of its content also is not news. About 70 per cent of the average newspaper is advertising and some of its editorial sections are explicitly designed to entertain. At most newspapers the proportion of the budget that goes into reporting is well below 20 per cent.[5] Calling television stations and newspapers *news* organizations exaggerates the importance of that function and distracts analysis from the media firm's other functions.

Within the news department a culture exists, a common set of understandings about how things are done. Although this culture differs with the department, in most newsrooms there are two sets of 'oughts', those of journalism—representing the interests of citizens; and those of business—representing the interests of investors. These govern the exchanges with parties outside the news department.[6]

The principal *norm of journalism*—whether broadcast or print—is public enlightenment: the most learning about consequential current issues and events for the largest number of persons. [. . .]

The principal *norm of business* is to maximize profits over an indefinite period.[7] Pushed by investors who seek maximum short-term returns and by pressures from mergers and buyouts, American corporations, including those in the news business, appear to be shortening the 'indefinite period' over which profits are to be maximized.[8]

Newsworkers includes all employees with a direct hand in creating news content, for example, news directors, managing editors, reporters, videographers, writers, copy editors, producers, directors, and so on.

News decisions are rarely made by consciously thinking through the components of business and journalism standards, but by reference to the organizational culture that integrates the two into practices that are rewarded, tolerated, or punished within a particular newsroom.[9] Key decisions occur at each of three stages of production.[10] The first stage of production—discovery—requires a series of decisions about how a news department shall deploy its resources to learn what is going on in the community that might be newsworthy. The second stage—selection—requires choices of which events and issues discovered in Phase 1 ought to be reported. The third stage—reporting—requires decisions about how to cover the events and issues selected in the previous step, for example, where to point the camera and whom to interview and which quotes and background to use to create a narrative account.

5 Squiers 1993.

6 Epstein 1973.

7 Main and Baird 1981.

8 Auletta 1991; Bagdikian 1990; Lambeth 1991; Shoemaker and Reese 1991; Squiers 1993.

9 Bantz 1985.

10 This is an expansion of Dimmick 1974.

In this model, newsmakers operate within constraints set by others.[11] Newsworkers are *employees* with few of the characteristics of semi-independent professionals such as doctors, engineers, lawyers, or tenured university professors. Newsworkers are not self-employed nor employed in professional partnerships. Nor are they certified or disciplined by organizations of professional peers. Nor do they elect top editors nor make policy by consensus. Nevertheless, newsworkers do have an influence over story production. Print journalists usually have more latitude than broadcast journalists because in most newspapers, reporters may originate ideas for stories, subject to approval by editors. At most stations, reporters are assigned stories by the assignment editor. Newsworkers also influence news production unconsciously because, like all humans, the 'lenses' of their personal histories and self-interest shape news. But both conscious and unwitting orientations must conform to the selection biases of the news department. There is little evidence that journalists who are out of step with the news selection orientation of their employers are tolerated.[12] [...]

News Sources News sources are the providers of the raw material of news. They include anyone reporters turn to for information—government and business officials, bureaucrats, witnesses of events, parties to issues, persons on the street.

Advertisers Advertisers are the providers of the income that fuels the enterprise. Local and national advertisers supply nearly 100 per cent of broadcast income,[13] and 70–90 per cent of newspaper revenues.[14]

News Consumers News consumers are individual viewers, and for newspapers, readers.

The General Public These are all those individuals in a society who do not consume news from the media firm under study.

Primary Relationships Given the nature of American culture and its market-based economy, commercial media firms must compete for necessary resources in four markets—one each for investors, sources of news, advertisers, and news consumers.

■ 1. Between Investors and Parent Corporation Turow defined this relationship as one where investors contribute capital to establish or upgrade the corporation and set general operating conditions. In return, investors expect profits. Because news creates the images of reality upon which people act, investors may also expect influence or prestige. Such influence could be broad—perhaps improving society by producing useful

11 Entman 1989: ch. 2.; Reese 1990; Soloski 1989; Weaver and Wilhoit 1986.

12 Breed 1955; Reese 1990; Sigalman 1973; Soloski 1989.

13 Local TV revenues come primarily from advertisements the station sells directly to local and national advertisers. Some national advertising revenues collected by the networks are also passed along to stations through 'clearance' fees—what the network pays for a local station to 'clear', or broadcast, network programmes. See Owen, Beebe, and Manning 1974.

14 Udell 1978.

goods or services—or more specific—perhaps gaining political or business advantage. The parent corporation sells its stock to investors for whatever the market will bear. If the profitability of the stock falls below the competition, so does its price and thus the amount of capital available to the corporation for expansion or improvement. Any fall in stock price, of course, also diminishes the wealth of current stockholders, including managers. Public trading also makes the corporation vulnerable to buyout by investors who believe they can generate larger profits than current management. Thus pressure on the firm to maximize profits is exerted from above not only by current investors, but also by prospective ones. The exchange between investors and the parent firm differs from all of the others in the production of commercial news in that investors gain explicit influence within the corporation.[15] The other three trading partners—news sources, advertisers, and consumers—exercise their influence from outside the corporate structure. In the investor–parent corporation relationship, ownership subordinates the purposes of management of the parent company to those of investors. In fact, management has a legal responsibility to serve the economic interest of owners.

■ **2. Between Parent Corporation and Media Firm**

Parent corporation management allocates capital and sets company policy under the broader dictates of the board of directors, and it chooses media firm executives. In return for direction and capital, the parent corporation collects revenues from the firm for disbursement either in profits to shareholders or to allocate to other business properties. The parent corporation also channels influence upward from the news department. As corporate executives act as subordinates to investors, local managers of firms are responsible to corporate headquarters and serve at its pleasure. The parent corporation can serve as a levelling agent for its corporate 'children'. One firm's profits can be siphoned off to aid a struggling sibling station or newspaper or company in a non-media business, or to pay off debts from mergers or expansions.[16]

■ **3. Between Media Firm and the News Department**

Besides hiring and firing the chief newsroom manager, the media firm's executive—in television the general manager and in newspapers the publisher—sets the news department's budget and audience goals. General news policy is also established.

In newspapers, the proportion of the media firm's revenues spent on the news department apparently has been falling over the past decade.[17] In television, however, news departments have become more important. Local newscasts affect the station's bottom line more than you might expect given the approximately 10 per cent of air time and 15 per cent of station revenues[18]

15 A few media firms, most notably The New York Times Company, have created two tiers of stock, voting and nonvoting, in an effort to maintain family control over company policy. Although offering some protection from hostile takeover, stock issued without voting rights has less value than that with such rights because it deprives the shareholder from exercising influence to maximize return.

16 Auletta 1991; Squiers 1993.

17 Squiers 1993.

18 Helregal 1991.

they consume. For stations affiliated with networks, local news is one of the few programming slots over which local management exercises much control. The content of network programming is decided in New York. For such programming, the station receives a clearance fee—a part of the advertising revenues the network collects for the show, and a limited number of open 'spots'—30-second periods that a station can sell to advertisers directly. The spots are usually more valuable than the clearance fees because the fees are shared with hundreds of other stations airing the network programme. For locally originated programmes such as news, however, all commercial time—usually about 16 minutes per hour (or 32 'spots') are sold by the station. Nothing has to be shared. An inexpensive and popular newscast, therefore, profits the station more than a similar amount of programme time turned over to the network.

A second reason why local newscasts disproportionately affect stations' profits is what broadcasters call the 'halo effect'. Viewers tend to identify the station with its news personalities, particularly its anchor men and women. Parasocial 'friendships' or trust relationships built with the news team appear to create an allegiance that carries over to the station's other programmes. As a result, the station whose newscasts attract the largest audiences may improve its ratings for the rest of the broadcast day as well.[19] Part of this 'halo' is explained by the position of news at noon and in the early evening. A popular newscast provides audience flow (viewers who watch a programme primarily because they were already tuned to that channel) to later entertainment programming on the same station.

A third reason for the economic importance of local news to a station is the growing competition for viewers. This rising competition has not affected local news and other—largely entertainment—programming equally. The addition of independent televisions stations, cable stations, and rental of videotapes has vastly expanded viewer choice everywhere but in local news. The Cable News Network and C-Span, for example, greatly expand choice for national and international news among cable subscribers. Sports lovers can now watch athletes compete day and night on ESPN and there are channels for pornography connoisseurs, for cartoon aficionados, rock music lovers, and many other segments of the viewership. By contrast, the competition in local news has increased only slightly. The variety of entertainment now available has reduced the audience share for the typical station's news programmes. But the spectrum of choice has drained a greater proportion of the viewership for entertainment programming because little local news comes through the cable and none from the VCR.[20]

Although many stations with unpopular newscasts still earn substantial profits,[21] local news has become the station's most important commodity.

■ **4. Between News Sources and News Department**

[…] From the exchange perspective, sources co-operate with reporters to the extent that sources believe they and/or their ideas will gain favourable public access. Sources can judge such access in three ways: character and quantity of

19 Sabreen 1985: 24.

20 Baldwin, Barrett, and Bates 1992.

21 Helregal 1991.

audience, character and quantity of content, and prestige of editorial environment. First, audience. Not only do sources usually want to reach as many people as possible, certain qualities of those persons are important. The most valuable are those readers or viewers in a position to help sources achieve their goals—people such as political constituents, potential supporters, customers, investors, and so on.[22] Second, content. Positively framed coverage beats neutral or critical reporting. A frame is the tone or spin or slant the story adopts—whether the sources quoted and the material supplied by the reporter without attribution is more supportive or critical. Quantity also counts; extended favourable or neutral quotes are likely to have more impact on the audience than a quick quote, or 'sound bite'. Third, editorial environment. Coverage in a prestige news product, such as *The New York Times*, may influence consumer attitudes toward a source more authoritatively than reportage in a less respected one. Coverage by prestige news departments also conveys a secondary audience when that department sets the agenda of other news departments. The tone adopted in the prestige coverage is also likely to be duplicated.[23] [...]

News departments, for their part, seek information that will interest and/or inform consumers at the least cost. The greater the volume and quality of such information a source controls at a given cost, the greater the motivation of reporters to use that source.[24]

■ **5. Between Advertisers and Media Firm**

Robert Picard, a media economist, described this relationship as an explicit exchange.[25] Advertisers pay for the public attention the media firm delivers based on independently gathered statistical estimates of the size, wealth, and stage in life of the consuming group. In general, the larger the audience, the greater their wealth, the greater the proportion in the highest consuming age bracket (those establishing or expanding homes), the more valuable the advertising space is to retailers and the higher the fees stations or newspapers may charge. Here again there is an environmental dimension. Advertisers value news environments that create what Bagdikian calls 'a buying mood'— a curiosity about and a desire to possess goods and services that is generated by purported news content.[26] Examples of such content are stories—or whole sections of newspapers—extolling the virtues of new automobiles, computers, the joys of home ownership, of gardening, of fashion, and so forth. As a corollary, a supportive environment would also exclude or downplay news that denigrated advertised products, services, or companies. Advertisers also value a second aspect of the news environment: Advertisements surrounded by news content that consumers find believable may gain credibility for their claims by association.[27]

22 Jamieson 1992.

23 Reese 1991.

24 Gans 1979.

25 Picard 1989.

26 Bagdikian 1990.

27 Meyer 1987.

■ **6. Between News Consumers and News Department**

This relationship is also based on an exchange. The consumer's attention is traded for information. Consider the advice a prominent news executive gave fellow local broadcasters:

> A marketing approach demands that we treat a newscast as a consumer durable good, a commodity that a viewer 'purchases' by spending time watching it. We must understand that when a viewer watches a specific television program, the viewer really is spending a precious resource: time. And time for many people is spent as carefully as money.[28]

Researchers have argued not only that viewers 'invest' their time in news, but that many apply a rudimentary cost-benefit analysis. The likelihood of a consumer choosing a particular news product is proportional to the amount or intensity of some expected reward—being informed and/or entertained—relative to the effort or cost thought to be required to gain the reward.[29] For its part, the news department seeks the attention of various audiences both for journalistic purposes and to sell to advertisers.[30] Newspapers differ from broadcast media in this exchange. In addition to their attention, subscribers must pay a direct charge for the newspaper, but almost always somewhat less than the actual cost because of the advertisers' subsidy.

■ **7. Between News Consumers and the General Public**

Not all members of the public watch or read the news from a particular media firm. So differences can arise between the consumers of one news department's products and those who consume another's or don't keep up with news. If the informational differences are significant, cultural and economic divisions can follow. The dotted line separating consumers from the rest of the public indicates that while the two groups differ in access to information, interpersonal news-telling creates a permeable boundary.

Who Has the Most Power?

If you look back at the model introduced as Figure 1, it may look a bit like a Rube Goldberg contraption: no pulleys, but lots of boxes and arrows. Where does one drop the pinball to get it all started? Is there one player that sets the conditions for all of the others? Scholars disagree. Robert Entman and Philip Meyer pointed to the consumers as the key players.[31] Herbert Gans said news media are caught in a tug-of-war between powerful sources and consumers.[32] J. Herbert Altschull argued that 'whoever pays the piper calls the tune'. In this case that would be the advertisers.[33] Joseph Turow also nominated the advertisers or 'patrons',[34] but later settled on the owners.[35]

---

28 Sabreen 1985: 24.

29 Rivers, Schramm and Christians 1980.

30 Picard 1989.

31 Entman 1989; Meyer 1987.

32 Gans 1979.

33 Altschull 1984.

34 Turow 1984.

35 Turow 1992.

Ben Bagdikian and news critic Robert Squiers fingered the owners and large investors.[36] Conservatives such as Robert Lichter, Stanley Rothman, and Linda Lichter argued that liberal reporters are in charge.[37] Critics from the left, such as Edward Herman and Noam Chomsky, pointed to the rich and powerful within society.[38]

Within the environmental framework of current US laws, culture, and technology, I would argue that the primary role is played by major investors[39] and owners. Of course commercial news departments must pay attention to consumer tastes. And to the degree that they are supported by advertisers, media firms must provide them competitive vehicles for their messages if they are to stay in business themselves. And news departments must maintain access to news sources. The degree of control exercised by these outside forces, however, rarely matches the influence investors/owners wield through top management. Of the four trading partners—consumers, advertisers, sources, and investors—only the last is also a boss. [. . .]

Conclusion   The present model suggests that primary news decisions—about how to learn what's going on outside the newsroom, about selecting from among those events and issues a subset to cover, about what to report in each story—are quite complex. In light of instructions from owners/investors and profit demand from the market for investors—which are channeled through corporate headquarters and media firm management—and guided by an organizational culture combining business and journalistic standards, the media firm competes in markets for investors, sources, advertisers, and consumers. Thus news, rather than the 'reflection of reality' that its producers have sometimes claimed it to be,[40] becomes a commodity to fit the market demands of a collection of special interests. As such, it is an elaborate compromise.

References   ALTSCHULL, J. H. (1984), *Agents of power* (New York: Longman).

AULETTA, K. (1991), *Three Blind Mice* (New York: Random House).

BAGDIKIAN, B. (1990), *The Media Monopoly* (Boston: Beacon).

BALDWIN, T. F., BARRETT, M., and BATES, B. (1992), 'Influence of Cable on Television News Audiences, *Journalism Quarterly*, 69: 651–8.

BANTZ, C. R. (1985), 'News Organizations: Conflict as a Crafted Cultural Norm', *Communication*, 8: 225–44.

BOZELL, L. B., and BAKER, B. H. (1990), *And that's the Way it Isn't: A Reference Guide to Media Bias* (Alexandria, Va.: Media Research Center).

---

36 Bagdikian 1990; Squiers 1993.

37 Lichter, Rothman, and Lichter 1986. See also Bozell and Baker 1990.

38 Herman and Chomsky 1988.

39 Major investors are defined by the federal Securities and Exchange Commission as 'insiders'. They hold 5 per cent or more of the corporation's outstanding shares of stock. Because of their powerful position, they and top executives are required to report their trading of the stock.

40 Epstein 1973, quoting the congressional testimony of CBS News president Frank Stanton, Ph.D.

DIMMICK, J. (1974), 'The gatekeeper: An uncertainty theory', *Journalism Monographs*, 37.

ENTMAN, R. M. (1989), *Democracy without Citizens* (New York: Oxford University Press).

EPSTEIN, E. J. (1973), *News from Nowhere: Television and the News* (New York: Random House).

GANS, H. J. (1979), *Deciding What's News* (New York: Pantheon).

HELREGAL, B. (ed.) (1991), *1991 Television Financial Report* (Washington, DC: National Association of Broadcasters).

HERMAN, E., and CHOMSKY, N. (1988), *Manufacturing Consent* (New York: Pantheon).

JAMIESON, K. H. (1992), *Dirty Politics* (New York: Oxford University Press).

LAMBETH, E. (1991), 'Gene Roberts: A Case for Leadership', *The Quill* (June): 14–24.

LICHTER, S. R., Rothman, S., and Lichter, L. (1986), *The Media Elite: America's New Powerbrokers* (Bethesda, Md.: Adler & Adler).

MAIN, R. S., and BAIRD, C. W. (1981), *Elements of Microeconomics* (2nd edn. St Paul, Minn.: West).

MEYER, P. (1987), *Ethical Journalism* (New York: Longman).

OWEN, B., BEEBE, J., and MANNING, W. (1974), *Television Economics* (Lexington, Mass.: D. C. Heath).

PICARD, R. G. (1989), *Media Economics* (Newbury Park, Calif.: Sage).

REESE, S. D. (1990), 'The News Paradigm and the Ideology of Objectivity: A Socialist at *The Wall Street Journal*', *Critical Studies in Mass Communication, 7*: 390–409.

—— (1991), 'Setting the Media's Agenda: A Power Balance Perspective', in J. A. Anderson (ed.), *Communication Yearbook 14* (Newbury Park, Calif.: Sage), 309–40.

RIVERS, W. L., SCHRAMM, W. L., and CHRISTIANS, C. G. (1980), *Responsibility in Mass Communication* (3rd edn. New York: Harper & Row).

SABREEN, R. (1985), 'News Is No Longer Enough', *Broadcasting* (26 Aug.): 24.

SHOEMAKER, P. J., and REESE, S. D. (1991), *Mediating the Message* (New York: Longman).

SIGALMAN, L. (1973), 'Reporting the News: An Organizational Analysis', *American Journal of Sociology, 79*: 132–51.

SOLOSKI, J. (1989), 'News Reporting and Professionalism: Some Constraints on the Reporting of News', *Media, Culture and Society,* 11: 207–28.

SQUIERS, J. D. (1993), *Read All about It* (New York: Random House).

TUROW, J. (1984), *Media Industries* (New York: Longman).

—— (1992), *Media Systems in Society* (New York: Longman).

UDELL, J. G. (1978), *The Economics of the American Newspaper* (New York: Hastings House).

21

World News Duopoly

Jeremy Tunstall

THE FLOW OF news around the world is dominated by two countries, the US and Britain, and in particular by the US Associated Press and the British Reuters. These two agencies are the leading news suppliers around the world, not only in text (aimed mainly at newspapers), but in still photographs, graphics, foreign video news for TV and also in financial news.

The United States is the world leader in terms of selling its foreign news—its daily world views and news—around the world. Depending upon the criteria adopted, either Britain or the rest of Europe would come second with the other third. There is no important candidate for fourth place; although the Japanese media are big gatherers of foreign news, they have few foreign customers for their world view.

Leading players in the US world news team include Associated Press and Cable News Network (CNN) but the special strength of the US lies in its major newspapers which also sell and syndicate news to other news organizations.

Britain has three world leaders in specific foreign news categories: Reuters (the largest of all foreign news operations), the BBC (probably the leading conventional broadcaster of foreign news) and the *Financial Times* (which claims the world's largest newspaper foreign correspondent team). On a lower level Britain has another four or five press groupings with some foreign news significance.

Western Europe is even more difficult to score. But it has in Eurovision the world's largest video news exchange—which spreads beyond Europe into Africa and Asia. No other continent has a collection of news agencies comparable to the world wide Agence France-Presse (AFP), the German DPA and the Spanish EFE (widely rated as first or first equal across all of Latin America). Western Europe is also unique in its high number of both newspapers and broadcast networks which each employ more than token numbers of foreign correspondents; Germany, France, Italy, Spain, and the Netherlands have some of the world's best foreign news, but very little of this foreign news is sold even to other European countries' media. Nevertheless, if western Europe is defined—in the most obvious way—as including

Source: Jeremy Tunstall, *The Anglo-American Media Connection* (Oxford: Oxford University Press, 1999).

Britain, then western Europe offers serious competition to the USA for the title of world news leader.[1]

All three leading British news players—Reuters, BBC, *Financial Times*—have increasingly oriented themselves towards Europe; with the break-up of the USSR, Europe (west and east) is the world's leading news market, and, although AP does offer a domestic German language service, AP is heavily outgunned within Europe by Reuters.

However, only the US and British news operators are genuinely world players. It is also evident that Agence France-Presse is really a French flag-carrier (subsidized by the French Government); but all of the Anglo-American world news players are the flag-carriers of larger media organizations. Reuters news carries the flag for Reuters financial data; BBC news carries the flag for BBC entertainment, the *Financial Times* carries the flag for the Pearson company.

In the United States this news flag-carrying for bigger commercial media operations has grown more pronounced. Along with the old newspapers and their owning families, we now see substantial elements of the Hollywood/Network combines using major news operations as corporate flag carriers. CNN is the proud prestige news operation of Time-Warner. Fox, NBC, and CBS all indicated in the 1990s their ambition to run international news networks.

This common view of news as corporate flag-carrier is only one of several elements in common between the leading American and British news players. There is a tendency, for example, to employ each others' citizens. London-based Reuters employs numerous Americans. Stephen Hess reports that of 400 American media foreign correspondents in 1992, some 32 were actually British citizens. Britain also seemed to be the only foreign country from which American media would accept foreign news. Stephen Hess found that in 1992 four large American dailies (average 323,000 circulation) took about 60 per cent of their longer foreign stories from AP, 20 per cent from the *New York Times* and 10 per cent from Reuters; all other sources (including their own correspondents) made up the final 10 per cent.[2]

When in the field, journalists tend to work in co-operation with colleagues from other news organizations. Because *New York Times* correspondents regard the Associated Press as a competitor, they often 'work with' Reuters correspondents in the field; in the past the *NYT* and other US newspapers actually transmitted their stories back home over Reuters facilities. This was the situation at the height of the Vietnam war in 1968. During the Tet offensive in 1968, American newspaper correspondents in general—and *New York Times* journalists in particular—used the Reuters office as a base for covering the street fighting in Saigon.[3]

1 Jeremy Tunstall, 'Europe as World News Leader', *Journal of Communication*, 42 (Summer 1992), 84–99.

2 Stephen Hess, *International News and Foreign Correspondents* (Washington: The Brookings Institution, 1996), 55, 93.

3 Peter Braestrup, *The Big Story* (Boulder, Colo.: Westview Press, 1977), i. 9–14, 47–51, 69–72, 104–17.

British Strength in Elite World News

Modern journalism was an Anglo-American invention.[4] France also played some part in this invention, especially through its news agency, Havas. But France lagged behind in the development of the élite newspaper; well into the twentieth century the leading French newspapers accepted corrupt subsidies from commercial interests and even from foreign governments.[5]

Elite journalism involved monitoring national and international politics and finance, and doing so without subsidy from government, from political party or from special interest. This pattern of élite journalism was largely invented by *The Times* of London in and around the 1840s. Some American newspapers after 1865 increasingly carried foreign news, although they initially did so in a more popular manner, for example by focusing on wars and somewhat fanciful accounts of heroic explorers.[6] Gradually, however, the *New York Times* drew level with *The Times* of London. Certainly by 1940 the US was the clear leader in world news.

Reuters used its position as the semi-official news agency of the British empire to become the world news leader between 1870 and 1914. But from 1914 right through to the 1960s Reuters struggled to compete with the American agencies; Reuters lacked the huge media home base of AP and its then domestic competitors (UP and INS). In 1942 Reuters and Associated Press signed a wartime news swapping agreement which effectively created a fresh news cartel controlled by the US and Britain. Reuters, in fact, in both world wars was embarrassingly dependent on the British government; well into the 1960s an effective subsidy was fed by the British government into Reuters via the BBC world service.[7] Reuters management in the 1960s decided to seek a new source of revenue; Reuters entered into computerized financial data, arguing that a big news event (such as the Kennedy assassination of 1963) was both a financial, and a general news, story. Reuters' computerized data activities were spectacularly successful especially in Europe, but also around the world.

The BBC is Britain's second world player in élite news. Like Reuters, BBC news has established a world reputation as perhaps the least biased and most reliable international news service in its field. Previous to the late 1980s the BBC had wastefully operated three largely separate networks of foreign correspondents—one set of foreign correspondents for domestic radio, one for domestic television and a third different team of foreign correspondents for the external radio service. The 1996 changes (see Table 1) incorporated all of these entities into a combined domestic UK and international news operation.

---

4 Jeremy Tunstall, *The Media Are American* (New York: Columbia University Press, 1977), 13–37.

5 Jean K. Chalaby, 'Journalism as an Anglo-American Invention', *European Journal of Communication*, 11/2 (September 1996), 303–26.

6 Beau Riffenburgh, *The Myth of the Explorer: the Press, Sensationalism and Geographical Discovery* (Oxford: Oxford University Press, 1993).

7 Donald Read, *The Power of News: the history of Reuters* (Oxford: Oxford University Press, 1992), 329–31.

TABLE 1. *BBC Foreign news correspondents (and producers), 1997*

Offices	Journalists
7 *Hub Bureaux* (Brussels, Washington, Moscow, Jerusalem, Hong Kong, Delhi, Johannesburg	33
8 *Second-Tier Bureaux* (New York, Paris, Geneva, Rome, Nairobi, Singapore, Beijing, Tokyo)	18
27 *'Stringer' Bureaux* (e.g. Abidjan, Amman, Ankara, Bangkok, Belgrade)	29
TOTAL:	80
World Regions	
Europe	27
Asia	22
USA	11
Africa	8
Mid-East	6
Latin America	4
Australia	2
TOTAL:	80

Source: BBC

The third British-based news player is the *Financial Times*, which now has much the largest British newspaper team of foreign correspondents. The *Wall Street Journal* is certainly the world's leading financial daily, but the *Financial Times* substantially outsells it on the continent of Europe. The *Wall Street Journal* prints each day in four European locations and four Asian locations. The *Financial Times* prints each day in five European locations outside Britain, in two Asian locations and in three US locations. These two financial dailies have quite a lot in common; both grew rapidly after 1950 with the expansion of the New York and London financial markets. The *Wall Street Journal* became the biggest selling US daily by printing in many locations across the continent. Both the *WSJ* and the *FT* were effective monopolies, growing, making profits and well aware of their power in their respective financial worlds. Both papers observed the electronic explosion of news agency activity from the 1960s. Both newspapers were cautious about jumping into the international market; then the *Wall Street Journal* suggested a combined *WSJ–FT* European financial daily. When these negotiations broke down, the *Wall Street Journal* initially avoided taking on the *FT* in Europe and launched a Hong Kong printed *Asian Wall Street Journal* in 1976, taking advantage of the US civilianization of space. The *Financial Times* began its first foreign printing in Frankfurt in 1979, initially flying copies from Frankfurt to the USA each night. Both papers found that additional local printings were quite cheap to launch; the main requirements for a new print were to generate some significant additional advertising and also to have some prospect of selling an extra 10,000 daily copies.

Anglo-American Video News for the Global Mass Audience

Most of the foreign video news shown on the world's TV screens comes from two video news agencies—one British-owned, one US-owned—both based in London. Probably well over one billion people each week around the world see at least a few minutes of these agencies' foreign news stories. This is the truly global, and truly mass market, TV foreign news service. These two agencies—Reuters TV and APTV—deliver each week at least a few minutes of video stories to over one billion people; CNN delivers bigger hunks (hours, not minutes) of news around the world to a much smaller niche audience, totalling at most a few tens of millions, or a few percent of the two agencies' much broader, but briefer, reach.

After 1991 the United States domestic TV audience watched less and less foreign news on the main TV networks. By 1996 each of the big three US networks' supposedly half hour evening news shows averaged just one foreign item per day or some 87 seconds of material 'filed by reporters with a foreign deadline' (The Tyndall Report). This amount had roughly halved since the big foreign news (1988–91) days of the Soviet break-up and the Gulf War. NBC, the most popular network in this period, was showing the least foreign news; and nearly half of all US adults seldom or never watched TV network news.

Each of the two 'global' video news services is in fact a relatively small news organization based in London. Each of the video news services is attached to a larger media organization. Reuters TV generates only about 2 per cent of the total revenue of Reuters; this agency has newsreel, British Commonwealth and BBC elements in its history and was called Visnews previous to being absorbed into Reuters. APTV is the video news operation of the other giant news agency, Associated Press of New York. A third video agency, WTN (Worldwide TV News) was in the past linked to the UPI news agency and was called UPITN; it was subsequently controlled by the ABC TV part of the Disney–ABC merged company. This latter connection led competitors to express surprise at Mickey Mouse's newfound interest in world news; such scepticism was shown to be valid, when in 1998 Disney–ABC gave up on WTN, which was merged into APTV.

Foreign news for television is costly to collect. Even the big American networks now have few foreign bureaux, because one TV bureau involves several people, high rents and living expenses, travel, extensive equipment, satellite links back home, and so on. Consequently all significant TV networks in the world (including the main US and European ones) rely upon the video agencies to supply a basic foreign news service. A London video agency typically supplies several TV networks in each of the main country markets; this is why viewers, switching between channels, can see the identical foreign material, edited in slightly different ways. Even a TV network which has its own correspondent and camera on the ground in the war zone, will still mix its own material together with video agency footage.

An agency like Reuters TV has over 400 client networks in the world to which it supplies satellite news feeds every day (in some cases several times a day). A typical Reuters satellite feed lasts 20 to 25 minutes and includes fifteen to twenty separate stories from perhaps a dozen separate countries. An American network might use only 20 seconds, while an African network might use 10 minutes or more on its evening news. Reuters TV sends out from London around fifteen to seventeen satellite feeds per day, scheduled for appropriate TV news timings in particular world regions; other Reuters feeds go out from regional hub offices. This totals between 100 and 150 satellite feeds per week, or perhaps 2,000 story-feeds per week.

A biggish receiving TV network might be paying $1 million or £500,000 for a year's supply of about 100 hours of foreign news film. As seen by the video agency this is an unrealistically low price, but a traditional news agency dilemma is evident here. Networks (like newspapers) are accustomed to getting agency news cheap.

Reuters TV and APTV originate the great bulk of their own video output; video journalists, operating from Reuters and AP offices around the world, generate video coverage which is passed back to London by satellite. In London the news receives substantial editing before being included in one or more world region feeds.

This international video news agency business is now in its third historical phase. In the first phase, up to the late 1970s, the news film travelled by air and Visnews was located in west London near to Heathrow airport and photographic laboratory back-up; in that era news film often took two or three days to reach its final destination. From the late 1970s there was a new era of videotape and satellite transmission, which allowed quicker and more complex patterns of distribution.

Until the mid-1990s the video news agency business was a relatively tranquil duopoly. There were numerous new network customers—many new commercial TV channels and a post-Communist TV boom in eastern Europe and Central Asia. All of this was good for the then two dominant companies, Reuters (Visnews) and WTN. However in 1994–5 a third player—Associated Press—entered the business; APTV brought significant competitive turbulence, because it initially charged low prices. It was accused by its competitors of predatory pricing, or of 'buying market share by giving the service away for free'. AP had left its entry to a surprisingly late date. AP was finally convinced that the new digital and Internet era would 'need multimedia services'.

APTV followed the approach of the other video agencies by dividing the world into three regions—the Americas, Asia, and Europe–Africa. London was chosen as the base location for what was intended to be a more international AP. Indeed the APTV service was centralized to an extreme degree, with even Latin American news being routed through, and edited in, London.

Meanwhile all three of these agencies found themselves experiencing fierce competition and facing unwelcome dilemmas. WTN was claiming to be the only profitable video news agency. WTN was engaging in a lengthy list of non-news commercial activities for British government departments, Mastercard Football and Merrill Lynch financial briefings. WTN also had a special daily entertainment feature service through which it was even recycling some material originating from its Disney parent. But in 1998

Disney–ABC gave up the video news agency business, which thus reverted to a familiar duopoly pattern.

All News TV Networks: For the News Addict and from the Large Media Organization

The non-stop all-news TV network is a prestige niche offering for the smallish numbers of all-news addicts. Consequently only the largest and most determined media organizations can be serious players of the all-news TV game.

All-news television was made possible by the explosion of channel capacity in the US around 1980. It was driven by the apparent success of Ted Turner's CNN; and it was subsequently sustained by big media companies' organizational urge to include all-news offerings in their emerging portfolios (or bouquets) of programming streams. The currently leading players in the all-news TV game are the largest American Hollywood-and-Network companies and the BBC.

CNN was modelled in part on the established all-news radio format. Turner borrowed the radio concept of repeating the news frequently during the day. Some people saw this as really a breakfast news show warmed up and served at all times in the 24 hours. CNN (and CNN Headline) became the prestige item within a bigger Turner package of entertainment offerings, including TBS and TNT. Turner exploited the Atlanta location, and the weakness of local trade unions, to pay much lower than New York salary levels. His timing was lucky in technology terms; satellite capacity was getting cheaper, and the television newsroom computer system was just coming on stream.

CNN by the later 1980s was in nearly all cable-subscribing American homes. But CNN remained the sole all-news TV channel in the world until 1989. The second such channel to appear was Sky News, offered as part of Rupert Murdoch's Sky package in Britain. Sky News also lost money, and was heavily subsidized both in its Sky form and then in its BSkyB form (after the late 1990 merger). Sky News was heavily dependent on WTN agency material, and on American ABC news; ABC's 8 a.m. breakfast news was served 'live' to British viewers at 1 p.m.

During the 1990s CNN faced all-news competition from NBC/CNBC, Fox, CBS, Bloomberg, and Dow Jones. CNN followed the common subdivision strategy, leading to CNN, CNN Headline, CNNfn (financial news), and CNNSI (sports news). Meanwhile after its Gulf War (1990–1) rating success, CNN found ratings falling, while its best audiences tended to be attracted by sensational murder cases (such as O. J. Simpson in 1995 and Karla Fay Tucker who was executed in Texas in 1998).

Nevertheless Time-Warner (and Ted Turner) were clearly determined to maintain the genre lead and to put extra pressure on their competitors by strong promotion of CNN International. Very soon after its 1980 launch, CNN began feeding its service to foreign broadcasters and to 'international' hotel rooms. CNN International formally launched as a separate entity in 1985. In part CNNI was simply building up the foreign bureaux which a credible domestic CNN news service needed. CNNI also relied heavily on Visnews/Reuters TV, CBC (Canada), and ITN (Britain).

Gradually during the 1990s CNN built up its European audiences and became (along with MTV and Eurosport) one of only three profitable pan-European networks. Nevertheless CNNI still faces a hard struggle in seeking to become a genuinely global operation.

The BBC is the leading non-American example of a media organization which is providing all-news both nationally and on a worldwide basis. By 1997 the BBC was carrying some news on each of twelve radio and TV networks:

- The radio (music) networks—BBC 1, 2, and 3—carried brief news summaries.

- Two radio networks (Radio 4 and BBC local radio) and three TV networks (BBC1, BBC2, and BBC Interactive) carried substantial amounts of news and comment.

- The BBC already had no less than four all-news networks. These were Radio 5 (news and sport), BBC World Service radio, BBC 24 (the domestic TV all-news service) and its international TV partner, BBC World.

This array of radio and TV as well as domestic and international networks means that—across these entire twelve networks—a single news story can be used and re-used several dozen times. By possessing so many networks, including its BBC1 and BBC2 domestic TV channels, the BBC has an unusual degree of flexibility; exceptional news events can receive the all-news treatment on one of the two domestic TV nets.

The Financialization of News

Financial news has, since the end of the Cold War, become more and more central to news and journalism. This trend plays to the strengths of the dozen leading international news suppliers. Three of these (Reuters, *Wall Street Journal, Financial Times*) specialize in financial news; a fourth, Associated Press, is involved with Dow Jones (owner of the *WSJ*) in the AP–Dow Jones financial service. In addition, most leading newspapers today follow the *New York Times* in devoting a substantial fraction of their pages to financial and business news.[8]

But the biggest changes have occurred at Reuters, at AP–Dow Jones, at NBC and with the insurgent Bloomberg company. Reuters in the 1970s and 1980s changed from being a news agency into an electronic financial data company. News (text, pictures, video) now generates about 7 per cent of Reuters' $5 billion annual revenue.

Michael Bloomberg launched his on-screen financial data company in 1982; the London office opened in 1987, with other offices following in most European countries. Bloomberg revenue reached $1 billion in 1997. The core of this company's business is the Bloomberg terminal on the desk of the financial market trader or analyst. The book, *Bloomberg by Bloomberg*[9] was a financial mogul demonstrating his skills as a bravura self-publicist; we also

---

8 For more detail on Britain, see: Jeremy Tunstall, *Newspaper Power* (Oxford: Oxford University Press, 1996), 354–73.

9 *Bloomberg by Bloomberg* (New York: John Wiley, 1997).

saw a fully qualified own-and-operate media mogul with a highly personal and belligerent management style. He explained why he decided also to enter the media—Bloomberg radio and television news, magazines, a financial pages service for newspapers, a news wire service, book publishing and, of course, the Bloomberg Web Site. The media publicity, the eternal media repetition of the Bloomberg name, would help to sell terminals.

Previous to Bloomberg's arrival, the financial data business had been dominated by Dow Jones and by Reuters. The main casualty of Bloomberg's arrival was the Dow Jones Telerate service. Following two decades of rapid and profitable growth, Reuters also was somewhat shaken by the appearance of new competitors in general and of Bloomberg in particular. But Reuters needed to stay in news for the same reason that Michael Bloomberg had wanted to get into news; news both for Reuters and Bloomberg was the visible few per cent of the iceberg.

Reuters' commitment to data has caused uneasiness among some Reuters journalists for at least two decades. The financialization of news has many strange consequences. Marxist-sounding phrases such as the 'commodification of news' are uttered by financial journalists with otherwise impeccably right-wing and free market views. There do seem to be genuine conflicts of interest. For example, Reuters makes much of its revenue from large-scale trading in shares and currencies; the more movement and insecurity in the financial markets, the more Reuters is taking commissions from (literally) hundreds of billions of dollars of weekly currency hedging and trading.

Dominating the World News: But for What?

Why are they doing all this? Senior people deny any complex non-profit motivation: 'When I hear the word Synergy I reach for my wallet,' and 'Nobody does anything for prestige any more.' One reason for a certain vagueness on these matters is that, if sums of money are being lost on, for example, the video news agencies, these sums are not big. The entire US and international news operations of both AP and Reuters combined still cost less than $1 billion annually in the late 1990s.

Another source of vagueness is the strong tendency towards Anglo-American duopoly. Associated Press and Reuters bestride the news agendas and news flows of the world. Each can be quietly happy about the other. Associated Press exerts a degree of dominance over domestic United States news which would not be tolerated in the cement business or even the movie business. But AP can happily point out that, in Reuters, it has a formidable competitor.

As the duopolistic wielders of a unique kind of power—'the power of news' around the world and in multiple fast news formats—the American AP and the British Reuters are almost entirely unregulated. Even if they normally behave with self-restraint, and normally justify their reputation for accuracy, AP and Reuters inevitably sometimes act out of narrow self-interest. One major blemish on their records is their treatment of UNESCO around 1976–82. The leaders of AP and Reuters helped to orchestrate an international media campaign, which soon led to both the US and Britain (and Singapore) leaving UNESCO. The AP and Reuters leaders accused UNESCO of supporting the kind of restrictive anti-media measures common under repressive third-world regimes. As an account of the main report in question—chaired by Sean McBride, a former foreign minister of Ireland—this was a travesty; the McBride committee included a former Editor of *Le Monde* and several other distinguished journalists and authors. The report's main thrust, much more French than third world, reflected common European-style centrist views.[10] Moreover much of the criticism of the Reagan/Thatcher decisions to punish UNESCO came from American, not third-world commentators.[11]

Even the brave new world of international all news video networks seems likely to be dominated by big American players with some less than lethal competition from BBC World. The *Financial Times*' attempt to emulate its half-brother *The Economist* (50 per cent Pearson-owned)—by selling more copies in the US—will not damage the huge domestic US sale of the *Wall Street Journal*. In fact the *Financial Times* and Dow Jones are co-operating against their joint enemy, Reuters, in several specialized financial TV news and database offerings. Meanwhile the US domestic daily market remains a *WSJ* preserve. The *Financial Times*' owners have quietly acquired the leading financial dailies of France and Spain; Europe has been tacitly agreed to be a *Financial Times*/Pearson financial daily newspaper preserve. The real benefit of the stronger *Financial Times* effort in the US is that it can build its general international strength and can especially consolidate its status as the leading financial newspaper voice of Europe.

There is then, much calculated vagueness about this domination of world news. Some of the vagueness is a defensive reluctance to admit duopoly. Some of it derives from waiting-to-see-if-the-interactive-future-actually-arrives, although Reuters and AP–Dow Jones have been profitably mining some of the digital and data 'future' since the 1970s. One thing is certain. This low-key vagueness is very Anglo-American.

AP and Reuters will doubtless survive for many more decades, but the same cannot be said for the dozen or so American, British and European organisations which in the 1990s staked a claim to being serious players in world news. Twelve players makes for a very crowded market. However, the news service is often intended as one offering within a portfolio or bouquet of satellite-and-cable services; the big media organization will not want to drop its prestige news service.

Two predictions seem safe. First there will in the future be less than the present number of major world news players. Second, the majority of the survivors will be American or British.

10 Sean McBride (chairman) *Many Voices, One World* (London: Kogan Page/UNESCO, 1980).

11 This included the (Conservative) Freedom Forum of New York. See also: Mark D. Alleyne, *News Revolution* (New York: St Martin's Press, 1997), 64–88.

22

The Crisis at the Heart of Our Media

Anthony Sampson

I WOULD LIKE TO take a new look at the problem of power of the media—not so much in terms of their much-argued direct power over voters and politicians, but in terms of their underlying influence through providing the chief context for information and understanding for the public. I suggest that British democracy now has a real problem from the dangerous imbalance between media and parliament, and the media's ability to confuse news with entertainment, and deny the public ability to understand real problems.

Of course this complaint is nothing new. There has always been a confusion between entertainment, polemic and truth. The media grew out of gossip and propaganda. Over last summer I was reading the complete diaries of the 1660s of Samuel Pepys, who was an excellent gossip in a London which had heavy censorship and no newspapers in the modern sense. Much of Pepy's subject-matter was remarkably similar to that of the media today: royal scandals, Whitehall corruption, bad news from the Continent. But he was also a very serious public servant and administrator. And he had to be his own newspaper, picking up both truth and lies at court, in coffee-houses and at dinner-parties. On June 19 1661 he complained to his diary: 'I am now become the most negligent man in the world as to matter of news. Insomuch that nowadays I neither can tell any nor ask any of others.'

Coffee-houses were really the origins of the early newspapers which followed in the eighteenth century, when they were freed from licensing. But there was always a conflict between the scandal-sheets and serious news and discussion, which continues to this day.

As more popular newspapers grew up they horrified educated readers, and the use of pictures made them seem worse. Wordsworth wrote one of his worst sonnets, in 1846, called 'On Illustrated Books and Newspapers'.

> A backward movement surely have we here
> From manhood—back to childhood, for the age—
> Back towards caverned life's first rude career.
> Avaunt this vile abuse of pictured page!

Source: Anthony Sampson, 'The Crisis at the Heart of Our Media', *British Journalism Review*, 7/3 (1996), 42–51

It seems odd to realize that he was probably complaining about the marvellous engravings in the *Illustrated London News*. Coleridge had early deplored magazines for a more interesting reason, that they helped destroy the memory with their disconnected facts. As he lamented in the *Biographia Literaria*:

> The habit of perusing periodical works may be properly added to Averroes' catalogue of Anti-mnemonics, or weakeners of the memory (which included eating of unripe fruit, gazing on the clouds, riding among a multitude of camels, frequent laughter, and reading tombstones in churchyards).

What would Coleridge think now about the effects on the memory of the multiplicity of advertisements, images, impulses, and soundbites averaging 6.5 seconds in length?

There were far more worries from intellectuals in the late nineteenth century with the development of the halfpenny press, and a flood of disconnected facts and useless information in magazines like *Titbits* and *Answers*. As the mass market developed the press owners assumed less and less intelligence. As the American columnist H. L. Mencken judged: 'No-one ever lost money by underestimating the intelligence of the American public.'

Popular papers kept descending still lower in the twentieth century. They increasingly mixed truth with fantasy, and a new opportunity came with television which enabled them to confuse fact and fiction, actors with parts. The success of the *Sun* in the 1960s depended on TV-style entertainment, and forced its rival, the *Daily Mirror* to abandon its modest attempts to educate its readers with serious information. The *Sun* also felt much freer to break traditional British taboos—partly because its owner Rupert Murdoch was detached from the nation's society. He need not worry about what his peers thought of him if he was flying to Sydney or New York the next day.

Newspaper owners living outside the country—including Lord Rothermere of the *Daily Mail*, who lives in Paris—are likely to be more immune from tribal restraints. And they could more freely exploit the helpless British addiction to sexual scandals—which made them as vulnerable to foreign exploitation as the Chinese opium addicts in the nineteenth century. The breaking of taboos and the obsession with sex provided huge profits for the *Sun*, which effectively built up Murdoch's global empire. But the sexual scandals also gave tabloids a pernicious new political power: for their intrusions into privacy could increasingly terrorise the more vulnerable MPs. It was not so much what they printed as what they did not print. Tabloid editors love to boast of their secret files of scandals about politicians, waiting to be published. They speak with the authentic voice of the blackmailer, the wielder of information-power, of William Randolph Hearst or J. Edgar Hoover.

Broadsheets Tabloids have undoubtedly been transformed, and have increased their influence over the last thirty years, but the more striking change has been in the character of the broadsheets or quality papers. Up till the 1960s they took for granted that they had separate yardsticks from the tabloids, measured by factors like prestige, influence, and their place in history. Of course 'quality' journalists always felt some tension between truth and readability. But they despised tabloids for their sensationalism and lack of scruple, and never mentioned them in their columns. Many were deliberately non-sensational, and aspired to write the 'first draft of history'. They looked to *The Times* as the ultimate 'journal of record', with its avoidance of any vulgarity. It is hard to remember that until May 1966 its front page had only small ads. I don't advocate going back to the earlier stuffiness and pomposity of that time; only to suggest that quality papers then had their own separate standards, which had merits as well as dangers.

But since the 1980s the frontier between qualities and popular papers has virtually disappeared. The introduction of new technology since Wapping gave quality papers the opportunity to become much more profitable; but as the competition intensified, they looked for circulation downward. Some of them learnt the trick of making sensationalism look serious. The *Sunday Times* looked quite different from the *News of the World*, but could be surprisingly similar; and both were owned by Rupert Murdoch. Tabloids became more admired by the broadsheets, and constantly mentioned. They were competing for the same market, and sometimes for the same editors. Paul Dacre, the editor of the *Mail*, turned down the editorship of both *The Times* and *The Daily Telegraph*.

The British press can now certainly claim to be the most competitive in the world, with 10 papers with national circulations, engaged in cut-throat contest. It's in dramatic contrast with the American press, largely based on local monopolies. It's much more dynamic, innovative, and more exciting and livelier writing than the Americans. But how far does this competition provide real variety? In many ways, I believe, it has led to less choice. In particular the high ground of serious reporting, investigating and foreign coverage has been vacated.

Why did this happen? It's a contrast to the kind of competition I recall forty years ago, when *The Observer* and the *Sunday Times* were competing to attract educated readers, and becoming more interesting in the process. But in those days newsprint was strictly rationed and advertising was turned away. Today the broadsheets compete fiercely for advertising, which imposes its own conditions—still more in the present crisis of newspapers which have cut their prices while newsprint has become more expensive. The advertisers determine the allocation of space—the pages devoted to consumers, travel, entertainment—which look more and more alike. And they're not interested in foreign news, books, or investigation.

Investigation has been almost abandoned. There are no new Orwells or Priestleys, to inspect the rest of the country or to describe what happens behind the servants' entrance of the hotel or across the railway tracks. Instead there has been an explosion of columns providing comment without facts, discussing friends, parties, or other journalists. Newspapers are much less about history, more about conversation of the most basic kind: 'What did you do today?' 'I've been worrying this week about knick-knacks. Why don't I have any?', we were asked recently by Joan Smith in the *Independent on Sunday*. Scores of other columnists tell us what happened to them on the way to Sainsbury's, what their children did at school, how they enjoyed holidays. One wonders what there is left for these people to talk about at home.

The most serious change in the broadsheet papers, I believe, has been the fading of serious foreign news. The world is disappearing out of sight. Foreign correspondents—those that remain—are discouraged from serious analysis; and even in quality papers they are now liable to have their interpretation directed by the news editor at home, often with a heavy political slant. They are continually encouraged to write human interest stories, like novelists manqué, which may be quite entertaining, but which assume that there is more serious explanation of critical events somewhere else—which there usually isn't.

The retreat from the world is all the more worrying because the world since the cold war has never been more important to follow, more exciting, fast-changing and relevant to Britain's future. There's never been more need to analyse the changing patterns, or to give the context for Britain's trade and survival: to convey the massive shift of power and wealth to Asia, the uncertainties of Russia or the Middle East. Yet such explanations are still harder to find in the press.

Exceptions Of course there are important exceptions to this retreat: most notably the *Financial Times, The Economist*, the *International Herald Tribune*. But they are all primarily business papers, influenced by financial readers and writers who limit the social perspective. There has been a huge explosion of financial information round world over the last twenty years. But information and understanding about the broader political and social changes has hardly begun to catch up.

The same retreat from serious world reporting is all too visible on television. What happened to all those high aspirations embodied in the BBC's motto from the Book of Isaiah: 'Nation shall speak peace unto Nation?' What kind of distortion lies behind the TV images of turning worlds? TV can sometimes perform wonders of explanation and analysis, like Brian Lapping's programmes on Yugoslavia, or South Africa. But the regular news coverage of the world presents disconnections not connections. They won't report news without the cameras, or provide a commentary without a setting: so they exclude crucial countries like Saudi Arabia almost completely. And the cameras become still more restless, as they move from one trouble-spot to the next. They will conclude a crisis in Bosnia, say, with the words 'the next few days will tell . . .' But the next day they are off somewhere else, so they never do tell.

True, there is more and more television news, but it's presented more as a processed product—what Malcolm Muggeridge called Newzak—and pressed into still shorter-term snippets, which hardly vary between programmes, with no time to stand back. News is converted still further into entertainment, with one presenter talking to another to reduce crucial events into a cosy chat-show.

Radio remains a much more serious and credible purveyor of world news, with some excellent correspondents. And much of the most serious and unbiased foreign reporting has come from the BBC World Service, subsidized by the Foreign Office. But the recent reorganization of the BBC by Blane and Birt shows how little value is placed on this special credibility.

Does the triviality of the media really matter? Why shouldn't they entertain, if that is what people want? It does matter, above all because it affects the whole political process. A mature democracy depends on having an educated electorate, informed and connected through parliament. But as the media have become more pervasive and more entertaining, parliament itself is being marginalized in the national debate. Debates on television have increasingly taken over in public interest from Westminster. At best they can be much sharper than parliament's, with fiercer questions, sometimes backed up by filmed interviews and evidence. They can sometimes detect groundswells of public concern and revolt before they reach MPs' attention. Yet television debates provide no real answers, no solutions, no follow-up to legislation. They are most exciting when they are most negative, like hecklers. And they increasingly eclipse the discussions in parliament itself.

In the newspapers, the columnists rise while MPs fade out of sight. [...] In the broadsheets its very hard now to find any reports of parliamentary debates, and Jack Straw has revealed the rapid drop in coverage of parliament. Under Simon Jenkins's editorship *The Times* dropped parliamentary reports altogether because, as he explained to Tom King in a classic dismissal of the concept of a journal of record:

> I couldn't find anyone who read it apart from MPs. We are not there to provide a public service for a particular profession, or for that matter, for a particular legislative chamber. Newspapers are about providing people with news.

It is becoming still harder to find the actual text of even the most important speeches. You can find comments on what was said, suggestions on what should have been said, jokes and references to what was said, but not what was actually said. While the sketch-writer is thriving, the gallery reporter is dying, if not dead. The politicians themselves feel still more dependent on the media to give them recognition and publicity. Their alternative communications systems—whether families, country-houses, or Westminster itself—have been increasingly eclipsed, and they look to journalists for both information and reassurance. The Prime Minister anxiously rings up editors and columnists to try to obtain a good press.

The columnists—as many freely admit—cannot maintain the kind of consistent interest in developing policies that ministers and civil servants have to master. Columnists are competing with each other in entertainment, jokes, and controversy which will attract readers. They are paid to criticize, not to be constructive, or to propose alternative ideas. [...]

Danger   There's a more serious danger to parliamentary democracy in the power of tabloids, which has been expressing itself much more boldly. We saw how the *Daily Mail* suddenly saw the chance to stir up the public and a few MPs to stop the new Domestic Violence Bill which aimed to provide rights for women in unmarried homes, and turned the debate into an ignorant crusade against Living in Sin. We have also seen how the *Sun* and the *Mail* have end-lessly campaigned on the most emotive issues concerning law and order—demanding tougher sentencing, more people in prison, stricter restrictions on immigrants—and have defied all the research which warns against dehu-manizing prisons and purely punitive policies. [...]

What we see here are the mass media effectively by-passing Parliament, with its capacity for reasoned argument and moderating influences, to im-pose their own demagogy in direct alliance with ministers. Parliament, despite all its faults and occasional hysteria, has to listen to argument and consider legislation in a rational mood. But the tabloids have no such obliga-tion. They can enjoy themselves stirring up one-sided prejudices, encourag-ing half-truths and intolerance. The media *are* usurping Parliament as the forum for national debate. But they can't take over its role as the critical funnel of democracy, connecting the people with the Government. For they need never be held responsible for policies. They are set in a negative critical mode. And they see themselves outside the system, when they are really part of it.

Behind this I see a deeper misunderstanding. The media still believe that they are battling against the citadels of centralized power, of old boy nets, in the vague shape of The Establishment. But that really ceased to exist in the 1950s, after the aftermath of empire and world war. Jeremy Paxman, the most abrasive and alarming of TV inquisitors, himself wrote an entertaining book in 1990 about the Establishment, called *Friends in High Places.* He looked to find the ultimate centre of power, and found it in 'the men in leather armchairs in St James's', who were, he said, 'the true authors of the nation's malaise'. But that mythology really died with John Buchan, or at the latest Ian Fleming. In Clubland the media are far more effective in organiz-ing support for their colleagues to become members of prestigious clubs than the old aristocracy of Paxman's imagination. In fact the nearest thing I can find to an Establishment today—in terms of a network of information, con-tacts, looking after each other and terrifying others—is in the media, with a special dread accorded to inquisitors like Jeremy Paxman. Media people still love to batter at the citadels without realising that it is they, the batterers, who have the greater power.

I have tried to give some reasons why the media are so unrepresentative; the narrowness of their competition, the pressures of advertising, the cen-tralisation of their power. But I believe the greatest distortion of newspapers comes from their owners—who themselves are quite unrepresentative. They're an old bogey, of course. Press barons have always tried and some-times succeeded in dictating to politicians and even Prime Ministers; some-times in becoming cabinet ministers, like Lord Northcliffe or Lord Beaverbrook, who in 1931 launched his own half-baked empire crusade, which has some resemblance to Sir James Goldsmith's crusade today. But his power was punctured by his own arrogance and the public's apathy, which enabled Baldwin to attack him for 'his power without responsibility—the prerogative of the harlot throughout the ages!'

We mustn't exaggerate the direct influence of newspaper owners: they cannot go against the tides of public opinion, as Beaverbrook learnt in the

1945 election. Most British papers have been Conservative, but they haven't stopped Labour victories in 1945, 1964, or 1974, and TV and radio have given politicians more direct access to voters. Now a new bogey has emerged, dramatized by Tony Blair's flight to Australia to speak to editors summoned by Rupert Murdoch: the global owner. In fact I believe the danger of international groups is not so much personal power, as impersonal power. There is no simple answer to the question: what does Murdoch want? He wants first to extend his empire through deals with Governments; second to stir up as much trouble and excitement as possible, to sell newspapers. Yet he has no serious policies to put forward for Britain, or any other nation. Global combines distance their owners further from responsibility for any single country.

Fervour   Conrad Black, the owner of the *Telegraph* group, is more seriously concerned than Murdoch with British politics; but as a right-wing Canadian he is fiercely opposed to Britain coming closer to Continental Europe, as he reveals at private conferences like Bilderberg. Without being British he enjoys stirring up a patriotic fervour, while propagating extreme free-enterprise ideas from North America which are inapplicable to Britain.

The preponderance of foreign ownership in Britain helps to explain the disproportion of publicity given to relatively few anti-European Tory MPs, and to the ferocious critics of John Major on the right. And it explains the extraordinary expectation in June 1995 that Redwood would topple Major in the Conservative leadership elections—while Tory MPs were realizing that their own constituents were terrified of Redwood, who would more surely lose them the next election. The more serious damage from this massive anti-European bias is the lack of more serious discussion of the European predicament: the real problems of reaching any European consensus, of avoiding a disintegration into intolerance and misunderstanding, and of providing democratic oversight into the cynical bargains made in Brussels between Governments—including our own Government.

I believe that a more truthful and informative press depends on restricting foreign ownership. For international owners do not represent Britain's interests or realities. It is not a xenophobic argument, but the opposite; we must oppose a dangerous alliance between jingos and foreign owners who exploit them. I believe we must also move against multiple ownership and semi-monopolies—which inevitably limit diversity and create links between already powerful media. The excessive laxness of the Monopolies Commission dates back to the time when many newspapers were close to bankruptcy—including *The Times* when it was bought by the *Sunday Times*. But today newspapers are potentially much more profitable. The current heavy losses by some are caused by the price war launched by *The Times*—which can afford losses only because of its multiple ownership. It is using the predatory pricing which ever since Rockefeller in the 1880s has been used by the strong to defeat the weaker. And there is now no reason why individual quality papers cannot stand without tabloid support, if they compete on equal terms. But such break-ups will not be enough to reoccupy the high ground of serious unbiased information which is so desperately needed. We have to face the fact that only some form of public service or subsidy can offset the pressure to triviality and protect serious news from entertainment; and can rescue extra TV channels from more replays of Dallas and news soundbites, to provide the direct unbiased reporting on which our fair judgements depend.

In the meantime, how can more serious observers get their own informed and lively picture of the world, without pressures or filters from advertisers or proprietors, or libel lawyers? Perhaps we are forced back to the experience of Pepys, who had to be his own newspaper. The best elements of the media, I believe, have always arisen from natural talk, discussion, curiosity, and questions—as eighteenth-century papers grew out of coffee-houses. If mass-communication has become too distorted and corrupted, it may be that the Internet and e-mail will provide the new technologies to rescue from the old ones, to build up more reliable systems of information across the world.

23

Downsizing the News: Network Cutbacks in the Nation's Capital

Penn Kimball

Conclusions

WHAT IS GOING on in network television is a redefinition of news, driven by financial considerations and ratings. News is what networks feel they can afford to cover and what will get on the air as determined by ratings. The wall of separation between the business side and the news side, which had always been under siege, has now been significantly breached.

It used to be, the traditionalists say, that news consisted of the things the public in a self-governing democracy needed to be aware of in order to cope. Now, the pragmatists argue, the job is to get a dwindling audience into the tent. The marketeers are triumphing in an atmosphere where the very future of network television, let alone network news, is in doubt. Resources to cover the news as traditionally defined have been drastically reduced.

This curtailment of news-gathering energies at the networks is taking place at a time when there is a movement within the government power structure to reduce the status of those who provide liaison with the press. The downsizing of Washington news on TV has been accompanied by a downgrading among federal employees charged with helping the press.

President Clinton has been accused of bypassing the White House press corps. Democratic leadership in the Senate has limited access to a reduced number of TV congressional reporters. The press offices at the Pentagon and State Department no longer have the status within the agencies to intervene successfully on behalf of the working press. A new layer of bureaucracy has been placed between correspondents and their sources. Thus, the Washington press corps is more isolated than ever from what is really going on.

For their part, the networks have downgraded their coverage of the State Department at the very time when crucial changes are taking place in the Middle East, the Balkans, the former Soviet Union, and Africa, from North to South. The correspondents covering these regions on the spot have largely been withdrawn. In these circumstances, television news is like a blind man

Source: Penn Kimball, *Downsizing The News: Network Cutbacks in the Nation's Capital* (Baltimore and London: The Johns Hopkins University Press, 1994).

trying to alert the American people to how much they are at risk. Only when events explode into dramatic visuals does the television audience focus on what is happening on the scene, too late to comprehend the factors that have led up to the crisis and which an informed public might have helped to prevent.

The coverage of Congress has likewise been truncated, so that there is a diminished public sense of continuity in the legislative process. Politicians are held up to scorn consistently by commentators on television. The public is not exposed to the drudge work that makes the system function because it is not visually exciting. Popular impressions of the second branch of government are trivialized and scandalized by sporadic television reporting from Capitol Hill.

The focus on the presidency and the White House by television reports on the evening news distorts the balance of our Constitutional structure. It raises expectations among voters of what the president can accomplish on his own to unreasonable levels. It is hard for any president to succeed when bombarded continually by the Washington press for his alleged shortcomings.

At a time when access to accurate information is extremely limited, the television audience is exposed to growing amounts of unfiltered information from on high. The watchdog responsibility of the press to hold public officials accountable for their acts is impaired by obstacles to correspondent access. The television news audience is nightly exposed to 'news' reports from the White House, which, though brief and inadequate, tend to eclipse the attention received by Congress, the State Department, and other important divisions of government.

Cuts in the Washington bureaux of the major television networks have further diminished the coverage, never very thorough, of regulatory agencies and executive departments. The Supreme Court is no longer a regular beat on its own for all three networks—despite the fact that landmark changes in legal doctrine have been adopted and are still in the process of evolvement. The star system, by which a reduced number of Washington correspondents cover the news, means that the decision of what to air on the evening news is correspondent-driven rather than according to the merits of the substance of the news.

At the same time that network executives are allocating fewer resources to news originating in Washington, the persons who hold the reins of government power continue to seek to manipulate the flow of news in their own special interest. The president, cabinet members, and members of Congress are increasingly taking advantage of alternative opportunities to address constituents more directly, without filtering their proposals and viewpoints through a screen of critical analysis by independent journalists. Washington's TV press corps is caught between a network hierarchy with a weakening commitment to news and government sources anxious to evade their scrutiny. A headline news service out of Washington that skips over the more complex issues is inadequate in the best of times. When network news resources are curtailed, these shortcomings are magnified.

There is a tendency among journalists in this country when they report on government to put down politicians. This is sometimes attributed to ideological bias, a charge blunted by the fact that the press has been just as critical of the new Democratic administration as it was of its Republican predecessors. The line between scepticism and cynicism is thinly drawn. In their watchdog capacity, journalists tend to focus on the warts of the body politic and share a general popular mistrust of those who make a career out of working in government. The shorthand of television reinforces this negative view.

The tendency to report negatively about all branches of government has helped to generate public hostility or apathy about the actual performance of democratic institutions. Television was often blamed for the long slide of public participation in elections during the 1960s, 1970s, and 1980s. Yet television exposure undoubtedly played a role in the turnaround that took place in the proportions of the electorate, still not very large, who voted in 1992. It has not been verified how television *news* figured in this long-term trend or temporary reversal.

The highly critical fare seen on television news is partly responsible for the politics of disillusionment preached by so many. And because television is best at conveying simple ideas, there are a great number of oversimplified remedies being circulated supposedly to cure our ills.

In addition to its role in expanding public understanding, television news is supposed to help set the public agenda for which issues become the centre of popular attention. The main stories covered on television resonate nationally. They are picked up and expanded by newspapers and magazines. In television news, specific information is often less important than the image conveyed—such as the charge that the president is not sufficiently focused on a single programme or that Congress is incapable of resisting special interests. Communication researchers have long documented that the flow of information is a many-tiered process. One of the most important levels is word-of-mouth. People talk about what they see on the evening news.

In Washington, cutbacks in budgets and personnel have reduced the ability of network bureaux there to carry out even those stories that interest their market-driven superiors at corporate headquarters in New York. Correspondents are demoralized about the present and pessimistic about their future.

The future of the evening news on the major networks is endangered by the proliferation of prime-time magazine shows and the new emphasis on cheaper news feeds to local affiliates. We may be witnessing the end of an era in broadcast history. 'Cheap' news programming on cable subsidiaries—panel shows, talk programmes, syndicated tape from home and abroad—can be done at a profit not possible in traditional network news divisions. The big moneymakers are magazine shows, inexpensive to produce but reaching sufficiently large audiences to be attractive to advertisers. The needs of the consumers of serious news could be lost in the shuffle. As long as an unrestricted marketplace determines which programmes will survive, and as long as federal supervision of broadcast content as it relates to news and public affairs continues to be lax, the network evening news programmes will continue to be inadequate.

On the one hand, the networks are investing what resources are available into prime-time magazines where they hope to make a profit—instead of shoring up the gathering of daily news. New staffers are being hired, but they tend to be news packagers. At the same time, the networks are experimenting with comparatively inexpensive ways to keep their affiliates happy with some kind of national and foreign news service directly fed to local newsrooms. The familiar evening news broadcasts are caught in between these forces of change. Furthermore, new technologies such as cable and fibre optics are changing the structure of broadcasting generally, and the major networks have to make huge investments in order to survive in an unpredictable twenty-first century. The role of news in these unknown waters has yet to be defined.

The network evening news programmes at present may not be the all-encompassing fixture in American homes that they once were, but they are still a daily source of information, however imperfect, for some fifty million Americans. These viewers grumble about bias and violence; they like or abhor the individual anchors; they tune in from force of habit or because they like what precedes or follows on the same channel. But the fact is that these programmes continue to be watched by a substantial share of the American public.

Thanks to technological advances and the skills of broadcast professionals, network evening news programmes have never *looked* better. The audience can watch and listen to a nearly seamless performance night after night. Despite the critics, the evening news is still a household staple, part of the pattern of American family life.

The contents of the news programmes on the three major networks usually resemble each other to a larger degree than they differ. There is not a great deal of argument among news producers over the definition of major news events. During twenty-two and a half minutes of non-commercial time, there is not much room for vastly different priorities in what should be reported to the audience. The major opportunity to be different comes with the longer segments adopted as a permanent feature by all three network news programmes. To the casual viewer, the evening news on all three networks seems about the same. But variations do occur to a degree—largely noticed in the personalities of rival anchors—and the audience continues to vote its preferences by zapping the dial.

Why then the furore over recent changes in the network news divisions? What, as one network news executive remarked in this study, does it matter? If the complaints are merely the gripes of disgruntled employees of the news divisions in response to their corporate masters, what else is new in the media business? If the customers never believe the stories on the evening news fit their conceptions of reality, when has it been otherwise? If academics and other experts continually deplore the level of popular taste, when have they not? Previously, civilization was thought to be on the edge of destruction by movies, radio, or recorded music—and even by the crude programme efforts when television was in its infancy. Somehow, we have survived.

This does not alter the fact, however, that the downsizing of network news, most particularly that gathered in Washington and abroad, may have serious consequences for the consumers of television news in this country. The persons at the far end of the tube are the ones with the most at stake in the downsizing of network news. Old-fashioned news standards are turning out to be a luxury that commercial television can no longer afford. Perhaps more serious is the possibility that the vast majority of the television audience may not recognize the difference, or if they do, that they may not care.

4

PART FOUR

Sources of News

Introduction to Part IV: Sources of News

OVER THE LAST fifty years writers have assessed the relationship between journalists and their sources to gauge the balance of power existing between the two. Of crucial importance to the study of news sources are the relations between the media and the exercise of political and ideological power, specifically by governments who attempt to define and manage the flow of information. By analysing the relationship between journalists and sources, an understanding of the relationship of journalism to society at large can be gained. In the following pieces strong arguments are made for the idea that the views and the interests of authoritative sources are generally promoted by the way journalism is organized and practised.

The first article in Part 4 is by Walter Gieber, whose study conducted in the mid-1950s develops a more complex structure of newsmaking compared to the limited findings of White and the gatekeeper approaches. Gieber looks at how journalists or gatekeepers and the sources of news operate at different levels of discourse. Sources have little idea of the manner in which the press works and very little knowledge of the audience. Sources communicate in terms of their own values and take for granted the audience shares these values. Forty years on of course, more recent studies indicate the sophisticated nature of current source behaviour. Gieber finds reporters, whilst personally holding the same values as their sources, do not convey them in the same way. They tend to use denoted symbols rather than the qualitative terms in which the sources tend to communicate.

Leon Sigal's research on the politics of news making in Washington was published in the early 1970s. It is one of the first empirical studies that looks in detail at the relationship between journalists and their sources, in this particular case, the officials in Washington and reporters from the *New York Times* and *Washington Post*. Sigal's central argument is that news is the outcome 'of the relationship between the newsmen and their sources'. By investigating the routines of news production he shows the heavy reliance by journalists on authoritative sources in the US government in Washington. He provides evidence to show how sources develop tactics and strategies for the release of information and comes to the conclusion that the newspapers mainly offer news from these official sources released through the official channels. Sigal's study is extremely useful because it quantifies the dominance of official sources in the production of news.

The following article comes from *Deciding What's News*, one of the classic production studies of the 1970s. Herbert Gans conducted a study of CBS evening news, NBC nightly news, Newsweek, and Time. The first part provides a typology for clarifying the manner, and summary of different theories, of story selection. Gans views news as information transmitted from sources to audiences. The role of the journalist is to refine and change material made available from these sources and turn it into a product suitable and familiar for their audiences. Gans locates the relationship between sources and journalists according to four related factors: incentives, power, the supply of suitable information, and proximity to journalists. Whilst acknowledging that sources can come from anywhere, he shows that in practice, access to journalists reflects the 'hierarchies of nation and society'. He concludes by showing that source power, whilst not determining news values, provides values implicit in the information given to journalists.

Stuart Hall and colleagues provide a structural analysis of the social production of news by looking at crime coverage. The media is analysed in terms of a theory of ideological power and its role is defined by looking at the structured relationship between the media and powerful sources. Their argument is that certain social groups within society benefit from a special status because of their institutional power, representative standing, or claims to expert knowledge. These groups are labelled as the primary definers of particular topics because of the structured preference conferred on the opinions of these powerful people by the media. This enables them to have the primary interpretation of the story in question. In this analysis the media play a crucial secondary role in reproducing the definitions of those that have this privileged access and therefore stand in a position of structured subordination to the primary definers.

Schlesinger and Tumber in *Reporting Crime* call for a further opening up of the understanding of the way that sources operate. Alongside the analyses of how news organizations work and the relationship between journalists and their sources from the journalists' perspective, they argue for further studies to look at the way the relationship operates from the sources' perspective. In their research the information and public relations strategies of sources involved in the criminal justice system are examined. Whilst acknowledging authoritative sources or those in a position of power may play a key role, the way voluntary and pressure groups are able to transmit their views either directly to journalists or via their relationship with more powerful sources is also recognized. They argue for a rethinking of the methodology of empirical studies of source behaviour, extending the scope of production studies to include not only investigating the practices of newsrooms and newsgathering but also examining the perspectives from the sources.

Todd Gitlin's work of the 1980s provides a Gramscian approach of hegemony to understand the operations of the news media. Gitlin looks at the relationship between the students' movement prominent in the anti-war protest in the 1960s in the USA and the national news media. It is one of the few studies showing the workings of hegemony in journalism that provides examples of the media construction of news. Gitlin examines the student movement's relationship with the news media and how celebrities, manufactured from the leadership of the student groups, became authoritative sources for the news media. The news media's personalization of social groups and singling out of individuals led to leadership struggles within the movement. Gitlin shows the news organizations' methods for legitimizing the capitalist system as a whole through its codes of objectivity and balance often pull it in conflicting directions. Sometimes it can be pulled towards the institutions of political and economic power whilst at other times towards alternative, and in the case of the students, an opposition movement. In this way the news networks incorporate competing forces enabling them to maximize audiences and maintain legitimacy.

The final piece in Part 4 by Ericson, Baranek, and Chan is an extract from *Negotiating Control*, the second of their three-volume study on news production and content in Toronto, Canada. They look at the reporting of crime and deviancy in several institutions in Toronto including the courts, the police, the legislature, and private sector organizations. They examine the processes of negotiation between news media and these social institutions, showing how authoritative sources are able to control successfully the flow of information to the news media. The news media produce negative and scandal coverage, can deny access to sources and can represent an event or story unfavourable to a particular source. In a similar argument to Schlesinger and Tumber, they suggest the concentration by sociological studies on powerful institutional sources neglects the role non-official sources play in the process.

24

News is what Newspapermen Make It

Walter Gieber

INTEREST IN THE gatekeeper study is founded on what at first blush seems to be an utterly simple notion: news is what newspapermen make it. Well then, how do newspapermen make news? The answer is as complex as any attempt to assay a social institution and its resident occupations. [...]

It seems to me that the examination of the press must start where the news begins—*within* the institution of the press, *within* the walls of the newsroom or any other place where a newsman gets and writes his stories.

To a sensitive, thoughtful newspaperman, writing the news story is a singularly personal experience. For despite what 'professional' or 'ethical' controls he enforces upon himself, or for that matter, the bureaucratic controls that are thrust upon him, the news story is—or should be—a product of his disciplined perception and his evaluation of the environment, of the social arena from which the story and its characters come, and of the bureaucratic climate in which it is written. The contemporary literature of the newsman is rich in personal, informal insights into the intimate nature of news-gathering experience.[1] [...]

The gatekeeper study is an empirical, systematic examination of the behaviour of those persons who at various points control the fate of news stories. Who are the gatekeepers? They are the newsmen employed by a news-gathering bureaucracy; they are the sources of news outside of the news bureaucracies; they are the members of the audience who influence the reading of other members of the audience (recall the two-step flow of communications). All these persons are gatekeepers at some point. This paper, however, concentrates primarily on the newsmen and their sources. [...]

The methodology of the gatekeeper study was well adapted to White's purpose; for our purpose here, however, we prefer the techniques of the depth interview and participant-observation.

Source: Walter Gieber, 'News is what Newspapermen Make It', in Lewis A. Dexter and David M. White (eds.), *People, Society, and Mass Communications* (Toronto: Collier-Macmillan Ltd., 1964).

1 Only a few books can be mentioned here: Eric Sevareid, *Not So Wild a Dream*; Joseph and Stewart Alsop, *The Reporter's Trade*; Vincent Sheean, *Personal History*; Webb Miller, *I Found No Peace*; Kenneth Stewart, *News Is What We Make It.*

The goal of the gatekeeper study is hopefully to make a contribution toward a better understanding of the behaviour of mass-communications specialists, ultimately toward a sociology of the journalist. White's more immediate goal was an attempt to explain some of the facets of behaviour within the complexities of the networks of news gathering.

White's conclusion, 'how subjective news really is' poses the question 'how subjective?' Let's start with the telegraph editor, as did White. A press association, as a news network, provides a series of telegraph editors with a common budget of news items; the 'flow' of communications up to and through the gate area, the telegraph desk, can be measured; the behaviour (selection of items) of the editors can be compared and contrasted.

One can define 'subjectivity' in this case as the telegraph editor's perception of his own values, the values of the newsroom and the values of his audience, the newspaper readers. The gatekeeper's selection in accordance with 'subjective' value criteria is limited by the number of news items available, their size and the pressures of time and mechanical production.

In 1956, the author selected 16 Wisconsin dailies receiving only the Associated Press wire.[2] No major differences in news selection and newspage display were found among the wire editors. They did differ, however, in the explanations and rationalizations of their role behaviour.

But I also found that, in each case, it was possible to approach what was a prediction of selection. If the editor's selection was regarded as a sample, statistically speaking, of the incoming wire budget, his 'draw' was excellent. Moreover, through testing the editor's decisions on a group of 'test' news items and by watching his selection for several days, it was possible to project what he would do on a selected operational day.

Common to all the telegraph editors were the pressures exerted by the reality of the newsroom bureaucratic structure and its operation. The most powerful factor was not the evaluative nature of news but the pressures of getting the copy into the newspaper; the telegraph editor was preoccupied with the mechanical pressures of his work rather than the social meanings and impact of the news. His personal evaluations rarely entered into his selection process; the values of his employer were an accepted part of the newsroom environment.

In short, the telegraph editor was 'task oriented'; he was concerned with goals of production, bureaucratic routine and interpersonal relations within the newsroom.

Two bald, discomforting facts became apparent. First, in his communication behaviour, the telegraph editor was passive. He was playing no real and active role as a communicator; indeed, the press association was more instrumental in making the selection than the telegraph editor. An active communications role seemingly would cause the newsman to come to grips—what Joseph and Stewart Alsop call *engagé*—with the environment. There was some evidence that the telegraph editor, a desk-bound newspaperman, may have different motivations leading to the difference in

---

2 Walter Gieber, *The Telegraph Editors: A Study in Communication Behaviour*, Ph.D. dissertation, University of Wisconsin, 1956, and 'Across the Desk: A Study of 16 Telegraph Editors', *Journalism Quarterly*, 33 (Fall, 1956): 423–32.

occupational choice from that of the reporter. It may be that he was lazy or, more acutely, he became lazy because his executives did not encourage him to be otherwise. At any rate, he made no critical evaluation of the incoming wire news.

Second, as a communicator he had no real perception of his audience and, therefore, was not truly communicating to it. If the major function of the newspaper is the meaningful and purposeful surveillance of the environment for the reader and, thus, the fulfilment of his communications needs and expectations, then this function was only fortuitously met.

A discussion of 'subjectivity' in news selection must take into account the limitations imposed by bureaucratic pressures.

These conclusions, based on a study of small-city telegraph editors,[3] were discomforting. Several further questions remained because, first of all, telegraph news filters to the telegraph editor through a long series of news networks controlled by other gatekeepers who are responsive to the demands of a diversity of newspapers; second, the press association budget carries a wide range of stories and thus a large variety of socially meaningful symbols. Thus, the question arises: What 'subjectivity' would be found if local news items were involved and the variety of symbols restricted? To put the question another way: Can news stories which carry socially evaluative symbols exert the pressure to force their way through 'gate areas'? The opportunity to examine this question came with a study of the gatekeepers of local news of civil rights and liberties.[4]

Having made a content analysis of news of civil rights and liberties,[5] I had noted the relative paucity of *local* stories. This, in 1958, was at a time when local spokesmen for civil rights were proclaiming that, despite large regional events and major court and legislative actions, Western cities were not free of violations of civil rights and liberties. If this were true, what was happening to local stories on these issues? Obviously, content analysis could not explain the reasons for such missions.

In view of the marked social value given to symbols of civil liberties and rights—at least among a number of vocal publics—it seemed to me that relevant stories would create among gatekeepers a variety of strong evaluative (subjective) responses: The gatekeeper's values may be consonant or in conflict with (*a*) the values in the story, (*b*) the values of the newspaper—which in turn may be in conflict or consonant with the values of the story, (*c*) the perceived values of the audience—which in turn may be consonant or in conflict with the values of the newspaper.

Using the same set of stories, in this case persons involved in civil rights activities, I went to both the sources of the news and to the reporters; I found that the two 'gatekeepers' of this single channel (source to reporter) of news were operating at different levels of discourse.

3 The author replicated the Wisconsin study with a group of small-city dailies in Indiana. The results were not published; they were, if anything, slightly more discomforting.

4 Walter Gieber, *Gatekeepers of News of Civil Rights and Liberties: A Study of the Fate of Local News Stories* (Department of Journalism, University of California, 1958); 'How the "Gatekeepers" View Local Civil Liberties News', *Journalism Quarterly*, 37 (Spring, 1960): 199–205; 'Two Communicators of the News: A Study of the Roles of Sources and Reporters', *Social Forces*, 39 (October, 1960): 76–83.

5 The Civil Liberties and Rights Project of the Association of Education in Journalism.

The sources tended to communicate in connotative terms. Civil liberties and civil rights were discussed in a tone and context of great urgency; the *public had to know* about relevant events and attenuating symbols. But the sources had little notion of the ways in which the press works. And they had little knowledge of the mass-media audience. In essence, they were attempting to communicate in terms of their own values and assuming that the audience shared these values. They saw consonance among the stories, themselves and the public, and believed themselves frustrated by a dissonant press.

The reporters, with few exceptions, *personally* held the same general values as the sources but publicly did not so convey them. Moreover, news of civil liberties and rights had to compete with other stories. In handling relevant news stories, the reporters tended to use denotive symbols (names rather than values; action rather than meaning; controversy rather than consensus). Although the reporters also held a *rationale* of audience needs (that it needs to know the facts), they too had little knowledge of their readers. They appeared to be oriented primarily to problems of the craft and the newsroom.

The reporters' major complaint was the lack of opportunity to write *any* story the way they saw it. The reporters were cognizant of the social meaning of events which took place in the community. No matter how feeble their awareness of the news interests and needs of their audience happened to be, they were aware of numerous events which required full reporting even if only in purely denotative symbols. The sad fact was that although many reporters were aware of their environment and, both personally and professionally, had a wide knowledge of the background of civil rights events, they had little opportunity to report fully on them. They charged that their employers did not allow them sufficient time to write full reports, often because they were preoccupied with a frantic gathering of trivia, failing to distinguish items of broader social significance. The reporters could, then, only discuss these issues among themselves and, in a few instances, write on them for magazines of small circulation.

The reporters' major concern was with the 'climate' of the newsroom: they recognized themselves as employees of a news-gathering bureaucracy in which rewards came from their editors and colleagues. The value system of the newspaper (news policy) was not considered a problem; the reporters accepted it as part of bureaucratic structuring. They were more inclined to complain of inconsistency in or lack of policy. In fact, the main charge against their employers was the failure to give the reporters a chance to exploit their craft and the failure to actively maintain surveillance of the environment.

The fate of the local news story is not determined by the needs of the audience or even by the values of the symbols it contains. The news story is controlled by the frame of reference created by the bureaucratic structure of which the communicator is a member.

The reporters recognized the evaluative nature of symbols of civil rights and liberties items, but these were only one set of symbols among many demanding attention; moreover, they believed that transmission of relevant events is enhanced by denotative symbols, arguing that the readers would get the point if 'name' were given more attention than a 'principle'. (And they may well have a point.) Accordingly, they were unlikely to present fully an evaluative release. The reporters saw dissonance between themselves and the sources over the definition of news, and they saw incongruity between their own craft expectations and the reality of the newsroom.

The civil liberties study further explored a basic problem in the transmission of news—the problem of the bureaucratic frame of reference. The press holds a basic tenet that it must remain aloof from the influences of other institutions—sources, public relations experts and others desiring to reach, or to avoid, the 'public'. It is likewise well known that other institutions—and all persons eager to reach or avoid the 'public'—exert pressures on the press to get it to behave as they would like. Politicians and governmental bureaucrats are traditionally the most notorious for applying such pressures on the press.

In point of fact the press and its reporters have not remained pristine by any means. Indeed, one can envision three possible relationships between the sources of the news and the reporters: (*a*) the reporters remain independent of the sources; (*b*) the reporters and the sources find areas of collaboration for their mutual benefit; (*c*) the sources 'absorb' and dominate the reporters, or vice versa. With this in mind, the author studied the relationships between reporters and the elected and appointed officials in a small California city.[6]

Both sources and reporters hailed the press as the champion of democratic society. Both supported 'open' channels of communication. Both claimed a principled interest in the public weal; but it was at this juncture that basic differences arose. The sources saw themselves as *custodians* of the welfare of the community and its voters; the reporters saw themselves as *protectors* of the 'public.' (I may as well mention that both had hazy, stereotyped perceptions of the 'public'.) Each group developed its own perception of its public role, its own frame of reference for its communications, and claimed for itself the primary role of communicating to the public.

For the sources the frame of reference was the 'city'. Any communication reaching the public had to be cleansed of any information that might upset the community consensus. All communications had to enhance the consensus. Naturally, all attempts to 'protect' from publication the utterances and records of the individual source were well rationalized as contributions toward consensus.

Inasmuch as the press is the major communication artery to the voters, the sources' major objective was to assimilate the press into their frame of reference. Their method: suasion and sociability.

The reporters saw themselves in an independent 'distributive' role. Their frame of reference was the 'beat' which included themselves, the sources, and the 'public'. On the one hand, fiercely rationalizing their 'watchdog' function on government; on the other, the reporters, nonetheless, were passive; they rarely 'dug' for a story and remained content to accept releases or to record public meetings. They shared with their sources an admiration for 'efficient' city government and tended to avoid stories about latent conflicts

6 Walter Gieber, *The City Hall Reporter and His Sources*, a paper prepared for the Media Analysis Section, Association for Education in Journalism, August, 1960.

within the community. Overt conflict at a meeting between sources and voters, or among sources, was another matter—it was fair play. More important, the reporters had interpreted the symbol of the 'public' to apply narrowly only to a strong 'in-group' loyal to 'the city' as opposed to the broader community. Their best stories were written when the 'city' was in conflict with an 'outside' agency. Indeed, the reporters would co-operate—and did co-operate—with the sources in suppressing or postponing publication of a story in order to protect 'the city' from threats from 'outsiders'.

Thus, the reporters, by giving up any real independence of surveillance and critique and by allowing themselves the comfort of 'in-group' community loyalties, willy-nilly have moved into the area of collaboration with their sources.

This generalization can be made from our research: news does not have an independent existence; news is a product of men who are members of a news-gathering (or a news-originating) bureaucracy. But the question remains: how 'subjective' is the news? Very much so, in my opinion. This answer implies a particular definition of 'subjective'. If one means expression of the individuality of the communicator, the answer is that there is *some* subjectivity. It appears to me that the reporter's individuality is strongly tempered by extrapersonal factors. Although no one expects the newsman to have the freedom of the artist, the professional communicator often does see himself as a craftsman possessing the right to 'tell the story as he sees it'. But craft freedom, which would encourage individual role development and critical evaluation of the news, is controlled by the news-gathering bureaucracy. The 'splendid isolation' necessary to the craftsman does not exist for the newsman.

The press—and by delegation, the individual newsman—rightfully has the institutional licence to gather and make public the news. Society rightfully can expect the press to maintain critical surveillance of the social arena and to provide an independent appraisal of the environment. This requires, it seems to me, the press to remain free from undue influences from other social institutions. And it means that the individual reporter must remain independent from pressures from sources and free as far as possible from such pressures from the news bureaucracy which would interfere with his craft of full and critical reporting.

The ultimate *rationale* of the press—the reason for its licence—is to serve the audience. The news-gathering machinery and the news-gathering bureaucracy are the means; the audience needs are the goals. In the telegraph editor survey, the means all but replaced the goals. In the civil liberties study, both the sources and the reporters rationalized audience needs but neither seemed to know the audience; both communicators shared responsibility for a communications breakdown resulting from their antagonistic frames of reference; each was communicating thought by the means of his bureaucracy. In the city hall study, the communicator allowed himself to be caught in a frame of reference which was only in part of his own making; the proper goals were all but forgotten.

News is what newspapermen make it.

But until we understand better the social forces which bear on the reporting of the news, we will never understand what news is.

25

Reporters and Officials: The Organization and Politics of Newsmaking

Leon V. Sigal

ORGANIZATIONAL ROUTINES AND bureaucratic politics have a significant impact on the structure of newsgathering and on the shape of news content. At the *New York Times* and the *Washington Post*, reporters working in bureaux around the United States and overseas, as well as those covering beats in Washington, seem relatively free of newsroom constraints in gathering news. On the beat, however, efficiency dictates newsgathering through routine channels. Reporters cannot witness many events directly because they are few in number and must locate themselves in places where information is most likely to flow to them, and because their access to information is usually barred and control over disclosures centralized. The necessity of locating themselves at key points of information flow and the restriction of access both apply to reporters in Washington, where the two newspapers maintain sizeable staffs, but these factors are hardly peculiar to the nation's capital.

The foregoing analysis generates two principal hypotheses that lend themselves to testing by examining the content of newspapers:

- First, *most national and foreign news in the* New York Times *and the* Washington Post *comes to reporters through routine channels.*
- Second, *most non-local news, regardless of subject matter, comes from officials and agencies of the US government.*

Other researchers have found some indications of the importance of routine channels for news content. Two studies of Presidential press conferences, for instance, have concluded that over time, despite variations in the number of such press conferences, the total number of stories based on information from them has remained roughly constant.[1] Surveys of reporters

Source: Leon V. Sigal, *Reporters and Officials: The Organization and Politics of Newsmaking* (Lexington, Mass.: D. C. Heath, 1973).

1 Elmer E. Cornwell, Jr., 'The Presidential Press Conference', *Midwest Journal of Political Science*, 4/4 (Nov. 1960): 388; Delbert McGuire, 'Democracy's Confrontation: The Presidential Press Conference', *Journalism Quarterly*, 44/4 (Winter 1967): 638–44.

REPORTERS AND OFFICIALS **225**

have also turned up evidence for their reliance on routine channels of newsgathering.[2]

Another way to test these hypotheses is to count the channels and sources cited in a sample of stories in the *Times* and the *Post*. This procedure presents two main problems: (1) how to draw a sample that is, at best, unbiased or, at worst, biased against acceptance of the hypotheses; and (2) how to classify channels and sources which the story has only vaguely identified or has deliberately disguised.

Drawing a sample over a period of years permits an assessment of changes over time and differences among administrations. For economy of effort, five-year intervals were chosen: 1949, 1954, 1959, 1964, and 1969. To control as much as possible for variations by season and by day of the week, the same two weeks in each year, selected at random, are used: those beginning with the first Sunday in February and the second Sunday in December. On the assumption that more important stories are less routinely gathered, only stories beginning on page one are examined.[3] Stories less than two inches long are excluded. Since the study focuses on foreign and national news, other stories are eliminated if they meet *all three* of the following conditions: they have no dateline (i.e. *Times* stories written in New York and *Post* stories from Washington); the reporter works for any desk other than foreign or national; and the sources cited in the story are local.[4] This leaves 599 stories from the *Times* and 547 from the *Post* in the sample.

Channels, the paths by which information reached the reporter, are classified into three categories: routine, informal, and enterprise. *Routine* channels include (1) official proceedings such as trials, legislative hearings, and election tabulations; (2) press releases as well as reports monitored over official radio or from TASS; (3) press conferences, including daily briefings by 'official spokesmen' and broadcast interviews; and (4) non-spontaneous events, such as speeches, ceremonies, and staged demonstrations. *Informal* channels include (1) background briefings; (2) leaks; (3) non-governmental proceedings like association meetings or trade union conventions;[5] and (4) news reports from other news organizations, interviews with reporters, and newspaper editorials. *Enterprise* channels include (1) interviews conducted at the reporter's initiative; (2) spontaneous events which a reporter witnesses firsthand, like fires, riots, and natural disasters; (3) independent research involving quotations from books and statistical data; and (4) the reporter's own conclusions or analysis.

In stories that fail to specify the channels used, the critical choice is

---

2 Nimmo, *Newsgathering in Washington*, passim.

3 The *Post* uses mutt boxes and headlines on Page One which refer to stories on inside pages. Both newspapers occasionally use pictures on Page One but run the accompanying story inside. In the fifteen cases where this occurred, the stories are included.

4 Six stories that satisfied these criteria but dealt with international financial matters were nevertheless included.

5 Coverage of non-governmental proceedings can be quasi-routine: the *Times* and the *Post* cover many labour, agriculture, political party, and academic conventions with beat correspondents just as reporters assigned to Capitol Hill cover the sessions of Congress. Most of the time, however, this is not the case. The decision to include non-governmental proceedings in the informal rather than the routine category was, in the end, dictated by the need to bias the classification against the routine in order to strengthen the null hypothesis.

between enterprise and informal channels. The procedure adopted is to classify as coming from a background briefing the information that has little or no attribution but that appears in more than one paper the same day; thus, backgrounders, by definition, have more than one reporter in attendance. When unattributed information appears in one, and only one, newspaper on a given day, it is classified as having been obtained through an interview, unless independent evidence from subsequent news articles, historical studies or memoirs, or officials' and reporters' recollections indicates that it was a leak. The restrictiveness of the background briefing and leak categories is designed to bias the choice toward enterprise channels, to favour the null hypothesis.

Those individuals or organizations passing information through a channel, or *sources* as they are known, are classified into one of five categories: (1) US government officials; (2) foreign government officials, including officials of international agencies; (3) officials of state and local governments in the United States; (4) foreigners not in any government; and (5) private citizens of the United States. Even when a source was only vaguely identified, it still proved possible in almost every instance to place him in one of the broad categories.

■ **Channels for News**

For all stories at the *Times* and *Post* combined, routine channels outnumber enterprise channels by well over two to one (see Table 1). Editors at both newspapers rely on the wire services to cover some routine spot news. They

TABLE 1. *Channels of Information for News in the* Times *and* Post *Combined—All Stories (N = 2,850)*[a]

Routine	58.2	Official proceedings	12.0
		Press releases	17.5
		Press conferences	24.2
		Non-spontaneous events	4.5
Informal	15.7	Background briefings	7.9
		Leaks	2.3
		Non-governmental proceedings	1.5
		News reports, editorials, etc.	4.0
Enterprise	25.8	Interviews	23.7
		Spontaneous events	1.2
		Books, research, etc.	—
		Reporter's own analysis	0.9
Not ascertainable	0.3		

[a] Per cent of total channels; stories may have more than one channel. All figures given are percentages

also run occasional stories from Reuters and from other newspapers which their own staff did not obtain. When only stories by the staffs of the two newspapers are included, routine channels still outnumber enterprise channels by about two to one, regardless of the newspaper, as shown in Table 2.

TABLE 2. *Channels of Information in the* Times *and the* Post— *Staff Stories Only (figures expressed as percentages)*

	The Times $(N = 1,398)^a$	*The* Post $(N = 822)^a$	*Both Papers* $(N = 2,220)^a$
Routine	53.7	58.9	55.6
Informal	18.5	13.0	16.4
Enterprise	27.6	28.1	27.8
Not ascertainable	0.2	—	0.1

^{a} Total number of channels.

A count of channels cited is one indication of the routine in newsgathering. News stories in the sample average between two and three channels per story, so that counting total channels does not discriminate between the story that relies primarily on one channel and the story gathered through numerous channels. About one-third of all stories in the sample cited one channel only. For the stories with more than one channel, a distinction was drawn between the primary channel and secondary channels of information. The *primary* channel is defined as the channel for the information which (1) comprises the lead and/or the major portion of the story as a whole; and (2) accounts for the timing of its appearance in the news. A few stories had no identifiable channel that satisfied both criteria. In these cases, the second criterion was considered sufficient for purposes of classification.[6]

Single-channel stories, based entirely on information received from one channel, account for one-third of the stories sampled. The channels for such stories are predominantly routine. So, too, are the primary channels for multichannel stories (see Table 3). The implication of these findings is that stories usually emerge through routine channels. These channels thus determine when most stories happen to surface. In one out of three stories, moreover, newsgathering goes no further than a single channel. In the other two-thirds, the reporter subsequently follows up his initial information through other channels, frequently involving his own enterprise. Thus, the breakdown among secondary channels is 49.7 per cent routine, 13.3 per cent informal, and 36.5 per cent enterprise.

TABLE 3. *Channels of Information in Single- and Multi-Channel Stories (figures expressed as percentages)*

	Single-Channel Stories (N=405)	*Primary Channel for Multi-Channel Stories (N-741)*	*All Primary Channels (N=1,146)*
Routine	74.6	68.6	70.7
Informal	18.7	19.6	19.3
Enterprise	6.6	11.7	9.9

6 One caveat is worth mentioning here. The term *primary* does not necessarily mean that the information passed through that channel is the most important in the story to any reader. Reporters have a way of inserting sentences near the end of their stories which cast doubt on the information in the bulk of the preceding copy. The discerning reader may well consider that the most important part of the story.

Newsgathering in Washington, even with the larger staffs that both the *Times* and *Post* devote to it, relies as heavily on routine channels as newsgathering elsewhere, as Table 4 shows. The small bureaux in foreign capitals and around the United States, many of them one-man operations, might be expected to cover spot news routinely, just as undermanned bureaux covering Washington for regional and foreign newspapers do, monitoring other newspapers and following the most important story in their locale. A look at only those stories written by staff members supports this finding. *Times* and *Post* correspondents in London, for example, made greater use of news reports in other newspapers and background briefings for both primary and nonprimary channels of newsgathering, but did about as much interviewing in following up a story as did their Washington colleagues. The same applies to those stationed in the Paris and Bonn bureaux. The predominant use of routine channels in Washington news-gathering seems to reflect efforts of official news sources everywhere to con-fine the dissemination of news to routine channels, as well as reporters' reliance on them.

Defining the categories of channels in the way the study has done, and counting each channel without weighting it according to the space or place-ment of the information from it, may yield an over-representation of the importance of enterprise channels. Nevertheless, the evidence supports the proposition that most page-one news in both the *Times* and the *Post* derives from routine channels.

TABLE 4. *Channels of Information in Washington and Elsewhere (figures expressed as percentages)*

	Washington Dateline		Other US Datelines		Foreign Datelines	
	Primary Only (N = 548)	All Channels (N = 1,316)	Primary Only (N = 197)	All Channels (N = 492)	Primary Only (N = 397)	All Channels (N = 1,034)
Routine	72.3	60.2	68.0	56.5	70.3	56.4
Informal	20.1	13.3	16.2	8.1	19.9	19.0
Enterprise	7.7	26.2	15.7	35.3	9.8	24.0

■ **News Sources**   Numerically, the most important sources of information are officials of the US government. They account for nearly one-half of all the sources cited in the sample of *Times* and *Post* page-one stories (see Table 5). Although the category 'US official' subsumes officials in all three branches of government, officials in the Executive Branch predominate as news sources: the federal judiciary contributes about 2 per cent of all sources and the Congress 6 per cent, nearly all in the course of judicial and legislative proceedings.

When stories not written by *Times* and *Post* staff correspondents are excluded, American officials are still the dominant sources of information in both newspapers (see Table 6). The contrast between the two newspapers seems largely a function of the number of bureaux each has outside Washington. Until the early 1960s, the *Post* staff was heavily concentrated in Washington. During that decade, as the *Post* expanded its network of overseas and domestic bureaux, the differences in news sources between the two newspapers diminished.

TABLE 5. *Sources of Information in the* Times *and the* Post—*All Stories (N = 2,850)*

	% of Total Sources
US officials, agencies	46.5
Foreign, international officials, agencies	27.5
American state, local government officials	4.1
Other news organizations	3.2
Non-governmental foreigners	2.1
Non-governmental Americans	14.4
Not ascertainable[a]	2.4

[a] Not ascertainable includes stories in which the channel was a spontaneous event or the reporter's own analysis.

TABLE 6. *Sources of Information in the* Times *and the* Post—*Staff Stories Only (percentages)*

	The Times (N = 1,398)[a]	The Post (N = 822)[a]	Both Papers (N = 2,220)[a]
US officials	42.3	62.8	49.9
Foreign, international	31.4	13.5	24.7
State, local government	3.6	3.9	3.7
Other news organizations	3.6	2.2	3.1
Non-government foreigners	2.4	1.1	1.9
Non-government Americans	14.9	15.2	15.0
Not ascertainable	1.9	1.3	1.7

[a] Total number of sources.

The dominance of American official sources is even more pronounced in stories with only one source and among primary sources. American officials were the sole source in 56.3 per cent of the 405 single-source stories and were 53.8 per cent of all primary sources.

American officials, as expected, contribute the bulk of information for stories datelined Washington, but they also serve as sources for many stories from across the country and around the world (see Table 7). American officials, for instance, were 21.2 per cent of the sources of news out of London, 24.8 per cent out of Paris, 15.9 per cent out of Moscow, and 54.0 per cent out of Saigon.

The spread of bureaux around the country and overseas nevertheless counterbalances somewhat the dominance of US official sources. Reporters in domestic bureaux, to a much greater extent than those in Washington, get information from individuals and groups who do not work in the Federal government. Reporters in foreign bureaux, to a greater extent than those in Washington, get their stories from officials, but most are officials of foreign governments, with perspectives on the world that might be at variance with those of American officials.

TABLE 7. *Sources of Information in Washington and Elsewhere—Staff Stories Only (percentages)*

	Washington		Other US		Foreign	
	Primary Sources (N = 478)	All Sources (N = 1,183)	Primary Sources (N = 124)	All Sources (N = 334)	Primary Sources (N = 251)	All Sources (N = 696)
US officials	85.1	71.8	45.2	28.7	18.3	23.0
Foreign, inter-national officials	3.6	9.1	1.6	3.6	70.9	61.8
State, local officials	0.4	1.9	11.3	17.4	0.0	0.1
Other news organizations	1.5	2.1	0.0	1.8	2.4	5.3
Non-government foreigners	0.4	0.8	0.0	0.3	2.4	4.5
Non-government Americans	7.9	13.4	36.3	44.6	2.8	3.0
Not ascertainable	1.0	0.8	5.6	3.6	3.2	2.3

■ **Routine Channels, Official Sources**

Whatever the location of their bureaux and their beats, reporters rely mainly on routine channels to get information. The beat system of the *Times* and *Post* concentrates staff at routine channels set up by the US government—channels generally under the control of senior officials. *The routine channels for newsgathering thus constitute the mechanism for official dominance of national and foreign news in the two papers.*

One way to indicate this relationship is to count information 'transfers', defining a transfer as the passage of information from a single source through a single channel to a reporter. Of the 2,850 transfers in the sample, American officials using routine channels alone account for 31.4 per cent. An additional 17.6 per cent of all transfers involve officials in foreign governments and international agencies employing routine channels. By contrast, only 16.5 per cent of all transfers comes from nonofficial sources, whatever their channel.

Another way to point up the interdependence of routine channels and official sources in newsgathering is to contrast dominance of routine channels by American officials to the relatively equal accessibility of enterprise channels to foreign officials and non-governmental sources (see Table 8). To the extent that a reporter receives information through routine channels, he has a one-in-two chance of getting it from a source in the American government.

TABLE 8. *Official Dominance of Routine Channels (figures expressed as percentages)*

Sources	Channels			
	Routine (N = 1,658)	Informal (N = 361)	Enterprise (N = 823)	All Channels (N = 2,850)
US government officials	53.8	50.1	30.5	46.5
Foreign, inter-national officials	30.3	28.0	21.3	27.4
Non-government sources[a]	11.3	12.5	28.8	16.5

[a] Foreign plus American

Alternatively, while American officials are three times as likely to pass information to reporters through routine channels as through enterprise channels, non-officials are more likely to do so through enterprise channels than through the other two types of channels (see Table 9).

Official dominance of routine channels is particularly evident in the place where both the *Times* and *Post* concentrate their staffs—on beats in Washington. Of the 794 uses of routine channels sampled there, US officials were the sources of information 80.7 per cent of the time—ten times as frequently as either foreign officials or non-government sources. Of the 345 uses of enterprise channels, American officials were the sources for 52.5 per cent, foreign officials for 7.8 per cent, and private citizens 24.9 per cent. When only stories by *Times* and *Post* staff members are considered, the relationship still holds.

TABLE 9. *Routine Channels and Official Sources (figures expressed as percentages)*

	US Govt. Official (N = 1,365)	For., Intl. Official (N = 782)	State, Local Official (N = 116)	Non-govt. Foreigner (N = 60)	Non-govt. American (N = 410)
Channels:					
Routine	67.3	64.3	61.1	35.0	40.5
Informal	13.7	12.9	3.5	5.1	10.3
Enterprise	18.9	22.4	35.3	60.0	49.0
Not ascert-ainable	—	0.4	—	—	0.2

The combination of the beat system and reporter reliance on routine channels has affected the ability of Members of Congress to make news. As the beat system has expanded over time, relatively fewer correspondents on the *Times* and the *Post* assigned to the Capitol Hill beat. Legislators in pivotal positions in Congress have become more adept at disseminating information to the press, releasing reports on Saturday for Sunday papers, issuing press releases, and, in general, making themselves available to reporters.

Walter Pincus's experience in working for the chairman of the Senate Foreign Relations Committee, J. William Fulbright, is illustrative:

> In 1962–63, when I first worked for him, Senator Fulbright avoided private interviews with reporters. He was an infrequent visitor in the Senate television gallery studio for interviews. It was not that he didn't have things to say in those days—he did. But he confined his remarks primarily to statements made on the Senate floor, believing that the press would either hear him or have a chance the next day to read the *Congressional Record.* Advance texts of his speeches were rare, and a press release on his floor statements was rarer still. When I returned to the Committee [in 1970], there had been quite a change. Advance speech texts and press releases were the rule. The senator himself was well aware that in order to make the evening news shows it was wise to do the filming around noon—never after 4 p.m.—to permit the networks to plan for it.[7]

However adept they have become at using the press, Congressmen have not kept pace with the expansion of newsmaking capabilities in the Executive Branch. The consequence has been a decline over time in the proportion of Congressmen among official news sources for page-one stories in the *Times* and the *Post.*

The beat system, in concentrating staff at locations where news emerges through routine channels, underlies the predominance of these channels. Yet there are variations from beat to beat in reporters' reliance on routine channels, which seems due to the centralization of news dissemination rather than to reporters' specialization. Men on a beat have a wider circle of contacts in the agencies they cover than outsiders do. They have built up relations of trust with officials. They know which officials to seek out and what questions to ask them. Men on general assignment or on beats elsewhere in the capital do not have these advantages. They might be expected to rely much more heavily on routine channels than correspondents on the beat, and they do; but they do not do less enterprise reporting. Beat correspondents, while using routine channels less, turn instead to informal channels—backgrounders and leaks—channels less accessible to those who do not cover the beat regularly. Still, the variation from beat to beat is more pronounced than the differences among reportorial types.

On news emanating from the White House, for example, 71.8 per cent of all channels were routine, 18.0 per cent informal, and 10.4 per cent enterprise. These percentages may be considered an *average value* for use of the various channels on that beat. White House correspondents on the *Times* and *Post* staffs used routine channels in 70.0 per cent of the transfers, informal channels 26.6 per cent, and enterprise channels 3.3 per cent. General assignment reporters, gathering news at the White House, used routine channels in 54.0 per cent of the transfers, enterprise channels 21.6 per cent, and informal channels 24.3 percent, as indicated in Table 10. The data should be read with caution because in one out of five cases the reporter's assignment could not be ascertained. While differences among types of reporters

7 Walter Pincus, 'Before the Pentagon Papers: Why the Press Failed', *New York*, 4/39 (19 July 1971): 36.

do exist, they are slight compared to the differences between beats. News dissemination at the White House is much more centralized through routine channels than at the State Department.

TABLE 10. *Variation in Channel by Beat and Reportorial Assignment (figures expressed as percentages)*

	(a) White House			
	Average Value	White House Correspondents	Men on General Assignment	Correspondents from Other Beats
	(N = 173)	(N = 30)	(N = 37)	(N = 62)
Routine	71.8	70.0	54.0	75.7
Informal	18.0	26.6	21.6	14.9
Enterprise	10.4	3.3	24.3	9.5

	(b) State Department			
	Average Value	State Department Correspondents	Men on General Assignment	Correspondents from Other Beats
	(N = 138)	(N = 66)	(N = 12)	(N = 9)
Routine	50.7	39.4	50.0	33.3
Informal	29.6	36.4	16.7	44.4
Enterprise	18.8	24.2	33.3	22.2

■ Changes over Time

Despite the expansion of bureau networks and staff size at both the *Times* and the *Post* from 1949 to 1969, most patterns of channel and source use did not change markedly during the period. Over time there was little change in the dominance of American officials as sources for news—if anything, American officials increased overall as sources for news while non-government sources showed no change and foreign officials declined. In stories by staff reporters only, the *Times* increased its use of US officials as sources from 38.8 per cent in 1949 to 47.9 per cent by 1969, while the *Post* decreased its use, from over 80 per cent in 1949 down to 53.1 per cent by 1969. Foreign officials made page one less and less often in the *Times*, but more and more often at the *Post*, as it opened new bureaux abroad. Non-government sources registered little change in either paper. American officials increased their dominance of the routine channels of newsgathering over the period and increasingly dominated informal channels as well.

But one significant difference did emerge. Reporters' reliance on routine channels declined throughout the period 1949–69, and their use of enterprise channels showed a corresponding rise (see Table 11). The trend was not nearly as pronounced in primary channels. Over time, then, reporters have increasingly followed up information obtained through routine channels by interviewing other sources. Along with this change has come a slight rise in enterprise stories, stories which the reporter develops on his own initiative.

TABLE 11. *Channels of Information in the* Post *and the* Times, *1949–1969—All Stories*

Year	Routine (%)	Informal (%)	Enterprise (%)	N =
1949	65.9	11.7	21.4	(545)
1954	62.2	14.8	22.5	(502)
1959	57.9	11.6	30.5	(556)
1964	57.5	15.6	26.9	(534)
1969	50.1	10.6	39.1	(713)

These conclusions have two major corollaries. First, although the proportion of nonofficial sources showed no significant rise, it did register an increase in absolute terms, particularly in 1969, as the total number of sources and channels rose. Second, although the proportion of US official sources remained steady over the twenty-year period, the relative decline in the use of routine channels may have altered the ratio of stories from senior officials to stories from lower-echelon bureaucrats. The data bearing directly on this question point in this direction, but they are too sketchy to permit any firm generalization. It is nevertheless a reasonable inference that as reporters do more and more interviewing, they will obtain more information from 'permanent government' as opposed to 'Presidential government' officials. Career bureaucrats may have an institutional inclination to hew less closely to a given administration line than do political appointees. What both the Johnson and the Nixon Administrations perceived as increased hostility in the press, then, may have an explanation other than just a change in newsmen's political attitudes. At the *Times* and the *Post*, at least, it may also be a manifestation of longer-run trends in newsgathering away from channels dominated by senior officials, trends resulting from an expansion of news staffs and a proliferation of news bureaux and beats.

■ Routine News
as 'Certified' News

Imbedded in the words *news medium* is a connotation that aptly defines the function of the press: it mediates between the officialdom and the citizenry of the United States. Like a pipeline carrying water from a reservoir to a city, it has some effect on what arrives at the end of the line. Not all droplets that enter the pipeline end up in the same destination; some are routed elsewhere, others evaporate en route. Yet the effects of the pipeline are minor compared to the source of the water—the reservoir. Similarly, newsmen, by adhering to routine channels of newsgathering, leave much of the task of selection of news to its sources.

Adherence to routine channels allows newsmen to cope with the uncertain world of journalism. Newsmen cluster around these channels, each gathering much the same information as his colleagues. Uncertainty loves company: the similarity of their stories provides some reassurance that newsmen understand what is going on in their world. For men who do not and cannot know what the 'real' news is, the routines of newsgathering produce 'certified news'—information that seems valid insofar as it is common knowledge among newsmen and their sources.

26

Deciding What's News

Herbert J. Gans

The Organization of Story Selection

IN REPORTING THE news about a nation of over 200 million potential actors in news stories, journalists could, in theory, choose from billions of potential activities. In fact, however, they can learn about only a tiny fraction of actors and activities; and having limited air time and magazine space, they must select an even tinier fraction. More important, they cannot decide anew every day or week how to select the fraction that will appear on the news; instead, they must routinize their task in order to make it manageable.[1]

■ **Theories of Story Selection**

Many theories have been put forth about how the selection of stories is routinized. One type of theory is journalist-centred: it argues that the news is shaped by the professional news judgement of journalists. Messrs Nixon and Agnew applied a variant of this theory when they attacked the news media for choosing the news on the basis of deliberate ideological bias. Many politicians hold a somewhat similar view. Judging the news by its implications for their political careers, they blame journalistic bias when the news hurts them.

A second type of theory, favoured by social-science studies, locates the routinization in the news organization and shows how story selection is influenced by organizational requirements. Some organizational theories focus on the news firm and emphasize commercial imperatives; others are more concerned with the news organizations themselves and look at how their structures and division of labour affect story selection.[2] The theories

Source: Herbert J. Gans, *Deciding What's News* (Constable, London: 1980; originally published 1979).

1 For an insightful discussion of this point, see Gaye Tuchman, 'Making News by Doing Work: Routinizing the Unexpected', *American Journal of Sociology*, 79 (July 1974): 110–31.

2 One of the first organizational studies of the news was Warren Breed's now classic 'Social Control in the Newsroom', *Social Forces*, 33 (May 1955): 326–35. The best recent empirical studies of the news organization are Leon V. Sigal's book on the *Washington Post* and *The New York Times* entitled *Reporters and Officials: The Organization and Politics of Newsmaking* (Lexington, Mass.: D. C. Heath, 1973); and Edward J. Epstein's study of *NBC News* entitled *News from Nowhere* (New York: Random House, 1973). See also Bernard Roshco, *Newsmaking* (Chicago: University of Chicago Press, 1975); and Robert Darnton, 'Writing News and Telling Stories', *Daedalus* (Spring 1975): 175–94.
 Some studies of local and foreign news organizations are cited in the bibliography. I have also benefited from Paul Hirsch's sociological analysis of the economics of mass media as oligopolies. See e.g. Hirsch, 'Occupational, Organizational, and Institutional Models in Mass Media Research. Toward an Integrated Framework', in P. Hirsch, P. Miller, and F. Kline (eds.), *Strategies for Communication Research*, Sage Annual Reviews of Communication Research 6 (Beverly Hills, Calif.: Sage Publications, 1977), 13–42.

also vary by the degree of influence organizational requirements have on story selection. Some reify the organization at the expense of events, as if story selection were not affected by them; others forget that journalists, being professionals, also shape the organization and the news.[3]

A third approach is event-centred: the so-called mirror theory, which used to be popular among journalists, proposes that events determine story selection, with journalists simply holding a mirror to them and reflecting their image to the audience. Mirror theory began to weaken in the 1960s, as media critics pointed out what journalists did to, and with, events in transforming them into news, and called attention to events that failed to become news.

A final set of theories explains story selection with forces outside the news organization. Technological determinists, such as Marshall McLuhan, argue that the message is determined by the technology of the medium. Economic determinists view the national economy as moulding story selection; and some Marxists treat journalists as the public-relations agents of monopoly capitalism. Similarly, ideological determinists believe that journalists align the news to the political ideology of those holding power in the country. Cultural theorists extend this, seeing journalists as selecting stories which accord with the values of the national culture. A related approach centers on the audience, as expressed in the notion that 'we get the news we deserve'. Another type of externally centred theory suggests that the news is shaped, above all, by the sources on which journalists rely; or, as Molotch and Lester argue, by those groups in society powerful enough both to create what they call 'public events' and to gain access to journalists.[4]

These capsule descriptions of alternative explanations of story selection all contain some degree of truth. Journalists do apply news judgement, both as members of a profession and as individuals, but they are by no means totally free agents, and in any case, they rarely make selection decisions on overtly ideological grounds; rather, they work within organizations which provide them with only a limited amount of leeway in selection decisions, which is further reduced by their allegiance to professionally shared values.

Journalists do not hold up mirrors to events; nonetheless, mirror theory remains useful, for it reminds us that journalists do not make up the news but begin with what they deem an empirically graspable external reality. Phenomenologically inclined researchers have made a major contribution to understanding journalists and their work by showing that whatever the nature of external reality, human beings can perceive it only with their own concepts, and therefore always 'construct' reality.[5] Even before phenomenological theories became popular, sociologists had shown that the events

3 An organizational theory that leaves more leeway for individual journalists is David Manning White's gatekeeper theory, which visualizes the editor as opening and closing the newspaper's 'gate' to stories he selects. Gatekeeper theory is more easily applied to media which depend largely on wire-service news than to those which also search out their own news. David M. White, 'The "Gatekeeper": A Case Study in the Selection of News', *Journalism Quarterly*, 27 (Fall 1950): 383–90.

4 H. L. Molotch and M. J. Lester, 'News as Purposive Behavior', *American Sociological Review*, 39 (Feb. 1974): 101–12.

5 Peter Berger and Thomas Luckmann, *The Social Construction of Reality* (New York: Anchor Books, 1967). For some applications to the study of news, see Molotch and Lester, 'News as Purposive Behavior'; Gaye Tuchman, 'Objectivity as Strategic Ritual: An Examination of Newsmen's Notions of Objectivity', *American Journal of Sociology*, 77 (Jan. 1972): 660–70; as well as Tuchman, *Making News* (New York: Free Press, 1978).

journalists ostensibly cover are themselves journalistic constructs that frame chronologically and otherwise related phenomena.[6]

While print and electronic news media rest on different technologies, every news medium uses its technology primarily to compete against other news media, and it does so selectively.[7] Television could limit itself to tell stories if it did not have to compete against the newspaper or the radio. Besides, the stories which different news media select are sufficiently similar to suggest that technology is not a determining factor. Economic determinists are closer to the truth; but even if the news is critical of socialism, journalists are not merely public-relations agents for capitalism. Insofar as they express the dominant political ideology, they often do so unconsciously. They work inside a national culture; but nations are aggregates of subcultures, and a relevant cultural approach would ask which subcultures are reported and ignored in the news. We do not get the news we deserve because we, the audience, are not directly involved in choosing it. Sources, however, are crucial.

My Own Approach   I view news as information which is transmitted from sources to audiences, with journalists—who are both employees of bureaucratic commercial organizations and members of a profession—summarizing, refining, and altering what becomes available to them from sources in order to make the information suitable for their audiences. Because news has consequences, however, journalists are susceptible to pressure from groups and individuals (including sources and audiences) with power to hurt them, their organizations, and their firms. By 'sources', I mean the actors whom journalists observe or interview, including interviewees who appear on the air or who are quoted in magazine articles, and those who only supply background information or story suggestions. For my purpose, however, the most salient characteristic of sources is that they provide information as members or representatives of organized and unorganized interest groups, and yet larger sectors of nation and society.

Although the notion that journalists transmit information from sources to audiences suggests a linear process, in reality the process is circular, complicated further by a large number of feedback loops. For example, sources cannot provide information until they make contact with a member of a news organization; and that organization will choose the sources it considers suitable for the audience, even as it is chosen by sources who want to transmit information to the audience. Sources are also an important part of the audience, particularly in Washington. The audience is, moreover, not only an information recipient but a source of income for the news firm; and insofar as its allegiance must be maintained, its viewing and reading behaviour even affects, to some extent, the choice of sources by journalists. In effect, then, sources, journalists, and audiences coexist in a system, although it is closer to being a tug of war than a functionally interrelated organism.

---

6 The pioneering work by sociologists is Kurt and Gladys Lang's 1952 study of the reporting of the MacArthur Day parade in Chicago, in their 'The Unique Perspective of Television and Its Effect: A Pilot Study', *American Sociological Review*, 18 (Feb. 1953): 3–12.

7 The Langs point out, rightly that '[C]ontrary to the McLuhanites, . . . the way [television] appears depends on the way the men who employ the technology make use of it.' *Politics and Television* (New York: Quadrangle Books, 1968), 5–6.

Tugs of war, however, are resolved by power; and news is, among other things, 'the exercise of power over the interpretation of reality'.[8] Power is exercised by all participants in the transmittal of information; it is also in evidence inside the news organization, which is hierarchically organized.[9] Even readers and viewers have some power, expressed by protest against and refusal to accept what they read and see, which is why journalists often worry about their credibility.

Availability and Suitability

Since this book is based on a study of journalists and their organizations, I have chosen to cut into the circular process there. From this perspective, story selection is essentially composed of two processes: one determines the availability of news and relates journalists to sources; the other determines the suitability of news, which ties journalists to audiences. Sources and journalists, however, must have access to each other before information can become news; but that access is differentially distributed, depending in part on the social distance between sources and journalists, and even more so on their respective power. The economically and politically powerful can obtain easy access to, and are sought out by, journalists; those who lack power are harder to reach by journalists and are generally not sought out until their activities produce social or moral disorder news. In short, access reflects the social structure outside the newsroom; and because that structure is hierarchical, the extent to which information about various parts of America is available to journalists is hierarchically and differentially distributed. Even so, journalists almost always have more available information than they can use; consequently, they must also make suitability judgements, through which they winnow available information to select what they can cover with limited staffs and time, and what they can report in the equally limited amount of air time or magazine space.

The crucial word is 'limited', because what distinguishes journalism from literary and social-science studies of America is the deadline, which is immutable in television and can be extended at the magazines only by high additional expenditures. Lack of time and staff also require the use of quickly and easily applied methods of empirical inquiry, and limited air time and magazine space restrict the number of findings that can be presented. This is one reason why news is basically descriptive; temporal and other resources that social scientists can devote to complex analyses and explanations are not often available. [. . .]

Sources and Journalists

Journalists obtain the news from sources they observe or interview. A complete study of the news should therefore include an investigation of both the individuals who become sources and the 99 per cent of the population that does not. Since sources represent organized and unorganized groups (if not

8 Philip Schlesinger, 'The Sociology of Knowledge' (Paper presented at the 1972 meeting of the British Sociological Association, 24 March 1972), p. 4.

9 The role of power in story selection was already emphasized by Breed, 'Social Control in the Newsroom'.

always intentionally), the study would need to ask how and why they become sources, and how what they do and say as sources relate to the groups they represent. I have not carried out such a study, however; my observations are gleaned from what I learned about sources in studying journalists and from the sources I encountered during my fieldwork.

The relationship between sources and journalists resembles a dance, for sources seek access to journalists, and journalists seek access to sources. Although it takes two to tango, either sources or journalists can lead, but more often than not, sources do the leading. Staff and time being in short supply, journalists actively pursue only a small number of regular sources who have been available and suitable in the past, and are passive toward other possible news sources. In many cases, national news organizations depend on the wire services or other news media (local and national) to find them, after which they assign their own reporters to get another version of, or angle on, the story. In other instances, they wait for sources to make contact with a reporter, and to sell him or her a story idea. There are notable exceptions, of course, such as exposés, for which journalists will become exceedingly active in digging out sources; and the magazines compete in part by discovering new sources who can shed additional light on important stories of the week. But often, the national journalists follow the news.

■ **Availability: Source-Journalist Relations**

Journalists see people mainly as potential sources, but sources see themselves as people with a chance to provide information that promotes their interests, to publicize their ideas, or in some cases, just to get their names and faces into the news. In any event, sources can only make themselves available; it is the journalists who will decide if they are suitable. If so, the information offered is screened by the journalists' observations and interview questions. The source-journalist relationship is therefore a tug of war: while sources attempt to 'manage' the news, putting the best light on themselves, journalists concurrently 'manage' the sources in order to extract the information they want.

Looking at the tug of war from the perspective of sources suggests that their successful access to journalists is shaped by at least four interrelated factors: (1) incentives; (2) power; (3) the ability to supply suitable information; and (4) geographic and social proximity to the journalists. Of the four, the ability to provide suitable information is crucial, but the other three factors enhance that ability. In fact, Molotch and Lester have suggested that the news is determined largely by the power of sources to create suitable news.[10] Not all sources are as powerful as the ones they discuss; but in the end, power of one kind or another is highly instrumental, at least in the attempt to gain access.

Incentives: Eager, Agreeable, and Recalcitrant Sources

Since journalists must often let sources come to them, the news is weighted toward sources which are eager to provide information. Sources become eager either because they benefit from the widespread and legitimated publicity the news media supply or because they need the news media to carry out their duties.

10 Molotch and Lester, 'News as Purposive Behavior'.

Private firms can use advertising to obtain publicity, but even they prefer a news story about their activities, since it is more credible. Public agencies, voluntary and professional organizations, and most individuals either cannot afford or are not allowed to advertise; consequently, they depend on the news media for visibility. National politicians cannot long function without news publicity, while the power of federal agencies to command an increased share of the federal budget often depends on their ability to be in the news at the right time. The point is obvious: individuals and groups whose well-being is achieved and maintained by acting for, or on behalf of, constituencies must become eager sources in the hope of reaching their constituents as members of the audience. This helps explain why so much of the news centers on public and other agencies which serve constituencies.

Eager sources eventually become regular ones, appearing in the news over and over again. Most sources that appear intermittently are agreeable; they do not need the news to survive but enjoy the benefits, such as added prestige, that come from appearing in the national news media. Permanently recalcitrant sources are few, although many politicians and public officials who are normally eager sources will quickly become recalcitrant when the news hurts them or their cause.

Being a recalcitrant source is less a matter of incentive than of power to refuse access to reporters. Corporate officials and others who operate without public funds—and some who do—are often able to bar reporters, but public officials are legally required to be available for public inspection even if they try to circumvent the relevant laws. The privacy of private enterprise is less easily invaded, which is why the news contains fewer moral disorder stories about it than about the government. Still, even powerful recalcitrants, including private agencies, can bar journalists only at some risk, for nothing whets journalistic hunger for a good story as much as being denied access, which may result in the scheduling of an exposé.

The investigative reporting required for an exposé is expensive and not always productive, for reporters must usually be assigned to the story for weeks, if not months, thus making them unavailable for other stories; and sometimes, months of investigation may not produce a suitable story. As a result, most news media resort to investigative reporting only when they cannot obtain access any other way or, equally often, when they need a circulation or rating booster. However, some reporters who are refused access will work long overtime hours to pursue a recalcitrant source on their own.

The ability of recalcitrant sources to bar access is balanced by a countervailing process. Organizations often become recalcitrant because of internal controversy or turmoil, which may spawn sources inside the organization eager to leak information, anonymously, either to expose immoral behaviour or to publicize their side of the controversy. During Watergate, the more the White House tried to prevent leaks, the more it increased the eagerness of other officials to supply news about people whom they wanted exposed and forced out of the government.

The Power of Sources

I noted earlier that while in theory sources can come from anywhere, in practice, their recruitment and their access to journalists reflect the hierarchies of nation and society. The president of the United States has instantaneous access to all news media whenever he wants it; the powerless must resort to civil disturbances to obtain it.[11]

Of course, powerful sources rarely use their power to bully their way into story lists; indeed, they use their power to create suitable news. Nor are story selectors easily bullied; they retain the right to choose suitable sources, and even the president is sometimes not deemed sufficiently newsworthy. Also, story selectors have little contact with sources, powerful or powerless; in fact, top editors and producers are quite isolated. Magazine editors do meet powerful sources at special briefings with the president or high federal officials, the luncheons and dinners they hold for presidential candidates or other notables visiting New York, and the parties they attend after working hours. These occasions do not, however, seem to provide the powerful with useful access, as editors attending these functions often complain that they are a waste of time. Television producers seldom have the time to attend such occasions and may never meet their most newsworthy sources; as one producer pointed out: 'We work in hermetically sealed rooms.' Anchorpersons are somewhat freer to get out of the newsroom, however. Whenever the evening news originates from Washington, the anchorperson has probably been invited to a White House dinner or a personal interview with a high official.

The hierarchical structure of the news organization has a similarly isolating effect, for contact with sources, powerful or not, is almost entirely left to reporters. To be sure, the president, or a corporation president, can get on the telephone and suggest a story directly to a top editor or producer; but for status reasons alone, powerful people generally call the corporate heads of the news firms. The executives, however, are restrained by the organizational division of labour, and they pass on the story suggestion in such a way as to enable story selectors to ignore it.

At the national level, power is generally exercised by refusing access and is the primary form of censorship. The White House, the Pentagon, the State Department, and a few other agencies can plead 'national security'; although the plea has been abused by more than one government agency over the years, journalists still have to think twice before going ahead. During the Vietnam War, the military sometimes kept reporters away from battles which were going badly by withholding transportation to the war zone.[12] [...]

The more powerful a politician, the harder it is for a reporter to find someone who will talk; thus, one early indicator of Richard Nixon's declining power was the number of people ready and able to leak information. At the same time, reporters who come up with stories that are explicitly or implicitly critical of powerful sources must provide considerable evidence to substantiate their facts, for such stories will result in an angry call from the source, and executives cannot defend reporters whose evidence is not convincing.

11 The access problems of the powerless are described in detail in Edie N. Goldenberg's study of the Boston newspapers, *Making the Papers* (Lexington, Mass: D. C. Heath, 1975).

12 The Pentagon also discouraged television reporters from showing closeups of wounded or dead American soldiers because it wanted to inform the next-of-kin first; reporters complied willingly because they, too, wanted to spare relatives from the shock of unexpectedly seeing tragic news on television.

Sources with less power can normally gain access only with an unusually dramatic story; on the other hand, as power decreases, so does the ability to bar access. Reporters can intrude on the privacy of ordinary individuals who have been struck by tragedy to ask them what they are feeling; they dislike the practice but continue doing so only for fear that their competitors will scoop them. Very poor people can stave off access, however, because reporters, like other nonpoor people, are reluctant to go into poor neighborhoods. The inability of white reporters to enter the ghetto slums during the disturbances of the 1960s thus created instantaneous jobs for black reporters.

Ability to Supply
Suitable Information

Given the journalists' insatiable appetite for story ideas and stories, sources which are able to supply suitable news can overcome deficiencies of power. Even so, the ability to be newsworthy itself requires resources and skills, many of which go hand in hand with economic power, at least, and are possessed by only a few.

Perhaps the most able sources are organizations that carry out the equivalent of investigative reporting, offer the results of their work as 'exclusives', and can afford to do so anonymously, foregoing the rewards of publicity. The FBI has often supplied detailed information about the misdeeds of American politicians whose political careers it wanted to end. In 1977, a story about the alleged appointment of a new head of the Mafia turned out later to have been leaked by the Drug Enforcement Administration. According to one reporter, the DEA supplied the story 'because this is the hood they know a lot about, so when they bring him down, they can say: "Oh wow! What a catch we got here. This is the boss of all bosses!" '[13] The news which these agencies supply always serves their organizational self-interest in one way or another; journalists may know this, but in return, they initially secure a monopoly on a sensational story and can thereby scoop their competitors.

A related practice, sometimes called news saturation, is the proliferation of so much information by the source that some of it cannot help but turn into news, concurrently placing less well-organized sources with more accurate information at a disadvantage. The Washington and Saigon Pentagons were able to saturate the news media with inflated body counts and successes in winning the hearts and minds of the South Vietnamese population, whereas the anti-war movement lacked the resources to rebut more than a fraction of these reports, even when it had convincing evidence. [...]

Still, affluent organizations have an advantage in the competition to gain access to journalists, for they can preschedule their activities so as to satisfy the news organizations' continued need for anticipated stories. A similar advantage accrues to organizations that can supply either newsworthy spokespersons or sources who are able to make themselves available to reporters at short notice, give them the time and information they need, and do so at no cost to the journalists.

News organizations are unique among commercial firms in that the raw material from which they produce the news is itself obtained without charge; except in the rare instances of 'checkbook journalism', they do not pay their sources. Consequently, the news media are especially attractive to sources

---

13 Thomas Plate, 'The Making of a Godfather', *More* (June 1977), 22–3, quote at p. 22.

that need publicity but not money. Not paying sources for news thus produces an implicit class bias, although so would paying for the news. Journalists also object to helping publicity seekers, but if these persons can provide suitable stories, their motives are sometimes ignored. Public officials are not deemed to be publicity seekers unless they are unwise enough to supply information that only reflects glory on themselves. Because journalists do not pay sources, they often attract individuals and groups who are paid by someone else to be sources. Reporters try hard to avoid public-relations personnel, and instead gain access to agency heads and corporate executives, whose prime duty is also public relations.

Media Events
Sources also gain an advantage in the competition over access to journalists when they are sufficiently able and ingenious to create activities that exist solely, or mainly, to be covered by the news media—which are therefore called media events. However, not all media events are newsworthy; in addition, journalists object to being 'used' by sources. If they suspect that an event is being staged for their benefit, they may refuse to cover it. Anti-war groups were sometimes accused of scheduling demonstrations solely for the television cameras. As a result, producers grew suspect of all but the largest demonstrations. Conversely, they were less reluctant to cover press conferences, hearings, or campaign stops and other media events created by official agencies. Not only are these agencies regular sources, but the events they create are frequently judged to be important news. In recent years, however, journalists have expressed their resentment over the proliferation of media events by turning the creation of a media event into a story. As party conventions and campaign whistle stops have been designed first and foremost for television, journalists report how and why they have been so designed. Voters are increasingly exposed to election stories that show how politicians use the news media to seek their votes. [. . .]

A very different kind of media event occurs when journalists stage activities for their own benefit, either when they are short of news or are falling behind in the competition. Staging by journalists is strictly prohibited, and my impression is that it happens very rarely in the national news media. Reporters may occasionally resort to it when they think they cannot be detected; during the ghetto disturbances, they were accused of urging participants to throw stones for the benefits of the camera. Film editors usually can notice staging, and suspicious film is not used.[14] Hoaxes impair the journalists' credibility, and stagers are punished.

Geographic and Social Proximity
Sources may be eager, powerful, and ready to supply suitable information, but in order to gain access and overcome the isolation within which story selectors normally function, they must be geographically and socially close to the journalists. (Reporters must also be close to sources to which they want to gain access, but they are more mobile, at least physically, than sources.)

---

14 'D. C. Quiz on Staged News Events', *Variety*, 24 May 1972, pp. 31, 42. Conversely, television suffers from chronic staging by sources, for actors behave more dramatically when the camera appears, and film editors must routinely cut from the raw film footage people who wave or make faces at the camera.

Geographical proximity is achieved, both for sources and journalists, by the establishment of bureaux. In his study of NBC News, Epstein showed that domestic news came mainly from or near the cities in which NBC had bureaux.[15] However, bureaux tend to be located where the most suitable news is likely to be gathered, and new bureaux are established when a critical mass of stories has appeared on story lists. In addition, the wire services have created a far-flung geographical network of 'stringers', who fill many gaps left uncovered by bureaux. A mapping of all wire-service stringers would probably show that large areas of the country, especially rural sectors and low-income neighbourhoods, remain uncovered.

Still, even geographical proximity cannot guarantee social proximity. Powerful or skilled sources know how to make contact with reporters; but many people—perhaps most—lack this knowledge. Few even know how to contact reporters affiliated with their local news media, and the reporters serving the national news media are socially and otherwise far more distant. In fact, many of the features about ordinary people that appear in the national news are brought to the attention of story suggesters by local Chambers of Commerce and similar organizations skilled in getting in touch with journalists.

Social proximity is, moreover, influenced by all the structural and demographic factors that shape other social relationships, thereby enabling people of similar backgrounds and interests to make contact, and obstructing those who differ. After all, journalists are also members of society. Upper-middle-class sources, for example, are not likely to have difficulty reaching reporters and may even have a mutual friend; people of lower social status often do not know how to deal with professionals, and fear rejection to begin with. [. . .]

As a result, national journalists—but I suspect local ones as well—move within a relatively small and narrow aggregate of sources, which is dominated by the people they contact or who contact them regularly. [. . .]

Peer and Personal Sources

Peer sources are closest at hand, for story suggesters and selectors spend as much time as possible perusing other news media for their own use. Most often, they analyse an already published story for new 'angles', different ways of conceptualizing or covering it; then they assign the idea to their own reporters as a new story.

Peer sources are useful in two other ways. First, the prior appearance of a story elsewhere means that a peer has already judged its availability and suitability, thus eliminating the need for an independent decision. *The New York Times* is a primary peer source inasmuch as the size and quality of its editorial and reporting staff are taken as guarantors of the best professional news judgement; but the *Washington Post, The Wall Street Journal,* and a few southern, midwestern, and western papers are also used for story ideas. Second, prior publication is taken to be a sign that the topic has audience appeal. This applies especially to 'trend stories', which report the arrival of an up-and-coming politician, author, or entertainer; a new fad, lifestyle, or social problem.

Personal sources are primarily family members, other relatives, friends, neighbours, and people journalists meet at parties. If these people are talking

15 Epstein, *News from Nowhere*, 261.

excitedly about a new trend that has not yet been reported in the national media, a potential story is in the offing. Personal sources are useful in part because of their credibility which accrues from their close association with the journalist. They are also considered representative of the audience; consequently, their excitement about a new trend leads story selectors to assume that the audience will be interested once the story appears. [...]

Logistics and Availability

I should note that the foregoing analysis has emphasized the social aspects of source availability, but in a production process dominated by deadlines, sources are sometimes unavailable for a variety of logistic reasons. People who want to be in the news or whom journalists want to reach may be out of town; camera crews may not be in the right place at the right time, often because there are too few of them, especially in Washington. Cameras can break down, and film is sometimes overexposed or underexposed. [...]

The networks suffer more from such problems than do magazines, but from time to time, all news media lose stories they want because the sources are unavailable. These difficulties loom large for journalists, but they are rarely publicized, for admitting to them reflects on the journalists' ability to get the news. However, they do dominate the post-mortem discussions that journalists hold when they are finished with their work and can see what their competitors have done; if problems continue, people are fired and production processes are reorganized.

■ **Suitability:**
Source
Considerations

The suitability of available sources is determined by the journalists, who make their judgments on the basis of a number of interrelated source considerations. The considerations are interrelated because they have one overriding aim: efficiency. Reporters who have only a short time to gather information must therefore attempt to obtain the most suitable news from the fewest number of sources as quickly and easily as possible, and with the least strain on the organization's budget.

Source considerations come into play at the start of story selection, when little is as yet known about the stories but the sources relevant to them may be familiar and can be evaluated. Even so, these considerations are always applied in conjunction with others, especially story suitability. Altogether, I identified six major source considerations at the news media I studied.

1. Past suitability

If sources have provided information leading to suitable stories in the past, they are apt to be chosen again, until they eventually become regular sources. However, regulars are liable to supply repetitious information over time; as a result, journalists become 'bored' with some of them, dropping them from the news 'because we've seen them too often lately'. To be sure, story selectors cannot often be bored by the president of the United States, but they can be bored by sources representing single-purpose organizations, who must continually deal with the same issue. [...]

2. Productivity

Sources are judged by their ability to supply a lot of information without undue expenditure of staff time and effort. Although reporters do not shrink from whatever legwork is necessary, they and their superiors must keep logistics in mind; as a result, they try to minimize the number of sources to be consulted. This partially accounts for the predominance of high public officials in the news: as spokespersons for their agencies, they can spare journalists time and effort by eliminating the need to interview other agency members. Productivity also explains the emphasis on government plans and new policies in the news; these can be obtained from the official announcing them, whereas stories about the implementation and effects of policies require interviews with many people. Of course, if the story calls for a large number of interviews, they will be done, in which case, reporters will seek out central clearing houses that can quickly supply names. [. . .]

3. Reliability   Story selectors want reliable sources whose information requires the least amount of checking. However, if a story or a fact is controversial or not readily believed, reporters are then expected to gather proof from at least two separate and independent sources.

When reporters can explicitly attribute information to a source, they do not have to worry about reliability (and validity), the assumption being that once a story is 'sourced', their responsibility is fulfilled, and audiences must decide whether the source is credible. A magazine writer once pointed out that 'we don't deal in facts but in attributed opinions'. Nevertheless, an unreliable source can damage journalistic credibility.

4. Trustworthiness   When reliability cannot be checked quickly enough, story selectors look for trustworthy sources: those who do not limit themselves to self-serving information, try to be accurate, and, above all, are honest. Reporters keep a continuing check on the honesty of sources, remember when they have been lied to, and inform story selectors accordingly while selling them story ideas.

Much of the cynicism attributed to journalists is actually their distrust of sources, and the greatest distrust is felt for politicians, who are deemed to be inherently 'two-faced' and inconsistent.

Journalists often have difficulty in judging the trustworthiness of their sources. Those they talk with frequently can be evaluated over time, which is another reason why story selectors prefer regular sources. When they cannot get to know their sources and thereby get a 'feel' for them, they rely on other indicators. Sources who co-operate with journalists and treat them cordially are apt to be trusted more than others; so are sources who take reporters into their confidence and explain why they must be inconsistent. Sources in positions of formal authority are considered more trustworthy than others; beyond that, journalists apply the same criteria professionally that they and others use in everyday life, placing greater trust in people who are similar to them. Accordingly, conservatives and liberals are trusted more than ultraconservatives and socialists, pragmatists more than ideologists; upper-middle-class people more than others. This is why socially proximate sources, such as peers and friends, are so frequently used.

5. Authoritativeness   All other things being equal, journalists prefer to resort to sources in official positions of authority and responsibility.[16] They are assumed to be

---

16 Sigal, *Reporters and Officials*, 69–70.

more trustworthy if only because they cannot afford to lie openly; they are also more persuasive because their facts and opinions are official. When stories become controversial, journalists can defend themselves before news executives by having relied on authoritative sources. Moreover, story suggesters can sell stories from these sources more easily than from others.

6. Articulateness When sources are interviewees, they must be able to make their point as concisely, and preferably as dramatically, as possible. Television interviewers achieve conciseness to some extent by rehearsing; in fact, all interviewees, famous or otherwise, are normally 'fed' questions off-camera until they have formulated a concise answer. Television reporters also look for interviewees who speak in the standard (national middle-class) English dialect that most of the audience is thought to understand most easily; unless absolutely necessary, they try to stay away from sources using lower-class dialects.

The newsmagazines also look for articulate sources, but conciseness and standard English can be achieved through editing. Editors are allowed to alter quotes accordingly, a practice one of them called 'helping the quoted guy'. [. . .]

■ Sources and the News

The means by which sources gain access to journalists, source considerations, and the relationships between reporters and their sources feed into each other to create a cumulative pattern by which journalists are repeatedly brought into contact with a limited number of the same types of sources. Eager and powerful sources which need to appear in the news first become suitable because they can always supply information, and then because they satisfy the source considerations for authoritativeness and productivity. The most regular sources develop an almost institutionalized relationship with the news organization, for beat reporters are assigned to them. The beat reporters become virtual allies of these sources, either because they develop symbiotic relationships or identify with them in a process that anthropologists call going native. General reporters usually go to the same kinds of sources and are managed by them as a result of their own transience and lack of knowledge.

There are exceptions, to be sure. When breaking stories develop, general reporters are freed to find the most relevant sources; and when powerless sources can supply dramatic news, the standard source considerations are temporarily set aside. Agency beat reporters can occasionally alienate their sources without suffering a permanent loss of rapport. Even so, on a day-to-day basis, they must side with their sources. The Watergate scandals were not uncovered by White House correspondents but by general reporters, who were then given the time and resources to develop the exposé. And when Watergate later became a beat, the reporters assigned to it did not gather their facts at the White House. During this period, White House correspondents could do little more than report the denials that came from the Oval Office whenever a new scandal was uncovered.

The cumulative pattern that determines availability and suitability makes the public official the most frequent and regular source. I did not count the number of times he or she appeared in television and magazine news; but Sigal analysed the origin of 2,850 domestic and foreign stories that appeared in *The New York Times* and *Washington Post*, and found that public officials were the source of 78 per cent of the stories.[17]

17 Sigal, *Reporters and Officials*, Table 6.5. About 17 per cent of the stories originated with 'non-governmental foreigners and Americans' and 3 per cent with other news organizations.

27
Policing the Crisis

Stuart Hall, Chas Critcher, Tony Jefferson, John Clarke, and Brian Roberts

The Social Production of News

THE MEDIA DO NOT simply and transparently report events which are 'naturally' newsworthy *in themselves*. 'News' is the end-product of a complex process which begins with a systematic sorting and selecting of events and topics according to a socially constructed set of categories. As MacDougall puts it:

> At any given moment billions of simultaneous events occur throughout the world. . . . All of these occurences are potentially news. They do not become so until some purveyor of news gives an account of them. The news, in other words, is the account of the event, not something intrinsic in the event itself.[1]

One aspect of the structure of selection can be seen in the routine organization of newspapers with respect to regular types or areas of news. Since newspapers are committed to the regular production of news, these organizational factors will, in turn, affect what is selected. For example, newspapers become predirected to certain types of event and topic in terms of the organization of their own work-force (e.g. specialist correspondents and departments, the fostering of institutional contacts, etc.) and the structure of the papers themselves (e.g. home news, foreign, political, sport, etc.)[2]

Given that the organization and staffing of a paper regularly direct it to certain categories of items, there is still the problem of selecting, from the many contending items within any one category, those that are felt will be of interest to the reader. This is where the *professional ideology* of what constitutes 'good news'—the newsman's sense of *news values*—begins to structure the process. At the most general level this involves an orientation to items which are 'out of the ordinary', which in some way breach our 'normal' expectations about social life, the sudden earthquake or the moon-landing, for example. We might call this the *primary* or *cardinal news value*. Yet, clearly 'extraordinariness' does not exhaust the list, as a glance at any newspaper will reveal: events which concern élite persons or nations; events which are

Source: Stuart Hall *et al.*, *Policing the Crisis* (London: Macmillan, 1978).

1 C. MacDougall, *Interpretative Reporting* (New York: Macmillan, 1968), 12.

2 For a fuller account of the impact of these 'bureaucratic' factors in news production, see P. Rock, 'News as Eternal Recurrence', in S. Cohen and J. Young (eds.), *The Manufacture of News: Social Problems, Deviance and the Mass Media* (London: Constable, 1973).

dramatic; events which can be personalised so as to point up the essentially human characteristics of humour, sadness, sentimentality, etc.; events which have negative consequences, and events which are part of, or can be made to appear part of, an existing newsworthy theme, are all possible news stories.[3] Disasters, dramas, the everyday antics—funny and tragic—of ordinary folk, the lives of the rich and the powerful, and such perennial themes as football (in winter) and cricket (in summer), all find a regular place within the pages of a newspaper. Two things follow from this: the first is that journalists will tend to *play up* the extraordinary, dramatic, tragic, etc. elements in a story in order to enhance its newsworthiness; the second is that events which score high on a number of these news values will have greater news potential than ones that do not. And events which score high on *all* dimensions, such as the Kennedy assassinations (i.e. which are *unexpected* and *dramatic*, with *negative* consequences, as well as *human tragedies* involving *élite persons* who were heads of an extremely *powerful nation*, which possesses the status of a *recurrent theme* in the British press), will become *so* newsworthy that programmes will be interrupted—as in the radio or television news-flash— so that these items can be communicated immediately.

For our present purposes it is sufficient to say that news values provide the criteria in the routine practices of journalism which enable journalists, editors and newsmen to decide routinely and regularly which stories are 'newsworthy' and which are not, which stories are major 'lead' stories and which are relatively insignificant, which stories to run and which to drop.[4] Although they are nowhere written down, formally transmitted or codified, news values seem to be widely shared as between the different news media (though we shall have more to say later on the way these are differently *inflected* by particular newspapers), and form a core element in the professional socialisation, practice and ideology of newsmen.

These two aspects of the social production of news—the bureaucratic organization of the media which produces the news in specific types or categories and the structure of news values which orders the selection and ranking of particular stories within these categories—are only part of the process. The third aspect—the moment of the *construction* of the news story itself—is equally important, if less obvious. This involves the presentation of the item to its *assumed* audience, in terms which, as far as the presenters of the item can judge, will make it comprehensible to that audience. If the world is not to be represented as a jumble of random and chaotic events, then they must be identified (i.e. named, defined, related to other events known to the audience), and assigned to a social context (i.e. placed within a frame of meanings familiar to the audience). This process—identification and contextualization—is one of the most important through which events are 'made to mean' by the media. An event only 'makes sense' if it can be located within a range of known social and cultural identifications. If newsmen did

3 See J. Galtung and M. Ruge, 'Structuring and Selecting News' in Cohen and Young (eds.), *The Manufacture of News*.

4 See ibid; K. Nordenstreng, 'Policy for News Transmission', in D. McQuail (ed.), *Sociology of Mass Communications* (Harmondsworth: Penguin, 1972); W. Breed, 'Social Control in the Newsroom? A Functional Analysis', *Social Forces*, 33 (May 1955); and S. M. Hall, 'Introduction', in A. C. M. Smith *et al.* (eds.), *Paper Voices* (London: Chatto and Windus, 1975).

not have available—in however routine a way—such cultural 'maps' of the social world, they could not 'make sense' for their audiences of the unusual, unexpected and unpredicted events which form the basic content of what is 'newsworthy'. Things are newsworthy because they represent the changeful-ness, the unpredictability and the conflictful nature of the world. But such events cannot be allowed to remain in the limbo of the 'random'—they must be brought within the horizon of the 'meaningful'. This bringing of events within the realm of meanings means, in essence, referring unusual and un-expected events to the 'maps of meaning' which already form the basis of our cultural knowledge, into which the social world is *already* 'mapped'. The social identification, classification and contextualization of news events in terms of these background frames of reference is the fundamental process by which the media make the world they report on intelligible to readers and viewers. This process of 'making an event intelligible' is a social process—constituted by a number of specific journalistic practices, which embody (often only implicitly) crucial assumptions about what society is and how it works.

One such background assumption is the *consensual* nature of society: the process of *signification*—giving social meanings to events—*both assumes and helps to construct society as a 'consensus'*. We exist as members of one society *because*—it is assumed—we share a common stock of cultural knowledge with our fellow men: we have access to the same 'maps of meanings'. Not only are we all able to manipulate these 'maps of meaning' to understand events, but we have fundamental interests, values and concerns in common, which these maps embody or reflect. We all want to, or do, maintain basically the same perspective *on* events. In this view, what unites us, as a society and a cul-ture—its consensual side—far outweighs what divides and distinguishes us as groups or classes from other groups. Now, at one level, the existence of a cultural consensus is an obvious truth; it is the basis of all social communica-tion.[5] If we were not members of the same language community we literally could not communicate with one another. On a broader level, if we did not inhabit, to some degree, the same classifications of social reality, we could not 'make sense of the world together'. In recent years, however, this basic cul-tural fact about society has been raised to an extreme ideological level. Be-cause we occupy the same society and belong to roughly the same 'culture', it is assumed that there is, basically, only *one* perspective on events: that pro-vided by what is sometimes called *the* culture, or (by some social scientists) *the* 'central value system'. This view denies any major structural discrepancies between different groups, or between the very different maps of meaning in a society. This 'consensual' viewpoint has important political consequences, when used as the taken-for-granted basis of communication. It carries the as-sumption that we also all have roughly the same *interests* in the society, and that we all roughly have an equal share of power in the society. This is the essence of the idea of the political consensus. 'Consensual' views of society represent society as if there are no major cultural or economic breaks, no major conflicts of interests between classes and groups. Whatever disagree-ments exist, it is said, there are legitimate and institutionalized means for

5 L. Wirth, 'Consensus and Mass Communications', *American Sociological Review*, 13 (1948).

expressing and reconciling them.' The 'free market' in opinions and in the media is supposed to guarantee the reconciliation of cultural discontinuities between one group and another. The political institutions—parliament, the two-party system, political representation, etc.—are supposed to guarantee equal access for all groups to the decision-making process. The growth of a 'consumer' economy is supposed to have created the economic conditions for everyone to have a stake in the making and distribution of wealth. The rule of law protects us all equally. This consensus view of society is particularly strong in modern, democratic, organized capitalist societies; and the media are among the institutions whose practices are most widely and consistently predicated upon the assumption of a 'national consensus'. So that, when events are 'mapped' by the media into frameworks of meaning and interpret-ation, it is assumed that we all equally possess and know how to use these frameworks, that they are drawn from fundamentally the same structures of understanding for all social groups and audiences. Of course, in the forma-tion of opinion, as in politics and economic life, it is conceded that there will be differences of outlook, disagreement, argument and opposition; but these are understood as taking place within a broader basic framework of agree-ment—'the consensus'—to which everyone subscribes, and within which every dispute, disagreement or conflict of interest can be reconciled by dis-cussion, without recourse to confrontation or violence. [...]

Events, as news, then, are regularly interpreted within frameworks which derive, in part, from this notion of *the consensus* as a basic feature of everyday life. They are elaborated through a variety of 'explanations', images and dis-courses which articulate what the audience is assumed to think and know about the society. The importance of this process, in *reinforcing* consensual notions, has been recently stressed by Murdock:

> This habitual presentation of news within frameworks which are already
> familiar has two important consequences. First, it recharges and
> extends the definitions and images in question and keeps them
> circulating as part of the common stock of taken-for-granted
> knowledge.... Second, it 'conveys an impression of eternal recurrence,
> of society as a social order which is made up of movement, but not
> innovation'.[6] Here again, by stressing the continuity and stability of the
> social structure, and by asserting the existence of a commonly shared set
> of assumptions, the definitions of the situation coincide with and
> reinforce essential consensual notions.[7]

What, then, is the underlying significance of the framing and interpretive function of news presentation? We suggest that it lies in the fact that the media are often presenting information about events which occur outside the direct experience of the majority of the society. The media thus represent the primary, and often the only, source of information about many import-ant events and topics. Further, because news is recurrently concerned with

6 Rock, 'News as Eternal Recurrence'.

7 G. Murdock, 'Mass Communication and the Construction of Meaning', in N. Armistead (ed.), *Rethinking Social Psychology* (Harmondsworth: Penguin, 1974), 208–9; but see also S. M. Hall, 'A World at One with Itself', *New Society*, 18 June 1970; and J. Young, 'Mass Media, Deviance and Drugs', in P. Rock and M. McIntosh (eds.), *Deviance and Social Control* (London: Tavistock, 1974).

events which are 'new' or 'unexpected', the media are involved in the task of making comprehensible what we would term 'problematic reality'. Problematic events breach our commonly held expectations and are therefore threatening to a society based around the expectation of consensus, order and routine. Thus the media's mapping of problematic events within the conventional understandings of the society is crucial in two ways. The media define for the majority of the population *what* significant events are taking place, but, also, they offer powerful interpretations of *how* to understand these events. Implicit in those interpretations are orientations towards the events and the people or groups involved in them.

■ **Primary and Secondary Definers**

In this section we want to begin to account for the 'fit' between dominant ideas and professional media ideologies and practices. This cannot be simply attributed—as it sometimes is in simple conspiracy theories—to the fact that the media are in large part capitalist-owned (though that structure of ownership is widespread), since this would be to ignore the day-to-day 'relative autonomy' of the journalist and news producers from direct economic control. Instead we want to draw attention to the more routine *structures* of news production to see how the media come in fact, in the 'last instance', to *reproduce the definitions of the powerful*, without being, in a simple sense, in their pay. Here we must insist on a crucial distinction between *primary* and *secondary definers* of social events.

The media do not themselves autonomously create news items; rather they are 'cued in' to specific new topics by regular and reliable institutional sources. As Paul Rock notes:

> In the main journalists position themselves so that they have access to institutions which generate a useful volume of reportable activity at regular intervals. Some of these institutions do, of course, make themselves visible by means of dramatization, or through press releases and press agents. Others are known to regularly produce consequential events. The courts, sports grounds and parliament mechanically manufacture news which is . . . assimilated by the press.[8]

One reason for this has to do with the internal pressures of news production—as Murdock notes:

> The incessant pressures of time and the consequent problems of resource allocation and work scheduling in news organizations can be reduced or alleviated by covering 'pre-scheduled events'; that is, events that have been announced in advance by their convenors. However, one of the consequences of adopting this solution to scheduling problems is to increase the newsmen's dependence on news sources willing and able to preschedule their activities.[9]

The second has to do with the fact that media reporting is underwritten by notions of 'impartiality', 'balance' and 'objectivity'. This is formally enforced

---

8 Rock, 'News as Eternal Recurrence', 77.

9 Murdock, 'Mass Communication', 210.

in television (a near-monopoly situation, where the state is directly involved in a regulatory sense) but there are also similar professional ideological 'rules' in journalism.[10] One product of these rules is the carefully structured distinction between 'fact' and 'opinion'. The important point is that these professional rules give rise to the practice of ensuring that media statements are, wherever possible, grounded in 'objective' and 'authoritative' statements from 'accredited' sources. This means constantly turning to accredited representatives of major social institutions—MPs for political topics, employers and trade-union leaders for industrial matters, and so on. Such institutional representatives are 'accredited' because of their institutional power and position, but also because of their 'representative' status: either they represent 'the people' (MPs, Ministers, etc.) or organized interest groups (which is how the TUC and the CBI are now regarded). One final 'accredited source' is 'the expert': his calling—the 'disinterested' pursuit of knowledge—not his position or his representativeness, confers on his statements 'objectivity' and 'authority'. Ironically, the very rules which aim to preserve the impartiality of the media, and which grew out of desires for greater professional neutrality, also serve powerfully to orientate the media in the 'definitions of social reality' which their 'accredited sources'—the institutional spokesmen—provide.

These two aspects of news production—the practical pressures of constantly working against the clock and the professional demands of impartiality and objectivity—combine to produce a systematically structured *over-accessing* to the media of those in powerful and privileged institutional positions. The media thus tend, faithfully and impartially, to reproduce symbolically the existing structure of power in society's institutional order. This is what Becker has called the 'hierarchy of credibility'—the likelihood that those in powerful or high-status positions in society who offer opinions about controversial topics will have their definitions accepted, because such spokesmen are understood to have access to more accurate or more specialized information on particular topics than the majority of the population.[11] The result of this structured preference given in the media to the opinions of the powerful is that these 'spokesmen' become what we call the *primary definers* of topics.

What is the significance of this? It could rightly be argued that through the requirement of 'balance'—one of the professional rules we have not yet dealt with—alternative definitions do get a hearing: each 'side' *is* allowed to present its case. In point of fact, as we shall see in detail in the next chapter, the setting up of a topic in terms of a debate within which there are oppositions and conflicts is also one way of *dramatizing* an event so as to enhance its newsworthiness. The important point about the structured relationship between the media and the primary institutional definers is that it permits the institutional definers to establish the initial definition or *primary interpretation* of the topic in question. This interpretation then 'commands the

---

10 For a historical account of the evolution of those rules, as J. W. Carey, 'The Communications Revolution and the Professional Communicator', *Sociological Review Monograph*, 13 (1969).

11 H. Becker, 'Whose Side are We on?', in J. D. Douglas (ed.), *The Relevance of Sociology* (New York: Appleton-Century-Crofts, 1972).

field' in all subsequent treatment and sets the terms of reference within which all further coverage or debate takes place. Arguments *against* a primary interpretation are forced to insert themselves into *its* definition of 'what is at issue'—they must begin from this framework of interpretation as their starting-point. This initial interpretative framework—what Lang and Lang have called an 'inferential structure'[12]—is extremely difficult to alter fundamentally, once established. For example, once race relations in Britain have been defined as a 'problem of numbers' (i.e. how many blacks there are in the country), then even liberal spokesmen, in proving that the figures for black immigrants have been exaggerated, are nevertheless obliged to subscribe, implicitly, to the view that the debate is 'essentially' *about numbers*. Similarly, Halloran and his co-workers have clearly demonstrated how the 'inferential structure' of violence—once it became established in the lead-up period—dominated the coverage of the second Anti-Vietnam Rally and the events of Grosvenor Square, despite all the first-hand evidence directly contradicting this interpretation.[13] Effectively, then, the primary definition *sets the limit* for all subsequent discussion by *framing what the problem is*. This initial framework then provides the criteria by which all subsequent contributions are labelled as 'relevant' to the debate, or 'irrelevant'—beside the point. Contributions which stray from this framework are exposed to the charge that they are 'not addressing the problem'.[14]

The media, then, do not simply 'create' the news; nor do they simply transmit the ideology of the 'ruling class' in a conspiratorial fashion. Indeed, we have suggested that, in a critical sense, the media are frequently not the 'primary definers' of news events at all; but their structured relationship to power has the effect of making them play a crucial but secondary role in *reproducing* the definitions of those who have privileged access, as of right, to the media as 'accredited sources'. From this point of view, in the moment of news production, the media stand in a position of structured subordination to the primary definers.

It is this structured relationship—between the media and its 'powerful' sources—which begins to open up the neglected question of the *ideological role* of the media. It is this which begins to give substance and specificity to Marx's basic proposition that 'the ruling ideas of any age are the ideas of its ruling class'. Marx's contention is that this dominance of 'ruling ideas' operates primarily because, in addition to its ownership and control of the means of material production, this class also owns and controls the means of 'mental production'. In producing their definition of social reality, and the place of 'ordinary people' within it, they construct a particular image of society which represents particular class interests as the interests of all members of

12 K. Lang and G. Lang, 'The Inferential Structure of Political Communications', *Public Opinion Quarterly*, 19 (Summer 1955).

13 J. D. Halloran, P. Elliott, and G. Murdock, *Demonstrations and Communication: a Case Study* (Harmondsworth: Penguin, 1970).

14 See S. M. Hall, 'The "Structured Communication" of Events', paper for the Obstacles to Communication Symposium, UNESCO/Division of Philosophy (available from Centre for Contemporary Cultural Studies, University of Birmingham); J. Clarke *et al.*, 'The Selection of Evidence and the Avoidance of Racialism: A Critique of the Parliamentary Select Committee on Race Relations and Immigration', *New Community*, 111: 3 (Summer 1974).

society. Because of their control over material and mental resources, and their domination of the major institutions of society, this class's definitions of the social world provide the basic rationale for those institutions which protect and reproduce their 'way of life'. This control of mental resources ensures that theirs are the most powerful and 'universal' of the available definitions of the social world. Their universality ensures that they are shared to some degree by the subordinate classes of the society. Those who govern, govern also through ideas; thus they govern with the consent of the subordinate classes, and not principally through their overt coercion. Parkin makes a similar point: 'the social and political definitions of those in dominant positions tend to become objectified in the major institutional orders, so providing the moral framework for the entire social system.'[15]

In the major social, political, and legal institutions of society, coercion and constraint are never wholly absent. This is as true for the media as elsewhere. For example, reporters and reporting *are* subject to economic and legal constraints, as well as to more overt forms of censorship (e.g. over the coverage of events in Northern Ireland). But the transmission of 'dominant ideas' depends *more* on non-coercive mechanisms for their reproduction. Hierarchical structures of command and review, informal socialization into institutional roles, the sedimenting of dominant ideas into the 'professional ideology'—all help to ensure, within the media, their continued reproduction in the dominant form. What we have been pointing to in this section is *precisely how one particular professional practice ensures that the media, effectively but 'objectively', play a key role in reproducing the dominant field of the ruling ideologies.*

15 F. Parkin, *Class Inequality and Political Order* (London: MacGibbon & Kee, 1971), 83.

28

Reporting Crime: The Media Politics of Criminal Justice

Philip Schlesinger and Howard Tumber

Source–Media Relations

WE HAVE SET OUT to analyse the behaviour of political actors as news sources. Crucial to the study of news sources are the relations between the media and the exercise of political and ideological power, especially, but not exclusively, by central social institutions that seek to define and manage the flow of information in contested fields of discourse.[1] Inevitably, in the present study we focus on the institutions of the state's criminal justice apparatus and how these compete for media attention, both amongst themselves and with other, more or less institutionalized, sources of information. Although, as we shall show, official bodies do occupy a dominant position in shaping crime-reporting (as is the case in other journalistic fields), we shall also demonstrate that a fuller understanding of competition amongst sources requires us also to pose questions about non-official sources—a theme hitherto neglected.

News Sources as 'Primary Definers'?

Much cited in debate about the power of sources has been the concept of 'primary definition' proposed by Stuart Hall and his colleagues in an analysis of 'the social production of news' that centres upon crime coverage.[2] The media are analysed by Hall *et al.* in terms of a theory of ideological power underpinned by a Gramscian conception of the struggle for hegemony between dominant and subordinate classes in capitalist societies. According to them, 'It is this structured relationship—between the media and its [*sic*] "powerful" sources—which begins to open up the neglected question of the ideological role of the media. It is this which begins to give substance and

Source: Philip Schlesinger and Howard Tumber, *Reporting Crime: The Media Politics of Criminal Justice* (Oxford: Clarendon Press, 1994).

1 In personal correspondence reacting to an earlier version of this chapter, Herbert Gans notes: 'Emphasizing the role of sources is the best way, or perhaps the only one, to connect the study of journalism to the larger society . . .' (22 July 1988).

2 Hall, S., Clarke, J., Critcher, C., Jefferson, T., & Roberts, B., *Policing the Crisis* (London: Macmillan, 1978).

specificity to Marx's basic proposition that "the ruling ideas of any age are the ideas of its ruling class".[3]

Hall *et al.* argue that the media give access to those who enjoy 'accreditation'. This is a resource limited to certain social groups which enjoy a special status as sources in virtue of their institutional power, representative standing, or claims to expert knowledge. Specific examples given are government Ministers and Members of Parliament (MPs), and organized interest groups such as the Confederation of British Industry (CBI) or the Trades Union Congress (TUC). As a consequence of professional practices of ascertaining source credibility, the media are held to be structurally biased towards very powerful and privileged sources who become 'over-accessed'. [. . .]

Primary definition, then, involves a primacy both temporal and ideological. This is a very strong argument indeed. Taken at face value, its import is that the structure of access *necessarily* secures strategic advantages for 'primary definers', not just initially but also subsequently, for as long as a debate or controversy lasts. It also asserts that counter-definitions can never dislodge the primary definition, which consistently dominates.

The assumptions just discussed are open to various criticisms. Here we set them out as analytical points, but as the empirical findings of this and other studies show, our critique is grounded in the actual relations between news sources and news media.

First, the notion of 'primary definition' is more problematic than it seems. The broad characterization offered above does not take account of contention between official sources in trying to influence the construction of a story. In cases of dispute, say, amongst members of the same government over a key question of policy, who is the *primary* definer? Or—and it goes against the very logic of the concept—can there be more than one?[4]

Second, the formulation of Hall *et al.* fails to register the well-established fact that official sources often attempt to influence the construction of a story by using 'off-the-record' briefings—in which case the primary definers do not appear directly as such, in unveiled and attributable form.[5]

A third point concerns the drawing of the boundaries of primary definition. Do these shift, and if so, why? Hall *et al.* make reference to MPs and Ministers. Presumably, primary definition is intended to include all consensually recognized 'representative' voices. But access to the media is plainly not equally open to all members of the political class: Prime Ministers and Presidents routinely command disproportionate attention and politicians may also use media strategies to gain attention for themselves in competition

3 Hall *et al.*, *Policing the Crisis,* 58.

4 A classic instance of policy divisions within the state machine is illustrated in Daniel Hallin's study of the Vietnam war and the news media. See Hallin, D., *The 'Uncensored War': The Media and Vietnam* (Oxford: Oxford University Press, 1986). More recently David Miller has shown the problems of applying the concept of 'primary definition' to a divided officialdom in Northern Ireland. See Miller, D., 'Official Sources and "Primary Definition": The Case of Northern Ireland', *Media, Culture and Society*, 15 (1993), 385–406.

5 The story of the prime-ministerial voice of the Thatcher years, Bernard Ingham, offers some instructive insights in this regard. See Harris, R., *Good and Faithful Servant: The Unauthorized Biography of Bernard Ingham* (London: Faber & Faber, 1990).

with others.[6] There is nothing in the formulation of primary defining that permits us to deal with such inequalities of access amongst the privileged themselves.

Fourth, there is the unconsidered question of longer-term shifts in the structure of access. Writing in the late 1970s, it may have been obvious to talk of the CBI and TUC as major institutional voices. But with the disappearance of corporatism in Britain under successive Conservative governments, such interests have lost their one-time prominence. What this point reveals is the tacit assumption that certain forces are permanently present in the power structure. It is thus an atemporal model, underpinned by the notion that primary definers are simply 'accredited' to their dominant ideological place in virtue of an institutional location. But when these are displaced by new forces and their representatives, it becomes essential to explain their emergence. [. . .]

The media are characterized as a subordinate site for the reproduction of the ideological field; in effect, they are conceived as 'secondary definers'.

This now brings us to a fifth objection, which is that Hall *et al.* tend to overstate the passivity of the media as recipients of information from news sources: the flow of definitions is seen as moving uniformly from the centres of power to the media. Within this conceptual logic, there is no space to account for occasions on which media may themselves take the initiative in the definitional process by challenging the so-called primary definers and forcing them to respond. Relevant examples would be cases of investigative journalism dealing with scandals inside the state apparatus or in the world of big business, or when leaks by dissident figures force out undesired and unintended official responses, or when accidents occur and official figures are caught on the hop.[7] At times, too, it is the media that crystallize slogans or pursue campaigns that are subsequently taken up by the would-be primary definers because it is in their interests to do so.[8] Aside from seeing the media as excessively passive, this way of conceiving of their relations to news sources tends to elide the variations that exist within and between different news media. Access for 'alternative' viewpoints differs as between the press and television, and indeed, as between different newspapers.[9]

A sixth criticism concerns how the conception of 'primary definition' renders largely invisible the activities of sources that attempt to generate 'counter-definitions'. This rules out any analysis of the process of *negotiation*

6 See Seymour-Ure, C., 'Prime Ministers' Reactions to Television: Britain, Australia and Canada', *Media, Culture and Society*, 11 (1989): 307–25; Hinkley, B., *The Symbolic Presidency: How Presidents Portray Themselves* (New York: Routledge, 1990).

7 For relevant studies see Murphy, D., *The Stalker Affair and the Press* (London: Unwin Hyman, 1991); Molotch, H., and Lester, M., 'News as Purposive Behavior: On the Strategic Use of Routine Events, Accidents and Scandals', *American Sociological Review*, 39 (1974): 101–12; Tumber, H., ' "Selling Scandal" '.

8 e.g. the press campaign over the 'seal plague' and its political impact. See Anderson, A., 'Source Strategies and the Communication of Environmental Affairs', *Media, Culture and Society*, 13 (1991): 459–76.

9 For relevant studies see Curran, J., 'Culturalist Perspectives of News Organizations: A Reappraisal and a Case Study', in Ferguson, *Public Communication*, 114–34; McNair, B., *Images of the Enemy* (London: Routledge, 1988); Schlesinger, P., Murdock, G., and Elliott, P., *Televising 'Terrorism': Political Violence in Popular Culture* (London: Comedia, 1983).

about policy questions between power-holders and their opponents that may occur prior to the issuing of what are assumed to be primary definitions. As we shall see, thinking about such brokerage as taking place within a policy arena does complicate the picture, even though access to that political space is undoubtedly limited. The essentially structuralist approach of Hall *et al.*, however, is profoundly incurious about the processes whereby sources may engage in ideological conflict prior to, or contemporaneous with, the appearance of 'definitions' in the media. It therefore tends to ignore questions about how contestation over the presentation of information takes place within institutions and organizations reported by the media, as well as overlooking the concrete strategies pursued as they contend for space and time.

Although Hall *et. al.*'s approach fails to deal with a number of conceptual difficulties, there is still undoubtedly a strong case for arguing that the organization of journalistic practice *generally* promotes the views and interests of authoritative sources. This is a paramount finding of much of the sociology of journalism, which will be discussed in the next section. The key point is that because the conception of 'primary definition' resolves the question of source power on the basis of structuralist assumptions, it closes off any engagement with the dynamic processes of contestation in a given field of discourse.[10] It has the signal advantage of directing our attention to the exercise of definitional power in society, but it offers no account of how this is achieved as the outcome of strategies pursued by political actors. That is because 'primary definers' are seen as simply guaranteed access to the news media in virtue of their structural position. To sum up: 'primary definition', which ought to be an empirically ascertainable outcome, is held instead to be an a priori effect of privileged access.

However, the massive investments that have taken place in political public relations and marketing both by state agencies, and by a variety of other interests that aim to establish themselves as authoritative news sources, do require some explanation. Thinking of 'primary definition' as a resolved matter makes us incurious about source competition and what its implications for the workings of the public sphere might be.

The Production of News

The production of news is one of the most well-researched fields in media studies, with work ranging across the political economy of the media, through organizational studies, and into broader cultural concerns with the

---

10 Hall has maintained his views on 'primary definition'. In the opening essay in a critical collection aimed at giving an 'adequate understanding' of media power to those at the receiving end, he put the argument in a less qualified, and therefore more revealing way: 'Some things, people, events, relationships always get represented: always centre-stage, always in the position to define, to set the agenda, to establish the terms of the conversation. Some others sometimes get represented—but always at the margin, always responding to a question whose terms and conditions have been defined elsewhere: never "centred". Still others are always "represented" only by their eloquent absence, their silences: or refracted through the glance or the gaze of others', see Hall, S., 'Media Power and Class Power', in J. Curran, J. Ecclestone, G. Oakley, and A. Richardson (eds.), *Bending Reality: The State of the Media* (London: Pluto, 1986), 9. Although he concedes that some 'marginal categories get "accessed" all the time' (ibid.), this is basically seen as window-dressing and not as the outcome of source strategies.

form and content of news.[11] Most sociological research into news sources has failed to focus upon the source–media relation from the standpoint of sources themselves *as well as* from that of journalists. In other words, it has been predominantly media-centric.

Empirical studies generally stress the importance to journalistic work of official sources in government and administration, and there is widespread agreement that these play a crucial role in defining and shaping the news agenda through their interaction with the news production process. Consequently, it has been suggested that 'the story of journalism, on a day to day basis, is the story of the interaction of reporters and officials'.[12] Studies examining news-reporting have tended to concentrate on how reporters cover specific institutional areas, although very occasionally a range of different specialisms has been analysed and compared in the same study.[13] Not surprisingly, given its crucial importance, news coverage of the political system has been repeatedly examined. For instance, in the American context, the relations between reporters and officials in Washington has been a major focus of research, whereas in Britain studies have focused on the Westminster—Whitehall lobby system, and in Australia there has been work on media and politicians in the Federal and state capitals.[14]

This predominantly institutional focus has been followed in studies of areas other than political reporting. US studies have long shown how much reporting is routinely centred upon specific 'beats'.[15] Likewise, in British work, the political lobby has provided a general model for the official flow of information to the media in other areas of institutional activity. Hence, for instance, a number of studies have dealt with the relations between various types of reporters and official sources within the state machinery, but usually in terms of how journalists perceive these.[16]

The well-founded recognition of the crucial role of the state (in the form of government departments and the wider political class) as the major

11 For a useful recent survey of the field see Schudson, M., 'The Sociology of News Production Revisited', in Curran, J., and Gurevitch, M., *Mass Media and Society* (London: Edward Arnold; 1991): 141–59.

12 Ibid. 148.

13 The classical study of this kind is Tunstall, J., *Journalists at Work: Specialist Correspondents, their News Organizations, News Sources, and Competitor-Colleagues* (London: Constable, 1971). Ericson, R. V., Baranek, P. M., and Chan, J. B. L., *Negotiating Control: A Study of News Sources* (Toronto: University of Toronto Press, 1989) also compares different, but more closely related, specialist fields.

14 On the USA see Sigal, L. V., *Reporters and Officials: The Organization and Politics of Newsmaking* (Lexington, Mass.: D. C. Heath & Co., 1973); Hess, S., *The Washington Reporters* (Washington, DC: The Brookings Institution, 1981); Cook, T., *Making Laws and Making News: Media Strategies in the U.S. House of Representatives* (Washington, DC: The Brookings Institution, 1989). On Britain see Seymour-Ure, C., *The Press, Politics and the Public* (London: Methuen, 1968); Tunstall, J., *The Westminster Lobby Correspondents* (London: Routledge & Kegan Paul, 1970); Cockerell, M., Hennessy, P., and Walker, D., *Sources Close to the Prime Minister: Inside the Hidden World of the News Manipulators* (London: Macmillan, 1984); on Australia see Tiffen, R., *News and Power* (Sydney: Allen & Unwin, 1989).

15 An early example was Gieber, W. and Johnson, W., 'The City Hall "Beat": A Study of Reporter and Source Roles', *Journalism Quarterly*, 38 (1961): 289–97. For more contemporary approaches see Fishman, M., *Manufacturing the News* (Austin: University of Texas Press, 1980) and Hess, S., *The Washington Reporters* (Washington, DC: The Brookings Institution, 1981).

16 See e.g. Chibnall, S., *Law-and-Order News: An Analysis of Crime Reporting in the British Press* (London: Tavistock Publishing, 1977); Golding, P. and Middleton, S., *Images of Welfare: Press and Public Attitudes to Poverty* (Oxford: Martin Robertson, 1982); Morrison, D. and Tumber, H., *Journalists At War: The Dynamics of News Reporting during the Falklands Conflict* (London: Sage, 1988).

producer of information which defines 'the amount, timing and overall direction' of much news does not preclude acknowledgement of some of the further complexities of struggles to influence coverage.[17] The empirical sociology of journalism for the most part has shied away from endorsing a concept of primary definition, although analogous terms can be found in the literature. The pressure of detailed analysis of source activity has tended to result in an appreciation of divergencies within the official camp. The question of alternative views (even if they fall into quite a restricted ideological range) necessarily surfaces as a matter of importance, as does recognition of the fact that official status does not automatically ensure credibility. As Leon Sigal observes, 'The convention of authoritativeness may assure a hearing in the news for those in authority, but it is no guarantee of a "good press" so long as other sources are willing and able to talk to reporters.'[18] It is precisely this latter point that the concept of primary definition ignores: the credibility of given political actors may vary over time, as indeed may the scope for oppositional and alternative views to force their way onto the political agenda.[19] The scope of the public sphere is not fixed for all time, and its relative openness or closure is an outcome of political struggle. Consensual times may give way to those of extreme crisis, and vice versa.

Apart from producing a recognition of possible divergencies within the political establishment, engagement with the empirical realities of source–media relations may also enhance awareness of the significance of non-official sources, such as, for instance, of pressure groups which 'serve a twin function. On the one hand they act as research agencies, able to point out the inconsistencies or evasions in official versions of policy. On the other hand they provide hand-wringing reactions to the iniquities of government policy that can be used to "balance" a story.'[20] Although it has certainly not loomed large, built into the empirical sociology of journalism—irrespective of whether it has tended towards pluralism or Marxism—is the potential for investigating the social organization of non-official news sources and of assessing their relationships to the state. This analytical opening has implications for how we think about the wider functioning of the public sphere.

Various writers have tried to generalize about the relations between news media and their sources. Such theorizing or model-building has generally been closely allied to the empirical research at hand. A common formulation is that news sources and journalists are engaged in an 'exchange of information for publicity'[21] or in a relationship characterized as a 'tug of war' in which 'sources attempt to "manage" the news, putting the best light on themselves [and] journalists concurrently "manage" the source in order to extract the information they want'.[22]

17 The phrase is Golding and Middleton's in *Images of Welfare*, 121.

18 Sigal, L. V., 'Who? Sources Make the News', in R. K. Manoff and M. Schudson (eds.), *Reading the News* (New York: Pantheon, 1986), 37.

19 See Schudson, 'The Sociology of News Production Revisited', who notes in this connection the importance both of historical and comparative approaches.

20 Golding and Middleton, *Images of Welfare*, 119.

21 See the discussion in Tunstall, *The Westminster Lobby Correspondents*, 43–4.

22 Gans, H., *Deciding What's News: A Study of CBS Evening News, NBC Nightly News, Newsweek, and Time* (New York: Pantheon, 1979), 117.

At one level, this view presupposes that such interaction is akin to those based on an instrumental economic calculation, where each side weighs up the costs and benefits involved in an activity, and seeks to maximize its satisfactions or utilities.[23] Although an explanation in terms of the coincidence of self-interest on both sides of an exchange relationship is of importance, it does not tell the whole story. Sources and journalists often need to appeal to norms other than those that are purely economic, for they are engaged in a social process that goes beyond simple buying and selling. For instance, such non-economic considerations as trust and confidentiality come into the equation on many occasions. And yet, although personal liking and compatibility may certainly be important at times, such relations are not in any case purely and simply conducted between individuals. They operate at the interface between news organizations and news sources, who, almost invariably, are themselves members of organizations with collective goals to pursue.[24]

In this context, relevant questions concern the kinds of control that sources have over journalists and those that journalists, in turn, have over their sources.[25] A number of studies suggest that, on the whole, the advantage lies with sources, given the substantial passivity of the media in information-gathering.[26] Moreover, empirical research does give considerable support to the notion that there is a structured bias towards access for the politically powerful, a view somewhat epigrammatically summed up thus, by the US sociologist, Herbert Gans:

> While in theory sources can come from anywhere, in practice, their recruitment and their access to journalists reflect the hierarchies of nation and society. The President of the United States has instantaneous access to all news media; the powerless must resort to civil disturbances to obtain it.[27]

In addition, economic resources play an important role in offering a privileged basis for the routine provision of information. The fact that sources are not generally paid entails an implicit class bias both in terms of self-selection as an information-provider and in the media's selection of given individuals or groups. The social and geographical concentration of news-gathering also brings about routinization of media search procedures.

It is not surprising, then, that in empirical studies there is strong support for that part of the 'primary definition' argument which stresses how the media's use of 'authoritative and efficient sources' leads to a 'cumulative pattern that determines availability and suitability' and 'makes the public official the most frequent and regular source'.[28] Nor is it especially startling to conclude that 'habitual access is generally found among those with extreme

---

23 The most fully worked-out version of this position is in Gandy, jun., O. H., *Beyond Agenda Setting: Information Subsidies and Public Policy* (Norwood, NJ: Ablex Publishing Co., 1982).

24 See Tunstall, *Journalists at Work*, 185–6.

25 Ibid. 203.

26 A view taken by H. Gans, *Deciding What's News* (New York: Vintage Books), Golding and Middleton, *Images of Welfare*, and Sigal, *Reporters and Officials*.

27 Gans, *Deciding What's News*, 119.

28 Ibid. 145.

wealth or other institutionally-based sources of power', with the consequence that 'Routine access is one of the important sources and sustainers of existing power relationships.'[29]

To recognize that such advantages accrue to those possessed of advantaged positions, however, does not preclude the need to look *beyond* the powerful in order to see whether, and how, that might affect our understanding of source–media relations. The empirical sociology of journalism plainly shares insights with the structuralist view about the strategic advantages that political and economic power may secure for sources. But on the whole it holds back from characterizing this as primary definition, because it tends to be recognized that those seeking access to the media must engage in the active pursuit of definitional advantage. Powerful sources still have to pursue goal-oriented action to achieve access, even though their recognition as 'legitimate authorities' is already usually inscribed in the rules of the game. This contrasts with the structuralist notion of 'automatic', accredited access resulting in primary definition.

These considerations point to rethinking the methodology of empirical studies of how sources act, an issue that has attracted almost no critical attention at all so far. The available approaches fall into two: the internalist and the externalist. These are not mutually exclusive by any means, but treating them as distinct alternatives helps bring out their separate logics.

Internalists typically produce their analyses of source behaviour either by interpreting what sources do by a reading of media content, or by deriving conclusions from accounts given by journalists of their interactions with their sources, or by combining both. There is nothing wrong with this, but it has shortcomings. If we restrict ourselves to what appears in the media this plainly does not tell us much about the process whereby it comes to be there. Furthermore, if we restrict ourselves to journalists' accounts of how they have dealt with sources the optic is largely limited to how the media organize *their* information strategies.

These limitations can be circumvented by taking an externalist approach. This implies an analysis of the strategies and tactics of sources in relation to the media. Such work exists already, for instance, in the form of *post hoc* reconstructions of particular exercises in news management or censorship. Such evidence is usually based upon a mix of journalistic reflections on experience, published revelations based on leaks or the subsequent coming clean of participants, and the release of official documents long after the event. In short, for externalist accounts involving substantial reconstruction from diverse sources the passage of time is a great help, especially so where the weeders of public records or the feeders of shredders have lacked foresight.

Our argument here is that in addition to using internalist evidence we need to extend the scope of externalist evidence. Our step in this direction has been a simple one, namely systematically to interview news sources. Observational studies are an obvious complement to this approach.[30] All

29 Molotch and Lester, 'News as Purposive Behavior', 107.

30 See Ericson *et al.*, *Negotiating Control*.

such research, of course, is open to the usual problems such as incompleteness, verification, evaluation, and interpretation. Moreover, since the analysis of sources (like that of media production) is highly dependent upon the co-operation of those studied, serious problems of access or secrecy could arise.[31] Nevertheless, the attempt has seemed worthwhile to us, for not only has it gathered in a different kind of evidence from that normally found in media studies, it has also provoked some reconceptualization and refocusing of the sociological study of journalism.[32]

Source–Media Analysis

A number of significant studies have gone beyond the dominant media-centrism of the sociology of journalism to investigate the media strategies and tactics of news sources. However, such research has tended to be subsumed under the production study tradition without its originality of focus being clearly seen. By drawing attention to this persisting line of investigation, it is not our intention, as might erroneously be supposed, to replace media-centred studies with a 'source perspective', as that too would suffer from tunnel vision.[33]

The overall approach that we single out here may be termed 'source–media analysis'. This extends the now well-established focus on how news organizations work. The sociological study of news production developed, at least in part, because of the inadequacies of analysing news simply by looking at its content. Of course, the external analysis of news has much to tell us, for instance, about the textual construction of given stories, or the patterns of attention accorded to given types of reporting. However, as an approach used on its own, external analysis (whatever form it takes) does face the crucial limitation of only being able to make inferences about the production process. By offering an internal vantage-point, therefore, production studies have substantially enlarged the possibilities of studying the anatomy of journalism.

There is a comparable gain to be made by the further shift of focus that we advocate here. Whilst studying the practices of newsrooms and news-gathering has much to tell us about how media work, it still has the crucial shortcoming of offering only a partial view of the interrelations between the

31 As pointed out in Gandy, jun., O. H., 'Information in Health: Subsidized News', *Media, Culture and Society*, 2 (1980): 114.

32 This point has been particularly clearly recognized in two studies working within what is still a media-centric framework that both have pushed to its limits. See Murphy, D., *The Stalker Affair and the Press* (London: Unwin Hyman, 1991), which trenchantly challenges the dominant ideology thesis by using an example of official loss of control over news management. Also see Tiffen, R., *News and Power*, which lucidly demonstrates the role of political news sources in contending over control of the political arena. This second study is based on an internalist approach coupled with externalist reconstructions.

33 The phrase cited is Dennis McQuail's. See McQuail, D., *Media Performance: Mass Communication and the Public Interest* (London: Sage, 1992), 133. Restricted as it is to questions of news production and content, the present study does not constitute a comprehensive account of the process of public communication, nor, indeed, is it intended to. For one, it leaves out any analysis of media reception, although our approach may articulate with analyses of the reception process in which judgements about the sources of public communication by audience members are quite central. For a relevant account see Corner, J., Richardson, K., and Fenton, N., *Nuclear Reactions: Form and Response in Public Issue Television* (London: John Libbey, 1990).

news media and the social institutions, organizations, and groups on which they report. Just as research into news organizations has offered an important refocusing of attention from product to process, so has the study of news sources considerably extended the scope of production studies by adding the complicating factor of sources' perspectives.

29

The Whole World is Watching

Todd Gitlin

Media Routines and Political Crises

WHERE DO NEWS frames come from? How are they fixed into the appearance of the stable, the natural, the taken-for-granted? And how, despite this, are the prevailing frames disputed and changed? How are we to understand the systematic denigration of the New Left? [...]

What I seek here is not so much an *alternative* as a *more ample* theoretical domain within which to understand the framing process and the media-movement relationship. For this purpose I want an approach attuned to the particular procedures of journalism, yet sensitive to the fact that journalism exists alongside—and interlocked with—a range of other professions and institutions with ideological functions within an entire social system. I want an approach which is both structural and historical—that is, which can account for regularities in journalistic procedure and product, yet which at the same time can account for historical changes in both. Such an approach should encompass not only news and its frames, but movements and their identities, goals, and strategies; it should comprehend both news and movements as contending conveyors of ideas and images of what the world is and should be like. The most comprehensive theoretical approach can be found in recent developments of the Gramscian idea of hegemony.

■ Ideological Hegemony as a Process

There exists no full-blown theory of hegemony, specifying social-structural and historical conditions for its sources, strengths, and weaknesses.[1] But a certain paradigm has been developing during the 1970s, after the collapse of the New Left and the translation of Antonio Gramsci's prison writings[2] and it is this paradigm—a domain of concerns, sensitivities, and conclusions—that can help situate the history of media-movement relations. [...]

Source: Todd Gitlin, *The Whole World is Watching: Mass Media in The Making and the Unmaking of The New Left* (Berkeley, Los Angeles, and London: University of California Press, 1980).

1 The following paragraph is based on p. 251 of my 'Prime Time Ideology: The Hegemonic Process in Television Entertainment', *Social Problems*, 26 (Feb. 1979): 251–66.

2 Antonio Gramsci, *Selections from the Prison Notebooks*, ed. and trans. Quintin Hoare and Geoffrey Nowell Smith (New York: International Publishers, 1971). There is no single passage in which Gramsci unequivocally defines and applies the concept of hegemony; rather, it is a leitmotif throughout his entire work. But see esp. 12, 52, 175–82.

Gramsci's concept can be defined this way: hegemony is a ruling class's (or alliance's) domination of subordinate classes and groups through the elaboration and penetration of ideology (ideas and assumptions) into their common sense and everyday practice; it is the systematic (but not necessarily or even usually deliberate) engineering of mass consent to the established order. No hard and fast line can be drawn between the mechanisms of hegemony and the mechanisms of coercion; the hold of hegemony rests on elements of coercion, just as the force of coercion over the dominated both presupposes and reinforces elements of hegemony.[3] In any given society, hegemony and coercion are interwoven. [. . .] Further, hegemony is, in the end, a process that is entered into by both dominators and dominated.[4] Both rulers and ruled derive psychological and material rewards in the course of confirming and reconfirming their inequality. The hegemonic sense of the world seeps into popular 'common sense' and gets reproduced there; it may even appear to be generated *by* that common sense.

In liberal capitalist societies, no institution is devoid of hegemonic functions, and none does hegemonic work only. But it is the cultural industry as a whole, along with the educational system, that most coherently specializes in the production, relaying, and regearing of hegemonic ideology. The media of the culture industry are ordinarily controlled by members of top corporate and political elites, and by individuals they attempt (with varying success) to bring into their social and ideological worlds. At the same time, the ruling coalitions of 'class fractions' are to a great extent dependent on these ideology-shaping institutions (1) to formulate the terms of their own unity, and (2) to certify the limits within which all competing definitions of reality will contend. They structure the ideological field within which, as Hall says, 'subordinate classes "live" and make sense of their subordination in such a way as to sustain the dominance of those ruling over them'.[5] Because at any given moment there is not a unitary functioning 'ruling class', but rather an alliance of powerful groups in search of an enduring basis for legitimate authority, the particular hegemonic ideology will not be simple; 'the content of dominant ideology will reflect this complex interior formation of the dominant classes'.[6]

The hegemonic ideology will be complex for a deeper structural reason as well. The dominant economic class does not, for the most part, produce and

---

3 In an astute essay, Perry Anderson has shown with a close reading of Gramsci's *Prison Notebooks* that various major inconsistencies were built into Gramsci's own original usage of his term: specifically that Gramsci was ambiguous in how he positioned culture and hegemony vis-à-vis the State and force in his diagraming of society. (Perry Anderson, 'The Antinomies of Antonio Gramsci', *New Left Review*, 100 (Nov. 1976–Jan. 1977, 5–78, esp. 12–44.) These issues are not at the centre of my current concern, but further development of the theory of ideological hegemony should not overlook the clarifications of Anderson's essay.

4 See, by contrast, Georg Simmel's notion of domination as 'a form of interaction' in which the dominant 'will draws its satisfaction from the fact that the acting or suffering of the other . . . offers itself to the dominator as the product of *his* will' (Simmel, 'Domination', trans. Kurt H. Wolff, in Donald N. Levine (ed.), *Georg Simmel: On Individuality and Social Forms* (Chicago: University of Chicago Press, 1971), 96). In this sense, hegemony differs from domination: in hegemony, dominator and dominated alike believe that the dominated is consenting *freely*. I am grateful to Mark Osiel for calling my attention to Simmel's discussion.

5 Hall, 'Culture, the Media and the "Ideological Effect" ', 333.

6 Ibid., in J. Curran, M. Gurevitch, and J. Woollacott (eds.), *Mass Communication & Society* (London: Edward Arnold, 1977), 315–48.

disseminate ideology directly. That task is left to writers and journalists, producers and teachers, bureaucrats and artists organized for production within the cultural apparatus as a whole—the schools and mass media as a whole, advertising and show business, and specialized bureaucracies within the State and the corporations. Thus the corporate owners stand, as Alvin W. Gouldner points out, in marked contrast to previous ruling classes: 'Unlike the slave-owners of antiquity or the ruling nobility of feudalism, the dominant class under capitalism is actively and routinely engaged in the conduct of economic affairs.'[7] By itself it cannot directly command the political or the administrative or the cultural apparatus that conditions the consent of the governed, even should it desire to do so. Rather, distinct strata have emerged and solidified, charged with specialized responsibilities for the administration of the entire social order. The liberal capitalist political economy is layered as an economy and a polity which meet and interpenetrate at many levels but remain organized separately; the executives and owners of the cultural apparatus—the press, mass entertainment, sports, and arts—are also interlocked at high levels with the managers of corporate and political sectors. But these sectors operate according to different principles. [. . .]

The fact that power and culture in a modern social system are to some considerable degree segmented and specialized makes ideology essential: ideology comes to the fore as a potentially cohesive force—especially in a society segmented in all the realms of life experience, ethnically and geographically as well as politically and occupationally. At the same time, the relative autonomy of the different sectors legitimates the system as a whole. And crucially, as Gouldner points out, the economic elite now becomes dependent on other sectors for securing the allegiance of the whole society. [. . .]

The hegemonic ideology of liberal, democratic capitalist society is deeply and essentially conflicted in a number of ways. At the center of liberal capitalist ideology there coils a tension between the affirmation of patriarchal authority—currently enshrined in the national security State—and the affirmation of individual worth and self-determination. Bourgeois ideology in all its incarnations has been from the first a contradiction in terms, affirming the once revolutionary ideals of 'life, liberty, and the pursuit of happiness', or 'liberty, equality, and fraternity', as if these ideas were compatible, or even mutually dependent, at all times in all places. More recently, the dominant ideology has strained to enfold a second-generation set of contradictory values: liberty versus equality, democracy versus hierarchy, public rights versus property rights, rational claims to truth versus the arrogations of power. All opposition movements in bourgeois society—whether for liberation or for domination—wage their battles precisely in terms of liberty, equality, or fraternity (or, recently, sorority)—in behalf of one set of bourgeois values against another. They press on the dominant ideology in its own name.

And, indeed, the economic system routinely generates, encourages, and tolerates ideologies which challenge and alter its own rationale. For example, as corporate capitalism became dependent on an indefinite expansion of

---

7 Alvin W. Gouldner, *The Dialectic of Ideology and Technology: The Origin, Grammar, and Future of Ideology* (New York: Seabury Press, 1976), 229. A similar approach to relations between economic and political structures is contained in Anthony Giddens, *The Class Structure of the Advanced Societies* (New York: Harper and Row, 1973).

consumer goods and consumer credit, it began to commend and diffuse hedonist values which conflicted with the older values of thrift, craft, and productivity. Workers are now told to be self-sacrificing and disciplined for eight hours a day and to relish their pleasurable selves for the next eight: to give themselves over to the production interests of the company or the office during the week and to express their true, questing, consuming selves over the weekend. Inevitably, hedonism and self-affirmation spill over from the realm of consumption into the realm of production, disrupting workplace efficiency and provoking managerial response: this whole process is central to what Daniel Bell rightly calls 'the cultural contradictions of capitalism'.[8]

But contradictions of this sort operate within a hegemonic framework which bounds and narrows the range of actual and potential contending world views. Hegemony is an historical process in which one picture of the world is systematically preferred over others, usually through practical routines and at times through extraordinary measures. Its internal structures, as Raymond Williams writes, 'have continually to be renewed, recreated and defended; and by the same token . . . they can be continually challenged and in certain respects modified'.[9] Normally the dominant frames are taken for granted by media practitioners, and reproduced and defended by them for reasons, and via practices, which the practitioners do not conceive to be hegemonic. Hegemony operates effectively—it does deliver the news—yet outside consciousness; it is exercised by self-conceived professionals working with a great deal of autonomy within institutions that proclaim the neutral goal of informing the public.[10] Does hegemony take place within journalism as a totality of techniques, assumptions, and choices?

■ The Workings of Hegemony in Journalism

As Ben Bagdikian puts it, news outside regular beats usually results from three stages in selection: (1) an editor decides that a certain scene should be looked at as the site of a newsworthy event; (2) a reporter decides what is worthy of notice on that scene; and (3) editors decide how to treat and place the resulting story.[11] Behind this process stands the institutional structure of

8 Daniel Bell, *The Cultural Contradictions of Capitalism* (New York: Basic Books, 1976). On deliberate corporate attempts to define popular happiness as the consumption of mass-produced goods, and to bring workers to identify themselves as consumers, see Stuart Ewen, *Captains of Consciousness: Advertising and the Roots of the Consumer Culture* (New York: McGraw-Hill, 1976).

9 Raymond Williams, 'Base and Superstructure in Marxist Cultural Theory', *New Left Review*, 82 (1973): 3–16, at p. 8; later reworked and extended in *Marxism and Literature* (New York: Oxford University Press, 1977), 108–14.

10 In a 1971 national survey of over four thousand journalists (including editors), a little over three-quarters said that they had 'almost complete freedom in deciding which aspects of a news story should be emphasized'; 60 per cent said that they had 'almost complete freedom in selecting the stories they work on' (though only 48 per cent of editorial employees in the larger organizations, those employing over 100 persons, claimed freedom of selection); and 46 per cent said that they made their own story assignments (as opposed to only 36 per cent in the larger news organizations). See John W. C. Johnstone, Edward J. Slawski, and William W. Bowman, *The News People: A Sociological Portrait of American Journalists and Their Work* (Urbana: University of Illinois Press, 1976), 222. Asked to rank aspects of their jobs in importance, the journalists in this sample placed public service first, followed, in descending order, by autonomy, freedom from supervision, job security, pay, and fringe benefits (p. 229). Such ordering is roughly what sociologists find among the professionals generally, though journalists differ from other professionals in lacking a generally agreed-upon training programme and credential.

11 Interview, Ben H. Bagdikian, 2 May 1979.

the media, and above all the managers who set overall corporate policy, though hardly with utter freedom. (In the argument to come, I shall single out national commercial television, but the argument about print media would not be essentially different.) By socialization, by the bonds of experience and relationships—in other words, by direct corporate and class interest—the owners and managers of the major media are committed to the maintenance of the going system in its main outlines: committed, that is to say, to private property relations which honor the prerogatives of capital; committed to a national security State; committed to reform of selected violations of the moral code through selective action by State agencies; and committed to approving individual success within corporate and bureaucratic structures.

The media élite want to honour the political-economic system as a whole; their very power and prestige deeply presuppose that system. At the same time, they are committed, like members of any other corporate elite, to their own particular economic and political advantage. The networks above all—far more than prestigious newspapers like the *New York Times*—play for high profit stakes. The resulting conflicts—between particular corporate interests and what the networks take to be the interests of the corporate system as a whole—constitute one irreducible source of strain within the system as a whole. Even a news organization's methods for legitimizing the system as a whole, its code of objectivity and balance, pull it in conflicting directions: at one moment toward the institutions of political and economic power, and at another toward alternative and even, at times, oppositional movements, depending on political circumstance. Organized as a distinct pyramid of power, the network develops the strategy of neutralization, incorporating the competing forces in such a way as to maximize its audiences and thus its profits, its legitimacy, and its stature. It claims and earns legitimacy (Harris Polls show TV news to be the most credible of *all* American institutions, though it shares in the general relative decline) in part by sanctioning reliable routines of objectivity; yet those very routines of objectivity sometimes permit—indeed, may insist on—the entry of challenging social movements into the public ideological space. The network's claim to legitimacy, embodied in the professional ideology of objectivity, requires it, in other words, to take a certain risk of undermining the legitimacy of the social system as a whole. The network's strategy for managing this contradiction is to apply the whole apparatus of techniques precisely to tame, to contain, the opposition that it dares not ignore.

After all, the legitimacy of a news operation rests heavily on the substantial—if bounded—autonomy of its employees. The audience must believe that what they are viewing is not only interesting but true, and the reporters must be permitted to feel that they have professional prerogatives to preserve. To avoid a reputation for having an axe to grind, the top media managers endow their news operations with the appearance, and a considerable actuality, of autonomy; their forms of social control must be indirect, subtle, and not at all necessarily conscious. Their standards flow through the processes of recruitment and promotion, through policy, reward, and the sort of social osmosis that flows overwhelmingly in one direction: downward. The editors and reporters they hire are generally upper-middle-class in origin, and although their personal values may be liberal by the conventional nomenclature of American politics, they tend to share the *core* hegemonic assumptions of their class: that is, of their managers as well as their major sources.[12] [. . .] Their common approach to the world infuses their homogenized cadence and tone: the news voice conveys the impression that the world is unruly because of deviations from a normally adequate and well-managed social order.[13] [. . .]

In the force field of intersecting political pressures—from the White House, the FCC, Congress, and the affiliates—the networks test the boundaries of the permissible; they carve out an ideological sphere in which they are free to move as they please. With documentaries especially, where the total air time and budget are so limited to start with, choices of subject and slant will depend most directly on the larger interests (in both the economic and the ideological sense) of the media elites. These interests, in turn, will of course take into account larger ideological currents in the society, and decisions will be made to amplify some and to dampen others. With the network's mass market mentality, 'controversial' decisions—that is, decisions to broadcast anything of political substance—are not taken lightly. [. . .]

Day to day, political and corporate pressures have not changed much: they go on setting unspoken outer limits for the routines that journalists are trained for and believe in. Once hired and assigned, reporters customarily form strong bonds with the sources (especially in Washington) on whom they depend for stories. They absorb the world views of the powerful. They may also contest them: when one institutional source disputes another (the General Accounting Office against the White House, say, or the Environmental Protection Agency against the Department of Energy); or when they come to believe that the powerful are violating the going code of conduct;[14] or when they develop, consciously or not, their own interest (as when their spouses and children actively opposed the Vietnam war); or, on occasion, when they resent, and organize to protest, one of their publishers' more outspoken editorial opinions.

But even when there are conflicts of policy between reporters and sources, or reporters and editors, or editors and publishers, these conflicts are played out within a field of terms and premises which does not overstep the hegemonic boundary. Several assumptions about news value serve, for the most part, to secure that boundary: that news involves the novel event, not the underlying, enduring condition; the person, not the group; the visible conflict, not the deep consensus; the fact that 'advances the story', not the one that explains or enlarges it.[15] Only where coverage under these rules flies in

12 H. J. Gans, *Deciding What's News* (New York: Vintage Books, 1979), 209; Johnstone *et al.*, *The News People*, 25–8.

13 There has not been much discussion of the meanings and impact of style and format in television news. See my 'Spotlights and Shadows: Television and the Culture of Politics,' *College English* 38 (April 1977): 789–801; Tuchman, *Making News*, chap. 6; and Gans, *Deciding What's News*, Part 1.

14 Gans, *Deciding What's News*, 60.

15 Some of the historical constancies throughout the 150 years of mass commercial newspapers are underscored in Helen M. Hughes, *News and the Human Interest Story* (Chicago: University of Chicago Press, 1940), and Darnton, 'Writing News and Telling Stories.' The concept of 'advancing the story' comes from Cindy Samuels, Assistant Manager of the New York Bureau of CBS News, who defines it qualitatively: 'If you have a story, and it gets bigger, then something else happens that moves it forward, you say it moved forward and it got bigger, you don't say it got bigger and it moved forward' (interview, 13 Nov. 1976).

the face of immediate institutional interest, or might be construed to be at odds with it, or wanders into some neutral zone where interests have not yet been clearly defined, is there ground for conflict between reporters and media elites over the integrity of the news operation. When outside political powers complain, top news executives mediate between them and the reporters; they may ask the staff to document their factual claims, for example. In news-paper rooms, national and foreign editors mediate between the top editors who are their superiors and the reporters who work beneath them.[16] [. . .]

Finally, there are organizational factors that in a lesser way constrain the news. Budget ceilings, for example, lead to shortages of bureaux, corres-pondents, and crews, all of which increase television news's dependence on a few big stories, preferably the *dramatic* and the *metropolitan*.[17] For the same reasons, many major newspapers have been shutting down their expensive out-of-town bureaux, especially abroad, and increasing their dependence on the wire services and on the *New York Times* and *Los Angeles Times—Washington Post* services.

The work of hegemony, all in all, consists of imposing standardized as-sumptions over events and conditions that must be 'covered' by the dictates of the prevailing news standards. [. . .]

The professional insistence that objective journalism is desirable, and that objective determinations of newsworthiness are possible, arose during the nineteenth century, albeit fitfully, as part of the sweeping intellectual move-ment toward scientific detachment and the culturewide separation of fact from value.[18] From time to time, as in the 1960s, the value of objectivity gets questioned; it always returns, virtually by default. 'Opinion' will be reserved to editorials, 'news' to the news columns; whatever was in the minds of the ideologues of objectivity, generations of journalists have aspired to that value, even enshrined it. And the aspiration does have the effect of insulating reporters greatly—though far from perfectly—from the direct political pres-sures of specific advertisers, politicans, and interest groups, and even, in the more prestigious news institutions, from the prerogatives of interfering pub-lishers.[19] Journalists are trained to be desensitized to the voices and life-worlds of working-class and minority people;[20] they are also trained in locating and treating 'the news' so that it is 'credible' and, by their own lights, 'important'. 'Credibility', 'importance', 'objectivity'—these elusive cat-egories are neither arbitrary nor fixed. They are flexible enough to shift with the expectations and experience of news executives and high-level sources,

---

16 L. V. Sigal, *Reporters and Officials* (Lexington, Mass: D. C. Heath, 1973), 19.

17 See Epstein, *News from Nowhere*, pp. 105–112, and Gould, 'The Trials of Network News', *More*, 3 (May 1973): 8–11. For example, in Nov. 1976, the Northeast bureau of CBS News, located in New York and responsible for the territory from Maryland through Maine, had a total of five camera crews.

18 Michael Schudson, *Discovering the News: A Social History of American Newspapers* (New York: Basic Books, 1978).

19 Of course, publishers went on ensuring that their immediate economic interests would be protected. Newspapers do not ordinarily cover antitrust suits against themselves, for example, and their coverage of downtown business developments tilts toward the downtown businesses that are their advertising mainstays. The closer to home the affected interest, the greater the strictures on news coverage.

20 Thelma McCormack, 'Establishment Media and the Backlash,' paper read to meetings of the American Sociological Association, Washington, DC, 1970, pp. 32–3.

yet definite enough to justify journalists' claims to professional status and standards. [...] Journalists' ideals are fluid enough to protect them from seeing that their autonomy is bounded: that by going about their business in a professional way, they systematically frame the news to be compatible with the main institutional arrangements of the society. Journalists thus sustain the dominant frames through the banal, everyday momentum of their routines. Their autonomy keeps within the boundaries of the hegemonic system.

■ **The Limits of Hegemonic Routine**

Still, traditional methods of news-gathering often contradict the demands that interested publics make for 'credibility' and 'responsibility' as their needs and expectations develop and shift. As oppositional groups and movements make claims for coverage, reporters may change their images of their audience or even of the world, and, too, their 'instincts' about what is 'newsworthy', 'interesting', or 'important'. These changes may be more or less subtle, more or less conscious: reporters may be influenced even as they resist overt pressures to report an issue in this or that way. Their vulnerability depends on many things: personal life-experience, specific organizational arrangements, and the shifting boundaries of the ideologically permissible in the wider society as well as within the newsroom. But this vulnerability also begins with the fact that reporters have only sparse contacts with their actual readers and viewers; their everyday sense of audience cannot be strong enough to insulate them against specific, focused pressures. And media managements cannot entirely overcome the symbiosis between reporters and their movement beats, even when they wish to, since the organization's ability to generate the commodity called 'news' depends on the reporter's ability to achieve rapport with a client group.

When movements mobilize, then, reporters may be pulled into the magnetic fields generated by their alternative or oppositional world views. Now the routines of objectivity prove somewhat adaptable. For normally, in the course of gathering news, reporters tend to be pulled into the cognitive worlds of their sources. Whatever their particular *opinions*, for example, Pentagon correspondents define military issues as generals, admirals, and Pentagon bureaucrats define them: as a choice between this missile system and that, not as a choice between the arms race and disarmament. When movements become newsworthy, reporters who cover them steadily are subject to a similar pull. Indeed, they may use the rhetoric and practices of objectivity to justify covering the movement sympathetically and to protect their work from editorial dampening.[21] Or further: when opposition is robust and compelling, reporters may even go so far as to jeopardize their mainstream careers. For although the main sources of news are official, the media also need other sources: they must survey the society for signs of instability, they must produce dramatic news, and thus they are vulnerable to the news-making claims of unofficial groups. Because the idea of 'objectivity' and the standards of 'newsworthiness' are loose, the hegemonic routines of news coverage are vulnerable to the demands of oppositional and deviant groups. *Through the everyday workings of journalism, large-scale social conflict*

---

21 G. Tuchman, *Making News: A Study in the Construction of Reality* (New York: Free Press, 1978), 100 ff.

is imported into the news institution and reproduced there: reproduced, however, in terms derived from the dominant ideology. Discrepant statements about reality are acknowledged—but muffled, softened, blurred, fragmented, *domesticated* at the same time.

That is, the vulnerability of the news system is not neutrality. The news routines are skewed toward representing demands, individuals, and frames which do not fundamentally contradict *the dominant hegemonic principles: the legitimacy of private control of commodity production; the legitimacy of the national security State; the legitimacy of technocratic experts; the right and ability of authorized agencies to manage conflict and make the necessary reforms; the legitimacy of the social order secured and defined by the dominant élites; and the value of individualism as the measure of social existence.* The news routines do not easily represent demands, movements, and frames which are inchoate, subtle, and most deeply subversive of these core principles. Political news is treated as if it were crime news—what went wrong today, not what goes wrong every day. A demonstration is treated as a potential or actual disruption of legitimate order, not as a statement about the world. These assumptions automatically divert coverage away from critical treatment of the institutional, systemic, and everyday workings of property and the State. (In 1977, for example, the *New York Times* hired its first investigative reporter assigned to business.) And secondly, the needs and values of sources, constituencies, and journalists alike are structured within the dominant ideology as a whole. Journalists and audiences collaborate in preferring media products which ratify the established order of commodity production and State power. Within these real limits, and only within them, the media may work out a limited autonomy from the expressed interests of political and corporate command posts; they may even affect the ways in which the elites understand their own immediate choices.

When the *New York Times* published parts of the Pentagon Papers in 1971, it risked legal penalties for relaying evidence that several administrations had lied about what they were doing in Vietnam. It did not report that the Papers confirmed some of what anti-war activists had been saying about the war for years. Editorial Page Editor Max Frankel told me that he compared the Pentagon Papers and the *Times*'s war coverage, and 'discovered we didn't do so badly. If you read the papers carefully, the press didn't do all that badly, given what we knew. Though true, it was hard for the general reader to put it all together.'[22] The anti-war movement, researching and writing outside the *Times*'s conventions for objectivity, had presented over the years a range of views that rather successfully 'put it all together,' amassing a strong case that American policy was systematically neocolonial, racist, and criminally targeted on the civilian population; but the *Times* did not cover these revelations and analyses at the time, and it would not have been seemly, in 1971 or since, for the *Times* to endorse the world view of the radical opposition, even retroactively. The solution to these unfortunate matters had to be left in the hands of duly constituted authorities; the *Times* could not criticize its own conventions or comprehend its own blind spots. [. . .]

Thus, in brief: sources are segmented and exist in history; journalists'

22 Telephone interview, Max Frankel, 23 March 1979.

values are anchored in routines that are at once *steady* enough to sustain hegemonic principles and *flexible* enough to absorb many new facts; and these routines are bounded by perceptions of the audience's common sense and are finally accountable to the world views of top managers and owners. These factors shape the news; even centralized manipulations by the State have to respect these limits. Everyday frames and procedures suffice to sustain the legitimacy of the economic-political system as a whole.

Yet the hegemonic system for regulating conflict through judgements of newsworthiness presupposes a certain minimum of political stability. When political crises erupt in the real world, they call into question whether the hegemonic routines, left to themselves, can go on contributing to social stability. Now some of the opposition movement's claims about reality seem to be verified by what mainstream reporters and editors discover about the world. *Then the hegemonic frame begins to shift.* Thus, in 1968, editors at the *New York Times* and other establishment news organizations turned sympathetic to moderate anti-war activity. The Tet offensive shattered the official rationale that the war should be pursued because it was not only just but winnable. The observed and reported facts of Tet subverted the Johnson administration's own claims—precisely the claims which had structured the media's dominant frame. At the same time, amidst what they experienced as economic and political crisis, the foreign policy élite (the 'Wise Men') began to turn against Johnson's war policy. The élite media amplified their critique of the war—a critique itself lodged within the hegemonic assumption that the United States had a right to intervene against revolutions everywhere— just as business and political authorities influenced media executives to shift positions on the war. But the political crisis was not confined to a back-and-forth process between sealed-off élites; the élites experienced political crisis precisely because of the upwelling of opposition—both radical-militant and liberal-moderate—throughout the society. That opposition made its way simultaneously into the newsrooms. Younger reporters had already begun to share in their generation's rejection of the war. And crucially, editors, like other members of their class, worried about their sons' draftability and were influenced by their anti-war children and spouses (wives, mostly). Ben Bagdikian, former national editor of the *Washington Post*, remembers this complaint by Executive Editor Ben Bradlee: 'We tell reporters not to march in a demonstration. But what can you do when their wives march in demonstrations?'[23] Reporters wheeling around to see the war differently were obviously more inclined to frame the anti-war movement differently. After the Chicago police riot of August 1968, they were still less inclined to assume that the police were the legitimate enforcers of a reasonable social order.

If editors had not shifted away from administration war policy—if élite authorities had not turned against the war—it is hard to know how far the journalists would have been able to stretch their frames for anti-war activity. Frames are in effect negotiated among sources, editors, and reporters; how they will emerge in practice is not preordained. But as the anti-war frame changed, the formulae for denigrating New Left actions remained in force; now they were clamped onto the *illegitimate* movement. The media were

23 Interview, Ben Bagdikian, 2 May 1979.

now at pains to distinguish acceptable from unacceptable opposition. Respectful treatment of the moderate anti-war activists, including the Moratorium, was clamped within the newly adjusted hegemonic frame: the war is unsuccessful, perhaps wrong; but ending it is the task of responsible authorities, not radical movements.

This adjusted frame presented problems for the media, the State, and the movement alike. The hegemonic routines had been amplifying—and distorting—an opposition movement. Legitimate authorities were not coping smoothly with the economic and political crisis; willy-nilly, they were firing up opposition; they were now widely seen as incompetent managers. At this point, *the normal routines for constructing news and reproducing hegemony became, from the point of view of much of the political élite, unreliable.* Opposition seemed to dominate the news and to contest routine management of the frames for war and anti-war news. Top media managers bridled at the normal results of hegemonic routines; therefore, from 1968 through 1973, and especially (but not only) under pressure from the Nixon White House, they interfered more directly in the news-gathering process. The forms of direct intervention are hard to smoke out. They are singular (by definition they are not routine), they may be idiosyncratic, and news of them is embarrassing: after all, they fly in the face of the hegemonic claim to professional journalistic autonomy. [. . .]

But precisely because the media have established some independence from the State, top political officials may feel threatened enough by amplified dissidence, however domesticated, to crack down directly. The State can intervene in media operations most subtly by withholding interviews, by preferring competitors, or by feeding false information to reliable reporters. The President can reward compliant editors and writers with prestigious political jobs or the President and other officials can alternately scold and cajole insufficiently docile media powers, or try to intimidate them directly. [. . .]

The media, finally, are corporations of a peculiar type. It is not only that broadcasters are regulated, directly and not, by the State; so are many other industries. (In any event, newspapers and news magazines are not directly regulated, and their framing procedures and the frames that result are not vastly different from those of the networks.) More to the point, the product that the networks sell is the attention of audiences; their primary market is the advertisers themselves. (Newspapers, too, draw the bulk of their income from advertising.) To assemble the largest and richest possible audiences, for whose attention advertisers will pay the highest rates, the media may risk offending particular corporate interests. They see themselves exercising a general steering function for the entire political economy. But the networks' profit interests are, in general, perfectly compatible with their journalists' routines for achieving objectivity. The 'good story' in traditional journalistic terms is also appealing to a mass audience: 'common sense' ratifies the hegemonic frames. The news organization therefore has two reasons to reward the production of 'good stories': for the network, good journalism is good business; but more, the media have a general interest in stabilizing the liberal capitalist order as a whole, and it is this interest, played out through all the hegemonic routines, which stands behind the dominant news frames. The whole hegemonic process in journalism operates in a reformist key: it exposes particular business and State violations of the core hegemonic principles. Precisely for that reason, the relations among media, corporations, and the State are intrinsically thick with conflict.[24]

So it is hardly surprising that businessmen regularly complain that the networks are biased against them.[25] In the first issue of a closed-circulation magazine called *Chief Executive*, for example, Walter Cronkite urges businessmen to make themselves more available to reporters in order to respond to charges against corporate practice. Cronkite argues that businesses need a reliable press to satisfy their own intelligence function, and he tries to enlist them in the networks' contest with the State over press freedoms and the First Amendment. He defends the bond between business and the news media as 'something known in the biological sciences as symbiosis':

> Newspapers, broadcasting outlets and networks survive on the advertising revenues that come from business. Journalism can thrive only so long as the business community remains healthy enough to provide these funds. Business, on the other hand, depends upon journalism to foster its own growth—through the dissemination of information through news and advertising.[26]

This is what the 'Dean of the World's Broadcast Journalists' (the magazine's blurb) urges upon an audience of top business, government, and other executives. Campaigning for symbiosis, as other top media people have also been doing, Cronkite acknowledges implicitly that it is far from an accomplished fact. On the other hand, the fact that he takes the trouble to spell out the goal reveals that the media élite is defensive. It is media strategy to *accomplish* symbiosis with the corporations as a whole, to guide that symbiosis, and in the process to guide the whole society toward a stable environment in which the media corporations may flourish. Just as the networks must be careful not to offend core interests of the State, so they must take care not to violate the most central premises of the business system as a whole: they must sanction the right of private control over investment and production, just as they sanctify their own right to control the space within which public communication takes place. The business practices exposed in the news—bribes,

24 See Gans, *Deciding What's News*, 68–69, 203–6, on the muckraking Progressivism of American journalism.

25 Business critiques of the news media are legion. Among the more articulate versions are 'Business and the Press—Independent or Interdependent?' a speech by Donald S. MacNaughton, Chairman and Chief Executive Officer, the Prudential Insurance Company of America, November 4, 1975, excerpted in the *New York Times*, Business Section, March 7, 1976, p. 12; 'The Values That Can Serve Mankind', Remarks by David Rockefeller, Chairman of the Board, the Chase Manhattan Bank, before the Northern California Region of the National Conference of Christians and Jews, April 7, 1976; and the discussion in Leonard Silk and David Vogel, *Ethics and Profits* (New York: Simon and Schuster, 1976), 104–16, drawing on comments from many executives who are members of the Conference Board. Media responses include 'Business and the Press: Who's Doing What to Whom and Why?' Remarks of Arthur R. Taylor, President, CBS Inc., before the Financial Executives Institute, October 21, 1975; and 'Businessmen Can Look Better If They Try', by Dan Cordtz, economics editor at ABC, in the *New York Times*, Business Section, July 18, 1976, p. 12. The tone of these latter two articles is strikingly similar to Cronkite's appeal, below, for a symbiotic division of labour: the media have *their* jobs to do, business has *its* job to do, and businessmen should learn how to make more effective use of the existing media system. In other words, the media spokesmen are defending a functional division of labour between economic and cultural-legitimation spheres.

26 *Chief Executive* 1 (July–Sept. 1977): 26. Weirdly enough, the role of the young heiress-terrorist in the film *Network* was played by Walter Cronkite's daughter Kathy.

sudden health hazards, damage to the environment—are precisely the exceptional; and the frames generally cushion the impact of these reports by isolating exceptional corporations, by blaming 'the public', by speaking from the angle of consumers and not workers, and by refraining from attempts at general explanation and radical solution. Yet, in this weakly reformist process, the media set terms for discourse which, corporations believe, threaten the legitimacy of the corporate system as a whole. *The media seek symbiosis with the corporate system precisely through the bounded routines of 'objective' journalism.* This drive is utopian; it does not cease, though it is always, in the end, unconsummated.

30

Negotiating Control: A Study of News Sources

Richard V. Ericson, Patricia M. Baranek, and Janet B. L. Chan

The Relative Autonomy of Sources: Regions and Closures

MOST RESEARCHERS HAVE concluded that institutional and organizational ties leave journalists in a state of dependency with respect to sources (e.g. Chibnall 1977; Hall *et al.* 1978; Fishman 1980; see Lane 1923, and Fraser 1956, for historical examples). Confronted with a bureaucratically constructed universe, the journalist can only reproduce bureaucratic constructs for public consumption. Simply by working within the constraints of his job the journalist functions as a conduit pipe for the flow of prefigured signs from his sources. As Sir John A. Macdonald once remarked, 'When you see what a journalist will write unbribed, why then, there's no need to bribe them, is there?' (cited by Black 1982: 215).

Just as sources face the problem of obtaining access to the news rather than mere coverage, so journalists have the problem of obtaining access to a source organization rather than the opportunity for mere coverage. There is a great difference between being in a position to give coverage to a source organization's event, process, or state of affairs, and having access that allows for the story the journalist needs for his news organization's purposes. Sources effect varying degrees of restriction on access to the back regions of their organization, and even their front regions are controlled in time, space, and social arrangements. Concomitantly, the knowledge available in the front regions is subject to degrees of closure.

Every human being and organization requires a workable level of privacy, defined as 'those places, spaces, and matters upon or into which others may not normally intrude without the consent of the person or organization to whom they are designated as belonging' (Reiss 1987: 20; see also Bok 1982: 10–11). Indeed, privacy is a necessary condition for the possibility of an organization's arising in the first instance (Rock, 1990), and for its continuation.

Our subsequent analyses are centrally concerned with how sources work to protect their organization against intrusion by journalists, while concomitantly achieving favourable publicity, which is seen as an important means of maintaining control over the organizational environment. This work is extremely complex and difficult because of the porosity of

Source: R. V. Ericson, P. M. Baranek, and J. B. L. Chan, *Negotiating Control: A Study of News Sources* (Milton Keynes: Open University Press, 1989), ch. 1, 'Negotiating the News'.

bureaucratic organizations, the volume of knowledge available, the elusive nature of knowledge, and the fact that knowledge can be taken without ever leaving its place. In order to capture the complexity of this work we have devised the model presented as Figure 1. This model is inspired by the pioneering work of Goffman (especially Goffman 1959), and the subsequent refinements of Giddens (1984: 122–6). However, Goffman and Giddens were primarily concerned with the individual's preservation and presentation of self by relying upon spatial preserves of privacy alternating with public places for the staging of appearances. In addition to this social-psychological framework, we are interested in the sociological level of how organizations protect and present their activities by policing spatial regions and knowledge.

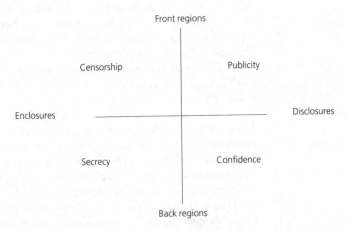

Figure 1.
Regions and closures

Figure 1 represents the possibilities for journalists' physical access to regions and sign access to knowledge in source organizations. The back regions are spaces where organizational work transpires and decisions are taken but which are open only to the purview of those who are officially authorized to be there. Excluded are not only those who do not have an official role in the organization, but also those whose official role is limited to some regions and not others. For example, in the courts key decisions are taken in the Crown attorney's office as the police, Crown attorney, and defence lawyer make plea-bargaining deals to settle criminal cases without trial. The accused and victim are routinely excluded from this setting where the 'real trial' occurs, as are other members of the public, including the reporter (Ericson and Baranek 1982). Judges' chambers are even more exclusive, as even other court officials are excluded except as the judge might summons them to discuss a case.

The front regions consist of those areas where the public business of the organization is transacted. In normal circumstances not only those with an official role, but also those who wish to do business with the organization, are allowed access to front regions. In many public bureaucracies members of the public can attend these spaces merely as spectators, without any official business. For example, in courts and legislatures designated public-gallery sections are normally open to any member of the public, including journalists.

Enclosure refers to efforts to circumscribe or extinguish the signs that are given off in various regions. An effort to keep signs or knowledge from others is an attempt at secrecy. An obvious way to maintain secrecy is to exclude from back regions those persons whom one wants to keep knowledge away from. For example, in the courts we studied, the reporters were excluded from plea-bargaining sessions in the Crown attorney's office. Enclosure is not restricted to back regions. '[T]he differentiation between front and back regions by no means coincides with a division between the enclosure (covering up, hiding) of aspects of the self and their disclosure (revelation, divulgence). These two axes of regionalization operate in a complicated nexus of possible relations between meanings, norms and power' (Giddens 1984: 126). For example, there are provisions in law that allow a judge to censor even that which transpires in the public forum of the courtroom. Censorship is a restriction on publicizing more broadly that which is made public in one narrower context. Thus, there are occasional publicity bans on what transpires in the courtroom.

Disclosure entails efforts to communicate signs in various regions. An effort to communicate to the unauthorized that which is normally communicated only to the authorized, and the expectation that it is not to be made known to others, is a confidence. Confidence, the revelation of private matters with mutual trust, normally pertains to work activities that transpire in the back regions. For example, a Crown attorney might tell a reporter that an accused decided to plead guilty as a result of a plea bargain involving the withdrawal of some charges and a favourable sentence recommendation, but expect the reporter not to include that in his filed story. Disclosure in the front regions is the normal condition of publicity. What is said in the courtroom, in interviews in the corridors of the courthouse, or through 'proper channels' over the telephone has been prefigured and preformulated for public consumption. Here the source organization works hard to give off signs that make it appear to be doing what interested publics think it should be doing.

There is considerable variation in access to source regions and knowledge, depending on the type of source organization involved, and the type of knowledge being sought within a given source organization. For example, prisons are relatively closed institutions for the purposes of news. It is rare to find a regular 'prison beat' reporter, the exceptions being communities where prisons are dominant (as with the *Whig–Standard* in Kingston, Ontario) or where there are special ties between the prison administration and a particular local news outlet (as occurred in Chicago over a twenty-five-year period—see Jacobs 1977). Prisons are run in terms more of administrative discretion than of external review and public accountability, and this veil of administrative decency has effectively kept out the news media. This observation is borne out by content studies that indicate that stories emanating from prisons, or about prisons, are rare statistically compared to court coverage and especially police coverage (Graber 1980; Garofalo 1981; Ericson *et al.* forthcoming).

Courts are relatively less closed. Reporters are given an office and develop ongoing relations with reporters from other news organizations, and with sources, in a distinctive beat culture. However, they are restricted to particular public physical spaces (e.g. the courtroom, but not the Crown attorney's office during plea-bargaining sessions), and to particular organizational documents. This restriction emanates from a combination of formal source control (including the law), work expediency, and norms of propriety that evolve among journalists and their sources (Epstein 1975; Fishman 1980; Dreschel 1983). Key actors in the court are reluctant to divulge knowledge because they are legally restricted from doing so, or have been socialized into being reticent about talking to the news media about their cases. This case especially applies to judges, who will not 'second-guess' their decisions to a reporter and are even reluctant to talk about issues on a regular basis for fear of tainting the image of their office as independent. The reporter is left to convey what the court organization has pre-established as public information, knowable through its presentation in public-display settings such as the courtroom.

The police have become relatively more open. Unlike the courts, they often have full-time public-relations specialists and news-media officers who are proactive in disseminating knowledge and arranging for 'media events'. While this aspect of openness may be taken as a sign that efforts are being made to exert more control over the news media, it is also a sign that the police recognize the need to be more open and accommodative to perpetual demands for news-media coverage (Hickling-Johnston 1982). In the face of being used at the forefront of public debates about the relation between the individual and the state, and as a sign of governmental accountability, the police recognize the importance of allowing reasonable access to the news media and the accountability allowed by its discourse (Brogden 1982; Jefferson and Grimshaw 1984; Reiner 1985). An additional consideration is that the membership of a police bureaucracy is very large, and varied in functions and sub-unit loyalties. In contrast to the small-city situation studied by Fishman (1980), the large urban police organization is open to multiple communication channels because of its size (often several thousand members), and internal divisions, which make control through guidelines and official contexts (news releases, the press room) only partial (Chibnall 1977).

Political beats appear relatively most open. In this sphere public accountability must be shown routinely, and the news media are seen as the most significant vehicles for displaying it. Political beats are characterized by myriad full-time media-relations personnel and consultants whose job is to represent political interests through gaining news access. Politicians and senior civil servants recognize the importance of the news media not only to the authority of their office, but also to their ability to stay in office (Sigal 1973; Cockrell *et al.* 1985; Golding *et al.* 1986). Access means maximizing their sources and objects, magnifying their coherence and hegemony; mere coverage can have the effect of the news media's minimizing their sources and objects, magnifying their incoherence and fragmentation. In the interest of maximizing their access while relegating the opposition to mere coverage, political interests expend enormous resources through a variety of proactive media strategies, and allow considerable access to some back-region settings.

It is wrong to say 'reporters expose themselves *only* to settings in which formally organized transactions of official business occur' (Fishman 1980;

emphasis added). Reporters' *primary* exposure may be in such front-region settings, but these are not the exclusive settings of their work (Ericson *et al.* 1987). Moreover, it is not just a matter of what reporters expose themselves to, but of what sources allow them to be exposed to. Even back-region access may not yield reportable material because relevant information is still enclosed (secrecy) or disclosed with the understanding it will not be published (confidence). Front-region access may not yield reportable material because what is presented there is enclosed (legally or otherwise restricted) or is a highly structured, mediated, and partial account. The nature and degree of exposure is always at issue, varying in time and place within a source organization, and by the type of source organization.

References   BLACK, E. (1982), *Politics and the News: Political Functions of the Mass Media* (Toronto: Butterworth).

BOK, S. (1982), *Secrets: On the Ethics of Concealment and Revelation* (New York: Pantheon).

BROGDEN, M. (1982), *The Police: Autonomy and Consent* (London: Academic Press).

CHIBNALL, S. (1977), *Law-and-Order News* (London: Tavistock).

COCKRELL, M., HENNESSY, P., and WALKER, D. (1985), *Sources Close to the Prime Minister: Inside the Hidden World of the News Manipulators* (London: Macmillan).

DRECHSEL, R. (1983), *News Media in the Trial Courts* (New York: Longman).

EPSTEIN, E. (1975), *Between Fact and Fiction* (New York: Vintage).

ERICSON, R., and BARANEK, P. (1982), *The Ordering of Justice* (Toronto: University of Toronto Press).

ERICSON, R., BARANEK, P. and CHAN, J. (forthcoming), *Acknowledging Order: A Study of News Content.*

FISHMAN, M. (1980), *Manufacturing the News* (Austin: University of Texas Press).

FRASER, P. (1956), *The Intelligence of the Secretaries of State and Their Monopoly of Printed News 1660–1688* (Cambridge: Cambridge University Press).

GIDDENS, A. (1984), *The Constitution of Society* (Cambridge: Polity).

GOFFMAN, E. (1959), *The Presentation of Self in Everyday Life* (New York: Doubleday).

GOLDING, P., MURDOCK, G., and SCHLESINGER, P. (1986), *Communicating Politics* (Leicester: University of Leicester Press).

GRABER, D. (1980), *Crime News and the Public* (New York: Praeger).

HALL, S., CRITCHER, C., JEFFERSON, T., CLARKE, J., and ROBERTS, B. (1978), *Policing the Crisis* (London: Macmillan).

HICKLING-JOHNSTON (1982), *Metropolitan Police Management Study Final Report: Managing Change within the Metropolitan Toronto Police* (Toronto: Hickling-Johnston).

JACOBS, J. (1977), *Stateville* (Chicago: University of Chicago Press).

JEFFERSON, T., and GRIMSHAW, R. (1984), *Controlling the Constable: Police Accountability in England and Wales* (London: Frederick Muller / The Cobden Trust).

LANE, J. (1923), *Muddiman: The Kings' Journalist 1659–1689* (London: Bodley Head).

REINER, R. (1985), *The Politics of the Police* (Brighton: Wheatsheaf Books).

REISS, A. (1987), 'The Legitimacy of Intrusion into Private Space', in C. Shearing and P. Stenning (eds.), *Private Policing* (Beverly Hills: Sage), 19–44.

ROCK, P. (1990), 'On the Birth of Organizations', *Canadian Journal of Sociology*, 13.

SIGAL, L. (1973), *Reporters and Officials* (Lexington, Mass.: D. C. Heath).

5

Objectivity and Ideology of News

Introduction to Part V: Objectivity and Ideology of News

THE PIECES IN this section provide an insight into debates about objectivity and ideology of news. Each article focuses on a different aspect. The first by Michael Schudson, traces the development of objectivity as an ideal in the American press from the beginning of the century. He provides an explanation of the change from partisanship to factual news and why objective reporting did not become the accepted norm in journalism in the late nineteenth century despite the growth of the news agencies. At the beginning of the twentieth century journalists did not see a sharp divide between facts and values. Schudson labels them naïve empiricists because they saw facts not as human statements but as comments about aspects of the world itself. It was the development of social sciences and philosophy from the 1920s onwards that saw journalists beginning to think about the subjectivity of perception. After the First World War in the 1920s and 1930s journalists began to distrust facts, and this led to a more sophisticated ideal of objectivity based on established rules and procedures of the profession. Schudson sees objectivity as the ideal that legitimizes the journalistic profession.

Gaye Tuchman, writing in the early 1970s, examines ideas of objectivity as professional rules and rituals used by journalists in order to process facts about social reality. She examines three separate factors determining reporters' ideas of objectivity, namely the form, content, and interorganizational relationships. Tuchman investigates the use of these ritual procedures, illustrating how they protect the reporter from criticism and libel, for example in the use of quotation marks. Tuchman's article although written nearly thirty years ago is still very relevant today in relation to current debates about objectivity and professionalism. Tuchman shows how objectivity is used defensively by reporters as a strategic ritual protecting them from mistakes as well as critics.

John Soloski describes how professionalism in news journalism affects the gathering and reporting of the news. News organizations maintain control over the way their reporters and editors operate by the use of professionalism. Alongside the rules and procedures comprising part of the profession, news policies are developed by organizations to control the behaviour of their employees. Soloski conducted participant observation noting news organizations' enforcement of these news policies. He found the relative autonomy of journalists requires employees to find the means to 'make the use of discretion predictable'. It is the use of professionalism and particularly ideas of objectivity that relieves a news organization from the responsibility of developing control mechanisms. He concludes that whilst journalists may not report the news in a way that consciously supports the capitalist system, it is their professional norms which provide the framework for producing stories implicitly maintaining the existing order. These professional norms legitimize the current system by making it appear 'normal'.

Maxwell McCombs and Donald Shaw demonstrate in their classic piece about the 1968 US Presidential election how journalists and editors play a vital role in setting the news agenda for the audience by reflecting what the candidates discussed during the campaign. In their analysis they show how readers of newspapers learnt about the campaign issues and also the amount of importance attached to each issue. Their hypothesis, developed further since their original Chapel Hill study, argues that the mass media set the agenda for each political campaign, influencing the salience of attitudes toward the political issues.

Daniel Hallin provides a critique of the thesis of an opposition media during the period of the Vietnam War—the myth that it was the media who caused America to lose the war in Vietnam. Hallin argues that from an examination of television news, there was no dramatic shift in the basic ideology and news gathering routines of American journalism. The routines of objective journalism persisted virtually unchanged throughout the period of the Vietnam War. The media relied heavily on official sources during the course of the war and the critical coverage eventually ensuing did not extend to criticism of either the political system or to general consensus ideals. Hallin questions why television more than the major newspapers tended to stick to consensus journalism on Vietnam, or as he terms it the narrowest kind of journalism. He suggests the immaturity of the television news media may be an answer. Hallin explains that as the war progressed the journalists were inclined to report information critical of political policy. The media's changing level of support during the war was bound up, ironically, in their constant commitment to the ideology and routines of objective journalism. It was the collapse of the consensus on foreign policy amongst the ruling élite reflected in the journalists' coverage that led to the perception that the news media were changing their stance against the policy in Vietnam. Stories and points of view not treated as legitimate news stories now became acceptable. It was this changed political environment that eventually led to a difference in the reporting of news. His conclusion is that whether the media tend to support or criticize government policies depends on the degree of consensus those policies enjoy amongst the political establishment.

Barbie Zelizer uses the notion of critical incidents or events to frame the manner of working norms. She looks at how the Gulf War offered a place for journalists to discuss their concerns about their own profession and claims the conflict can be viewed as another potential critical incident in line with other famous events in journalism history, such as the Kennedy assassination and the Vietnam War. It is these critical incidents which highlight rules and conventions about journalistic practice, and often their authority. In the case of the Gulf War, issues of professionalism arose from the outset, particularly concerns about censorship, editorial integrity, economic viability, and the establishment of authority for what Zelizer calls reportage in real time. The

Gulf War enabled journalists to reconsider ideas about their own professional practice and the boundaries of the journalistic authority.

Robert Picard summarizes the controversies and criticisms about the role of the news media and other communication systems in the developed and developing world. He traces the origins of the global communications arguments emerging from the developing nations as independence was granted and nationalist movements arose after the Second World War. Concerns expressed about the monopolization of international information by the Western news media, in particular by the big four news agencies was later extended to criticisms about the domination of the television news media. These issues were discussed in forums such as UNESCO, The International Telecommunications Union and other organizations. Out of these debates, proposals emerged and calls made for a New World Information and Communications Order (NWICO). Some of the issues concerned the control of the technology by Western countries and organizations and the content of the news from the developing world portraying a negative picture focusing on disasters and conflicts. The emphasis on Western definitions of news created the image of the developing world that did not portray accurately economic and social life.

Davis Merritt's piece on public journalism and public life discusses the recent calls for a change in the operation of journalists and news organizations. Within a framework of an analysis that trust in all institutions and particularly journalism is in decline, Merritt and other key figures recently produced a body of work setting out their ideas about how the growing gap between the citizen and the government may be bridged by a new or different kind of journalism. The state of disillusionment existing not only amongst the general public, but also within the journalistic profession stems in part from the crisis in the economic structures that support journalism. Merritt sees no coincidence in the decline in journalism mapping the decline in public life. Merritt and others in the public journalism movement argue that journalism is a major contributor to the malaise in public life. The failure of the profession is leading to calls for new forms of reporting requiring a change in the profession necessary for journalism once again to be a primary force in the revitalisation of public life. The public journalism movement believes that journalism is suffering a fundamental loss of authority and regaining that authority must be journalism's first step towards revitalizing itself. Explicit in the attacks on conventional journalism by the public journalism movement is the professional idea of objectivity. The principle of balance removes any obligation and indeed risk that people with different views would be offended. In addition the idea of objectivity and balance provides an element of conflict, whether real or contrived into the story. It is the framing of stories in this way that Merritt claims creates a deficiency of accuracy by polarising stories to the extremes. It leaves most people out of discussion of particular stories.

The final piece by Jo Bardoel asks some very pertinent questions about the future of journalism in relation to the information society. There is a singular lack of theorizing and empirical studies about the relationship to journalism and the new technologies, particularly in regard to the internet, and we await the classic pieces to compare with the production studies of twenty or thirty years ago. Bardoel discusses the way the new information technologies affect the traditional task of journalism. Is the development of news via the internet from direct sources making the old style journalist redundant and how will the public itself view this new form of news? If the new interactive services provide an increase in communications between citizens and their leaders what will be the role of journalists in this unmediated landscape? Bardoel sees the position of journalism as a unified profession no longer tenable. The new media formats will lead to two types of journalism. First, orientating journalism where background commentary and explanation are given to the general public and second, instrumental journalism that provides functional and specialized information to interested customers. The new information services require mostly these new kinds of journalists or 'information brokers' while the classical media would seek all journalists. Within this media sector segmentation the call for a new type of journalist will expand, whereas the need for the old type of classical journalism may die out.

31

Discovering the News: A Social History of American Newspapers

Michael Schudson

Introduction: The Ideal of Objectivity

AMERICAN JOURNALISM HAS been regularly criticized for failing to be 'objective'. Whether it was Democrats in 1952 complaining of a one-party press biased against Adlai Stevenson or the Nixon–Agnew administration attacking newspapers and television networks for being too liberal, the press has repeatedly been taken to task for not presenting the day's news 'objectively'.

But why do critics take it for granted that the press *should* be objective? Objectivity is a peculiar demand to make of institutions which, as business corporations, are dedicated first of all to economic survival. It is a peculiar demand to make of institutions which often, by tradition or explicit credo, are political organs. It is a peculiar demand to make of editors and reporters who have none of the professional apparatus which, for doctors or lawyers or scientists, is supposed to guarantee objectivity.

And yet, journalists, as well as their critics, hold newspapers to a standard of objectivity. Not all journalists believe they should be objective in their work, but the belief is widespread,[1] and all journalists today must in some manner confront it. But why? What kind of a world is ours and what kind of an institution is journalism that they sustain this particular ideal, objectivity? That is the problem this book addresses. I shall not ask here the familiar question: are newspapers objective? I shall ask, instead, why that question is so familiar.

The question assumes special interest when one learns that, before the 1830s, objectivity was not an issue. American newspapers were expected to present a partisan viewpoint, not a neutral one. Indeed, they were not expected to report the 'news' of the day at all in the way we conceive it—the idea of 'news'

Source: Michael Schudson, *Discovering The News: A Social History of American Newspapers* (New York: Basic Books, 1978).

1 John W. C. Johnstone, Edward J. Slawski, and William M. Bowman, 'The Professional Values of American Newsmen', *Public Opinion Quarterly* 36 (Winter 1972–1973): 522–40; and, by the same authors, *The News People* (Urbana: University of Illinois Press, 1976).

itself was invented in the Jacksonian era. If we are to understand the idea of objectivity in journalism, the transformation of the press in the Jacksonian period must be examined. That is the task of the first chapter, which will interpret the origins of 'news' in its relationship to the democratization of politics, the expansion of a market economy, and the growing authority of an entrepreneurial, urban middle class.

There is an obvious explanation of why the idea of news, once established, should have turned into nonpartisan, strictly factual news later in the century. This has to do with the rise of the first American wire service, the Associated Press (AP). The telegraph was invented in the 1840s, and, to take advantage of its speed in transmitting news, a group of New York newspapers organized the Associated Press in 1848. Since the Associated Press gathered news for publication in a variety of papers with widely different political allegiances, it could only succeed by making its reporting 'objective' enough to be acceptable to all of its members and clients. By the late nineteenth century, the AP dispatches were markedly more free from editorial comment than most reporting for single newspapers.[2] It has been argued, then, that the practice of the Associated Press became the ideal of journalism in general.[3]

While this argument is plausible, at first blush, there is remarkably little evidence for it and two good reasons to doubt it. First, it begs a key question: why should a practice, obviously important to the survival of the institution of the wire service, become a guiding ideal in institutions not subject to the same constraints? It would be just as likely, or more likely, that newspapers would take the availability of wire service news as licence to concentrate on different kinds of reporting. *If* the AP style became a model for daily journalists, one would still have to account for its affinity with their interests and needs. But this brings us to the second, still more serious problem: objective reporting did *not* become the chief norm or practice in journalism in the late nineteenth century when the Associated Press was growing. As I will show in the second and third chapters, at the turn of the century there was as much emphasis in leading papers on telling a good story as on getting the facts. Sensationalism in its various forms was the chief development in newspaper content. Reporters sought as often to write 'literature' as to gather news. Still, in 1896, in the bawdiest days of yellow journalism, the *New York Times* began to climb to its premier position by stressing an 'information' model, rather than a 'story' model, of reporting. Where the Associated Press was factual to appeal to a politically diverse clientele, the *Times* was informational to attract a relatively select, socially homogeneous readership of the well to do. As in the Jacksonian era, so in the 1890s, changes in the ideals of journalism did not translate technological changes into occupational norms so much as make newspaper ideals and practices consonant with the culture of dominant social classes.

---

2 Donald L. Shaw, 'News Bias and the Telegraph: A Study of Historical Change', *Journalism Quarterly* 44 (Spring 1967): 3–12, 31.

3 Shaw suggests this in Shaw, 'News Bias and the Telegraph' and in 'Technology: Freedom for What?' in Ronald T. Farrar and John D. Stevens, *Mass Media and the National Experience* (New York: Harper and Row, 1971), pp. 64–86. James W. Carey cautiously voices the same position in 'The Communications Revolution and the Professional Communicator', *Sociological Review Monograph* 13 (1969): 23–38. Bernard Roscho espouses the same view in *Newsmaking* (Chicago: University of Chicago Press, 1975), p. 31.

But into the first decades of the twentieth century, even at the *New York Times*, it was uncommon for journalists to see a sharp divide between facts and values.[4] Yet the belief in objectivity is just this: the belief that one can and should separate facts from values. Facts, in this view, are assertions about the world open to independent validation. They stand beyond the distorting influences of any individual's personal preferences. Values, in this view, are an individual's conscious or unconscious preferences for what the world should be; they are seen as ultimately subjective and so without legitimate claim on other people. The belief in objectivity is a faith in 'facts', a distrust of 'values', and a commitment to their segregation.

Journalists before World War I did not subscribe to this view. They were, to the extent that they were interested in facts, naïve empiricists; they believed that facts are not human statements about the world but aspects of the world itself. This view was insensitive to the ways in which the 'world' is something people construct by the active play of their minds and by their acceptance of conventional—not necessarily 'true'—ways of seeing and talking. Philosophy, the history of science, psychoanalysis, and the social sciences have taken great pains to demonstrate that human beings are cultural animals who know and see and hear the world through socially constructed filters. From the 1920s on, the idea that human beings individually and collectively construct the reality they deal with has held a central position in social thought.[5]

Before the 1920s, journalists did not think much about the subjectivity of perception. They had relatively little incentive to doubt the firmness of the 'reality' by which they lived. American society, despite serious problems, remained buoyant with hope and promise. Democracy was a value unquestioned in politics; free enterprise was still widely worshipped in economic life; the novels of Horatio Alger sold well. Few people doubted the inevitability of progress. After World War I, however, this changed. Journalists, like others, lost faith in verities a democratic market society had taken for granted. Their experience of propaganda during the war and public relations thereafter convinced them that the world they reported was one that interested parties had constructed for them to report. In such a world, naïve empiricism could not last.

This turning point is the topic of my fourth chapter. In the 1920s and 1930s, many journalists observed with growing anxiety that facts themselves, or what they had taken to be facts, could not be trusted. One response to this discomfiting view was the institutionalization in the daily paper of new genres of subjective reporting, like the political column. Another response

---

4 From the seventeenth century until the past several decades, Wayne Booth wrote in 1974, 'it grew increasingly unfashionable to see the universe or world or nature or "the facts" as implicating values'. But he argues that it is only in the twentieth century that 'the fact-value split became a truism *and* that the split began to entail the helplessness of reason in dealing with any values but the calculation of means to ends'. (See Wayne C. Booth, *Modern Dogma and the Rhetoric of Assent* [Chicago: University of Chicago Press, 1974], pp. 14–15.) Booth argues forcefully against a radical disjunction of facts and values as does the philosopher Alasdair MacIntyre in *A Short History of Ethics* (New York: Macmillan, 1966) and *Against the Self-Images of the Age* (New York: Schocken Books, 1971), especially the essay, 'Hume on "Is" and "Ought" ', pp. 109–124.

5 Two influential recent statements regarding the social construction of reality are Thomas Kuhn, *The Structure of Scientific Revolutions* (Chicago: University of Chicago Press, 1962); and Peter Berger and Thomas Luckmann, *The Social Construction of Reality* (Garden City, N.Y.: Doubleday, 1966).

turned the journalists' anxiety on its head and encouraged journalists to re-place a simple faith in facts with an allegiance to rules and procedures created for a world in which even facts were in question. This was 'objectivity'. Object-ivity, in this sense, means that a person's statements about the world can be trusted if they are submitted to established rules deemed legitimate by a professional community. Facts here are not aspects of the world, but consen-sually validated statements about it.[6] While naïve empiricism has not disap-peared in journalism and survives, to some extent, in all of us, after World War I it was subordinated to the more sophisticated ideal of 'objectivity'.

Discussion of objectivity as an ideal (or ideology) in science, medicine, law, the social sciences, journalism, and other pursuits tends to two poles: either it seeks to unmask the profession in question or to glorify it. It is either debunking or self-serving. Debunkers show that the claims of professionals about being objective or expert or scientific are really just attempts to legit-imate power by defining political issues in technical terms. This is often true. But, first, why is 'objectivity' the legitimation they choose, and, second, why is it so often convincing to others? When professionals make a claim to au-thoritative knowledge, why do they base the claim on their objectivity rather than on, say, divine revelation or electoral mandate? Debunking by itself does not provide an answer.

The opposite stance is to Whiggishly identify objectivity in journalism or in law or other professions with 'science', where science is understood as the right or true or best path to knowledge. This is the point at which science, generally understood as opposed to ideology, threatens to become ideology itself. But that, in a sense, is just what interests me here—not the internal de-velopment of science as an institution or a body of knowledge and practices, but the reasons the *idea* of science and the *ideal* of objectivity are so resonant in our culture. Even if science, as we know it today, is in some sense getting us nearer to truth than past systems of knowledge, we can still inquire why twentieth-century Western culture should be so wise as to recognize this. And that is a question that glorifications of science and objectivity do not answer.

It should be apparent that the belief in objectivity in journalism, as in other professions, is not just a claim about what kind of knowledge is reliable. It is also a moral philosophy, a declaration of what kind of thinking one should engage in, in making moral decisions. It is, moreover, a political commit-ment, for it provides a guide to what groups one should acknowledge as rele-vant audiences for judging one's own thoughts and acts. The relevant audiences are defined by institutional mechanisms. Two mechanisms of social control are frequently said to underwrite objectivity in different fields. First, there is advanced education and training. This is supposed to provide

6 This is the leading version of objectivity in science. Israel Scheffler has defined it as follows: 'Commitment to fair controls over assertion is the basis of the scientific attitude of impartiality and detachment; indeed, one might say that it constitutes this attitude. For impartiality and detachment are not to be thought of as substantive qualities of the scientist's personality or the style of his thought; scientists are as variegated in these respects as any other group of people. . . . What is central is the acknowledgment of general controls to which one's dearest beliefs are ultimately subject.' (Israel Scheffler, *Science and Subjectivity* [Indianapolis: Bobbs-Merrill, 1967], p. 2.)

trainees with scientific knowledge and an objective attitude which helps them set aside personal preferences and passions. Thus the training of physicians enables them to sustain detached attitudes at times when persons without such training would submit to panic or despair at the human agony they face. Law students are taught to distinguish 'legal' questions (generally understood to be technical) from 'moral' issues (generally understood to be outside the proper domain of legal education and legal practice).

A second basic form of social control is insulation from the public. Technical language or jargon is one such insulating mechanism. Others may be institutional. For instance, legal scholars argue that courts are able to be more objective than legislatures because judges are institutionally further removed from the pressures of electoral politics than are legislators. Objectivity in the professions is guaranteed, then, by the autonomy of professional groups— the collective independence of professions from the market and from popular will, and the personal independence of professionals, assured by their training, from their own values.

In this context, the notion of objectivity in journalism appears anomalous. Nothing in the training of journalists gives them licence to shape others' views of the world. Nor do journalists have esoteric techniques or language. Newspapers are directly dependent on market forces. They appeal directly to popular opinion. Journalism is an uninsulated profession. To criticize a lawyer, we say, 'I'm not a lawyer, but—' and to question a doctor, we say, 'I'm no expert on medicine, but—.' We feel no such compunction to qualify criticism of the morning paper or the television news. I do not subscribe to the view that journalism is thereby inferior to other professional groups; I simply mean to identify the problem of objectivity in the case of journalism. How is it that in an occupation without the social organization of self-regulated authority there is still passionate controversy about objectivity? Of course, one answer is that the less a profession is seen to be self-evidently objective, the more passionate the controversy will be. But this is not answer enough. Why, in journalism, where none of the features that guarantee objectivity in law or medicine exist or are likely to exist, should objectivity still be a serious issue? Why hasn't it been given up altogether?

By the 1960s, both critics of the press and defenders took objectivity to be the emblem of American journalism, an improvement over a past of 'sensationalism' and a contrast to the party papers of Europe. Whether regarded as the fatal flaw or the supreme virtue of the American press, all agreed that the idea of objectivity was at the heart of what journalism has meant in this country. At the same time, the ideal of objectivity was more completely and divisively debated in the past decade than ever before. In the final chapter, I will examine how changing subject matter, sources of news, and audience for the news precipitated this debate in journalism. Government management of the news, which began to concern journalists after World War I, became an increasingly disturbing problem with the rise of a national security establishment and an 'imperial' presidency after World War II. In the Vietnam war, government news management collided with a growing 'adversary culture' in the universities, in journalism, in the government itself, and in the population at large. The conflagration that followed produced a radical questioning of objectivity which will not soon be forgotten and revitalized traditions of reporting that the objective style had long overshadowed. The ideal of objectivity has by no means been displaced, but, more than ever, it holds its authority on sufferance.

I originally conceived this work as a case study in the history of professions and in the genesis of professional ideology. I saw objectivity as the dominant ideal that legitimates knowledge and authority in all contemporary professions. If I could excavate its foundations in one field, I could hope to expose its structure in all. While this book has not entirely outgrown that ambition, it came to be moved equally by another. I grew fascinated by journalism itself and convinced there were important questions, not only unanswered but unasked, about the relationship of journalism to the development of American society as a whole. Where standard histories of the American press consider the social context of journalism only in passing, this work takes as its main subject the relationship between the institutionalization of modern journalism and general currents in economic, political, social, and cultural life.

With two such ambitions, I know my reach has exceeded my grasp. If I have not achieved as much here as I would like, I hope nonetheless to have engaged the reader's interest in the quest and the questions.

32

Objectivity as Strategic Ritual: An Examination of Newsmen's Notions of Objectivity[1]

Gaye Tuchman

T O A SOCIOLOGIST, the word 'objectivity' is fraught with meaning. It invokes philosophy, notions of science, and ideas of professionalism. It conjures up the ghosts of Durkheim and Weber, recalling disputes in scholarly journals concerning the nature of a 'social fact' and the term 'value free'.

The social scientist's frequent insistence upon objectivity is not peculiar to his profession. Doctors and lawyers declare objectivity to be the appropriate stance toward clients. To journalists, like social scientists,[2] the term 'objectivity' stands as a bulwark between themselves and critics. Attacked for a controversial presentation of 'facts', newspapermen invoke their objectivity almost the way a Mediterranean peasant might wear a clove of garlic around his neck to ward off evil spirits.

Newspapermen must be able to invoke some concept of objectivity in order to process facts about social reality. This paper will examine three factors which influence the newsman's notion of objectivity: form, interorganizational relationships, and content. By form, I mean those attributes of news stories and newspapers which exemplify news procedures, such as the use of quotation marks. By content, I mean those notions of social reality which the newspaperman takes for granted. Content is also related to the newsman's interorganizational relationships, for his experiences with those

Source: Gaye Tuchman, 'Objectivity as Strategic Ritual: An Examination of Newsmen's Notions of Objectivity', *American Journal of Sociology*, 77/4 (1972), 660–79.

1 A shorter version of this chapter was delivered at the 1971 American Sociological Associated meetings. I benefited from the comments of Charles Perrow. Kenneth A. Feldman, Rose L. Coser, and Florence Levinsohn helped me edit.

2 Jacobs (1970) challenges comparisons between newsmen and sociologists, pointing out that sociologists gather more data for a different purpose. She notes that her editor's first rule was 'Get the facts' and his second, 'Don't let the facts interfere with the story'. Contemporary newspapers, including those for which Jacobs worked, have cast aside this second dictum. The quantity and purpose of gathered information do not detract from my argument.

organizations lead him to take for granted certain things about them. Finally, I shall suggest that the correct handling of a story, that is, the use of certain procedures discernible to the news consumer, protects the newspaperman from the risks of his trade, including critics.

Everett Hughes (1964) suggests that procedures that serve this purpose may be seen as 'rituals'. A ritual is discussed here as a routine procedure which has relatively little or only tangential relevance to the end sought. Adherence to the procedure is frequently compulsive. That such a procedure may be the best known means of attaining the sought end does not detract from its characterization as a ritual. [...]

Unlike social scientists, newsmen have a limited repertoire with which to define and defend their objectivity. In Radin's terms (1957, 1960), the social scientist is a 'thinker'; the newsman, a 'man of action'. That is, the social scientist may engage in reflexive epistemological examination (Schutz 1962: 245 ff.); the newsman cannot. He must make immediate decisions concerning validity, reliability, and 'truth' in order to meet the problems imposed by the nature of his task—processing information called news, a depletable consumer product made every day. Processing news leaves no time for reflexive epistemological examination. Nonetheless, the newsmen need some working notion of objectivity to minimize the risks imposed by deadlines, libel suits, and superiors' reprimands.

Unless a reporter has drawn an extended investigatory assignment, he generally has less than one working day to familiarize himself with a story's background, to gather information, and to write his assignment.[3] The reporter knows that his written work will pass through an organizational chain consisting of hierarchically arranged editors and their assistants. [...]

In sum, every story entails dangers for news personnel and for the news organization. Each story potentially affects the newsmen's ability to accomplish their daily tasks, affects their standing in the eyes of their superiors, and affects the ability of the news organization to make a profit. Inasmuch as the newspaper is made of many stories, these dangers are multiplied and omnipresent.

The newsmen cope with these pressures by emphasizing 'objectivity', arguing that dangers can be minimized if newsmen follow strategies of newswork which they identify with 'objective stories'. They assume that, if every reporter gathers and structures 'facts' in a detached, unbiased, impersonal manner, deadlines will be met and libel suits avoided.

The newsman navigates between libel and absurdity by identifying 'objectivity' with 'facts' which he or other newsmen observed or which may be verified. Verification entails the use of, or the possibility of using, appropriate

---

3 The reporter has less than one working day because he may also be asked to accomplish such routine tasks as writing obituaries and rewriting accounts of events telephoned to the city room by the newspaper's correspondents. Also, a reporter may not be assigned a story, such as a fire, until after a considerable portion of his working day has already passed. The task is somewhat different for the 'beat' reporter, since he already has some background information at his disposal. However, he will be asked to write more than one story a day, and he must keep up routine contacts with his news sources.

procedures, such as telephoning a marriage license bureau to determine whether Robert Jones had married Fay Smith. If verification is necessary but cannot be obtained, the newsmen may follow other strategies.

Besides verifying 'facts', the following four strategic procedures, exemplified as the formal attributes of a news story, enable the newsman to claim objectivity.

1. Presentation of Conflicting Possibilities

Newspapermen must be able to identify 'facts', even though some truth-claims are not readily verifiable. For instance, a US senator may claim that America lags behind the Soviet Union in the development of a specific type of missile. A reporter certainly cannot check that claim in time to meet his deadline, and it is even possible that he could never locate adequate information with which to assess the extent to which the claim is a 'fact'. The reporter can only determine that the senator stated 'A'. Newspapermen regard the statement 'X said A' as a 'fact', even if 'A' is false.

This creates problems for both the reporter and the news organization. First, the news consumer supposedly wants to know whether statement 'A' is a 'fact', and one function of news is to tell the news consumer what he wants and needs to know. Second, since the senator's claim to truth cannot be verified, the news consumer may accuse both the reporter and the news organization of bias (or of 'favouring' the senator) if an opposing opinion is not presented. For instance, if the senator is a Democrat and the president is a Republican, the news consumer might accuse the newspaper of bias favouring the Democrats, because the only 'fact' reported was that the Democratic senator said 'A'. The newsman would feel his ability to claim 'objectivity' in the face of anticipated criticism had been endangered.

Although the reporter cannot himself confirm the truth of the senator's charge, he can contact someone who can. For instance, he can ask the Republican secretary of defence whether the senator's charge is true. If the secretary of defence states the charge is 'false', the reporter cannot prove that the secretary's assessment is 'factual'. He can, however, write that the secretary of defence stated 'B'. Presenting both truth-claim 'A' attributed to the senator and truth-claim 'B' attributed to the secretary of defence, the newsman may then claim he is 'objective' because he has presented 'both sides of the story' without favouring either man or political party.[4] Furthermore, by presenting both truth-claims, the 'objective' reporter supposedly permits the news consumer to decide whether the senator or the secretary is 'telling the truth'.

Calling this practice a procedure fostering objectivity is problematic. In this simple example, it could equally well be labelled 'providing a sufficient number of data for the news consumer to make up his mind'. The procedure

---

4 Speaking of television practices, Benet (1970: 113), an advocate of first-person or interpretive journalism, points out that, if one statement is filmed, the rebuttal must also be filmed, not spoken by the television reporter. TV and 'ink' newsmen recognize one problem with presenting conflicting possibilities. Since news concerns conflict (Rovere 1960), a charge is more newsworthy than a denial. Thus, the charge placed at the beginning of a story (because it is more newsworthy, important, etc.) might receive more attention from the news consumer than the denial placed toward the bottom of the story. Rovere (1960) reports Joseph McCarthy's skill at using this rule to maximize his own news exposure.

may grow increasingly complex. For instance, while asserting truth-claim 'B', the secretary of defence may charge the senator is playing politics with national defense. The chairman of the House Arms Committee, a Democrat, may then counter the secretary's charge, stating that the Republican administration is endangering national safety through inadequate intelligence and cavalier treatment of the military budget for arms development. The next day, the national chairman of a peace group may call a press conference to accuse all parties to the controversy of militarism, overemphasizing weapons development to the detriment of a determined exploration of a diplomatic search for world peace and security. A spokesman for the president may then condemn the leader of the peace group as a Communist sympathizer trying to undermine the American political process.

At this point, there are five persons (the senator, the secretary, the committee chairman, the peace group leader, the presidential spokesman) making non-verifiable truth-claims, each representing one possible reality. Analysing the marijuana controversy, Goode (1970: 50–68) refers to such a morass of opinions purporting to be facts as the 'politics of reality'. While this notion is sociologically relevant, it is useless to newsmen faced with the dilemma of identifying and verifying 'facts'. However, by pairing truth-claims or printing them as they occur on sequential days, the newsmen claim 'objectivity'. As the newsmen put it, the news consumer may not be presented with all sides of a story on any one day, but he will receive a diversity of views over a period of time.

As a forum airing the 'politics of reality', the newspapermen's definition of the situation goes beyond the presentation of sufficient data for the news consumer to reach a conclusion. A morass of conflicting truth-claims, such as those hypothetically introduced, might more profitably be viewed as an invitation for the news consumers to exercise selective perception, a characteristic reaction to news. Indeed, the invitation to selective perception is most insistent, for each version of reality claims equal potential validity. Inasmuch as 'objectivity' may be defined as 'intentness on objects external to the mind', and 'objective' as 'belonging to the object of thought rather than the thinking subject' (both dictionary definitions), it would appear difficult to claim—as newspapermen do—that presenting conflicting possibilities fosters objectivity.

2. Presentation of Supporting Evidence

Of course, there are occasions when the newspapermen can obtain evidence to support a truth-claim. Supporting evidence consists of locating and citing additional 'facts', which are *commonly accepted as 'truth'*. This insistence upon supporting 'facts' is pervasive, running throughout the editors' criticisms of reporters as well as the reporters' criticisms of editors.

For instance, one evening the assistant managing editor asked for 'more objective obits' after reading an obituary which described the deceased as a 'master musician'. He asked, 'How do we know' the deceased was a 'master musician' as opposed to a 'two-bit musician' playing with the town band? He was told that, several paragraphs into the story, one learns the deceased had played with John Philip Sousa. The additional 'fact', the editor agreed, justified the term 'master musician'.

Similarly, a reporter criticized the news editors for 'bad' non-objective editing, when a published story referred to 'Communist propaganda' seen at a specific location. He claimed the article should have included more 'facts', such as the titles of specific observed works. While recognizing that the label 'Communist propaganda' might not be an accurate characterization of each individual piece of literature, he insisted that such a presentation would be more 'objective'. It would offer 'facts' (titles) supporting the initial truth-claim. Furthermore, the titles would presumably enable the reader to assess the degree to which the description 'Communist propaganda' was accurate and thus 'factual', just as noting the deceased musician's association with Sousa would enable the reader to decide for himself whether the label 'master musician' was warranted.[5]

The newsmen's assertion that 'the facts speak for themselves' is instructive. This saying implies an everyday distinction between the 'speaking facts' and the reporter (speechmaker, gossiper, etc.) speaking for the 'facts'. If the reporter were to speak for the 'facts', he could not claim to be objective, 'impersonal', 'without bias'. Of course, it is sociological commonplace that 'facts' do not speak for themselves. For instance, Shibutani (1966) demonstrates that the assessment and acceptance of 'facts' is highly dependent upon social processes.

3. The Judicious use of Quotation Marks

The newsmen view quotations of other people's opinions as a form of supporting evidence. By interjecting someone else's opinion, they believe they are removing themselves from participation in the story, and they are letting the 'facts' speak, as shown in the editors' discussion of the following incident.

A slum building, owned by an absentee landlord, had been without heat for several days in a near-zero degree temperature. The landlord claimed someone was fixing the furnace at that moment. When Smith, the local news editor, called the building, no one was working on the heating unit, a 'fact' Smith added to the reporter's story. Checking the story, Jones, the assistant managing editor, told his subordinate Smith to contact more tenants of the building and to increase the number of names mentioned in the story.

> Jones says, 'If you can get me more [quotations from tenants] we'll [print] it.' [After a while] Jones repeated that he wants more people quoted, because 'I've had too much trouble.' Without supporting evidence, the story may be libelous.

Adding more names and quotations, the reporter may remove his opinions from the story by getting others to say what he himself thinks. [...]

4. Structuring Information in an Appropriate Sequence

Structuring information in an appropriate sequence is also a procedure to denote objectivity which is exemplified as a formal attribute of news stories. The most important information concerning an event is supposed to be presented in the first paragraph, and each succeeding paragraph should contain

5 One might quite properly object that 'piling fact upon fact' presupposed a sophisticated news consumer conversant with diversified fields. On the one hand, newsmen assume that presenting supporting evidence enables the news consumer to decide for himself whether an allegation or description is 'factual'. On the other hand, newsmen occasionally complain about and denigrate the intelligence of their readers. In fact, on several occasions, editors made a special point of teaching me to read between the lines of newspaper accounts so that I could assess the 'facts' correctly. These contradictory assumptions might explain Ellul's insistence (1966: 76) that the man who believes himself to be knowledgeable and hungers for news is readily propagandized, especially if he adheres to the myths dominant in technological societies.

information of decreasing importance. The structure of a news story theoretically resembles an inverted pyramid.

This is the most problematic formal aspect of objectivity for the newsman. Discussing the other three formal attributes, the newsman may state that he presented conflicting truth-claims; that the supplementary evidence existed, and he merely collected it; that quotations and items in quotation marks represent the opinions of others, not his opinions. However, even though a reporter may unconsciously second guess his editors as he chooses a lead paragraph, and so bow to company policies, he is the person responsible for the story's lead. He cannot claim the choice belongs to someone else. The reporter can only invoke professionalism and claim the lead is validated by his news judgement.

Invoking news judgement (professional acumen) is an inherently defensive stance, for 'news judgement' is the ability to choose 'objectively' between and among competing 'facts', to decide which 'facts' are more 'important' or 'interesting'. 'Important' and 'interesting' denote content. In other words, discussing the structuring of information, the newsman must relate his notions of 'important' or 'interesting' content.

To some extent the newsman's difficulties are mitigated by the familiar formula that news concerns 'who, what, when, where, why, and how'. These 'five w's' are called the most 'material facts' about a story. Thus, if the newsman can claim he has led with the 'most material things', he can claim he has been 'objective'. For example, explaining how he would write the story about the anti-war, anti-draft demonstration, the reporter said,

> First I'll lead with the most material things.... How many people were there—that's the story... the number of draft cards turned in.... In the second [paragraph], I'll set the tone. Then I'll go into the speeches. The hard facts go first.

Yet newspapers and reporters may not concur on the identification of material facts. This same reporter had skimmed an account of the demonstration in another paper and had called it 'biased'. He complained that 'there were thousands of people [at the demonstration], and maybe all but a few were peaceful, yet the afternoon paper led with an incident about violence'. Obviously, the reporter from the afternoon newspaper would counter that his account was 'objective', that the violence was 'the most material thing', the 'who, what, where, when, why, and how' of the story. As amply demonstrated in the literature, newspapers differ in their choice of material 'facts', their news policies,[6] but all claim to be 'objective'.

If the newsmen have trouble identifying 'material facts' even within the bounds of their newspaper's policy, they may practise another option. Instead of discussing the formal attributes of an individual news story, they may describe the formal attributes of a newspaper.

A newspaper is divided into section and pages. The first pages contain 'straight objective' general stories. Specialized news, such as sports, women's and financial news, appear on clearly delineated pages placed together in a

---

6 Perhaps the best comparison of two newspapers is to be found in Matthews (1959).

section. General stories which are not 'objective' are placed on either the editorial page or the 'Op Ed' (the page opposite the editorial page). There are only two exceptions to this rule. One is the feature story. Despite telling arguments that the feature story is a news story (H. Hughes 1940), newsmen insistently distinguish between the two forms (e.g. Mott 1962). On some newspapers this distinction is formalized. For instance, the *New York Times* runs features on the first page of the second section. The other exception is 'news analysis' which may be published on the 'straight objective' general pages if it is accompanied by the distinct[7] formal label 'news analysis'.

The newsmen use the label 'news analysis' to place a barrier between the problematic story and the other stories on the general pages. Just as quotation marks theoretically establish a distance between the reporter and a story and signal that the materials enclosed may be problematic, 'news analysis' indicates that accompanying materials neither represent the opinions of the management nor are necessarily 'true'. These materials are the reporter's interpretation of the 'facts'. Readers should trust and accept the reporter's information according to their assessment of his qualifications and attitudes as revealed in his general work and previous news analyses.

Yet, the invocation of news analysis to suggest objectivity also presents difficulties. The question 'How is objective reporting different from news analysis?' turned out to be the most difficult for respondents to answer of all the questions asked during two years of research.[8] One editor had this to say after he had rambled for 10 minutes without being able to focus on the subject:

> News analysis implies value judgments. Straight news has no value judgements whatsoever. . . . You can't eliminate the label 'news analysis' and say anything. No, I'd say an alarm goes off in the editor's mind who thinks this is loaded and I want to get off the hook. [Although] the reader thinks the label . . . [is] weighty and ponderous, the key point is the number and degree of value judgements undocumented at the time.

Although the editor delineated a formal technique to alert the reader, he could not say what determines the 'number and degree of value judgements undocumented at the time'. Furthermore, the editor recognizes the discrepancy between the reason for his action and the news consumer's interpretation of that action. Faced with this dilemma, the newsman again invokes his professional news judgement—meaning his experience and common sense which enable him to assess 'important' and 'interesting' 'facts'.

It would appear that news judgement is the sacred knowledge, the secret ability of the newsman which differentiates him from other people. The newsman's experience with inter-organization relationships, his dealings with his

---

7 The words 'news analysis' are printed in a distinct type, different from those used in the headline, by-line, lead paragraph, and body of the article.

8 Several reporters and an assistant city editor said they did not know. The managing editor of the Sunday paper smiled and patted the local news editor on the back when he heard me ask the latter this question. For a text on the topic, see MacDougall (1968).

own and other organizations enables him to claim this news judgement as well as 'objectivity'. He makes three generalizations:

1. Most individuals, as news sources, have an axe to grind. To be believed, an individual must prove his reliability as a news source through a process of trial and error.[9]
2. Some individuals, such as committee chairmen, are in a position to know more than other people in an organization. Although they may have an axe to grind, their information is probably more 'accurate' because they have more 'facts' at their disposal.
3. Institutions and organizations have procedures designed to protect both the institution and the people who come into contact with it. The significance of either a statement or a 'no comment' must be assessed according to the newsman's knowledge of institutional procedures.

The newsmen tend to lump these three generalizations together by speaking of the extent to which 'something makes sense'. [...]

Exploring the newsman's notion of objectivity, I have thus far examined (1) news procedures as formal attributes of news stories and newspapers, (2) judgements based upon inter-organizational relationships, and (3) common sense as the basis for assessing news content. Although the formal attributes of news stories and newspapers may present problems to the newsman, they enable him to claim objectivity, and his claims may be assessed by the reader.

Because of the diverse pressures to which the newsman is subject, he feels that he must be able to protect himself, to state, 'I am an objective professional.' He must be able to develop strategies which enable him to state, 'This story is objective, impersonal, detached.' Similarly, the editors and newspaper management feel that they must be able to state that the news columns are 'objective' and that news policy and editorial policy are distinct from one another. Because readers do not have news judgement and, when challenging newsmen, tend to act as though they do,[10] claiming objectivity based upon news judgement may not satisfy critics.

However, citing formal attributes of news stories and of newspapers, including those which may be problematic (such as *Das Kapital* justifying the term 'Communist propaganda'), the newsmen can point to proof that they have distinguished between what they think and what they report. They may claim to have (1) presented conflicting possibilities related to truth-claims, (2) presented supplementary evidence to support a 'fact', (3) used quotation marks to indicate that the reporter is not making a truth-claim, (4) presented the most 'material facts' first, and (5) carefully separated 'facts' from opinions by using the label 'news analysis'. It would appear that *news procedures exemplified as formal attributes* of news stories and newspapers *are actually strategies through which newsmen protect themselves from critics and lay professional claim*

9 Shibutani (1966) notes that two reporters missed exclusive stories concerning Marshall Goering's suicide because the news source—a prison guard—had not proven his reliability.

10 Since newsmen are not surrounded by a technical mystique, it looks as though almost anyone could do the newsman's job. After all, almost everyone gossips. For a comparison of news and gossip, see Shibutani (1966) and Park and Burgess (1967).

to objectivity, especially since their special professional knowledge is not sufficiently respected by news consumers and may indeed even be the basis of critical attack. Although such procedures may provide demonstrable evidence of an attempt to obtain objectivity, they cannot be said to provide objectivity. Indeed, it has been suggested that such procedures (1) constitute an invitation to selective perception, (2) mistakenly insist the 'facts speak for themselves', (3) are a discrediting device and a means of introducing the reporter's opinion, (4) are bounded by the editorial policy of a particular news organization, and (5) mislead the news consumer by suggesting that 'news analysis' is weighty, ponderous, or definitive. In sum, there is a distinct discrepancy between the ends sought and those achieved. Nor is there a clear relationship between the ends sought (objectivity) and the means used (the described news procedures).

This interpretation has several interesting theoretical implications. First, it supports Everett Hughes's contention (1964: 94–8) that occupations develop ritualized procedures to protect themselves from blame. He notes, 'In teaching', an occupation like journalism, 'where ends are very ill-defined— and consequently mistakes are equally so—where the lay world is quick to criticize and to blame, correct handling becomes ritual as much as or even more than an art. If a teacher can prove that he has followed the ritual, blame is shifted from himself to the miserable child or student; and failure can be and is put upon them' (pp. 96, 97). Examining the ritualistic behaviour of such second-rank professionals as pharmacists and nurses, Hughes continues, 'We get a hint of what may be the deeper function of the art, cult and ritual of various occupations. *They may provide a set of emotional and even organizational checks and balances against both the subjective and objective risks of the trade*' (p. 197; emphasis added). From this point of view, the formal attributes of news stories and of newspapers would appear to entail strategic rituals justifying a claim to objectivity. They enable a newsman to say, pointing to his evidence, 'I am objective because I have used quotation marks.'

Second, these findings may have bearing on notions of objectivity used by other professionals. As previously suggested, social scientists distinguish between themselves and others by noting their own proclivity toward reflexive examination of philosophic assumptions. Yet Gouldner (1970: 249), joining C. Wright Mills in speaking of 'transpersonal replicability', suggests, 'In this notion, objectivity simply means that a sociologist has described his procedures with such explicitness that others employing them on the same problem will come to the same conclusions. In effect, then, this is a notion of objectivity as technical routinization and rests, at bottom, on the codification of the research procedures that were employed. At most, however, this is an *operational* definition of objectivity which presumably tells us what we must *do* in order to justify an assertion that some particular finding is objective. It does not, however, tell us very much about what objectivity *means* conceptually and connotatively.' In sum, Gouldner accuses sociologists of ducking epistemological problems by hiding behind formal techniques. He paints a picture of sociological objectivity as *strategic ritual*.[11]

---

11 Other statements by sociologists seem to support this charge. Speaking of sociologists' reactions to studies of premarital behaviour, Udry (1967) claims (although he does not offer supporting evidence) that sociologists quote studies with conclusions they approve, but challenge the methodology of articles whose findings offend their own values. Reynolds (1970) challenges footnoted scientific facts

Other professions and occupations equate objectivity with the ability to remain sufficiently impersonal to follow routine *procedures* appropriate to a specific case. For instance, the lawyer's objective stance provides the everyday saying, 'The lawyer who has himself for a client is employed by a fool.' The rule that doctors cannot operate on family members supposedly protects both the doctor and patients from his mistakes. Involved emotionally, it is felt, the doctor might not follow appropriate medical *procedures*.[12]

In all these examples, objectivity refers to routine procedures which may be exemplified as formal attributes (quotation marks, levels of significance, legal precedents, X-rays) and which protect the professional from mistakes and from his critics. It appears the word 'objectivity' is being used defensively as a strategic ritual. However, while my findings substantiate this conclusion concerning the newsman's use of the word 'objectivity', generalizations to other professions and occupations must await a systematic examination of their use of the word 'objectivity' in the context of their work.[13]

References

BENET, JAMES (1970), 'Interpretation and Objectivity in Journalism', in Arlene K. Daniels and Rachel Kahn-Hut (eds.), *Academics on the Line* (San Francisco: Jossey-Bass).

ELLUL, JACQUES (1966), *Propaganda* (New York: Knopf).

EMERSON, JOAN (1970), 'Behaviour in Private Places: Sustaining Definitions of Reality in Gynecological Examination', in Hans P. Dreitzel (ed.), *Recent Sociology, No. 2* (New York: Macmillan).

GOODE, ERICH (1970), *The Marijuana Smokers* (New York: Basic).

GOULDNER, ALVIN (1970), 'The Sociologist as Partisan: Sociology and the Welfare State', Larry T. Reynolds and Janice M. Reynolds (eds.), *The Sociology of Sociology* (New York: David McKay).

HUGHES, EVERETT C. (1964), *Men and Their Work* (Glencoe, Ill.: Free Press).

HUGHES, HELEN M. (1940), *News and the Human Interest Story* (Chicago: University of Chicago Press).

JACOBS, RUTH (1970), 'The Journalistic and Sociological Enterprises as Ideal Types', *American Sociologist*, 5: 348–50.

KLAPPER, JOSEPH (1960), *The Effects of Mass Communication* (New York: Free Press).

MACDOUGALL, C. D. (1968), *Interpretive Reporting* (New York: Macmillan).

MATTHEWS, T. S. (1959), *The Sugar Pill* (New York: Simon & Shuster).

by tracing the natural history of a perpetuated 'scientific' fiction. Goode (1970) discusses research on marijuana in the context of the 'politics of reality'. Gouldner feels (1970: 254) 'the realm of objectivity is the realm of the *sacred* in social science'.

12 Doctors insist their attitude is 'objective' or 'medical' when dealing with procedures fraught with more personal meaning, such as gynaecological examinations. Although Emerson (1970) does not report that doctors use the word 'objectivity', she does state (1970, p. 78), an 'implication of the medical definition is that the patient is a technical object to the staff. It is as if the staff worked on an assembly line for repairing bodies; similar body parts roll by and the staff have a particular job to do on them.' In other words, the medical staff emphasizes an impersonal *procedure*.

13 The recognition of objectivity as a strategic ritual also raises other problems pertinent to the study of mass media, particularly to the study of their effects. Do strategic rituals enhance the credibility of news reports? Does their use modify individuals' predilections to behave in one way or another? What is the interaction if any, between these strategies and content? If there is an interaction, does it affect the audience's reaction? Such questions have both political and sociological significance, but except for studies of the effect of presenting opposing views (reviewed by Klapper 1960: 113–17), they have yet to be explored.

MOTT, FRANK L. (1962), *The News in America* (Cambridge, Mass: Harvard University Press).

PARK, ROBERT, and ERNEST BURGESS (1967), *The City* (Chicago: University of Chicago Press).

RADIN, PAUL (1957), *Primitive Man as Philosopher* (New York: Dover).

—— (1960), *The World of Primitive Man* (New York: Grove).

REYNOLDS, LARRY T. (1970), 'A Note on the Perpetuation of a Scientific Fiction', in Larry T. Reynolds and Janice M. Reynolds (eds.), *The Sociology of Sociology* (New York: David McKay).

ROVERE, RICHARD (1960), *Senator Joe McCarthy* (New York: Meridian).

SHIBUTANI, TAMOTSU (1966), *Improvised News* (New York: Bobbs-Merrill).

TUCHMAN, GAYE (1969), 'News, the Newsman's Reality', Ph.D. dissertation, Brandeis University.

UDRY, J. RICHARD (1967), *Social Context of Marriage* (New York: Lippincott).

WEINSTEIN, EUGENE (1966), 'Toward a Theory of Interpersonal Tactics', in Carl Backman and Paul Second (eds.), *Problems in Social Psychology* (New York: McGraw-Hill).

33

News Reporting and Professionalism: Some Constraints on the Reporting of the News

John Soloski

THE ROMANTIC VISION of journalism is that of a crusading reporter who, much to the consternation of a cantankerous but benevolent editor, takes on one of the more villainous politicians in the city, and after some hard work and a bit of luck, catches the politician 'red-handed', helps to send him to jail and betters the lives of the downtrodden and helpless. This myth has many versions, some less grand but all of them more or less the same. Embedded in these myths are many of the professional norms and values of journalism as it is practised in the US. To fully understand the process by which events are selected for presentation as news, it is necessary to examine news professionalism. Much ink has been spilled over arguments about whether journalism is a bona-fide profession. Even more ink has been used by scholars who have attempted to identify the criteria that make an occupation a profession. But, as Hughes (1958: 45) points out, it is not important to argue about which occupations qualify as professions; what is important is to ask what it means for an occupation to claim it is a profession. With this as a jumping-off point, this chapter will attempt to show how journalistic professionalism affects the gathering and reporting of the news. Specifically, the chapter argues that professionalism is an efficient and economical method by which news organizations control the behaviour of reporters and editors. But news organizations (or for that matter any business organization) cannot rely just on professional norms to control the behaviour of its professional employees; to further limit the discretionary behaviour of journalists, news organizations have developed rules—news policies. News organizations rely on the interplay of news professionalism and news

Source: John Soloski, 'News Reporting and Professionalism: Some Constraints on the Reporting of the News', *Media, Culture and Society* (London, Newbury Park, and New Delhi: Sage, 1989), 207–28. The author would like to thank Michael Schudson, University of California, San Diego, and Hanno Hardt, University of Iowa, for their comments on early drafts of this chapter.

policies to control the behaviour of journalists. The second part of this chapter reports the results of a participant-observation study that examined how one news organization enforces its news policies.[1]

Since US journalists work within profit-making business organizations, news organizations need to develop techniques for controlling the behaviour of their professional employees. If the news organization is conceptualized as an open system (Perrow 1970; Thompson 1967) composed of subsystems that are interrelated and interconnected with one another, and with the larger organization, then the problem of control becomes clearer. [...]

The news department as a subsystem of a news organization must deal with a highly unpredictable environment—news. Decisions about news coverage must be reached rapidly, with little time for discussion or group decision-making. Thus the structure of the news department must be fluid enough to deal with a constantly changing news environment. Reporters and editors must have considerable autonomy in the selection and processing of the news. Controlling the behaviour of its journalists could be a difficult problem for management of a news organization, especially since reporters spend most of their time outside of the newsroom and out of sight of supervisors. One method management could use to control its journalists would be to establish elaborate rules and regulations. This bureaucratic form of administration would not be very efficient because (1) the rules would have to cover all possible situations that journalists might encounter, including rules to deal with situations not covered by the rules; (2) elaborate rules are prescriptive and would limit a journalist's ability to deal with the unexpected, which is the essence of news; and (3) the news organization's management would have to establish an expensive and time-consuming system for teaching its journalists the rules and regulations. A more efficient method for controlling behaviour in non-bureaucratic organizations, such as news organizations, is through professionalism. Professionalism '*makes the use of discretion predictable*. It relieves bureaucratic organizations of responsibility for devising their own mechanisms of control in the discretionary areas of work' (Larson 1977: 168) (emphasis in original).

Ideology of Professionalism

The vast literature on professionalism is preoccupied with two major historical-sociological pursuits: (1) attempts to define what a profession is, usually based on an historical analysis of the rise of medicine and law; and (2) examinations of the relationships between professionals and bureaucratic business organizations that employ them. The first pursuit is the older of the two and is responsible for much of the literature on professionalism. The second approach recognizes the inadequacy of the model of professionalism that was built on the older, free professions like medicine and law, since the newer, dependent professions—such as engineering, accountancy, and journalism—operate within profit-making business organizations. This second theme will be the primary concern of this chapter. [...]

---

1 Although most of the references in this chapter are to the print medium, the arguments can be applied to the electronic media.

In monopoly capitalism, new professions arose that were unable to exercise as much control over the work situation as the free professions could. Engineering, accountancy and journalism depend on large business organizations for their employment. Work assignments and the choice of clients are, for the most part, out of the hands of these professionals. But these professionals have been able to achieve social status through financial compensation, upward mobility and distinctive work tasks that require special skills. To facilitate control in the work place, management has come to rely on professionalism to control the behaviour of its key employees. Professionalism, then, must be seen as an efficient and rational means of administering complex business organizations.

In summary, professionalism and the bureaucratic business organization cannot be conceived of as being opposite poles on a continuum of freedom and control. Both bureaucratic business organizations and professionalism 'belong to the same historical matrix: they consolidated in the early twentieth century as distinct but nevertheless complementary modes of work organization' (Larson 1977: 199). And the type of administration (bureaucratic or professionalism) used by an organization will depend on the work situation: the less stable the work environment, the greater the reliance on professionalism (Stinchcombe 1959).

News Professionalism

News professionalism controls the behaviour of journalists in two related ways: (1) it sets standards and norms of behaviour, and (2) it determines the professional reward system.

Since news professionalism establishes norms of conduct for journalists, it is unnecessary for individual news organizations to arbitrarily establish elaborate rules and regulations for staff members. Also, there is no need for news organizations to establish expensive and time-consuming training programmes for new journalists since all journalists come to the organization with a certain amount of professional training. But unlike engineering or accountancy, there are a number of educational paths that lead to careers in journalism (Johnstone et al. 1976: 35–7). Journalism, then, cannot rely just on controlling professional education to achieve cognitive standardization necessary for professionalism. It is through formal professional education, on-the-job professional training or, as is usually the case, a combination of these (Johnstone et al. 1976: 65), that journalists come to share the cognitive base of news professionalism. The norms of behaviour that emanate from news professionalism constitute a *trans*-organizational control mechanism. Since the behaviour of journalists is rooted—to a great extent—in shared professional norms, this minimizes the problem of how news organizations are able to maintain control over journalists. But shared professional norms do not eliminate completely the problem of organizational control because (1) professionalism provides journalists with an independent power base that can be used to thwart heavy-handed interference by management in the professional activities of the news staff, and (2) professionalism provides too much freedom for journalists, and thus news organizations must adopt procedures that further limit the professional behaviour of their journalists. By

examining some professionalism norms, we can show how news professionalism guides the behaviour of journalists.

**Professional
Norms**

For journalists in the United States, objectivity is the most important professional norm, and from it flows more specific aspects of news professionalism
such as news judgement, the selection of sources and the structure of news
beats. Objectivity does not reside in news stories themselves; rather it resides
in the behaviour of journalists (Roscho 1975: 55). Journalists must act in
ways that allow them to report the news objectively. For journalists, objectivity does not mean that they are impartial observers of events—as it does
for the social scientist—but that they seek out the facts and report them as
fairly and in as balanced a way as possible. As Phillips notes, by having
journalists define objectivity as being the balanced reporting of the facts,
the question of whether or not objectivity is possible in its scientific sense
is neatly side-stepped. 'By definition, then, journalists are turned into
copying machines who simply record the world rather than evaluate it'
(Phillips 1977: 68). This makes it incumbent on the journalist to seek out the
facts from all 'legitimate' sides of an issue, and then to report the facts in an
impartial and balanced way. It would be an oversimplification to suggest that
the selection of issues to cover and the choice of sources to present to the
public in news stories is politically motivated. While it is true that news legitimizes and supports the existing politico-economic system, it is not true that
journalists' selection of news stories reflects a conscious desire on their part
to report the news in such a way that the status quo is maintained.

Objectivity, as practised by journalists, is an eminently practical—and apparently highly successful—way of dealing with the complex needs of journalists, news organizations, and audiences. Events can be safely presented as
a series of facts that require no explanation of their political significance. By
presenting the news as a series of facts, news organizations are protected in
at least two ways. The first and most obvious way is that since journalists need
to rely on sources to provide them with the facts about events, sources and
not journalists are responsible for the accuracy of the facts. To a limited
degree this helps to insulate both journalists and their news organization from
charges of bias and inaccurate reporting (Tuchman 1972). Being duped by a
news source is embarrassing to the news organization but, provided it does
not happen often, the integrity of the news organization is not threatened.
The news organization's position in the marketplace is directly linked to its
ability to maintain the integrity of its news operation. And this brings us to
the second advantage objectivity has for news organizations: it helps to secure their monopoly position in the marketplace.[2] If the news were to be reported in an overtly political or ideological manner, the market would be
ripe for competition from news organizations that held opposing political or
ideological points of view. By reporting the news objectively, reader loyalty
to a newspaper is not a function of the ideology of that newspaper. It is rather

---

2 The term 'monopoly' is being used in its economic and ideological senses. For a discussion of
monopoly in this context, see Owen 1975.

based on the thoroughness of the news coverage, subscription costs, delivery services or some other tangible factor that a newspaper can control. Therefore, as long as news organizations report the news objectively, monopoly control of the marketplace will not be seen as being much of a problem by audiences, journalists, advertisers, and media owners.

Journalists are non-ideological in the sense that they do not report the news according to an ideological perspective that is consciously shared by the members of the profession. Therefore, the natural place to find newsworthy sources will be in the power structure of society because journalists see the current politico-economic system as a naturally occurring state of affairs (Tuchman 1978; Gans 1979). News sources, then, are drawn from the existing power structure; therefore news tends to support the status quo. But journalists do not set out to consciously report the news so that the current politico-economic system is maintained. The selection of news events and news sources flows 'naturally' from news professionalism. This does not mean that news judgements do not change; nor does it mean that journalists do not differ in their news judgements, but differences are worked out within a specific frame of reference, namely that of the prevailing norms of news professionalism. Furthermore, news judgement requires that journalists share assumptions about what is normal in society, since an event's newsworthiness is related to its departure from what is considered to be normal. By concentrating on the deviant, the odd and the unusual, journalists implicitly support the norms and values of society. Like fables, news stories contain hidden morals.

While the selection and presentation of news events and sources are determined by news professionalism, the news organization for which a journalist works will also influence this process. For instance, in an effort to maximize its return on its economic investment, the news organization routinizes news coverage through the establishment of news beats (Tuchman 1978: 44–5). The choice of beats results from the interplay of news professionalism and the resources of the news organization. News professionalism will determine the legitimacy and value of news beats, but the news organization, through its control over the news department's budget, will determine the number of beats that can be covered. News professionalism identifies more legitimate news beats than can be covered by journalists on the staff.

The Professional Ladder

In addition to specifying norms of behaviour for journalists, news professionalism establishes a reward system for journalists. That is, journalists will look to their profession for recognition of professional success. However, a reward system that is determined by criteria outside direct management control would, on the surface, appear to be another source of conflict between professionals and business organizations (Goldner and Ritti 1967). The assumption is that professional employees will look to the profession and not to their business organization for rewards. In other words, the ideals of the profession will be more of a concern to professionals than are the goals of the organization.

The dilemma, then, for management is how to reward professionals for outstanding professional performance even if that performance does not result in any significant benefits for the business organization. [...]

The structure of the news department permits management to promote successful journalists without having to bring them into the organization's decision-making process. As successful journalists move up the professional ladder in the news department, they have more individual freedom to pursue stories without carrying more responsibility for decisions concerning the allocation of scarce organizational resources. By providing opportunities for upward movement, the news organization is able to maintain the loyalty of key professionals without providing access to the actual power hierarchy of the organization. Although some journalists move onto the management ladder and into key management positions, most journalists use the professional ladder as their gauge of success, and movement on that ladder will be determined by professional norms. The viability of the professional ladder as a measure of success is the result of journalists' professional training, and it is part of the romantic lore of the profession. Journalism schools, stories about crusading journalists and journalists themselves have all contributed to making the professional ladder a means of measuring success.

| Intra-Organizational Controls | From the point of view of management, news professionalism is an efficient and effective means for both controlling and rewarding journalists. Although professionalism makes the use of discretion predictable, it does not dictate specific behaviour for journalists, rather professionalism establishes guidelines for behaviour. Even so, professionalism provides journalists with more freedom in the selection, reporting and editing of news stories than most news organizations can permit. To further limit journalists' discretionary behaviour, news organizations have established news policies. [...] |

Just as news professionalism can be seen as a trans-organization control mechanism, the idiosyncratic news policies of individual news organizations can be seen as an *intra*-organizational control mechanism. Together, these two control mechanisms direct the actions of journalists. Since the norms of news professionalism are shared by all journalists, the news organization needs only to concentrate on teaching journalists its own news policies, and needs only to develop techniques for ensuring that its journalists adhere to the policies. To examine how news policy works and how a news organization enforces its policies, I undertook a participant-observation study at a medium-sized daily.[3] The results of this study form the basis for the remainder of this chapter.

Both news professionalism and news policy are used to minimize conflict within the news organization. That is, professional norms and a news

---

3 As a participant observer I worked as an editor on the copy desk, which provided an exceptionally good vantage point to observe how news policies are enforced. Unlike nearly all of the so-called participant observer studies of the newsmaking process, I actually joined the staff of the paper with the specific purpose of studying its news operation. As a researcher/journalist I was able to see and understand behaviour that would have been unavailable to a researcher who relied on observing and interviewing.

organization's news policies are accepted by journalists and only in rare in-stances are either professional norms or news policies a point of disagree-ment among the staff of the news organization. Like a game, professional norms and news policies are rules that everyone has learned to play by; only rarely are these rules made explicit, and only rarely are the rules called into question.

News professionalism is a double-edged sword. Since news professional-ism is independent of any one news organization, it provides journalists with an independent power base that can be used in confrontations with a news or-ganization's management because the tenets of news professionalism limit the ability of management to be directly involved in the newsmaking process. A publisher who continually intervenes in news coverage would run the risk of undercutting the professionalism of his or her journalists and, if the inter-vention resulted in biased reporting, would hurt the reputation of the news-paper and potentially damage the newspaper's position in the marketplace. News professionalism makes it taboo for management to continually inter-fere in the newsmaking process. Of course, this does have some benefits for management because it is a good argument to put off advertisers, politicians or others who may want management to intervene in news coverage.

To some extent, news professionalism shields journalists from the inter-vention of management by allowing journalists to deflect management's de-sires without jeopardizing their position in the news organization. For example, the publisher of the paper under study wanted the news depart-ment to follow up on a series of stories on drug trafficking in the city that had appeared in a newspaper published in a nearby city. Both the editor and the city editor[4] believed that there was nothing to the stories, and that they did not warrant assigning a reporter to follow them up. During a meeting of the paper's editors the city editor said, 'We've gone through this before, doesn't he [the publisher] believe us when we tell him there is nothing there?' The edi-tor responded saying '[The publisher] says that if the [other paper's] stories are not true that we've got to get the city manager, the mayor or [another civic leader] to say so.' The editor decided not to assign a reporter to the story, saying that it was not worth following up the story just to satisfy the publisher. Later, when the publisher was interviewed about the amount of attention his story suggestions received from the editor, he said that he had talked to the editor a number of times about story ideas but he cannot get the editor to follow up on his ideas. The publisher went on to say that this has caused considerable friction between the editor and him. None of the jour-nalists could recall any instance when the publisher bypassed the editor and ordered reporters to follow up his story ideas. [...]

Within any business organization that employs professionals, there is at least one administrator between management and the professional employ-ees. The underlying tension in this position is the need, on the one hand, to protect professional employees from interference by management and, on the other hand, to direct the work of the professional employees according to the goals and interest of the organization (Kornhauser 1963: 60). In the news

---

4 The editor is the executive in charge of the news department. The other editors will be referred to as junior editors, or by their titles, in order to distinguish them from the editor.

organization it is the editor who functions both as a professional and as a member of the news organization's management. Any examination of news policies must therefore focus on the editor as the executive in charge of the news operation. At the paper I studied, the editor uses a variety of methods to ensure that his journalists followed the paper's news policies. These included editorial meetings, story assignments, reprimands, and supervision of the paper's production.

During the editorial meeting the editor selects stories for the newspaper from news budgets prepared by the junior editors, and tells the city editor which reporters to assign to various stories. He also uses the meeting to criticize the work of the news staff, which takes the form of marking up a copy of yesterday's paper, pointing out poor layout, reporting problems, and the lack of editing poorly written stories. The criticisms are couched in terms of improving the professional competence of the news staff. Although the criticisms can be severe, the editor rarely criticizes a reporter directly, preferring to have the news editor pass on his criticisms to the reporter.

Also during the editorial meeting, the editor acts as arbiter of disputes among the junior editors. At this particular newspaper the news editor, the city editor and the sports editor all have about equal authority in the news department, although technically the news editor ranks next in authority after the editor. In disputes among the junior editors they attempt to gain the support of the editor. Instead of settling disagreements among themselves, the junior editors rely on the editor to decide the dispute. This procedure avoids open conflict in the news department and allows the junior editors to maintain a friendly work atmosphere in the newsroom. On the other hand, it provides the editor with an opportunity to arbitrate differences according to the paper's news policy. In effect, disputes among junior editors act as an early-warning system to potential policy violations.

The editorial meeting is also crucial for understanding how the editor controls the content of the newspaper because it is during these meetings that he decides which stories to cover or ignore. The editor is not heavy-handed in making story decisions; nor will he not assign a reporter to a story because it may have policy implications. But his involvement in the story selection process minimizes confrontations with reporters over policy issues. It is easier for the editor to control story assignments than to have to kill or tone down a story after it has been written. Reporters see story assignments as part of the editor's professional responsibilities, but they perceive heavy-handed editing as the editor's bowing to the interests of management. By controlling assignments, the editor ensures that the more important stories, which are more likely to have policy implications, are covered by the more trustworthy reporters.

Even so, quite a few stories deal with controversial issues that have policy implications. Although the editor is not involved in the day-to-day editing process, he does edit all stories that deal with controversial issues. During an interview the editor said, 'I like to see all sensitive stories and [potentially] libelous stuff especially. A lot of copy goes across my desk for approval. I like to keep my hands in the newsroom.'

Reporters who have had their stories changed have strong feelings about the editor and why he changed their stories. Often they believe it is because the editor is bowing to pressure from management to keep the paper out of controversy, and not to upset important advertisers. [...]

Reprimands, or the threat of being reprimanded, offer yet another method of controlling the news staff. Although I witnessed only a few reprimands, the ones I did witness, and the ones staff members told me about, were severe. Usually just the fear of being reprimanded is enough to keep most staff members in line. Reprimands help to establish policy not only for the journalists who receive them, but for those who witness or hear of them. In some cases the policy established by a reprimand may not actually be part of the newspaper's policy at all. For example, a junior editor had heard the editor reprimand another junior editor for using the word 'Soviet' in a headline. The junior editor who had overheard the remark had interpreted it to mean that 'Soviet' must not be used anywhere in the paper, and he would change 'Soviet' to 'Russian' in all stories he edited. When I asked the editor if I should change 'Soviet' to 'Russian' in stories I edited, he said that he had no objections to the word in stories but that it should not be used in headlines because it was not accurate. The junior editor had assumed that the newspaper had a policy that prohibited the use of the word.

The final control over the content of the newspaper lies in overseeing the production of the paper. The editor makes it a point to check all pages before they are removed from the production area, but he pays particularly close attention to the front page and the late page.[5] In fact, neither the front page nor the late page can be taken from the production area without the editor's permission; and even though it is difficult to change stories or headlines once copy is set and pasted on the pages, it was not uncommon for the editor to order some last-minute changes. [...]

Although all of the journalists working for the newspaper had complaints about the editor, none said that the editor was professionally inept or that he had sold out to management. On the contrary, the journalists thought that the editor was in a no-win situation, being caught between management and the news department. And most of the journalists thought that the editor did a good job of protecting them from managerial interference. Yet the editor must walk a fine line between management and news professionalism. To be successful he must convince his staff that the newspaper's policies do not conflict with news professionalism. By examining two incidents involving policy, we can see that news policy has been incorporated into the news professionalism of the paper's journalists.

Part of the newspaper's news policy reflects management's decision to define the paper as a family newspaper. One aspect of this policy affects selection of photographs. A junior editor said 'The editor has a policy on pictures. No bloody photos like accidents are used. It's policy.' Another junior editor said '[The newspaper] is a family newspaper. Once in a while I get called on the carpet for doing something which management doesn't like. I consult with the editor whenever something is possibly upsetting. Nothing of bad taste—sex, immoral, bodies—gets in unless it is really necessary. We ran

---

5 The late page is the last news page to be produced. Late-breaking stories that do not warrant remaking the front page are placed on this page.

a picture of a student beating a hung [sic] body in Thailand once, but I consulted with the editor before using it.'

When Pope Paul VI died, the Associated Press Wirephoto service carried many pictures of the pope lying in state. The front page of the newspaper was 'dummied' with a photo of the Pope lying in state surrounded by his guards and church officials. Because the page contained a photo of a body, the junior editor brought the dummy to the editor for his approval, and he was turned down. The junior editor said, 'We don't run pictures of bodies on the front page.' In its place the paper used a photograph taken a month earlier of the pope blessing a crowd. But because the death was such a big news story, the paper did run photographs of the pope lying in state on some inside pages.

In the second incident a man convicted of murdering a 10-year-old girl had had his conviction overturned by the US Supreme Court. A new trial was ordered and it was held in a nearby city. The newspaper did not send a reporter to cover the trial but relied on the Associated Press coverage. The defence rested its case on whether or not the accused had sexually assaulted the girl, and much of the wire stories about the trial dealt with the sexual assault. One day a junior editor showed me what he had edited out of the story. Almost every sentence that had contained the words 'vagina', 'rectum' or 'sperm' had been deleted from the story. The junior editor said that he had given the story to the editor to check and he had cut even more out of the story. The junior editor said, 'A lot of our readership don't care to see those words used in the paper. This is a family newspaper. I know that's how the editor thinks. On other papers I would have used it but not here in [this newspaper].' During an interview, the editor was asked about the editing of the trial stories. He said, 'The reason parts of the stories were edited out is because I would not want to have to define the terms used in the stories to my 10-year-old son, if I had one. [This newspaper] is a family newspaper which goes into people's homes and youngsters read it. The editing of the stories did not do readers a disservice because the stuff edited out wasn't necessary to show [the man's] defense.'

During interviews with the paper's journalists they were asked about these and other incidents involving the paper's policy of not publishing potentially offensive material. None of them believed that the policy affected the ability of the newspaper to inform its readers. All of the journalists had accepted the policy, and it had become part of their professional task. A few of them provided examples of where they thought that the policy had gone too far and had affected the news that was reported. But when other journalists were asked about these examples they tended to stress personality differences between a reporter and the editor, and not issues involving professional norms. Except for those involved in the incidents, most of the journalists believed that the editor had been right to reject or edit stories because the reporters had acted in an unprofessional manner. The journalists at this newspaper are convinced that the policy of protecting readers from potentially offensive material does not interfere with the norms of news professionalism, and they have come to accept the paper's news policy as a natural part of their jobs.

Conclusion   Drawing upon organizational theory and the literature of professionalism, this chapter argues that news professionalism is an efficient and effective means for controlling the professional behaviour of journalists. The chapter attempts to show how the norms of news professionalism determine the legitimate arenas and sources of news in the US. Although journalists do not set out to report the news so that the existing politico-economic system is maintained, their professional norms end up producing stories that implicitly support the existing order. In addition, the professional norms legitimize the existing order by making it appear to be a naturally occurring state of affairs. The tenets of news professionalism result in news coverage that does not threaten either the economic position of the individual news organization or the overall politico-economic system in which the news organization operates. Also, news professionalism produces news stories that permit news organizations to maximize audience size and to maintain firm control over the marketplace. In the final analysis, news professionalism biases news at a societal level.

Since news professionalism is independent of any one news organization, news professionalism provides journalists with an independent power base that can be used against management. To minimize the potential for conflict, management has established news policies that further limit the professional behaviour of its journalists. Although the specific nature of these policies will vary from organization to organization, the purpose of the policies does not. News policies lessen the potential conflict between journalists and management, and there is no reason to assume that an organization's policies will be a source of tension between management and journalists (Sigelman 1973). As long as news policy does not force journalists to violate the norms of news professionalism, there is no reason to assume that journalists will see news policy as a constraint on their work, even though it does limit the type of stories that can be reported.

The organizational nature of news is determined by the interplay between the trans-organizational control mechanism represented by news professionalism and the intra-organizational control mechanisms represented by news policy. Together, these control mechanisms help to establish boundaries for the professional behavior of journalists. It would be wrong to assume that these boundaries dictate specific actions on the part of journalists; rather these boundaries provide a framework for action. The boundaries are broad enough to permit journalists some creativity in the reporting, editing and presentation of news stories. On the other hand, the boundaries are narrow enough so that journalists can be trusted to act in the interest of the news organization.

References   GANS, H. J. (1979), *Deciding What's News* (New York: Pantheon).

GOLDNER, F. H., and RITTI, R. R. (1967), 'Professionalization as Career Immobility', *American Journal of Sociology*, 72: 489–502.

HALL, R. E. (1968), 'Professionalization and Bureaucratization', *American Sociological Review*, 33: 92–104.

HUGHES, E. C. (1958), *Men and Their Work* (Glencoe, Ill.: Free Press).

JOHNSTONE, J. W. C., SLAWSKI, E. J., and BOWMAN, W. W. (1976), *The News People* (Urbana, Ill.: University of Illinois Press).

KORNHAUSER, W. (1963), *Scientists in Industry: Conflict and Accommodation* (Berkeley, Calif.: University of California Press).

LARSON, M. S. (1977), *The Rise of Professionalism: A Sociological Analysis* (Calif.: University of California Press).

OWEN, B. (1975), *Economics and Freedom of Expression* (Cambridge, Mass.: Ballinger).

PERROW, C. (1970), *Organizational Analysis: A Sociological View* (Monterey, Calif.: Brooks/Cole).

PHILLIPS, E. B. (1977), 'Approaches to Objectivity: Journalistic vs. Social Science Perspectives', in P. M. HIRSCH, P. V. Miller, and F. G. KLINE (eds.), *Strategies for Communication Research* (Beverly Hills, Calif.: Sage).

ROSCHO, B. (1975), *Newsmaking* (Chicago: University of Chicago Press).

STINCHCOMBE, A. L. (1959), 'Bureaucratic and Craft Administration of Production: A Comparative Study', *Administrative Science Quarterly*, 4: 168–87.

THOMPSON, J. D. (1967), *Organizations in Action* (New York: McGraw-Hill).

TUCHMAN, G. (1972), 'Objectivity as Strategic Ritual: An Examination of Newsmen's Notions of Objectivity', *American Journal of Sociology*, 77: 660–79.

—— (1978), *Making News: A Study in the Construction of Reality* (New York: Free Press).

WIEBE, R. H. (1967), *The Search for Order: 1877–1920* (New York: Hill and Wang).

34

The Agenda-Setting Function of Mass Media

Maxwell E. McCombs and Donald L. Shaw

I**N OUR DAY,** more than ever before, candidates go before the people through the mass media rather than in person.[1] The information in the mass media becomes the only contact many have with politics. The pledges, promises, and rhetoric encapsulated in news stories, columns, and editorials constitute much of the information upon which a voting decision has to be made. Most of what people know comes to them 'second' or 'third' hand from the mass media or from other people.[2]

Although the evidence that mass media deeply change attitudes in a campaign is far from conclusive,[3] the evidence is much stronger that voters learn from the immense quantity of information available during each campaign.[4] People, of course, vary greatly in their attention to mass media political information. Some, normally the better educated and most politically interested (and those least likely to change political beliefs), actively seek information; but most seem to acquire it, if at all, without much effort. It just comes in. As Berelson succinctly puts it: 'On any single subject many 'hear' but few "listen".' But Berelson also found that those with the greatest mass media exposure are most likely to know where the candidates stand on different issues.[5] Trenaman and McQuail found the same thing in a study of the 1959 General Election in England.[6] Voters do learn.

Source: Maxwell E. McCombs and Donald L. Shaw, 'The Agenda-Setting Function of Mass Media', *Public Opinion Quarterly*, 36 (Summer 1972), 176–85. This study was partially supported by a grant from the National Association of Broadcasters. Additional support was provided by the UNC Institute for Research in Social Science and the School of Journalism Foundation of North Carolina.

1 See Bernard R. Berelson, Paul F. Lazarsfeld, and William N. McPhee, *Voting* (Chicago: University of Chicago Press, 1954), 234. Of course to some degree candidates have always depended upon the mass media, but radio and television brought a new intimacy into politics.

2 Kurt Lang and Gladys Engel Lang, 'The Mass Media and Voting', in Bernard Berelson and Morris Janowitz (eds.), *Reader in Public Opinion and Communication* (2nd edn. New York: Free Press, 1966), 466.

3 See Berelson *et al.*, *Voting*, 223; Paul F. Lazarsfeld, Bernard Berelson, and Hazel Gaudet, *The People's Choice* (New York: Columbia University Press, 1948), xx; and Joseph Trenaman and Denis McQuail, *Television and the Political Image* (London: Methuen and Co., 1961), 147, 191.

4 See Bernard C. Cohen, *The Press and Foreign Policy* (Princeton: Princeton University Press, 1963), 120.

5 Berelson *et al.*, *Voting*, 244, 228.

6 Trenaman and McQuail, *Television and The Political Image*, 165.

They apparently learn, furthermore, in direct proportion to the emphasis placed on the campaign issues by the mass media. Specifically focusing on the agenda-setting function of the media, Lang and Lang observe:

> The mass media force attention to certain issues. They build up public images of political figures. They are constantly presenting objects suggesting what individuals in the mass should think about, know about, have feelings about.[7]

Perhaps this hypothesized agenda-setting function of the mass media is most succinctly stated by Cohen, who noted that the press 'may not be successful much of the time in telling people what to think, but it is stunningly successful in telling its readers what to think *about*'.[8] While the mass media may have little influence on the direction or intensity of attitudes, it is hypothesized that *the mass media set the agenda for each political campaign, influencing the salience of attitudes toward the political issues.*

Method   To investigate the agenda-setting capacity of the mass media in the 1968 presidential campaign, this study attempted to match what Chapel Hill voters *said* were key issues of the campaign with the *actual content* of the mass media used by them during the campaign. Respondents were selected randomly from lists of registered voters in five Chapel Hill precincts economically, socially, and racially representative of the community. By restricting this study to one community, numerous other sources of variation—for example, regional differences or variations in media performance—were controlled.

Between 18 September and 6 October, 100 interviews were completed. To select these 100 respondents a filter question was used to identify those who had not yet definitely decided how to vote—presumably those most open or susceptible to campaign information. Only those not yet fully committed to a particular candidate were interviewed. Borrowing from the Trenaman and McQuail strategy, this study asked each respondent to outline the key issues as he saw them, regardless of what the candidates might be saying at the moment.[9] Interviewers recorded the answers as exactly as possible.

---

7 Lang and Lang, 'The Mass Media and Voting', 468. Trenaman and McQuail warn that there was little evidence in their study that television (or any other mass medium) did anything other than provide information; there was little or no attitude change on significant issues. 'People are aware of what is being said, and who is saying it, but they do not necessarily take it at face value.' See *Television and the Political Image*, 168. In a more recent study, however, Blumler and McQuail found that high exposure to Liberal party television broadcasts in the British General Election of 1964 was positively related to a more favourable attitude toward the Liberal party for those with medium or weak motivation to follow the campaign. The more strongly motivated were much more stable in political attitude. See Jay G. Blumler and Denis McQuail, *Television in Politics: Its Uses and Influence* (Chicago: University of Chicago Press, 1969), 200.

8 Cohen, *The Press and Foreign Policy*, 13.

9 See Trenaman and McQuail, *Television and the Political Image*, 172. The survey question was: 'What are you *most* concerned about these days? That is, regardless of what politicians say, what are the two or three *main* things which you think the government *should* concentrate on doing something about?'

Concurrently with the voter interviews, the mass media serving these voters were collected and content analysed. A pre-test in spring 1968 found that for the Chapel Hill community almost all the mass media political information was provided by the following sources: *Durham Morning Herald*, *Durham Sun*, *Raleigh News and Observer*, *Raleigh Times*, *New York Times*, *Time*, *Newsweek*, and NBC and CBS evening news broadcasts.

The answers of respondents regarding major problems as they saw them and the news and editorial comment appearing between 12 September and 6 October in the sampled newspapers, magazines, and news broadcasts were coded into fifteen categories representing the key issues and other kinds of campaign news. Media news content also was divided into 'major' and 'minor' levels to see whether there was any substantial difference in mass media emphasis across topics.[10] For the print media, this major/minor division was in terms of space and position; for television, it was made in terms of position and time allowed. More specifically, *major* items were defined as follows:

1. Television: Any story 45 seconds or more in length and/or one of the three lead stories.
2. Newspapers: Any story which appeared as the lead on the front page or on any page under a three-column headline in which at least one-third of the story (a minimum of five paragraphs) was devoted to political news' coverage.
3. News Magazines: Any story more than one column or any item which appeared in the lead at the beginning of the news section of the magazine.
4. Editorial Page Coverage of Newspapers and Magazines: Any item in the lead editorial position (the top left corner of the editorial page) plus all items in which one-third (at least five paragraphs) of an editorial or columnist comment was devoted to political campaign coverage.

Minor items are those stories which are political in nature and included in the study but which are smaller in terms of space, time, or display than major items.

Findings

The overall *major* item emphasis of the selected mass media on different topics and candidates during the campaign is displayed in Table 1. It indicates that a considerable amount of campaign news was *not* devoted to discussion of the major political issues but rather to *analysis of the campaign itself*. This may give pause to those who think of campaign news as being primarily about the *issues*. Thirty-five per cent of the major news coverage of Wallace was composed of this analysis ('Has he a chance to win or not?'). For Humphrey and Nixon the figures were, respectively, 30 per cent and

---

10 Intercoder reliability was above 0.90 for content analysis of both 'major' and 'minor' items. Details of categorization are described in the full report of this project. A small number of copies of the full report is available for distribution and may be obtained by writing the authors.

25 per cent. At the same time, the table also shows the relative emphasis of candidates speaking about each other. For example, Agnew apparently spent more time attacking Humphrey (22 per cent of the major news items about Agnew) than did Nixon (11 per cent of the major news about Nixon). The overall *minor* item emphasis of the mass media on these political issues and topics closely paralleled that of major item emphasis.

TABLE 1. *Major Mass Media Reports on Candidates and Issues, by Candidates (expressed as percentages)*

	Quoted Source (%)						
	Nixon	Agnew	Humphrey	Muskie	Wallace	Lemay[a]	Total
The issues							
Foreign policy	7	9	13	15	2	—	10
Law and order	5	13	4	—	12	—	6
Fiscal policy	3	4	2	—	—	—	2
Public welfare	3	4	(*)[b]	5	2	—	2
Civil rights	3	9	(*)[b]	0	4	—	2
Other	19	13	14	25	11	—	15
The campaign							
Polls	1	—	—	—	1	—	(*)[b]
Campaign events	18	9	21	10	25	—	19
Campaign analysis	25	17	30	30	35	—	28
Other candidates							
Humphrey	11	22	—	5	—	—	—
Muskie	—	—	—	—	—	—	—
Nixon	—	—	11	5	3	—	5
Agnew	—	—	(*)[b]	—	—	—	(*)[b]
Wallace	5	—	3	5	—	—	3
Lemay	1	—	1	—	4	—	1
Total per cent	101[c]	100	99[c]	100	100	—	98[c]
Total number	188	23	221	20	95	11	558

[a] Coverage of Lemay amounted to only 11 major items during the 12 September–6 October period and are not individually included in the percentages; they are included in the total column.
[b] Less than .05%.
[c] Does not sum to 100% because of rounding.

Table 2 focuses on the relative emphasis of each party on the issues, as reflected in the mass media. The table shows that Humphrey/Muskie emphasized foreign policy far more than did Nixon/Agnew or Wallace/Lemay. In the case of the 'law and order' issue, however, over half the Wallace/Lemay news was about this, while less than one-fourth of the Humphrey/Muskie news concentrated upon this topic. With Nixon/Agnew it was almost a third—just behind the Republican emphasis on foreign policy. Humphrey of course spent considerable time justifying (or commenting upon) the Vietnam War; Nixon did not choose (or have) to do this.

The media appear to have exerted a considerable impact on voters'

TABLE 2. *Mass Media Report on Issues, by Parties (expressed as percentages)*

Issues	Republican Nixon/Agnew			Democratic Humphrey/Muskie			American Wallace/Lemay		
	Major	Minor	Total	Major	Minor	Total	Major	Minor	Total
Foreign policy	34	40	38	65	63	64	30	21	26
Law and order	26	36	32	19	26	23	48	55	52
Fiscal policy	13	1	6	10	6	8	—	—	—
Public welfare	13	14	13	4	3	4	7	12	10
Civil rights	15	8	11	2	2	2	14	12	13
Total per cent[a]	101	99	100	100	100	101	99	100	101
Total number	47	72	119	48	62	110	28	33	61

[a] Some columns do not sum to 100% because of rounding.

judgements of what they considered the major issues of the campaign (even though the questionnaire specifically asked them to make judgements without regard to what politicians might be saying at the moment). The correlation between the major item emphasis on the main campaign issues carried by the media and voters' independent judgements of what were the important issues was + 0.967. Between minor item emphasis on the main campaign issues and voters' judgements, the correlation was + 0.979. In short, the data suggest a very strong relationship between the emphasis placed on different campaign issues by the media (reflecting to a considerable degree the emphasis by candidates) and the judgements of voters as to the salience and importance of various campaign topics.

But while the three presidential candidates placed widely different emphasis upon different issues, the judgements of the voters seem to reflect the *composite* of the mass media coverage. This suggests that voters pay some attention to all the political news *regardless* of whether it is from, or about, any particular favoured candidate. Because the tables we have seen reflect the composite of *all* the respondents, it is possible that individual differences, reflected in party preferences and in a predisposition to look mainly at material favourable to one's own party, are lost by lumping all the voters together in the analysis. Therefore, answers of respondents who indicated a preference (but not commitment) for one of the candidates during the September–October period studied (45 of the respondents; the others were undecided) were analysed separately. Table 3 shows the results of this analysis for four selected media.

The table shows the frequency of important issues cited by respondents who favoured Humphrey, Nixon, or Wallace correlated (*a*) with the frequency of *all* the major and minor issues carried by the media and (*b*) with the frequency of the major and minor issues oriented to *each party* (stories with a particular party or candidate as a primary referent) carried by each of the four media. For example, the correlation is 0.89 between what Democrats see as the important issues and the *New York Times*'s emphasis on the issues in *all* its major news items. The correlation is 0.79 between the Democrats' emphasis on the issues and the emphasis of the *New York Times* as reflected *only* in items about the Democratic candidates.

If one expected voters to pay more attention to the major and minor

TABLE 3. *Intercorrelations of Major and Minor Issue Emphasis by Selected Media with Voter Issue Emphasis*

Selected Media	Major Items		Minor Items	
	All News	News Own Party	All News	News Own Party
New York Times				
Voters (D)	0.89	0.79	0.97	0.85
Voters (R)	0.80	0.40	0.88	0.98
Voters (W)	0.89	0.25	0.78	−.53
Durham Morning Herald				
Voters (D)	0.84	0.74	0.95	0.83
Voters (R)	0.59	0.88	0.84	0.69
Voters (W)	0.82	0.76	0.79	0.00
CBS				
Voters (D)	0.83	0.83	0.81	0.71
Voters (R)	0.50	0.00	0.57	0.40
Voters (W)	0.78	0.80	0.86	0.76
NBC				
Voters (D)	0.57	0.76	0.64	0.73
Voters (R)	0.27	0.13	0.66	0.63
Voters (W)	0.84	0.21	0.48	−0.33

issues oriented to their own party—that is, to read or view *selectively*—the correlations between the voters and news/opinion about their own party should be strongest. This would be evidence of selective perception.[11] If, on the other hand, the voters attend reasonably well to *all* the news, *regardless* of which candidate or party issue is stressed, the correlations between the voter and total media content would be strongest. This would be evidence of the agenda-setting function. The crucial question is which set of correlations is stronger.

In general, Table 3 shows that voters who were not firmly committed early in the campaign attended well to *all* the news. For major news items, correlations were more often higher between voter judgements of important issues and the issues reflected in all the news (including of course news about their favoured candidate/party) than were voter judgements of issues reflected in news *only* about their candidate/party. For minor news items, again voters more often correlated highest with the emphasis reflected in all the news than with the emphasis reflected in news about a favoured candidate. Considering both major and minor item coverage, 18 of 24 possible comparisons show voters more in agreement with all the news rather than with news only about their own party/candidate preference. This finding is better explained by the agenda-setting function of the mass media than by selective perception.

11 While recent reviews of the literature and new experiments have questioned the validity of the selective perception hypothesis, this has nevertheless been the focus of much communication research. For example, see Richard F. Carter, Ronald H. Pyszka, and Jose L. Guerrero, 'Dissonance and Exposure to Arousive Information', *Journalism Quarterly*, 46 (1969), 37–42; and David O. Sears and Jonathan L. Freedman, 'Selective Exposure to Information: A Critical Review', *Public Opinion Quarterly*, 31 (1967), 194–213.

Although the data reported in Table 3 generally show high agreement between voter and media evaluations of what the important issues were in 1968, the correlations are not uniform across the various media and all groups of voters. The variations across media are more clearly reflected in Table 4, which includes all survey respondents, not just those predisposed toward a candidate at the time of the survey. There also is a high degree of consensus among the news media about the significant issues of the campaign, but again there is not perfect agreement. Considering the news media as mediators between voters and the actual political arena, we might interpret the correlations in Table 5 as reliability coefficients, indicating the extent of agreement among the news media about what the important political events are. To the extent that the coefficients are less than perfect, the pseudo-environment reflected in the mass media is less than a perfect representation of the actual 1968 campaign.

TABLE 4. *Correlations of Voter Emphasis on Issues with Media Coverage*

	Newsweek	Time	New York Times	Raleigh Times	Raleigh News and Observer
Major Items	0.30	0.30	0.96	0.80	0.91
Minor Items	0.53	0.78	0.97	0.73	0.93
	Durham Sun	Durham Morning Herald	NBC News	CBS News	
Major Items	0.82	0.94	0.89	0.63	
Minor Items	0.96	0.93	0.91	0.81	

Two sets of factors, at least, reduce consensus among the news media. First, the basic characteristics of newspapers, television, and newsmagazines differ. Newspapers appear daily and have lots of space. Television is daily but has a severe time constraint. Newsmagazines appear weekly; news therefore cannot be as 'timely'. Table 5 shows that the highest correlations tend to be among like media; the lowest correlations, between different media.

Second, news media do have a point of view, sometimes extreme biases. However, the high correlations in Table 5 (especially among like media) suggest consensus on news values, especially on major news items. Although there is no explicit, commonly agreed-upon definition of news, there is a professional norm regarding major news stories from day to day. These major-story norms doubtless are greatly influenced today by widespread use of the major wire services—especially by newspapers and television—for much political information.[12] But as we move from major events of the

12 A number of studies have focused on the influence of the wire services. For example, see David Gold and Jerry L. Simmons, 'News Selection Patterns among Iowa Dailies', *Public Opinion Quarterly*, 29 (1965), 425–30; Guido H. Stempel III, 'How Newspapers Use the Associated Press Afternoon A-Wire', *Journalism Quarterly*, 41 (1964), 380–4; Ralph D. Casey and Thomas H. Copeland Jr., 'Use of Foreign News by 19 Minnesota Dailies', *Journalism Quarterly*, 35 (1958), 87–9; Howard L. Lewis, 'The Cuban Revolt Story: AP, UPI, and Three Papers', *Journalism Quarterly*, 37 (1960), 573–8; George A. Van Horn, 'Analysis of AP News on Trunk and Wisconsin State Wires', *Journalism Quarterly*, 29 (1952), 426–32; and Scott M. Cutlip, 'Content and Flow of AP News—From Trunk to TTS to Reader', *Journalism Quarterly*, 31 (1954), 434–46.

TABLE 5. *Intercorrelation of Mass Media Presidential News Coverage for Major and Minor Items*

	Newsweek	Time	New York Times	Raleigh Times	Raleigh News & Observer	Durham Sun	Durham Morning Herald	NBC	CBS
					Major Items				
Newsweek		.99	.54	.92	.79	.81	.79	.68	.42
Time	.65		.51	.90	.77	.81	.76	.68	.43
New York Times	.46	.59		.70	.71	.66	.81	.66	.66
Raleigh Times	.73	.66	.64		.85	.89	.90	.72	.62
Raleigh News and Observer	.84	.49	.60	.74		.84	.93	.82	.60
Durham Sun	.77	.47	.47	.70	.80		.94	.91	.77
Durham Morning Herald	.89	.68	.68	.80	.93	.73		.89	.76
NBC News	.81	.65	.38	.87	.73	.84	.75		.82
CBS News	.66	.60	.83	.88	.79	.76	.78	.72	
					Minor Items				

campaign, upon which nearly everyone agrees, there is more room for individual interpretation, reflected in the lower correlations for minor item agreement among media shown in Table 5. Since a newspaper, for example, uses only about 15 per cent of the material available on any given day, there is considerable latitude for selection among minor items.

In short, the political world is reproduced imperfectly by individual news media. Yet the evidence in this study that voters tend to share the media's *composite* definition of what is important strongly suggests an agenda-setting function of the mass media.

Discussion

The existence of an agenda-setting function of the mass media is not *proved* by the correlations reported here, of course, but the evidence is in line with the conditions that must exist if agenda-setting by the mass media does occur. This study has compared aggregate units—Chapel Hill voters as a group compared to the aggregate performance of several mass media. This is satisfactory as a first test of the agenda-setting hypothesis, but subsequent research must move from a broad societal level to the social psychological level, matching individual attitudes with individual use of the mass media. Yet even the present study refines the evidence in several respects. Efforts were made to match respondent attitudes only with media actually used by Chapel Hill voters. Further, the analysis includes a juxtaposition of the agenda-setting and selective perception hypotheses. Comparison of these correlations too supports the agenda-setting hypothesis.

Interpreting the evidence from this study as indicating mass media influence seems more plausible than alternative explanations. Any argument that the correlations between media and voter emphasis are spurious—that they are simply responding to the same events and not influencing each other one way or the other—assumes that voters have alternative means of observing the day-to-day changes in the political arena. This assumption is not plausible; since few directly participate in presidential election campaigns, and fewer still see presidential candidates in person, the information flowing in interpersonal communication channels is primarily relayed from, and based upon, mass media news coverage. The media are the major primary sources of national political information; for most, mass media provide the best— and only—easily available approximation of ever-changing political realities.

It might also be argued that the high correlations indicate that the media simply were successful in matching their messages to audience interests. Yet since numerous studies indicate a sharp divergence between the news values of professional journalists and their audiences, it would be remarkable to find a near perfect fit in this one case.[13] It seems more likely that the media have prevailed in this area of major coverage.

---

13 Furthermore, five of the nine media studied here are national media and none of the remaining four originate in Chapel Hill. It is easier to argue that Chapel Hill voters fit their judgements of issue salience to the mass media than the reverse. An interesting study which discusses the problems of trying to fit day-to-day news judgements to reader interest is Guido H. Stempel III, 'A Factor Analytic Study of Reader Interest in News', *Journalism Quarterly*, 44 (1967), 326–30. An older study is Philip F. Griffin, 'Reader Comprehension of News Stories: A Preliminary Study', *Journalism Quarterly*, 26 (1949), 389–96.

35

The 'Uncensored War': The Media and Vietnam

Daniel C. Hallin

The 'Uncensored War', 1965–1967

As we shift from print to television, the mode of exposition of this study must change: rather than following Vietnam coverage in detail day by day, as we did in examining print coverage, we will push chronology into the background for most of the present chapter, and examine themes which persisted in television coverage throughout the period from the deployment of large-scale ground forces in the summer of 1965 until the Tet offensive in January 1968. In part, this change of style is necessary because of the sheer volume of coverage during this period, compared with 1961–5, when Vietnam was in the news more sporadically. But it is also appropriate to the nature of television coverage, which was less the 'first draft of history' that the press is supposed to provide than a series of more or less timeless images of men—or, more precisely, of Americans—at war.

More than half of television's coverage in these early years was concerned with military operations, the rest being divided among various forms of politics—the policy debate in Washington, the development of the antiwar movement, the political conflicts that continued to rock South Vietnam, and diplomatic activity. So this chapter will focus primarily on the 'uncensored war' that Americans saw so often on their television screens. We will begin, however, with the policy debate in Washington, where we can start to get a sense of how network television coverage might differ from the 'prestige press' coverage we have examined to this point.

Unfortunately, Washington coverage is one of the areas for which the Defence Department Kinescopes are incomplete. It will be impossible, therefore, to provide a fully representative picture of the networks' Washington coverage throughout the 1965–7 period. There is, however, one important episode for which the kinescopes do contain extensive Washington coverage: the 'peace offensive' which began on 24 December 1965, intended by the administration to prepare public opinion for an expansion of the war. The reporting of the peace offensive cannot be taken as typical of television's Washington reporting throughout 1965–7; on the contrary, as we explore television's response to the growing conflict over the war, we shall see that there is good reason to assume that the networks moved gradually away from

Source: Daniel C. Hallin, *The 'Uncensored War': The Media and Vietnam* (Berkeley, Los Angeles, and London: University of California Press, 1986).

the kind of 'patriotic' journalism we are about to encounter. But the peace offensive will show us where television stood in relation to official policy at the war's beginning, and provide us with a model of journalism very different from anything we have seen in our reading of the *New York Times*. [...]

■ **The Peace Offensive and the Boundaries of Objectivity**

The decision of July 1965 to raise the level of American troops in Vietnam to 175,000 was intended as the first of two phases, with approval of the second phase expected early in 1966. Phase II was originally planned to involve 112,000 additional US troops. But the North Vietnamese were matching US escalation. By November 1965, it had become clear that infiltration from North Vietnam had increased substantially, and Phase II had to be revised upward. By December, force levels of up to about 400,000 were being discussed for the end of 1966. Vietnam was going to be a big war. Political support would be a problem, and there was considerable sentiment in the administration that an escalation of this magnitude should not be undertaken without some major new peace effort which would, if nothing else, convince world and American public opinion that diplomatic channels had been fully explored. At the end of November, Secretary McNamara wrote to the president:

> It is my belief that there should be a three- or four-week pause in the programme of bombing the North before we either greatly increase our troop deployments to Vietnam or intensify our strikes against the North. The reasons for this belief are, first, that we must lay a foundation in the mind of the American public and in world opinion for such an enlarged phase of the war, and, second, we should give North Vietnam a face-saving chance to stop the aggression.[1]

So on Christmas Eve 1965, a thirty-seven-day pause in the bombing of North Vietnam began. It was accompanied by a moderately serious, secret contact with the North Vietnamese through their mission in Rangoon, Burma, which was broken off for reasons we will examine later. It was also accompanied by a massive public peace offensive, aimed at both US and world opinion. W. Averill Harriman, Vice President Humphrey, and other officials were dispatched to various capitals to carry the message of American willingness to negotiate; Arthur Goldberg did this at the United Nations; Secretary Rusk released the first formal statement of American peace proposals, known as the Fourteen Points. Not everyone was convinced by the peace offensive. Perhaps most important, J. William Fulbright, chairman of the Senate Foreign Relations Committee and at one time the president's key Capitol Hill supporter on foreign policy, went public with his opposition to US policy in Vietnam, holding hearings in February which could be considered the first major congressional debate on the war. But on television, the peace offensive was an unqualified success.

In order to understand television's reporting from Washington during this period, we need to consider a more complex view of American journalism. The television journalist presented himself, in this case, not as a

1 *Pentagon Papers*, Senator Gravel, ed. (Boston: Beacon Press, 1971), iv. 33.

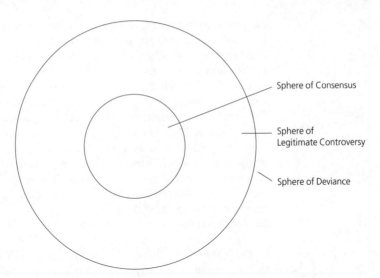

Sphere of Consensus

Sphere of
Legitimate Controversy

Sphere of Deviance

Figure 1.
Spheres of consensus,
controversy, and deviance.

disinterested observer, but as a patriot, a partisan of what he frequently referred to as 'our' peace offensive. It is useful to imagine the journalist's world as divided into three regions, each of which is governed by different journalistic standards.[2] These regions can be represented by the concentric circles shown in Figure 1. The province of objectivity is the middle region, which can be called the Sphere of Legitimate Controversy. This is the region of electoral contests and legislative debates, of issues recognized as such by the major established actors of the American political process. The limits of this sphere are defined primarily by the two-party system—by the parameters of debate between and within the Democratic and Republican parties—as well as by the decision-making process in the bureaucracies of the executive branch. Within this region, objectivity and balance reign as the supreme journalistic virtues.

Bounding the Sphere of Legitimate Controversy on one side is what can be called the Sphere of Consensus. This is the region of 'motherhood and apple pie'; it encompasses those social objects not regarded by the journalists and most of the society as controversial. Within this region journalists do not feel compelled either to present opposing views or to remain disinterested observers. On the contrary, the journalist's role is to serve as an advocate or celebrant of consensus values.

And beyond the Sphere of Legitimate Controversy lies the Sphere of Deviance, the realm of those political actors and views which journalists and the political mainstream of the society reject as unworthy of being heard. It is, for example, written into the FCC's guidelines for application of the Fairness Doctrine that 'it is not the Commission's intention to make time available to Communists or to the Communist viewpoints'.[3] Here neutrality once again falls away, and journalism becomes, to borrow a phrase from Talcott

2 See Daniel C. Hallin, 'The Media, the War in Vietnam and Political Support: A Critique of the Thesis of an Oppositional Media', *Journal of Politics*, 46: 1 (Feb. 1984).

3 Quoted in Edward Jay Epstein, *News From Nowhere* (New York: Vintage, 1974), 64.

Parsons, a 'boundary-maintaining mechanism':[4] it plays the role of exposing, condemning, or excluding from the public agenda those who violate or challenge the political consensus. It marks out and defends the limits of acceptable political conflict.

It should be added that each 'sphere' has internal gradations, and the boundaries between them are often fuzzy. Within the Sphere of Legitimate Controversy, for example, the practice of objective journalism varies considerably. Near the border of the Sphere of Consensus, journalists practise the kind of objective journalism, where objectivity involves a straight recitation of official statements. Farther out, as the news deals with issues on which consensus is weaker, the principle of balance is increasingly emphasized, and then, still farther out, the 'adversary' ideal of the journalist as an independent investigator who serves to check the abuse of power. We will see these other faces of objective journalism increasingly as this account moves toward the era of polarization over Vietnam.

Which of these various models of journalism prevails depends on the political climate in the country as a whole. But there is also considerable variability within American journalism. And at the beginning of 1966 there was a dramatic contrast between television and the 'prestige' print media in Vietnam coverage. The prestige press, for the most part, continued to practise the kind of objective journalism that lies just outside the Sphere of Consensus, though there had perhaps been a little movement outward within the Sphere of Legitimate Controversy in the eleven months since Pleiku. Most press reports, particularly on the front page, still simply reported official statements at face value. There were, however, considerably more front page reports on congressional criticism of administration policy. There were more stories in which a number of different sources, some from inside the administration and some from outside (almost always in Congress), were used more or less coequally, with the journalist constructing a synthesis. And non élite opposition was beginning to be reported in a 'straight' way, that is, stories on opposition figures, like those on the administration, would be centred around the sources' own statements.[5]

On television, on the other hand, the peace offensive appeared as a kind of morality play: while the coverage of a paper like the *Times* had a dry and detached tone, television coverage presented a dramatic contrast between good, represented by the American peace offensive, and evil, represented by Hanoi. In part, the effectiveness of the peace offensive in creating a powerful television image of American virtue might be considered a result of the familiar ironies of objective journalism, somewhat modified by the nature of television presentation. It has often been observed that American television coverage is more 'thematic' than print reporting.[6] Because television news is

---

4 Talcott Parsons, *The Social System* (New York: Free Press, 1951).

5 These stories were almost always inside the paper, but at least one had a significant political impact. A widely reported statement by Staughton Lynd, a radical historian who with two other dissenters had made his own peace mission to Hanoi (the *Times* still put *peace* in quotation marks in this context; here we were on the *outer* edge of the Sphere of Legitimate Controversy), that the United States had not contacted Hanoi directly led the administration to disclose the secret contact in Rangoon. John D. Pomfret, 'Hanoi Accepted Secret U. S. Note, Washington Says', *NYT*, 11 Jan. 1966, p. 1.

6 Paul Weaver, 'Newspaper News and Television News', in Douglass Cater and Richard P. Adler (eds.), *Television as a Social Force* (New York: Praeger, 1975); Michael J. Robinson and Margaret A. Sheehan,

organized in time rather than space, the television audience must be 'carried along' from the beginning of the story to the end. It cannot be allowed—as a newspaper audience can—to shift its attention from story to story. A definite theme or story line is therefore essential to a television report (or even, at times, will structure a whole broadcast) in a way it is not for a newspaper article.

Some recent critics have described the thematic quality of television news as a factor that pushes it toward a more openly 'adversarial' stance *vis-à-vis* political authority.[7] And under certain conditions that can be true. A good example, if the reader will permit a digression a decade and half past 1965, would be the reporting of the Gulf of Sidra incident early in the Reagan administration, in 1981. Two Libyan jets had attacked US planes off the Libyan coast, during exercises described by the administration as 'routine', and were shot down. Information was available to reporters, however, that the manoeuvres were not routine at all, but were considered likely—if not actually intended—to produce some sort of response from Libya. The parallel with the Gulf of Tonkin incident was so clear, and contrasting information had so recently come out, that many press reports were quite skeptical. In the *Washington Post*, for example, the lead story (which was generally an 'objective' presentation of the various official statements) was accompanied by a long news analysis which was—if one put together the various facts it presented— quite damning to the official version of events.[8] The *Post*'s analysis, however, was presented simply as a discussion of the background to the conflict and did not focus explicitly on the contrast between official statements and background information. In television reports, by contrast, information that in the *Post* was dispersed was joined together into a single package of stories, and the contrast between the administration's public statements and what reporters knew (mostly from officials speaking off the record) jumped to the foreground. CBS, for example, cut directly from a statement by presidential aide Edwin Meese denying that the United States had been challenging Libya to correspondent Leslie Stahl, who reported:

> However, *Newsweek* magazine ran an item before the incident [video: still of *Newsweek* article] that the Reagan administration was choosing the Gulf of Sidra for the exercises specifically to challenge Qaddafi as a way of 'neutralizing' him. And CBS News has been told that the engagement was—quote—'not unanticipated . . . it did not come out of the blue'.[9]

In 1966, however, when contrasting interpretations were rarely being reported, what jumped to the foreground in television's simple, thematic presentation was the administration's own rhetoric. Television's version of objective reporting looked something like this:

Over The Wire and on TV: UPI and CBS in Campaign '80 (New York: Russell Sage Foundation, 1983); Daniel C. Hallin and Paolo Mancini, 'Speaking of the President: Political Structure and Representational Form in US and Italian TV News', *Theory and Society*, 13:6 (Nov. 1984).

7 e.g. Michael J. Robinson, 'American Political Legitimacy in an Age of Electronic Journalism', in Cater and Adler (eds.), *Television as a Social Force*.

8 Michael P. Getler, 'U.S. Navy Fighters Shoot Down Two Libyan Jets', Don Oberdorfer, 'U.S. Has Sought to Pressure Quaddafi', both *Washington Post*, 20 Aug. 1981, p. 1.

9 CBS, 19 Aug. 1981. All references are to the evening news unless otherwise indicated.

David Brinkley. President Johnson's peace campaign continues, and there has been no bombing of North Vietnam for more than ten days now. But radio Hanoi called the whole campaign a swindle and there is no public sign of any peace talks. [Hubert Humphrey is then shown speaking at a news conference, after which Brinkley 'wraps up'.] What Humphrey did was to deliver a brief, simple list of this country's efforts to end the war and a quick explanation of what the United States is after in Vietnam. It says among other things: the US wants no bases there, will happily pull out its troops, will give economic aid to all sides, will accept a neutral Vietnam if that is what the people there freely decide they want. In short, Humphrey said, we have offered to put everything into the basket of peace except the surrender of South Vietnam. As yet, again, there has been no favourable response from the North.[10]

What Brinkley does here is not so different from what a newspaper reporter might do: he structures the story around the vice president's remarks. The difference is that on television the story is boiled down to a single image, the contrast between the American peace offensive—'everything in the basket of peace except surrender'—and North Vietnamese failure to respond, an image sharpened by Brinkley's simple, expressive language.

Television, moreover, tends to 'thematize'—that is, to simplify and unify—not only within a particular story or broadcast, but over time as well. Television tends, in other words, to pick out a limited number of ongoing stories and cover them day in and day out. This may in part explain (I will offer some other possible explanations, or parts of the explanation, below) why television focused much more heavily on the peace offensive than did the press. In the major papers, coverage of Vietnam policy shifted among a number of subjects, including the administration's developing plans for further increases in the US commitment and the growing debate in Congress over the prospect of escalation. On television, however, the peace offensive was the single major theme of Vietnam coverage as long as it went on, and was in the foreground of coverage on most days. CBS used daily graphics showing how long the bombing pause had lasted.

But in drawing the contrast between America and its enemies—between good and evil—television journalists did not always confine themselves to reporting the official proceedings of the peace offensive. Their role was much more active: they moved back and forth between 'straight' reporting and commentary; their language was peppered with phrases strongly charged with moral and ideological significance. Television treated the peace offensive largely as a matter of consensus, to which the injunctions of objective journalism did not apply. Here are a few excerpts.

ABC, 4 January 1966, Peter Jennings. Hanoi, commenting for the first time on the halt in US bombing of North Vietnam, snapped that the US had no right to make any conditions for ending the war except on Hanoi's terms. Ambassador Goldberg talked again of negotiating peace.

10 NBC, 3 Jan. 1966.

NBC, 21 January 1966, David Brinkley. As for the peace campaign, the Communist side has repeatedly called it a sham. If it is, they could come to the bargaining table and expose it. But they haven't.

Chet Huntley. The Communists in Vietnam demonstrated today that they attach no more solemnity to a truce than to their politics. [Huntley then reported on charges of violations of the Tet truce, which received prominent and dramatic coverage on all three networks that day. On the cease-fire, the *New York Times* reported, 'Most cease-fire violations have been of "minor significance", a United States military communiqué said, and casualties suffered by allied forces have been light.'[11]

ABC, 1 February 1966, Jennings (making a transition between a report from the UN and another from Paris). The uncompromising position of North Vietnam was also made clear today in a different quarter . . .

Following the 1 February report from Paris, Jennings continued, 'The stubborn defiance of the North Vietnamese leadership in Hanoi is often evident in the Communist prisoners captured in the South.' Jennings then reported on North Vietnamese prisoners, being returned to the North in an exchange, who had thrown into the river packages given them as a 'goodwill' gesture by the South Vietnamese. This kind of connection between different stories usually does not exist in newspaper coverage. It is one of the things that makes television a more ideological medium than the newspaper: television forces much more of the news into the unity of a story line—and therefore of a world view.

Why should television have been more inclined than major newspapers to stick to consensus journalism on Vietnam, or to the narrowest kind of objective journalism? In part, it may simply have been the immaturity of a medium that was just beginning to be taken seriously, and to take itself seriously, as a major part of the journalistic profession. Most of television's Washington coverage during the peace offensive was not reported by correspondents with regular beats in the State Department, White House, and so on.[12] The typical report on Vietnam policy would consist of lengthy film clips of public statements by officials, introduced and wrapped up by the anchor, who relied primarily on wire service material. Perhaps this is one reason television tended to take official rhetoric so often at face value, and to fall back on sterotypes: a great deal of the news was put together by anchors, producers, and newswriters in the New York office, people who did not have the familiarity with particular areas of policy that reporters covering a beat normally will have. There is a 'gee whiz' quality to much television coverage that suggests very limited awareness of the background to official rhetoric. This lack of background knowledge can be seen in reports of 4 and 5 January on NBC and CBS, respectively. On 4 January David Brinkley reported, 'So the United States is willing to go anywhere, anytime and negotiate anything.' In fact, the United States was not willing to negotiate the one thing that mattered to the

---

11 'U.S. Officers Killed in Blast During Truce', *NYT*, 22 Jan. 1966, p. 1.

12 Av Westin recounts a struggle for time at CBS between New York newswriters, who preferred for Cronkite to tell the news, and the film and tape people, in *Newswatch: How TV Decides the News* (New York: Simon and Schuster, 1982), 72–3.

North Vietnamese and the NLF: political power in the South. Debate in Congress was beginning to broach the issue of what the US attitude should be toward Vietcong participation both in peace talks and in the future government in Vietnam, and this issue received some attention in the press;[13] it received almost none on television. As it turned out, it was probably the central issue of the negotiating process. The North Vietnamese broke off the Rangoon contact early in February, in response, US analysts believed, not to the resumption of bombing that occurred then, but to the Honolulu Declaration issued after a meeting between US and South Vietnamese officials, which reaffirmed that the United States considered the GVN the 'sole legitimate representative' of the South Vietnamese people.[14] The following day Walter Cronkite began dramatically, 'Good evening. The United States is offering to decelerate the pace of the Vietnam War as a prelude to peace talks.' The following Sunday, 9 January, the *Times*'s Week in Review closed its discussion of Vietnam by quoting the Senate majority and minority leaders, each of whom said the possibility of negotiations was remote and a decision on escalation would have to be made soon.

One of the most striking differences between television and prestige press coverage of Vietnam policy early in 1966 is that television reporting centred around public press conferences while newspaper reporting was based primarily on background contacts with officials. A difference in focus naturally accompanied the difference in sources. When major officials spoke publicly, they focused on the peace offensive. Privately the talk of Washington was the growing debate about what to do when, as expected, it did not lead to promising diplomatic results. Among the *Times*'s headlines during peace offensive:

> *5 Jan.* '$12 Billion More Sought by Johnson for Vietnam'
> *13 Jan.* 'Army Due to Gain Up to 50,000 Men'
> *18 Jan.* 'McNamara to Ask 113,000 More Men for the Military'
> *22 Jan.* 'Vietnam Buildup to 400,000 Troops Expected in Year'
> *30 Jan.* 'US Aides Said to Feel War May Last 6 or 7 Years'

Little of this talk of escalation was covered on television.

But I do not think the immaturity of television news in the mid-1960s is adequate by itself to explain the more 'patriotic' character of its Vietnam coverage. Television news has 'grown up' a great deal since 1966. Its Washington coverage is no longer a mere summary of wire reports, backed by film of press conferences. The reporter, with his or her established beat and inside contacts, now provides most of television's coverage of national politics. Yet TV journalism is still often moralizing journalism, either of the condemnatory or the celebrating variety. Two good recent examples would be the Korean airliner incident and the invasion of Grenada. I will suggest here two possible explanations.

It may be, in the first place, that television's very power—or reputation for power—has the ironic consequence of making the medium particularly

---

13 Max Frankel, 'Elusive Peace Keys', *NYT*, 1 Jan. 1966, p. 2; Drew Middleton, 'Thant Suggests a Vietcong Role in Future Regime', *NYT*, 21 Jan. 1966, p. 1.

14 George C. Herring (ed.), *The Secret Diplomacy of the Vietnam War: The Negotiating Volumes of the Pentagon Papers* (Austin: University of Texas Press, 1983), 121–2.

sensitive about the boundaries of legitimate controversy. Television seems to generate much more intense political reactions than other media. In part this may be because of its reputation for immense influence over the public. In part I suspect it is because of the nature of television's presentation, which is both unsubtle, because of its thematic simplicity, and very personal. When the invisible—and in this case anonymous—writer of the *Times* Week in Review notes in the middle of a long article that 'the weakness of the [peace] offensive seemed to be . . . in the nature of the message conveyed. . . . Official sources gradually made clear that the message contained no new substantive offer',[15] the *Times* need not worry terribly about charges it is aiding and abetting the enemy. If Cronkite had come on and said, 'Good evening. The United States has offered a new plan for peace in Vietnam. But CBS has learned the proposal contains little that is new,' the reaction might have been quite strong. By the time of the progress offensive television had already been 'burned' once on Vietnam, the previous August when Morley Safer's report from Cam Ne (discussed below) had generated a major public controversy; events like Cam Ne were reported routinely in the newspapers without any significant reaction.[16] Later, when boundaries of the Sphere of Legitimate Controversy began to shift and become themselves a subject of debate, so that it was no longer clear where they lay, the networks would have such problems often, as they did, for instance, with their portrayal of the police at the Democratic National Convention in 1968.[17] So perhaps television people, consciously or not, were particularly wary of treating as controversial things many people might regard as belonging properly to the Sphere of Consensus.

Television, moreover, seems to have a positive attraction to the role of moralist. This I believe is true for two interrelated reasons, the first having to do with television's audience, the other with its presentation. The papers we have been comparing with television news, particularly the *Times* and *Post*, are written for an audience most of which follows politics relatively closely. Television's audience is diverse, but compared with élite newspapers it is a long way 'down-market': older, less educated, much more heavily a working-class audience. And television people often say that they assume the audience to be uninformed about and uninterested in politics. As for presentation, television merges information and entertainment far more than an élite newspaper does. This is related to the nature of the audience: readers of the *Times* are assumed to want the news for information, television viewers, for entertainment. (Newspapers with audiences similar to television's also merge the functions of entertainment and news reporting. Vietnam coverage in the New York *Daily News* was much more like television coverage than like the reporting of the *Times*.) And it is also related to the 'time-embeddedness' of television's presentation: the evening news is an integral part of the 'audience flow' which builds up to the real heart of television's product, prime-time entertainment. Television cannot separate its entertainment and

15 *NYT*, 2 Jan. 1966.

16 e.g. Jack Langguth, 'Brutality Is Rising on Both Sides in South Vietnam', *NYT*, 7 July 1965, p. 7.

17 John P. Robinson, 'Public Reaction to Political Protest: Chicago, 1968', *Public Opinion Quarterly*, 34: 1 (Spring 1970).

information-providing functions as easily as a newspaper can, with its spatial dispersion of separate stories and sections.

The argument is often made that because television news is inescapably also entertainment, and therefore takes the form of *drama*, television is constantly searching for conflict and controversy, with the result that it portrays social and political institutions in a particularly negative light.[18] But that is much too glib. Television does love drama, on the news as well as in prime time, and drama does require conflict, but what that conflict will be about, what characters will be the 'good guys' and 'bad guys', what kind of resolutions and morals will be deemed appropriate—none of this is determined by the dramatic nature of the medium itself. It depends on the prevailing ideology of the society as well as on the particular historical conjuncture, which brings certain elements of that ideology to the fore and pushes others into the background.

American political ideology is deeply ambivalent about politics and authority (perhaps this is true, in different ways, about the political culture of any society). Americans have always had a suspicion of power and those who seek and wield it; power is often portrayed in American popular culture as the enemy of the Individual, who is of course the basic American hero. Exposés of abuse of power and tales of individuals who resist oppression by it are indeed a favoured source of drama for American journalism and in particular for television. But there is also in American political culture a deep desire for order and unity. The institution that represents Community in its 'good' form, in most popular culture, and which makes the Individual a part of society and therefore not a threat, not 'evil' in his or her individualism, is the Family. Almost all prime-time TV entertainment sets its characters within a family or (especially in the late 1970s and early 1980s) a substitute family of some sort. In politics, the Nation tends to be treated as a Family writ large; suspicion of power therefore coexists with a deep belief in loyalty to the political family and harmony within it. And those who hold political authority, though they can be treated as seekers of power, that is, Individuals breaking the limits of Community or usurping its functions, can also be treated as paternal representatives of Community itself.

It is by no means always true that the dramas of television news focus on disharmony or place established institutions or authorities in a negative light. Television loves, in fact, to find stories that allow it to celebrate the unity of the National Family. These are essential to the dramatic structure of the news: Evil must stand in contrast to Good, disharmony to the ideal of harmony. And the medium not surprisingly likes to identify itself with Good. It is interesting here to think what kinds of stories television has dignified and identified itself with by sending the anchor to cover them in person. Until a recent move to make the anchor a reporter as well, almost all were in some sense ceremonies of national unity. They included national political conventions and elections, which involve conflict, but of an especially controlled and sanctified kind; space shots, which are symbolic of national accomplishment; presidential trips abroad, in which the Nation, in its dealings with

---

18 For example, Michael J. Robinson, 'Public Affairs Television and the Growth of Political Malaise: The Case of "The Selling of the Pentagon" ', *American Political Science Review*, 70: 2 (June 1967); and 'American Political Legitimacy'.

other countries, becomes personified; and the Kennedy funeral. In only a single case, so far as I know, had an anchor covered personally a story that lacked this ceremonial quality: Cronkite's trip to Vietnam during the Tet offensive. As for stories of conflict, those that are the best material for television drama are the ones in which Good and Evil can be represented as clear and separate, where the source of conflict can be located outside the National Family.

Because of their different audiences, then, and because of television's special need for drama, TV and the prestige press perform very different political functions. The prestige press provides information to a politically interested audience; it therefore deals with *issues*. Television provides not just 'headlines', as television people often say, nor just entertainment, but ideological guidance and reassurance for the mass public. It therefore deals not so much with issues as with symbols that represent the basic values of the established political culture. This difference is certainly not absolute. Newspapers too can play the role of moralist; much of the *Times*'s coverage of Vietnam in the early 1960s, before Vietnam had moved into the Sphere of Legitimate Controversy, did this, albeit in a more sophisticated way for its more sophisticated audience. And television has always been torn between a desire to belong to the inner circle of serious journalism and its other identity as storyteller-moralist. Since the mid-1960s the balance in television has shifted considerably toward 'serious journalism', and the contrast between television and the press has narrowed. But in 1966 it was still very great, and it was therefore natural for television to focus on the good moral tale of the peace offensive, while the élite papers gave their attention to the growing policy debate.

36

CNN, the Gulf War, and Journalistic Practice

Barbie Zelizer

THE WORLD OF journalism is cluttered with practices that should generate questions about newsworkers' ability to act as authoritative reporters of events of the 'real world'. From news gathering to news presentation, a journalist's authority often derives from the fact that the public cannot verify what he or she has done. This situates the establishment of journalistic authority within the hands of journalists, and their authority is informed by their own decisions about how, why, and in what way they turn ordinary events into news stories. Such decisions in turn become the topic of discussions among journalists.

This is even more the case with major events, like the Gulf War. While the war's central events were unraveled in the eye of the media, their telling was accompanied by extensive discourse among journalists and news organizations about who put those events into narrative form, and in what way. This discourse particularly centered on the Cable News Network (CNN), the value of satellite-fed communication, and the advantages and disadvantages of reporting a war in 'real time'. In discussing the Gulf War, journalists thereby turned war stories into a forum for discussing issues of concern to the professional community.

This article considers how this took place—how journalists entwined stories about CNN, satellite-fed technology, and 'real-time' war reporting with Gulf War discourse. The article uses what Glaser and Strauss (1967) call a 'strategically chosen example' to track down journalistic mediated and professional discourse about covering the Gulf War. Analysis is based on systematic examination of the public discourse by which reporters discussed their part in covering the Gulf War, as it appeared in the printed press, television news, professional reviews, and trade journals.[1] In so doing, it addresses the emergence of the Gulf War as a critical incident for journalism professionals, which helped journalists redefine boundaries of appropriate practice.

Source: Barbie Zelizer, 'CNN, the Gulf War, and Journalistic Practice', *Journal of Communication* 42: 1 (Winter 1992), 66–81.

1 Discussions of Gulf War coverage appeared between January and August 1991 and were located via the *Current Guide to Periodical Literature*. The *New York Times*, *Philadelphia Inquirer*, and select television programmes were also scanned during the same time period, as was the trade press (*Columbia Journalism Review*, *Washington*, *Journalism Review*, *The Quill*, and *Electronic Media*) and newsletters of professional organizations (ASNE *Bulletin* and the Associated Press's *AP Log*).

Regardless of what they call them, journalists have long used critical incidents as a way to frame the hows and whys of journalistic practice. Critical incidents are what Levi-Strauss once called 'hot moments', phenomena or events through which a society or culture assesses its own significance (Levi-Strauss 1966: 259). Gerbner coined the term 'critical incident' in his discussion of decision-making processes in media organizations (Gerbner 1973: 562). He allowed that critical incidents give organizational members a way to defuse challenges to recognized authority. When employed discursively, critical incidents refer to those moments by which people air, challenge, and negotiate their own boundaries of practice. For journalists, discourse about critical incidents suggests a way of attending to events that are instrumental for the continued well-being of the journalistic community.

A number of events in journalism history can be seen as having functioned as critical incidents. Watergate—the scandal that journalists uncovered—displayed the appropriate boundaries of investigative journalism (Schudson, 1978; Woodward and Bernstein 1976). The Kennedy assassination allowed the journalistic community to negotiate its response to the ascent of television news (Zelizer 1990, 1993). The Vietnam War helped journalists rethink the hows and whys of televisual reporting and journalistic responsibility during wartime (Arlen 1969; Braestrup 1977). Critical incidents of different kinds illuminate different rules and conventions about journalistic practice and authority.

At the heart of critical incidents is discourse about more general topics at issue for journalism professionals. The Kennedy assassination, for example, emerged at a time when the professionalization of journalists was uppermost and the legitimation of television news questionable. Journalists used assassination stories to address both agendas (Zelizer 1993). Using discourse in this way helps journalists attend to different notions about journalistic practice by telling and retelling the stories of major public events.

Critical incidents are generally shaped by discourse about two features: technology and archetypal figures. Technology, or the devices that shape an incident into news, offers a stage for journalism professionals to experiment with new ways of achieving work-related goals. During the Vietnam War, journalists were given the opportunity to append filmed pictures to words in reporting the war on television, even if a certain time lag was involved (Braestrup 1977). At the time of the Kennedy assassination, live television gave the American public its first live televisual experience of a major public event. The shooting of Kennedy's presumed assassin, Lee Harvey Oswald, on television prompted reporters to consider the advantages—and disadvantages—of live coverage (Zelizer 1993). Changes in technology thereby form the backdrop against which a critical incident is acted out, and made meaningful for those involved in its relay.

Archetypal figures, or the individuals who successfully use the technology of news reporting, are an instrumental part of a critical incident's development. They provide the faces behind the technological devices. The Kennedy assassination produced the Walter Cronkites and Dan Rathers, reporters who covered the story in what came to be referenced as exemplary television journalism (Zelizer 1993). Watergate generated the Bob Woodwards and

Carl Bernsteins (Woodward and Bernstein 1976), both of whom were seen as exemplar investigative journalists.

Within this context, the Gulf War can be seen as a potentially critical incident for journalism professionals. As *Time* magazine opined: 'Like the Kennedy assassination or the space-shuttle disaster, the outbreak of war in the Gulf was one of those historic events destined to be remembered forever in the terms by which television defined it' (Zoglin 1991*a*: 69). Called by one trade journal 'the biggest news story in decades' (Boot 1991: 23), it problematized for journalists the hows and whys of the newest dimension of news-gathering technology—the satellite-fed television news report. At the same time, it offered a forum for negotiating the response of the journalistic community to that same technology, as it was already being successfully employed by CNN.

Live from the Gulf

From the onset, the Gulf War offered a forum for journalists to discuss concerns about the profession. For most journalists, covering the Gulf War exemplified the ultimate dilemma of wartime reporting, which, in *Time*'s view, involved 'how to communicate events fairly and accurately, without revealing confidential military information' (Zoglin 1991*c*: 44). The growing availability of live satellite-fed television communication from within enemy territory made war-time reporting particularly visible to the public, in all its negative and positive aspects. It 'opened up the news-gathering process to millions of people' (Osborne 1991: 2), and showed them how 'disorganized, sloppy and unappetizing the process can be' (Greenfield 1991: 7).

It also made the war a 'real-time' story. As US viewers watched air raid alerts of SCUD attacks in real time, so did the Iraqis. Reporting real-time war constituted an unprecedented professional challenge for many journalists, who needed to act fast, 'professionally', in unknown territory—and all in the eye of the camera. This generated the feeling that 'for much of American journalism, especially broadcasting, the implications of the gulf war will be as far reaching as they are for the Middle East' (Katz 1991: 29).

Yet once the war began, news organizations moved to accommodate unusually large audiences. Newsstand sales of *Newsweek* doubled (Diamond 1991*b*), and dailies like the *Philadelphia Inquirer* and the *Boston Globe* sold up to 20,000 more copies per day (Zoglin 1991*b*: 78). Newspapers printed second editions, supplements, and wraparound sections ('The Persian Gulf Explodes', 1991). Television offered news coverage that clarified the war effort (i.e., 'Meet the Press', 1991). Special issues of the trade press and proceedings of professional forums were devoted to war coverage.

Journalists' fundamental unfamiliarity with the reporting of modern wartime technology, however, gave coverage the aura of a Nintendo game. As media critic Peter Braestrup saw it:

> A new generation of journalists is learning about war and they're
> learning about the military . . . They're ahistorical; they can't remember
> any precedents for anything. They keep discovering the world anew.
> They either concentrate on high-tech stories or on what an ABC

producer described as 'boo-hoo journalism', that is, asking 'How do you feel?' not 'What do you know?' . . . They're yuppies in the desert (quoted in Valeriani 1991: 26).

Time lamented the scarcity of 'reliable, objective information about the war's progress' (Zoglin 1991*c*: 44). Journalists were faulted for surrendering to governmental attempts at censorship (Boot 1991), providing what Hodding Carter called 'essentially phony coverage' (quoted in Valeriani 1991: 28), toeing the government line (Massing 1991; Schanberg 1991). *US News & World Report* claimed that all the press corps had to show for its coverage was 'a big black eye' (Gergen 1991: 57). Television addiction, said the editor, had turned into a 'sour distaste for journalists'. A critic for *The Progressive* went further in commenting that journalists were 'on call 24 hours a day to report that they know nothing' (Landau 1991: 26).

Perhaps as a means of compensating for insufficient reportage, reporters entwined the war story with the story of those doing the reporting. Television networks began to offer programmes that concentrated on the media and the Gulf (i.e. *The Press Goes to War*, 1991; *The Media and the Military*, 1991). *TV Guide* tracked journalistic celebrities who became famous for their war coverage (Lieberman, Stein, and Collins 1991) and relayed reporters' experiences at war, as if journalists, not soldiers, were the privileged tellers of tales from the front (Stein 1991). As one critic wryly observed, 'the United States has nearly 500,000 troops in the Gulf Region, and the only people you see in jeopardy are reporters . . . the process of reporting had become the story' (Rosenberg 1991: 17–18).

In the spring of 1991, *Newsweek* published a special commemorative war issue, which hailed reporters' co-operation with each other and their ability to overcome professional challenges like desert heat or censorship restrictions ('The Story Behind the Story', 1991: 3). The more innovative the activity, the more attention it received: One journalist shaved his head to spare himself the effort of grooming while reporting the war; another lost 15 pounds during his seven weeks in the region. *Newsweek*'s reporting was lauded (by the magazine's own staff) as 'prescient', 'heroic', and 'tremendous'. It brought journalists 'as close to writing history as journalism goes' ('The Story Behind the Story', 1991: 3). Because it introduced a story about Americans at war, this article placed journalists at the forefront not only of efforts to tell the story but of the war effort itself.

Television journalism provided a particularly fertile forum for reporters' war discourse. Television became the 'proscenium of the theater of war', said veteran newsperson Fred Friendly (quoted in *The Media and the Military*, 1991), in that many activities took place before its cameras. The war's onset seemed to have been timed to coincide with the networks' evening news programmes, and night after night Americans were treated to action that heated up as prime time neared. Television networks broke into scheduled programmes with live shots of reporters under SCUD attack. Even radio borrowed or purchased television audio in order to keep up with the story (Collins 1991: 29). From gas-masked reporters to teary Iraqis outside a bombed shelter to scenes of Kuwaitis hanging up American flags made of old pyjamas, the war for most Americans 'ended as it had begun—on television' (Diamond 1991*a*: 26).

The war's emplottment thus favored the television journalist. One reporter offered the view that the 'dearth of uncensored, firsthand information about the war [forced] the press—especially television—to focus on the few parts of the story reporters can witness' (Zoglin 1991*c*: 45). This made the eyewitness accounts of television reporters one of the few authoritative relays of the war coverage. As one press reporter recalled, 'a friend took a picture of me the other day taking notes in front of a television set. That's what being a war correspondent has come to' (quoted in Zoglin 1991*b*: 78).

An emphasis on television news sometimes turned non-newsworthy events into news, largely because television technology was there to report them. 'To have technology is to use it', said David Halberstam, as he lamented the widening gap between the immediacy offered by satellite-fed technology and the instantaneous journalism it created, and the time needed to make reliable news judgements (Halberstam 1991: 1). One bizarre recasting of events 'came not when General Powell unveiled his diagrams of damaged Iraqi targets, but when CNN's Charles Jaco scrambled for his gas mask on the air in Saudi Arabia' (Zoglin 1991*c*: 45). Called the 'biggest gaffe' of the war by one account, it nonetheless was reported by nearly every news organization. The incident not only displayed the emotional toll of reporting war in real time, accompanied by a technology that superseded one's ability to gain composure, but it called on journalists to consider establishing new boundaries of appropriate behaviour.

Network news organizations could not adopt the setup required of reporting the war in real time for long. The story called for reporters to be constantly on call, cramming 'three years' worth of stories into three weeks' (Diamond 1991*b*: 33). The breaking story, one reporter said, was 'old by dinner-time. Satellite-linked stations and CNN, serving 58.9 million homes, can and do give the viewers the day's hot news well before the network newscasts crank up' (Sharbutt 1991: 5D). By contrast, CNN's 'ubiquity, mobility and hustle seemed to leave [its] network competitors paralyzed' (Katz 1991: 29). The cost of covering breaking news had generated a situation whereby the 'networks [couldn't] afford to be in the breaking news business anymore' (Katz 1991: 29). As the cost of coverage rose, they were unable to continue covering the story, no longer competent to run it in its most developed technological form. *Newsweek* went so far as to claim that the night the war began was 'the night the networks died' (Alter 1991: 41).

From the beginning, then, journalists linked issues of professionalism with discourse about war coverage. Stories of the Gulf War raised questions about the preferred form of journalistic practice, that addressed not only long-standing concerns about censorship, editorial integrity and economic viability but a specific issue related to the Gulf War—how to establish authority for reportage in real time.

The Ascendancy of CNN

Discussions of the Gulf War focused on CNN for its successful usage of the newest news-gathering technology, the satellite-fed communication. CNN not only distributed news by satellite but brought portable satellite uplinks, called 'flyaway dishes', to the front line. This enabled journalists to collect news by satellite, introducing faster news transmission and generating a continuous stream of news copy from diverse locations. Because CNN had successfully employed this technology, the story of Gulf War coverage became entwined with the story of CNN's technological mastery and its emergence as a viable news organization.

Network news was vividly contrasted with cable news during the initial shelling of Baghdad, when ABC, NBC, and CNN all succeeded in transmitting reports for their correspondents. Within minutes, only CNN was left with an operable line, and its three reporters provided what *Time* called 'an exceptional, and perhaps unprecedented, live account of the start of war from inside an enemy capital' (Zoglin 1991a: 69). Journalists and news organizations uneasily watched what CNN would do next:

> The CNN team had what every other American news organization—
> the oldline networks, the newspapers, and the wire services—wishes it
> had: implicit recognition on the part of Iraqi authorities that it is the
> preeminent news-gathering force in the world, a continuing and
> officially sanctioned presence in the Iraqi capital, and the technology that
> allows its reporters to get their stories out (Diamond 1991b: 30).

CNN possessed the ability to present, transmit, and distribute news 24 hours a day, making it the sole news organization capable of 'keeping up' with satellite-fed communication.

As the war progressed, other media began to notice CNN's coverage. Local stations signed on to carry CNN affiliates and bypass the other traditional networks (Mott 1991). On one night, over 200 news directors at local affiliates abandoned their own network's feed to acquire CNN material (Cooper 1991). NBC anchor Tom Brokaw interviewed CNN's Bernard Shaw from Shaw's hotel room in Baghdad. CNN became 'the unpaid news service for papers' (Bernard Gwertzman, quoted in Colin 1991: 31), which adapted traditional formats to include more graphics and visual layouts (Colin 1991; Diamond 1991a). Audiences also began to pay attention and CNN's ratings increased fivefold (Cooper 1991; Kamen 1991; Gannett Foundation 1991).

CNN's triumph was seen by many reporters as an about-face on the part of what had been considered a second-rate news organization. In one view, CNN went from being the 'Chicken Noodle Network' to having public credibility (Diamond 1991b: 35). Often this was relayed through war terminology: *US News & World Report* observed that 'January 16 will be remembered as the night [producer Bob] Furnad and his CNN colleagues carpet-bombed the competition' (Cooper 1991: 44). Headlines like 'CNN Wins' or 'CNN Hits Its Target' were strewn across the print media, as was mention of the 'collateral damage' inflicted on CBS, NBC, and ABC (Katz 1991). War terminology suggests the extent to which CNN was originally seen as part of the opposition, a second-rate news organization, and helps explain why journalists needed to link CNN's legitimation with an event like the Gulf War. In a sense, the magnitude of events that underscored CNN's triumph softened the blow of being positioned as members of the losing side.

Thus CNN was largely hailed across media in statements that linked its ascendancy with the war. *Time* called CNN its 'undisputed star', which 'affirmed its credibility and worldwide clout with new authority' (Zoglin 1991a: 69). *US News & World Report* called CNN a network that 'shows how to cover a war' (Cooper 1991: 44). And *Newsweek*, applauding a 'new television order', commented already in January that CNN was 'changing the news business forever' (Alter 1991: 41). The Gulf War offered the kind of news story that portrayed CNN's technological advantages in their best light (Diamond 1991b: 35). Its coverage thus somewhat changed expectations of wartime reporting.

In the eyes of CNN insiders, however, war coverage adapted itself to the form of reportage that CNN did best. As one CNN executive said, 'we handled the big story hour after hour, taking incoming materials from satellites, but that's what we do all the time' (John Baker, quoted in Diamond 1991b: 34). Wartime coverage played into 'CNN's traditional strengths: its unquenchable lust for the breaking story, its willingness to feed a story in contradictory fragments to an audience hooked on drama and the very ambiguities of life' (Polman 1991: 27). On these grounds, CNN executives claimed to offer 'a new kind of journalism', which presented 'the unfolding story . . . live' (Ed Turner, quoted in Polman 1991: 26).

Shortly after the war began, CNN's publicity department distributed a pamphlet entitled 'War in the Gulf' (*War in the Gulf*, 1991). The pamphlet was telling for how it incorporated the Gulf War into CNN's publicity effort. Alongside a map of the Gulf region, its front cover hailed CNN as 'the world's news leader'. Inside, it recorded the sentiments of CNN's main players—Peter Arnett, Bernard Shaw, and John Holliman—as well as a daily accounting of the war's main events. Shaw conveyed how he, Arnett, and Holliman had 'cheated death' on the first day of the war. 'The world benefited,' he said, 'CNN was there. History was served' (ibid. 1). The pamphlet also recounted the praise of key public officials and media organizations throughout its 23 pages of text and pictures: Dick Cheney lauded CNN for the 'best reporting' (ibid. 11), while foreign newspapers praised it for being more objective than other networks (ibid. 13). The pamphlet concluded with the following statement: 'No one will ever doubt . . . that CNN is the most important network in the world. This is the most important journalism story of the decade' (ibid. 23).

CNN's so-called 'overnight success'—which *The Quill* called a 'quantum leap into the broadcasting big leagues in only a matter of hours' (Mott 1991: 15)—did not take place in one night. It had actually been in the making for nearly ten years. Years earlier, CNN's coverage of events like the Challenger shuttle disaster or the shooting of Ronald Reagan had already hinted at the advantages to be had in continuous live coverage, and recognition of those parameters prompted CNN executives to negotiate for the installation of an overseas telephone link in Iraq in case of emergency power failure (Mott 1991). Even before the war there were hints of public legitimacy, such as a *Washington Journalism Review* readers' poll conducted in October that gave CNN the title of Best Network for News ('Best in the Business', 1991).

So why was CNN's ascendancy linked with the Gulf War? Such a linkage was necessary for the negotiation and successful recognition of altered parameters of journalistic professionalism. By narratively reworking the tale of CNN's legitimation via Gulf War discourse, journalists were able to couch it in terms that made its ascendancy more understandable and less threatening to existing boundaries of journalistic practice. It also gave CNN itself a marker through which it could claim its own legitimation. 'New King of the Hill' was how *The Quill* pronounced CNN's newfound status (Mott 1991), and it was a cry echoed by mediated and professional forums alike, however true a recounting it was. Journalists' discussions came to underscore the central role of CNN in mastering the technology that gave the Gulf War story its form.

The Peter Arnett Phenomenon

Left unresolved in discussions of CNN's ascendancy, however, were concerns about the reporter. One professional forum offered the view that reporters were 'hardly needed' in much of CNN's coverage 'other than as a relay point along the transmission line' (Haarsager 1991: 3). Journalists questioned whether they had been displaced by satellite-fed communications, whether the reporter had become 'less important than the satellite dish that he's standing next to' (Yaari 1991). While CNN coverage was described by one trade journal as 'technologically ingenious and dramatic' (Katz 1991: 29), these were hardly adjectives favoured by hard-boiled reporters. The idea that a reporter was created from one night of saturation footage did not bode well for definitions of professional activity.

Questions remained about the authority of the reporter *vis-à-vis* that of the portable satellite uplink, creating a need for stories that might help journalists deal with their own mastery over the satellite-fed news item. Thus, journalists used the archetypal figure as a way of negotiating their mastery of the satellite-fed story, and they positioned Peter Arnett as the archetypal figure of Gulf War discourse. Arnett was seen as the reporter who met newly-defined professional challenges despite great personal risk and hardship. By staying behind enemy lines to report the story, he exemplified what was needed of a reporter in an age of satellite-fed communication. Within these parameters, an image of him was constructed that addressed questions among journalists about their authority within such an age.

The media labelled Arnett the 'last American correspondent left in Baghdad' (Zoglin 1991c: 45). They likened his dispatches to the legendary reportage of Edward R. Murrow during World War II. Newspaper columns outlined his performance in Baghdad (i.e. Heller 1991). Reporters like David Halberstam, Marvin Kalb, and Malcolm Browne went on national media to remind viewers of Arnett's reportorial competence and experience, which had won him a Pulitzer Prize for his Vietnam reportage (Browne 1991; Granger 1991; *The Media and the Military*, 1991). He had, said Halberstam, 'an almost unique ability to operate in an environment that most reporters would have found unendurable' (quoted in Halonen 1991: 6). CNN executives praised Arnett as a 'seasoned combat correspondent, who has been tested by time and in so practicing his craft received the highest honors journalism can bestow' (Ed Turner, quoted in Halberstam 1991: 31).

While public figures levelled criticism at the reporter for relaying Iraqi-censored reports, for not being overtly loyal to America, for insisting on staying behind enemy lines, journalists spoke almost to a person in his defence. When Arnett reported that the allies had bombed a plant producing infant formula, and not biological weapons as the US insisted, and public fears intensified that his dispatches were being used for propaganda purposes, journalists spoke out in his behalf. The *Philadelphia Inquirer* called him an 'endangered species' (Heller 1991: D1). At one point lawmakers pressed for control over his broadcasts (Halberstam 1991: 1), and the *Washington Journalism Review* called the attempts 'Malice in Wonderland' (Monroe 1991: 6). Interestingly, these comments addressed the appropriateness of a reporter's actions within the expanded boundaries of coverage offered by satellite-fed communiques. In other words, discourse about Arnett explored whether adjusting the boundaries of appropriate coverage was necessary to suit the newest news-gathering technology.

Nearly all of the trade press—including *Washington Journalism Review, Columbia Journalism Review,* and *Electronic Media*—ran articles praising Arnett's performance. The *New York Times Magazine* traced his personal history under the title 'If There's a War, He's There' (Prochnan 1991: 30). One editorial called Arnett the 'anti-hero hero of Baghdad' (Monroe 1991: 6). The logistics of Arnett securing his interview with Saddam Hussein were tracked by *Electronic Media*, whose front-page headline proclaimed that 'CNN's Secret Journey Ends in Exclusive Hussein Broadcast' (Shaw 1991: 1). The *Washington Journalism Review* defended Arnett with the phrase, 'observe the legend taking shape—the legend of Peter Arnett, go-to-hell war correspondent' (Monroe 1991: 6). He was:

> the hero that journalists deserve, sent by the Lord to comfort us in our time of affliction and gross unpopularity . . . [he was] the perfect symbol of the beleaguered press in the Scudded world of February 1991. He lives and breathes the story (Monroe 1991: 6).

As American forces began their pullout from the region, the *Columbia Journalism Review* ran a special article about war coverage that was simply titled 'Arnett'. In part, it went as follows: 'By turns defiant and defensive, [Arnett] upheld his role even as he acknowledged that the sort of journalism he had practiced, or been permitted to practice, had been severely circumscribed' (Goodman 1991: 29). Such remarks underscored that reporting a war in real time called for a change in reportorial practice. In many reporters' eyes, Arnett had become 'the first war correspondent of the global village' (Halonen 1991: 7).

The controversy surrounding Arnett's coverage did not go unnoticed by the reporter himself. In a speech to the National Press Club shortly after he returned to the US, he claimed that the same public figures who criticized him for being too soft on Saddam Hussein had upbraided him before the war began for being too critical (Rosenstiel 1991). He also claimed that his ability to conduct unrehearsed question-and-answer sessions with his CNN anchors was what 'saved [his] reputation'; those sessions showed that he was not simply 'reading material that I was forced to write' (Rosenstiel 1991: 12A). The response of the journalistic community was overwhelmingly supportive. He was called upon to address other professional forums on the same issue, including the Knight Fellows at Stanford and the American Society of Newspaper Editors (Collins 1991). He also signed a contract to write his memoirs.

For an understanding of appropriate boundaries of journalistic practice, Arnett's activities were instrumental in illustrating the need for a change. His response confirmed his authority as a reporter through the spontaneous and unplanned nature of reporting in real time. Casting journalistic practice in this way upheld the need for changing the boundaries of reportage in an age of satellite-fed communication. His remarks thereby not only underscored his own stature and that of CNN, but also that of the technology of satellite-fed communication that made his reportage possible. It is significant that he was a reporter who had previously proved himself in the print media, and his ascendancy as CNN's star illustrates a peculiar, but workable, wedding of the old and new in American journalism. By being filmed sitting next to the satellite, he also signified the connection between the archetypal figure and the new preferred technology of news gathering.

It is worthwhile to contrast Arnett with another journalistic personality who was central to stories about the Gulf War: CBS's Bob Simon. Simon was captured by the Iraqis when he abandoned pool arrangements and went on his own in search of a story. He spent weeks in captivity. Simon emerged as the mirror image of Arnett, the reporter who defied military restrictions to investigate the scene and was then taken captive for his efforts. Simon was portrayed as having walked away from the technology of transmission (and losing the story), while Arnett was seen as having prevailed for remaining alongside that same technology (and winning the story). In a semiotic sense, this signified the importance of remaining alongside the satellite, regardless of what one saw, did, or heard.

In this way, discourse about Arnett as the archetypal reporter underscores the journalist's mastery of satellite-fed communication. Such a pattern is found in other critical incidents. Discourse about Woodward and Bernstein constitutes a personalized way of telling the story of Watergate (Woodward and Bernstein 1976), and stories about Edward R. Murrow mark discourse about World War II (Monroe 1991). Stories about Arnett thus humanize Gulf War discourse, lending a human element to tales that hail the advent of satellite-fed technology.

Has Journalism Changed?

In response to the Gulf War, the journalistic community has adapted to altered boundaries of journalistic practice in two ways: imitation and surrender. Discourse about CNN and Peter Arnett has made clear to members of the journalistic community that altered boundaries of appropriate practice are inevitable. It has called on them to consider new ways of adapting. Certain journalists and news organizations have chosen to imitate the news as it is produced by satellite-fed technology. They in effect have 'redefined themselves':

> During the opening days of the gulf war, viewers were never in need of greater cool, clear, informed reporting and analysis. . . . Yet for years now the networks have been busily tossing onto the streets the very researchers, producers, commentators and staff that could have helped carry out such a role (Katz 1991: 29).

For the first days of the war, the networks expanded their evening broadcasts to one hour, providing their version of what one journalist called 'saturation coverage': 'expanding their evening newscasts, preempting prime-time entertainment lineups and rushing stories onto the air as soon as possible' (Lieberman 1991: 14). Newspapers used eye-catching graphics, sidebars, boxes, maps, and special pull-out sections—a response to the increasing centrality of the visual element in news (Colin 1991). Even the *AP Log*, the in-house organ of the Associated Press, appended its own full page of graphics to its monthly newsletter ('The Persian Gulf Explodes', 1991).

Such practices persist today in expanded forms. Newspapers continue to favour the more visual packaging and informative graphics that many adopted during the war. On the international front, Sky News in Britain, the BBC's World Service Television, and the European Broadcasting Union's Euronews Channel offer versions of television news along lines suggested by CNN (Goodwin 1991). Veteran CBS producer Don Hewitt called for a general television news service, much like a visual wire service, that would supply the networks with the basic visual and factual frame of each news story (Alter 1991). A recent plane crash over a suburban Philadelphia school generated six hours of live television broadcasting, which, as one local journalist said, 'we might not have necessarily done without the lessons learned from CNN' (Guttman, 1991). Imitation suggests that CNN's rendition of the news has come to be seen as a viable, and worthwhile, form of transmission.

Other news organizations have elected to surrender to the demands suggested by CNN coverage. While CNN recently said it would spend over $2 million to open new bureaux in Amman, Rio de Janeiro, and New Delhi (Sharbutt 1991), network news organizations are closing bureaux. One NBC executive admitted that his network is no longer able to cover breaking news: 'We're not going back to covering everything that breaks. . . . We're not running after bus crashes. We're relying on our affiliates and our owned stations to cover that kind of story' (Sharbutt 1991: 5D). Interestingly, this gives CNN exclusivity on breaking news, as do attempts to explain shutdowns and other moves of adaptation as a recasting of journalistic practice.

Since the war ended, journalists' discussions of war coverage have taken on an increasingly critical stance. The Associated Press convened a special panel discussion on the Gulf War at its annual meeting, where it featured Peter Arnett as one of its speakers ('AP Annual Meeting', 1991). The American Society of Newspaper Editors' (ASNE) president used its monthly newsletter to ponder the effect of judging war correspondents 'on the basis of how they behave on television' (Osborne 1991: 2). The Association for Education in Journalism and Mass Communication published two divisional newsletters that separately pondered journalists' authority alongside ever-present television cameras and CNN's evolution as a 'new genre of news' (Atwood 1991; Haarsager 1991). All of this suggests that journalists have begun to use discussions about the Gulf War as a critical marker of appropriate journalistic practice, much like stories about the Kennedy assassination, Watergate, and Vietnam were used in earlier decades.

Two lines of thought continue to punctuate Gulf War discourse. One line still debates long-standing journalistic concerns about the appropriate boundaries of censorship, viability of pool arrangements, and degree of appropriate opposition to governmental curbs ('AP Annual Meeting', 1991; Hentoff 1991; Lewis 1991; McMasters 1991; Nathan 1991). Such discourse might have been appended to a number of conflicts in which the United States has been involved, including Grenada, Vietnam, or Panama.

But a second line of thought is specific to the Gulf War. It addresses the potentially dangerous liaison that has formed between CNN and the Gulf War, by which the war and CNN are seen to legitimate each other (Diamond 1991*a*; Malik 1991). Characterizations of the war—'the television war' (*Meet the Press*, 1991), the 'real-time war' (Kinsley 1991: 80), 'war in video *verité*' (Osborne 1991: 43), or the 'CNN war' (Capuzzo and Shister 1991: 14A)—are conflated with labels about CNN—'news without end' (Polman 1991: 26), a 'new kind of journalism' (quoted in Polman 1991: 26), or 'instantaneous journalism' (Kamen 1991: 27)—in discussions about the contemporary practices of American journalists.

CNN's role in the war has generated suggestions that its mode of news gathering signals an end to recognized journalistic practice and the beginning of a new era of journalism. While CNN insiders would certainly favor such a view, this article suggests that what is different about CNN's mode of news gathering is simply a matter of degree: CNN does not offer 'new' journalism, just faster, more continuous, less polished, and less edited journalism. Journalists continue to engage in generally the same activities of news gathering, although they may emphasize and reveal different aspects of the process for public viewing.

This discussion also suggests that viewing CNN's mode of news gathering as new journalism is historically myopic. Response to CNN's modes of news gathering parallels response to the ascent of television news 30 years ago (Zelizer 1990, 1993) and to expanded boundaries of investigative journalism a decade later (Schudson 1993). This suggests a need to attend more closely to the role of technology in generating journalistic authority. While technology provides a logical extension of the appropriate practices of journalism, reporters are able to negotiate their response to it through their discussions about critical incidents, yet maintain their professional identities. This means that rather than regard the Gulf War as an end to recognized forms of journalism, we need to accept the role of the Gulf War in providing a stage for journalists to reshape their professional practices in accordance with new preferred forms of technology. The Gulf War extends, rather than deadens, journalism as we know it.

It is within such a context that the Gulf War constitutes the beginnings of a critical incident for American journalists. Discussing the Gulf War offers reporters a stage on which to evaluate, negotiate, and ultimately reconsider ideas about professional practice and appropriate boundaries of journalistic authority. The American journalistic community is thereby using the Gulf War to choreograph tales of its own adaptation to satellite-fed communication. Only time will tell the extent to which that adaptation is beneficial, or dangerous—for CNN, for network television news, and for the journalistic community.

References   ALTER, J. (1991), 'When CNN Hits its Target', *Newsweek*, 28 Jan., 41.

AP Annual Meeting (13 May 1991). *AP Log*.

ARLEN, M. (1969), *Living-room war* (New York: Viking).

ATWOOD, R. (1991), 'War Provides case study re "objectivity"', *Clio: Among the Media* (Newsletter of History Division of AEJMC; Spring): 2.

'Best in the business: CNN best network for news' (1991). *Washington Journalism Review* (March): 44.

BOOT, W. (1991), 'Covering the Gulf War: The Press Stands Alone', *Columbia Journalism Review* (March/April), 23–4.

BRAESTRUP, P. (1977), *Big Story* (Boulder, Colo: Westview).

BROWNE, M. W. (1991), 'The military vs the press', *New York Times Magazine* (3 March): 27–30.

CAPUZZO, M., and SHISTER, G. (1991), '"The CNN war": Cable underdog scoops the big three', *Philadelphia Inquirer* (18 Jan.): 14A.

COLIN, T. J. (1991), 'As Television Glanced off the Story, Newspapers Surrounded It', *Washington Journalism Review* (March): 31–3.

COLLINS, M. (1991), 'News-Hungry Turn to Radio—It's a (S)hell of a Medium', *Washington Journalism Review* (March): 29.

COOPER, M. (1991), 'The Very Nervy Win of CNN', *U.S. News & World Report* (28 Jan.): 44.

DIAMOND, E. (1991a), 'Who Won the Media War?' *New York Magazine* (18 March): 26–9.

—— (1991b), 'How CNN Does It', *New York Magazine* (11 Feb.): 30–9.

Gannett Foundation (1991), *The Media at War: The Press and the Persian Gulf Conflict* (New York: Gannett Foundation Media Center).

GERBNER, G. (1973), 'Cultural Indicators: The Third Voice', in G. Gerbner, L. Gross, and W. Melody (eds.), *Communications Technology and Social Policy: Understanding the New 'cultural revolution'* (New York: Wiley).

GERGEN, D. (1991), 'Why America Hates the Press', *U.S. News & World Report* (11 March): 57.

GLASER, B., and STRAUSS, A. (1967), *The Discovery of Grounded Theory* (Chicago: Aldine).

GOODMAN, W. (1991), 'Arnett', *Columbia Journalism Review* (May/June): 29–31.

GOODWIN, P. (1991), 'News for the Taking', *TV World* (April): 31–3.

GRANGER, R. (1991), 'Media Defend News from Iraq', *Electronic Media* (25 Feb.): 1.

GREENFIELD, J. (1991), 'America Rallies Round the TV Set', *TV Guide* (16 Feb.): 4–7.

GUTTMAN, S. (1991), Interview with Michael Groulmin (30 April).

HAARSAGER, S. (1991), 'The Press and the Gulf War', *QS News* (Newsletter of the Qualitative Studies Division of AEJMC; Summer): 3.

HALBERSTAM, D. (1991), 'Where's Page 2 in TV News?' *New York Times* (21 Feb.): 1, 31.

HALONEN, D. (1991), 'Cronkite Calls for Greater Access, More Censorship', *Electronic Media* (25 Feb.): 3, 6–7.

HELLER, K. (1991), 'For CNN Reporter Peter Arnett, It's a Life on the Front Lines', *Philadelphia Inquirer* (1 Feb.): D1.

HENTOFF, N. (1991), 'When it was Time to Challenge the Military, where were the "Lords of the Press"?' *ASNE Bulletin* (May/June): 38–9.

KAMEN, J. (1991), 'CNN's Breakthrough in Baghdad: Live by Satellite (Censored)', *Washington Journalism Review* (March): 26–9.

KATZ, J. (1991), 'Covering the Gulf War: Collateral Damage to Network News', *Columbia Journalism Review* (March/April): 29.

KINSLEY, M. (1991), 'Trusting Ourselves with the News', *Time* (25 Feb.): 80.

LANDAU, S. (1991), 'The Real Nintendo Game', *The Progressive* (March): 26–8.

LEVI-STRAUSS, C. (1966), *The Savage Mind* (Chicago: University of Chicago Press).

LEWIS, C. J. (1991), 'The "City Editor" of the Persian Gulf was a Colonel', *ASNE Bulletin* (May/June): 14–23.

LIEBERMAN, D. (1991), 'With Its Desert Stand, CNN Charts the Course for TV News' Future', *TV Guide* (9 Feb.): 14–16.

LIEBERMAN, D., STEIN, L., and COLLINS, M. (1991), 'On the Firing Line, a Handful of Reporters Stake their Claim to Stardom', *TV Guide* (23 Feb.): 8–11.

MALIK, R. (1991), 'The Media's Gulf War: Notes and Issues', *Intermedia* (March/April): 4–7.

MASSING, M. (1991), 'Another front', *Columbia Journalism Review* (May/June): 23–4.

McMASTERS, P. (1991), 'Journalists Aren't Winning their Gulf War', *The Quill* (March): 8.

The Media and the Military (1991). PBS (21 Feb.).

Meet the Press (1991). NBC News Division, (27 Jan.).

MONROE, B. (1991), 'Peter Arnett: Anti-Hero of Baghdad', *Washington Journalism Review* (March): 6.

MOTT, P. (1991), 'New King of the Hill', *The Quill* (March): 14–16.

NATHAN, D. (1991). Just the Good News, Please', *The Progressive* (Feb.): 25–7.

OSBORNE, B. (1991). 'With Friends Like Us in the Press, the First Amendment Doesn't Need Any Enemies', *ASNE Bulletin* (March): 2, 43.

'The Persian Gulf Explodes' (2 Jan. 1991). *AP Log.*

POLMAN, D. (1991), 'News without End', *Philadelphia Inquirer Magazine* (19 March): 25–30.

The Press goes to War (with Bill Moyers) (1991). CNN Productions (26 Jan.).

PROCHNAN, W. (1991), 'If There's a War, He's There', *New York Times Magazine* (3 March): 30–4.

ROSENBERG, H. (1991), 'TV and the Gulf War', *The Quill* (March): 17–19.

ROSENSTIEL, T. (1991), 'Arnett Defends Baghdad Reporting', *Philadelphia Inquirer* (20 March): 12A.

SCHANBERG, S. H. (1991), 'Censoring for Political Reasons', *Washington Journalism Review* (March): 23–6.

SCHUDSON, M. (1978), *Discovering the News* (New York: Basic Books).

—— (1993), *Watergate in American Memory: How we Remember, Forget and Reconstruct the Past* (New York: Basic Books).

SHARBUTT, J. (1991), 'Cable News is on the Rise, while the Networks Retrench', *Philadelphia Inquirer* (26 July): 5D.

SHAW, R. (1991), 'Secret CNN Journey Ends in Exclusive Hussein Broadcast', *Electronic Media* (4 Feb.): 1.

STEIN, L. (1991), 'Tales from the Front: The Glitches and Hitches in Bringing the War to your Living Room', *TV Guide* (16 Feb.): 8–11.

'The Story behind the Story' (1991). *Newsweek*, Special Commemorative Issue on 'Americans At War' (Spring/Summer): 3.

VALERIANI, R. (1991), 'Covering the Gulf War: Talking back to the Tube', *Columbia Journalism Review* (March/April) 24–8.

War in the Gulf (1991). CNN promotional pamphlet (March): 1, 11, 13, 23.

WOODWARD, B., and BERNSTEIN, C. (1976), *The Final Days* (New York: Simon and Schuster).

YAARI, E. (1991), 'The Role of the Media in the Gulf War. Roundtable Discussion at the International Symposium on the Media, Protest and Political Violence, Jerusalem, Israel (12 June).

ZELIZER, B. (1990), 'Achieving Journalistic Authority through Narrative', *Critical Studies in Mass Communication* 7(4): 37–48.

—— (1993). '*Covering the Body*': *The Kennedy Assassination and the Establishment of Journalistic Authority* (Chicago: University of Chicago Press).

ZOGLIN, R. (1991a), 'Live from the Middle East', *Time* (28 Jan.): 69–71.

—— (1991b), 'How Dailies Cover a TV War', *Time* (11 Feb.): 78.

—— (1991c), 'Volleys on the Information Front', *Time* (4. Feb.): 44–5.

37

Global Communications Controversies

Robert G. Picard

THE GROWING INTERNATIONALIZATION of communications during the twentieth century, combined with the emergence of new nations in search of autonomy and identity, has resulted in extensive discussions and criticisms of the roles of media and other communications systems in domestic and international life worldwide. [...]

Much of the criticism from emerging and developing nations in Africa, Asia, and Latin America has focused on the preponderance of information and its control by firms from developed nations, especially private companies in Western nations. These criticisms began to spread rapidly as the breakdown of the colonial system progressed in the three decades after World War II, spurred by independence and nationalist movements in Africa, Asia, and Latin America. The success of such movements brought about the establishment of scores of new countries whose government structures, as well as educational, communications, and other cultural institutions, had been established during colonial times to serve the interests of the colonizing country and its citizens.

The newly emerged countries faced the choice of continuing existing institutions, altering and expanding those institutions to meet new needs, or establishing entirely new institutions to meet government, educational, communications, and cultural needs. [...]

Emerging Nations and the NWICO

As governments began to attempt to use communications systems to carry out national social, political, and economic goals, it became evident that significant hurdles lay in their paths. Problems included the lack of necessary communications technology, the lack of frequencies for broadcast communications because they were already occupied by communications systems in developed countries, the inability of existing media to meet the new needs of the nations, and the overwhelming nature and effects of external communications systems. Differences in ideology about the roles and functions of

Source: Robert G. Picard, 'Global Communications Controversies', in John C. Merrill (ed.), *Global Journalism*, 2nd edn. (New York and London: Longman, 1991).

various media in society, the financial support available for communications systems, and the nature of government and social controls worldwide also became apparent.

At the same time, the actual and potential applications of increasingly sophisticated electronic technology worldwide concerned both developing and developed nations. The ability to transmit communications across borders using shortwave and other frequencies and to reach large regions from direct-broadcast satellites gave all with access to technology the ability to engage in significant external and internal broadcasting. National sovereignty and other international issues relating to rights to send such broadcasts, to control their reception, to regulate propaganda, and to interfere with other broadcasts arose as a result of the new capabilities.

Such problems set off significant discussions in the International Telecommunication Union (ITU), the United Nations Educational, Scientific, and Cultural Organization (UNESCO), and other organizations. These issues were subsumed in discussions of proposals that are now known as the New World Information and Communications Order (NWICO), the New International Information Order (NIIO), or the New World Information Order (NWIO), and these discussions have included vociferous debates involving news gathering and dissemination by media as well.

Basic Criticisms of the Present Order

The primary criticism of journalistic information contained in the NWICO has been the near monopolization of international information by the Associated Press, United Press International, Reuters, and Agence France-Presse. Because of the unavailability of other news services, or their inability to provide sufficient information about events worldwide, media across the globe were forced in the 1950s, 1960s, and 1970s to subscribe to the services of the major news agencies. A similar dominance existed in television news, where two major Western suppliers provided news video worldwide. Visnews, owned by the British Broadcasting Corp. and Reuters, and UPITN, owned by Independent Television News and United Press International, provided most of the world's television with video for use in news shows.

Developing world media and newly independent governments have been highly critical of this situation, arguing that coverage from the major services contains ethnocentric occidental values that affect its content and presentation. Coverage from these media most often include political, economic, Judeo-Christian religious, and other social values that are not universal. Thus, critics argued, news from these services became a form of cultural imperialism. In addition, developing world media and governments have argued that Western ethnocentrism creates an unequal flow of information by providing a large stream of information about events in the developed world but only a very small flow from the developing world.

A related criticism has been that when news is conveyed from the developing world, it invariably conveys negative images because it focuses on the unusual, on disasters, on corruption, or on conflict. Critics argued that little information was conveyed on progress in national development, and most nations never appeared in the news. Observers in developing world nations argued that Western definitions of news and the emphasis on reporting isolated events thus created perceptions and images of nations and citizens that did not accurately portray reality and harmed efforts to improve economic and social life. These critics argued that this problem was especially critical because of the developing nations' dependence on the major wire services for news about themselves and their neighbours.

At the same time, news media and others in Western nations voiced their own criticism of international communications. A primary complaint was that Western journalists' abilities to cover much of the developing world and developed communist nations has been impeded by the lack of access resulting from government restrictions and by direct efforts to censor reports. Attacks on journalists, arrests and detentions, visa denials and expulsions, and harassment have been, and continue to be, common means used by governments worldwide to halt or restrict coverage deemed harmful to their interests.

The increasing reliance of developed world media on high-technology communications systems, such as satellite uplinks, cellular telephones, and computer systems requiring data-quality transmission lines, has also created tension between foreign media and governments worldwide. Because every government has its own national policies and regulations on the use of electromagnetic spectrum and electronic technology, conflicts occur over the use and control of such equipment as journalists move about the world. Western media, which have had the opportunity to adopt these technologies faster than media in other parts of the world, have been especially critical of governments that have restricted the use of such equipment.

Actions to Address Criticisms

A variety of national and international efforts, both public and private, have been instituted in response to some of the difficulties and problems plaguing communications in developing and developed nations.

A result of the criticisms of dependence on Western news organizations has been the growth of interest in and use of non-Western news services and news exchanges. Two news services created specifically to overcome the objections of developing nations are the Non-Aligned News Agency (NANA) and Inter-Press Service (IPS). NANA was created in 1976 to link the national news agencies of non-aligned nations into a news pool that provides news with non-Western perspectives and values. The agency is operated for the non-aligned nations by Tanjug, the national news agency of Yugoslavia. Its staff gathers material from the participating national news agencies, translates stories, and then distributes the combined worldwide news back to participating news agencies. IPS was started in 1964 by Latin-American media interested in gaining information on government programmes and policies worldwide, especially those dealing with development issues. Similar efforts to promote new exchange among television systems have developed, including an exchange programme operated by the Broadcasting Organization of the Non-Aligned Countries.

A significant number of regional news exchanges similar to the NANA and IPS have developed, including the Pan-African News Agency (PANA), Caribbean News Agency (CANA), and Asian-Pacific News Network (ANN).

Many joint efforts have resulted from international regional broadcasting organizations such as the Arab States Broadcasting Union (ASBU), Asian Broadcasting Union (ABU), European Broadcasting Union (EBU), International Radio and Television Organization of Eastern Europe (OIRT), and Union of National Radio and Television Organizations of Africa (URTNA). A number of existing news agencies in the developed and developing world have also benefited from the increased interest in non-Western media, including TASS, the agency of the Soviet Union; Xinhua, the Chinese news agency; and the Egyptian-based Middle East News Agency (MENA). Several Western agencies that had not previously been widely used also have benefited from the criticism of news control by the so-called Big Four agencies. Agencia EFE, the Spanish news agency, has become a major supplier of news throughout Latin America, and Deutsche Presse-Agentur of West Germany has also been well received worldwide.

Although the development and maturation of new types of news agencies and news exchanges have provided alternative sources of material based on and containing some different values and news definitions, thus altering and increasing information worldwide, these new services have tended to provide coverage that focuses on hard news events and political stories, just as traditional news agencies have. In addition, the major criticisms of major Western and developed world media continue to be voiced, and their norms and types of coverage have changed very little. As a result, international communications continues to provoke controversy and generate efforts to affect the flow of information.

Major Participants in Communications Debates

A variety of international organizations and journalistic associations have played, and continue to play, important roles in the discussions about international communications and journalism. Organizations representing journalists, publishers, and broadcasters have been deeply involved, and groups representing various ideologies have also been active. Although each group has had its own purposes, much of their involvement in international communication issues has revolved around efforts by UNESCO to deal with criticism and problems in the developing world for the past two decades.

Important participants in these international communications discussions have included the Inter American Press Association, International Federation of Journalists, International Federation of Newspaper Publishers, International Organization of Journalists, International Press Institute, ITU, Movement of Non-Aligned Countries, UNESCO, and World Press Freedom Committee. [...]

The Key Controversy: NWICO

No international communication issue has generated more controversy in the past two decades than efforts by members of MNAC and UNESCO to promulgate the New World Information and Communication Order. NWICO is not a unified, well-defined programme for change in communications but rather a philosophical approach to the role of communications

that has become manifest in various international discussions and documents. It is based on the idea that unless communication capabilities are significantly improved, less developed nations cannot accomplish meaningful
economic, political, and social development that will improve the standard
of living of their citizens. Proponents of the concept have argued that successful development is dependent on improvements in two areas, international communications and domestic communications.

Proponents of the NWICO argue that the economic interdependence of
nations, recognized only in the second half of the twentieth century, gives advantages to nations that have strong international communications capabilities involving telephone, data transmission, and satellite communications.
The ability of citizens of nations rapidly to gather and transmit information
of all kinds, including news, affects their ability to participate in world commerce and political and cultural life.

Leaders of the non-aligned nations began studying needs and objectives.
Because of policies of developed nations and private ownership of much
communications technology worldwide, they quickly understood that access or equal access to international communications technology and capabilities was required.

Development officials also understood the need to develop internal communications capabilities, ranging from telephone to broadcasting systems. A
significant focus of MNAC and international development discussions soon
became developing broadcast and print media that would be used primarily
for educational and informational purposes, rather than entertainment. In
addition, they envisioned use of these media to help build national unity and
a sense of community.

The basic philosophical tenet of NWICO is that each nation must become
self-reliant in communications capabilities so that it is not dependent on
other nations and thus cannot be held subservient. The NWICO also adheres
to the ideal that in developing domestic communications capabilities, each
nation has the right to determine what the communications system within its
boundaries will be, what should be communicated, and to what end. Implicit
in this ideal is the view that there are differences in communications functions in nations and that the differences are particularly evident in less developed nations that wish consciously to use media as tools to promote national
economic growth, to develop and preserve national culture, and to create a
cohesive national identity among diverse and often antagonistic ethnic,
tribal, and religious groups.

Efforts by MNAC to draw UNESCO into efforts to promote and achieve
such international communications changes have resulted in an international struggle in that worldwide organization that has pitted many Western
nations against nations in MNAC and the Eastern bloc. The concept of using
media and communications systems in such a fashion conflicted with Western liberal views of press freedom and desires to limit government influence
on and control of communications. As a result, Western nations, especially
the United States and others with highly commercialized, non-
governmental communications systems, responded to some NWICO ideas
and developments negatively.

During the late 1970s and early 1980s, much of the discussion became couched in cold war rhetoric that included charges that the NWICO was Soviet-inspired and -supported. The Soviet Union and its allies admittedly supported the concepts behind the NWICO and provided assistance to MNAC nations in helping to make it a significant UNESCO issue. It is clear, however, that MNAC was the instigator of the concept. Support from the Soviet Union, Eastern bloc nations, China, and other communist nations came because communist philosophy embraces the use of communications as an agent for social change and ideological development. These nations were also unwilling to oppose the NWICO's philosophy of self-determination, which they, along with the United States, support but have rarely followed.

The outlines of the NWICO began to emerge in the 1960s as the decolonized nations were established. By the early 1970s, the director general of UNESCO, Amadou-Mahtar M'Bow of Senegal, suggested that the organization begin supporting the MNAC efforts to formulate national communication policies. When the general conference of UNESCO was held in 1972, the Soviet Union presented the 'Draft Declaration on the Use of the Mass Media', which supported the use of media as a tool of the state instead of its operation as an independent institution. In 1974, discussion of the issue became highly politicized, and the United States and three dozen nations, mostly Western, boycotted discussions when UNESCO delegates voted to place in the preamble to the declaration language equating Zionism with racism.

Action on the declaration was delayed for several years as the leadership of UNESCO consulted and mediated disputes between the West and the developing and Eastern nations. The result was the establishment of UNESCO's International Commission for the Study of Communications Problems, popularly known as the McBride Commission because it was led by the respected Irish diplomat Sean McBride.

UNESCO's 1978 Declaration

While the commission's work was under way, UNESCO's general conference in 1978 agreed on the 'Declaration of Fundamental Principles concerning the Contribution of the Mass Media to Strengthening Peace and International Understanding, to the Promotion of Human Rights, and to Countering Racialism, Apartheid and Incitement of War'. The declaration was viewed as a victory by Western, Eastern, and non-aligned nations alike. Western nations were pleased that it removed earlier indications that the press should be controlled by the state. Eastern and Communist states were pacified because it did not contain criticisms of the use of journalism to promote political agendas. Non-aligned nations supported the declaration because it included promises of technical assistance in the development of communications.

News of UNESCO's efforts gained the attention of Western news agencies and publishers' organizations, especially the International Press Institute and International Federation of Newspaper Publishers, which began organizing and pressuring their governments for not taking a strong stance against certain elements emerging from the discussion of international communication policy. Western journalists' groups argued that UNESCO's activities were merely a means of legitimizing government control of media and that the organization was paying too much attention to the power and use of the press and not enough attention to freedom of the press. Leading these critics was the International Federation of Journalists. In order to monitor developments and organize opposition more effectively, the publishers', broadcasters', and journalists' organizations joined together to form the World Press Freedom Committee.

The McBride Commission Report

In 1980, the general conference of UNESCO in Belgrade, Yugoslavia, heard the findings of the McBride Commission on contemporary communications problems and international and domestic communications issues. The report made eighty-two recommendations related to the human right to communicate, needs for diversity of opinion, free flow of information, and access to news. It included recognition of the need for each nation to develop comprehensive national communication policies and structures including news agencies, broadcasting networks, book publishers, and communications training institutions, and warned nations against dependence on foreign information sources.

Some Western nations, led by the United States, were troubled by elements in the report that urged governments to set up communications agencies and showed a bias against private communications media. Although agreeing that concentration of ownership and media mortality due to the competitive economic system were undesirable elements of commercialized media, representatives of some Western nations argued that these negative elements were balanced by the political freedom obtained by not having a state monopoly on media.

Despite such reservations, the Belgrade conference unanimously passed a resolution that set down the principles of the NWICO. The resolution called for media to be responsible and for a balanced flow of information worldwide. The resolution and NWICO are based on the view that the major Western news services dominate coverage of the world, set the world news agenda, and distort the picture of the world by focusing on news in developed nations. In addition, it embraced the view that dominance of the world's communication by Western information and entertainment media threatens national identity and slows development because it is based on Western attitudes and interests. The NWICO also criticizes the definition of news used by Western media for its focus on negative developments such as political instability, natural disasters, and policy failures. This emphasis, NWICO supporters argued, harms efforts to foster social, economic, and political values that promote development and to convey information on domestic and international programs designed to improve education, family planning, agricultural practices, and industrialization.

Western Reactions

Although the Belgrade resolution received wide support, few people were happy with it in its entirety. Western diplomats, especially those from the Federal Republic of Germany, the United Kingdom, and the United States, disagreed with phrases that the developing world and Soviet bloc interpreted as giving UNESCO the right to regulate news organizations and acknowledging news as a commodity that governments could control. They also perceived the concept of a balanced flow of information as conflicting with the free flow of information. Developing nations and the Soviet bloc were unhappy with watered-down provisions that did not provide funds for procurement of communications technology for developing nations or provide significant cost advantages in the use of international communications systems.

The unease of Western nations about UNESCO's efforts increased in 1981 when the organization sponsored a meeting to discuss a proposal for a commission for the protection of journalists. Although representatives of the West were concerned about attacks on journalists worldwide and agreed that international standards for identifying and protecting journalists might be helpful, they disagreed with proposals that the commission set regulations for journalists, be empowered to investigate reporters' conduct, and revoke identification cards of journalists not adhering to international standards.

Concern about the possible creation of such a commission led representatives of news media and journalistic organizations from Western nations and their supporters to meet in Talloires, France, at the invitation of the WPFC and Tufts University to organize opposition to UNESCO plans. As part of their meeting they issued the 'Declaration of Talloires', which upheld press freedom and the right to be informed as basic human rights, expressed concerns about censorship, and indicated opposition to international and national efforts that elevated government interests above individual interests by requiring journalists to obtain licenses or to adhere to codes of ethics or behaviour.

The Western media groups involved in the NWICO discussions gave heavy coverage to the declaration, as they had to UNESCO meetings dealing with the concepts during the late 1970s and early 1980s. The coverage focused significantly on perceived threats to their abilities to cover world events and press freedoms. Several reviews of coverage, including one by the US National News Council, revealed that the coverage of UNESCO's activities was highly distorted and biased.

Efforts to counteract the Western media attack on NWICO were launched by journalists' organizations in countries associated with MNAC and the Eastern bloc. The International Organization of Journalists, Federation of Arab Journalists, Federation of Latin American Journalists, and others asserted that the NWICO and its provisions were not intended to support censorship or control of communications but to improve communications. The campaign did not comfort or dissuade opponents from their positions, however.

The news coverage and pressure from Western media and journalists' groups soon gained significant support from the Reagan administration in the United States and the Thatcher administration in the United Kingdom, due in part to their strong anti-government ideologies. Concurrently, criticism of the growth of the bureaucracy of UNESCO and the unwillingness or inability of its leadership to control its expenses was rising within the international community. In 1983, the United States responded by withdrawing from UNESCO, followed by the United Kingdom in 1984, citing the body's ideological outlook on communications as inappropriate and the failure of the organization to manage its finances. The withdrawal cost the organization more than $50 million annually; the United States had been its largest financial contributor.

The financial crisis created by the departure of the two Western members and other pressing matters held the attention of UNESCO's staff through the mid-1980s, and implementation of the International Programme for the Development of Communications (IPDC) kept staff and others interested in communications from reviving the NWICO debate significantly. By the late 1980s, the impetus for using UNESCO to promote NWICO had waned, and the new secretary general, Federico Mayor, promulgated a communication plan that did not include most of the elements that have disturbed Western nations and journalists.

References BOYD-BARRETT, OLIVER, *The International News Agencies* (Newbury Park, Calif.: Sage, 1980).

BROWNE, DONALD, *International Radio Broadcasting* (New York: Praeger, 1982).

DESMOND, ROBERT W., *The Information Process: World News Reporting in the Twentieth Century* (Ames: Iowa State University Press, 1978).

FENBY, JONATHAN, *The International News Services* (New York: Schocken Books, 1986).

GARBO, GUNNAR, *A World of Difference: The International Distribution of Information: The Media and Developing Countries* (Documents on Communication and Society, No. 15. Paris: UNESCO, 1985).

GERBNER, GEORGE (ed.), *Mass Media Policies in Changing Cultures* (New York: Wiley, 1977).

—— and MARSHA SIEFERT (eds.), *World Communications: A Handbook* (White Plains, NY: Longman, 1984).

HACHTEN, WILLIAM, *The World News Prism: Changing Media, Clashing Ideologies*, 2nd edn. (Ames: Iowa State University Press, 1987).

HEAD, SYDNEY W., *World Broadcasting Systems: A Comparative Analysis* (Belmont, Calif.: Wadsworth, 1985).

HORTON, PHILIP C. (ed.), *The Third World and Press Freedom* (New York: Praeger, 1981).

HOWELL, W. J., Jr., *World Broadcasting in the Age of the Satellite* (Norwood, NJ: Ablex, 1986).

International Commission for the Study of Communication Problems. 'Many Voices, One World' (New York: Unipub, 1980).

JAMIESON, DEAN T., and MCANANY, EMILE G., *Radio for Education and Development* (Newbury Park, Calif.: Sage, 1978).

KATZ, ELIHU, and WEDELL, GEORGE, *Broadcasting in the Third World: Promise and Performance* (Cambridge, Mass.: Harvard University Press, 1977).

KATZ, ELIHU, and SZECSKO, TAMAS (eds.), *Mass Media and Social Change* (Newbury Park, Calif.: Sage, 1981).

LEE, CHIN-CHAUN, *Media Imperialism Reconsidered* (Newbury Park, Calif.: Sage, 1980).

MARTIN, L. JOHN, and CHAUDHARY, ANJU GROVER (eds.), *Comparative Mass Media Systems* (White Plains, NY: Longman, 1983).

MARTIN, L. JOHN, and HIEBERT, RAY ELDON, *Current Issues in International Communication* (White Plains, NY: Longman, 1990).

McPhail, Thomas L., *Electronic Colonialism: The Future of International Broadcasting and Communication*, 2nd edn. (Newbury Park, Calif.: Sage, 1987).

Mowlana, Hamid, *International Flow of Information: A Global Report and Analysis* (Reports and Papers on Mass Communication, No. 99. Paris: UNESCO, 1985).

—— *Global Information and World Communication* (White Plains, N.Y.: Longman, 1986).

Murphy, Sharon, Atwood, E., and Bullion, S. (eds.), *International Perspectives on News* (Carbondale: Southern Illinois University Press, 1982).

Nordenstreng, Kaarle, *The Mass Media Declaration of UNESCO* (Norwood, NJ: Ablex, 1984).

—— and Schiller, Herbert I., *National Sovereignty and International Communication* (Norwood, NJ: Ablex, 1979).

Picard, Robert G., 'Discipline of Foreign Correspondents', *FOI Center Report*, 448 (1981).

—— 'Private Mass Communications, Development Aid: An Analysis of Projects of Three Western Organizations', In Mekki Mtewa (ed.), *Perspectives in International Development* (New Delhi: Allied Publishers, 1986), 229–39.

Righter, Rosemary, *Whose News? Politics, the Press and the Third World* (New York: Times Books, 1978).

Rogers, Everett, *Communication of Innovations*, 3rd edn. (New York: Free Press, 1985).

Smith, Anthony, *The Geopolitics of Information: Problems of Policy in Modern Media* (London: Macmillan, 1978).

Schiller, Herbert I, *Communication and Cultural Domination* (Armonk, NY: Sharpe, 1976).

Sreberny-Mohammadi, Annabelle, Nordenstreng, Kaarle, Stevenson, Robert L., and Ugboajah, Frank, *Foreign News in the Media: International Reporting in 29 Countries* (Reports and Papers on Mass Communication, No. 93. Paris: UNESCO, 1985).

Twentieth-Century Fund Taskforce on the International Flow of News. *A Free and Balanced Flow* (Lexington, Mass.: Lexington Books, 1978).

Wiio, Osmo A., *Open and Closed Mass Media Systems and Problems of International Communication Policy* (Tokyo: Studies of Broadcasting, NHK, 1977).

Wildman, Steven S., and Siwek, Stephen E., *International Trade in Films and Television Programs* (Cambridge, Mass.: Ballinger (American Enterprise Institute Trade in Services Series), 1988).

World Press Freedom Committee. *The Media Crisis* (Miami, 1980; 2nd edn., Washington, DC, 1982).

38

Public Journalism and Public Life: Why Telling the News Is Not Enough

Davis Merritt

Introduction

■ **This Should Scare You. . . .**

A SURVEY FROM THE *Yankelovich Monitor* asked citizens 'In which of these do you find that you have great confidence?'

	1988 (%)	1993 (%)
Doctors	71	63
Federal government	18	12
State government	12	9
Local government	15	10
Advertising	8	8
Religious leaders	38	26
News reports on TV	55	25
News in newspapers	50	20
News in magazines	38	12

(Yankelovich Partners 1993: 20)

In a time of declining trust in virtually all institutions, journalism's decline is by far the steepest. The respondents to a survey such as this have no way of knowing whether the news they read and hear is accurate or not, but they know it is not useful. People will not place trust in something they feel is not helpful to them in solving their problems.

Similarly, a 1994 national survey from The Times-Mirror Center for The People and The Press asked 'Which of the following two statements about the news media do you agree with more . . . (a) "The news media helps society to solve its problems" [25%] or (b) "The news media gets in the way of society solving its problems" [71%]' (Times-Mirror 1994: 121). One could hardly conjure up a more devastating negative judgement about any institution—that it stands in the way of improving life in America.

These two surveys produced other results worth serious thought. In 1988,

Source: Davis Merritt, *Public Journalism and Public Life: Why Telling The News Is Not Enough* (Hillsdale, NJ: Lawrence Erlbaum Assocs., 1995).

55 per cent of Americans said they were dissatisfied with the way things were going in the nation. By 1993, that number had risen to 75 per cent. In both those years, however, 68 per cent agreed with the statement, 'As Americans, we can always find a way to solve our problems' (p. 135).

■ **This Should Give You Ideas . . . and Hope**

In dozens of towns and cities across America from 1992 to 1994, the journalists who produce newspapers decided that telling the news was not enough. Many of them had been telling, for years, even decades, the news of unresolved local and national problems, of a political system in disrepair and disrepute, of a society relentlessly withdrawing into narrow personal concerns. Their response to the feelings reflected in the chilling statistics previously discussed was to re-examine their traditional role as the detached teller of news, to imagine ways in which their unique place in American society and law gave them leverage to contribute more than information.

This was not a small step. For decades, the pervasive model of American journalism has been one of distance, of the deliberate disconnection between journalists and the events and people they write about. Moving beyond that detachment required their rethinking some of the cultural axioms under which they operate.

In Akron and Dayton, in Charlotte and San Francisco, in Boston and Tallahassee and Norfolk and Bremerton and dozens of other places, editors and reporters discovered that the communities in which they newspapered in fact contained the will and brains to address those long-standing problems, but lacked the tools and capacity to do so. Those newspapers thus moved beyond cool neutrality and detachment, acted as if they belonged where they were and cared about that place, began treating people as citizens rather than consumers, risked the approbation—if not condemnation—of many of their peers, and helped make things better. None of them solved 'the crime problem' or revolutionized education or helped reach economic or racial nirvana, but by adopting a purposefulness beyond merely telling the news, they began the long and testing process of revitalizing public life in their communities. That revitalization is the only hope for eventual progress on those and other seemingly perpetual ills.

The journalists and their newspapers were not taking that step onto barren ground. The Yankelovich Monitor for 1994—2-hour, personal interviews with 4,000 Americans—seemed to be picking up slight but potentially significant indications of a shift away from some of the toxic attitudes that characterized the American psyche in the 1980s and 1990s. Although the budding trends are subject to both further analysis and to change by sudden circumstances, the survey indicated:

A potential lessening of:
    Distrust
    Victim syndrome
    Relentless stress
    Gender warfare
And hints of:
    Optimism
    Bottoming out of cynicism

A new demand for accountability
Less whining about life in general

The survey also detected an increase in the acknowledgement of a personal obligation to make a contribution to the community, a growing realization of personal responsibility for outcomes, and, interestingly, an inclination toward fun, to explore 'the up side' of life. If those indications are real, they represent an even greater, and unexpected, opportunity for journalists. The issue for journalism in America, and in a consequential way for America as a whole, however, is how to respond to the beliefs and attitudes reflected in all of the above findings. [. . .]

Why Change?   Begin with the proposition that public life—the way in which our democracy is expressed and experienced—is not going well. Our formal politics, which is only one part of public life, is sodden and largely ineffective. Many Americans view it as being a world apart from their realities, as already subjected to a hostile takeover by special interests and professional politicians. The other part of public life—our civic ethic—is largely inward-looking, as Americans isolate themselves in their own narrow concerns and seek safety and solace in insular communities and activities.

The gap between citizen and government has grown. Citizens do not trust their governments to properly tend to important matters (see the introduction), but are increasingly less inclined because of the pressures of their personal lives to tend to them themselves.

Meanwhile, the dispiriting list of long-standing national problems such as crime, a lagging educational system, dysfunctional families, and environmental deterioration grows rather than shrinks. Discussions about solutions degenerate into shouting matches across an ideological gap that is a false construct of extremes designed by politicians and perpetuated by journalists. Such false framing leaves citizens little hope for resolution of their problems, and, worse, virtually insures that nothing good can happen. This occurs because the presentation of issues as having only extreme solutions attracts some citizens to one or the other of the poles, whereas it convinces others, the majority who tend toward the middle ground on most issues, that they and their more moderate views are not and cannot be part of the debate. Either way, true deliberation that can lead to consent about important issues is foreclosed; so the problems persist year after year, decade after decade.

As a result, in the 1980s, a majority of Americans expressed for the first time the opinion that their children would inherit a society less livable, more dangerous, and offering less opportunity than they had. It was an unprecedented negative judgement—far more profound and devastating than mere pessimism.

Not coincidentally, for the first time since 1924, only half of the nation's registered voters bothered to vote for president in 1988. Furthermore, in 1994, The Times-Mirror Center for the People and the Press reported that 71 per cent of Americans agreed with the statement 'The news media gets in the way of society solving its problems.' Only 25 per cent agreed that the news media 'helps society solve its problems' (p. 178).

Economics formed a part of citizens' unease with the future, but forces less cyclical and more corrosive than a lax economy were at work on the citizens' mind and soul. Various commentators diagnosed the slide toward the precipice from their particular points of view, including a slackening of religious and moral values; government gridlock; the restructuring of traditional family life; the dissolution of community spawned by short-sighted, auto-based sprawl; the yen; the deutsche mark; even vibrations from a rogue comet, still unseen, hurtling toward the earth.

Any one of the dozens or hundreds of theories is as spinnable as any other, for each winds up dealing with only one dimension of a multidimensional problem: Public life—democracy—is not fulfilling its historic promise.

Like other Americans, many journalists are troubled. Many of the people who entered newspaper journalism in the mid-20th century, and most of those who succeeded at it, shared a vision. Journalism, we sensed, mattered; it was an integral part of the democratic process; it had purpose. That core importance gave substance and meaning to an otherwise low-paying trade.

By 1993, one in five working journalists told pollsters that they would probably leave the field within five years, a number twice that of figures found in 1982 and 1983 (Weaver and Wilhoit 1992). These numbers reflect an increasing decline in job satisfaction. Journalism, the respondents are saying, will not matter enough in the future. Its core importance is eroded and its purposefulness lost, making it simply one literary and visual trade among many.

Part of this disillusionment stems from the state in which journalism and the economic structures that support journalism find themselves. By nearly every measure, the journalistic product—newspapers, broadcast news, magazines—is not believed and our motives not trusted. The economic bases—primarily advertising—of the business structures that support journalism are disintegrating.

It is no coincidence that the decline in journalism and the decline in public life have happened at the same time. In modern society, they are codependent: public life needs the information and perspective that journalism can provide, and journalism needs a viable public life because without one there is no need for journalism.

Thus journalism and the people in the field face a challenge. If we are to leave our country a better place than we found it and secure our profession's future, a great deal must change.

My biases should be understood at the outset. I believe:

- Journalism in all its forms ignores its obligations to effective public life.
- That failure has been a major contributor to the resultant malaise in public life.
- Journalism should be—and can be—a primary force in the revitalization of public life.
- However, fundamental change in the profession—cultural, generational change—is necessary for that to occur.

I do not contend that journalists alone can be—or should be—the primary moving force, just as we were not the sole actors in the decline. People in general and politicians in particular were co-conspirators. Nor do I suggest that most of present journalistic practice needs to be abandoned. Our modern practices are not so much defective as they are insufficient. The reporting, sorting, and analysing of news are important functions; they simply are not the only—or even the most important—ones for us.

Journalism contains, at least for now, the power either to cultivate or thwart a healthy public life. Without fundamental change within the profession, the latter will continue.

There is, of course, a possible alternative. By remaining on its present insufficient and restricted course, journalism will make itself wholly irrelevant. A society that considers journalism to be only an irritating appurtenance or a negative burden rather than an interested stakeholder will look elsewhere for ways of getting the information necessary for that society to function. The Information Superhighway clearly suggests that possibility, while offering journalists an opportunity to re-establish the profession's core importance and authority that should be its contribution to public life.

To do this, we must clarify our own values, realize the true context of our work, and begin to look at ourselves in a different way. This book thus argues for a redefinition of journalism.

I suggest the revitalization of public life as a broad purpose for journalism and journalists. For no matter the state of individual morals, the efforts of government, the structure of families, the rise or fall of the yen and the Deutschmark, the course of a menacing comet—if public life does not go well, if communities cannot act collectively and effectively to solve problems, Americans' fears about the future will surely be realized. And no matter what we do as journalists, if people are not attentive to public life, if they continue to retreat into only private concerns, they will have no need for journalists or journalism.

Conversely, we can help revitalize public life and restore the core importance to our profession by becoming fair-minded participants in public life rather than detached observers. ('Fair-minded participant' does not mean wholesale involvement in the affairs that we cover. It is a much more limited concept.)

I do not propose a formula; if one exists, it has yet to be discovered. Based on recent trends in journalism, we need to be extremely sceptical of quick fixes that do not involve fundamental change.

So this is not a 'how to' manual, it is a 'why' discussion. I try to imagine a journalism that is extended—one that has purpose beyond merely 'telling the news'—and an audience that intelligently uses a revitalized journalistic product to help public life go well. How that idea is made concrete depends on the courage and imagination of the wonderfully varied, fiercely independent minds who make it their job to keep people informed.

My purpose is not to try to describe or encourage a particular device or set of practices. To do so would, in itself, limit the possibilities. Rather, my purpose is to stimulate thoughtful, serious discussion both inside and outside the profession about journalism's true place in a democracy. The aim isn't to provide, even if I could, immediate and specific answers. Journalism and public life did not reach their points of present decline quickly, and they will not recover quickly. Those specific answers will have to be found over time and through earnest experimentation. Recovery, however, is possible, and, as the end of the twentieth century approaches, there are reasons for optimism.

Americans' general disgust with and withdrawal from public life nevertheless includes some early signs of maturing into a determination to change the way things presently work. The emerging communitarian movement, changes in corporate processes to empower workers, experimentation in new ways to operate public schools, growing discussion of new ways of organizing living places and communities, increased pressure for community policing, and the founding of support groups are all signs of an awakening, although it seems ever so slight, of America's civic ethic.

Such movement will continue to occur, with or without journalism's recognition and help. It will go much better, however, accomplish more in a shorter time, and advance into more areas of public life if journalists recognize the importance of such movement, validate it as newsworthy (which it most certainly is by any but the most pinched definition), and understand how it coincides with the self-interests of journalists in all their roles—as citizens and practitioners, and partners in an economic venture. Getting to such a point will be a difficult, contentious, and, most surely, indirect journey, but we must begin.

■ Journalism's Role in Democracy

In order to begin, it is necessary to understand the appropriate role of journalism in a modern democracy. Participatory democracy is a function of community. One person alone could not conceive of democracy and, indeed, would have no need of it. However, two or more people with common interests—a community—require democracy if they are to exist in freedom and equity.

Jointly deciding about things—and that is the purpose of democracy—is a dynamic that requires three fundamentals:

1. Shared, relevant information.

2. A method or place for deliberation about the application of that information to public affairs.

3. Shared values on which to base decisions about that information.

If any one of these is missing, democratic decision-making cannot occur and the democratic community cannot progress. Some call it gridlock.

The last years of the twentieth century provide disturbing indications that the necessary shared information and a common place for discussing it are no longer givens. Without those components, values are mere shibboleths that are likely to define and perpetuate differences rather than take advantage of commonalities.

■ What 'Information' . . . ?

Perversely, the component of shared information is endangered by the very pervasiveness of information itself. In the 1990s, we are nearing a state of paralysis caused by the gush of information—raw data—that technology makes possible. The paralysis arises not in the nature of the information flow itself, for it is benign even if overwhelming. Rather, it arises out of the culture of society caught in its rush. The crush of information encourages a self-granted immunity from responsibility born of impotence. [...]

And as if the sheer volume were not daunting enough, when the information constitutes public issues it arrives at our eyes and ears packaged in hopeless insolubility. It is framed by both politicians and journalists as black-and-white contests, presented through the words of experts and absolutists. Each of the framers has a stake in continuing the argument; none has a stake in resolving it. Those who do have such a stake—average citizens—are frustrated by the crush of contextless information and the polarized presentation of issues. The packages seem to have no handles, no place for well-intentioned citizens to begin the search for solutions. [...]

■ ... And What 'Agora'?

The second requirement of the democratic dynamic is a place or method for deliberation to occur. In ancient Greece, the agora was more than a marketplace. Goods often ranked second in importance to shared information and public deliberation. In Europe and the early United States, the docks and their environs provided an agora of a more informal sort, but nevertheless a place where fresh information was received and the possibilities for its use discussed. When presses became free and commonplace, pamphlets, newspapers, magazines, and books provided a physically dispersed but common, public, and potentially effective agora.

It became theoretically possible for the agora to function at large and without limits. The increasing availability of information, the enhancement of communication, and the mobility provided by mechanical transportation freed human interaction of physical restraints. But something perverse happened: Rather than connecting us, the burgeoning miracles of information, communication, and transportation separated us. In our rush to take advantage of our liberation from the constraints of time and place, we left behind the primary advantage those constraints had dictated: the local community as the centre of life; the geographic place where affinity, proximity, and tenure made the solution to problems both mandatory and possible.

And the retreat into determined isolation may be only beginning. The Information Superhighway of the twenty-first century, which, in its rawest form, is the antithesis of an agora, may further erode the concept of community where democracy is nurtured. That is still an open question. Interconnectivity provides the opportunity for building virtual communities of various sorts, but early experience indicates those nongeographic communities are extremely specialized in their makeup and concerns. The lack of new and effective agoras joins with information overload to render public deliberation aimed at deciding things difficult, if not impossible.

■ Objectives and Objections

How can an increasingly uninvolved and disconnected public maintain the level of public life that is essential to a democracy? At what point in the explosion of raw data can shared relevance be identified and turned to productive use? Who will do that? What will be the origin and form of the crucial agoras where that information is discussed and turned into democratic action?

I believe that most of the answers to these questions can be provided by journalists, but that can occur only if we develop an expanded role, a broader vision of our contribution to public life.

Certainly, present journalistic practices are not suited to the task of providing relevance and the agora. Simply 'telling the news' of a complex society does little to help solve basic problems, for we have spent years carefully detailing them, analysing them, and raising alarms about them, but still they persist.

Yet many journalists reject the suggestion that there is, or should be, a broader journalistic role than the one we have played. The public, their philosophy declares, must simply take the divinely defined and delivered news and do the best it can. Journalists, they contend, must maintain a pristine distance, a contrived indifference to outcomes, else the news product be contaminated. This is usually called *objectivity* and in its traditional context places an impossible burden on journalism.

So pinched a view ignores a practical reality: Our profession's very existence depends on the viability of public life. A public that does not attend to public affairs, that retreats deeply into private life and concerns, has no need of journalists and journalism, for such a public cannot and will not heed either the news or the needs of public life beyond its most immediate surroundings. So journalists have at least as large a stake in viable public life as anyone else. And we have, for now, the ability to affect that viability.

'For now' is an important qualifier. No one can seriously question that journalism in all its manifestations—newspapers, broadcast, periodicals—is in serious trouble with the public. By every measure of circulation, penetration, reach, respect, ratings, revenue generation, and credibility, the vehicles of journalism are, at best, spinning their wheels.

Some journalists argue that the declines are the fault of the audiences; that for the most part everything is fine within the profession—it's those annoying, stubbornly uninterested and increasingly semiliterate 'people out there' who must change. Others argue that the problem is simply that journalism has not caught up with the technological explosion, but most surely will as better technologies are developed. This 'it's just over the horizon' attitude assumes, incorrectly, that the journalism of the old technology can effortlessly become the journalism of the new technology by putting on spiffy new clothes.

Still others contend that the gap between journalists and the shrinking consumer pool is simply a matter of discovering the right formula: a magical new colour weather map, just the right mauve-and-off-white news set, a tightly targeted demographic niche. Find that, they say, and a chagrined public will reappear gratefully on your doorstep. All three arguments, although containing bits of truth, trivialize the problems that are inherent in all of the foreboding numerical and behavioural trends that research uncovers about audiences.

Those troubles did not grow out of a string of small, wrong-headed media operational decisions along the way and cannot be reversed merely by making different operational decisions. The loss of attention and authority has arrived on a steadily building tide of discontent bred in Postman's (1985) 'neighborhood of strangers and pointless quantity' and fed by an increasingly introverted journalism caught in the same discontent. Rather than accurately diagnosing the problem and devising a useful remedy, however, journalists set out in frantic pursuit of the departing audiences. Concerned about our weakening commercial franchise, we ignored our truer and far more valuable franchise: the essential nexus between democracy and journalism, the vital connection with community, and our role in promoting useful discourse rather than merely echoing discontent.

The result is that journalism has suffered a fundamental loss of authority; that is, as Rosen (1993) put it, 'the right to be heard, the right to be taken seriously, the ability to be persuasive in your account of things' (p. 51). Regaining that authority, that authenticity, must be journalism's first step toward revitalizing itself and public life, but that requires fundamental change, and journalism's deeply embedded culture is resistant to such change.

Understanding a Peculiar Culture

Worry first about the connections, and the separations you need to make will become clear over time.

(Jay Rosen 1994)

■ **Separations and Connections**

As the nation, and its newspapers, grew and prospered, political and commercial considerations gave rise to the notion of 'objectivity' as a foundation of US journalism. Some attribute its ascendancy to an attempt by art to emulate science: the dominance of scientific thought and methods in Western civilization sanctified the most distanced observer as being the most reliable. Others attribute it to a crasser impetus: the need of publishers to move away from highly politicized, opinionated coverage so as to please a larger audience and offend fewer advertisers.

That is an academic argument that will not soon be agreeably settled, but its resolution is not necessary now. However foggy the reasons for the rise of the notion of objectivity in journalism, its impact on the journalistic culture of today is clear.

The perceived need for objectivity created what Rosen (1994) called 'separation fever'. Journalists have constructed a long list of separations that guide our attitudes, thoughts, and reactions—all are driven by the notion of detachment as an overriding value, a primary virtue. Our operational ethics require that editorial functions are separate from advertising functions; news from opinion; facts from values; reality from rhetoric. The newspaper is separated from other institutions by its duty to report on them, journalists are expected to separate their professional identity from their personal identity, and truth telling is separated from the consequences of truth telling so that we can 'tell it like it is'. How the journalist feels about something must be separated from how the journalist reports on it. Newsmakers must be separate from those who report the news. In sum, Rosen (1994) concluded that 'the journalist's mind is separated from the journalist's soul'.

The objective tradition declares that these separations are crucial because they underlie our claim to authority: if we maintain the proper separations, then surely our product is pure and will be perceived as such; its 'objectivity' is insured.

Separation fever runs at various temperatures. Some journalists, in an effort to maintain complete distance from the politics they cover, do not even register or vote. Most newsrooms have policies that range from complete noninvolvement by staffers in any citizen-related activities to less stringent rules that prohibit staffers from engaging in any activity that they or their colleagues might need to write about.

In our effort to get the separations right and persuade ourselves and others that we are properly detached, we engage in endless, arcane hair splittings and rationalizations that strike most citizens not as simply difficult but humanly impossible.

How, citizens properly wonder, can people who profess to not care what happens be trusted to inform us? Why should the public value the perspectives on the importance of events offered by people who insist they have no stake in those events? The journalistic determination to be properly detached also feeds into other cultural traits that have negative ramifications for journalism and public life:

- It not only supports but encourages transience. When caring about a place or circumstance is considered a negative, roots cannot be comfortably put down or useful relationships established; familiarity breeds professional discomfort.

- It insures that certain important things will not be seen as important, or perhaps not seen at all. Determined detachment leads to a kind of blindness about particular things, a trained incapacity to understand part of our environment and the people in it.

- It insures that more will be reported about what is going wrong than what is going right. Reporting on something wrong involves no risk, requires no extension of faith. But reporting on something right involves the risk that it can always go wrong. Detachment allows us to avoid that risk.

■ Does A + Z = Balance?

25,890 Airplanes Land Safely; One Crashes in NYC
(A perfectly balanced headline)

The notion of objectivity carries with it a requirement for something called 'balance'. The idea is that journalists, being conduits, should carefully offer 'both sides' of virtually any matter under discussion. Every assertion more arguable than that the earth is round must be matched by a contending assertion. Invoking this axiom supposedly removes any obligation—and risk—on the part of the reporter that people with different views will be offended or left out of the discussion. Problems with the principle of balance arise, however, in real-world applications.

If a source, for instance, asserts 'A', the reporter is obliged to seek balance. This almost always means finding an expert to assert 'Z', and reporters with more than passing knowledge of their beats know exactly where to find such a person. He or she is almost always an absolutist on the matter, or else the reporter would not have known to call that particular person.

Seeking 'Z' serves two cultural imperatives: It provides the necessary journalistic 'balance' and, important to tradition, it inserts a clear element of conflict into the story. Conflict, real or contrived, is the highest coin in the journalistic realm. Journalists love it and defend their ardour on the grounds that readers also relish it. Clearly, people are drawn to conflict, but where obviously contrived or transparently partisan conflict stands in the way of resolution of important problems, citizen tolerance for it—and those who convey it—becomes strained.

Seeking balance works perfectly well in those situations where the issue is one-dimensional. Of course, that is not most situations. More often than not, 'A' and 'Z' provide a falsely simplistic frame, for many of the other 24 letters would provide nuances reflecting the whole array of opinion.

Framing the issue at the extremes creates more than the deficiency of inaccuracy. On issues of more than one dimension, it defines most people out of the discussion. 'If that's what the argument is about', they say, 'I'm not in it; my views aren't reflected'—they thus opt out. The quoted sources (and the journalist who presents them) become participants in a closed cycle.

Significantly, Weaver and Wilhoit (1992) found that fewer than half of the journalists they surveyed believe that giving ordinary people a chance to express their views on public affairs is 'extremely important' (p. 11).

■ The Adversary Axiom

If your mother says she loves you, check it out.
(Journalism professor John Bremner)

The other value that Weaver and Wilhoit (1992: 11) found that a majority of journalists consider 'extremely important' is 'investigating government claims'. Historic origins help explain that relationship. The purpose of the First Amendment's hands-off admonition to government was to insure that criticism of authority could not be foreclosed.

In today's world, whether or not government or journalism is comfortable with the idea, the watchdog role implicit in the First Amendment locks government and journalism into a symbiotic relationship. Neither can get along without the other; neither can survive if the other becomes dominant. Such a healthy symbiosis between government and journalism is essential and life sustaining not only for the partners but for a third entity—democracy.

Our aim as journalists should be to ensure that Americans understand the true choices they have about issues so they can see themselves, their hopes, and their values reflected in the democratic process. Because the relationship is symbiotic, we cannot accomplish that aim if either partner abandons or poisons the relationship.

The watchdog role that inexorably springs from the First Amendment has served journalism (and democracy) well in dealing with government. Journalists routinely and casually refer to their relationship with government as 'adversarial,' and contend that it is naturally and properly so. But, as Lambeth (1986: 99) pointed out:

There is a real sense in which an uncritical embrace [of the adversarial posture] forecloses the critical thinking needed in moral reasoning.

There is a sense in which an adversarial posture becomes an ideology that prevents the sensitive interpretation and application of the principles of humaneness, truth telling, justice, freedom/independence, and the stewardship of free expression.

Rather, Lambeth argued, *scepticism* is the useful posture; adversarialism, with its many limiting factors, can sometimes, and unavoidably, result from healthy scepticism, but the relationship should not begin there.

Unfortunately, journalism's determined adversarial relationship with government is not confined to that; it reaches into—and damages—our relationship with all authority, and even beyond to our dealings with regular citizens. This has proven to be less than helpful. The downside of the fists-up, gnarly attitude that we have cultivated in dealing with officialdom is clear when a journalist identifies himself or herself on the phone to an average citizen unaccustomed to dealing with us. You can hear the hesitation at the other end, almost feel the concern: 'Uh oh, this can't be anything good.' Yet the late Kansas University journalism Professor John Bremner's oft-quoted admonition, 'If your mother says she loves you, check it out,' is an important one. There are many good reasons for being wary and checking it out, not all of them cynical. For instance, somebody may simply be mistaken. When a relentless adversarial attitude becomes an end in itself, however, a prime directive, useful communication is then threatened and often foreclosed. This has important ramifications, many of them negative, for journalists, their sources, and their audiences. [. . .]

Is that All there Can Be?

This is not an argument against such useful cultural traits as *proper* separations or an appropriate scepticism-driven position in relation to government—it is not a plea for that most dreaded of journalistic conditions; namely, softness. Journalism's birth in a defensive crouch is unavoidable—and useful—history. I do, however, suggest that when proper separations mutate into unconcerned aloofness and determined toughness becomes a singular aim and attribute, things go fundamentally wrong for both journalism and public life. Fixing them will require rethinking journalism's culture and the how and why of its development. It will require opening our minds to additional elements in the definition of 'good journalism'.

Because journalism operates with no external proscriptions or rules for participation or other legal requirements, excesses are not only possible but inevitable. To fend against the threats to the First Amendment that such excesses spawn, the mainstream journalism community has, over time, developed certain conventions, generally agreed-on ways of operating. Although these mores are self-generated and adherence to them is voluntary, they take on the patina of membership requirements, sometimes even of canons. Those who subscribe to them believe that 'good journalism' is that which adheres to the generally accepted mores and anything else is less than 'good journalism'.

From time to time, and usually in response to the public's concerns about excesses, various groups within the mainstream profession have attempted to codify those mores. However, such efforts at establishing codes of ethics or canons of behaviour have always fallen short of universal acceptance because of the fiercely independent bent of the people who are attracted to journalism.

One result of journalism's self-conscious defensiveness about its great latitude is that mainstream journalism is reluctant to question and slow to change those mores that, through general acceptance and long use, approach the status of canons. Yet, the practices that underlie those canons constantly change.

Fifty years ago, presidents were not quoted directly unless they made a formal speech; the conventions of White House coverage absolutely forbade it. Even thirty-five years ago, circumspection had its place. In the midst of the Vietnam war, President Lyndon Johnson sought to force North Vietnam to the peace table with a bomb-and-talk strategy. A visiting group from Charlotte, where I was city editor at the *Observer*, met with him in the Rose Garden on a steamy July afternoon. Clearly weary and troubled, the president lapsed into eerie monologue.

He had been up almost all night conferring with his military people in Washington and Saigon, he said, and he was frustrated. 'I bombed 'em last week and nothing happened. So I hit 'em again last night,' he said. The stunning personalization by the most powerful man in the world never got into print. Editors at the *Observer* felt that it was off-limits despite the absence of acknowledged ground rules and the fact that some ninety citizens of Charlotte heard it. Today, properly, every presidential word, nuance, and slip is fair game, not simply to pass along, but to analyse, comment on, and archive for later use.

Forty years ago, news stories routinely referred to the race of the people involved—if they were other than White, of course. It was, in the eyes of many, a convention to help a predominantly White audience sort out perceived importance. In most news operations today, racial references appear only where they are directly pertinent to the circumstances.

Thirty years ago, routine stories always included an address of the person involved; it was basic, required by convention. A rookie reporter who came back without a specific address risked at least a stern lecture. In today's privacy-conscious atmosphere, stories include specific addresses only when unusual circumstances require it.

In each case, reasons emerged that most journalists considered sufficient to warrant change. Again, the purpose here is not to debate the merits of those changes. Rather, it is to demonstrate that today's 'rules' may not be tomorrow's; that journalism, like any other institution, finds reasons to change even the small things.

Importantly, however, journalism's changes, large or small, are almost always self-generated. The congenital defensive crouch, although useful in some ways and historically unavoidable, is limiting in others. It deprives us of the possibility of seeing our role in public life from a fresh perspective, because it makes us reflexively intolerant of 'outside' criticism. We view most serious criticism not as potentially helpful but as threatening to our unfettered status (and we casually dismiss what we consider nonserious criticism). This low tolerance for serious outside criticism creates an interesting contradiction when considered in relation to journalism's traditional attachment to 'objectivity'.

We dismiss many of our critics on the grounds that they are laypersons not washed in the waters of our culture, and therefore, knowingly or not, likely to put our independence at risk through the changes they propose. If they really understood our culture and the history and dynamics of journalism, we argue, they could never recommend such changes. Yet much of our own journalistic effort is based in our being 'outside' critics of such institutions as government. In that case, we insist that our detachment, or noninvolvement, is precisely what legitimizes our criticism, yet we argue that a similar detachment from journalism on the part of our critics invalidates their criticism. That contradictory attitude comes very close to defining a priesthood, and it is one of the less endearing attributes that we show to citizens concerned about our influence.

References   LAMBETH, E. B. (1986), *Committed journalism* (Bloomington: Indiana University Press).

POSTMAN, N. (1985), *Amusing ourselves to death* (New York: Penguin Books).

ROSEN, J. (1993), 'Beyond Objectivity', *Nieman Reports, 47*(4): 48–53.

—— (1994), '*Getting the Connections Right.* Presentation to Project on Public Life and the Press, American Press Institute, Reston, Va. (March).

Times-Mirror Center for The People and The Press (1994), *The People, the Press & Politics: The New Political Landscape* (Washington, DC: Author).

WEAVER, D., and WILHOIT, G. C. (1992), *The American Journalist in the 1990s* (Arlington, Va.: The Freedom Forum).

YANKELOVICH PARTNERS (1993), *The Yankelovich Monitor 1993.* Prepared for Knight-Ridder Newspapers.

39

Beyond Journalism: A Profession between Information Society and Civil Society

Jo Bardoel

IS JOURNALISM BECOMING redundant? Is the profession, slowly but surely, losing its prominent place in communication between the citizen and government? Over the past years, it has repeatedly been said that the function of journalism is gradually being eroded. Underlying such concerns are the changes that have taken place in the journalistic dissemination of news as a result of new media technology. [...]

The advent of new, interactive communication services such as the Internet, 'free nets' and 'digital cities' has given rise to expectations that in the future journalistic intervention in political communication will no longer be necessary. Mitchell Kapor, founder of the American digital citizens' movement Electronic Frontier Foundation, gives the example of vice-president Al Gore's appearance on *Compu-Serve*:

> It was the first live interactive news conference by the vice-president. The *New York Times* observed: This actually might be like when Franklin Roosevelt went on television at the New York World Fair in 1939. Symbolically it could be marking the beginning of an era, in which public officials are available to discuss and interact in real time. (Wiering and Schröder 1994)

These developments pose questions as to the significance of the new information technology for the traditional task of journalism. What will the information society mean for the position of journalists in political communication? Will they become redundant, as some have suggested? Will the advance of the direct registration of news smother the journalism that seeks to explain its background? Or might it be the other way round? Will individuals lose their way on the information highway and feel a greater need for journalistic direction? In this context we are of course less interested in

Source: Jo Bardoel, 'Beyond Journalism: A Profession between Information Society and Civil Society', *European Journal of Communication*, 11/3 (1996), 283–302.

the changes in the day-to-day working routines of journalists that might occur (see Bardoel 1993) than in the broader mission that is attributed to the profession in relation to political democracy and social integration in any society. Although the latter function of comment and critique is all too often identified with the written press, the same holds true, in principle, for the 'workers of the word' in audiovisual and electronic media.

Will Journalism Become Redundant?

The gradual but inexorable *shift* in the current media landscape from *print to audiovisual means* (Sociaal en Cultureel Planbureau 1994) is not doing the profession any good, so the first assumption goes. Because of the written word and the greater level of abstraction and selectivity, the journalistic surplus-value of the old print media is, it is argued, almost by definition greater than that of the audiovisual media. Television prefers easy-to-follow problems and short 'sound bites' (Rosenblum 1993). Shocking images make a greater impression than deep debate on the underlying problems. These substantive objections against television journalism will carry even more weight as people come to rely more on television for information on 'serious' subjects. Politicians make use of television's strong position in order to address the electorate directly, circumventing the (critical) press. Over the past few years there have been some telling examples: Ross Perot, Bill Clinton, and Silvio Berlusconi. Perot's sudden success fuelled a debate in the United States on what Sandel (1992) has called 'electronic bonapartism'. In Europe, a comparable discussion on 'tele(vision-demo)cracy' took place after the meteorite-like rise of Silvio Berlusconi and his electoral association Forza Italia.

As well as shifts within the existing media—from print to audiovisual—there is also the impact of new technology. First, we notice the *explosion of information* as more new information is produced and the accessibility of existing sources of information, such as databases, increases. Within this growing flow of information, the part played by journalistic products will decrease proportionately, the assumption being that the 'communication pressure' it creates reduces both journalism's scope and the citizen's accessibility.

A primary element of this increasing communication pressure is the *amount of information*, the increase in the volume of information. By now it is well known that the supply of information is expanding explosively, while the amount of time available to the receiver remains more or less constant (Van Cuilenburg *et al.* 1992: 51–68). In order not to lose track, or to miss as little as possible, consumers have taken refuge in increasingly impatient communication behaviour of which 'zapping' has become the symbol.

But there is more. The *speed* at which news and information circulate in society is also assumed to be steadily increasing (Sociaal en Cultureel Planbureau 1994: 427). News circulates ever faster and the public adjusts its pattern of expectations accordingly. For the journalist, faster reporting means less time for selection and processing. Across the board, the time difference between event and report is decreasing, those involved are allowed less time to give their reactions (Van der Donk and Tops 1992: 54) and increasingly, moreover, it is the public's opinion that is sought through instant opinion polls, 'The politicians reach the people via television; the people reach the politicians via polls' (see Abramson *et al.* 1988: 90). The life of public issues is shortened as the publicity process speeds up. This whirling communication carousel of immediate action and reaction within the publicity process decreases rather than increases the scope for journalistic signification.

Finally, increased opportunities for telematic communication also lead to a greater concentration, a greater *density* (Münch 1993: 262–3; Weischenberg *et al.* 1994: 27) of available information. In principle, each message can now reach everyone and, in principle, be received by everyone. Journalists are finding it increasingly difficult to attract the public's attention within this densely packed public space. There is a parallel increase in employment opportunities for professional attracters of attention such as government information officials and public relations (PR) officers, the natural antipodes of journalists. Recent research in the Netherlands shows that the first group already outnumbers the latter by 2:1 (Van Ruler and de Lange 1995: 24).

When we wish to summarize the preceding trends into a formula, the 'communication pressure' in society consists of a multiplication of volume, speed of circulation and density of public communication:

Communication pressure = Volume × Speed of circulation × Density.

The most distinguishing feature of the new communication services based on telematics, *interactivity* (Bardoel 1993: 57), undermines the position of journalism yet again. The emphasis shifts from 'allocution' to 'consultation' (Bordewijk and Van Kaam 1982; McQuail 1987: 41), from undirected dissemination to a directed search for information. Increasingly, it is the receiver to whom the task of selection falls. Although it is fair to say that only a limited public, as yet, will actually make use of such (inter)active opportunities, as a matter of principle their significance is considerable, for they infringe on the exclusive access to many different sources that journalists have enjoyed up till now.

Interactive services may also provide an incentive for increased communication between citizens, for *horizontal communication* in society. It has been predicted that this development will be at the expense of the existing vertical communication between the state and the citizen, in which journalism has traditionally played such an important part. The advance of what Abramson *et al.* (1988: 113) refer to as 'unmediated media' may exert extra pressure on the position and the filtering effect of the established media. Moreover, the combination of computers and networks provides additional opportunities for communication in fields of social life hitherto practically untouched by the media. We are already seeing the emergence of many new circles of communication, bound together by common interest, through services such as the Internet. The 'media gap' (Neuman 1991: 9–10) between interpersonal communication and mass communication is gradually being closed. In other words, 'civil society' is also being 'mediatised' (Bardoel 1993: 57). There is, however, little or no journalistic intervention involved in these new, direct forms of media communication.

The existing *vertical communication* between citizens and the state is also expected to become easier and to bypass such traditional intermediaries as political parties and journalists. Many observers have remarked that the modern technological opportunities for direct interaction with citizens and direct democracy are even a panacea for the limitations of representative democracy. [. . .] Tops *et al.* (1995: 106) conclude that the use of new information and communication technologies creates the possibility of 'unmediated politics', 'in which information about politicians and political parties is no longer coloured by interpretations of independent journalists'. Electronic 'push button democracy' (Abramson *et al.* 1988: 120) is within reach, according to these technological optimists.

The position of journalism is not only under debate as a direct result of the trends in technology, such as the advance of (satellite) television, the surplus of information and the advent of interactive media. These are also reflected in wider developments in society that are equally threatening to the journalist's position.

This technology reinforces the tendency both to decentralization through horizontal communication and to centralization in the form of a globalized communication flow. As new and old media are linked in a global network, the individual journalist is reduced to just a cog in an ever widening 'communication machine'. Of course, the globalization of the communication structure began long ago with the advance of internationally operating press agencies. But the pace of development is increasing with the advent of worldwide news stations such as CNN, databases and expert systems. Separate media and individual journalists are increasingly helpless in the face of this global flow of information Münch (1993: 276) compares the modern journalist with a disc jockey playing their choice of music for a dancing public. The material is produced elsewhere; the disc jockey's job is simply to select and present.

A further threat is presented by the *erosion of the nation-state*, until now an important breeding ground and source of support for the journalistic profession. This traditional centre of political power and sovereignty is losing powers in two directions, to more central and to more decentralized centres of power: on the one hand to Europe, on the other to regional and local entities. [. . .]

Globalization and the diminishing significance of the nation-state have both tangible and psychological implications. The development of individual lifestyles on the one hand and global connections on the other, leads to a sociocultural 'Umwertung aller Werte', in which politics are given a different, more modest role to play. These changes have been defined in such terms as *postmodern culture* and cultural value-relativism. [. . .] It puts an end to several old certainties, without offering a new, normative basis to replace them. This applies to both (ideas on) politics and culture in general and more specifically to journalism. In today's culture, for example, politics occupy a less prominent place, the significance of norms and values is more relative, and the borders between once divided domains (such as information and entertainment, high and low culture) are being blurred.

At the same time, there are fewer objections to *commercial exploitation*— once widely held in the field of the media—and less fear of monopolization, so that there is also less justification providing public amenities to the media. Solutions based on liberal ideas and market conformity apparently provide the foundations for an emerging 'new consensus' on new media policies, both in the United States and in Europe (McQuail 1993: 196). This (post)modern (media) culture may also have implications for the special social status and protection upon which the profession of journalism has always been able to count.

Will Journalism Remain?

Now that technology has rendered journalistic intervention less necessary, the future of the profession will depend more than ever on other *social factors* and considerations. The development of a global system of communication and growing 'communication autonomy' of the citizen outlined above, offer new opportunities, but also create new dilemmas and problems. Against this backdrop, these developments and their significance remain, to a certain extent, questionable—both empirically and normatively.

First, it should be noted that the advance of CNN—which indeed prompted many a sombre thought—seems to have passed its zenith. The original agitation around CNN is reminiscent of the unease that accompanies each new technological development upon which new and more direct forms of reporting are based. We may expect the new direct and global television reporting to carve itself a niche alongside—and not primarily instead of—existing forms of journalism. More international news stations will join CNN in providing the daily menu of television. At a national and local level too, comparable news stations will emerge, as has long been the case in the United States.

In general, the shifts in media use outlined above, *from print to audiovisual*—including their assumed disadvantages to journalism—are less impressive than they appear at first sight. Research from the Dutch Social and Cultural Planning Agency (Sociaal en Cultureel Planbureau 1994) shows that 'loss of reading' occurs mostly in relation to 'popular newspapers, regional papers and the tabloid press', in short 'newspapers and magazines that, in their presentation and simplicity, address the same broad public as broadcasting stations' (Knulst 1994: 334–5). The generalizing and depreciating approach of television in the recent debate on the 'loss of reading culture' completely ignores the professionalization that television journalism has gone through in the last decades.

Moreover, the first articulated fears that the public would literally be flooded out by the rising tide of information are disappearing. It is becoming clear that receivers develop their own strategies for dealing with the flow. At the same time, technology—itself partly responsible for the flood in the first place—also provides solutions. Artificial memories such as the answering machine, video recorder, fax and personal computer (PC) afford an escape from the pressure of permanent accessibility and direct communication and allow messages to be received later—or not at all. According to Van Cuilenburg (1994: 146–54), in the midst of this surfeit, the modern citizen has an increasing need to be 'absently present', to reserve the right of non-communication. The increase of directed consultation and interaction services at the expense of undirected 'allocutive' communication also provides a defence against an embarrassment of unsolicited communication. The increase in segmentation and 'targeting' may prove a social anomaly. The well-known 'information gap', the inequality between citizens in terms of access to information and participation in the political process, is increasing, and reinforces existing social and political inequality.

Again, the suggestion that the new technology provides a solution for a different gap—the participation gap in democracy, is at least questionable. The technological opportunities for self-representation allow citizens to participate directly in political debate and decision-making and are said to negate the reason for the existence of *intermediary agencies* such as political parties and the mass media. While the first experimental experiences have shown that electronic meetings may contribute to sociopolitical debate, they cannot replace representative democracy (Van Dijk 1991: 80–90). Via electronic networks citizens are approached separately, without there being a common identity or a shared signification system. The handling of the agenda proves to be a problem in electronic meetings. This direct democracy lacks the mechanisms of common consideration and compromising that are inherent in representative democracy.

The nature of direct, electronic communication is often elusive: it is well suited to consumerism marketing (in politics too), but does not provide an alternative to existing forms of opinion formation and decision-making. According to Van Dijk (1994: 9), it is primarily populist political movements such as that of Ross Perot and short-lived campaign organizations (*à la* Clinton) that make use of media and information technology.

The assumption that the individual citizen will make the most of all of the political and personal opportunities that unlimited information affords, is also receiving more and more criticism. The most important consequence of the new media situation may well lie, as is increasingly acknowledged, in the field of social integration and political participation (Weischenberg *et al.* 1994). In an electronic and individualized society such notions as 'community' and 'debate' will inevitably be less self-evident. Abramson *et al.* (1988) point to the function that the national media have had as an important source of common civic culture, in which the goals are a common political vocabulary, a common political agenda and the formation of public opinion. Indeed, one of the paradoxes of the new technology is that, in principle, it greatly increases the opportunities for getting together, but in practice decreases the chances of that happening accordingly. At best, once stable communities evaporate into 'shared moments' (Tracey 1993: 14–16).

The transformation from traditional, physical community to a modern, abstract public sphere (*Öffentlichkeit*) renders the organization of social debate increasingly difficult. The concept of 'debate' itself suggests still a unity of time, place and action that is, in the modern media reality, 'stretched out' to a process of—in relation to time and place—scattered contributions to the discussion. Nevertheless, terms such as 'conversation' (Hallin 1992: 10) or 'debate' remain the dominant metaphors in relation to the public sphere, a position that the 'market' metaphor holds in the economic sector.

Despite the reduced chance of getting together, modern society shows an increasing need for common orientation and debate. Absolute norms and values, derived from conviction or religion, are less and less functional. More and more, we live according to relative guidelines, permanently redetermined and adapted in mutual debate. Knapen (1994: 362) has concluded correctly: 'Whoever is unable or unwilling to draw socio-political guidance from the Bible, from Allah or the Pope, will have to get it from mutual discourse.'

■ **New journalistic practices**

Within this framework, individualization of communication can be seen as a threat to social dialogue. Habermas (1992: 438) emphasizes the importance of a *discursive public sphere* that is more than a mere statistical majority. The social basis for an active political *Öffentlichkeit* in this sense is 'civil society' (Dekker 1994). This concept has become increasingly popular in social science over the past years. It stands for the organizations, societies and movements that, at an intermediate level, determine political democracy and social cohesion in a given society. It presupposes an open and pluralistic field of voluntary organizations and informal groups, as an alternative to relationships between people that are governed by market forces or a hierarchical, state-dominated model of opinion formation and power blocs (Edwards 1994: 317). In a notion of 'civil society', a certain involvement is expected of the citizen, and in that sense there is a link with recent debate in the Netherlands on *citizenship and civic consciousness*. More generally, there are arguments in favour of broadening the concept of 'citizenship', from its classical, rational-political content to a more (post)modern, sociocultural interpretation.

According to Habermas (1992: 461), the power of the civic society, that he defines as peripheral to the political centre, lies in its sensitivity to new social issues. He points to recent examples such as the arms race, nuclear energy, the environment, the Third World, feminism and ethnicity: all issues that were not introduced by the political centre. He paints a social pattern of communication in which issues are launched from the periphery (by intellectuals and other advocates, involved or self-appointed) and taken up by journals or associations, after which they develop into social movements or new subcultures and, finally reaching the general public via the mass media, make it on to the *public and political agenda*.

Concepts such as 'public sphere' and 'civil society' allow us to reach a more well-considered conclusion on the effect of the new media on public communication and the position of journalism within these developments. Taking the concept of civil society as a starting point, the new technology is easily recognized as a facilitating device for social contact and relationships at a meso-level, positioning between traditional mass media and person-to-person communication. We have already seen that this technology, based on computers and networks, is likely to affect society at a meso-level most, a domain that as yet is barely 'mediatized' (Bardoel 1993: 57), overcoming the limitations of distance/space and time and offering more opportunity for horizontal communication between citizens. If it is true that, to paraphrase Peters (1993: 566), that mass media are splendid in representation but horrid for participation, the opposite may hold for the new information and communication technology. According to Tops *et al.* (1995: 104–5), the use of this new technology opens up opportunities for forms of direct democracy and for a more 'responsive' representational democracy. Although we should be very cautious not to fall into the trap of technological determinism we must acknowledge that certainly there are new opportunities. The extensive interest in the Internet could be possibly interpreted as the first sign of this development.

However, it is a very different matter to assume that new opportunities for communication will make the old intermediary frameworks (like mass media and political parties) superfluous. Inevitably, they will be somewhat crowded, but not crowded out, for in general we may assume that *new relationships* will *add to* rather than replace old ones. Both old and new media will assist in recognizing and defining the problems that politics must address. Compared to the new communication technology and information services, the mass media and political parties mainly operate at a different stage of social issue formation. It is possible to represent the mechanism of public and political debate graphically. Unlike Habermas, who seems to think of social communication in terms of concentric circles (he refers to it as centre and periphery), our figure (Fig. 1)—following McQuail's (1987: 6) figure of 'communication processes in society'—contains a *communication pyramid*.

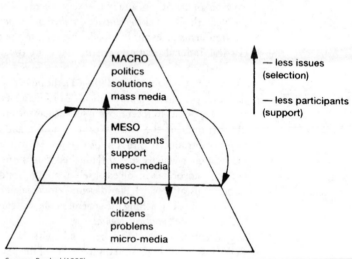

Figure 1.
Communication
pyramid-public/political
debate.

Source: Bardoel (1995)

The shape of a pyramid has been chosen to illustrate the bottom-up process of problem selection and definition by citizens and the top-down process of producing decisions, measures and solutions by the political establishment. Going up in the pyramid means more support and fewer issues (issue filtration). It shows the position of the mass media (and therefore also of journalists) and of political parties as 'higher up' in the pyramid than the new interactive communication technology. If new technological developments further down in the pyramid—so the assumption goes—lead to greater opportunities for mediated communication on the meso-level, the selection and filtering of relevant issues higher up in the pyramid may be expected to gain in significance. Journalism will therefore, in my view, continue to play a crucial part in recruiting and processing relevant issues from the growing plurality of public spheres towards the political centre (Habermas) or towards the top (in my model). Therefore the function of journalism as a director of social debate will be more essential than ever in a society in which the pressure of communication is steadily increasing. Journalism will not, as in the era of mass media, control the public debate, but can take the lead in directing and defining the public agenda. As journalists are no longer the indispensable intermediaries between the outside world and the public, they must prove their position in this respect. It is important that journalists take this aspect of their intermediary task more seriously than they seem to do at present.

As well as—and not primarily instead of—the existing media, modern communication technology will lead to new information services and to *new journalistic practices*. These will not be 'the same old journalism but with better tools' (see Koch 1991: xv, xxiii). As is always the case at the start of major technological innovations, only first ideas and experiments provide a glimpse now of what the future may hold. In the beginning, new services are apt to resemble the old and it will take some time before they are applied according to their own functionality. The first automobiles were coaches without horses and for a long time, television was regarded—and still is by some—as a mixture of radio, cinema and theatre. If we look at the first experiments with the 'electronic newspaper', we see two prototypes. Following Van Kaam (1988: 32–4; 1991: 150–1), I call them the 'fax paper' and the 'PC paper'. Knight Ridder's 'news tablet' seems to be an example of the former, MIT's 'Fish Wrap' of the latter. In this way, the new communication technology has already led to product differentiation in the public dissemination of information, filling the gap between direct communication and mass communication. New information services are being developed for new publics (or, if you prefer: new product/market combinations) that offer new forms of employment in information processing professions. Let us, for the time being, call these workers 'information brokers'. Meanwhile, users have an increasingly wide choice, at least in a formal sense. They may opt for information that has been selected and processed by journalists or for information that other professionals (in PR and documentation) have collected, or they may choose to consult any one of a number of information files directly. This changes the journalist from an unavoidable to an avoidable link in the chain of information provision.

Orientating and Instrumental Journalism

The position of journalism as a 'unified' profession that encompasses many very different activities at very different levels, seems no longer tenable. The advent of new media formats, based on multimedia applications and the increasing (inter)activity of the user, make this presumption less realistic then it already was. Ideal-typically, I see two sorts of journalism developing (Bardoel 1993: 117–20). First, there is *orientating journalism* whose job it is to provide a general orientation (background, commentary, explanation) to a general public. Second, there is *instrumental journalism*, geared to providing information (functional, specialistic) to interested customers. (I gladly leave to the reader the question of whether all of these activities should be called journalism.)

The main differences between these journalistic ideal-types are indicated in Figure 2. It will be clear that the new information services require mostly 'new' journalists (or information brokers), while the classical media seek 'old' journalists. As we have said, these are ideal-types; all sorts of mixtures are possible.

We can see, therefore, that as the media sector segments, the integrating, centripetal task gains in importance as well. There will be employment for journalists in both fields in the future. The difference is that the first task will expand while the second will shrink, and thus journalistic intervention will be threatened, both in quantitative and qualitative terms.

	ORIENTATING	INSTRUMENTAL
Goal:	orientation	action
Function:	stage, forum	file, memory
Emphasis:	attention	information
User:	public/citizens	individual/role player
Info-mode:	one way/'allocution'	interactive/'consultation'
Product:	'fax paper'	'PC paper'
Profession:	'old' journalism	'new' journalism

Figure 2.
Ideal-types of journalism.

Source: compare Bardoel (1993: 119).

What will happen to *classical journalism*? In a society held together less by geographical and physical relationships than by medial and symbolic links, the good journalist functions as a conductor of social debate and a broker of social consensus. Peters' (1993: 550) thesis that—referring to Bentham and Mill—the press functions as the 'social superego' and the 'moral regulator' for the coordination of society contains more truth then ever before. In the new surfeit of information, the traditional task of journalism will evolve from sending messages to offering orientation to the citizen and the emphasis will shift from 'content' to 'context'. We have already suggested that the emphasis in journalistic intervention will shift from 'getting' information to 'bringing' information (Bardoel 1989: 49). Within the profession itself, however, the emphasis is still very much on collecting information (the traditional 'Tin Tin romanticism' in journalism) and less on directing the social flow of information and public debate. More than ever, the task of journalism will lie in filtering relevant issues from an increasing supply of information in a crowded public domain and its fragmented segments. Journalism evolves from the provision of facts to the provision of meaning. In the new ocean of information, 'navigation' is desperately needed. Information in itself is less important than information shared with others. Communication rather than information becomes the key word, and journalists have a long tradition in bringing minds together. In fulfilling this function the—higher educated—public expects the journalist to put aside all traces of old-fashioned paternalism.

At the same time, it should be noted that journalism does not seem adequately equipped to deal with this new task. Blumler (1992: 104) has said: 'A threading suture of these analyses is that a weakened political sphere confers on journalism functions and responsibilities that it is at best half-equipped to assume: agenda definition, interest aggregation, civic correlation, and sense-making.' The recent increase in news 'hypes' in the Netherlands and elsewhere—as a result of the speeding up, competition and concentration in the dissemination of news—shows that journalistic ethics and practice *vis-à-vis* its role in public communication are lagging behind. The new challenges require responsibilities beyond traditional journalism.

On the other hand, the new media offer scope for 'instrumental journalism'. As yet there are no clear professional profiles or training requirements in this field. The new information broker appears to be an unspecialized Jack-or-Jane-of-all-trades. The emphasis will be, for the time being, on exploring and developing new techniques in the direction of meaningful and profitable exploitation by information services (product development). A knowledge of the technology, of layout (computer graphics) and of the compact, brief and sequential presentation of information via menus and trees, is essential. Of course, basic journalistic skills remain important. Moreover, information and database management—skills thus far mostly found among documentation professionals—will gain in importance, while knowledge of and orientation towards target groups are basic conditions. Indeed, the individual user pays the piper and calls the tune, thanks to direct feedback via interactive techniques and paying per unit used. Journalism and marketing will have more to do with each other than many an old press dog would wish.

A number of these changes will have repercussions for journalism in general. Digital techniques join previously separate flows of information in networks and increase the options for users. The importance of *journalistic distinction*, the recognizable surplus value of journalism *vis-à-vis* the products of documentation professionals (such as documentalists) and publicity professionals (such as PR agents) is increasing, not in the last instance because journalistic information has its price.

Moreover, the journalist's work will be increasingly less bound to specific media. 'Single source, multiple media' is a term often heard in this connection. This means that journalists will find themselves more frequently on publishing desks, together with layout and marketing staff, and that they will work individually and from a distance as modern teleworkers. This threatens the *collective culture* of the editorial desk, always an important factor in and guarantee for the transfer of professional skills and values. The threat will increase as the different provisions that have always served to protect editorial space against commercial and political interests, come under pressure. Public broadcasting is in deep water here, both as a matter of principle (legitimation) and of practice (finance). The scope of responsible journalism—in practice especially the press—in the market sector, is increasingly dependent on a decreasing number of owners. There is a risk that the 'enlightened' media owner of yesteryear, with their understanding of journalism's specific position, will be replaced by owners with an eye to 'return on investment' only. The risk increases as new players flow in from 'outside' as a result of the convergence of media and telecommunication, but by definition lacking all affinity with media culture. In that light, it may be necessary to create new guarantees or to develop new media ethics (Dennis, 1994; Harwood Group, 1995). Training and education should play an important role here.

At the end of the 20th century, journalism must once again seek its place in a changing society. A society that is secular, open, more dependent on media, transnational and whose members are relatively well educated. This implies that the profession can be bypassed more easily, but it makes journalism more valuable at the same time. The concerns outlined in the introduction are legitimate. There *is* ever more direct, unmediated television reporting—both worldwide and local. There *are* ever more interactive communication media. The social dissemination of information *is* increasingly individual and it *is* increasingly difficult to organize getting together and debate. 'Journalism'—if it ever existed as such—is falling apart. On the one hand, there is a need for information brokers, on the other, for directors and conductors of the public debate.

The function of classical journalism will probably shift to the latter position, also because the profession is one of the last strongholds of generalism in an increasingly specialized and fragmented society (Bardoel, 1988: 157). Greater individual freedom for citizens produces, more than ever, the need for common orientation. This might be the most important mission for journalists in the future—a mission that calls for responsibilities and skills beyond the present journalistic practice.

References

ABRAMSON, J. B., ARTERTON, F. C., and ORREN, G. R. (1988), *The Electronic Commonwealth. The Impact of New Technologies upon Democratic Politics* (New York: Basic Books).

BARDOEL, J. (1988), 'Nieuwe informatietechnologie en journalistiek domein', in L. Heinsman, and J. Servaes (eds) *Hoe nieuw zijn de nieuwe media? Een mediabeleid met een perspectief* (Leuven and Amersfoort: ACCO), 149–67.

—— (1989), 'Journalistiek en nieuwe informatietechnologie', in J. Bardoel (ed.), *De krant van morgen. De elektronische toekomst van de schrijvende pers* (Amsterdam: Stichting 'Het Persinstituut'), 41–55.

—— (1993), *Zonder pen of papier. Journalistiek op de drempel van een nieuwe eeuw* (Amsterdam: Otto Cramwinckel Uitgever).

BLUMLER, J. G. (1992), 'News Media in Flux: An Analytical Afterword', *Journal of Communication*, 42(3): 100–8.

BORDEWIJK, J. L., and VAN KAAM, B. (1982), *Allocutie. Enkele gedachten over communicatievrijheid in een bekabeld land* (Baarn: Bosch en Keuning).

DEKKER, P. (1994), *Civil Society. Verkenningen van een perspectief op vrijwilligerswerk.* (Rijswijk and Den Haag: Sociaal en Cultureel Planbureau/VUGA), i. 42–9.

DENNIS, E. E. (1994) 'An Ethic for a New Age', *Media Studies Journal* (Freedom Forum Media Studies Center), 8(1): 143–53.

EDWARDS, A. R. (1994), 'Informatisering, demokratie en staatsburgerrol', in A. Zuurmond, J. Huigen, P. H. A. Frissen, I. Th. M. Snellen, and P. W. Tops (eds.), *Informatisering in het openbaar bestuur. Technologie en sturing bestuurskundig beschouwd* ('s-Gravenhage: VUGA Uitgeverij), 309–21.

HABERMAS, J. (1992), *Faktizität und Geltung. Beiträge zur Diskurstheorie des Rechts und des demokratischen Rechtsstaats* (Frankfurt am Main: Suhrkamp).

HALLIN, D. C. (1992), 'We Keep America on Top of the World. Television Journalism and the Public Sphere', *Journal of Communication* 3(4): 14–26.

HARWOOD GROUP (1995), *Timeless Values. Staying True to Journalistic Principles in the Age of the New Media* (Reston: American Society of Newspaper Editors).

KNAPEN, B. (1994), 'Hoe au courant is de krant?', *De Gids* (May): 356–65.

KNULST, W. (1994), 'Omroep en publiek', in H. Wijfjes (ed.) *Omroep in Nederland. Vijfenzeventig jaar medium en maaatschappij, 1919–1994* (Zwolle: Waanders), 300–38.

KOCH, T. (1991), *Journalism in the 21st Century. Online Information, Electronic*

Databases and the News (Twickenham: Adamantine Press).

McQuail, D. (1987), *Mass Communication Theory; An Introduction* (London: Sage).

—— (1993), 'Informing the Information Society; The Task for Communication Science', in P. Gaunt (ed.), *Beyond Agendas. New Directions in Communication Research* (Westport and London), 185–99.

Münch, R. (1993), 'Journalismus in der Kommunikationsgesellschaft', *Publizistik,* 38(3): 261–80.

Neuman, W. R. (1991), *The Future of the Mass Audience* (Cambridge: Cambridge University Press).

Peters, J. D. (1993), 'Distrust of Representation: Habermas on the Public Sphere', *Media, Culture and Society* 15(4): 541–71.

Rosenblum, M. (1993), *Who Stole the News?* (New York: Wiley).

Sandel, M. (1992), *De Volkskrant* 19 October. (The article was first published in *New Perspectives Quarterly.*)

Sociaal en Cultureel Planbureau (1994), *Sociaal en Cultureel Rapport 1994* (Den Haag: VUGA).

Tops, P. W., Schalken, C. A. T., and Zouridis, S. (1995), 'ICT en veranderende relatiepatronen tussen burgers en bestuur', in I. Baten and J. Ubacht (eds.), *Een kwestie van toegang. Bijdragen aan het debat over het publieke domein van de informatievoorziening* (Amsterdam: Otto Cramwinckel Uitgever (with Rathenau Instituut, Den Haag)).

Tracey, M. (1993), 'A Ceremony of Innocence. An Interpretation of the Condition of Public Service TV', in W. Stevenson (ed.), *All our Futures. The Changing Role and Purpose of the BBC* (The BBC Charter Review Series; London: BFI), 39–65.

Van Cuilenburg, J. J. (1994), 'Een toekomst vol informatie en communicatie', in A. C. Zijderveld (ed.), *Kleine geschiedenis van de toekomst: 100 thesen over de westerse samenleving op weg naar de eenentwintigste eeuw* (Kampen: Kok Agora), 146–54.

Van Cuilenburg, J. J., Scholten, O., and Noomen, G. W. (1992), *Communicatiewetenschap* (Minderburg: Dick Coutinho).

Van der, Donk, W. B. H. J., and Tops, P. W. (1992), 'Informatisering en demokratie: Orwell of Athene?', in P. H. A. Frissen *et al.* (eds.), *Orwell of Athene? Democratie en informatiesamenleving* (Den Haag: SDU/NOTA), 33–75.

Van Dijk, J. A. G. M. (1991), *De netwerkmaatschappij. Sociale aspecten van nieuwe media* (Houten: Bohn Stafleu Van Loghum).

—— (1994), 'De programma's dreigen het van de kiezers te verliezen', *NRC-Handelsblad* (15 April): 9.

Van Kaam, B., (1989), 'Hoe dichtbij is de elektronische krant?', in J. Bardoel *De krant van morgen. De elektronische toekomst van de schrijvende pers* (Amsterdam: Stichting 'Het Persinstituut').

Van Ruler, B., and de Lange, R. (1995) 'Kwantiteit is geen probleem kwaliteit nog. Onderzoek onder 700 bedrijven schetst helder communicatiebranche', *Communicatie* 1(1): 24–5.

Weischenberg, S., Attmeppen, K. D., and Löffelholz, M. (1994), *Die Zut Journalismus* (Opladen: Westdeutscher Verlag.).

Wiering, F., and Schröder, R. (1994), 'Beeldstorm', transcript of a television documentary 'Van McLuhan tot Virtual Reality', broadcast by Nederland 3, 4 September 1994. Hilversum: VPRO.

Index

Note: Page numbers in **bold** indicate chapters. People mentioned only *once* in footnotes have generally been omitted, except where they are quoted in the text above.